THIRD LATIN BOOK

Fig. 1. The Appian Way

THIRD LATIN BOOK

BY

B. L. ULLMAN, Ph.D.

PROFESSOR OF LATIN
UNIVERSITY OF CHICAGO

WITH THE COLLABORATION OF

NORMAN E. HENRY, M.A.

PEABODY HIGH SCHOOL, PITTSBURGH

AND

DORRANCE S. WHITE, M.A.

STATE UNIVERSITY OF IOWA

THE MACMILLAN COMPANY
NEW YORK

TO THE TEACHER

This book conforms to the suggestions and requirements of the Report of the Classical Investigation, the College Entrance Examination Board, the Syllabus in Ancient Languages (1928) of the State of New York, and other recent courses of study. These new requirements are the result of long-continued demands by Latin teachers for an enriched curriculum, for greater freedom in determining a course of reading, and for emphasis on the acquisition of power to read Latin. The sharp drop in the Latin enrollment of the third year as compared with that of the second shows the need for a course that will prove attractive and worth while. Without detracting from the importance of Cicero as an author and as material for third-year study, it is clearly undesirable, under present-day conditions, to begin the year with the study of Rome's great orator. Nor is it desirable to devote a whole year to his orations.

This book contains much more material than can be covered in one year in order that the teacher may have available a wide range of material to draw from, may have a chance to vary the course from time to time, and may have abundant material for sight translation and for use with superior pupils. In this way individual differences may be taken care of.

Enough material from Cicero is offered to fill an entire year, but in making up a course of study it is suggested that two or three months be devoted to the selections from Pliny and Gellius in Part II before beginning the reading of Cicero in Part III. The introductory lessons in Part III should by all means be included, as they prepare the pupil to understand the peculiarities of Cicero's style. The speeches against Catiline (two in complete form) and the speech for Archias are sufficient to represent Cicero's oratory. The rest of the year may be spent in reading Cicero's *Letters* or Ovid.

A better understanding of the purposes of the book may be gained from examining the various parts in detail:

Part I. — The ten passages from Caesar's *Civil War* are intended for use with those classes which need a review of second-year Latin. The material is arranged in lessons, with assignments of review work in forms and syntax and with accompanying composition exercises. Many teachers will prefer to omit this part, especially if their pupils have read much Caesar in the second year.

Part II. — The popularity of the selections from Pliny's *Letters* given in the *Second Latin Book* of this series has led to the inclusion of additional letters from this source. Most of the other selections are from Aulus Gellius. Only portions of this part can be read in any one year. Particularly desirable are Selections 6, 7, 10, 12, 13, 16, 17, 20–23, 28, 29, 34, 36, 37, 41, 43. The selections from Petronius (47–51) will be found amusing for sight reading, and Cicero's jokes (Selection 53) may well be read at sight before or along with the orations.

Part III. — The main difficulty in reading Cicero is caused by his style. To obviate this difficulty, the chief peculiarities of his style are developed in eight lessons based on carefully selected portions of Cicero's speech on the Consular Provinces — a speech which deals with a subject familiar to all pupils: Caesar's conquest of Gaul.

The first and third speeches against Catiline are given in full. The second speech is represented by those chapters which are important for an understanding of the conspiracy of Catiline. There is also a short selection from the fourth. The selections from Sallust were made with the thought of supplementing and throwing an interesting light on Cicero's account of the conspiracy.

Cicero's speech for Archias is included in full, and most teachers will no doubt wish to read this favorite. The speech for the Manilian Law is given *in toto*, but portions are printed in smaller type as a suggestion that they be omitted or read very rapidly. Some teachers will prefer to omit the entire speech.

Some of the Letters should by all means be read for their human interest, especially 1–3, 10–12, 14–16, 20–26.

Part IV. — The selections from Ovid are included for those teachers who wish to introduce their pupils to Latin poetry in the third year. The stories of Daedalus, Midas, Pyramus, and Atalanta are particularly suitable.

In other respects the present book continues the features made familiar by the first two books of this series. These are:

1. Comprehensiveness. — This book contains not only the regular reading material for the third year but also all that will be required for supplementary work, all the necessary composition exercises, and all the grammar (both forms and syntax) which the pupil will need for study and consultation. Thus this single book is all that is needed during the year.

2. Notes. — The notes are brief and simple and are placed at the foot of the page. Their aim is to give help in understanding the text and to bring out interesting points about Roman life and history and comparisons with modern conditions. Grammatical points are elucidated but not overemphasized. For those who desire full grammatical discussion there are frequent references to the grammatical appendix. There are few cross-references to other notes.

3. Word Study. — The study of Latin and English word formation, which plays so prominent a part in the other books of the series, is a regular feature of all four parts of this book. At the end there is a summary of prefixes and suffixes.

4. Vocabulary Drills. — The vocabulary drills scattered throughout Parts I–III include the words required for the third year in the Word List of the College Entrance Examination Board. Many of them are repeated from time to time as found in the reading in order that the omission of parts of the book may not result in failure to acquire a basic vocabulary. The College Board words and those of the New York Syllabus are grouped together on page 519.

5. Comprehension. — The reading of the Latin for comprehension is emphasized by review questions in Part III and by occasional thought questions in the notes. The teacher will do well to extend the plan.

6. Grammar. — Drill on the essentials of grammar is provided by the composition exercises. The Summaries of Inflection and Syntax are constantly referred to in the notes.

7. Collateral Reading. — Definite assignments of reading in English are made in various parts of the book. A bibliography will be found in **255**.

8. Composition. — English sentences and passages for translation into Latin are based on Parts I, II, and III. Like the Latin passages, these exercises are more numerous than can be covered in any one year. The teacher can select such exercises as are based on the Latin material read. There is constant drill on the fundamentals of syntax.

9. Illustrations. — The illustrations supplement other phases of the book in presenting aspects of Roman life and civilization and are to be considered an essential portion of the teaching material in the book.

CONTENTS

ix

CONTENTS

Nescire autem quid antequam natus sit acciderit, id est semper esse puerum.

— CICERO, *Orator*. 120

THIRD LATIN BOOK

PART I

SECOND YEAR REVIEW

Selections from Caesar's *Civil War*

1. **Introduction**

In 60 B.C. Caesar, Pompey, and Crassus had formed the first triumvirate (combination of three) for the purpose of keeping all political power in their own hands. As a result of this agreement, Caesar had gone to Gaul with his army. But on the death of Crassus and of Julia, the daughter of Caesar and wife of Pompey, these two men drifted apart. They were now the two foremost men of the Roman world. Pompey had conquered Mithridates and the East, Caesar the Gauls and the Germans.

It was not uncommon for a proconsul's political

FIG. 2. JULIUS CAESAR

1

enemies to bring charges against him on his return from his province. To avoid this, Caesar asked that he be allowed to run for the consulship before giving up his proconsulship; for after his election he would be immune from prosecution. This the aristocratic senate, under Pompey's influence, refused to do. But the common people favored Caesar. Every conceivable political trick was tried by both men and their political "machines" to gain their ends. Each was too suspicious of the other to yield his point of view. The senate tried to pass various measures aimed at Caesar, but some of the tribunes friendly to Caesar blocked this action. When the consuls threatened violence, these tribunes fled to Caesar. This act enabled Caesar to pose as the defender of the constitution in that the senate had violated the sacred office of tribune and the right of veto.

The following passages from the *Civil War* will serve as a summarized account in Caesar's own words, describing that stupendous struggle between Rome's two outstanding military and political leaders which plunged their country into four years of civil strife, doomed the free Republic, and paved the way for the Empire of the Caesars.

2. I. The Die Is Cast — Caesar Prepares to Cross the Rubicon

Quīnque prīmīs diēbus[1] quibus habērī senātus potuit,[2] dē imperiō Caesaris et dē amplissimīs virīs, tribūnīs plēbis, gravissimē acerbissimēque dēcernitur.[3] Profugiunt statim ex urbe[4] tribūnī plēbis sēsēque ad Caesarem cōnferunt. Is eō tempore erat Ravennae[5] exspectābatque suīs lēnissimīs postulātīs[6] respōnsa.

Proximīs diēbus habētur extrā urbem senātus. Pompeius eadem illa quae per Scīpiōnem ostenderat agit[7]; senātūs virtūtem cōnstantiamque collaudat; cōpiās suās expōnit: legiōnēs habēre sēsē parātās x; praetereā cognitum compertumque sibi[8] aliēnō esse animō[9] in Caesarem mīlitēs neque iīs posse persuādērī[10] utī[11] eum dēfendant aut sequantur.

Quibus rēbus cognitīs, Caesar apud mīlitēs cōntiōnātur. Hortātur ut eius imperātōris exīstimātiōnem dignitātemque ab inimīcīs dēfendant cuius ductū

---

[1] For case see **344**.

[2] *i.e.* when there were no legal holidays. The date was January, 49 B.C.

[3] *decrees are passed.* What literally?

[4] " The City " in Latin writers is always Rome unless otherwise stated.

[5] For case see **351**. Ravenna was about twenty-one miles north of the Rubicon, hence within Caesar's own province.

[6] Dative with **respōnsa**: *answers to his demands.*

[7] *proposes.*

[8] Supply **esse** before **sibi**, which is dative of agent with **compertum** (**317**).

[9] With **aliēnō**: *unfriendly* (**342**).

[10] *they could not be persuaded* (**313**, *a*).

[11] Long form of the conjunction **ut**. Distinguish from **ūtī**, infinitive of **ūtor**.

VIIII annīs rem pūblicam fēlīcissimē gesserint [1] plū-
rimaque proelia secunda fēcerint, omnem Galliam
Germāniamque pācāverint. Conclāmant mīlitēs le-
20 giōnis XIII, quae aderat (hanc enim initiō tumultūs

FIG. 3. THE SQUARE IN RIMINI

In the foreground is the monument with the inscription mentioned in section 3.

ēvocāverat ; reliquae nōndum convēnerant), sēsē parātōs esse imperātōris suī tribūnōrumque plēbis iniūriās
dēfendere.

Cognitā mīlitum voluntāte, Arīminum [2] cum ea

---

[1] For mood see **388**.

[2] About twelve miles south of the Rubicon, which marked the southern boundary of Caesar's province.   His act in thus crossing the Rubicon with an army was equivalent to a declaration of war upon Rome.
Plutarch graphically describes Caesar's indecision and mingled emotions
as he pauses on the bank of the Rubicon to reflect upon the consequences
of civil strife.   At last, with heroic resolve, he exclaims, " The die is
cast ! " and makes the fateful plunge.   So to-day a man is said to cross
the Rubicon when he makes an irrevocable decision.

legiōne proficīscitur ibique tribūnōs plēbis, quī ad eum 25
cōnfūgerant, convenit ; reliquās legiōnēs ex hībernīs
ēvocat et subsequī iubet.   (I. 5–8)

3.   Caesar at Ariminum

In the center of the town of Rimini (the ancient Ariminum) there is a monument in a picturesque square
on the spot from which, according to tradition, Caesar
addressed his troops. The inscription, dated 1555,
reads as follows :

C. CAESAR   SUGGESTUM
DICT.   HUNC
RUBICONE   VETUSTATE
SUPERATO   COLLAPSUM
CIVILI BEL.   COSS. ARIM.
COMMILIT.   MENSIUM
SUOS HIC   NOVEMBRIS
IN FORO AR.   ET DECEMB.
ADLOCUT.   MDLV
                  RESTIT.

With the abbreviations expanded this would be :

C. Caesar dictātor, Rubicōne superātō, cīvīlī bellō,
commīlitōnēs suōs hīc in forō Arīminēnsī [1] adlocūtus [2]
est. Suggestum [3] hunc vetustāte collāpsum cōnsulēs
Arīminēnsēs [1] mēnsium [4] Novembris et Decembris
MDLV restituērunt.

---

[1] Adjective : *of Ariminum.*

[2] For **allocūtus :** *addressed.*

[3] *platform.*

[4] The " consuls," or highest officials, were changed every few months.

4. Vocabulary Drill

apud	imperium	persuādeō
cognōscō	initium	praetereā
comperiō	legiō	statim
hīberna	lēnis	subsequor
hortor	pācō	voluntās

5. Form Review

Conjugate **possum** in full (**280**).

6. Syntax Review

Use of the reflexive pronoun (**288**). Volitive substantive clauses (**370**). Ablative absolute (**335**).

Find all examples of these constructions in the preceding passage.

7. Latin Composition

To the Teacher. — For English-to-Latin exercises to accompany the lessons of Part I see page 434. The exercises there given form a corporate part of the lessons as numbered and should therefore be used in direct connection with them.

FIG. 4. A ROMAN ORNAMENTAL DESIGN

8. II. Caesar's Clemency at Corfinium

After crossing the Rubicon, Caesar swept southward along the east coast. There was consternation at Rome, and the consuls and most of the magistrates fled to Capua. Pompey himself left for Apulia and began to mobilize his forces at Brundisium in order to transport them to Greek soil if necessary. Meanwhile Caesar, with Brundisium as his objective, advanced triumphantly. After seizing Asculum, he proceeded to Corfinium and laid siege to it. Domitius in vain sought aid from Pompey, who left the town to its fate, although the Pompeian force there numbered more than thirty cohorts, besides a large number of Roman senators and knights.

Litterīs perlēctīs, Domitius dissimulāns[1] in cōnsiliō prōnūntiat Pompeium celeriter subsidiō[2] ventūrum hortāturque eōs nē animō[3] dēficiant, quaeque ūsuī[2] ad dēfendendum oppidum sint[4] parent.[5] Ipse arcānō cum paucīs familiāribus suīs colloquitur cōnsiliumque 5 fugae capere cōnstituit. Cum vultus Domitī cum ōrātiōne nōn cōnsentīret, atque omnia trepidantius timidiusque ageret quam superiōribus diēbus cōnsuēsset,[6] multumque cum suīs cōnsiliandī causā sēcrētō praeter cōnsuētūdinem colloquerētur, concilia con- 10 ventūsque hominum fugeret, rēs diūtius tegī dissimulārīque nōn potuit. Pompeius enim rescrīpserat[7] sēsē rem in summum perīculum dēductūrum[8] nōn esse, neque suō cōnsiliō aut voluntāte Domitium sē in oppidum Corfīnium contulisse. 15

---

[1] *concealing the truth.*   [2] For case see **310.**
[3] For case see **345.**   [4] For mood see **388.**
[5] Supply **ut** from the preceding **nē.**
[6] Contracted form of **cōnsuēvisset.** For mood see **388.**
[7] See line 1 above and note force of prefix. Domitius had sent messengers to Pompey in Apulia, requesting reinforcements.
[8] *he would not bring the matter into.*

Dīvulgātō Domitī cōnsiliō, mīlitēs quī erant Corfīnī[1]
vesperī sēcessiōnem faciunt. Omnēs ūnō cōnsiliō Domitium prōductum[2] in pūblicum circumsistunt et
custōdiunt lēgātōsque ex suō numerō ad Caesarem
20 mittunt : sēsē parātōs esse[3] portās aperīre quaeque[4]
imperāverit facere et L. Domitium vīvum in eius potestātem trādere.

Caesar omnēs senātōrēs senātōrumque līberōs, tribūnōs mīlitum equitēsque Rōmānōs ad sē prōdūcī iubet.
25 Hōs omnēs prōductōs ā contumēliīs mīlitum convī-
ciīsque prohibet ; pauca apud eōs loquitur, quod sibi
ā parte eōrum grātia relāta nōn sit[5] prō suīs in eōs
maximīs beneficiīs ; dīmittit omnēs incolumēs.

(I. 19, 20, 23)

9.   **Vocabulary Drill**

aperiō	cōnsuēscō	parō
beneficium	dēficiō	praeter
celeriter	familiāris	subsidium
colloquor	fuga	superior
cōnsentiō	imperō	ūsus

[1] For case see **351.**

[2] Translate by a clause.

[3] Indirect statement ; the verb of saying is implied in lēgātōs . . .
mittunt.

[4] Note that **imperō** takes the direct object of the thing (**quae**) ; only
the person ordered is put in the dative.

[5] Subjunctive because the reason here given is that which Caesar
presented at that time (**389**). While some of these officers and men
appreciated Caesar's clemency so far as to enlist in his army, others
broke their parole and later joined Pompey in Macedonia. But Caesar
maintained his policy of clemency throughout the Civil War.

10.   Form Review

Formation and declension of participles; future passive participle and gerund (**276, 277, 265**).

11.   Syntax Review

Uses of participles (**395–397**). Uses of the gerund (**399**). Uses of the future passive participle (**398**). Subjunctive in **cum** causal clauses (**383**).

Find all examples in the Latin text of this lesson.

12.   Latin Composition

See section **7** and page 434.

FIG. 5.   BRUTUS AND CAESAR AT RAVENNA

Brutus has just delivered the ultimatum of the senate. (From "Julius Cæsar.")

13.   III. Strategy versus Courage

After the fall of Corfinium, Pompey secretly sailed from Brundisium for Greece, eluding Caesar, who had planned to establish a blockade. Caesar could not follow because he lacked transports. He therefore resolved to crush Pompey's armies in Spain. He first, however, dispatched forces to seize Sicily and Sardinia, the two chief sources of Rome's grain-supply. He himself marched northward, prepared to lay siege to Marseilles, then hastened on to Spain and appeared before Ilerda. Certain Spanish tribes joined him. The Pompeian leaders, Afranius and Petreius, decided to retreat. By a skillful maneuver Caesar cut them off from their supplies and gained a bloodless victory.

Caesar in eam spem vēnerat[1] sē sine pugnā et sine vulnere suōrum rem cōnficere posse, quod rē frūmentāriā[2] adversāriōs interclūsisset. Cūr etiam secundō proeliō aliquōs ex suīs[3] āmitteret[4]? Cūr vulnerārī
5 paterētur optimē meritōs dē sē mīlitēs? Cūr dēnique fortūnam perīclitārētur,[5] praesertim cum nōn minus esset imperātōris[6] cōnsiliō superāre quam gladiō? Movēbātur etiam misericordiā cīvium, quōs interficiendōs[7] vidēbat; quibus[8] salvīs atque incolumibus, rem
10 obtinēre mālēbat. Hoc cōnsilium Caesaris plērīsque nōn probābātur;[9] mīlitēs vērō palam inter sē loquē-

---

[1] *had conceived the hope.*

[2] Ablative of separation (**327**).

[3] See **300, Note** (*b*).

[4] Deliberative subjunctive (**375**) in indirect discourse. Translate *Why should he lose;* so also paterētur and perīclitārētur.

[5] Cf. perīculum.

[6] Predicate genitive : *the part of a commander.*

[7] *would have to be killed.* What is the form?

[8] Connecting relative (**293**).

[9] *was not acceptable to.* Note the difference of construction below in line 31.

bantur, quoniam tālis occāsiō victōriae dīmitterē-
tur,[1] etiam cum vellet[2] Caesar, sēsē nōn esse pugnātūrōs.

Posterō diē ducēs adversāriōrum perturbātī, quod 15
omnem reī frūmentāriae flūminisque Hibērī spem

Fig. 6. Caesar at the Rubicon
(From " Julius Caesar.")

dīmīserant, dē reliquīs rēbus cōnsultābant. Vāllum ex
castrīs ad aquam dūcere incipiunt. Id opus inter sē
Petreius atque Afrānius partiuntur ipsīque perficiendī
operis causā longius prōgrediuntur.   20

---

[1] For mood see **389**.   [2] For mood see **387**.

Quōrum discessū līberam nactī mīlitēs colloquiōrum facultātem vulgō prōcēdunt, et quem quisque in Caesaris castrīs nōtum aut mūnicipem habēbat, conquīrit atque ēvocat.[1] Sē statim signa trānslātūrōs
25 cōnfirmant lēgātōsque dē pāce prīmōrum ōrdinum[2] centuriōnēs ad Caesarem mittunt. Erant plēna laetitiā[3] et grātulātiōne omnia, et eōrum[4] quī tanta perīcula vītāsse[5] et eōrum quī sine vulnere tantās rēs cōnfēcisse vidēbantur, magnumque frūctum suae prīs-
30 tinae lēnitātis omnium iūdiciō Caesar ferēbat, cōnsiliumque eius ā cūnctīs probābātur. (I. 72–74)

14.   Vocabulary Drill

facultās	nancīscor	quisque
gladius	patior	quoniam
incolumis	plērīque	rēs frūmentāria
interclūdō	posterus	sine
lēnitās	prīstinus	vulnerō

15.   Form Review

Conjugate **volō, nōlō,** and **mālō** (**283**).

16.   Syntax Review

Indirect statements (**402**). Causal clauses (**389**). Find all examples in the preceding Latin passage.

---

[1] Such fraternizing among soldiers of opposing armies was common during lulls in the fighting in the World War.

[2] These were the six centurions of the first cohort, who outranked all the others. Cf. our sergeants-major (" top sergeants ").

[3] Ablative with **plēna**: *Joy was full to overflowing.*

[4] *both (on the part) of those.*

[5] For **vītāvisse.**

17.　　IV. A Peace Conference

As a result of Caesar's operations near Ilerda the entire Spanish peninsula submitted to him without further opposition. He generously gave all the captives, officers and men, their freedom.

In the Second Book of his *Civil War* Caesar describes the siege of Marseilles, which held out for about six months under Trebonius and Decimus Brutus, both of whom had served brilliantly under Caesar in Gaul. When the city fell, Caesar granted a general pardon. Meanwhile Caesar's cause suffered a severe blow in Africa, where Curio, one of his ablest generals, was overwhelmingly defeated by the Numidian allies of Varus.

In the Third Book of the *Civil War* Caesar describes his preparations against Pompey in the East. He crossed over to Greece with seven legions, January 4–5, 48 B.C. Vibullius, one of Pompey's officers who had twice fallen into Caesar's hands and had been kindly treated, had been commissioned by him to proceed to Pompey with proposals of peace. Meanwhile Pompey cut Caesar off from Dyrrachium and both armies went into winter-quarters on opposite banks of the Apsus. Pompey finally rejected Caesar's peace proposals.

Dēmōnstrāvimus L. Vībullium Rūfum, Pompeī praefectum, bis in potestātem pervēnisse Caesaris atque ab eō esse dīmissum, semel ad Corfīnium, iterum in Hispāniā. Hunc prō suīs beneficiīs Caesar idōneum iūdicāverat quem cum mandātīs ad Cn. Pompeium 5 mitteret[1] eundemque apud Cn. Pompeium auctōritātem habēre intellegēbat. Erat autem haec summa mandātōrum: dēbēre utrumque pertināciae fīnem facere et ab armīs discēdere neque amplius fortūnam perīclitārī. Satis esse magna utrimque incommoda 10 accepta: illum[2] Italiā[3] expulsum, āmissā Siciliā et

---

[1] The clause depends on **idōneum**: *a fit man to send* (**381**).

[2] *i.e.* Pompey.　　　　[3] For case see **328**.

Sardiniā duābusque Hispāniīs et cohortibus in Italiā
atque Hispāniā cīvium Rōmānōrum c atque xxx;
sē[1] morte Curiōnis et dētrīmentō Āfricānī exercitūs
15 tantō mīlitumque dēditiōne ad Curictam. Proinde
sibi[2] ac reī pūblicae parcerent.[3]

Vībullius, adhibitō Libōne et L. Lucceiō et Theo-
phane,[4] quibuscum commūnicāre dē maximīs rēbus
Pompeius cōnsuēverat, dē mandātīs Caesaris agere
20 īnstituit. Quem ingressum in sermōnem Pompeius
interpellāvit et loquī plūra prohibuit. " Quid mihi,"
inquit, " aut vītā[5] aut cīvitāte opus est, quam beneficiō Caesaris habēre vidēbor? " Bellō perfectō, ab
iīs Caesar haec facta cognōvit quī sermōnī[6] interfuē-
25 runt; cōnātus tamen nihilō minus est aliīs ratiōnibus
per colloquia dē pāce agere. (III. 10, 18)

18.   Vocabulary Drill

alius	cōnor	potestās
āmittō	dētrīmentum	ratiō
amplius	idōneus	summa
bis	inquit	tamen
colloquium	īnstituō	uterque

---

[1] *i.e.* Caesar. Supply **accēpisse satis magna incommoda** from above.

[2] For case see **313.**

[3] *they should spare.* In direct address this would be volitive subjunctive.

[4] Lī'bo was one of the commanders of Pompey's fleet. Lucceius
(Lucsē'yus) had a reputation as an historian — so much so that his
services were sought by Cicero as his biographer in a letter which is still
preserved. Theophanes (Thēof'anēz), a Greek, later was Pompey's
biographer. It was he who advised Pompey, after the defeat at Phar-
sā'lus, to seek refuge in Egypt.

[5] Ablative with **opus est**: *need of life*, etc.

[6] For case see **314.**

19.   Syntax Review

Dative of possession (**316**).   Volitive subjunctive
(**366**).   Subjunctive in indirect questions (**386**).
Find all examples in the preceding passage.

FIG. 7.   CAESAR IN THE TEMPLE OF SATURN AT ROME
On his arrival in Rome Caesar seized government funds to pay his troops.
(From " Julius Caesar.")

20.   V. Obeying Orders

Caesar made another overture for peace, but it was rejected.
The rest of Caesar's fleet crossed safely from Brundisium.
Antony joined Caesar and dispatched ships to Brundisium for
the rest of Caesar's army. Pompey's son destroyed Caesar's
warships at Oricum and Lissus. Since Caesar was unable to
draw Pompey into a general battle, he decided to establish a
blockade and shut him off from his base of supplies at Dyrrachium. Both armies suffered untold hardships from lack of food.

Interim certior factus P. Sulla,[1] quem discēdēns
castrīs praefēcerat Caesar, auxiliō cohortī[2] vēnit cum
legiōnibus duābus; cuius adventū facile sunt repulsī
Pompeiānī. Neque vērō cōnspectum aut impetum
5 nostrōrum tulērunt, prīmīsque dēiectīs, reliquī sē ver-
tērunt et locō cessērunt. Sed īnsequentēs nostrōs, nē
longius prōsequerentur, Sulla revocāvit. At plērīque
exīstimant, sī ācrius īnsequī voluisset,[3] bellum eō diē
potuisse fīnīrī. Cuius[4] cōnsilium reprehendendum[5]
10 nōn vidētur. Aliae[6] enim sunt lēgātī partēs atque
imperātōris: alter omnia agere ad[7] praescrīptum, alter
līberē ad summam rērum cōnsulere dēbet. Sulla ā
Caesare castrīs relīctus, līberātīs suīs, hōc fuit contentus
neque proeliō dēcertāre voluit (quae rēs tamen fortasse
15 aliquem reciperet[8] cāsum), nē imperātōriās sibi partēs

---

[1] A nephew of Sulla, the dictator. He seems to have had a " shady "
record as a politician, having been kept from the consulship because
found guilty of bribery. Later he was tried for complicity in Catiline's
conspiracy but was acquitted through Cicero's eloquent plea, though
presumably guilty

[2] Dative of reference (**311**). Avoid the literal translation. This one
cohort had held out for several hours against four of Pompey's legions,
until Sulla came to its relief.

[3] For mood see **320**. II.   [4] *i.e.* Sulla.   [5] Supply **esse.**   [6] *different.*
according to.   [8] *which might perhaps have involved some risk* (**377**).

sūmpsisse vidērētur. Pompeiānīs magnam rēs ad
receptum difficultātem afferēbat. Nam ex inīquō prō-
gressī locō in summō cōnstiterant : sī per dēclīve
sēsē reciperent, nostrōs ex superiōre īnsequentēs locō
verēbantur ; neque multum ad sōlis occāsum temporis 20
supererat ; spē enim cōnficiendī negōtī prope in noctem
rem dēdūxerant.[1] Ita necessāriō atque ex tempore[2]
captō cōnsiliō, Pompeius tumulum quendam occu-
pāvit, quī tantum aberat ā nostrō castellō ut tēlum
tormentō missum adigī nōn posset. Hōc cōnsēdit 25
locō atque eum commūnīvit omnēsque ibi cōpiās
continuit. (III. 51)

21.   **Vocabulary Drill**

adigō	fīniō	prōsequor
adventus	impetus	sē recipere
alter . . . alter	īnsequor	sūmō
certiōrem facere	occāsus	supersum
dēiciō	praeficiō	vereor

22.   **Form Review**

Conjugation of **ferō** (**281**).

23.   **Syntax Review**

Datives of purpose and reference (**310, 311**). Purpose clauses with **ut** and **nē** (**367**). Result clauses
with **ut** and **ut nōn** (**378**). Subordinate clauses in
indirect discourse (**387**).

Find all examples of these constructions in the above
passage.

---

[1] *had prolonged the struggle.*
[2] *according to the necessity of the moment.*

24.   VI.   Graft and Ingratitude

Pompey made an attack upon Caesar's lines and was repulsed
with heavy losses.   Caesar rewarded his men for their gallantry.
Pompey, who had now retired to his former position, refused to
be drawn into battle.   At last, however, his supplies gave out
and, as his position was becoming intolerable, he attempted to
break through Caesar's lines.

Erant apud Caesarem in equitum numerō Allobrogēs duo frātrēs, Roucillus et Egus, Adbucillī fīliī,
quī prīncipātum in cīvitāte multīs annīs obtinuerat,
singulārī virtūte hominēs, quōrum operā[1] Caesar
5 omnibus Gallicīs bellīs optimā fortissimāque erat
ūsus.   Hīs domī[2] ob hās causās amplissimōs magistrātūs mandāverat.   Hī propter virtūtem nōn sōlum apud
Caesarem in honōre erant, sed etiam apud exercitum
cārī habēbantur ; sed frētī amīcitiā[3] Caesaris et stultā
10 ac barbarā arrogantiā ēlātī dēspiciēbant suōs stīpen-
diumque equitum fraudābant[4] et praedam omnem
domum[5] āvertēbant.   Quibus illī[6] rēbus permōtī
ūniversī Caesarem adiērunt palamque dē eōrum iniūriīs
sunt questī.
15 Caesar neque[7] tempus illud animadversiōnis esse
exīstimāns et multa virtūte eōrum concēdēns rem tōtam
distulit ; illōs sēcrētō castigāvit quod quaestuī equitēs

---

[1] From **opera,** not **opus (337).**

[2] *i.e.* in their own country (**351**).   [3] For case see **339.**

[4] Caesar evidently employed these men as paymasters in his Gallic
cavalry.   They were grafters of the worst type who not only systemat-
ically robbed the soldiers of a portion of their pay but even drew the
wages of the dead by failing to report all the casualties.   They also
appropriated the booty which fell to the lot of the cavalry.

[5] *i.e.* to themselves (**320**).   [6] *i.e.* the cavalrymen.

[7] = et nōn.

habērent, monuitque ut ex suā amīcitiā omnia exspectā-
rent et ex praeteritīs suīs officiīs reliqua[1] spērārent.
Magnam tamen haec rēs illīs offēnsiōnem et contemp- 20
tiōnem ad[2] omnēs attulit. Quō pudōre adductī

FIG. 8. THE ROMAN BRIDGE AT RIMINI
This bridge, still in use, was built by Augustus.

discēdere ab nōbīs et novam temptāre fortūnam no-
vāsque amīcitiās experīrī cōnstituērunt.

Quōs Pompeius, quod erant honestō locō[3] nātī et
īnstrūctī līberāliter magnōque comitātū et multīs 25
iūmentīs[4] vēnerant virīque fortēs habēbantur et in
honōre apud Caesarem fuerant, omnia sua praesidia[5]
circumdūxit atque ostentāvit. Nam ante id tempus
nēmō aut mīles aut eques ā Caesare ad Pompeium

---

[1] *future rewards in accordance with his past favors.*
[2] *among.*   [3] For case see **329**.
[4] Supply **cum** with both nouns. The phrase explains **īnstrūctī**.
[5] Depends on **circum** in **circumdūxit**.

30 trānsierat, cum paene cotīdiē ā Pompeiō ad Caesarem
perfugerent mīlitēs.   (III. 59–61)

25.   Vocabulary Drill

adeō *(verb)*	eques	singulāris
amplus	experior	stīpendium
āvertō	magistrātus	temptō
concēdō	nāscor	ūniversus
dēspiciō	opera	ūtor

26.   Form Review

Conjugation of eō and its compounds (**282**).

27.   Syntax Review

Genitive and ablative of description (**299, 342**).
Adversative (concessive) **cum** clauses (**384**).

Find all examples in the preceding passage.

28. VII. Overconfidence: Pride Goeth before a Fall

After much severe fighting, Caesar's men retreated with heavy loss, narrowly escaping annihilation. The Pompeians rejoiced as if they had now triumphed. Caesar raised the drooping spirits of his men by assuring them that their defeat would finally turn to victory. He then retreated, pursued by Pompey. The theater of war now shifted to Thessaly. Domitius joined Caesar and they took Gomphi by storm. The rest of Thessaly then submitted. Caesar pitched camp on the plain of Pharsalus. Pompey, joining Scipio, encamped near Caesar. His men were so sure of victory that they quarreled over the anticipated spoils and disputed with one another about the offices at Rome.

Pompeius paucīs post diēbus[1] in Thessaliam pervēnit cōntiōnātusque apud cūnctum exercitum suīs[2] agit grātiās, Scīpiōnis mīlitēs cohortātur ut, partā iam victōriā,[3] praedae ac praemiōrum velint esse participēs. Auctīs cōpiīs Pompeī duōbusque magnīs exercitibus 5 coniūnctīs, prīstina omnium cōnfirmātur opīniō et spēs victōriae augētur adeō ut, quicquid intercēderet temporis,[4] id morārī reditum in Ītaliam vidērētur[5] et, sī quandō quid Pompeius tardius aut cōnsīderātius[6] faceret, ūnīus esse negōtium diēī, sed illum dēlectārī 10 imperiō[7] et cōnsulārēs praetōriōsque servōrum habēre numerō[8] dīcerent. Iamque inter sē palam dē praemiīs

---

[1] For case see **341**.

[2] *his own (troops)*, in contrast with Scipio's.

[3] *as if the victory had already been won.*

[4] The clause means: *the intervening time.* What literally?

[5] For mood see **378**; for that of interc**ē**deret, **388**.

[6] *If Pompey ever did anything somewhat slowly or deliberately.* Both **quandō** and **quid** are indefinite (**275, Note**). For subjunctive see **387**.

[7] Ablative with **dēlector** (**340**).

[8] *treated as slaves.* What literally?

ac dē sacerdōtiīs contendēbant in annōsque¹ cōnsulātum dēfīniēbant, aliī domōs bonaque eōrum quī in
15 castrīs erant Caesaris petēbant.

Iam dē sacerdōtiō² Caesaris Domitius, Scīpiō,
Spinthērque Lentulus³ cotīdiānīs contentiōnibus ad

FIG. 9.   ROMAN SOLDIERS   *Wide World*
A parade in York, Pennsylvania.

gravissimās verbōrum contumēliās palam dēscendērunt,
cum Lentulus aetātis honōrem ostentāret,⁴ Domitius

---

¹ *for years ahead.*   The enclitic -que is rarely attached to prepositions;
therefore it is attached here to **annōs** instead of **in.**

² Caesar was pontifex maximus or high priest of the state religion.
Since priests held their offices for life, Caesar's enemies evidently did
not intend to spare him if he fell into their hands.

³ Domitius (not to be confused with Caesar's most trusted officer
of the same name) and Lentulus Spinther had been captured at Corfinium by Caesar, pardoned, and allowed to go free, only to fight against
him again under Pompey, as we see here.   The Scipio here mentioned
was Pompey's father-in-law.

⁴ *proclaimed the honor due his age.*

urbānam grātiam dignitātemque iactāret, Scīpiō af- 20
fīnitāte [1] Pompeī cōnfīderet. Postrēmō omnēs aut
dē honōribus suīs aut dē praemiīs pecūniae aut dē
persequendīs inimīcitiīs agēbant, nec quibus ratiōnibus
superāre possent, sed quem ad modum ūtī victōriā
dēbērent cōgitābant.   (III. 82–83)   25

29.   Vocabulary Drill

adeō (*adv.*)	coniungō	moror
aetās	cōnsulātus	opīniō
cōgitō	contumēlia	quem ad modum
cohortor	dignitās	superō
cōnfīdō	inter sē	videor

30.   Form Review

Indefinite pronouns (**275**).

31.   Syntax Review

General review of ablative constructions (**326** ff.).
Classify all ablatives in the preceding passage.

---

[1] For case see **346**.

32.   VIII.   THE GENERALS SPEAK

Caesar tried repeatedly to draw Pompey into battle. Since he had less than a thousand horsemen with which to combat Pompey's cavalry force of seven thousand, he augmented their fighting strength by having his fleetest infantry deploy and co-operate with them. This strategic move resulted in victory when Pompey launched an attack upon this previously exposed flank. Caesar had given up the hope of being able to induce Pompey to attack him, and with column formed was about to march forth to another position, when Pompey decided to fight.

Tunc Caesar apud suōs, cum iam esset agmen in portīs, " Differendum est," inquit, " iter in praesentiā nōbīs et dē proeliō cōgitandum, sīcut semper dēpoposcimus. Animō[1] sumus ad dīmicandum parātī ; nōn
5 facile occāsiōnem posteā reperiēmus "; cōnfestimque expedītās cōpiās ēdūcit.

Pompeius quoque, ut[2] posteā cognitum est, suōrum omnium hortātū[3] statuerat proeliō dēcertāre. " Persuāsī equitibus nostrīs," inquit, " (idque mihi factūrōs
10 cōnfirmāvērunt)[4] ut dextrum Caesaris cornū ab latere apertō aggrederentur et, circumventā ā tergō aciē, prius[5] perturbātum exercitum pellerent quam ā nōbīs tēlum in hostem iacerētur. Ita sine perīculō legiōnum[6] et paene sine vulnere bellum cōnficiēmus. Id autem
15 difficile nōn est, cum tantum equitātū valeāmus."

---

[1] With parātī (345).   [2] With indicative ut means *as*.

[3] Ablative of cause : *owing to*.

[4] In the light of what happened there is grim humor in Pompey's " persuading " the cavalry to carry out this maneuver and in their solemn promise to do so — as if they alone could decide the matter.

[5] Translate with quam by one word.

[6] Objective genitive : *to the legions*.

Hunc Labiēnus[1] excēpit et, cum Caesaris cōpiās dēspiceret,[2] Pompeī cōnsilium summīs laudibus efferret, " Nōlī,"[3] inquit, " exīstimāre, Pompeī,[4] hunc esse exercitum quī Galliam Germāniamque dēvīcerit.[5] Omnibus interfuī proeliīs. Perexigua pars illīus exerci- 20 tūs superest ; magna pars dēperiit, multōs autumnī pestilentia[6] in Italiā cōnsūmpsit, multī domum discessērunt, multī sunt relīctī in continentī.[7] An nōn audīstis[8] ex iīs quī per causam valētūdinis remānsērunt cohortēs[9] esse Brundisī factās? Hae cōpiae quās 25 vidētis ex dīlēctibus hōrum[10] annōrum in citeriōre Galliā sunt refectae, et plērīque sunt ex colōniīs Trānspadānīs. Ac tamen quod fuit rōboris[11] duōbus proeliīs Dyrrachīnīs interiit." Haec cum dīxisset, iūrāvit sē nisi victōrem in castra nōn reversūrum reliquōsque 30 ut idem facerent hortātus est. Hoc laudāns Pompeius idem iūrāvit ; nec vērō ex reliquīs fuit quisquam quī iūrāre dubitāret.[12]   (III. 85–87)

---

[1] This is the famous T. Labienus, Caesar's trusty officer during the Gallic War. During the Civil War he joined Pompey and became one of Caesar's bitterest enemies.

[2] *while he,* etc.

[3] A negative command (lit., *be unwilling to think*) : *don't think.*

[4] Vocative.   [5] For mood see **387.**

[6] Malaria, at its height in the early autumn, was the most common of Roman diseases. Its cause (infection through the bite of a certain kind of mosquito) was not known until a few years ago.

[7] *i.e.* Italy.   [8] For **audīvistis.**

[9] Whole cohorts had remained behind in Italy, ostensibly on account of their health, but in reality (Labienus hints) because they did not want to serve against Pompey.

[10] *recent.*

[11] *whatever strength* (**300**).

[12] A descriptive relative clause (**380**). As some one has said, such oaths are made to be broken.

33. **Vocabulary Drill**

aciēs	cōnfirmō	quoque
aggredior	cōnsūmō	tēlum
agmen	cornū	tergum
cohors	equitātus	reperiō
cōnfestim	latus (*noun*)	revertor

34. **Syntax Review**

Ablative of respect (**345**). Descriptive **cum** clauses (**382**). Dative of agent with future passive participle and **sum** (**317**). Subjunctive in anticipatory clauses (**385**).

Find all examples of these constructions in the preceding passage.

Fig. 10. Bronze Railing

From the houseboat of the Emperor Caligula found at Lake Nemi (cf. Fig. 32).

35. IX. The Battle of Pharsalus and the Defeat of Pompey

Pompey and Caesar marshaled their forces for the impending struggle, destined to prove one of the decisive battles of the world. After addressing his army, Caesar gave the signal for battle. A veteran soldier led the charge.

Erat Crāstinus ēvocātus in exercitū Caesaris, quī superiōre annō apud eum prīmum pīlum in legiōne x dūxerat,[1] vir singulārī virtūte. Hic, signō datō, " Sequiminī[2] mē," inquit, " manipulārēs meī quī fuistis, et vestrō imperātōrī quam cōnstituistis operam 5 date.[3] Ūnum hcc proelium superest ; quō cōnfectō, et ille suam dignitātem et nōs nostram lībertātem[4] recuperābimus." Simul respiciēns Caesarem, " Faciam," inquit, " hodiē, imperātor, ut aut vīvō mihi aut mortuō grātiās agās.[5] " Haec cum dīxisset, prīmus ex 10 dextrō cornū prōcucurrit, atque eum ēlēctī mīlitēs circiter cxx voluntāriī eiusdem centuriae sunt prōsecūtī.

In eō proeliō nōn amplius cc mīlitēs dēsīderāvit,[6] sed centuriōnēs, fortēs virōs, circiter xxx āmīsit. Interfectus est etiam fortissimē pugnāns Crāstinus, cuius 15 mentiōnem suprā fēcimus, gladiō in ōs[7] adversum coniectō. Neque id fuit falsum quod ille in pugnam proficīscēns dīxerat. Sīc enim Caesar exīstimābat, eō

---

[1] *had led the first maniple of the first cohort in the tenth legion* (Caesar's favorite).

[2] Imperative. [3] *render the service which.*

[4] Their liberty was threatened by Pompey.

[5] Substantive result clause, object of **faciam**: *I shall make you thank.*

[6] *i.e.* Caesar.

[7] *having received a sword (thrust) full in the face.*

proeliō excellentissimam virtūtem Crāstinī fuisse, opti-
20 mēque eum dē sē meritum iūdicābat.

Ex Pompeiānō exercitū circiter mīlia xv cecidisse
vidēbantur, sed in dēditiōnem vēnērunt amplius mīlia
xxiiii (namque etiam cohortēs quae praesidiō in
castellīs fuerant sēsē Sullae dēdidērunt), multī prae-
25 tereā in fīnitimās cīvitātēs refūgērunt, signaque mīli-
tāria ex proeliō ad Caesarem sunt relāta clxxx et
aquilae viiii.[1] L. Domitius ex castrīs in montem
refugiēns, cum vīrēs eum lassitūdine[2] dēfēcissent, ab
equitibus est interfectus. (III. 91, 99)

36. Vocabulary Drill

adversus	dēdō	proficīscor
castellum	enim	respiciō
centuriō	fīnitimus	simul
circiter	pīlum	suprā
coniciō	praesidium	vīs

37. Form Review

Personal pronouns (270).

38. Syntax Review

General review of dative constructions (309 ff.). General review of the infinitive tenses and uses (400-403).

Classify all datives in the preceding passage.

---

[1] Each legion had its eagle or legionary standard. Caesar captured
those of nine out of eleven of Pompey's legions.

[2] On account of weariness.

39.   X. POMPEY'S DEATH

The battle of Pharsalus had resulted in the utter rout of the Pompeians and the capture of their camp with all its luxurious appointments. Pompey made no effort to rally his demoralized troops but, stripping off his decorations and uniform, he mounted the first horse he could find and with thirty followers rode madly toward the coast, where, finding a grain vessel, he embarked. Pompey's men, thus deserted, surrendered the next day and were kindly treated by Caesar, who then pursued Pompey. The latter sailed from Amphipolis, stopped at Mitylene long enough to take on board his wife and younger son, and finally reached Pelusium at the mouth of the Nile, where he sought the protection of the young king, whose father he had placed upon the throne.

FIG. 11. AQUILAE

Roman soldiers with standards.

Pompeius Pēlūsium pervēnit. Ibi cāsū rēx erat Ptolemaeus, puer aetāte, magnīs cō-5 piīs cum sorōre Cleopātrā[1] bellum gerēns, quam paucīs ante mēnsibus

---

[1] Later the famous charmer of Antony (cf. Shakespeare's *Antony and Cleopatra*), who for her sake became a traitor to his country. She was

10 per suōs propinquōs atque amīcōs rēgnō expulerat;
castraque Cleopātrae nōn longō spatiō ab eius castrīs
distābant. Ad eum Pompeius mīsit, ut prō hospitiō
atque amīcitiā patris[1] Alexandrīā[2] reciperētur atque
illīus opibus in calamitāte tegerētur. Sed quī ab eō
15 missī erant, cōnfectō lēgātiōnis officiō, līberius cum
mīlitibus rēgis colloquī coepērunt eōsque hortārī ut

suum officium Pompeiō
praestārent nēve eius
fortūnam dēspicerent.

20   Hīs tunc cognitīs
rēbus, amīcī rēgis, quī
propter aetātem eius in
prōcūrātiōne erant rēg-
nī, sīve timōre adductī,
25 ut posteā praedicābant,
sollicitātō exercitū rēgiō,
nē Pompeius Alexan-
drīam   Aegyptumque
occupāret,[3] sīve dē-
30 spectā eius fortūnā, ut
plērumque in calami-
tāte ex amīcīs inimīcī

FIG. 12. POMPEY

exsistunt, iīs quī erant ab eō missī palam līberāliter
respondērunt eumque ad rēgem venīre iussērunt; ipsī,
35 clam cōnsiliō initō, Achillam, praefectum rēgium, singu-

---

now nineteen, six years older than her brother Ptolemy Dionysus.   The
young king's guardian had expelled her from the country, but she had
just returned from Syria with an army to regain the throne.

[1] Ptolemy's father had enjoyed the hospitality of Pompey in Rome.

[2] *into Alexandria.*

[3] The clause depends upon **timōre**: *the fear, (caused) by the instigation
of the king's army,* etc.

lārī hominem audāciā, et L. Septimium,[1] tribūnum mīlitum, ad interficiendum Pompeium mīsērunt. Ab hīs līberāliter ipse appellātus et quādam nōtitiā Septimī prōductus,[2] quod bellō praedōnum apud eum ōrdinem dūxerat, nāviculam parvulam cōnscendit cum paucīs 40 suīs; ibi ab Achillā et Septimiō interficitur.[3]   Item L. Lentulus comprehenditur ab rēge et in custōdiā necātur. (III. 103–104)

40.   Vocabulary Drill

calamitās	ineō	ops
clam	item	praestō
coepī	lēgātiō	propinquus
comprehendō	mēnsis	tegō
cōnscendō	necō	timor

41.   Syntax Review

Final review of participles (**395–398**) and subjunctive constructions (**366** ff.).   Tense sequence (**359**). Classify all subjunctives in the preceding passage.

---

[1] A centurion in Pompey's army in his war against the pirates nineteen years before this, now serving under the Egyptian king.

[2] *led on by acquaintance of a sort with Septimius.*

[3] Plutarch (*Pompey*, 77 ff.) says that Pompey as he stepped ashore was stabbed in the back by Septimius before the very eyes of his wife and son, who had not yet come ashore.   We are told that Caesar shed bitter tears when shown the head of his former son-in-law and later political foe, for Caesar cherished no personal hatred against Pompey, who had aided him in his rise to power and had married his beloved Julia.

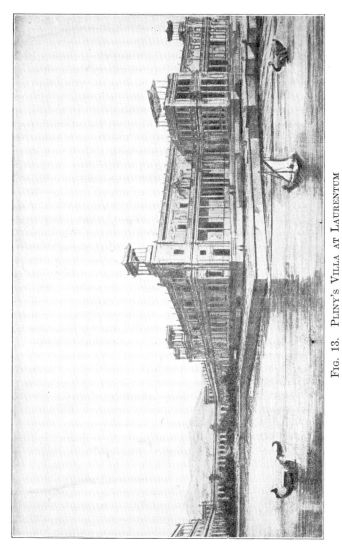

Fig. 13. Pliny's Villa at Laurentum

As restored by Canina from Pliny's description. (From *The Villas of Pliny the Younger*, by Helen H. Tanzer, Columbia University Press.)

PART II

42. PLINY

Pliny, called the Younger to distinguish him from his uncle, is known to us chiefly as the author of a volume of letters of remarkable interest for the light they throw on conditions in the Roman Empire of his time and for the revelation which they afford of his own character. We are made to feel that he and his fellow-Romans were real human beings like ourselves. We may occasionally laugh at him for taking himself too seriously, but we cannot help admiring him for his high ideals.

Pliny's letters belong chiefly to the reign of Trajan (98–117 A.D.). They fall into two groups. The larger group consists of letters which he himself selected and prepared for publication ; the smaller group consists of letters interchanged by Pliny and Trajan while the former was a provincial governor. Among his most famous letters are two which tell of the eruption of Mt. Vesuvius in the year 79, when he was in his 'teens.[1]

Pliny was a man of importance in his day. He held the highest public offices. His reputation as an orator seems to have been noteworthy. At any rate, he

---

[1] These letters are to be found in the *Second Latin Book* of this series.

prided himself on his orations and hoped to achieve immortality through them. It is characteristic of fate, ever tricky, that all but one of his orations have disappeared, while his letters, which he took much less seriously, have survived. His one ambition was to be like Cicero, Rome's greatest orator.

43. Aulus Gellius

Aulus Gellius was born at Rome about 130 A.D. We know little about his life and depend for that little upon what he says about himself in his " Attic Nights " (**Noctēs Atticae**), a huge scrapbook in which he jotted down anecdotes, bits of history and snatches of poetry and dissertations on various phases of philosophy, geometry, and grammar.

This scrapbook, so Gellius tells us in the preface, was written in Attica during the winter evenings for the amusement of his children. Some of it, indeed, is almost too childish to read. But it also contains information about Roman public and private life not found elsewhere in Latin literature. For example, he has given us extracts from a great number of Greek and Roman writers, mentioning 275 by name, whose works have been wholly or in great part lost. He frequently mentions Cicero and Virgil and speaks of them with great respect.

Selections from other sources than Pliny and Gellius are grouped at the end of Part II. Information about their authors will be found in footnotes on the text.

44.   1. Drop Me a Line

Ōlim mihi nūllās epistulās mittis.[1] "Nihil est," inquis,
"quod scrībam."[2] At hoc ipsum scrībe, nihil esse quod
scrībās, vel sōlum illud unde incipere priōrēs solēbant:
"sī valēs, bene est; ego valeō."[3] Hoc mihi sufficit;
est enim maximum. Lūdere mē putās? Sēriō petō.[5]
Fac sciam[4] quid agās,[5] quod sine sollicitūdine summā
nescīre[6] nōn possum. Valē. (I. 11)

45.   2. How to Grow Old Gracefully

Magnam cēpī voluptātem, cum ex commūnibus
amīcīs cognōvī tē, ut sapientiā[7] tuā dignum est, et
dispōnere ōtium et ferre,[8] habitāre amoenissimē, et nunc[10]
terrā,[9] nunc marī[9] corpus agitāre,[10] multum disputāre,
multum audīre, multum lēctitāre, cumque[11] plūrimum
sciās, cotīdiē tamen aliquid addiscere.[12] Ita senēscere
oportet virum quī magistrātūs amplissimōs gesserit,[13]
exercitūs rēxerit, tōtumque sē reī pūblicae obtulerit.[15]
Nam et prīma[14] vītae tempora et media[14] patriae,

---

[1] As with **iam diū,** the present tense is used with **ōlim.** English idiom
calls for the present perfect.

[2] Descriptive clause (**330**): *nothing to write.*

[3] This was one of the formulas so frequently found in letters, like
"Dear Sir," "Sincerely yours," etc. It had gone out of fashion over a
century before, as **priōrēs solēbant** suggests, like such phrases as "I am,
Sir, your humble and obedient servant," so common in Washington's day.

[4] *Let me know.* What literally? One would expect **ut,** but it is often
omitted in such substantive clauses.

[5] *how you are.*   [6] *be in ignorance (about you).*   [7] For case see **349.**

[8] *make good use of.*   [9] Ablative of place (**343**).   [10] *take exercise.*

[11] The precise meaning is revealed by **tamen.**

[12] *learn something new.* Note the emphasis on the prefix **ad.**

[13] Descriptive clause (**380**).

[14] *i.e.* youth and middle age as opposed to **extrēma,** old age.

extrēma nōbīs impertīre dēbēmus, ut ipsae lēgēs mo-
nent, quae maiōrem annīs[1] ōtiō reddunt. Quandō
mihi licēbit, quandō per aetātem honestum erit imitārī

Fig. 14. Roman Baths at Bath, England

Wherever the Romans went they introduced their elaborate bathing estab-
lishments.

istud pulcherrimae quiētis exemplum? Quandō sēces-
5 sūs[2] meī nōn dēsidiae nōmen sed tranquillitātis ac·
cipient? Valē. (IV. 23)

46.   3.   Sick Folks Are Good Folks

Nūper mē cuiusdam amīcī languor admonuit optimōs
esse nōs, dum īnfirmī sumus. Quem enim īnfirmum
aut avāritia aut libīdō sollicitat? Nōn amōribus
10 servit, nōn appetit honōrēs, opēs neglegit et quantu-

---

[1] Ablative of respect depending on **maiōrem**: *one somewhat advanced
in years.*

[2] Plural: *my retirement.*

lumcumque ut relictūrus satis habet.[1] Tunc deōs,[2] tunc hominem esse sē meminit, invidet nēminī, nēminem mīrātur, nēminem dēspicit ac nē sermōnibus[3] quidem malignīs aut attendit aut alitur : balinea imaginātur[4] et fontēs. Haec summa cūrārum, summa 5 vōtōrum, mollemque[5] in posterum et pinguem, sī contingat ēvādere,[6] hoc[7] est innoxiam beātamque dēstinat vītam. Possum ergō quod plūrimīs verbīs, plūrimīs etiam volūminibus philosophī docēre cōnantur ipse breviter tibi mihique praecipere,[8] ut tālēs esse sānī[9] 10 perseverēmus quālēs nōs futūrōs profitēmur īnfirmī. Valē. (VII. 26)

Vocabulary Drill (1–3). — soleō, nesciō ; voluptās, habitō, agitō ; nūper, admoneō, avāritia, invideō.

47.   4. Friends and Favors

Calestrium Tīrōnem familiārissimē dīligō, et prīvātīs mihi et pūblicīs necessitūdinibus implicitum. Simul mīlitāvimus, simul quaestōrēs Caesaris[10] fuimus.   Ille 15 mē in tribūnātū līberōrum iūre[11] praecessit, ego illum in praetūrā sum cōnsecūtus,[12] cum mihi Caesar annum

---

[1] *he is satisfied with ever so little, as if on the point of giving up (even that).*

[2] Supply esse.

[3] Both dative and ablative, since it depends on both verbs.

[4] *he dreams of.* The daily bath, so important an institution among the Romans, is missed by the sick man ; country life is alluded to by fontēs.

[5] Modifies vītam, object of dēstinat *(promises himself).*

[6] *i.e.* from death.   [7] Cf. id est, English *i.e.*

[8] *lay down a precept which* (quod), explained by the ut clause, namely, *that we should continue,* etc.

[9] *(when) well.*   [10] *Emperor,* as usually in Pliny.

[11] *by the privilege gained through having children.* Men with children had special privileges and exemptions.

[12] *caught up with.*

FIG. 15. THE ANIO RIVER AT TIVOLI

Many Romans had their summer villas near Tibur (Tivoli), in the hills
eighteen miles east of Rome.

remīsisset.[1] Ego in vīllās eius saepe sēcessī, ille in domō
meā saepe convaluit. Hic nunc prō cōnsule[2] prōvinciam Baeticam per Tīcīnum est petītūrus.[3] Spērō,
immō cōnfīdō facile mē impetrātūrum ut ex itinere
5 dēflectat ad tē, sī volēs vindictā[4] līberāre quōs proximē
inter amīcōs manūmīsistī. Nihil est quod[5] vereāris

---

[1] *i.e.* allowed him to hold office a year earlier than the regulations
permitted.

[2] *as proconsul.*   [3] *set out for.*

[4] *by the staff,* i.e. *formally.* Fabatus, to whom Pliny addresses this
letter, had freed some slaves in the presence of witnesses, but citizenship
could be granted them only by a magistrate.

[5] *there is no reason for which you should.* For the mood of **vereāris**
see **380**, of **sit** see **373**.

nē sit hoc illī molestum, cui orbem terrārum circumīre[1]
nōn erit longum meā causā. Proinde nimiam istam
verēcundiam pōne[2] tēque quid velīs cōnsule. Valē.

(VII. 16)

48.   5. A WOMAN OF COURAGE

Angit mē Fanniae valētūdō. Contrāxit hanc dum
assidet[3] Iūniae virginī,[4] sponte prīmum (est enim[5]
affīnis), deinde etiam ex auctōritāte[5] pontificum.
Nam virginēs, cum vī morbī ātriō[6] Vestae cōguntur
excēdere, mātrōnārum cūrae custōdiaeque mandantur.
Quō mūnere[7] Fannia dum sēdulō fungitur, hōc discrīmine implicita est.[8] Īnsident febrēs, tussis incrēscit, [10]
summa maciēs, summa dēfectiō ; animus tantum[9] et
spīritus viget, Helvidiō[10] marītō, Thraseā patre dig-
nissimus ; reliqua lābuntur[11] mēque nōn metū tantum
vērum etiam dolōre cōnficiunt. Doleō enim fēminam
maximam ēripī oculīs cīvitātis, nesciō an aliquid simile [15]
vīsūrīs.[12] Quae castitās illī ! quae sānctitās ! quanta
gravitās ! quanta cōnstantia ! Bis marītum secūta in
exsilium est, tertiō ipsa propter marītum relēgāta.

Eadem quam iūcunda, quam cōmis, quam dēnique
(quod paucīs datum est) nōn minus amābilis quam [20]
veneranda ! Eritne quam posteā uxōribus nostrīs

---

[1] Subject of **erit**.   [2] *lay aside.*   [3] *i.e.* as a nurse.
[4] Supply **Vestālī.**   [5] *by order of.*
[6] The " convent " in which the Vestals lived, near the temple of Vesta.
[7] Depends on **fungitur,** which, like **ūtor,** regularly governs the ablative.
[8] *she contracted this serious illness.* What literally ?
[9] *only.*   [10] For case see **349.**   [11] *her other (powers) are ebbing away.*
[12] *which will perhaps never see any woman like her.* What is the literal
meaning of **nesciō an ?**

ostentāre[1] possīmus? erit ā quā virī[2] quoque fortitūdinis exempla sūmāmus, quam sīc cernentēs audien-
tēsque mīrēmur ut illās[3] quae leguntur?

In hīs eram[4] cūrīs cum scrīberem ad tē; quās sī
5 deus aliquis in gaudium verterit, dē metū nōn querar.
Valē. (VII. 19)

49. 6. The Pen Is Mightier than the Hunting Sword

Rīdēbis, et licet rīdeās.[5] Ego ille quem nōstī[6]
aprōs trēs et quidem pulcherrimōs cēpī. " Ipse? "[7]

Fig. 16. A Boar Hunt
From an ancient sarcophagus.

---

[1] *point out*, as a model.

[2] In apposition with **nōs**, the implied subject of **sūmāmus**.

[3] *as we do those that are read about, i.e.* in the histories. What famous Roman women can you name?

[4] The writer of a letter sometimes put himself in the place of the receiver and used past tenses instead of the present.

[5] The subjunctive (without **ut**) instead of the more common infinitive: *and well you may*. What literally?

[6] Contracted form of **nōvistī**. Such omissions of **vi** in the perfect tenses are very common.

[7] The first **Ipse** is for **Tū ipse**; the second, for **Ego ipse**.

inquis. Ipse ; nōn tamen ut[1] omnīnō ab inertiā meā et quiēte discēderem. Ad rētia[2] sedēbam : erat in proximō nōn vēnā-bulum[3] aut lancea, sed stilus et pugil-lārēs : meditābar[4] aliquid ēnotābam-que, ut, sī manūs vacuās, plēnās tamen cērās[5] reportārem. Nōn est quod[6] con-temnās hoc studendī genus. Mīrum est ut[7] animus agitāti-ōne mōtūque corpo-ris excitētur. Iam undique silvae et sōlitūdō ipsumque illud silentium quod vēnātiōnī datur magna cōgitātiōnis incitāmenta sunt. Proinde cum vēnā-

FIG. 17. DIANA

---

[1] (*in such a way*) *that.*

[2] The method of hunting referred to is that of " beating " (cf. " beat about the bush "), in which the animal is driven toward a central spot. Nets were used to prevent escape from the circle.

[3] *hunting spear,* for thrusting.

[4] *I was composing;* no doubt he means verse, or possibly a speech. He prided himself on both. This verb is often used in the sense of *practice, i.e.* doing a thing over and over.

[5] *notebooks;* lit., *wax.* The **pugillārēs** were covered with wax.

[6] *There is no reason why you should.* For subjunctive see **380.**

[7] *how.*

bēre,[1] licēbit, auctōre[2] mē, ut[3] pānārium[4] et laguncu-
lam[5] sīc etiam pugillārēs ferās. Experiēris nōn Diā-
nam[6] magis montibus quam Minervam iner-
5 rāre. Valē. (I. 6)

Read Johnston, section 391.

Vocabulary Drill (4–6). — necessitūdō, praetūra, vīllā; virgō, morbus, discrīmen, lābor (*verb*); pulcher, inertia, sedeō.

50. 7. VACATION TIME

Bene est mihi, quia tibi bene est. Habēs uxōrem tēcum, habēs fīlium; fruēris[7] marī, 10 fontibus, viridibus,[8] agrō, vīlla amoenissimā. Neque enim dubitō esse amoenissimam, in quā sē composuerat homō 15 fēlīcior[9] ante quam fēlī-

FIG. 18. MINERVA

In art Minerva is regularly represented as the goddess of war.

---

[1] Future, second person singular.
[2] Ablative absolute: *on my authority.*
[3] With **sīc:** *not only . . . but also.* What literally?
[4] *lunch basket.*   [5] *bottle of wine.*
[6] Diana was the goddess of hunting, Minerva of wisdom.
[7] This verb, like **ūtor** and **fungor,** takes the ablative.
[8] Used substantively: *green things* (grass, trees, etc.).
[9] This is thought to refer to the emperor Nerva, who was happier

cissimus fieret. Ego in Tuscīs[1] et vēnor et studeō,[2] quae interdum alternīs,[3] interdum simul faciō, nec tamen adhūc possum prōnūntiāre utrum sit difficilius capere aliquid an scrībere. Valē. (V. 18)

51. Word Study

Review the prefixes ad-, con-, dē-, dis-, ex-, in-, in-(negative), re- (411).

Find three examples of each in Selections 1–7. Give English derivatives from as many as you can.

Note the intensive force of the prefix in cōnficiō (do "up"), convalēscō, incrēscō. Point out five examples of assimilation.

52. 8. SEE ITALY FIRST

Ad quae[4] nōscenda iter ingredī, trānsmittere mare 5 solēmus, ea sub oculīs posita neglegimus, seu quia ita nātūrā comparātum[5] ut proximōrum[6] incūriōsī longinqua sectēmur, seu quod omnium rērum cupīdō languēscit cum facilis occāsiō,[7] seu quod differimus tamquam saepe vīsūrī quod datur[8] vidēre quotiēns velīs[9] cernere. 10

---

before he became emperor, a position which, according to popular opinion, made him the happiest of men. Pliny's thought may be compared with the saying: "Uneasy lies the head that wears a crown."

[1] *on my Tuscan estate* (in the mountains).

[2] Cf. the preceding letter.   [3] Supply **vicibus**: *alternately*.

[4] The antecedent is **ea**: *those things to learn which.*

[5] Supply **est**: *we are so constituted.* What literally?

[6] Substantive; depends on **incūriōsī**.

[7] *i.e.* for satisfying it. Supply **est**.

[8] *it is possible.* What literally?

[9] The subjunctive is often used in place of the indicative when the subject is the indefinite second person singular (" you " in the sense of " one ")

Quācumque dē causā, permulta in urbe nostrā iūxtāque
urbem nōn oculīs modo[1] sed nē auribus quidem nōvi-
mus, quae sī tulisset Achaia, Aegyptus, Asia aliave
quaelibet mīrāculōrum ferāx terra, audīta, perlēcta,
5 lūstrāta habērēmus.[2]

Ipse certē nūper quod nec audieram ante nec vīderam
audīvī pariter et vīdī. Exēgerat prōsocer[3] meus ut
Amerīna praedia sua īnspicerem. Haec[4] perambulantī mihi ostenditur subiacēns lacus nōmine Vadimō-
10 nis; simul quaedam incrēdibilia nārrantur. Pervēnī
ad ipsum.[5] Nūlla in hōc nāvis (sacer enim), sed
innatant īnsulae, herbidae omnēs harundine et iuncō.[6]
Interdum iūnctae cōpulātaeque et continentī similēs
sunt, interdum discordantibus ventīs dīgeruntur, nōn
15 numquam dēstitūtae[7] tranquillitāte singulae fluitant.
Saepe minōrēs maiōribus velut cumbulae[8] onerāriīs
adhaerēscunt, saepe inter sē maiōrēs minōrēsque quasi
cursum certāmenque dēsūmunt.

Haec tibi scrīpsī quia nec minus ignōta quam mihi nec
20 minus grāta crēdēbam. Nam tē quoque, ut mē, nihil
aequē ac[9] nātūrae opera dēlectant.[10] Valē. (VIII. 20)

53. 9. The Fate of a Cruel Master

Rem atrōcem nec tantum epistulā[11] dignam Larcius
Macedo, vir praetōrius, ā servīs suīs passus est, super-

---

[1] For nōn modo nōn: *not only not . . . but not even.*

[2] Almost like the English perfect tense formed with *have: we would
have heard of them,* etc. For the mood see **390,** II.

[3] *my wife's grandfather.*   [4] Object of **perambulantī.**

[5] *i.e.* la**cum.**   [6] *reeds and rushes.*

[7] *sometimes becalmed.* What literally?   [8] *small boats.*

[9] *as,* the usual meaning after **aequē** and similar words.

[10] Agrees with **opera** instead of **nihil.**   [11] Ablative with **dignam.**

bus alioquī[1] dominus et saevus et quī servīsse patrem
suum parum,[2] immō nimium meminisset.[3] Lavābātur
in vīllā Formiānā : repente eum servī circumsistunt :
alius faucēs invādit, alius ōs verberat, alius pectus et
ventrem contundit ; et cum exanimem putārent, 5
abiciunt in fervēns pavīmentum,[4] ut experīrentur an
vīveret. Ille, sīve quia nōn sentiēbat, sīve quia sē
nōn sentīre simulābat, immōbilis et extentus fidem
perāctae mortis implēvit.[5] Tum dēmum quasi aestū
solūtus[6] effertur, excipiunt servī fidēliōrēs, concubīnae 10
cum ululātū et clāmōre concurrunt. Ita et vōcibus
excitātus et recreātus locī frīgore, sublātīs[7] oculīs
agitātōque corpore, vīvere sē (et iam tūtum erat)
cōnfitētur.[8] Diffugiunt servī ; quōrum magna pars
comprehēnsa est, cēterī requīruntur. Ipse paucīs 15
diēbus aegrē focilātus nōn sine ultiōnis sōlāciō dēces-
sit, ita vīvus vindicātus ut occīsī solent. Vidēs quot
perīculīs, quot contumēliīs, quot lūdibriīs sīmus obnoxiī.[9] (III. 14)

Read Johnston, sections 129–175.

Vocabulary Drill (7–9). — quia, fruor, interdum ; longinquus,
tamquam, quotiēns, auris, exigō, certāmen ; atrōx, tantum,
serviō, dominus, parum.

[1] *to be sure.*

[2] Parum is contrasted with nimium and modifies meminisset. The
thought is that Larcius' own slave ancestry should have made him more
lenient, but it worked the other way.

[3] Note how this descriptive clause is coördinate with descriptive
adjectives.

[4] In the hot room of the bath.

[5] *confirmed the belief that he was actually dead.* What literally?

[6] *suffocated.*

[7] *raising, i.e.* opening (ablative absolute).

[8] *reveals.*   [9] *exposed to.*

54.   10.   A Kind-Hearted Master

Videō quam molliter tuōs habeās;[1] quō[2] simplicius tibi cōnfitēbor quā indulgentiā meōs trāctem.   Est mihi semper in animō hoc nostrum[3] " pater 5 familiae."[4]   Quod sī essem[5] nātūrā asperior et dūrior, frangeret[6] mē tamen īnfirmitās lībertī meī Zōsimī, cui 10 tantō maior hūmānitās exhibenda est, quantō[7] nunc illā[8] magis eget. Homō probus, officiōsus, litterātus; et ars 15 quidem eius et quasi īnscrīptiō[9] comoedus, in quā plūrimum facit. Nam prōnūntiat[10] ācriter, sapienter, aptē, de 20 center etiam; ūtitur et

Fig. 19.   Apollo with Cithara

[1] *treat your (servants).*

[2] Ablative of measure of difference: *all the more frankly.*

[3] *this (expression of) ours.*

[4] The older form **pater familiās** is still used in English.   In this sense the **familia** included the slaves.

[5] Contrary to fact condition (**390**, II).

[6] Cf. the expression " to be all broken up."   Freed slaves often remained in the service of the former master.

[7] With **tantō**: *all the more since.*   Cf. Note 2.   [8] For case see **327.**

[9] *his label, so to speak,* like the label on a bottle or book, or perhaps the tag placed on a slave offered for sale.   Supply **est.**

[10] *he speaks, enunciates.*

citharā perītē, ultrā quam comoedō necesse est. Īdem
iam commodē ōrātiōnēs et historiās et carmina legit ut
hoc sōlum didicisse videātur.

Haec tibi sēdulō exposuī, quō[1] magis scīrēs quam
multa ūnus mihi et quam iūcunda ministeria praestāret. 5
Accēdit longa iam cāritās hominis, quam ipsa perīcula
auxērunt. Est enim ita nātūrā comparātum ut nihil
aequē amōrem incitet et accendat quam carendī metus,[2]
quem ego prō hōc nōn semel[3] patior. Nam ante
aliquot annōs, dum intentē īnstanterque prōnūntiat, 10
sanguinem reiēcit,[4] atque ob hoc in Aegyptum missus
ā mē, post longam peregrīnātiōnem cōnfirmātus rediit
nūper. Deinde dum per continuōs diēs nimis imperat[5]
vōcī, veteris īnfirmitātis tussiculā[6] admonitus, rūrsus
sanguinem reddidit. Quā ex causā dēstināvī eum 15
mittere in praedia tua quae Forō Iūlī[7] possidēs. Audīvī enim tē saepe referentem esse ibi et āera salūbrem
et lac eius modī cūrātiōnibus[8] accommodātissimum.
Rogō ergō scrībās[9] tuīs ut illī vīlla, ut domus pateat,
offerant[10] etiam sūmptibus eius sī quid opus erit ; 20
erit autem opus modicō.[11] Est enim tam parcus et
continēns ut nōn sōlum dēliciās vērum etiam necessi-
tātēs valētūdinis frūgālitāte restringat. Ego pro-

---

[1] See **369**.   [2] *the fear of losing.*   [3] *i.e.* more than once.

[4] He evidently had tuberculosis.   [5] *put a strain upon.*   [6] *a slight cough.*

[7] **Forum Iūlī** is the name of a city, now Fréjus, in southern France.
It is just west of what is now known as the Riviera, a stretch of coast
famous for its mild winter climate.

[8] Milk and sunshine still constitute the favorite treatment for tuberculosis.

[9] For mood see **370**.

[10] The subject is implied from **tuīs**, the object is the **sī** clause
(= *whatever*) ; **sūmptibus** is ablative of price : *at his expense.*

[11] Supply **sūmptū** ; for the case see **338**.

ficīscentī[1] tantum viāticī dabō quantum sufficiat euntī
in tua. Valē. (V. 19)

55.   11. ABUSE OF THE SECRET BALLOT[2]

Scrīpseram tibi verendum esse nē ex tacitīs suffrāgiīs
vitium   aliquod   exsisteret.   Factum   est.   Proximīs
5 comitiīs in quibusdam tabellīs multa ioculāria atque
etiam foeda dictū,[3] in ūnā vērō prō candidātōrum
nōminibus suffrāgātōrum[4] nōmina inventa sunt.   Excanduit senātus magnōque clāmōre eī quī scrīpsisset[5]
īrātum prīncipem est comprecātus.[6]   Ille tamen fefellit
10 et latuit, fortasse etiam inter indignantēs fuit.   Quid
hunc putāmus domī facere, quī in tantā rē tam sēriō
tempore tam scurrīliter lūdat, quī dēnique omnīnō[7]
in senātū dicāx et urbānus et bellus est?[8]   Tantum
licentiae prāvīs ingeniīs adicit illa fīdūcia " quis enim
15 sciet?"[9]   Poposcit[10] tabellam, stilum accēpit, dēmīsit

---

[1] Supply eī.

[2] Election of magistrates took place in the senate at this time.
Shortly before this the method of voting had been changed from *vivo
voce* to the secret ballot.

[3] The ablative of the supine expresses respect (**405,** *b*).

[4] *supporters, i.e.* those who had nominated or spoken for the candidates.

[5] Why subjunctive?   See **387.**

[6] *invoked the anger of the emperor upon him,* etc.   What literally?

[7] With **in senātū:** *of all places.*   What would Pliny say if he saw two
of our Congressmen actually pommeling each other during an alter-
cation!

[8] Note the shift from subjunctive to indicative.   The descriptive
feeling had faded out when **est** was reached.

[9] The quotation is in apposition with **fīdūcia.**

[10] The subject of these verbs is the man who in jest wrote the wrong
name on the ballot.

caput, nēminem verētur, sē contemnit. Inde ista lūdibria scaenā et pulpitō[1] digna. (IV. 25)

56. Word Study

Review the prefixes **ob-, per-, sub-** (411) and the suffixes **-ānus, -ia** (-tia, etc.), **-iō** (-tiō), **-ium** (-cium), **-tās** (412).

Find three examples of each prefix and suffix in Selections 8–11. Give English derivatives of some of these words.

Give English derivatives of **oculus, auris, patior.**

57. 12. SPRING POEMS AND VERY HUMAN ROMANS

Magnum prōventum[2] poētārum annus hic attulit. Tōtō mēnse Aprīlī nūllus ferē diēs quō nōn recitāret aliquis.[3] Iuvat mē quod vigent studia, prōferunt sē 5 ingenia hominum et ostentant, tametsī ad audiendum pigrē coitur.[4] Plērīque in statiōnibus[5] sedent tempusque audiendī fābulīs conterunt ac subinde sibi nūntiārī[6] iubent an[7] iam recitātor intrāverit, an dīxerit praefātiōnem, an ex magnā parte ēvolverit[8] librum. 10 Tunc dēmum, ac tunc quoque lentē cūnctanterque veniunt; nec tamen permanent, sed ante fīnem recē-

---

[1] *stage.* Our word *pulpit* comes from it. For the construction see **349.**

[2] *crop.*

[3] The custom of reciting one's literary efforts in a private home or a hired hall had become so common as to constitute a nuisance. It was difficult to refuse to attend the recitations of one's friends.

[4] Impersonal: *people assemble.*

[5] *lounging places,* such as the public porticoes, baths, etc.

[6] *i.e.* by their slaves.　　　　　　[7] *whether . . . or.*

[8] *finished.* What literally? Remember that the Roman book was a roll.

dunt, aliī dissimulanter et fūrtim, aliī simpliciter et
līberē. At hercule[1] memoriā parentum Claudium[2]
Caesarem ferunt,[3] cum in Palātiō spatiārētur audīs-
setque clāmōrem,[4] causam requīsīsse, cumque dictum
5 esset recitāre Nōniānum, subitum recitantī inopīnā-
tumque vēnisse. Nunc ōtiōsissimus quisque[5] multō
ante rogātus et identidem admonitus aut nōn venit
aut, sī venit, queritur sē diem, quia nōn perdiderit,
perdidisse. Sed tantō magis laudandī probandīque
10 sunt quōs ā scrībendī recitandīque studiō haec audītō-
rum vel dēsidia vel superbia nōn retardat. Equidem
prope nēminī dēfuī.[6] Erant sānē plērīque amīcī;
neque enim est ferē quisquam quī studia, ut nōn simul
et nōs amet.[7] Hīs ex causīs longius quam dēstināveram
15 tempus in urbe cōnsūmpsī.[8] Possum iam repetere
sēcessum et scrībere aliquid quod nōn recitem,[9] nē
videar, quōrum[10] recitātiōnibus adfuī, nōn audītor
fuisse sed crēditor.[11] Nam ut in cēterīs rēbus ita in
audiendī officiō perit grātia, sī reposcātur. Valē. (I. 13)

Read Johnston, sections 393–398.

---

[1] *by Hercules;* cf. our English expressions "by Jove," "by George."

[2] The emperor Claudius (41–54 A.D.).

[3] *they say.*   [4] *i.e.* in applause.

[5] This idiom is best remembered as the " **optimus quisque** idiom "
(literally, *each best;* freely, *all the best*). What with **ōtiōsissimus**?

[6] *I have failed* (with dative), *i.e.* in attendance on recitations. Pliny
had a real New England conscience.

[7] **amet** belongs to both the **quī** clause and the **ut** clause, which is one
of result.

[8] Note that ordinarily Pliny would go to his summer home as early
as April.

[9] For mood see **380**.   [10] Supply **eōrum** as antecedent.

[11] Mr. A attended the recitations of Mr. B, Mr. C, etc., in order that
they might feel bound to attend his.

Vocabulary Drill (10–12). — trāctō, egeō, ars, quasi, discō; suffrāgium, vitium, exsistō, comitia, tabella; recitō, ingenium, tametsī, liber, tunc, equidem.

58. 13. WEAK EYES BUT GOOD APPETITE

Pāreō, collēga[1] cārissime, et īnfirmitātī oculōrum, ut iubēs, cōnsulō.[2] Nam et hūc tēctō vehiculō undique

FIG. 20. ANCIENT WRITING MATERIALS

Wax tablets, styli, inkwell, and fragment of pottery with Greek spelling exercise.

inclūsus, quasi in cubiculō, pervēnī et hīc nōn stilō modo vērum etiam lēctiōnibus difficulter, sed abstineō[3]

---

[1] They had held office together.

[2] Distinguish the two meanings of cōnsulō: with accusative, *consult;* with dative, *take care of.*

[3] From the English point of view we should expect: lēctiōnibus abstineō (difficulter, sed abstineō).

sōlīsque auribus[1] studeō. Cubicula obductīs vēlīs
opāca nec tamen obscūra faciō. Cryptoporticus[2]
quoque, adopertīs īnferiōribus fenestrīs, tantum um-
brae[3] quantum lūminis habet. Sīc paulātim lūcem
5 ferre condiscō. Balineum assūmō, quia prōdest, vīnum,
quia nōn nocet, parcissimē tamen. Ita assuēvī, et
nunc custōs[4] adest. Gallīnam, ut ā tē missam, libenter
accēpī; quam satis ācribus oculīs, quamquam adhūc
lippus,[5] pinguissimam vīdī. Valē. (VII. 21)

59. 14. There Was Method in His Madness

10 Mīrificae reī nōn interfuistī: nē ego quidem; sed
mē recēns fābula excēpit.[6] Passennus Paulus, splendidus eques Rōmānus et in prīmīs ērudītus, scrībit elegōs.
Gentīlicium[7] hoc illī: est enim mūniceps Propertī[8]
atque etiam inter maiōrēs suōs Propertium numerat.
15 Is cum recitāret, ita coepit dīcere: " Prīsce, iubēs."[9]
Ad hoc Iavolēnus Prīscus (aderat enim, ut[10] Paulō
amīcissimus): " ego vērō nōn iubeō." Cōgitā quī rīsus
hominum, quī iocī. Est omnīnō Prīscus dubiae sānitā-
tis, interest tamen officiīs,[11] adhibētur cōnsiliīs[12] atque

---

[1] *i.e.* he has a slave read to him.   [2] *covered portico.*

[3] For case see **300.**   [4] Presumably the doctor or the nurse.

[5] *half-blind.*   [6] *met me, i.e.* everywhere I went.

[7] *runs in the family.*

[8] An illustrious writer of " elegies " (chiefly love poems in those days)
in the age of Augustus. He was probably born at Assisi, later famous
as the home of St. Francis.

[9] These were the opening words of a poem. The Priscus referred to
by the poet was of course not Javolenus Priscus. The latter was probably tired of the boresome recitations (cf. **57**).

[10] *as being.*

[11] *functions* of all kinds, private and public. For case see **314.**

[12] *consultations* with judges.

etiam iūs cīvīle pūblicē respondet:¹ quō magis quod²
tunc fēcit et rīdiculum et notābile fuit. Interim
Paulō aliēna³ dēlīrātiō aliquantum frīgoris⁴ attulit.
Tam sollicitē recitātūrīs⁵ prōvidendum est nōn sōlum
ut sint⁶ ipsī sānī, vērum etiam ut sānōs adhibeant. 5
Valē. (VI. 15)

60.   15. Rain and Flood

Num⁷ istīc⁸ quoque immīte et turbidum caelum?
Hīc assiduae tempestātēs et crēbra dīluvia. Tiberis
alveum excessit et dēmissiōribus⁹ rīpīs altē super-
funditur. Quamquam fossā,¹⁰ quam prōvidentissimus 10
imperātor fēcit, exhaustus, premit vallēs, innatat
campīs. Vīdērunt¹¹ quōs excelsiōribus terrīs illa tempestās dēprehendit alibi¹² dīvitum apparātūs et gravem
supellectilem,¹³ alibi īnstrūmenta rūris, ibi bovēs,
arātra,¹⁴ rēctōrēs, hīc solūta et lībera armenta, atque 15
inter haec arborum truncōs aut vīllārum trabēs, variē
lātēque fluitantia. Ac nē illa¹⁵ quidem malō¹⁶ vacā-
vērunt ad quae nōn ascendit amnis. Nam prō¹⁷

---

¹ *hands down decisions on the civil law.*
² Supply id as antecedent of **quod** and subject of **fuit.**
³ *i.e.* that of Javolenus.
⁴ *chilly reception, " frost."* For case see **300.**
⁵ Dative; supply **eīs** (**317**).   ⁶ For mood see **370.**
⁷ Introduces a question expecting a negative answer: *you are not
having . . . , are you?*
⁸ *where you are.* Iste and istīc often refer to the second person.
⁹ *lower.*
¹⁰ *canal.* Even to-day, in spite of high embankments, the Tiber
occasionally overflows.
¹¹ The subject is the implied antecedent of **quōs.**
¹² *in some places . . . in others.*   ¹³ *furniture.*
¹⁴ *plows.*   ¹⁵ Supply **loca.**   ¹⁶ For case see **327.**   ¹⁷ *instead of*

amne imber assiduus et dēiectī nūbibus turbinēs,[1]
prōruta opera[2] quibus pretiōsa rūra cinguntur, quas-
sāta atque etiam dēcussa monumenta. (VIII. 17)

Vocabulary Drill (13–15). — collēga, cārus, obscūrus; dubius,
cīvīlis, frīgus; caelum, assiduus, quamquam.

61. 16. Pliny Budgets His Time

Quaeris quem ad modum in Tuscīs[3] diem aestāte
5 dispōnam. Ēvigilō cum libuit, plērumque circā hōram
prīmam,[4] saepe ante, tardius rārō; clausae fenestrae
manent. Mīrē enim silentiō et tenebrīs ab iīs[5] quae
āvocant abductus et līber et mihi relīctus, nōn oculōs
animō sed animum oculīs sequor, quī eadem quae mēns
10 vident, quotiēns nōn vident alia.[6] Notārium vocō et,
diē admissō, quae fōrmāveram dictō; abit rūrsusque
revocātur rūrsusque dīmittitur. Ubi[7] hōra quārta
vel quīnta (neque enim certum dīmēnsumque tempus),
ut diēs suāsit, in xystum[8] mē vel cryptoporticum[9]
15 cōnferō, reliqua meditor et dictō. Vehiculum ascendō.
Ibi quoque idem[10] quod ambulāns aut iacēns. Dūrat
intentiō[11] mūtātiōne ipsā refecta; paulum redormiō,[12]
dein ambulō, mox ōrātiōnem Graecam Latīnamve

---

[1] *cloud-bursts.* Supply **sunt,** as also with the following participles.

[2] *dikes.*   [3] See page 43, note 1.

[4] *i.e.* at daybreak or soon after. The period of daylight was divided
into twelve periods, called " hours," which varied from 45 to 75 minutes
according to the season.

[5] = **eīs (272)**; neuter.

[6] *i.e.* when the eyes are shut the mind does not wander.

[7] Supply the verb.   [8] *terrace.*   [9] *covered portico.*

[10] Supply **faciō** here and in the **quod** clause.

[11] *power of concentration.*

[12] The afternoon siesta, still indulged in in Italy and other southern
countries, especially in hot weather.

clārē et intentē, nōn tam vōcis causā quam stomachī
legō. Pariter tamen et[1] illa firmātur. Iterum ambulō, ungor, exerceor, lavor.[2] Cēnantī mihi, sī cum
uxōre vel paucīs, liber legitur; post cēnam comoedus
aut lyristēs;[3] mox 5
cum meīs[4] ambulō,
quōrum in numerō
sunt ēruditī. Ita
variīs sermōnibus
vespera extendi- 10
tur, et quamquam[5]
longissimus diēs
cito conditur. Nōn
numquam[6] ex hōc
ōrdine aliqua mū- 15
tantur. Nam sī
diū iacuī vel am-
b u l ā v ī , p o s t
somnum dēmum
lēctiōnemque nōn 20
v e h i c u l ō s e d
(quod[7] brevius,
quia vēlōcius) equō
gestor. Interveni-
unt amīcī ex proxi- 25

Fig. 21. A Villa near Rome

An ancient villa garden must have resembled
this modern one at Frascati.

mīs oppidīs partemque diēī ad sē trahunt interdum-
que lassō mihi opportūnā interpellātiōne subveniunt.

---

[1] = etiam, as often in Pliny.
[2] The passive verbs are used in a reflexive sense.
[3] *musician* (nominative).   [4] Supply amīcīs.
[5] *however*, with longissimus.
[6] With nōn: *sometimes*. What literally?
[7] The antecedent is the whole clause · *a thing which is.*

Vēnor aliquandō, sed nōn sine pugillāribus,[1] ut, quamvīs nihil cēperim, nōn nihil[2] referam. Datur et colōnīs,[3] ut vidētur ipsīs, nōn satis temporis, quōrum mihi
agrestēs querēlae litterās[4] nostrās et haec urbāna opera
5 commendant.[5] Valē. (IX. 36)

62. Word Study

Review the prefixes **ab-, inter-, prō- (411)** and the
suffixes **-idus, -īlis, -men, -mentum, -or, -or (-tor),
-ōsus (412)**.

Find three examples of each prefix and two of each
suffix in Selections 12–16. Give English derivatives
of some of these words.

Remember that in compounds short **-a-** or short **-e-**
changes to short **-i-** before a single consonant except **-r-:**
ad-hibeō from **habeō**, **dif-ficilis** from **facilis**, **abs-tineō**
from **teneō**. Similarly **-ae-** changes to long **-ī-** and
-au- to long **-ū-:** **re-quīrō** from **quaerō**, **in-clūdō** from
claudō. Illustrate further from English derivatives of
faciō, quaerō, claudō.

63. 17. Modern Philanthropy in Ancient Rome

Salvum tē in urbem vēnisse gaudeō ; vēnistī autem,
sī quandō aliās,[6] nunc maximē mihi[7] dēsīderātus.
Ipse pauculīs adhūc diēbus[8] in Tusculānō[9] commorā-

---

[1] Cf. **49**.   [2] With **nōn:** *something.* What literally ?
[3] *tenant farmers.*   [4] *literary pursuits.*
[5] *i.e.* make them seem much pleasanter by comparison.
[6] Adverb contrasted with **nunc**.   [7] For case see **317**.
[8] The ablative of time sometimes expresses duration of time.
[9] A country home near Tusculum, fifteen miles south-east of Rome.

bor, ut opusculum quod est in manibus[1] absolvam.
Interim quod[2] sum praesēns petītūrus hāc quasi
praecursōriā[3] epistulā rogō. Sed prius accipe causās

Ewing Galloway, N. Y.

Fig. 22. Lake Como

Pliny's home town, Comum, was on its shores. He had several villas there.

rogandī. Proximē cum in patriā[4] meā fuī, vēnit ad
mē salūtandum mūnicipis[5] meī fīlius praetextātus.[6] Huic ego " studēs? " inquam. Respondit " etiam."[7]

---

[1] *in hand, i.e.* under way. He refers to a literary work, probably a speech.

[2] Supply **id** as antecedent and as object of **rogō**.

[3] Get the meaning of the word from its derivation.

[4] *home town.* Patriotism was more local than national in those days. The town was Comum, on the beautiful Lake Como in northern Italy.

[5] *fellow-townsman.*

[6] The toga praetexta, which had a colored border, was worn by boys before they came of age.

[7] *yes.*

" Ubi? "   " Mediōlānī."[1]   " Cūr nōn hīc? "   Et pater eius (erat enim ūnā[2] atque etiam ipse addūxerat
puerum) " quia nūllōs hīc praeceptōrēs habēmus."
" Quārē nūllōs? nam vehementer intererat vestrā,[3]
5 quī patrēs estis," et opportūnē complūrēs patrēs audiēbant, " līberōs vestrōs hīc potissimum discere. Ubi
enim aut iūcundius morārentur quam in patriā aut
pudicius continērentur quam sub oculīs parentum aut
minōre sūmptū quam domī? Quantulum est ergō,
10 collātā pecūniā, condūcere praeceptōrēs, quodque[4]
nunc in habitātiōnēs, in viātica, in ea quae peregrē
emuntur (omnia autem peregrē emuntur) impenditis
adicere mercēdibus![5] Atque adeō ego, quī nōndum
līberōs habeō, parātus sum prō rē pūblicā nostrā, quasi
15 prō fīliā vel parente, tertiam[6] partem eius quod cōnferre vōbīs placēbit dare. Tōtum etiam pollicērer,[7]
nisi timērem nē hoc mūnus meum quandōque ambitū[8]
corrumperētur, ut accidere multīs in locīs videō, in

---

[1] See **351**. This city (now Milan) was about twenty-five miles from Comum.

[2] Adverb.

[3] *it would be to your interest.* The imperfect indicative is sometimes used for greater vividness instead of the subjunctive in the conclusion of a contrary to fact condition (**390**, II); cf. **morārentur** below. For case **vestrā** see **347**.

[4] Supply **id** as antecedent of **quod** and object of **adicere,** which is the subject of **est.**

[5] *fees.* The money saved by not going to college in another city could be used for the salaries of the professors in a local institution.

[6] What per cent of the total does he offer to pay?

[7] For mood see **390**, II.

[8] *by " pull."* Originally **ambitiō** and **ambitus** had the same meaning, " going around " looking for votes. By a process of differentiation **ambitiō** came to be used of legitimate methods of office seeking and eventually became our word *ambition,* whereas **ambitus** was used of corrupt methods and meant *bribery, " pull."*

quibus praeceptōrēs pūblicē condūcuntur. Huic vitiō occurrī ūnō remediō potest,[1] sī parentibus sōlīs iūs condūcendī relinquātur īsdemque religiō[2] rēctē iūdicandī necessitāte collātiōnis addātur. Nam quī fortasse dē aliēnō[3] neglegentēs, certē dē suō dīligentēs erunt 5 dabuntque operam[4] nē ā mē pecūniam nisi dignus[5] accipiat, sī acceptūrus et[6] ab ipsīs erit. Proinde cōnsentīte, cōnspīrāte, maiōremque animum ex meō sūmite, quī cupiō esse quam plūrimum quod dēbeam[7] cōnferre. Nihil honestius praestāre līberīs vestrīs, 10 nihil grātius patriae potestis. Ēducentur[8] hīc quī hīc nāscuntur statimque ab īnfantiā nātāle solum amāre, frequentāre cōnsuēscant. Atque utinam tam clārōs praeceptōrēs indūcātis[9] ut fīnitimīs oppidīs studia hinc petantur, utque[10] nunc līberī vestrī aliēna in loca, ita 15 mox aliēnī in hunc locum cōnfluant!" (IV. 13)

64.　　　　18. A GENEROUS FEE[11]

Proxima īnfirmitās mea, domine,[12] obligāvit mē Postumiō Marīnō medicō; cui parem grātiam referre beneficiō tuō possum, sī precibus meīs ex cōnsuētūdine bonitātis tuae indulseris. Rogō ergō ut propinquīs 20 eius dēs cīvitātem. (X. 11)

---

[1] Impersonal. In English we would make **vitiō** the subject. For case of **vitiō** see **314**.

[2] *duty.*　　　　　　　　　　[3] *about another's money.*

[4] The idiom **operam dare** is very common: *see to it.*

[5] With **nē . . . nisi:** *only a deserving person.*　　[6] *also.*

[7] For mood see **388**.　　　　[8] From **ēducāre**, not **ēdūcere**.

[9] A wish, as shown by the introductory particle **utinam:** (*I wish*) *that you might* (**376**).　　　　[10] *and as.*

[11] This and the following letters were exchanged by Pliny and Trajan while the former was governor of the province of Bithynia in Asia Minor.　　　　[12] The Emperor Trajan: *Sir.*

Vocabulary Drill (16–18). — tenebrae, suādeō, iaceō, iterum, sermō, querēla; salvus, gaudeō, adhūc, hīc (*adv.*), potissimum; ergō.

65.   19. The Administration of Justice[1]

Meminerīmus[2] idcircō tē in istam prōvinciam missum, quoniam multa in eā ēmendanda appāruerint.

Erit autem hoc vel maximē corrigendum, 5 quod[3] quī damnātī ad poenam erant nōn modo eā[4] sine auctōre, ut scrībis, līberātī sunt, sed etiam in con- 10 diciōnem probōrum ministrōrum retrahuntur. Quī igitur intrā hōs proximōs decem annōs damnātī nec ūllō 15 idōneō auctōre līberātī sunt, hōs oportēbit poenae suae reddī: sī quī[5] vetustiōrēs invenientur et senēs ante 20 annōs decem damnātī, distribuāmus illōs in

Fig. 23. Trajan

---

[1] Pliny had written to Trajan, asking him what to do about criminals who had escaped punishment for the crimes for which they had been convicted, and had even obtained government positions. Modern parallels are not infrequent.

[2] *let us remember* (**366**).   [3] *the fact that.*

[4] Supply **poenā**. For case see **327**.   [5] Meaning? See **275, Note**.

ea ministeria quae nōn longē ā poenā sint. Solent enim eius modī[1] ad balineum, ad pūrgātiōnēs cloācārum,[2] item mūnītiōnēs viārum et vīcōrum darī.

(X. 32)

66. 20. PROPOSED ORGANIZATION OF A FIRE DEPARTMENT

Cum dīversam partem prōvinciae circumīrem, Nīcomēdīae vāstissimum incendium multās prīvātōrum domōs et duo pūblica opera, quamquam viā interiacente, Gerūsian et Īseon,[3] absūmpsit. Est autem lātius sparsum prīmum violentiā ventī, deinde inertiā hominum, quōs satis cōnstat ōtiōsōs et immōbilēs tantī malī spectātōrēs perstitisse; et aliōquī nūllus usquam in pūblicō sīphō,[4] nūlla hama,[5] nūllum dēnique īnstrūmentum ad incendia compescenda. Et haec quidem, ut iam praecēpī, parābuntur. Tū, domine, dispice an īnstituendum putēs[6] collēgium[7] fabrōrum dumtaxat[8] hominum CL. Ego attendam nē quis nisi faber recipiātur nēve iūre[9] concessō in aliud[10] ūtātur; nec erit difficile custōdīre tam paucōs. (X. 33)

---

[1] Supply **hominēs.** [2] *sewers.*

[3] Greek accusative forms, because the chief language of the province was Greek, and Pliny naturally lapses into it: *the Old Men's Home and the Temple of Isis.*

[4] *fire engine* (nominative). What English derivative?

[5] *bucket.* [6] For mood see **386.**

[7] *brigade.* [8] *only.* [9] For case see **337.**

[10] *for any other purpose.* This indicates why the question was referred to the emperor. Elsewhere it was common practice to have regular fire departments, but the unsettled political condition of this province made it unwise to allow the formation of any associations or groups which might become the center of political intrigue. The law forbade clubs of all kinds.

67.   21. Trajan's Disapproval

Tibi quidem secundum[1] exempla complūrium in mentem venit posse collēgium fabrōrum apud Nīcomēdēnsēs cōnstituī. Sed meminerīmus prōvinciam istam et praecipuē eās cīvitātēs eius modī factiōnibus esse 5 vexātās. Quodcumque nōmen ex quācumque causā dederimus iīs quī in idem[2] contrāctī fuerint, hetaeriae[3] brevī fīent. Satius itaque est comparārī ea quae ad coercendōs ignēs auxiliō esse possint admonērīque dominōs praediōrum ut et ipsī inhibeant, ac sī rēs 10 poposcerit, accursū[4] populī ad hoc ūtī. (X. 34)

Vocabulary Drill (19–21). — meminī, idcircō, damnō; usquam, attendō; praecipuē, vexō.

68.   22. Graft in Public Contracts

In aquaeductum, domine, Nīcomēdēnsēs impendērunt HS x̅x̅x̅ cccxviii,[5] quī imperfectus adhūc relīctus atque etiam dēstrūctus est; rūrsus in alium ductum ērogāta[6] sunt c̅c̅.[7] Hōc quoque relīctō, novō impendiō[8] est 15 opus, ut aquam habeant quī tantam pecūniam male perdidērunt. Ipse pervēnī ad fontem pūrissimum, ex quō vidētur aqua dēbēre perdūcī, sīcut initiō temptātum

---

[1] Preposition : *following.*

[2] *for a common purpose.*   [3] *political clubs.*

[4] *i.e.* the spectators were to be appealed to for help. Ordinarily that efficient administrator Trajan would have favored so excellent a plan as the organization of a fire department. His rejection of the plan shows how much fear he had of political clubs.

[5] HS stands for **sēstertiī** (*sesterces*, worth about five cents each). The " box " around xxx shows that this represents hundred thousands; the line above the rest indicates thousands. The total, therefore, is 3,318,000, about $165,000.

[6] *spent.*

[7] 200,000 sesterces.   How many dollars?   [8] For case see **338.**

erat, arcuātō[1] opere, nē tantum[2] ad plāna cīvitātis[3] et humilia perveniat. Manent adhūc paucissimī arcūs; possunt et ērigī quīdam lapide quadrātō, quī ex superiōre opere dētrāctus est; aliqua pars, ut mihi vidētur,

FIG. 24. THE CLAUDIAN AQUEDUCT NEAR ROME

testāceō opere[4] agenda erit; id enim et facilius et[5] vīlius. Et in prīmīs necessārium est mittī ā tē vel aquilegem[5] vel architectum, nē rūrsus ēveniat quod

---

[1] *of arches*, the type familiar to us from remains near Rome and elsewhere.

[2] *only.* The Romans knew that water seeks its level, but the use of cement-lined conduits on top of arches instead of on or under the ground reduced the "ups and downs" and thus kept down the leakage and had other advantages. Pliny seems not to be aware of the real facts.

[3] = **urbis**, like the English derivative. With **plāna** and **humilia** supply **loca.**

[4] *brick work.*   [5] *hydraulic engineer.*

accidit. Ego illud ūnum affirmō, et ūtilitātem operis et pulchritūdinem saeculō[1] tuō esse dignissimam. (X. 37)

69. 23. Trajan's Reply

Cūrandum est ut aqua in Nīcomēdēnsem cīvitātem perdūcātur. Vērē crēdō tē eā quā dēbēbis dīligentiā 5 hoc opus aggressūrum. Sed medius fidius[2] ad eandem dīligentiam tuam pertinet inquīrere quōrum vitiō ad hoc tempus tantam pecūniam Nīcomēdēnsēs perdiderint, nē, cum inter sē grātificantur, et inchoāverint aquaeductūs et relīquerint.[3] Quid itaque compererīs 10 perfer in nōtitiam meam. (X. 38)

70. **Word Study**

Review the prefixes **bene-, circum-, prae-** (**411**) and the suffixes **-ālis, -ārius, -icus, -ilis** (**412**).

Find examples of each in Selections 17–23 and give English derivatives.

Verbs that are derived from nouns or adjectives are called denominatives. Most of them belong to the first conjugation : **cūrō** (**cūra**), **līberō** (**līber**). Give the nouns or adjectives from which the following are derived : **cōnfirmō, labōrō, spērō, pācō.**

---

[1] For case see **349.**

[2] *most certainly;* derived from **meus deus Fidius** (cf. **fidēs**). Cf. the English " my word ! " The usually calm and practical Trajan becomes excited by Pliny's tale of graft. It is familiar enough to American readers. Almost any day a similar story of graft may be found in the newspapers.

[3] *so that they will not keep on beginning and abandoning aqueducts while doing favors to one another, i.e.* by " fixing things." The exceptional use of the perfect subjunctive in purpose clauses is due to the attraction of **perdiderint.**

71.　24. Happy Birthday — and Many of Them!

Optō, domine, et hunc nātālem et plūrimōs aliōs quam fēlīcissimōs agās aeternāque laude flōrentem virtūtis tuae glōriam incolumis et fortis aliīs super alia operibus[1] augeās.　(X. 88)

72.　25. Thanks!

Agnōscō vōta tua, mī Secunde[2] cārissime, quibus 5 precāris ut plūrimōs et fēlīcissimōs nātālēs flōrente statū reī pūblicae[3] nostrae agam.　(X. 89)

Vocabulary Drill (22–25). — perdō; optō, aeternus; flōreō.

73.　26. Help for a Thirsty City

Sinōpēnsēs, domine, aquā dēficiuntur;[4] quae vidētur et bona et cōpiōsa ab sextō decimō mīliāriō[5] posse perdūcī.　Est tamen statim ab capite[6] paulō amplius 10 mīlle passibus locus suspectus et mollis, quem ego interim explōrārī modicō impendiō iussī, an recipere et sustinēre opus[7] possit.　Pecūnia, cūrantibus nōbīs, contrācta[8] nōn deerit, sī tū, domine, hoc genus operis et salūbritātī et amoenitātī valdē sitientis colōniae 15 indulseris.　(X. 90)

---

[1] *by one accomplishment on top of another.*

[2] Pliny's full name was C. Plinius Caecilius Secundus.

[3] Pliny's good wishes had been for Trajan's personal welfare; Trajan accepts them as applying to the state.

[4] *are short of.*

[5] *milestone, i.e.* from a distance of sixteen miles.

[6] *at the source.*　　　　[7] *i.e.* the arches of an aqueduct.

[8] *collected through my efforts.*

74. 27. Approved

Ut coepistī, Secunde cārissime, explōrā dīligenter
an locus ille quem suspectum habēs sustinēre opus
aquaeductūs possit. Neque enim dubitandum putō
quīn[1] aqua perdūcenda sit in colōniam Sinōpēnsem,
5 sī modo id vīribus[2] suīs assequī potest, cum plūrimum
ea rēs et salūbritātī et voluptātī eius collātūra sit.

(X. 91)

75. 28. The Problem of the Christians[3]

Sollemne est mihi, domine, omnia dē quibus dubitō
ad tē referre. Quis enim potest melius vel cūnctā-
tiōnem meam regere vel ignōrantiam īnstruere? Cog-
10 nitiōnibus dē Chrīstiānīs interfuī numquam; ideō
nesciō quid et quātenus[4] aut pūnīrī soleat aut quaerī.
Nec mediocriter haesitāvī sitne[5] aliquod discrīmen
aetātum an quamlibet[6] tenerī nihil ā rōbustiōribus
differant, dētur paenitentiae venia an eī quī omnīnō
15 Chrīstiānus fuit dēsīsse[7] nōn prōsit, nōmen[8] ipsum, sī flāgitiīs[9] careat, an flāgitia cohaerentia nōminī pūniantur.

---

[1] *that* (372). [2] *resources.* The subject of **potest** is **colōnia.**
[3] This is one of Pliny's most famous letters. His difficulty with the
Christians was due to the law against clubs (see **66**) and the refusal of
the Christians to take the oath of allegiance to the emperor. To the
Romans this seemed treason. Yet Pliny and Trajan realized that many
of those who called themselves Christians were innocent of wrongdoing.
But the law was the law, and to allow flagrant violations of it was to
encourage those whose motives were not so innocent. Pliny and
especially Trajan deserve praise for their attempt to be lenient.
[4] *to what limits.* [5] For the double indirect questions see **386,** *a.*
[6] Adverb modifying **tenerī:** *the very young.*
[7] From **dēsinō;** subject of **prōsit.**
[8] *i.e.* of Christian. The question was whether a man was to be
punished for being a Christian or for the crimes which he committed.
[9] For case see **327.**

Pliny's Attempts to Handle the Situation

Interim in iīs quī ad mē tamquam Chrīstiānī dēferē-
bantur hunc sum secūtus modum. Interrogāvī ipsōs
an essent Chrīstiānī. Cōnfitentēs iterum ac tertiō interrogāvī, supplicium minātus : perseverantēs dūcī[1] iussī.
Neque enim dubitābam. quālecumque esset[2] quod 5
fatērentur, pertināciam certē et īnflexibilem obstinā-
tiōnem[3] dēbēre pūnīrī. Fuērunt aliī similis āmentiae
quōs, quia cīvēs Rōmānī erant, adnotāvī[4] in urbem
remittendōs.

The Problem Becomes More Complicated

Mox ipsō trāctātū,[5] ut fierī solet, diffundente sē 10
crīmine, plūrēs speciēs incidērunt.[6] Prōpositus est
libellus sine auctōre[7] multōrum nōmina continēns.
Quī negābant esse sē Chrīstiānōs aut fuisse, cum,
praeeunte mē,[8] deōs appellārent et imāginī tuae, quam
propter hoc iusseram cum simulācrīs nūminum afferrī, 15
tūre ac vīnō supplicārent,[9] praetereā maledīcerent[10]
Chrīstō, quōrum nihil posse cōgī dīcuntur[11] quī sunt

---

[1] *i.e.* to punishment (death).   [2] *no matter what the thing was.*

[3] To Pliny it was incomprehensible that people should persist in calling themselves Christians when the one word " No " would save them
from death.

[4] *i.e.* on the record of the case. Roman citizens could appeal to
Rome. In the age of Nero the apostle Paul, who was a Roman citizen,
went to Rome for trial (Acts XXV, 11).

[5] *in the mere handling (of the cases).*

[6] *various types came to light.*   [7] With **sine:** *anonymously.*

[8] Ablative absolute : *as I recited (the formula).*

[9] To Pliny this was merely an act of patriotism, like taking off one's
hat when the flag passes ; to the Christians it was, of course, idolatry.

[10] *reviled.*

[11] *none of which things, it is said, they can be forced (to do) who,* etc.

rē vērā Chrīstiānī, dīmittendōs[1] esse putāvī. Aliī ab
indice nōminātī esse sē Chrīstiānōs dīxērunt et mox
negāvērunt : fuisse quidem, sed dēsīsse, quīdam ante
triennium, quīdam ante plūrēs annōs, nōn nēmō[2]
5 etiam ante vīgintī. Hī quoque omnēs et imāginem
tuam deōrumque simulācra venerātī sunt et Chrīstō
maledīxērunt. Affirmābant autem hanc fuisse summam vel culpae suae vel errōris, quod essent solitī
statō diē[3] ante lūcem convenīre carmenque Chrīstō
10 quasi deō dīcere sēcum in vicem,[4] sēque sacrāmentō
nōn in scelus aliquod obstringere, sed nē fūrta, nē
latrōcinia, nē adulteria committerent,[5] nē fidem
fallerent, nē dēpositum appellātī[6] abnegārent ; quibus
perāctīs, mōrem sibi discēdendī fuisse, rūrsusque
15 coeundī ad capiendum cibum,[8] prōmiscuum tamen
et innoxium ;[9] quod ipsum facere dēsīsse post ēdictum
meum, quō, secundum mandāta tua, hetaeriās[10] esse
vetueram. Quō magis[11] necessārium crēdidī ex duābus
ancillīs, quae ministrae[12] dīcēbantur, quid esset vērī et[13]

---

[1] Modifies eōs, the implied antecedent of quī (in preceding line).

[2] With nōn: *some*.   [3] *i.e.* Sunday.   [4] *responsively.*

[5] Substantive clause depending upon sacrāmentō obstringere.

[6] *on demand.* The mention of this matter in the present context
seems rather strange to us and may indicate that repayment of a loan
was less common than to-day. This would account in part for the
high rates of interest then current.

[7] Gerund or future passive participle? How do you know?

[8] The early Christian " love feast."

[9] *common and harmless.* The Christians were charged with eating
human flesh and drinking the blood of children.

[10] *clubs* (see **67**).   [11] *all the more.*

[12] As the language of the country was Greek, he means this as a translation of the Greek word διακόνισσαι (diakonissai) from which " deaconess " is derived.

[13] = etiam.

per tormenta¹ quaerere. Nihil aliud invēnī quam superstitiōnem prāvam, immodicam.

In Despair Pliny Appeals to the Emperor

Ideō dīlātā cognitiōne, ad cōnsulendum tē dēcurrī. Vīsa est enim mihi rēs digna cōnsultātiōne,² maximē propter perīclitantium numerum. Multī enim omnis 5 aetātis, omnis ōrdinis, utrīusque sexūs etiam, vocantur in perīculum et vocābuntur. Neque cīvitātēs³ tantum sed vīcōs etiam atque agrōs superstitiōnis istīus contāgiō pervagāta est; quae vidētur sistī et corrigī posse. Certē satis cōnstat prope iam dēsōlāta templa coepisse 10 celebrārī et sacra sollemnia diū intermissa repetī pāstumque venīre⁴ victimārum, cuius adhūc rārissimus ēmptor inveniēbātur. Ex quō facile est opīnārī quae turba hominum ēmendārī possit, sī sit paenitentiae locus. (X. 96) 15

Vocabulary Drill (27–28). — assequor; pūniō, venia, dēsinō, prōsum, flāgitium, careō, minor, fateor, crīmen, imāgō, vīnum, index, culpa, fūrtum, latrōcinium.

76. ### 29. Action Approved

Āctum⁵ quem dēbuistī, mī Secunde, in excutiendīs⁶ causīs eōrum quī Chrīstiānī ad tē dēlātī fuerant secūtus

---

¹ This was used only on slaves.   ² See **349.**   ³ *cities.*

⁴ From **vēneō:** *is being sold, is in demand.* The demand for animals for sacrifice and for feed created an important market for the farmers. The spread of Christianity lessened the demand to such an extent that many farmers were threatened with ruin.

⁵ *procedure.*

⁶ *investigating;* literally *shaking out,* as one shakes a garment to see what is concealed in it. How did " discuss " come to have its present meaning?

es. Neque enim in ūniversum[1] aliquid quod quasi certam fōrmam habeat cōnstituī potest. Conquīrendī nōn sunt; sī dēferantur et arguantur, pūniendī sunt, ita tamen ut quī negāverit sē Chrīstiānum esse idque

5 rē ipsā manifestum fē-
cerit, id est suppli-
candō dīs nostrīs,
quamvīs suspectus in
praeteritum,[2] veniam
10 ex paenitentiā impe-
tret. Sine auctōre
vērō prōpositī libellī in
nūllō crīmine[3] locum
habēre dēbent. Nam
15 et pessimī exemplī[4]
nec nostrī saeculī est.
(X. 97)

Fig. 25. Trajan

77. Word Study

Verbs of the first conjugation ending in -tō (-sō) or -itō express repeated action and are called frequentatives. They are formed from other verbs, usually from the past participle: **haesitō** (**haereō**), *keep on sticking, hesitate;* **dictō** (**dīcō**), *keep on saying, dictate;* **ostentō** (**ostendō**), *keep on showing, show off.* Many English words are derived from frequentatives. Give the simple and frequentative forms of the verbs from which the following are derived: *habitation, incessant, spectator, agitation, visitation.*

---

[1] With **in**: *in general.*   [2] *in the past.*   [3] *charges.*
[4] *precedent.* The genitives are in the predicate; **nec** = et nōn.

78. 30. ROMAN GEOMETRY[1]

Figūrārum, quae σχήματα[2] geōmetrae appellant, genera sunt duo, plānum et solidum. Plānum est quod[3] in duās partīs[4] sōlum līneās habet, quā[5] lātum est et quā longum; quālia sunt triquetra et quadrāta, quae in āreā fīunt, sine altitūdine. Solidum est quandō[5] nōn longitūdinēs modo et lātitūdinēs plānās[6] numerī līneārum efficiunt, sed etiam extollunt altitūdinēs. Līnea autem ā nostrīs dīcitur quam γραμμὴν[7] Graecī nōminant. Eam M. Varrō ita dēfīnit: " Līnea est," inquit, " longitūdō quaedam sine lātitūdine et altitū- 10 dine." Εὐκλείδης[8] autem brevius, praetermissā altitūdine: " γραμμή,[9] " inquit, " est μῆκος ἀπλατές."[10]

(I. 20)

79. Word Study

Make up a list of English words used in geometry which are derived from the Latin words in Selection 30. Name some other English geometrical terms which are derived from Latin.

---

[1] Selections 30 to 46 are from Aulus Gellius (cf. **43**).

[2] **schēmata** in Latin letters. What English derivative? For the Greek alphabet see **256**.

[3] *that which.*

[4] Accusative plural: *directions.*

[5] Adverb.

[6] *in a plane.*

[7] **grammēn;** accusative (nominative, **grammē**). The literal meaning is *writing.* What derivative in English?

[8] **Eukleidēs** (**Euclīdēs**), *Euclid,* subject of **dīxit** understood. A celebrated professor of mathematics at Alexandria about 280 B.C. His book is the basis of the geometry which you have studied.

[9] **grammē,** as above.

[10] *breadthless length,* as it were.

80. 31. A Snake Story

Tūberō in historiīs scrīptum relīquit, bellō prīmō
Poenicō[1] Atīlium Rēgulum[2] cōnsulem in Āfricā,
castrīs apud Bagradam flūmen positīs, proelium grande[3]
atque ācre fēcisse adversus ūnum serpentem in illīs
5 locīs stabulantem[4] invīsitātae immānitātis,[5] eumque
magnā tōtīus exercitūs cōnflīctiōne ballistīs[6] atque
catapultīs[6] diū oppugnātum,[7] eiusque interfectī corium[8]
longum pedēs[9] centum et vīgintī Rōmam mīsisse. (VII. 3)

81. 32. The Quarrel of the Grammarians

Dēfessus ego quondam diūtinā commentātiōne[10]
10 laxandī levandīque animī grātiā in Agrippae campō[11]
ambulābam. Atque ibi duōs forte grammaticōs cōn-
spicātus nōn parvī[12] in urbe Rōmā nōminis, certātiōnī[13]
eōrum ācerrimae adfuī, cum alter in cāsū vocātīvō 'vir
ēgregī' dīcendum contenderet, alter 'vir ēgregie.'
15 Ratiō autem eius quī 'ēgregī' oportēre dīcī cēnsē-
bat huiusce[14] modī fuit: "Quaecumque," inquit,
"nōmina seu vocābula rēctō[15] cāsū numerō singulārī

---

[1] 264-241 b.c.

[2] This is the famous Regulus who, after being sent with an embassy
from Carthage to effect an exchange of prisoners, despite the entreaties
of the Romans, returned to Carthage and met a horrible death.

[3] *long.* [4] *which had an abode.* [5] With **serpentem.**

[6] Can you describe these from their use in Caesar?

[7] Supply **esse.** [8] *hide.* What does the English *excoriate* mean?

[9] Accusative of extent with **longum.** [10] *continued study.*

[11] At the edge of the Campus Martius, north of the Capitoline Hill.
Agrippa was one of Augustus' chief generals and advisers.

[12] *of no small reputation.* [13] For case see **314.**

[14] A stronger form of **huius.**

[15] *nominative,* the "upright" case, as opposed to the "oblique"
cases.

' us ' syllabā fīniuntur, in quibus ante ultimam syllabam posita est ' i ' littera, ea omnia cāsū vocātīvō ' i '
litterā terminantur, ut ' Caelius-Caelī,' ' modius-modī,'
' tertius-tertī,' ' Accius-Accī,' ' Titius-Titī ' et similia
omnia ; sīc igitur ' ēgregius,' quoniam ' us ' syllabā in 5
cāsū nōminandī fīnītur eamque syllabam praecēdit ' i '
littera, habēre dēbēbit in cāsū vocandī ' i ' litteram
extrēmam et idcircō ' ēgregī,' nōn ' ēgregie,' rēctius
dīcētur."

Hoc ubi ille alter audīvit, " ō," inquit, " ēgregie 10
grammatice vel, sī id māvīs, ēgregissime, dīc, ōrō
tē, ' īnscius ' et ' impius ' et ' sōbrius ' et ' ēbrius ' et
' proprius ' et ' propitius ' et ' ānxius ' et ' contrārius,'
quae ' us ' syllabā fīniuntur, in quibus ante ultimam
syllabam ' i ' littera est, quem cāsum vocandī habent? 15
Mē enim pudor et verēcundia tenent[1] prōnūntiāre ea
secundum[2] tuam dēfīnitiōnem." Sed cum ille paulisper
oppositū[3] hōrum vocābulōrum commōtus reticuisset
et mox tamen sē collēgisset[4] eandemque illam quam
dēfīnierat rēgulam[5] retinēret et prōpugnāret, eaque 20
inter eōs contentiō longius dūcerētur, nōn arbitrā-
tus ego operae pretium[6] esse eadem istaec diūtius
audīre, clāmantēs compugnantēsque illōs relīquī.[7]

(XIV. 5)

Vocabulary Drill (29–32). — manifestus, quamvīs, exemplum ;
quālis, quandō ; quondam, lĕvō, igitur, rēctē, proprius, pudor,
pretium.

---

[1] *prevent me from.*   [2] Preposition.   [3] *hostile array.*
[4] *had regained his composure.*   What literally?
[5] *rule.*   [6] With **operae**: *worth while.*   What literally?
[7] Can you mention a point in English grammar about which there is
a difference of opinion?

82.   Word Study

Make up a list of English words used in grammar
which are derived from the Latin words in Selection
32. Name some other English grammatical terms
which are derived from Latin.

83. 33. THE HORSE THAT BROUGHT BAD LUCK

Gāvius Bassus in commentāriīs suīs, item Iūlius
Modestus in secundō[1] quaestiōnum cōnfūsārum his-
toriam dē equō Seiānō trādunt dignam memoriā[2]
atque admīrātiōne: Gnaeum Seium quempiam[3] scrībam
5 fuisse eumque habuisse equum nātum Argīs in terrā
Graeciā, dē quō fāma cōnstāns[4] esset tamquam dē
genere equōrum prōgenitus foret[5] quī Diomēdis[6]
Thrācis fuissent, quōs Herculēs, Diomēde occīsō, ē
Thrāciā Argōs[7] perdūxisset. Eum equum fuisse dīcunt
10 magnitūdine invīsitātā, cervīce arduā, colōre poeniceō,[8]
flōrā et comantī iubā,[9] omnibusque aliīs equōrum laudibus[10] quoque longē praestitisse; sed eundem equum
tālī fuisse fātō[11] sīve fortūnā[11] ferunt,[12] ut, quisquis habēret[13] eum possidēretque, is cum omnī domō, familiā,

---

[1] Supply librō.   [2] For case see **349.**
[3] = quendam.   [4] *persistent.*
[5] = esset: *that* (lit., *as if*) *it was descended from.*
[6] Predicate genitive of possession : *which had belonged to.* Hercules
slew Diomedes in battle after he had stolen the latter's horses as his
eighth labor in the service of Eurystheus.
[7] For case see **320.**
[8] *deep-red.* So called from the dye extracted by the Phoenicians
(**Poeni**) from a shell-fish.
[9] *a shining, long-haired mane.*
[10] *all other good qualities of horses.*   [11] Ablative of description.
[12] *they say.* It is also understood with the following sentence.
[13] For the subjunctive see **388.**

fortūnīsque omnibus suīs ad intern[e]ciōnem dēperīret. Itaque prīmum illum Gnaeum Seium, dominum eius, ā M. Antōniō, quī posteā triumvirum[1] reī pūblicae cōnstituendae fuit, capitis[2] damnātum, miserandō suppliciō affectum esse; eōdem tempore Cornēlium [5] Dolābellam cōnsulem in Syriam proficīscentem[3] fāmā istīus equī adductum[3] Argōs dēvertisse cupīdineque habendī eius exārsisse ēmisseque eum sēstertiīs centum mīlibus; sed ipsum quoque Dolābellam in Syriā bellō cīvīlī obsessum atque interfectum esse; mox eundem [10] equum,[4] quī Dolābellae[5] fuerat, C. Cassium, quī Dolābellam obsēderat, abdūxisse. Eum Cassium posteā satis nōtum est, victīs partibus[6] fūsōque exercitū suō, miseram mortem oppetīsse, deinde Antōnium post interitum Cassī, partā[7] victōriā, equum illum [15] nōbilem Cassī requīsīsse et, cum eō[8] potītus esset, ipsum quoque posteā victum atque dēsertum, dētestābilī[9] exitiō interīsse. Hinc prōverbium dē hominibus calamitōsīs: " ille homō habet equum Seiānum."

Eadem sententia est illīus quoque veteris prōverbī [20] quod ita dictum accēpimus: " aurum Tolōsānum."[10] Nam cum oppidum Tolōsānum in terrā Galliā Quīntus Caepiō cōnsul dīripuisset multumque aurī in eius oppidī templīs fuisset, quisquis ex eā dīreptiōne aurum attigit miserō cruciābilīque exitū periit. (III. 9) [25]

---

[1] *was (one) of the triumvirs for,* etc. This was the formal title of power conferred upon Octavian, Antony, and Lepidus in 43 B.C.

[2] *condemned to death;* genitive of the punishment (307).

[3] Do not translate as participles.

[4] Object of abdūxisse.   [5] Dative of possessor (316).

[6] *party;* the so-called Liberators, slayers of Caesar, who were defeated by Octavian and Antony at Philippi in 42 B.C.

[7] From pariō.   [8] For case see 337.

[9] *ignominious* rather than *detestable.*   [10] Tolosa is now called Toulouse.

84. **34.** THE FIRST PUBLIC LIBRARY

Librōs[1] Athēnīs disciplīnārum[2] līberālium pūblicē ad legendum praebendōs[3] prīmus posuisse dīcitur Pīsistratus tyrannus. Deinceps studiōsius accūrātiusque ipsī Athēniēnsēs auxērunt;[4] sed omnem illam posteā librō-

FIG. 26. THE FORUM OF TRAJAN AS IT WAS

The low building at the right is one of the two public libraries, Greek and Latin, built by Trajan. The tall building is a court house. At the left is a temple.

5 rum cōpiam Xerxēs,[5] Athēnārum[6] potītus, urbe ipsā praeter arcem incēnsā, abstulit[7] asportāvitque in Persās. Eōs porrō librōs ūniversōs multīs post tempestātibus[8]

---

[1] Why placed first? Note carefully the order of the entire sentence.
[2] = **artium,** depending on **Librōs.**   [3] With **Librōs**: *to be offered.*
[4] From **augeō.** Supply **librōs** as object.
[5] The Persian king who invaded Greece in 480 B.C.
[6] With **potītus;** for the more usual ablative.
[7] From **auferō.**
[8] An old and poetic substitute for **annīs.** How do you account for the case? See **341.**

Seleucus rēx, quī Nīcānor appellātus est, referendōs Athēnās cūrāvit.[1]

Ingēns posteā numerus librōrum in Aegyptō ab Ptolemaeīs rēgibus vel conquīsītus vel cōnfectus[2] est ad mīlia fermē volūminum septingenta ; sed ea omnia 5 bellō priōre[3] Alexandrīnō, dum dīripitur ea cīvitās, nōn sponte neque operā cōnsultā,[4] sed ā mīlitibus forte auxiliāriīs incēnsa sunt.   (VII. 17)

Vocabulary Drill (33–34). — quaestiō, cervīx, tālis, fātum, quisquis, possideō, exitium, hinc, templum ; legō (-ere), arx, auferō.

85.   35. The Origin of the Ring Finger

Veterēs Graecōs ānulum habuisse in digitō accē-pimus[5] sinistrae manūs quī[6] minimō est proximus. 10 Rōmānōs quoque hominēs aiunt sīc plērumque ānulīs ūsitātōs.[7]   Causam esse huius reī Āpiōn in librīs Aegyptiācīs[8] hanc[9] dīcit, quod, īnsectīs apertīsque hūmānīs corporibus, ut mōs in Aegyptō fuit, quās Graecī ἀνατομὰς[10] appellant, repertum est nervum quen- 15 dam tenuissimum ab eō ūnō digitō dē quō dīximus ad cor hominis pergere ac pervenīre ; proptereā nōn īnscītum[11] vīsum esse eum potissimum digitum tālī honōre[12] decorandum.   (X. 10)

---

[1] *arranged to be brought back.*

[2] *written, i.e.* copied from other manuscripts.

[3] 48 B.C.   [4] *by deliberate effort.*   [5] *I have heard.*

[6] How do you know that the antecedent is not **manūs**?

[7] = **solitōs esse ūtī (337)**.   [8] The title of Apion's book.

[9] Predicate to **causam.**   The **quod** clause is in apposition.

[10] **anatomās ;** lit., *cutting up.*   Use the English derivative in trans-lating.   For the Greek alphabet see **256.**

[11] With **nōn :** *sensible.*   [12] *i.e.* with the ring.

86.   36. The Cipher Code of Julius Caesar

Librī sunt epistulārum C. Caesaris ad C. Oppium
et Balbum Cornēlium, quī rēbus eius absentis cūrābant.[1]
In hīs epistulīs quibusdam[2] in locīs inveniuntur litterae
singulāriae, quās tū putēs[3] positās inconditē;[4] nam
5 verba ex hīs litterīs cōnficī nūlla possunt. Erat autem
conventum inter eōs clandestīnum dē commūtandō
sitū litterārum, ut in scrīptō quidem alia aliae[5] locum
et nōmen tenēret, sed in legendō locus[6] cuique suus et
potestās[7] restituerētur; quaenam vērō littera prō quā
10 scrīberētur, ante[8] īs,[9] sīcutī dīxī, placēbat quī hanc
scrībendī latebram[10] parābant. Est adeō Probī gram-
maticī commentārius satis cūriōsē factus dē occultā
litterārum significātiōne in epistulārum C. Caesaris
scrīptūrā. (XVII. 9)

87.   37. Senatorial Procedure

15 Ante lēgem quae nunc dē senātū habendō[11] obser-
vātur, ōrdō rogandī[11] sententiās varius fuit. Aliās[12]
prīmus rogābātur quī prīnceps ā cēnsōribus[13] in senātum

---

[1] Takes the dative: *looked after the affairs.*

[2] Modifies **locīs.**

[3] *one would think.* The subjunctive is used in subordinate clauses
when the indefinite second person singular is used.

[4] *at random.*   [5] Genitive singular (rare form).

[6] *position.*   [7] *force.*   [8] Adverb.

[9] = **eīs.** Dative with **placēbat**; it is the antecedent of **quī.**

[10] *this secret code of writing.* The historian Suetonius (second century A.D.) states that Caesar transposed the letters of words by writing
d for *a, e* for *b*, etc. Try a code of this sort.

[11] Gerund or future passive participle?

[12] **aliās . . . aliās:** *at one time . . . at another.*

[13] For their duties see **116.**

lēctus fuerat, aliās quī dēsignātī[1] cōnsulēs erant; quīdam ē cōnsulibus, studiō aut necessitūdine aliquā adductī, quem[2] īs vīsum erat honōris grātiā extrā ōrdinem sententiam prīmum rogābant.[3] Observātum[4]

Fig. 27. Roman Senators
(From "Julius Caesar.")

tamen est, cum extrā ōrdinem fieret, nē quis quemquam 5 ex aliō quam[5] ex cōnsulārī locō sententiam prīmum

---

[1] Elected, but awaiting the opening of their term of office. Since they would be intrusted with the responsibility of carrying out a measure when in office, their opinions were sought first.

[2] *whomever it seemed best to them* (īs = eīs).

[3] Imperfect of customary action.

[4] *care was taken.* Its subject is the nē clause.

[5] *than* (with aliō)

rogāret. C. Caesar in cōnsulatū,[1] quem cum M. Bibulō gessit, quattuor sōlōs extrā ōrdinem rogāsse sententiam dīcitur. Ex hīs quattuor prīncipem rogābat M. Crassum; sed postquam fīliam Cn. Pompeiō 5 dēsponderat, prīmum coeperat Pompeium rogāre.

Eius reī[2] ratiōnem reddidisse eum[3] senātuī Tīrō[4] Tullius, M. Cicerōnis lībertus, refert, itaque sē ex patrōnō suō audīsse scrībit. Id ipsum Capitō Ateius in librō quem dē officiō senātōriō composuit scrīptum 10 relīquit.

In eōdem librō Capitōnis id quoque scrīptum est: " C.," inquit, " Caesar cōnsul M. Catōnem sententiam rogāvit. Catō rem, quae cōnsulēbātur, quoniam nōn ē rē pūblicā[5] vidēbātur, perficī[6] nōlēbat. Eius 15 reī dūcendae[7] grātiā longā ōrātiōne ūtēbātur[8] eximēbatque[9] dīcendō diem. Erat enim iūs senātōrī, ut sententiam rogātus dīceret[10] ante quicquid vellet aliae reī[11] et quoad vellet. Caesar cōnsul viātōrem[12] vocāvit eumque, cum fīnem nōn faceret, prēndī loquentem[13] et 20 in carcerem dūcī iussit. Senātus cōnsurrēxit[14] et

---

[1] 59 B.C.   [2] *procedure.*   [3] Caesar.

[4] Cicero's secretary, a man of high accomplishment. He was the inventor of a system of shorthand writing. We owe to him the preservation, arrangement, and publication of part of Cicero's correspondence.

[5] *for the public good.*   [6] With **rem**: *motion to be carried.*

[7] *dragging out.*   [8] *delivered.*

[9] An imperfect of attempted action: *tried to,* etc. What do you know about the cloture rule in the United States Senate? How much like the Roman practice is that of the United States?

[10] *talk first on any other subject he wished.*

[11] Genitive of the whole with **quicquid; aliae** is an unusual genitive form.

[12] *messenger,* a sort of sergeant-at-arms.

[13] *in the midst of his speech.*

[14] From **cōnsurgō.** What is the force of the prefix here?

prōsequēbātur Catōnem in carcerem. "Hāc," inquit,[1]
" invidiā factā,[2] Caesar dēstitit et mittī[3] Catōnem
iussit." (IV. 10)

Vocabulary Drill (35–37). — aiō, hūmānus, tenuis ; quisquam ;
varius, cēnsor, cōnsulātus, carcer, invidia.

88. 38. THE MORE YOU GET, THE MORE YOU WANT

Vērum est[4] profectō, quod, observātō rērum ūsū,[5]
sapientēs virī dīxēre,[6] multīs[7] egēre[8] quī multa habeat,[9] 5
magnamque indigentiam nāscī nōn ex inopiā magnā,
sed ex magnā cōpiā : multa enim dēsīderārī ad multa
quae habeās tuenda. Quisquis igitur multa habēns
cavēre atque prōspicere velit, nē quid egeat[10] nēve quid
dēsit,[10] iactūrā opus esse,[11] nōn quaestū. (IX. 8)   10

89.   Word Study

Review the suffixes **-āris, -īnus, -īvus, -tūdō, -ūra**
(**412**).

Find examples of each in selections 30–38 and give
English derivatives.

---

[1] Capitō is subject.

[2] *Owing to the indignation thus aroused.*

[3] *to be set free.*

[4] Supply **id** as subject and as antecedent of **quod.**

[5] With **rērum** : *the way things go,* i.e. *life.*

[6] = **dīxērunt.**   [7] Why not **multa** ? See **327.**

[8] Supply **eum** as subject and as antecedent of **quī.**

[9] There are two reasons for this mood (**380, 387**).

[10] Volitive substantive clause, object of **prōspicere.** **Nēve** is regularly
used for **et nē.**

[11] *needs* (with ablative). The infinitive depends on **dīxēre** of
line 2.

90. 39. Bitter Enemies Sometimes Become Warm Friends

P. Āfricānus superior et Tiberius Gracchus, Tiberiī et C. Gracchōrum pater, rērum gestārum magnitūdine et honōrum atque vītae dignitāte illūstrēs virī, dissēn-sērunt saepe numerō[1] dē rē pūblicā et eā[2] sīve quā aliā 5 rē nōn amīcī fuērunt. Ea simultās cum diū mānsisset et sollemnī diē[3] epulum Iovī lībārētur atque ob id sacrificium senātus in Capitōliō epulārētur, fors fuit ut apud eandem mēnsam duo illī iūnctim[4] locārentur.[5] Tum, quasi diīs immortālibus arbitrīs in conviviō Iovis 10 optimī maximī[6] dextrās eōrum condūcentibus,[7] repente amīcissimī factī. Neque sōlum amīcitia incepta, sed affīnitās simul īnstitūta ; nam P. Scīpiō fīliam virginem habēns iam virō mātūram,[8] ibi tunc[9] eōdem in locō dēspondit eam Tiberiō Gracchō.

15 Aemilius quoque Lepidus et Fulvius Flaccus, nōbilī genere amplissimīsque honōribus ac summō locō in cīvitāte praeditī, odiō inter sēsē gravī et simultāte diūtinā cōnflīctātī sunt. Posteā populus eōs simul cēnsōrēs[10] facit. Atque illī, ubi vōce praecōnis renūn-20 tiātī sunt,[11] ibīdem in campō[12] statim, nōndum dīmissā

---

[1] With **saepe** = **saepissimē**.   [2] *for that or for some other reason.*

[3] On September 13, the anniversary of the founding of the Capitoline temple.

[4] *side by side.*   [5] For mood see **379 ; fors est** = **accidit.**

[6] As these adjectives are commonly used together as epithets of the Jupiter worshiped in this temple, no conjunction is used.

[7] *joining;* ablative absolute with **diīs**. Use a clause : *as if the gods . . . had joined their hands.*

[8] With **virō :** *of a marriageable age.*

[9] *then and there.*   [10] For their duties see **116.**

[11] *i.e.* when the result of the election was announced to the people.

[12] The Campus Martius, where the elections took place.

cōntiōne, ultrō uterque[1] et paiī voluntāte coniūnctī complexīque sunt, exque eō diē et in ipsā cēnsūrā et posteā iūgī[2] concordiā fīdissimē amīcissimēque vīxērunt. (XII. 8)

91.   40. TELEVISION

Quō[3] C. Caesar et Cn. Pompeius diē per cīvīle bellum 5 signīs collātīs[4] in Thessaliā cōnflīxērunt, rēs accidit Patavī in Trānspadānā Italiā memorārī[5] digna. Cornēlius quīdam sacerdōs, et nōbilis et sacerdōtiī[6] religiōnibus venerandus et castitāte vītae sānctus, repente, mōtā mente,[7] cōnspicere sē procul dīxit pugnam ācerrimam 10 pugnārī, ac deinde aliōs cēdere, aliōs urgēre, caedem, fugam, tēla volantia, īnstaurātiōnem[8] pugnae, impressiōnem,[9] gemitūs, vulnera, proinde ut[10] sī ipse in proeliō versārētur, cōram vidēre sēsē vōciferātus est ac posteā subitō exclāmāvit Caesarem vīcisse. (XV. 18)   15

Vocabulary Drill (38–40). — profectō, caveō, quaestus; illūstris, convīvium, praeditus, cōntiō, concordia; sacerdōs, sānctus, urgeō, proinde.

92. 41. SCIENTIA LINGUĀRUM EST POTESTĀS

Quīntus Ennius tria corda habēre sēsē dīcēbat, quod loquī Graecē et Oscē[11] et Latīnē scīret.   Mithridātēs

---

[1] In apposition with illī (line 19).

[2] Ablative of the adjective iūgis: *permanent.*

[3] = eō diē quō.

[4] With cōnflīxērunt: *engiged in battle.* What literally?

[5] A poetic use of the infinitive with **digna.**

[6] *office.*   [7] *in an inspired moment.*

[8] *renewal.* The nouns are objects of **vidēre,** as are the preceding infinitives.

[9] *charge.*   [10] *as.*

[11] Oscan was a language related to Latin, spoken in southern Ita y

autem, Pontī atque Bithyniae rēx inclutus, quī ā Cn. Pompeiō bellō superātus est, quīnque et vīgintī gentium quās sub diciōne habuit linguās percalluit[1] eārumque omnium gentium virīs haud umquam[2] per interpretem
5 collocūtus est, sed ut[3] quemque ab eō appellārī ūsus[4] fuit, proinde linguā et ōrātiōne ipsīus nōn minus scītē quam sī gentīlis[5] eius esset,[6] locūtus est. (XVII. 17)

93. 42. A BARGAIN IN SECOND-HAND BOOKS

Cum ē Graeciā in Italiam redīrēmus et Brundisium īrēmus ēgressīque ē nāvī in terram in portū illō inclutō
10 spatiārēmur, fascēs[7] librōrum vē-
nālium expositōs vīdimus.
Atque ego avidē statim pergō ad
librōs. Erant autem istī omnēs
librī Graecī mīrāculōrum fābulā-
15 rumque plēnī, rēs inaudītae, in-
crēdulae,[8] scrīptōrēs veterēs nōn
parvae auctōritātis. Ipsa autem
volūmina ex diūtinō sitū[9] squā-
lēbant et habitū aspectūque
20 taetrō erant. Accessī tamen
percontātusque pretium sum et,
adductus mīrā atque īnspērātā vīlitāte, librōs plūrimōs
aere paucō emō eōsque omnīs[10] duābus proximīs noctibus cursim[11] trānseō; atque in legendō carpsī exinde

FIG. 28. FASCIS LIBRŌRUM

---

[1] *knew well.* From **percalleō**. [2] With **haud = numquam**.
[3] *when.* [4] = **opus**. [5] *fellow countryman.*
[6] For mood see **390**, II.

[7] *bundles.* It should be remembered that the Roman **liber** was rolled like a scroll. Note **volūmina** below.

[8] = **incrēdibilēs**. [9] *lying about.* [10] Accusative plural.
[11] *hastily.* From **currō**, *run*. He read them *on the run*.

ʠuaedam et notāvī mīrābilia et scrīptōribus[1] ferē nostrīs intemptāta.

Erant igitur in illīs librīs scrīpta huiusce[2] modī: Scythās illōs penitissimōs, quī sub ipsīs septentriōnibus aetātem agunt, corporibus[3] hominum vēscī et ἀνθρωπο- 5 φάγουs[4] nōminārī; item esse hominēs sub eādem regiōne caelī[5] ūnum oculum in frontis mediō habentēs, quī appellantur Arimaspī, quā fuisse faciē Cyclopas poētae ferunt;[6] aliōs item esse hominēs apud eandem caelī plagam[7] singulāriae vēlōcitātis, vēstīgia pedum 10 habentēs retrō porrēcta, nōn, ut cēterōrum hominum,[8] prōrsum spectantia; praetereā trāditum esse memorātumque, in ultimā quādam terrā, quae Albānia[9] dīcitur, gignī hominēs quī in pueritiā cānēscant[10] et plūs cernant oculīs per noctem quam interdiū; item esse 15 compertum et crēditum Sauromatās, quī ultrā Borysthenēn[11] flūvium longē colunt, cibum capere semper diēbus tertiīs,[12] mediō abstinēre.

Id etiam in īsdem librīs scrīptum offendimus, quod posteā in librō quoque Plīniī Secundī[13] nātūrālis his- 20

---

[1] Dative of agent, with the perfect participle.

[2] A stronger form of huius.

[3] Ablative depending on vēscī (337).

[4] anthrōpophāgous, man-eaters, accusative. What English derivatives from anthrōpos? For the Greek alphabet see 256.

[5] With regiōne: latitude.

[6] of the same appearance which poets say the Cyclopes had.

[7] Like regiōne above.   [8] Supply vēstīgia.

[9] Not modern Albania, but a country near the Caspian Sea.

[10] whose hair turns white. Why subjunctive? See 380.

[11] Accusative (Greek form). It is now called the Dnieper.

[12] every other day. The Romans counted the first and last day of the period reckoned. Hence not two days, but one intervened.

[13] The older Pliny, who lost his life during the eruption of Vesuvius in 79 A.D.

toriae septimō lēgī, esse quāsdam in terrā Āfricā
hominum familiās vōce atque linguā effascinantium,[1]
quī[2] sī impēnsius forte laudāverint pulchrās arborēs,
segetēs laetiōrēs,[3] īnfantēs amoeniōrēs,[4] ēgregiōs equōs,
5 pecudēs pāstū atque cultū opīmās, ēmoriantur repente
haec omnia. (IX. 4)

Vocabulary Drill (41–42). — haud; avidus, plēnus, notō,
penitus, vēstīgium, colō, laetus.

94. 43. A Roman Always Keeps His Word

Iūs iūrandum apud Rōmānōs inviolātē sānctēque
habitum servātumque est. Id et mōribus lēgibusque
multīs ostenditur, et hoc quod dīcēmus eī reī nōn
10 tenue[5] argūmentum esse potest. Post proelium Can-
nēnse Hannibal, Carthāginiēnsium imperātor, ex cap-
tīvīs nostrīs ēlēctōs[6] decem Rōmam mīsit mandāvitque
eīs pactusque[7] est, ut, sī populō Rōmānō vidērētur,[8]
permūtātiō fieret captīvōrum. Hoc, priusquam prō-
15 ficīscerentur, iūs iūrandum eōs adēgit,[9] reditūrōs esse in
castra Poenica, sī Rōmānī captīvōs nōn permūtārent.

Veniunt Rōmam decem captīvī. Mandātum Poenī
imperātōris in senātū expōnunt. Permūtātiō senātuī
nōn placita. Parentēs, cognātī, affīnēsque captīvōrum
20 amplexī[10] eōs postlīminiō[11] in patriam redīsse dīcēbant

---

[1] *working spells.*

[2] Introduces **ēmoriantur** but is subject of **laudāverint:** *if they . . .
then all these things,* etc.

[3] *bountiful.*   [4] *charming.*

[5] *no slight.* An example of litotes, *i.e.* instead of affirming a thing,
to deny the opposite.   [6] Translate as if **ēlēgit et.**   [7] From **pacīscor.**

[8] *seemed best.* Why subjunctive? See **388.**

[9] *forced upon them.*   [10] From **amplector.**

[11] *by the recovery of their civil rights,* according to law.

statumque eōrum integrum incolumemque esse, ac nē
ad hostēs redīre vellent ōrābant. Tum octō ex hīs
postlīminium iūstum nōn esse sibi[1] respondērunt, quoniam dēiūriō[2] vīnctī[3] forent, statimque, uti iūrātī
erant, ad Hannibalem profectī sunt. Duo reliquī 5
Rōmae mānsērunt solūtōsque esse sē ac līberātōs
religiōne[4] dīcēbant, quoniam, cum ēgressī[5] castra
hostium fuissent, commenticiō[6] cōnsiliō regressī eōdem,
tamquam sī ob aliquam fortuitam causam, īssent atque
ita iūre iūrandō satisfactō rūrsum iniūrātī[7] abīssent. 10
Haec eōrum fraudulenta calliditās tam esse turpis
exīstimāta est ut contemptī vulgō discerptīque[8] sint,
cēnsōrēsque eōs posteā et damnīs et ignōminiīs af-
fēcerint, quoniam, quod factūrōs dēierāverant, nōn
fēcissent.[9]   15
Cornēlius autem Nepōs[10] in librō exemplōrum
quīntō id quoque litterīs mandāvit, multīs in senātū
placuisse ut hī quī redīre nōllent,[11] datīs custōdibus,[12]
ad Hannibalem dēdūcerentur, sed eam sententiam
numerō plūrium,[13] quibus id nōn vidērētur, superātam ; 20
eōs[14] tamen quī ad Hannibalem nōn redīssent usque
adeō invīsōs fuisse ut taedium vītae cēperint[15]
necemque sibi cōnscīverint. (VI. 18)

---

[1] With iūstum.   [2] *by an oath.*   [3] From vinciō ; forent = essent.
[4] *obligation;* ablative of separation.
[5] Transitive, as if relīquissent ; fuissent is for essent.
[6] *feigned.*   [7] *freed from the oath.*
[8] *criticized;* lit., *torn to pieces;* from discerpō. For sequence see 378 (*b*).
[9] Why subjunctive? See 389.
[10] A friend of Cicero, author of Dē Virīs Illūstribus.
[11] Subjunctive by attraction (388).
[12] *under guard.* What literally?   [13] With numerō : *majority.*
[14] The indirect discourse is continued.
[15] *became weary of life.* What literally?

95. ## Word Study

The suffix -**ēnsis** (-**iēnsis**) is attached chiefly to names of towns in order to form adjectives : **Athēn-iēnsis.** Find two examples in the preceding selection. In English it has the form -*ese* and is used freely : *Bosıon-ese, Pekin-ese.*

The Latin word **religiō** is said to be derived from **ligō,** *bind.* This literal meaning is well illustrated in the preceding selection. It then came to mean *religious restraints,* or *scruples.*

Distinguish **liber, līber, lībra** and their derivatives. From **liber** we have *library;* from **līber,** *liberal;* from **lībra,** the abbreviation *lb.* (first letter of each syllable) for *pound,* and the abbreviation £ for *pound sterling.*

96. 44. THE TRUE MEANING OF CULTURE

Quī verba Latīna fēcērunt quīque hīs[1] probē[2] ūsī sunt, hūmānitātem[3] nōn id esse voluērunt quod vulgus exīstimat quodque ā Graecīs φιλανθρωπία[4] dīcitur et significat dexteritātem[5] quandam benevolentiamque 5 ergā omnīs hominēs prōmiscuam, sed hūmānitātem appellāvērunt id propemodum[6] quod Graecī παιδείαν[7] vocant, nōs ērudītiōnem īnstitūtiōnemque in bonās artīs dīcimus. Quās[8] quī sincēriter cupiunt appetuntque, hī sunt vel[9] maximē hūmānissimī. Huius

---

[1] Supply **verbīs.**   [2] *correctly.*

[3] The English order is **nōn voluērunt** (*i.e.* **putāvērunt**) **hūmānitātem esse id quod,** etc.

[4] **philanthrōpia.** The prefix **phil-** means *loving;* **anthrōpos,** *man.*

[5] *willingness* (to do a good turn or favor).   [6] *very nearly.*

[7] **paideian,** a Greek accusative ending for the Latin -**am.** The same stem is seen in English *pedagogy.*   [8] Translate as if **Hī quī hās.**

[9] Strengthens **maximē :** *in the highest degree.*

enim scientiae cūra et disciplīna ex ūniversīs animanti-
bus ūnī hominī data est idcircōque hūmānitās appellāta
est.

Sīc igitur eō verbō veterēs[1] esse ūsōs et cum prīmīs[2]
M. Varrōnem[3] Mārcumque Tullium,[4] omnēs fermē librī 5
dēclārant. (XIII. 17)

97. 45. Christmas Dinner in a Foreign Country

Sāturnālia[5] Athēnīs agitābāmus[6] hilarē prōrsum ac
modestē.[7] Conveniēbāmus autem ad eandem cēnam
complūsculī,[8] quī Rōmānī in Graeciam vēnerāmus
quīque eāsdem audītiōnēs eōsdemque doctōrēs colē- 10
bāmus. Tum quī et cēnulam ōrdine[9] suō cūrābat
praemium solvendae quaestiōnis pōnēbat, librum[10]
veteris scrīptōris vel Graecum vel Latīnum et corōnam
ē laurō plexam, totidemque rēs quaerēbat quot hominēs
istīc erāmus; cumque eās omnīs exposuerat, rem lo- 15
cumque dīcendī sors dabat.[11] Quaestiō igitur solūta
corōnā et praemiō dōnābātur,[12] nōn solūta autem trā-
mittēbātur ad eum quī sortītō successerat. (XVIII. 2)

---

[1] *the ancients.*   [2] With **cum**: *especially.*

[3] The most learned of Roman scholars; a contemporary of Cicero.

[4] *i.e.* Cicero, the orator.

[5] An important festival held in December. Some of its customs
have survived in our Christmas festivities.

[6] *we used to spend.*

[7] *right merrily but with decency.* Gellius' restraint need not be interpreted to apply to all Romans.   [8] *a good many (of us).*

[9] Each diner, it seems, took his turn in managing the dinner.

[10] In apposition with **praemium.**

[11] *determined the subject and order of speaking.*

[12] He means, of course, that the person answering the question received the prize.

Vocabulary Drill (43–45). — argūmentum, parēns, patria, solvó, ignōminia, nex; benevolentia, ērudītiō. appetō, dēclārō: sors.

98.   46. A Matter of No Importance

Mīra et prope adeō[1] rīdicula dīversitās fābulae apud Graecōs poētās dēprēnditur[2] super[3] numerō Niobae[4] fīliōrum.

Nam Homērus puerōs
5 puellāsque eius bis
sēnōs[5] dīcit fuisse,
Euripidēs[6] bis septē-
nōs, Sapphō[7] bis no-
vēnōs, Bacchylidēs et
10 Pindarus[8] bis dēnōs,
quīdam aliī scrīptōrēs
trēs fuisse sōlōs dīxē-
runt. (XX. 7)

99. Word Study

Find English deriv-
atives of the Greek
word roots in Selec-
tions 30–46.

Fig. 29. Homer

---

[1] *actually almost.*   [2] *is noted.*   [3] *about.*

[4] The story of Niobe and her children will be found in **205**. Many ancient scholars interested themselves in and quarreled over such trifling matters as that discussed here.

[5] Distributive numeral: *six each.*

[6] An Athenian of the fifth century B.C., one of the world's greatest tragic poets.

[7] A Greek poetess of the seventh century B.C.

[8] These two were lyric poets of the fifth century B.C.

100. 47. Lucky Fortunata[1]

Uxor Trimalchiōnis Fortūnāta appellātur, quae nummōs modiō mētītur. Et modo, modo[2] quid fuit?
Nōluissēs[3] dē manū illīus pānem accipere. Nunc, nec
quid nec quāre,[4] in caelum[5] abiit et Trimalchiōnis
topanta[6] est. Ad summam, merō[7] merīdiē sī dīxerit 5
illī tenebrās esse, crēdet.[8] Ipse nescit quid habeat,
adeō sāplūtus[9] est; sed haec lupatria[10] prōvidet omnia
et ubi nōn putēs. Est sicca, sōbria, bonōrum cōnsiliōrum, est tamen malae linguae. Quem amat, amat;
quem nōn amat, nōn amat. (37)   10

101. 48. The Disadvantages of Wealth[11]

Plānē interpellāvit saltātiōnis libīdinem āctuārius,
quī tamquam urbis ācta[12] recitāvit: " VII Kalendās[13]

---

[1] Selections 47–51 are taken from a novel written by Petronius during
the reign of Nero. Only parts of it have been preserved, including a
description of a dinner party given by an immensely rich parvenu,
named Trimalchio. The work is delightful for its character sketches
and satire. In this selection one of the guests tells his neighbor at
table about Fortunata, Trimalchio's wife.

[2] *just recently.* The word is repeated for emphasis — a common practice in ordinary speech in ancient times, as in modern Italian.

[3] *You would have been unwilling.*   [4] *without why or wherefore.*

[5] Figuratively, of course. She had risen in the world.

[6] A noun derived from the Greek, literally, *the all.* Translate: *she
means everything to.*

[7] *high* (lit., *pure*).   [8] The subject is Trimalchio.

[9] *very rich.*   [10] *sharp-eyed woman.*

[11] After some dancing between courses of the dinner, a clerk (**āctuārius**) comes in and makes a report on Trimalchio's business affairs.

[12] The **ācta diurna,** an official newspaper.

[13] *the seventh (day before) the first of,* i.e. July 26. The Romans counted
in both ends. It was usual to reckon the days of the month by counting
back from the first and certain other fixed days (**410**).

Sextīlēs in praediō Cūmānō quod est Trimalchiōnis:
nātī sunt puerī[1] xxx, puellae[1] xl; sublāta in horreum ex āreā trīticī mīlia modium[2] quīngenta; bovēs
domitī quīngentī. Eōdem diē: Mithridātēs servus in

Fig. 30. Hortus
A garden at Pompeii.

5 crucem āctus est, quia Gāī[3] nostrī geniō[4] maledīxerat.
Eōdem diē: in arcam relātum est, quod collocārī[5] nōn
potuit, sēstertium centiēs.[6] Eōdem diē: incendium
factum est in hortīs Pompeiānīs, ortum ex aedibus
Nastae   vīlicī."   " Quid? "   inquit   Trimalchiō.

---

[1] *i.e.* slaves.   [2] Genitive plural of **modius.**   [3] Trimalchio.

[4] *the guardian angel,* and therefore the man himself.

[5] *invested.*   Trimalchio's income was so huge that investments could
not be found for it all and some of it had to be put into a safe.

[6] *A hundred times (a hundred thousand) sesterces, i.e.* 10,000,000,
about $500,000.

" Quandō mihi Pompeiānī hortī ēmptī sunt? " " Annō priōre," inquit āctuārius, " et ideō in ratiōnem nōndum vēnērunt."[1] Excanduit Trimalchiō et " quīcumque," inquit, " mihi fundī ēmptī fuerint, nisi intrā sextum mēnsem scierō, in ratiōnēs meās īnferrī vetuō."[2] (53) 5

102.   49. TRIMALCHIO'S VERSION OF THE TROJAN WAR[3]

" Diomēdēs et Ganymēdēs duo frātrēs fuērunt. Hōrum soror erat Helena. Agamemnon illam rapuit et Diānae[4] cervam subiēcit.[5] Ita nunc Homēros[6] dīcit quem ad modum inter sē pugnent Trōiānī et Parentīnī.[7] Vīcit[8] scīlicet et Īphigenīam, fīliam suam, 10 Achillī dedit uxōrem." (59)

103.   50. ENJOYING LIFE AFTER DEATH

Trimalchiō " amīcī," inquit, " servī hominēs sunt et aequē[9] ūnum lactem[10] bibērunt, etiam sī illōs malus

---

[1] *have not yet been entered in the accounts.* So numerous and vast were the business transactions made on Trimalchio's behalf that he knew nothing about them until a year later.

[2] = **vetō**, a colloquial form.

[3] Trimalchio's education, like that of many a self-made man to-day, was nothing to brag about. His comical confusion about the Trojan War has its modern counterparts. There is one mistake in the first sentence, one in the second, etc. Can you correct them?

[4] Dative of reference, expressing disadvantage.

[5] *substituted.*   [6] Greek form of the nominative.

[7] The selection of the name of the people of an insignificant town as the opponents of the Trojans heightens the humorous effect.

[8] Trimalchio seems to be thinking of Agamemnon.

[9] With **ūnum:** *just the same as we did.*

[10] Trimalchio's Latin was very bad — almost as bad as that of some high school freshmen to-day. Here he uses the wrong gender, as also in **fātus.** What are the correct forms?

fātus oppressit. Tamen, mē salvō,⁴ cito aquam lī-
beram² gustābunt. Ad summam,³ omnēs illōs in tes-
tāmentō meō manūmittō. Philargyrō etiam fundum
lēgō⁴ et contubernālem suam. Cāriōnī quoque ïnsu-
5 lam⁵ et vīcēsimam⁶ et lectum strātum.⁷ Nam Fortūnātam meam hērēdem faciō et commendō illam omnibus amīcīs meīs. Et haec ideō omnia pūblicō, ut
familia⁸ mea iam nunc sīc mē amet tamquam
mortuum." Grātiās agere omnēs indulgentiae coepe-
10 rant dominī, cum ille oblītus nūgārum exemplar tes-
tāmentī iussit afferrī et tōtum ā prīmō ad ultimum,
ingemēscente familiā, recitāvit. Respiciēns deinde
Habinnam " quid dīcis," inquit, "amīce cārissime?
Aedificās monumentum meum, quem ad modum tē
15 iussī? Valdē tē rogō, ut secundum pedēs statuae meae
catellam pōnās et corōnās et unguenta et Petraïtis⁹
omnēs pugnās, ut mihi contingat tuō beneficiō post
mortem vīvere; praettereā ut sint in fronte pedēs
centum, in agrum¹⁰ pedēs ducentī. Omne genus¹¹
20 enim pōma volō sint circā cinerēs meōs, et vīneārum¹²
largiter. Valdē enim falsum est vīvō¹³ quidem domōs
cultās esse, nōn cūrārī eās ubi diūtius nōbīs habitandum
est. Et ideō ante omnia adicī volō : ' Hoc monumentum

---

¹ Lit., *while I am alive*, meaning *if I have anything to say about it.*
This is a sort of Irish bull, as the realization of his plan depends on his
being dead, not alive.   ² *the water of freedom.*

³ *In short.*   ⁴ *bequeath.*   ⁵ *apartment house.*

⁶ Supply **partem.** The twentieth part (5%) of the slave's value was
paid as a tax.   ⁷ *a bed made up, i.e.* one with bedding

⁸ *i.e.* the slaves.   ⁹ A gladiator.

¹⁰ *in depth,* lit., *into the field,* from the road on which the tomb faced.
¹¹ *fruits of all kinds.*

¹² Genitive of the whole, depending on **largiter:** *plenty of.*

¹³ Dative of reference.

hērēdem nōn sequātur.'[1] Tē rogō ut nāvēs etiam in
monumentō meō faciās plēnīs vēlīs euntēs, et mē in
tribūnālī sedentem praetextātum cum ānulīs aureīs
quīnque et nummōs in pūblicō dē sacculō effundentem;

FIG. 31. A ROMAN TOMB
On the Via Latina near Rome.

scīs enim quod[2] epulum dedī, bīnōs dēnāriōs.[3] Faciā- 5
tur,[4] sī tibi vidētur, et trīclīnia. Hōrologium in mediō,
ut quisquis hōrās īnspiciet, velit nōlit,[5] nōmen meum
legat. Īnscrīptiō quoque vidē dīligenter sī haec satis

---

[1] *shall not go to*, a phrase frequently found on tombstones, to prevent
an heir from appropriating the monument for himself.

[2] The use of a **quod** clause instead of the infinitive after **sciō** is a
colloquialism.

[3] In apposition with **epulum**: *a dinner (costing) two denarii per person.*

[4] What two grammatical errors in this word?

[5] *willy-nilly.*

idōnea tibi vidētur : ' C. Pompeius Trimalchiō Maecēnātiānus hīc requiēscit. Pius, fortis, fidēlis, ex parvō
crēvit, sēstertium relīquit trecentiēs,[1] nec umquam
philosophum audīvit.[2] Valē : et tū.' "[3]   (71)

Vocabulary Drill (48–50). — plānus, libīdō, aedēs, vetō ;
soror, scīlicet ; pius.

104. 51. TRIMALCHIO STAGES A COME-BACK[4]

5   " Concupīvī negōtiārī. Nē multīs vōs morer,[5]
quīnque nāvēs aedificāvī, onerāvī vīnum, mīsī Rōmam.
Putārēs[6] mē hoc iussisse : omnēs nāvēs naufragārunt ;
factum, nōn fābula. Ūnō diē Neptūnus trecentiēs
sēstertium[7] dēvorāvit. Putātis mē dēfēcisse ? Nōn
10 meherculēs mī[8] haec iactūra gustī[9] fuit, tamquam
nihil factī.[10]   Alterās[11] fēcī maiōrēs et meliōrēs et fēlī-
ciōrēs, ut nēmō nōn mē virum fortem dīceret. Scītis,
magna nāvis magnam fortitūdinem habet. Onerāvī
rūrsus vīnum, lardum, fabam, sēplasium,[12] mancipia.
15 Hōc locō Fortūnāta rem piam fēcit ; omne enim aurum
suum, omnia vestīmenta vēndidit et mī[8] centum
aureōs in manū posuit. Hoc fuit pecūliī meī fermen-

---

[1] About $1,500,000.

[2] *i.e.* he never went to college. The "hard-boiled" Trimalchio is
well satisfied with himself.

[3] *Farewell, (stranger) : you too, (Trimalchio).* Such exchanges of
greetings between the dweller in the tomb and the traveller passing along
the road are common on Roman tombs.

[4] Trimalchio is telling the story of his life.

[5] *Not to burden you with many details;* a purpose clause.

[6] *You would have thought.*   [7] See note 1.

[8] = mihi.

[9] Genitive : *was not tasted* (i.e. *noticed*) *by me.*

[10] Genitive of the whole : *as if nothing had happened.*

[11] Supply nāvēs.   [12] *perfume.*

tum.   Cito fit[1] quod dī volunt.   Ūnō cursū centiēs sēstertium corrotundāvī.[2]   Statim redēmī fundōs omnēs

FIG. 32.   THE ROMAN SHIP AT LAKE NEMI

This is one of two houseboats which the Emperor Caligula had on Lake
Nemi, near Rome.   By partial drainage of the lake in 1929 the boat became
visible.   See Figs. 10, 34, 35.

quī patrōnī[3] meī fuerant.   Aedificō domum, coemō
iūmenta;   quicquid tangēbam,   crēscēbat   tamquam
favus."[4]   (76)   5

105.   52. WORDS OF WISDOM[5]

Illud autem vidē nē ista lēctiō auctōrum multōrum
et omnis generis volūminum habeat aliquid vagum

---

[1] Supply id as subject of fit and antecedent of quod.

[2] I rounded out (or cleared) ; see p. 92, note 6.

[3] Predicate genitive, referring to his former master.

[4] honeycomb.

[5] Selections from the letters on philosophical subjects which Seneca
wrote to his friend Lucilius.   Seneca played an important part in the

et īnstabile. . . . Nusquam est quī ubīque est. . . .
Distringit librōrum multitūdō. (2. 2–3)

Nōn quī parum habet, sed quī plūs cupit, pauper est.
(2. 6)

Diū cōgitā an[1] tibi in amīcitiam aliquis recipiendus
5 sit. Cum placuerit fierī, tōtō illum pectore admitte.

. . . Utrumque enim
vitium est, et[2] omni-
bus crēdere[3] et nūllī.
(3. 2, 4)

Nūllīus bonī[4] sine
10 sociō iūcunda possessiō
est. (6. 4)

Nōn sunt ad caelum
ēlevandae manūs nec
exōrandus aedituus[5] ut
15 nōs ad aurem simulā-
crī,[6] quasi magis exau-
dīrī possīmus, admit-
tat. Prope est ā[7] tē
deus, tēcum est, intus
20 est.[8] (41. 1)

Fig. 33. Seneca

government of the Roman Empire during the early years of the reign of
Nero (54–68 A.D.). Because of alleged participation in a plot against
the emperor he was forced to commit suicide. His philosophical teachings are based on those of the Greek Stoics. The first selection advises
intensive rather than extensive reading of books.

[1] *whether*.   [2] *both*.

[3] In apposition with **Utrumque**.

[4] Substantive, depending on **possessiō**; **iūcunda** is predicate adjective.

[5] *priest*.   [6] *i.e.* of God.

[7] With **prope**: *near you*. Note difference of idiom.

[8] Many of Seneca's sentiments are strikingly Christian in tone, due in
part to the fact that Christianity adopted many Stoic teachings.

Sīc cum īnferiōre vīvās[1] quem ad modum tēcum superiōrem velīs vīvere. . . . Vīve cum servō clēmenter, comiter quoque et in sermōnem illum[2] admitte et in cōnsilium et in convīctum. . . . Quem ad modum stultus est quī equum ēmptūrus nōn ipsum īnspicit, [5] sed strātum eius ac frēnōs, sīc stultissimus est quī hominem aut ex veste aut ex condiciōne, quae vestis modō[3] nōbīs circumdata est, aestimat. . . . " Servī sunt."[4] Immō hominēs. " Servī sunt." Immō contubernālēs.[5] " Servī sunt." Immō humilēs amīcī. [10] " Servī sunt." Immō cōnservī. (47. 11–16, 1)

" Mūs[6] syllaba est. Mūs autem cāseum rōdit: Syllaba ergō cāseum rōdit." . . . " Mūs syllaba est. Syllaba cāseum nōn rōdit : Mūs ergō cāseum nōn rōdit." . . . Vīs scīre quid philosophia prōmittat [15] generī hūmānō? Cōnsilium. (48. 6–7)

Nōn ut diū vīvāmus cūrandum est,[7] sed ut satis. . . . Longa est vīta sī plēna est. . . . Quaeris quod sit amplissimum vītae spatium? Usque ad sapientiam vīvere. Quī ad illam pervēnit attigit nōn longissimum [20] fīnem sed maximum. (93. 2, 8)

Imperāre sibi maximum imperium est. (113. 30)

---

[1] Subjunctive used as imperative : *So live . . . as you would wish.*

[2] *him.*

[3] *like a garment.* What literally?

[4] With such words some people justify the harsh treatment of slaves. Seneca's answer (rhetorically phrased) in effect means that " all men are created free and equal."

[5] *comrades;* lit., *tent-companions.*

[6] The two quotations are examples of absurd reasoning on the part of some philosophers. Seneca attacks these useless philosophical tricks and then sets forth his own conception of the mission of philosophy: to give good counsel.

[7] *We ought not to care;* the **ut** clause depends upon it.

106.   53.   A CICERO JOKE BOOK[1]

Sed mīror omnēs vōs ioca[2] tacuisse Cicerōnis, in quibus fācundissimus, ut in omnibus, fuit. Cicerō, cum apud Damasippum cēnāret et ille, mediocrī[3] vīnō positō, dīceret: " Bibite Falernum[4] hoc; annōrum 5 quadrāgintā est," " Bene," inquit, " aetātem fert."[5]

Īdem cum Lentulum, generum suum, exiguae statūrae hominem, longō gladiō accīnctum vīdisset, " Quis," inquit, " generum meum ad gladium alligāvit? "

Nec Q. Cicerōnī frātrī[6] pepercit.   Nam cum in eā 10 prōvinciā quam ille[7] rēxerat vīdisset imāginem eius[8] ingentibus līneāmentīs usque ad pectus ex mōre pictam (erat autem Quīntus ipse statūrae parvae), ait: " Frāter meus dīmidius[9] maior est quam tōtus."

In cōnsulātū Vatīniī, quem paucīs diēbus[10] gessit, 15 notābilis Cicerōnis urbānitās circumferēbātur.   " Magnum ostentum,"[11] inquit, " annō Vatīniī factum est, quod, illō cōnsule, nec brūma nec vēr nec aestās nec autumnus fuit."[12]

---

[1] Chiefly from Macrobius (II. 3), a writer of the fifth century. He presents a number of Cicero's jokes, which he took from a collection made by Cicero's secretary, Tiro.   The last two paragraphs are from Quintilian (VI. 31. 73), a writer of the first century.

[2] Object of **tacuisse.**

[3] *indifferent;* the word is important for the joke.

[4] A fine Italian wine.

[5] *it carries its age well,* or, *it doesn't show its age.*   Old wine is better than new.   [6] For the case see **313.**

[7] Marcus Cicero.   [8] Quintus Cicero.

[9] *half of my brother,* in reference to the painting which showed simply the head and shoulders, while **tōtus** refers to Quintus himself.

[10] The ablative of time is used here to express extent of time.

[11] *miracle.*

[12] Because the period of his consulship was so short.

Querentī deinde Vatīniō, quod gravātus esset[1] ad
sē īnfirmum venīre, respondit: " Voluī in cōnsulātū
tuō venīre, sed nox mē comprehendit."

Dē Canīniō quoque Rebilō, quī ūnō diē cōnsul fuit,
Cicerō dīxit: " Vigilantem[2] habēmus cōnsulem Canī-[5]
nium,[3] quī in cōnsulātū suō somnum nōn vīdit."

FIG. 34.   LAKE NEMI AND CALIGULA'S GALLEY
The boat was built in much the same way that boats are built to-day.   See
Fig. 32.

Pompeius Cicerōnis facētiārum impatiēns fuit.   Cum
Cicerō ad Pompeium[4] vēnisset, dīcentibus[5] sērō eum
vēnisse respondit: " Minimē sērō vēnī: nam nihil hīc

---

[1] he (Cicero) had been reluctant.

[2] wide-awake.   [3] (in) Caninius.

[4] During the Civil War Cicero had remained in Italy after Pompey
left.   He hesitated a long time before joining Pompey.

[5] Supply eīs (dative).

parātum videō." Deinde interrogantī Pompeiō ubi gener eius Dolābella[1] esset, Cicerō respondit: " Cum socerō tuō." Et cum dōnāsset Pompeius trānsfugam cīvitāte Rōmānā: " Ō hominem bellum,"[2] inquit; 5 " Gallīs[3] cīvitātem prōmittit aliēnam,[4] quī nōbīs nostram nōn potest reddere."[5]

Cum Laberius[6] in fīne lūdōrum ānulō[7] aureō honōrātus ā Caesare ē vēstīgiō[8] in quattuordecim[9] ad spectandum trānsiit, violātō ōrdine, et cum dētrec- 10 tātus est eques Rōmānus, ait Cicerō praetereuntī Laberiō et sedīle quaerentī: " Recēpissem tē, nisi angustē sedērem,"[10] simul et illum respuēns et in novum senātum iocātus, cuius numerum Caesar suprā fās auxerat. Nec impūnē. Respondit enim Laberius: 15 " Mīrum, sī angustē sedēs, quī solēs duābus sellīs sedēre."[11]

Īdem Cicerō aliās[12] facilitātem Caesaris in allegendō senātū irrīsit palam. Nam cum ab hospite suō P.

---

[1] He had joined Caesar. Pompey knew this and taunted Cicero with the disloyalty of a member of his own family. In his " come- back " Cicero neatly reminded Pompey that the latter was no more loyal to his father-in-law (Caesar) than Dolabella to his.

[2] *A fine fellow;* accusative of exclamation.

[3] Evidently the **trānsfuga** of the preceding sentence was a Gaul.

[4] *i.e.* not rightly their own.

[5] The allusion is to Pompey's inability to conquer Caesar and to restore Roman liberty.   [6] A dramatist and actor.

[7] *ring.* A sign of admission to the class of knights (**equitēs**).

[8] *at once.*

[9] Supply **ōrdinēs.** The first fourteen rows in the theater were reserved for the knights.

[10] *if I were not sitting in close quarters.*

[11] In allusion to Cicero's hesitation during the Civil War to decide whether to throw in his lot with **Caesar** or with **Pompey.**

[12] Adverb: *at another time.*

Malliō rogārētur ut decuriōnātum[1] prīvignō eius expedīret, dīxit: " Rōmae, sī vīs, habēbit; Pompeīs difficile est."

Cicerō, cum Pīsō gener eius mollius incēderet, fīlia autem 5 concitātius, ait fīliae: " Ambulā tamquam vir."[2]

Cicerō Cūriō multum dē annīs aetātis suae mentientī dīxit: " Tum ergō cum ūnā 10 dēclāmābāmus[3] nōn erās nātus." Īdem, Fabiā dīcente trīgintā sē annōs habēre,[4] " Vērum est," inquit; " nam hoc illam[5] vīgintī annīs 15 audiō."

Cum Vatīnius pedibus aeger[6] vellet vidērī commodiōris valētūdinis factus[7] et dīceret sē iam bīna[8] mīlia passuum ambulāre, Cicerō 20 dīxit: " Diēs enim longiōrēs sunt."

Vocabulary Drill (52–53). — īnstabilis, nusquam, iūcundus, clēmēns, stultus, immō; taceō, somnus, dōnō, lūdus, violō, praetereō, fās, palam.

---

[1] A *senatorship* in a small town (in this case Pompeii).

[2] A two-edged thrust, one at the masculine gait of the wife, the other at the feminine steps of the husband: *like your husband.*

[3] *we were students together.* Curius tried to make out that he was younger than he was.

[4] What is the corresponding English idiom?

[5] Subject of **dīcere**, to be supplied.

[6] *crippled in his feet,* probably from gout.

[7] *wished to (have it) appear (that he was) restored to health.* What literally? [8] *two each (day).*

FIG. 36. THE FORUM FROM THE PALATINE HILL

PART III

Introduction

107.　　　　　CICERO[1]

The lives of literary men, like the annals of the poor, are mostly devoid of stirring incident. But Cicero, while preëminently great as a master of prose and the arbiter of literary style for all time, is an exception to the rule, for he was an orator and statesman as well, an associate of such men as Pompey, Caesar, and the young Augustus. There was no more stirring period in the history of the ancient world than the first century B.C. which culminated in the fall of the Roman Republic with

Fig. 37.　Cicero

its glorious traditions, and the rise of the Empire of the Caesars. Surrounded on every hand by graft, corruption, and the unmistakable evidences of civic decay, Cicero remained personally honest throughout his career. He was, however, no impractical theorist, but

---

[1] For books about Cicero see **255.**

felt that the game of politics was one of give and take, and that compromise and concession were often necessary in order to gain a desirable result. With a love for the glorious past, he longed for a return to the purity, the lofty ideals, and the simplicity of earlier

Near East Research, University of Michigan

FIG. 38.   ARPINUM

Looking from road leading up from the probable site of Cicero's home.

Rome, and was eager to have a large share in its restoration.

Cicero was born near Arpinum January 3, 106 B.C., and was therefore six years older than Caesar. His family was a prosperous and honored one in Arpinum. This small town, sixty miles southeast of Rome, was already famous as the birthplace of Marius. Cicero spent his boyhood on his father's farm — or perhaps we should dignify it by calling it a country estate — with his younger brother Quintus, who later became

one of Caesar's leading generals in Gaul.   The father
decided that his sons should receive the best education
possible and so took them to Rome.   In those days
higher education prepared boys for law and public life,
though the course of study was a broad one.   So Cicero
studied rhetoric, poetry, and philosophy under the best
teachers available, some of them Greek, such as Archias,
whom he later defended in court in a much admired
speech (**166**).   He went to the law courts to hear the
famous orators and he studied law.   During the Social
War (90–88 B.C.) he was in the army and completed
the military service which was a prerequisite to a public
career.   On his return he continued his studies and
began to act as lawyer in court.

Cicero's earliest extant speech was made in 81 B.C.
(**Prō Quīnctiō**).   But his first real success was achieved
the following year as defense attorney in a murder case
(**Prō Rosciō**).   His indirect yet brave attack upon the
all-powerful Sulla in this speech, when no other man in
Rome dared to open his lips, showed clearly that the
obscure young lawyer was a man of remarkable courage.   Having won his case, Cicero found it advisable
to leave Italy at once for an extended tour of Greece
and Asia Minor, where he perfected himself in oratory
and philosophy under Greek masters at Athens and
Rhodes.   Upon his return to Rome, two years later,
he married Terentia, a woman of wealth and position.
They had two children, a daughter Tullia, who was
her father's great pride, and a son Marcus, who proved
to be a sore disappointment to his father.

Cicero's oratorical gifts and the reputation gained
by his bold defense of Roscius won for him immense

popularity. Only two years after his return to Rome he was elected to the quaestorship, the first step in the **cursus honōrum** (" official career ") and was sent to Sicily. The downtrodden Sicilians were pleasantly surprised by his fair-dealing in contrast with the extortionate methods of his predecessors. Cicero was very proud of his success, but his pride suffered a rude shock when on his way home he met some Romans who did not even know that he had left Rome. Four years later the Sicilians employed him to prosecute the notorious Verres, who as praetor had enriched himself by plundering and murdering the helpless provincials. The eloquent Hortensius, the foremost lawyer in Rome, defended Verres in the proceedings, but Cicero in his opening speech brought such convincing evidence against Verres that the latter at once went into voluntary exile. That did not prevent Cicero, however, from working up the unused evidence in the form of five great orations, which were then published as political pamphlets. His position as the leading lawyer and orator in Rome was now assured.

His blameless record as a public servant, combined with his unrivaled oratorical gifts, led to his rapid rise through all the steps of office. As praetor in 66 B.C. he made his first purely political speech in favor of the Manilian Law, which aimed to make Pompey commander in chief in the war against Mithridates. It was his strong plea for the bill which brought about its passage (**168**).

In the elections of 64 B.C. Cicero was chosen consul for the following year in spite of the fact that he was a **novus homō** — a " new man " in politics, for none of his ancestors had ever held a high office. It was rare indeed for such a man to achieve the consulate. The explanation of Cicero's election is that many conservative senators voted for Cicero, the **novus homō,** in order to defeat the radical Catiline. The result was that Cicero leaned more and more toward the senatorial party, away from the more liberal tendencies of his youth. He was very proud of his success in bringing about a coalition of the senators and knights in political matters. The outstanding event in Cicero's consulship was his suppression of the Catilinarian conspiracy (**158**).

After Cicero's consulship the political situation changed. In the year 60 B.C. Pompey, Crassus, and Caesar formed the First Triumvirate, a three-man combination intended to keep all political power in their own hands. Cicero had a chance to join this group but refused on principle. The coalition of senators and knights, in which Cicero took so much pride, was now broken. Then Cicero incurred the enmity of a powerful politician, Clodius, who eventually, with the tacit consent of the triumvirs, succeeded in securing Cicero's banishment for having put to death without due process of law five of the participants in the conspiracy of Catiline (58 B.C.). This was the most crushing blow that Cicero ever received. He had been enormously proud of his achievements as consul and of the acclaim which he received. Now the bubble of his conceit (for it must be admitted that his pride sometimes had the appearance of conceit) had been pricked. The complaining letters which he wrote during this period leave a bad impression on the reader who does not make allowance for the seriousness of the wound to Cicero's pride.

After his recall the following year Cicero brightened perceptibly as a result of the enthusiastic reception the people of Rome gave him. But on account of the power of the triumvirs he could play no important part in politics. In the year 51 he went to Cilicia in Asia Minor as governor. Instead of enriching himself and his friends by graft, as most governors did, he astonished the Roman world by his honesty. On his return at the end of the following year Cicero found that the two remaining triumvirs, Pompey and Caesar (Crassus had died several years before), had quarreled, and that civil war was imminent. When this broke out in 49 B.C., he tried to mediate. But he was unsuccessful and finally joined Pompey's forces at Dyrrachium. After Pompey's defeat at Pharsalus (48 B.C.) Cicero was allowed by Caesar to return to Rome (47 B.C.). Political activity was impossible, and he retired to his books. But he was not to have happiness. In the year 46 he divorced Terentia as a result of quarrels over her management of their property during his exile. He married again, but the marriage was short-lived. In 45 B.C. he lost his daughter Tullia, who had inherited much of her father's talent and who was sympathetic with his interests and ambitions. Her death left him heart-broken.

After Caesar's assassination in 44 B.C. Cicero once more became one of the leading figures in the Roman world, but only for a few months. The senators saw in the death of Caesar a chance to regain their power. With Cicero at their head they defied Mark Antony, who had seized the reins of power. Cicero delivered against Antony a series of fourteen bitter speeches, known as Philippics. Whatever we may think of Cicero's weakness during his exile, we cannot but admire him for his courage and patriotism in this last attempt to restore the constitution of the Republic. The hostility aroused by these attacks led Antony to demand his life as soon as the Second Triumvirate (Octavian, Antony, and Lepidus) was formed. On December 7, 43 B.C., Cicero was beheaded by Antony's soldiers on his estate at Formiae.

So much for Cicero the man. Great statesman that he was, his chief claim to fame is as a writer and speaker. Among orators only the Greek Demosthenes can be mentioned in the same breath. Over fifty of his speeches have come down to us. He also wrote several treatises on the history and theory of oratory. We have too a number of his essays on philosophical subjects. Finally there are his letters, of which more than eight hundred are extant (**171** ff.). They afford us interesting and intimate glimpses of the great men and events of his day and place Cicero at the head of all letter writers. All these works have profoundly influenced succeeding generations even to our own time.

" He created a language which remained for sixteen centuries that of the civilized world, and used that language to create a style which nineteen centuries have not replaced, and in some respects have scarcely altered. He stands in prose, like Virgil in poetry, as the bridge between the ancient and modern world." [1]

---

[1] J. W. Mackail, *Latin Literature*, p. 62.

108.   Questions for Discussion

1. Does Cicero remind you of any American statesmen? 2. What American orator might be compared with Cicero? 3. Do you think that vanity is a rare characteristic of great men? 4. Should a statesman stick to his ideals under all circumstances, or should he be willing to make concessions? 5. After reading some of his works, do you admire Cicero?

109.   ROMAN GOVERNMENT IN CICERO'S DAY

Rome was the law-giver of the world. Many features of the Roman constitution have profoundly influenced modern ideas of government, and Rome's success in handling her political problems in the course of her development from a city-state into a world empire has many a lesson for us. It should be remembered, however, that Rome had no written constitution like that of the United States. What amounted to a constitution was a collection of laws passed at various times which defined the rights of citizens. The first written laws, the Twelve Tables, dating from the fifth century B.C., served as the core of this collection.

110.   CITIZENS

After the Social War (90–88 B.C.) all free male inhabitants of Italy who had assumed the **toga virīlis** (at the age of about sixteen) were citizens. Before that most of the communities outside of Rome had only a restricted citizenship (**Latīnitās**), as was still true in the provinces. Foreigners and slaves were not citizens.

Originally the Roman state consisted of two classes of people, patricians and plebeians, of whom the latter did not have the right to hold office. In the course of centuries, however, they succeeded in obtaining practically every political right possessed by the pa-

FIG. 39. TOGA-CLAD ROMANS

tricians. In Cicero's day, therefore, the distinction between the two had little political significance. But in the course of time a new division into three classes had taken place :

1. The term **plēbs** was now given to the great mass of voters. Within this **ōrdō plēbeius** a distinction was made between freemen (**ingenuī**) and ex-slaves (**lībertīnī**), who had the right to vote but not to hold a magis-

tracy. Their children became full-fledged **ingenuī**. The plebs in Cicero's day rose little above the level of an idle mob, living largely at the public expense.

2. The knights (**equitēs**) were originally the cavalry of Rome, as their name indicates. But at this time the cavalry consisted of foreigners. In the political sense the **equitēs** were the men of wealth. Any free citizen of Rome who acquired 400,000 sesterces (about $20,000) became an **eques** and was entitled to wear a gold ring and a tunic with a narrow purple stripe and was allowed to sit in the first fourteen rows of seats in the theater immediately behind the senators, who sat in the orchestra. The **ōrdō equestris** dominated commerce, trade, and banking and hence constituted an aristocracy of wealth. One of their important sources of income came from their government contracts for the collection of taxes. Cicero was an **eques** by birth and was supported by this order during his consulship.

3. The third group of Roman citizens composed the governing class (**ōrdō senātōrius**), numbering 600, all of whom were ex-magistrates or descendants of men who had held one of the higher (curule) offices. Such descendants were known as **nōbilēs**. The senate therefore was practically a hereditary nobility. Its members monopolized the offices as truly as the **equitēs** monopolized the wealth and trade. They were addressed collectively as **patrēs cōnscrīptī** (usually translated as " conscript fathers "). This term, which stands for **patrēs et cōnscrīptī,** no longer had any special significance. It went back to the time when the first plebeians were admitted to the senate as " enrolled " or " added " members in distinction from the patrician

members called **patrēs.** As a mark of distinction senators wore tunics with a broad purple stripe and special high shoes, and occupied the choicest seats in the orchestra of the theater.

111. POLITICAL PARTIES

Strictly speaking, there was no party system like ours, but there was a well-defined division between conservatives and radicals. Most of the senators were conservatives (**optimātēs, bonī**), most of the plebs radicals (**populārēs,** or **improbī,** as their opponents called them). Cicero from the time of his consulship was an ardent supporter of the **optimātēs;** Caesar, although belonging to the **optimātēs** by birth and rank, became the champion of the **populārēs.**

112. THE POPULAR ASSEMBLIES

All administrative and legislative power in Republican Rome was supposed (in theory, at least) to emanate from various assemblies of the people called **comitia,** of which two were of importance in Cicero's day :

1. The **comitia centūriāta,** originally military in its character, later became a voting body and elected the higher magistrates — consuls, praetors, and censors. All citizens were grouped into centuries or " hundreds," and each century voted as a unit, casting but one vote collectively.

2. The **comitia tribūta** was an assembly by tribes, so called, each with one vote, the plebeians having the preponderance of power. It had become the

chief legislative body and elected tribunes, quaestors, aediles, and minor officials. There were thirty-five tribes.

To vote in either assembly a citizen had to come to Rome. There was no such thing as representative government in these bodies. The politicians did not want to let the legislative and electoral power get out of the hands of the people of the city of Rome.

There was no speech-making in these assemblies. If a magistrate wished to speak on some subject before the people, he could call a mass-meeting (**contiō**). A magistrate also called and presided over meetings of the assemblies.

113   THE SENATE

See **110**, 3. The senate was originally merely an advisory board of older men (**senēs**) consulted by the kings. Later it became an advisory board consulted by the magistrates. The advisory nature of the body is shown by the term applied to a decision of the senate (**senātūs cōnsultum**). In Cicero's time it had become the highest administrative body of the Republic by usurping rights and powers originally belonging to the assemblies and magistrates. Its members held office for life, in contrast with the magistrates, most of whom held office for a year. Furthermore, since the higher magistrates could look forward to membership in the senate at the close of their terms, they would be less inclined to act counter to the wishes of that body while in office. Moreover, the senate discussed and formulated laws to be presented by the magistrates to the assemblies for action.

Broadly speaking, the senate was chiefly concerned with questions of finance, foreign affairs, and matters of religion, and had sole jurisdiction over the provinces. In times of great danger it could pass the **cōnsultum ultimum,** which suspended all ordinary laws and placed dictatorial powers in the hands of the consuls. The senate alone had the power to declare war and make peace, so that its authority came to be respected throughout the world.

One of the consuls usually called and presided at meetings of the senate, which were generally held in a special building (called the **cūria**) but sometimes in a temple. Senators spoke only when called upon by the chairman to give their opinions (**sententiae**). They could then talk at length on anything. When the discussion was over, the chairman asked for a division, *i.e.* those favoring the proposed action went to one side of the house, the opponents to the other.

114. ROMAN OFFICIALS

Under the Roman Republic military, judicial, and administrative powers were divided among magistrates elected by the assemblies of the people (**112**). The order of offices (**cursus honōrum**) was fixed by law and custom, and the term of office (with the exception of censor and temporary officials) was one year. Elections took place in July. All officials assumed office January 1, except the quaestors (December 5) and tribunes (December 10). An interval of two years had to elapse before a citizen could pass to the next highest office, and usually ten years between terms in the same office. In every office there were at least two men of equal powers, *e.g.* two consuls. All these provisions were intended as checks on the usurpation of power by an individual. Only certain officials held the **imperium** or supreme executive authority, military and civil. These were the consuls, praetors, dictator, and his **magister equitum.** The other officials who were without the **imperium** possessed merely civil authority (**potestās**) and could not lead armies.

Roman officials served without salary but as ex-magistrates they were usually assigned to the provinces, where they had many opportunities for both grafting and legitimate profit. The higher magistrates were honored with certain insignia or marks of distinction.

FIG. 40. SELLA CURŪLIS

Consuls, censors, praetors, and curule aediles wore a white toga with a purple border (**toga praetexta**). While transacting public business they sat on a carved ivory chair known as the **sella curūlis;** hence these officials were called " curule " magistrates. The curule chair was a sort of elaborate camp chair which could be folded up and carried about. Whenever a dictator, consul, praetor, or quaestor appeared on the street on affairs of state, he was preceded by lictors (varying in number according to the importance of the official) carrying the fasces (bundle of rods) as a sign of his power (Fig. 41). The rods were originally used for flogging but had become merely symbols.

The powers and duties of the various officials are briefly enumerated below.

115. *Consuls*

Two, elected annually by the *comitia centuriata.* Required age 43. Prerequisite : praetorship. They possessed equal powers, each acting as a check upon the other. Attended by twelve lictors.

Their duties were :

1. To preside over the senate and the assemblies.
2. To bring bills before the assemblies, usually after approval by the senate.
3. To take the auspices and to look after other religious matters of a political nature.
4. To take charge of the chief elections.
5. To perform the duties of censors during the three and a half year period when there were no censors.

They possessed the *imperium* but seldom led armies after 146 B.C.

At the close of their term of office they were usually appointed governors of provinces as proconsuls.

FIG. 41. FASCES

The ax was carried only outside of Rome ; it symbolized the power of life and death.

116. *Censors*

Two, elected by the *comitia centuriata* every five years for a term of eighteen months. They were usually ex-consuls.

Their duties were:

1. To assess property and to classify the citizens by tribes, etc.
2. To fix the eligibility of senators.
3. To raise revenue and make disbursements for public works.
4. To maintain high standards of private and public morality.

In Cicero's day the office of censor lost its power and dignity.

117. *Praetors*

Eight, elected by the *comitia centuriata*. Required age 40. Prerequisite: quaestorship. Attended by two lictors (six outside of Rome).

They possessed the *imperium*.

Their chief duties were to act as judges in civil and criminal courts.

The **praetor urbānus** was the chief justice and in the absence of the consuls was the chief magistrate in Rome.

After their term of office, the praetors were appointed governors of provinces as propraetors.

118. *Plebeian Tribunes*

Ten, elected annually by the *comitia tributa*. As direct representatives of the people, by their power of veto, they originally protected the plebs from the arbitrary acts of consuls and other magistrates. They therefore became the most powerful officials in the state. The mere threat of a veto was usually sufficient to prevent an action by the assemblies, senate, or magistrates. They were considered " sacrosanct " ; therefore anyone who assaulted a tribune could be put to death without trial.

119. *Aediles*

Four, elected annually by the *comitia tributa,* two being plebeian and two curule.

Their duties were :

1. To provide funds for, and supervise the public games and festivals.
2. To look after the care of the streets, fire protection, water, and public works in general.
3. To see to the importation and sale of grain at low prices and in general to supervise business transactions.

120. *Quaestors*

Twenty, elected annually by the *comitia tributa.* Required age 31. Two remained in Rome as public treasurers and collected all money due the state and paid it out to the proper officers. Eighteen served in the provinces or as paymasters in the armies.

121. *Other Officials*

A dictator was appointed by the consuls in emergencies at the request of the senate to serve for six

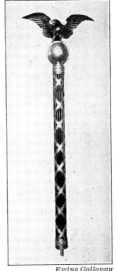

Ewing Galloway

Fig. 42. Mace

Symbol of the House of Representatives. Copied from the fasces and the Roman eagle.

months (or less) with absolute power. He selected his own Master of Horse (**magister equitum**). The dictatorships of Sulla and Caesar in Cicero's day were irregular, being usurpations of monarchical power.

Religious officials included the fifteen **pontificēs** (priests), the chief of whom was the **pontifex maximus.** They had charge of the calendar as well as of religious affairs. There were also fifteen augurs, in charge of the auspices. The six Vestal Virgins kept the fire burning in the temple of Vesta.

There were also many minor officials and clerks.

122. Questions for Discussion

1. Can you think of any American " nobiles," *i.e.* high officials who are descendants of high officials? 2. What differences are there between the senate of Rome and that of the United States? 3. Is there anything like a **cursus honōrum** in our country? 4. What important public offices have the last six or eight presidents of the United States held before becoming president? 5. Is there an age requirement for public office in this country? 6. Do any of our officials serve without pay? 7. Which of our officials have duties similar to those of the aediles? 8. What officials now have some of the powers of the tribune?

A COMPARISON OF ROMAN AND AMERICAN POLITICS

123. CAMPAIGN METHODS

The study of Cicero gives an excellent opportunity for a comparison between Roman and American poli-

tics, for the climax of the politics of the Roman Republic came in Cicero's time.

We may begin with the political significance of certain Latin words. The English word " candidate,"
from the Latin **candidātus,** literally means the " man

FIG. 43. CLEANERS AND DYERS AT POMPEII

The wearing of white togas made this a profitable business. From a wall
painting.

in white," for, although all Roman citizens wore the
white toga, the candidate for office made it a particular
point to see to it that he wore one that had just come
from the cleaner's. With this attempt to make himself
conspicuous by his clothing, we may compare the fancy
clothes and loud jewelry of the traditional ward politician. Then there is the English word " ambition "
from the Latin **ambitiō** — " going about " looking for

votes. In classical times the only ambition worth while was that of holding office. The **ambitiō** consisted of meeting and talking to the voters, and in connection with it the word **prēnsātiō** was used, which means " catching hold," and may be paraphrased as a " hand-shaking tour." Then there is the word **ambitus,** which originally meant the same as **ambitiō,** but came to be differentiated from it. **Ambitiō** was legitimate canvassing, **ambitus** illegitimate, and thus became the regular word for bribery — and bribery was always a conspicuous campaign method of the Romans. An excellent example is furnished by the Murena case, which was intimately connected with the conspiracy of Catiline. In the year 63 B.C., when Catiline made his last attempt to obtain the consulship, the opposing party of conservatives passed additional laws against bribery to make it more difficult for Catiline to win. But both sides used bribery very freely. As a result, one of the conservatives, Sulpicius, was so disgusted with his own party that he brought charges of bribery against Murena, the winning candidate of the conservative party. Cicero's speech in defense of Murena is still extant.

124. Intimidation of Voters

Another campaign " method " of which the Romans were very fond was violence. In this same year 63, the elections were postponed in order to diminish Catiline's chances, and when they were held, Cicero appeared on the scene in " shining armor," fearing, or pretending to fear, violence at the hands of Catiline. As a matter of fact, bloodshed was not at all uncommon

in Roman elections. To-day, on the eve of important
elections in certain districts of our largest cities, rioting
often occurs at the polls, and occasionally thugs and
gunmen are imported to intimidate peaceful voters.

125. ELECTION POSTERS

The election posters of Pompeii throw a flood of
light on the devious ways by which votes were won.
A typical poster is the following: **P. Fūr**(*ium II*)
v(*irum*) **v**(*irum*) **b**(*onum*) **ō**(*rō*) **v**(*ōs*) **f**(*aciātis*),[1] " Publius
Furius for duovir. A good man. I ask you to vote for
him." These phrases were so stereotyped that they were
usually abbreviated. One poster promises that a certain candidate will watch the treasury: **Bruttium
Balbum II vir. Gen**(*iālis*) **r**(*ogat*) **hic aerārium cōn-
servābit.** This reminds us of our own former " watch-
dog of the treasury." Another advertises a certain
candidate as delivering good bread: **pānem bonum
fert.** Other posters ask for the support of a particular
class, as the fishermen and even the ballplayers. It
seems to have been customary for the opposition to put
up fake posters: thus one poster proclaims that all
the sneakthieves (**fūrunculī**) support So-and-So; another that all the late-drinkers (**sēribibī ūniversī**) support him; still another promises the support of all the
sleepers (**dormientēs ūniversī**). At the end of a poster
we find the pleasant remark: **Invidiōse quī dēlēs aegrō-
tēs,** " May the malicious person who erases this sign
get sick." In their enterprise the Roman politicians
even put posters on tombstones, a fact which will be a

---

[1] The letters within parentheses are expansions of abbreviations.

surprise to those of us who think that in advertising we are in a class by ourselves. On one tombstone near Rome we find, not the phrase current with us, " Post no bills under penalty of law," but the far more effective prayer that candidates who put up their posters there may fail of election.

126. LIMITING THE FRANCHISE

Why is it that a " new man " like Cicero had so much difficulty in being elected to office? The explanation may be found in the fact that the Romans did not have the individual equal ballot. They voted by classes, and the number of persons in the various classes varied considerably, with the result that the votes of certain individuals were far more valuable than those of others. This restriction of the franchise made it possible for a small group to keep control of the government. Cicero was one of the few men not in the group to break through this ring. The situation was exactly that existing in Prussia before the World War, where 15% of the voters had a vote which was worth twice as much as that of the other 85%. Nor was it only in Germany that this situation existed. Not many years ago a great general strike was declared in Belgium to protest against class voting, and legislation was finally passed to effect reforms.

127. THE LAND QUESTION

The campaign issues of the Romans differed somewhat from ours. The tariff did not get into politics. The big issue was the agrarian problem. The public lands in Italy had been acquired in one way or another by a small group of men. The problem was to get a better distribution. Different solutions were offered by different men. Some were in favor of confiscation, others of purchase. It was a problem that was especially prominent as a political issue from the time of the Gracchi. In Russia since the seventeenth century the democratic slogan has been " Land and Freedom." Much of the trouble in Ireland was due to the control of large estates by a comparatively small number of absentee landlords. America has in general been alert to prevent the exploitation of public land.

128.   THE HIGH COST OF LIVING

Connected with the agrarian problem was the high cost of living, a political issue then as (to some extent) now. The example of Rome warns us to keep this question out of politics as a party issue. In Rome the various grain laws that were passed ultimately had a bad effect. First grain was sold at cost, in later years it was sold for less than cost, and finally it was given free to thousands of Roman citizens. The end of it all is summed up in Juvenal's remark that the Roman populace cared for nothing except **pānem et circēnsēs,** which we may paraphrase as a " square meal and a baseball game." The warning of Rome became especially significant to us in the days of government food control during the World War. We did not come to the point of selling provisions at less than cost price. In England the sum of $200,000,000 was appropriated by the government in the first three years of the war to make up for the difference between the cost and the selling price of bread. If the political parties should vie with one another in promising to sell provisions for less than cost price, we should have a situation analogous to that of Rome.

129. EXTENSION OF THE FRANCHISE

The question of the extension of the franchise was another political issue. The people of Italy outside of Rome did not have the full rights of Roman citizens until after the Social War, which was not a " society affair " but the war with the **socii,** or allies of Rome, over this question of the franchise. Before that time the matter was a party issue in Rome. In this country the question of restriction or extension of the franchise was a big issue in the days of the Know-Nothing party years ago. In 1916 as a result of the agitation about " hyphenated " Americans, bills were introduced in Congress to make naturalization more difficult.

130. WOMAN SUFFRAGE

Woman suffrage was never a campaign issue, but it came very near being one. In the year 195 B.C. the women protested because the sumptuary laws directed against the display of jewelry and fine clothing had not been repealed. The stern old-fashioned Cato was of course opposed to the women, and in the course of a speech made the following remarks: " Tell me, if you allow the women to seize and wrest privileges from you one by one, and finally to become your equals, do you think that you can stand them? As soon as they have begun to be your equals, they will be your superiors." A century and a half later a surtax was levied on the incomes of certain rich women, and one of them made the following speech: "Why should we pay taxes when we have no part in the honors, the commands, the statecraft, for which you contend against one another with such harmful results?" This argument was much used in the United States by the advocates of woman suffrage because the same argument led to the independence of our nation.

131. Questions for Discussion

1. Do you recall cases of violence at elections in this country? 2. Do you know of any situations in this country in which one man's vote is worth more than that of another? 3. Have public lands in our country ever been exploited? 4. How has our government tried to keep down the cost of living?

132. How to Prepare the Lesson

1. From the review lesson try to imagine what the writer is going to say. If you can forecast the trend of thought in this way, you are well on your way through the advance lesson.

2. Read the first paragraph *aloud in the Latin* and you will find that the words will group themselves into *thought units* (adjective or genitive with noun, preposition with object, etc.), and after some practice you will find yourself pausing naturally at the end of such thought units, whether punctuated or not. If the thought of any part is not clear, re-read aloud the entire sentence so as to be able to guess at the meaning from the sense of the whole. (Remember that intelligent guessing is a very important and legitimate step in all foreign language study.) As you do so you will prob-

ably be conscious of sound effects which escaped you the first time, such as those to be discussed in the following pages. You will notice, too, especially in Cicero, that the longer sentences possess a certain rhythm, particularly toward the end, and that the final syllables seem to form a musical cadence.

3. If you have read and re-read the sentence or paragraph in the Latin word order and any part of it is not yet clear, consult your notes to see whether any help is given there. Perhaps it is an unfamiliar word — one that suggests no related Latin word or English derivative — that holds the key to the meaning of the sentence. If so, this is the time to look it up — but not before. Remember that the vocabulary at the back of the book is to be used only as a last resort.

4. Sometimes you will find an unusually long sentence in which one word group follows another, phrase upon phrase, clause upon clause, without a governing verb until the end is reached. When you meet one of these ponderous, yet stately and sonorous sentences, attack it as it stands and you will see that it falls regularly into successive word groups of about equal length, each forming a complete thought unit. Take for instance the last sentence of Cicero's first speech against Catiline; parallel lines have been inserted merely to show the natural pauses which divide this elaborate sentence into fourteen members:

Tū, Iuppiter, ‖ quī īsdem quibus haec urbs auspiciīs ‖ ā Rōmulō es cōnstitūtus, ‖ quem Statōrem huius urbis atque imperī vērē nōmināmus, ‖ hunc et huius sociōs ‖ ā tuīs cēterīsque templīs, ‖ ā tēctīs urbis ac moenibus, ‖ ā vītā fortūnīsque cīvium omnium arcēbis ‖ et hominēs bonōrum inimīcōs, ‖ hostīs patriae, ‖ latrōnēs Italiae ‖ scelerum foedere inter sē ac nefāriā societāte coniūnctōs ‖ aeternīs suppliciīs ‖ vīvōs mortuōsque mactābis.

5. When, however, you come to translate a long, involved sentence like the above, it is usually best to break it up into several short sentences, avoiding such un-English expressions as a literal rendering of the Latin double dative and the ablative absolute would give. You will now see why translating from the Latin has been called a practical exercise in English composition.

133. How Cicero Ties His Sentences Together

Coherence, as you probably know from your English theme work, requires the use of certain fixed words and expressions, such as " now," " therefore," " as a result," to tie the sentences together and make the transition from one to another easy.

Latin likewise has its store of transitional words and phrases, to say nothing about its constant use of the relative pronoun at the beginning of a sentence to connect it with the preceding sentence (**293**). Examine at random any page of Cicero's speeches and you will find at least a half-dozen different transitional devices. The following are the most common :

age nunc, *come now*
age vērō, *well then*
dēnique, *in short, in a word*
hīc *(adv.), in view of this, under these circumstances*
iam tum, *even then*
iam vērō, *moreover*

igitur, *then, as I was just saying*
itaque, *accordingly*
nam, *for*
nē longum sit, *to be brief*
nunc, *as it is*
nunc vērō, *but as it is*
postrēmō, *finally, at last*
quae cum ita sint, *and since this is so*
quam ob rem, *and for this reason, and therefore*
quamquam, *and yet, however*
quārē, *and for that reason, therefore*
quid, *tell me, again* (calling attention to a question to follow)
quid igitur, *what then*
quid quod, *what of the fact that*
quid vērō, *what is more, furthermore*
quod sī, *but if;* occasionally, *if then*
sīn autem, *but if, on the other hand*

CICERO ON CAESAR'S CONQUEST OF GAUL[1]

It was customary for the senate to decide annually before the elections what provinces were to be assigned to the outgoing consuls. In 56 B.C. there was some talk of making Gaul, which Caesar was then subduing, one of the consular provinces. Cicero opposed this and in the course of his speech praised Caesar.

I

134. *Cicero Drops Political Differences and Supports Caesar*

19. Bellum in Galliā maximum gestum est ; domitae sunt ā Caesare maximae nātiōnēs, sed nōndum lēgibus, nōndum iūre certō, nōndum satis firmā pāce dēvīnctae. Ego senātor (inimīcus,[2] sī ita vultis, hominī),[3] amīcus esse, sīcut semper fuī, reī pūblicae dēbeō. **20.** Quid 5 sī ipsās inimīcitiās dēpōnō reī pūblicae causā, quis mē tandem[4] iūre reprehendet? **22.** An[5] ego possum huic esse inimīcus, cuius litterīs,[6] fāmā, nūntiīs celebrantur[7] aurēs cotīdiē meae novīs nōminibus gentium, nātiōnum, locōrum? **23.** Ārdeō, mihi crēdite, patrēs 10

---

[1] Selections from the speech **Dē Prōvinciīs Cōnsulāribus.** The numbers in the text are those of the sections in the complete speech.

[2] In politics Cicero always represented the senatorial or aristocratic party and Caesar the popular or democratic party.

[3] *i.e.* Caesar ; depends on **inimīcus**, as **reī pūblicae** depends on **amīcus**.

[4] In questions **tandem** = *tell me*.

[5] *Or* (introducing the second member of a double question).

[6] Caesar's dispatches to the senate, as well as the vast numbers of war prisoners sold as slaves in Italy, introduced the Romans to names of Gallic tribes and places which they had never heard of before.

[7] *are filled.*

FIG. 44. THE ROMAN FORUM DURING THE EMPIRE

Looking toward the east. At the right, the Basilica Julia, a courthouse built by Julius Caesar; at the left, the Basilica Aemilia; in the center background, the temple of Julius Caesar.

cōnscrīptī[1] (id quod vōsmet[2] dē mē exīstimātis et
facitis ipsī), incrēdibilī quōdam amōre patriae; quī
mē amor subvenīre ōlim[3] impendentibus perīculīs
maximīs coēgit.   Hic mē meus in rem pūblicam animus
prīstinus ac perennis cum C. Caesare redūcit, recon- 5
ciliat, restituit in grātiam.   **24.** Quod volent dēnique
hominēs exīstiment;[4] nēminī ego possum esse bene
merentī dē rē pūblicā nōn amīcus.[5]

26. Sed quid est quod[6] in hāc causā maximē hominēs
admīrentur et reprehendant meum cōnsilium, cum ego 10
īdem anteā multa dēcrēverim[7] quae magis ad hominis
dignitātem quam ad reī pūblicae necessitātem pertinērent? Supplicātiōnem quīndecim diērum dēcrēvī
sententiā meā.   Reī pūblicae satis erat tot diērum quot
C. Mariō;[8] dīs[9] immortālibus nōn erat exigua eadem 15
grātulātiō quae[10] ex maximīs bellīs.   Ergō ille cumulus
diērum hominis est dignitātī tribūtus.

135.	**Vocabulary Drill**	
ārdeō	patrēs cōnscrīptī	reprehendō
celebrō	quot	supplicātiō
-met		tandem

---

[1] *senators* (see **110**, 3).

[2] Forms of **tū** and **ego** are strengthened by attaching -met to them:
vōsmet = *you yourselves.*

[3] During Catiline's conspiracy (see **158**).

[4] Volitive subjunctive: *let*, etc.

[5] *I cannot be other than a friend to one*, etc.

[6] *why is it that.*   [7] *voted for.*

[8] Supply *as were granted.*   Marius had been voted a **supplicātiō** of
five days; Caesar was honored with one which lasted fifteen days, hence
cumulus below.

[9] Dative plural of **deus**: *in the eyes of.*

[10] Supply *resulted.*

136.　　Characteristics of Cicero's Style

Anaphora. — Cicero is fond of repeating a word at the beginning of successive phrases and clauses for emphasis. See **nōndum** (p. 133, line 2), which is used three times in the same sentence for rhetorical effect. Such repetition is called anaphora.[1] It is a substitute for a conjunction. Watch for examples in the following lessons.

Alliteration and Assonance. — Alliteration is the repetition of the same letter at the beginning of words which follow each other at short intervals; such as *m*ē *m*eus, *p*ūblicam *p*rīstinus *p*erennis (p. 135, line 4). When this repetition is made to include the whole syllable at the beginning of successive words, it is called assonance, as in *re*dūcit, *re*conciliat, *re*stituit (p. 135, line 5).

The best example of alliteration in the Latin language is a line from the poet Ennius, which carries the principle to absurd lengths:

Ō *T*ite *t*ūte *T*atī, *t*ibi *t*anta *t*yranne *t*ulistī

An example in English is:

Peter Piper picked a peck of pickled peppers, etc.

Another Latin example is:

*S*ōsia in *s*ōlāriō *s*oleās *s*arciēbat *s*uās,
Sosia was sewing his shoes in the solarium.

---

[1] The names of such rhetorical figures are not important, but it is interesting as well as helpful to recognize these devices, all of which are employed by speakers to-day.

II

137. *Military Reasons Demand that Caesar Be Kept
at the Front*

29. At ego īdem[1] nunc in prōvinciīs dēcernendīs interpellor, cum mē nihil aliud nisi ratiō bellī, nisi summa
ūtilitās reī pūblicae moveat.[2]   Nam ipse Caesar, quid
est cūr in prōvinciā commorārī velit, nisi ut ea quae
per eum affecta sunt perfecta reī pūblicae trādat? 5
Amoenitās[3] eum, crēdō, locōrum, urbium pulchritūdō,
hominum nātiōnumque illārum hūmānitās et lepōs,
victōriae cupiditās, fīnium imperī prōpāgātiō retinet.
Quid illīs terrīs[4] asperius, quid incultius oppidīs, quid
nātiōnibus immānius, quid porrō tot victōriīs praestā- 10
bilius, quid Ōceanō longius invenīrī potest?   An reditus
in patriam[5] habet aliquam offēnsiōnem?   Utrum[6]
apud populum ā quō missus, an apud senātum ā quō
ōrnātus est?   An diēs[7] auget eius dēsīderium, an magis
oblīviōnem, ac laurea illa[8] magnīs perīculīs parta[9] 15

---

[1] *also.*   [2] See **334.**

[3] The central and northern parts of Gaul were covered in many
places by dreary swamps and gloomy forests.   The Gauls were fierce
and warlike, and there were no picturesque hamlets and gay cities such
as one finds to-day in sunny France.   We can thus appreciate the irony
of Cicero's words.

[4] For case see **331.**

[5] Cicero had returned to Rome from political banishment less than
two years before; he is here no doubt thinking of his own longing then
to return to the capital and to fling himself once more into its busy life
and strife.

[6] Supply *I ask you,* to introduce the double question **Utrum . . . an.**

[7] *time.*

[8] Following its noun **illa** is here emphatic: *and does that famous victorious laurel, gained,* etc.

[9] From **pariō.**

āmittit longō intervāllō viriditātem?   Quārē, sī quī[1]
hominem nōn dīligunt, nihil est quod eum dē provinciā
dēvocent[2];   ad glōriam dēvocant, ad triumphum, ad
grātulātiōnem, ad summum honōrem senātūs, equestris
5 ōrdinis grātiam, populī cāritātem.

138.   Vocabulary Drill

dīligō	immānis	triumphus
grātulātiō	ōrnō	utrum . . . an
	pariō	

139.   Characteristics of Cicero's Style

Wordplay.[3] — When a play on words is used humorously, we call it punning :

> " They went and *told* the sexton and
>   The sexton *tolled* the bell."

Cicero often uses it for serious effect.   By it he sets over
against each other words of similar sound but different
meaning, as in **affecta, perfecta** (p. 137, line 5).

Irony. — Cicero occasionally, as in lines 6–8, p. 137,
indulges in a kind of grim humor or sarcasm whereby
he really means just the opposite of what he says.   Such
ironical passages are often accompanied by **crēdō,** *I
suppose*, **scīlicet** or **vidēlicet,** *of course*.

Review. — Find three examples of anaphora in the
above passage.

---

[1] *if any.*   After **sī** (also **nisi, nē,** and **num**) **quis** and **quī** = *some, any.*

[2] *there is no reason why they should* (**380**).

[3] Sometimes called paronomasia.

III

140. *Lasting Peace on the Gallic Frontier*
Should Be Our Aim

30. Ego vērō sīc intellegō, patrēs cōnscrīptī, nōs hōc tempore in prōvinciīs dēcernendīs perpetuae pācis[1] habēre oportēre ratiōnem. Nam quis hoc nōn sentit, omnia alia[2] esse nōbīs[3] vacua ab omnī perīculō atque etiam suspīciōne bellī? **31.** Iam diū mare vidēmus[4] illud immēnsum, cuius fervōre[5] nōn sōlum maritimī cursūs, sed urbēs etiam et viae mīlitārēs iam tenēbantur, virtūte Cn. Pompeī[6] sīc ā populō Rōmānō ab Ōceanō[7] usque ad ultimum Pontum[8] tamquam ūnum aliquem portum tūtum et clausum tenērī; nātiōnēs eās, quae numerō[9] hominum ac multitūdine ipsā poterant in prōvinciās nostrās redundāre, ita ab eōdem esse partim recīsās, partim repressās, ut Asia,[10] quae imperium anteā nostrum terminābat, nunc tribus novīs prōvinciīs[11] ipsa cingātur. Possum dē omnī regiōne, dē omnī genere hostium dīcere. Nūlla gēns est quae nōn aut ita sublāta sit[12] ut vix exstet, aut ita domita ut quiēscat, aut ita pācāta ut victōriā nostrā[13] imperiōque laetētur.

---

[1] Objective genitive (**302**) with **ratiōnem habēre:** *have regard for.*

[2] *everything else*, explained by the next sentence.

[3] See **311.**

[4] *we have seen;* so regularly with **iam diū.**

[5] *through whose disturbed state voyages . . . were blocked.*

[6] In his speech on the Manilian Law (**168**), Cicero states that Pompey cleared the Mediterranean of pirates in forty-nine days.

[7] *i.e.* the Atlantic.

[8] Find on the map, opposite p. 132.

[9] For case see **340.**   [10] Asia Minor.

[11] Bithynia, Pontus, and Syria.   [12] *weakened* (from **tollō**).

[13] For case see **340.**

141. Word Study

Ārdeō literally means to *burn,* **ferveō,** to *boil.* The former is used metaphorically in **134,** the latter in the preceding passage. Their English derivatives, *ardent* and *fervent,* are likewise metaphorical. What does *effervescent* mean? Give derivatives of **impendeō, subveniō, prīstinus, redundō, cingō,** and **perennis.** Note that in **perennis,** derived from **annus, a** changes to **e,** as in **perfectus** from **faciō.**

142. Chracteristics of Cicero's Style

Correlatives. — Pairs of introductory words or phrases which are regularly used together in a balanced arrangement are called correlatives. The following are used frequently by all Latin authors and should be memorized.

> **cum** (or **etsī**) . . . **tamen,** *although* . . . *nevertheless.*
> **cum(tum)** . . . **tum,** *not only* . . . *but also.*
> **nōn modo** . . . **vērum etiam,** *not only* . . . *but also.*
> **nōn sōlum** . . . **sed (etiam),** *not only* . . . *but also* (p. 139, line 6).
> **partim** . . . **partim,** *in part* (or *partly*) . . . *in part* (or *partly*). See p. 139, line 12.
> **sīve** . . . **sīve,** *if* . . . *or if.*
> **tot** . . . **quot,** *so many* . . . *as* (*many*).

Review **et** . . . **et, neque** (**nec**) . . . **neque** (**nec**), **aut** . . . **aut,** and **vel** . . . **vel.**

Metaphor. — A metaphor is an implied comparison. In a metaphor one person or thing is identified with another.

Metaphors are the most common of all figures, and

form an inseparable part of the language of emotion. Cicero is especially fond of them. In **fervōre** (p. 139, line 6) he employs a metaphor which suggests a *troubled* sea, for **fervor** here clearly does not have its literal meaning of *boiling* but is to be taken in the metaphorical sense of the sea in an *excited* and therefore *unsafe* state, caused by pirate raids. Again, in **nātiōnēs . . . redundāre** (p. 139, line 10), the surrounding nations are likened to *waters* which threaten to *overflow* the Roman provinces; in **recīsās** (p. 139, line 13) the metaphor changes and Pompey is represented as *lopping* or *cutting off* these nations like the branches of a vine or tree.

Review. — Find one example of alliteration in the above passage. Find a metaphor in **134.**

From " Ben Hur "

FIG. 45.   ROMAN WARSHIPS IN ACTION

IV

143. *In the Past We Have Warded Off Attacks*

32. Bellum Gallicum, patrēs cōnscrīptī, C. Caesare imperātōre, gestum est,[1] anteā tantummodo repulsum. Semper illās nātiōnēs nostrī imperātōrēs refūtandās potius bellō quam lacessendās putāvērunt. Ipse ille
5 C. Marius, cuius dīvīna atque eximia virtūs magnīs populī Rōmānī lūctibus fūneribusque[2] subvēnit, īnfluentīs[3] in Italiam Gallōrum maximās cōpiās repressit, nōn ipse ad eōrum urbīs sēdīsque penetrāvit. Modo ille meōrum labōrum, perīculōrum, cōnsiliōrum socius,[4]
10 C. Pomptīnus, fortissimus vir, ortum repente bellum Allobrogum atque hāc scelerātā coniūrātiōne excitātum proeliīs frēgit, eōsque domuit quī lacessīverant; et eā victōriā[5] contentus, rē pūblicā metū līberātā, quiēvit.

Caesar Has Carried the War into the Enemy's Country

C. Caesaris longē aliam videō fuisse ratiōnem. Nōn
15 enim sibi sōlum cum iīs[6] quōs iam armātōs contrā populum Rōmānum vidēbat bellandum esse dūxit,[7] sed tōtam Galliam in nostram diciōnem esse redigendam.
33. Itaque cum ācerrimīs nātiōnibus et maximīs Germānōrum et Helvētiōrum proeliīs fēlīcissimē dē-
20 certāvit[8]; cēterās conterruit, compulit, domuit, imperiō populī Rōmānī pārēre assuēfēcit, et quās re-

---

[1] Here = **cōnfectum est.**   [2] For case see **314.**

[3] The accusative plural in -**īs** instead of -**ēs** is common in ī-stem nouns and adjectives.

[4] As praetor in helping Cicero suppress the Catilinarian conspiracy. The war referred to occurred when Pomptinus was governor of Gaul.

[5] Depends on **contentus.**   [6] For **eīs.**

[7] Here (as often) *consider.*   [8] *fought with the greatest success.*

giōnēs[1] quāsque gentīs nūllae nōbīs[2] anteā litterae, nūlla vōx, nūlla fāma nōtās fēcerat,[3] hās noster imperātor nosterque exercitus et populī Rōmānī arma peragrārunt.[4]

144.   **Vocabulary Drill**

contentus	fēlīx	quiēscō
dīvīnus	potius	scelerātus
eximius		sēdēs

145.   Characteristics of Cicero's Style

Antithesis. — Cicero frequently contrasts words or ideas by placing them in corresponding positions in successive clauses or sentences. This contrast of words and ideas is called antithesis. Note **gestum est . . . repulsum** (p. 142, line 2) and **refūtandās . . . lacessendās** (p. 142, line 3). Find another example in this paragraph.

Asyndeton. — The omission of the connectives "and" and "but" in a series of words or phrases gives a pointed or sharp effect and is called asyndeton ("not bound together"). Cicero employs asyndeton in order to call sharp attention to each statement in the series, as in line 20.

Review. — What figure in **īnfluentīs . . . cōpiās repressit** (line 7)? In the second paragraph point out an example of anaphora and one of correlatives. Find an example of antithesis in **134.**

---

[1] When the relative clause stands first, as here, the antecedent (here **regiōnēs** and **gentēs**) is often placed within the relative clause. Translate the antecedent nouns first.   [2] Depends on **nōtās** below.

[3] Agrees in number with the nearest subject.

[4] For **peragrāvērunt (236).**

V

146. *We Had Merely a Pathway to Spain through Gaul Before*

33. Sēmitam[1] tantum Galliae tenēbāmus anteā, patrēs cōnscrīptī; cēterae partēs ā gentibus aut inimīcīs huic imperiō aut īnfīdīs aut incognitīs aut certē immānibus et barbarīs et bellicōsīs tenēbantur; quās
5 nātiōnēs[2] nēmō umquam fuit quīn[3] frangī domārīque cuperet; nēmō sapienter dē rē pūblicā nostrā cōgitāvit quīn[3] Galliam maximē timendam huic imperiō[4] putāret; sed propter vim ac multitūdinem gentium illārum numquam est anteā cum omnibus dīmicātum.
10 Restitimus semper lacessītī. Nunc dēnique est perfectum ut imperī nostrī terrārumque illārum idem esset[5] extrēmum.[6]

One or Two More Summers Yet Needed to Complete the Conquest

34. Alpibus Italiam mūnīverat anteā Nātūra, nōn sine aliquō dīvīnō nūmine; nam sī ille aditus Gallōrum
15 immānitātī multitūdinīque patuisset,[7] numquam haec urbs summō imperiō domicilium ac sēdem praebuisset.

---

[1] The southern part of Gaul along the Mediterranean had been conquered by the Romans before Caesar's time.

[2] Subject of **frangī domārīque**, depending on **cuperet**.

[3] Here = **quī nōn**, introducing a relative clause of description (**380**).

[4] For case see **317**. Until Caesar conquered them in 58–49 B.C., the Gauls from earliest times had been a constant menace to Rome, and in 390 B.C. they had captured and burned the city. Fresh hordes from beyond the Alps kept invading Italy from time to time. It remained for Julius Caesar to remove the fear of another invasion by subduing Gaul north of the Alps.

[5] Translate as if present. For mood see **379**.

[6] Noun: *frontier.*   [7] A condition contrary to fact (**390, II**).

Ewing Galloway

Fig. 46. Alpibus Italiam Mūnīverat Nātūra

Mt. Blanc, highest of the Alps, as seen from Italy.

Quae iam licet cōnsīdant![1] Nihil est enim ultrā illam
altitūdinem montium usque ad Ōceanum quod sit
Italiae pertimēscendum. Sed tamen ūna atque altera
aestās[2] vel metū vel spē vel poenā vel praemiīs vel
armīs vel lēgibus potest tōtam Galliam sempiternīs 5
vinculīs astringere. **35.** Quārē sit[3] in eius tūtēlā
Gallia cuius[4] virtūtī, fideī, fēlīcitātī commendāta est.

---

[1] *They* (the Alps) *may now disappear!* For the construction of
cōnsīdant see **370,** *b*.

[2] The sequel showed that Cicero was too optimistic, for instead of
" one or two summers," it required four more years for Caesar *to bind
all Gaul with lasting chains.*

[3] For mood see **366.**

[4] The antecedent is **eius:** *of that man* (*i.e.* Caesar) *to whose,* etc.

147. Vocabulary Drill

commendō	domicilium	sapienter
dēnique	nūmen	vinculum
	pertimēscō	

148. Characteristics of Cicero's Style

Pairs and Groups of Three. — A very important feature of Cicero's style is the arrangement of words, phrases, and clauses in two's or three's. Note the two clauses in line 5, p. 144 (**nēmō . . . quīn**), the three nouns in line 7, p. 145 (**virtūtī, fideī, fēlīcitātī**), and the two pairs of nouns in line 15, p. 144 (**immānitātī multitūdinīque, domicilium ac sēdem**). When there are more than three units, they are naturally grouped in pairs or three's. Note the four qualities in line 3 which fall into two groups, the first (**inimīcīs, īnfīdīs**) representing the result of contact with Rome, the other two (**incognitīs, immānibus**) not involving such contact. The last quality is subdivided into three parts (**immānibus, barbarīs, bellicōsīs**). Some such elaboration is a common indication that it is the last of the series. In line 4, p. 145, the six nouns are clearly to be taken in pairs : " fear and hope," " reward and punishment," " arms and laws."

(The common balancing of connectives has already been discussed in **142**.)

Polysyndeton. — Sometimes, as in line 4, p. 145, the speaker desires to produce a smooth, connected effect by tying a series of words together through the repetition of the conjunction. This repetition of connectives is called polysyndeton (" much bound together "). Contrast asyndeton (**145**).

Review. — Find one metaphor, one case of alliteration, and one of asyndeton in **146**. Analyze the first paragraph of **143** for pairs and groups of three.

FIG. 47.   ARCH OF AUGUSTUS, SUSA

It is interesting to see that only a few years after Cicero's speech this town in the foothills of the Alps was sufficiently Romanized to set up such a characteristically Roman monument as this.

VI

149. *The Senate Should Restore Caesar to Its Confidence*

38. Ego vōs intellegō, patrēs cōnscrīptī, multōs dē-
crēvisse eximiōs honōrēs C.
Caesarī, et prope singulārīs.
Nēminem umquam est hic
5 ōrdō[1] complexus honōribus
et beneficiīs suīs quī[2] ūllam
dignitātem praestābiliōrem
eā[3] quam per vōs esset
adeptus[4] putārit.[5] Nēmō
10 umquam hīc potuit esse
prīnceps quī māluerit esse
populāris.[6] Sed hominēs
aut propter indignitātem
suam diffīsī ipsī sibi,[7] aut
15 propter reliquōrum obtrec-
tātiōnem ab huius ōrdinis[8]
coniūnctiōne dēpulsī, saepe
ex hōc portū sē in illōs
flūctūs[9] prope necessāriō
20 contulērunt. Quī sī ex illā

Fig. 48. A Roman Orator
Said to be Cicero.

---

[1] The senate.
[2] The antecedent is **Nēminem**.
[3] For case see **331.**
[4] From **adipīscor**. The tense depends on the past idea in **putārit**.
[5] For mood see **380**; for form, **236.**
[6] *democratic.* See p. 133, footnote 2.
[7] For case see **346.**   [8] Translate *with*, etc.
[9] Note that the metaphor introduced by **ex hōc portū . . . flūctūs**
is continued by **iactātiōne cursūque** in the next sentence.

iactātiōne cursūque populārī.[1] bene gestā rē pūblicā,
referunt aspectum[2] in cūriam atque huic amplissimae
dignitātī[3] esse commendātī volunt, nōn modo nōn re-
pellendī sunt, vērum etiam expetendī.

Let Us Not Dim His Glory Nor Cool His Ardor toward Us through Our Jealous Fears

39. Monēmur ā fortissimō virō atque optimō post 5
hominum memoriam cōnsule[4] ut prōvideāmus nē citerior
Gallia, nōbīs invītīs, alicui[5] dēcernātur post eōs cōnsulēs quī nunc erunt dēsignātī, perpetuōque posthāc ab iīs
quī hunc ōrdinem oppugnent populārī ac turbulentā ratiōne teneātur.[6] Quam ego plāgam etsī nōn contemnō, 10
patrēs cōnscrīptī, praesertim monitus ā sapientissimō
cōnsule et dīligentissimō custōde pācis atque ōtī, tamen
vehementius arbitror pertimēscendum,[7] sī hominum
clārissimōrum ac potentissimōrum aut honōrem minu-
erō aut studium ergā hunc ōrdinem repudiārō.   15

150.   **Vocabulary Drill**

adipīscor	dēsignō	ōtium
clārus	ergā	repudiō
complector	necessāriō	vērum (conj.)

Idiom: **post hominum memoriam**, *since the memory of man.*

---

[1] *after being buffeted about in their quest for popular favor.*

[2] *show their faces again in the senate hall.*

[3] *approved by* (lit., *agreeable to*) *this most honorable body.*

[4] This is probably Lentulus, one of the two consuls. Cato also
feared that Caesar would ultimately hand over his proconsular power to
a successor of his own choosing. We are told that he even interrupted
Cicero on the floor of the senate during the course of this speech, in order
to voice his suspicions.

[5] *i.e.* to some **populāris** (*democrat*).   [6] With **nē** above.

[7] *still I think that there is an evil to be dreaded even more,* etc.

151. Characteristics of Cicero's Style

Periodic Style. — The older English writers, such as Milton, Samuel Johnson, and Macaulay, delighted in heaping up sonorous phrases and clauses which kept the thought suspended until the end of the sentence was reached. A complex sentence of this sort, with a series of introductory clauses leading to a final subject and predicate, is known as a period.

Cicero employs the periodic style frequently in his speeches. Observe the last two sentences of the first paragraph in the Latin text of this lesson. Learn to grasp the meaning of each phrase and clause in its exact order, as just so many successive steps in the logical development of the speaker's thought. Imagine that you are taking in the words as they fall from the speaker's lips — phrase by phrase, clause by clause, until at last the full meaning of the sentence stands revealed as a sort of climax as you reach the end.

Review. — Find one example of correlatives in the above passage.

VII

152. *I Refused All of Caesar's Former Honors*
and Offices

40. Sed nōn aliēnum[1] esse arbitror explicāre breviter
quae mihi sit ratiō et causa cum Caesare.   Ac prīmum
illud tempus familiāritātis et cōnsuētūdinis quae mihi[2]
cum illō, quae frātrī meō, quae C. Varrōnī, cōnsobrīnō
nostrō, ab omnium nostrum adulēscentiā fuit, praeter- 5
mittō.   Posteā quam sum penitus in rem pūblicam[3]
ingressus, ita dissēnsī ab[4] illō ut in disiūnctiōne sententiae, coniūnctī tamen amīcitiā manērēmus.   **41.** Cōnsul ille ēgit eās rēs quārum mē participem esse voluit ;
quibus ego sī minus[5] assentiēbar, tamen illīus mihi 10
iūdicium grātum esse dēbēbat.   Mē ille ut quīnque-
virātum[6] acciperem rogāvit ;   mē   in   tribus   sibi
coniūnctissimīs cōnsulāribus[7] esse voluit ; mihi lēgā-
tiōnem quam vellem, quantō cum honōre vellem,
dētulit.   Quae ego omnia nōn ingrātō animō, sed 15
obstinātiōne quādam sententiae repudiāvī.   Quam
sapienter, nōn disputō (multīs enim nōn probābō[8]) ;
cōnstanter quidem et fortiter certē.   Sed nōn is sōlum
grātus dēbet esse quī accēpit beneficium, vērum etiam.

---

[1] *out of place.*

[2] See **316**; so also the following datives.

[3] *deeply engaged in public affairs.*

[4] What is the English idiom ?   [5] *not.*

[6] *an appointment on his board of five commissioners.*

[7] *among the three men of consular rank, i.e.* Pompey (Caesar's son-in-
law) and Crassus.   If Cicero had accepted, he would thus have become
most intimately associated with the three men who later formed the First
Triumvirate.

[8] *for in the eyes of many I shall not justify my course.*

is cui potestās accipiendī fuit.[1] Ego illa ōrnāmenta
quibus ille mē ōrnābat[2] decēre[3] mē et convenīre iīs
rēbus quās gesseram nōn putābam. Illum quidem
amīcō animō mē habēre eōdem locō quō[4] prīncipem
5 cīvium, suum generum, sentiēbam. **42.** Posteā mē
ut sibi essem lēgātus,[5] nōn sōlum suāsit, vērum etiam
rogāvit. Nē id quidem accēpī ; nōn quod aliēnum[6]
meā dignitāte arbitrārer,[7] sed quod tantum reī pūblicae[8] sceleris[9] impendēre ā cōnsulibus proximīs nōn
10 suspicābar.

153.   Vocabulary Drill

| cōnsulāris | impendeō | praetermittō |
| decet | | sceius |

154.   Characteristics of Cicero's Style

Praeteritio. — Under the pretext of passing over
certain matters, a speaker or writer will often really
emphasize them by parading them before the hearer

---

[1] A noble sentiment, worth remembering.

[2] *wanted to honor me.*

[3] Object of **putābam** ; its subject is **ōrnāmenta.**

[4] *held me in the same light as.*

[5] *his deputy (i.e. representative).*

[6] *inconsistent with.* The Roman constitution provided that a man
who had held the highest office in the gift of the people, namely, the
consulship, should afterwards serve under his successor in a subordinate
position (usually as proconsular governor of a province). This was a
wise provision, for it meant that the public was to continue to enjoy the
services of the men whom it had trained — a practice which the United
States might well adopt in the case of its ex-presidents, many of whom
are allowed to return to civilian life.

[7] The subjunctive is used in a rejected reason.

[8] For case see **314.**

[9] With **tantum :** *so much crime.*

or reader (line 5, p. 151).   This rhetorical device is known as praeteritio (from **praeter-eō,** *pass by*).

Chiasmus. — Occasionally, for the sake of sharp contrast or antithesis, Cicero employs a crisscross instead of a parallel order of words, called chiasmus (kī az'mus) from the crossed arms of the Greek letter *chi* (X).   See p. 137, line 6, and p. 151, line 19 :

a	*b*	*b*	*a*
amoenitās	locōrum	urbium	pulchritūdō
accēpit	beneficium	potestās	fuit

Review. — Find one example of anaphora and two of correlatives in the above passage.   Find an example of chiasmus in **149.**

VIII

155. *It Is My Duty to Support Caesar Now*

47. Extrēmum illud[1] est. Ego, sī essent[2] inimīcitiae mihi cum C. Caesare, tamen hōc tempore reī pūblicae cōnsulere, inimīcitiās in aliud tempus reservāre
dēbērem. Sed cum inimīcitiae fuerint numquam,[3]
5 opīniō iniūriae beneficiō sit exstīncta,[4] sententiā meā,
patrēs cōnscrīptī, sī dignitās agitur[5] Caesaris, hominī
tribuam[6]; sī honōs quīdam, senātūs concordiae cōn-
sulam; sī auctōritās dēcrētōrum vestrōrum, cōnstan-
tiam ōrdinis in eōdem ōrnandō imperātōre servābō; sī
10 perpetua ratiō Gallicī bellī, reī pūblicae prōvidēbō; sī
aliquod meum prīvātum officium, mē nōn ingrātum esse
praestābō.

156.   Word Study

In the preceding passage **exstinguō** is used meta
phorically; its literal meaning is seen in the English derivative *extinguish*. What does *extinct* mean
literally? Many derivatives contain metaphors which
we do not think of as such until we trace their origin.
They are *dead* metaphors until we give them *life* by
comparison with Latin.

Find metaphorical derivatives of **flūctus, ingredior,**
and **astringō.**

---

[1] *This is the last thing (which I have to say).*

[2] For mood see **390, II.**

[3] Supply **et** after this word to connect **fuerint** and **sit exstīncta.**

[4] *the feeling of being wronged has been destroyed by his kindness.*

[5] *is under discussion.* Supply also in the following clauses.

[6] Supply **dignitātem** as object : *I shall vote for it.*

157. Characteristics of Cicero's Style

Litotes. — Cicero often uses two negatives to express an affirmative, as in **nōn ingrātum** (p. 154, line 11). This figure of speech is called litotes (lī'totēs). Compare a " citizen of *no mean* city " (*i.e.* of a *famous* city).

Review. — Find two examples of litotes in **134**.

FIG. 49. THE TEMPLE OF JULIUS CAESAR

Mussolini, often compared to Caesar, is making a speech from the spot in the Forum where Caesar's body was burned and where a temple was later built in his honor.

158.   THE CONSPIRACY OF CATILINE

Ever since the period of the Gracchi there had been
a good deal of economic unrest in Rome, due to the land
question (**127**), the high cost of living (**128**), and the
general difficulty of carrying on business. Everyone
was in debt. Money rates were high and money was
scarce, for the big capitalists found it more profitable
to invest their money abroad than at home. It has
been asserted at times that similar conditions exist in
this country.

L. Sergius Catiline was a noble by birth and in his
early years was a follower of Sulla. But when the
reaction against the ultra-conservative government
brought the more liberal forces into prominence, Catiline shifted his political adherence to the radicals. He
was elected to the various offices in the **cursus honōrum,**
until finally he became a candidate for the consulship
in 66 B.C. But the conservatives brought charges
against him for graft in his management of a province
in order to prevent him from running for office. The
charges were no doubt justified but were brought as a
political move rather than in a spirit of reform. Catiline and another disappointed candidate, Autronius,
formed a plot to murder the consuls on January 1,
65 B.C., and to seize the reins of power. But the plot
was discovered and frustrated. At the elections held
in that year Catiline was again prevented from running
for office by the charges against him. Acquitted of
these charges through bribery, he became a candidate
in 64, when Cicero was running. At one time Cicero
thought of running with Catiline on the same ticket,

so to speak (**173**).   But nothing came of this.   As a result of the efforts of the nobles, Catiline was defeated by a narrow margin.   The next year (63) he turned up again as candidate.   His plan was to intimidate the voters by armed bands.   But Cicero the consul heard of this and appeared in armor with a strong guard. The conservative candidates, by a generous use of bribery, were elected.   Catiline now decided to use force.

Through all the years of his efforts to obtain the consulship, Catiline had the backing not only of the criminal classes but also of a large number of good citizens who were in debt and who felt that this condition was due to economic injustice.   Catiline's solution of the problem was the cancellation of all debts.   This was not a new thing in Rome.   Even in modern times this has been done in part in one form or another.   In his second speech against Catiline Cicero describes in detail the various classes of Catiline's followers (**160, 17 ff.**), and this passage gives us the best idea of the conspiracy and its causes.

Catiline began quietly to secure armed supporters in various parts of Italy.   October 27 was set as the day for the revolution.   But Cicero had an excellent secret service organization.   His chief source of information was a woman, Fulvia, who wheedled it out of her lover, Curius, one of Catiline's aids.   So Cicero exposed the plot in the senate on October 21.   A **cōnsultum ultimum** (**113**) was passed which gave the consuls full power to suppress the conspiracy.   Some of the conspirators began the revolution in Etruria as planned, but Catiline remained in Rome.   He finally decided to kill Cicero before leaving the city. Plans were completed at a meeting held November 6. Cicero was to be murdered early the next morning but was immediately forewarned and took precautions. He then called a meeting of the senate in the temple of Jupiter Stator on November 7, at which Catiline was present, and made the first speech against Catiline.[1] Its purpose was to force Catiline into the open. He dared not yet arrest him for lack of evidence. Cicero later refers to this speech as the one **cum Catilīnam ēmīsī.**

---

[1] Some, interpreting **superiōrem** in section 8 in the sense in which **superiōre** is used in section 1 (" night before last "), think that the speech was delivered November 8.

159.
M. TULLI CICERONIS
ORATIO
QUA L. CATILINAM EMISIT
IN SENATU HABITA

*Cicero Assails Catiline's Audacity and the
Consuls' Inaction*

I. 1. Quō[1] usque tandem[2] abūtēre,[3] Catilīna, patientiā[4] nostrā? quam diū etiam[5] furor iste[6] tuus nōs
ēlūdet? quem ad fīnem sēsē effrēnāta[7] iactābit audācia? Nihilne[8] tē[9] nocturnum praesidium Palātī,[10] nihil
urbis vigiliae, nihil timor populī, nihil concursus bonō- [5]
rum[11] omnium, nihil hic mūnītissimus habendī[12] senātūs locus,[13] nihil hōrum[14] ōra vultūsque[15] mōvērunt?
Patēre tua cōnsilia nōn[16] sentīs, cōnstrictam[17] iam

---

[1] These opening words and **Ō tempora, ō mōrēs!** below are as familiar
to Latin students the world over as the famous **Gallia est omnis dīvīsa
in partēs trēs** with which Caesar's *Gallic War* begins.

[2] *I ask*, or *tell me*. It gives an impatient tone to the question.

[3] Future second singular.   [4] For case see **337**.   [5] *still.*

[6] Often expresses contempt, as here.   [7] Why better than **magna?**

[8] = a strong **nōnne**. It is used six times. What figure? See **136**.
The six clauses are divided into three pairs according to the sense. Note
that the oration begins with three questions. See **148**.

[9] Do not forget to find a construction for tē.

[10] This hill had become the most fashionable quarter of the city, and
Cicero later had his residence there. Special guards were placed there
to protect the houses of the rich from the mob of "reds."

[11] *patriots.*   [12] Gerund or future passive participle?

[13] *this most secure place for holding.* Where was this speech delivered?

[14] *i.e.* the senators.   [15] *expression on the faces* (**406**).

[16] = **nōnne.**

[17] With **tenērī:** *held in check.* Note the emphasis on this word and
on **Patēre.**

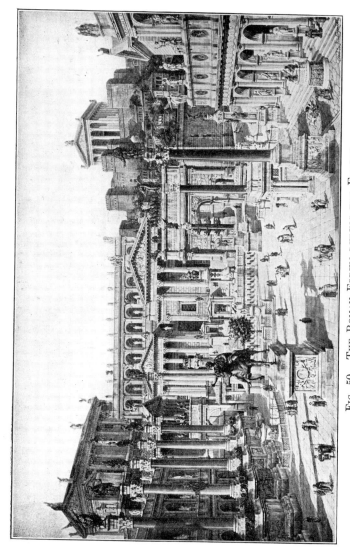

Fig. 50. The Roman Forum during the Empire

Looking toward the west. On the Capitoline Hill at the left, the temple of Jupiter; on the right, the temple of Juno; in between, the **tabulārium**, or record office. Below this, in the center, is the rostra.

hōrum omnium scientiā tenērī coniūrātiōnem tuam nōn
vidēs?   Quid proximā,[1] quid superiōre nocte ēgerīs,[2]
ubi fuerīs, quōs convocāverīs, quid cōnsilī[3] cēperīs
quem nostrum[4] ignōrāre arbitrāris?

FIG. 51. THE FORUM AND THE PALATINE

In the left background, on the slope near the arch of Titus, is the site of the
temple of Jupiter Stator, where the senate was meeting.

2. Ō tempora, ō mōrēs![5] Senātus haec intellegit,[5]
cōnsul videt; hic tamen vīvit. Vīvit? immō vērō[6]

---

[1] November 6, when the meeting at Laeca's house took place. But
others think that the speech was made November 8, and that **proximā**
refers to November 7.

[2] First of a series of indirect questions depending on **ignōrāre**. Keep
the word order in translating.

[3] *what plan* (**300**).   [4] Genitive of **nōs.**

[5] Accusative of exclamation (**324**).

[6] With **immō:** *or rather.*

etiam in senātum¹ venit, fit² pūblicī cōnsilī particeps,
notat et dēsignat oculīs ad caedem ūnum quemque
nostrum.³ Nōs autem, fortēs virī,⁴ satis facere reī
pūblicae vidēmur, sī istīus⁵ furōrem ac tēla vītāmus.
5 Ad mortem tē, Catilīna, dūcī⁶ iussū cōnsulis iam prīdem oportēbat, in tē cōnferrī pestem quam tū in nōs
omnīs iam diū māchināris.⁷ 3. An⁸ vērō vir amplissimus, P. Scīpiō, pontifex maximus,⁹ Ti. Gracchum
mediocriter labefactantem statum reī pūblicae prīvātus
10 interfēcit : Catilīnam orbem terrae caede atque incendiīs vāstāre cupientem nōs cōnsulēs perferēmus?¹⁰
Nam illa nimis antīqua praetereō,¹¹ quod¹² C. Servīlius

---

¹ Catiline as an ex-praetor had a right there.

² Note how the verb is shifted to first position in its clause, thus
coming immediately after the preceding verb.

³ *each one of us.*   ⁴ Irony (**139**).

⁵ *of that fellow* (Catiline).

⁶ Subject of **oportēbat.** Since the English word " ought " is
always felt as present, the dependent infinitive must be made to
show the tense; thus, *you ought . . . to have been led.* Notice the
striking word order, intended to make Catiline tremble : *to death, Catiline,* etc.

⁷ With **iam diū** the present is used where we use the perfect.

⁸ *Or is it that.* But in translating it is better to omit this and to
make the clause a statement, in contrast to the question beginning with
Catilīnam.

⁹ Though *high priest,* he was still a *private citizen,* because the priesthood was not a civil office. In 133 B.C. Gracchus while tribune of the
plebs had aroused the antagonism of the rich conservatives by his land
laws in aid of the poor. Scipio led a mob which killed him. Note the
chiastic ("crisscross") word order in **Scīpiō : Gracchum :: Catilīnam :
nōs.**

¹⁰ Contrasted with **interfēcit ;** so also **cōnsulēs** and **prīvātus.** By
pairing off words in this way, Cicero makes his meaning stand out in
bold relief.

¹¹ What is this figure called (**154**)?

¹² *the fact that ;* it explains **illa.**

Ahāla Sp. Maelium[1] novīs rēbus studentem manū suā occīdit. Fuit, fuit[2] ista quondam in hāc rē pūblicā virtūs ut virī fortēs ācriōribus suppliciīs cīvem perniciōsum quam acerbissimum hostem[3] coercērent. Habēmus senātūs cōnsultum[4] in tē, Catilīna, vehemēns et 5 grave, nōn deest reī pūblicae[5] cōnsilium neque auctōritās huius ōrdinis[6]: nōs, nōs, dīcō apertē, cōnsulēs dēsumus.

Vocabulary Drill. — patientia, ōs(ōris), **vultus, prīdem, pestis, orbis, nimis, acerbus, cōnsultum.**

Word Study. — No word has had a more interesting and thrilling history than the word *palace*, derived from Palatium. It epitomizes the whole history of the city of Rome. The Palatium, or Palatine Hill, is said to have been named after Pales, the goddess of the shepherds who built their rude huts on the hill. In Cicero's time the hill had become the most fashionable part of the city, and huge sums were spent for houses on it. It was natural therefore for Caesar and Augustus to establish themselves on this hill. In the course of time the emperors extended their buildings, private and public, over the whole hill, and Palatium became synonymous with palace. It was a long jump from the huts of the first shepherds to the magnificent buildings of the Empire.

---

[1] Whether Spurius Maelius, who distributed grain at his own expense among the poorer classes during a famine (439 B.C.), really *desired a revolution* (**novae rēs**) will never be known.

[2] The tense, the emphatic position, and the repetition alike show that such (**ista**) sense of virtue no longer exists in the state.

[3] Notice the chiastic order (**154**) of **cīvem perniciōsum** and **acerbissimum hostem.**

[4] On October 21 the senate had passed a special decree (**senātūs cōnsultum ultimum**) vesting supreme authority in the consuls, thereby giving Cicero dictatorial powers in dealing with Catiline. It corresponds in a sense to our declaration of martial law.

[5] Dative with **deest** (**313**).

[6] *i.e.* the senate.

Formerly Men Like Catiline Were Put to Death at Once. Reasons for Delay

II. **4.** Dēcrēvit quondam senātus utī L. Opīmius[1] cōnsul vidēret[2] nē quid rēs pūblica dētrīmentī[3] caperet : nox nūlla intercessit : interfectus est propter quāsdam sēditiōnum suspīciōnēs C. Gracchus,[4] clārissimō patre,[5]
5 avō, maiōribus, occīsus est cum līberīs M. Fulvius cōnsulāris. Similī senātūs cōnsultō C. Mariō et L. Valeriō cōnsulibus est permissa rēs pūblica : num[6] ūnum diem[7] posteā L. Sāturnīnum tribūnum plēbis et C. Servīlium praetōrem mors ac reī pūblicae poena[8] remorāta est?[9]
10 At vērō nōs vīcēsimum[10] iam diem patimur hebēscere aciem hōrum auctōritātis.[11] Habēmus enim eius modī

[1] The consul who in 121 B.C. was given special power by a **cōnsultum ultimum** and who killed Gracchus and 3000 of his followers. The language of this clause is that regularly used in such resolutions.

[2] A substantive volitive, not a purpose clause : *should see to it.*

[3] With **quid** : *any harm* (**300**). After **sī, nisi, nē,** and **num, quis** is indefinite.

[4] Younger brother of the Tiberius Gracchus mentioned in the preceding section. These are the two whom as boys their mother, Cornelia, referred to so proudly as " her jewels." Both were put to death by the senatorial party while attempting to enact legislation favorable to the masses.

[5] (*descended from*), etc. (**342**). His mother's father, Scipio Africanus, was the conqueror of Hannibal.

[6] Introduces a question the expected answer to which is *No.*

[7] Accusative of extent of time. In reality it was not the consuls who put these radical reformers to death (100 B.C.) but an angry mob of citizens.

[8] With **mors :** *death penalty;* hendiadys (**406**).

[9] *keep . . . waiting.* The proper nouns are the objects.

[10] Cicero uses a round number, a little larger than the truth. It was actually the eighteenth day (seventeen full days), or nineteenth if this speech was made November 8 (p. 158, n. 1).

[11] *the edge of the senate's authority.* The decree which has not been

senātūs cōnsultum, vērum inclūsum in tabulīs, tamquam in vāgīnā reconditum, quō ex¹ senātūs cōnsultō cōnfestim tē interfectum esse,² Catilīna, convēnit. Vīvis, et vīvis nōn ad dēpōnendam, sed ad cōnfirmandam audāciam.   Cupiō, patrēs cōnscrīptī,³ mē esse 5

FIG. 52.   FAESULAE (FIESOLE)

To-day Fiesole is but a small town, while Florence, in the valley below, is a large city.

clēmentem, cupiō⁴ in tantīs reī pūblicae perīculīs nōn dissolūtum⁵ vidērī, sed iam mē ipse inertiae⁶ nēquitiaeque condemnō.   **5.** Castra sunt in Italiā contrā

---

enforced but merely spread upon the minutes of the senate is compared to a sword *hidden away in its scabbard.*

¹ *in accordance with.*

² The perfect infinitive (instead of the present) with the perfect impersonal **convēnit** emphasizes the result: *you ought to have been,* etc. Cf. the similar use of *ought* (really the past tense of *owe*) in English.

³ *senators.*   See **110**, 3.

⁴ Notice the emphatic position and repetition (**136**).

⁵ *lax.*   ⁶ = **propter inertiam** (**307**).

populum Rōmānum in Etrūriae faucibus¹ collocāta,
crēscit in diēs singulōs² hostium numerus; eōrum
autem castrōrum imperātōrem³ ducemque hostium⁴
intrā moenia atque adeō in senātū vidētis intestīnam
5 aliquam cotīdiē perniciem reī pūblicae mōlientem.
Sī tē iam,⁵ Catilīna, comprehendī, sī interficī iusserō,⁶
crēdō,⁷ erit verendum mihi nē nōn hoc potius omnēs
bonī sērius ā mē quam quisquam crūdēlius factum esse
dīcat.⁸ Vērum ego hoc quod iam prīdem factum esse
10 oportuit certā⁹ dē causā nōndum addūcor ut faciam.
Tum dēnique interficiēre,¹⁰ cum iam nēmo¹¹ tam
improbus, tam perditus, tam tuī¹² similis invenīrī
poterit quī id nōn iūre factum esse fateātur.¹³ 6. Quam
diū quisquam erit quī tē dēfendere audeat,¹⁴ vīvēs, et
15 vīvēs ita ut¹⁵ nunc vīvis, multīs meīs et¹⁶ firmīs praesidiīs obsessus nē commovēre tē contrā rem pūblicam
possīs. Multōrum tē etiam oculī et aurēs nōn senti-

---

¹ At Faesulae (modern Fiesole), a strategic military point command-
ing the valley of the Arno, one of the routes into Cisalpine Gaul. Here
Manlius was collecting an army under Catiline's orders to march upon
Rome. See Fig. 52.

² *day by day.*   ³ Manlius or Catiline?

⁴ What figure? See **154.**   ⁵ *at once.*

⁶ Observe how much more accurate Latin is in its use of tenses than
English. We would naturally say *if I order you.*

⁷ Ironical: *I suppose* (**139**).

⁸ *I shall have to fear, not that all good citizens will say that this has been
done too late by me, but rather that some one may say that it was done too
cruelly.* **Dīcant** is to be supplied with **omnēs.** Since the passage is
ironical, Cicero means the opposite of what he says.

⁹ *definite;* explained by the next sentence.

¹⁰ Future.

¹¹ With **iam:** *no longer anyone.*

¹² For case see **305.** Note the climax.

¹³ Result (**380, Note**).   ¹⁴ Descriptive (**380**).

¹⁵ *just as.*   ¹⁶ Omit in translating.

entem,[1] sīcut adhūc fēcērunt, speculābuntur atque
custōdient.

Vocabulary Drill. — avus, tabula, nēquitia, crēscō, moenia,
perniciēs, mōlior, crūdēlis, improbus.

Catiline's Plans Are Fully Known

III.   Etenim quid est, Catilīna, quod iam amplius
exspectēs,[2] sī neque nox tenebrīs obscūrāre coetūs
nefāriōs nec prīvāta domus parietibus continēre vōcēs 5
coniūrātiōnis tuae potest, sī illūstrantur,[3] sī ērumpunt
omnia? Mūtā[4] iam istam mentem, mihi crēde,
oblīvīscere caedis[5] atque incendiōrum. Tenēris undique ; lūce[6] sunt clāriōra nōbīs tua cōnsilia omnia, quae
iam mēcum licet recognōscās.[7] **7.** Meministīne[8] mē 10
ante diem xii Kalendās Novembrīs[9] dīcere[10] in senātū
fore[11] in armīs certō diē, quī diēs futūrus esset[12] ante
diem vi Kal. Novembrīs, C. Mānlium, audāciae
satellitem atque administrum tuae?[13] Num mē fefel-

---

[1] *although you do not know it.*   [2] Descriptive (**380**).

[3] Translate with strict regard to the root meaning, for this verb continues the thought of **nox tenebrīs obscūrāre**, as **ērumpunt** continues
that of **parietibus**. Throughout the beginning of the speech Cicero
tantalizes Catiline by revealing bit by bit his knowledge of the conspiracy.

[4] Review the imperative, active and passive (**276, 277**).

[5] For case see **306**.   [6] For case see **331**.

[7] Subject of licet: *you may review.* What literally?

[8] -ne = nōnne.

[9] October 21.   For the Roman calendar see **410**.

[10] The perfect might be expected, but with **meminī** the present is
common.

[11] = **futūrum esse**. The subject is **Mānlium** below.

[12] Why subjunctive? Keep the strong future force (*was going to be*),
which could not be brought out by the plain subjunctive **esset**.

[13] Note the order of the last five words.

lit,[1] Catilīna, nōn modo rēs tanta, tam atrōx tamque incrēdibilis, vērum, id quod multō magis est admīrandum, diēs? Dīxī ego īdem[2] in senātū caedem tē optimātium[3] contulisse in[4] ante diem v Kalendās 5 Novembrīs, tum cum multī prīncipēs cīvitātis Rōmā

FIG. 53. PRAENESTE (NOW CALLED PALESTRINA)

nōn tam suī cōnservandī[5] quam tuōrum cōnsiliōrum reprimendōrum causā profūgērunt. Num īnfitiārī potes tē illō ipsō diē meīs praesidiīs, meā dīligentiā circumclūsum commovēre tē contrā rem pūblicam nōn potu-

---

[1] To keep the emphasis change to the passive: *I wasn't* (**Num**) *mistaken, was I, Catiline, not only in regard to the plot* (**rēs**), *but*, etc. Observe that **num** is used to introduce a question whose implied answer is *No*.

[2] *likewise.* It agrees with **ego**.

[3] The conservative party, largely **nōbilēs,** which was in power. See **111.**

[4] The phrase **ante diem . . . Novembrīs** (*the fifth day before the Calends of November*) is the object of **in.** What date? See **410.**

[5] Future passive participle, agreeing with **suī,** which in form is singular but in thought plural. It depends on **causā.** Cicero either is ironical or, as is more likely, he wants to deal as gently as possible with these cowardly senators because he needs their support.

isse, cum tū disœssū cēterōrum,[1] nostrā tamen quī [2] remānsissēmus [3] caede contentum tē esse dīcēbās? **8.** Quid? [4] cum tē Praeneste [5] Kalendīs ipsīs Novembribus occupātūrum nocturnō impetū esse cōnfīderēs, sēnsistīn [6] illam colōniam meō iussū meīs praesidiīs, 5 custōdiīs, vigiliīs esse mūnītam? Nihil agis, nihil mōlīris, nihil cōgitās quod nōn ego nōn modo audiam sed etiam videam plānēque sentiam.[7]

Vocabulary Drill. — etenim, nefārius, pariēs, oblīvīscor, meminī, atrōx.

The Plot against Cicero's Life. Why It Failed

IV. Recognōsce mēcum tandem[8] noctem illam superiōrem; iam[9] intellegēs multō mē vigilāre ācrius 10 ad salūtem quam tē ad perniciem reī pūblicae. Dīcō tē priōre[10] nocte vēnisse inter falcāriōs[11] — nōn agam ob-

---

[1] *on the departure of the rest,* or *though the rest had departed.*

[2] The antecedent is **nostrī** (genitive of **nōs**) implied in **nostrā,** which modifies **caede.**

[3] Why subjunctive? See **387.** But **dīcēbās** is indicative because it is not felt as belonging to the preceding indirect statement.

[4] *What about this?* Cicero employs this word frequently, often with **vērō,** almost like our colloquial " Listen ! " " Say ! " to attract attention to the following remark.

[5] About twenty miles southeast of Rome. Catiline planned to make this mountain stronghold his military base. See Fig. 53.

[6] For **sēnsistīne ; -ne** = **nōnne.**

[7] Descriptive (**380**). The three main verbs form an appropriate climax for the end of this vigorous chapter. What other figure is illustrated in the sentence?

[8] *I ask.* Cf. p. 159, note 2.   [9] How translated with the future?

[10] *last night* (cf. **illam superiōrem** above). But as these expressions more naturally mean *night before last* some think that this speech was delivered November 8, not 7.

[11] *to Scythemakers' Street.* Many of our street names originated in the same way.

scūrē[1] — in M. Laecae domum;[2] convēnisse eōdem[3] complūrīs eiusdem āmentiae scelerisque[4] sociōs. Num negāre audēs? Quid[5] tacēs? Convincam, sī negās. Videō enim esse hīc in senātū quōsdam[6] quī tēcum
5 ūnā[7] fuērunt. **9.** Ō dī immortālēs! ubinam gentium[8] sumus? quam rem pūblicam habēmus? in quā urbe vīvimus? Hīc, hīc sunt in nostrō numerō, patrēs cōnscrīptī, in hōc orbis terrae sānctissimō gravissimōque cōnsiliō, quī dē nostrō omnium[9] interitū, quī dē
10 huius urbis atque adeō dē orbis terrārum exitiō cōgitent.[10] Hōs ego videō cōnsul et dē rē pūblicā sententiam rogō,[11] et quōs ferrō trucīdārī oportēbat, eōs nōndum vōce vulnerō![12] Fuistī igitur[13] apud Laecam illā nocte, Catilīna, distribuistī partīs Italiae, statuistī
15 quō quemque proficīscī placēret,[14] dēlēgistī quōs Rōmae

---

[1] With **nōn** what figure? See **157.**

[2] **Ad** or **in** may be used with **domum** when it has an adjective or genitive modifier.

[3] Adverb.   [4] *your mad folly.* What figure? See **406.**

[5] = **cūr,** as often.

[6] This must have made certain guilty senators squirm in their seats for fear of being exposed.

[7] Adverb.

[8] *where in the world.* For case see **300.**

[9] We would say *of us all.*   [10] Why subjunctive? See **380.**

[11] *I ask their opinion.* Cicero as consul was the presiding officer of the senate.

[12] Both alliterative and metaphorical. Note the rhetoric in this section. He begins by calling upon the gods, continues with three rhetorical questions, repeats **hīc** for emphasis, and ends with alliteration and metaphor. Analyze for the pairs of words and groups of three.

[13] *you were, then (since you don't deny it),* resuming the thread of thought. Cicero fires these revelations at Catiline like bullets from a machine gun. Note that the seven verbs, all ending in **-stī,** come first in their clauses.

[14] *where you wanted each to go.* What literally?

relinquerēs,[1] quōs tēcum ēdūcerēs, discrīpsistī urbis partīs ad incendia, cōnfirmāstī[2] tē ipsum iam esse exitūrum, dīxistī paulum tibi esse etiam nunc morae,[3] quod ego vīverem.   Repertī sunt duo equitēs Rōmānī

FIG. 54.   ROMAN BATHS AT FIESOLE

The most extensive remains of ancient Faesulae are those of the baths here shown and of a theater.

quī tē istā cūrā līberārent[4] et sē illā ipsā nocte paulō[5] ante lūcem mē in meō lectō interfectūrōs esse pollicērentur.

10. Haec ego omnia vixdum[5] etiam coetū vestrō dīmissō comperī; domum meam maiōribus praesidiīs mūnīvī atque firmāvī, exclūsī eōs quōs tū ad mē salū-[10]

---

[1] Subjunctive of purpose.   [2] = cōnfirmā(vi)stī (**286**).

[3] With paulum (**300**): *a slight delay.*

[4] For mood see **368**.   [5] *almost before.*

tātum[1] māne mīserās, cum illī ipsī vēnissent quōs[2] ego iam multīs ac summīs virīs ad mē id temporis[3] ventūrōs esse praedīxeram.

Vocabulary Drill. — vigilō, obscūrus, taceō, sānctus, exitium.

Word Study. — The suffix -scō is attached to verb and adjective stems to form inceptive verbs, so called because they have the idea of *begin to* (from **incipiō**, *begin*) : **hebē-scō**, *begin to be dull.* Sometimes the inceptive force tends to disappear, as in **oblīvīscor.** What other examples of this suffix can you give?

Catiline Advised to Leave Rome

V.   Quae cum ita sint,[4] Catilīna, perge quō coepistī :
5 ēgredere aliquandō ex urbe ; patent portae ; proficīscere.   Nimium diū tē imperātōrem tua[5] illa Mānliāna castra dēsīderant.[6]   Ēdūc[7] tēcum etiam omnīs tuōs, sī minus,[8] quam plūrimōs ; pūrgā urbem.   Magnō mē metū līberāveris, modo[9] inter mē atque tē[10] mūrus

---

[1] *to greet* (**405,** *a*).   The early morning was the proper time for paying calls of respect on important people.

[2] Subject of **ventūrōs esse.**

[3] = **eō tempore ;** id is adverbial ; for **temporis** see **300.**

[4] One of Cicero's favorite expressions in making a transition : *since this is so,* or *consequently.*

[5] *of yours,* with sarcasm.   Manlius was at Fiesole (near Florence in northern Italy), organizing the army which Catiline was expected to lead against Rome.

[6] With **diū** the present is used where we use the present perfect.

[7] Imperative singular with final e dropped (so also **dīc, fac,** and **fer** and their compounds).   See **perge, ēgredere,** and **proficīscere** and review the imperative, active and passive (**276, 277**).

[8] = **nōn** (**omnēs**).

[9] *provided that* — a " proviso " clause (**374**).

[10] The Latin is logical in its use of the personal pronouns in that it always puts the first person ahead of the second, etc.   Translate according to English usage : *you and me.*

intersit. Nōbīscum versārī iam diūtius nōn potes;
nōn feram, nōn patiar, nōn sinam.[1] **11.** Magna[2] dīs

FIG. 55. THE TEMPLE OF JUPITER STATOR AS IT WAS

immortālibus habenda est atque[3] huic ipsī Iovī Sta-
tōrī,[4] antīquissimō custōdī huius urbis, grātia, quod

---

[1] Note anaphora. Not climax, as might be thought, but repetition
of ideas for emphasis.

[2] With **grātia**. The unusual separation emphasizes the adjective
and throws the noun immediately before the **quod** clause which explains it.

[3] With emphasis on what follows: *and especially.*

[4] With a gesture (implied in **huic**) Cicero points to a statue of Jupiter
the Stayer, in full view of his hearers, for this special session of the senate
was being held in the temple of that god. Legend said that Romulus
had vowed such a temple if Jupiter would *stay* the flight of the Romans
when they were retreating before the Sabines. This temple was not
erected until 294 B.C.

hanc[1] tam taetram, tam horribilem tamque īnfestam
reī pūblicae pestem totiēns iam effūgimus. Nōn est
saepius[2] in ūnō homine summa salūs perīclitanda reī
pūblicae. Quam diū mihi cōnsulī dēsignātō,[3] Catilīna,
5 īnsidiātus es, nōn pūblicō mē praesidiō, sed prīvātā
dīligentiā dēfendī. Cum proximīs comitiīs[4] cōnsulāribus mē cōnsulem in campō[5] et competītōrēs tuōs
interficere voluistī, compressī cōnātūs tuōs nefāriōs
amīcōrum praesidiō et cōpiīs, nūllō tumultū pūblicē
10 concitātō;[6] dēnique, quotiēnscumque mē petīstī, per
mē tibi obstitī, quamquam vidēbam perniciem meam
cum magnā calamitāte reī pūblicae esse coniūnctam.[7]
12. Nunc iam[8] apertē rem pūblicam ūniversam petis,
templa deōrum immortālium, tēcta urbis, vītam[9]
15 omnium cīvium, Italiam tōtam ad exitium et vāstitātem
vocās. Quārē, quoniam id[10] quod est prīmum, et
quod huius imperī[11] disciplīnaeque maiōrum proprium

---

[1] With **pestem**; translate first, followed by its modifiers: *this scourge*
(*i.e.* Catiline), *so vile*, etc.

[2] *too often.*

[3] *consul-elect.* Cicero had been elected in July, but his term of
office did not begin until January 1.

[4] *at the last election of consuls.* Note the alliteration (of *c*) in this
sentence.

[5] *the Campus Martius* (see Vocabulary), where the polling place was.

[6] *without making an official call to arms.* Cicero as the consul in
charge could have called out the troops to insure an orderly election, in
view of the threatened rioting.

[7] *involved great disaster to the state.* What literally? For **reī pūblicae**
see **302.**

[8] With **apertē:** *even openly.*

[9] We use the plural in English. Note that in this sentence there are
two verbs, two pairs of objects of the second verb, and two objects of **ad.**
To which pair of nouns does **exitium** refer?

[10] Object of **facere.**

[11] *this my authority* (conferred upon him by a decree of the senate).

est, facere nōndum audeō, faciam id quod est ad sevēri-
tātem¹ lēnius, ad commūnem salūtem ūtilius.   Nam
sī tē interficī iusserō, residēbit in rē pūblicā reliqua
coniūrātōrum manus; sīn tū, quod² tē iam dūdum
hortor,³ exieris, exhauriētur⁴ ex urbe tuōrum comitum⁵ ₅
magna et perniciōsa sentīna reī pūblicae.

13. Quid est,⁶ Catilīna? Num⁷ dubitās id, mē
imperante, facere quod iam tuā sponte faciēbās?⁸
Exīre ex urbe iubet cōnsul hostem.⁹   Interrogās mē,
num¹⁰ in exsilium?   Nōn iubeō, sed, sī mē cōnsulis, ₁₀
suādeō.

Vocabulary Drill. — **aliquandō, nimius, sinō, īnfestus, totiēns,
īnsidior, concitō, tēctum, comes, sīn, exsilium.**

Catiline's Criminal Past Reviewed

VI.   Quid est enim, Catilīna, quod tē iam in hāc urbe
dēlectāre possit?¹¹ in quā nēmō est extrā istam coniū-

---

¹ *with regard to.*   The phrase is really superfluous but put in to balance the next phrase.

² *as* (lit., *that which*).   ³ For tense see **361.**

⁴ *drained off.*   Note the emphatic position of the verb.   The reader
is kept in suspense as to the meaning of the strong metaphor until the
subject (**sentīna,** *sewage*) is reached at the end.

⁵ *the sewage* (*consisting*) *of your companions.*

⁶ *Look here, Catiline.*   A favorite device of Cicero's in introducing
a question.

⁷ In a direct question **num** anticipates a negative answer: *You don't
hesitate, do you?*

⁸ *were on the point of doing.*

⁹ Note both contrast and emphasis (at end of sentence).   Throughout these orations Cicero wants to impress upon his hearers that Catiline
is to be treated like a foreign enemy.

¹⁰ = *whether* (*I mean*) *into exile.*

¹¹ There are four more descriptive relative clauses in this chapter
(**380**).

rātiōnem perditōrum hominum quī tē nōn metuat,
nēmō quī nōn ōderit.[1] Quae nota domesticae turpi-
tūdinis nōn inusta[2] vītae tuae est? Quod prīvātārum
rērum dēdecus nōn haeret in fāmā? Quae libīdō ab
5 oculīs, quod facinus ā manibus umquam tuīs, quod
flāgitium ā tōtō corpore āfuit?[3] cui tū adulēscentulō[4]
quem corruptēlārum illecebrīs irrētīssēs[5] nōn aut ad
audāciam ferrum aut ad libīdinem facem praetulistī?
14. Quid vērō?[6] nūper cum morte[7] superiōris uxōris
10 novīs nūptiīs locum vacuēfēcissēs, nōnne etiam aliō
incrēdibilī scelere[8] hoc scelus cumulāvistī? Quod ego
praetermittō[9] et facile patior silērī, nē in hāc cīvitāte
tantī facinoris immānitās[10] aut exstitisse aut nōn vindicāta esse videātur. Praetermittō ruīnās fortūnārum

---

[1] Perfect with present force because ōdī has no present system.

[2] From inūrō. The letter " F " (for Fugitīvus) was often branded upon the forehead of a runaway slave when caught. What figure of speech? Why is the dative used?

[3] *Have your eyes ever been free from lust*, etc. What literally? Note the climax.

[4] Dative depending upon **praetulistī**: *Before what youth . . . have you not borne the sword for deeds of boldness or the torch for acts of passion?* By a bold metaphor Cicero compares Catiline, the corrupter of youth, to the slave who commonly preceded his master with torch and sword when he ventured forth at night through Rome's unlighted and unpoliced streets.

[5] Descriptive: *of the sort that you ensnared.*

[6] *look here!* Cf. **Quid est.**

[7] Not time when but means. What is the implication about the first wife's death?

[8] The murder of his only son, to please his second wife (according to Sallust, the historian).

[9] What figure? See **154.**

[10] In Latin an epithet is sometimes transferred or put for the thing itself, as here. Do not translate " the enormity of so great a crime " but *a crime of such enormity.* In all such cases follow the English idiom.

tuārum quās omnīs[1] proximīs Īdibus[2] tibi impendēre
sentiēs. Ad illa veniō quae nōn ad prīvātam ignōminiam vitiōrum tuōrum, nōn ad domesticam tuam
difficultātem ac turpitūdinem, sed ad summam rem
pūblicam[3] atque ad omnium nostrum vītam salū- 5
temque pertinent. **15.** Potestne tibi haec lūx, Catilīna,
aut huius caelī spīritus esse iūcundus, cum sciās esse
hōrum nēminem quī nesciat tē prīdiē[4] Kalendās Iā-
nuāriās, Lepidō et Tullō cōnsulibus, stetisse in comitiō[5]
cum tēlō,[6] manum[7] cōnsulum et prīncipum cīvitātis 10
interficiendōrum causā parāvisse, scelerī[8] ac furōrī
tuō nōn mentem[9] aliquam aut timōrem tuum sed
Fortūnam populī Rōmānī obstitisse? Ac iam illa[10]
omittō — neque enim sunt aut obscūra aut nōn multa[11]
commissa posteā[12] — quotiēns tū mē dēsignātum, quo- 15
tiēns vērō cōnsulem interficere cōnātus es! Quot ego
tuās petītiōnēs[13] ita coniectās ut vītārī posse nōn

[1] While agreeing with **quās, omnīs** logically goes with **ruīnās:** *the
complete ruin . . . of which.*

[2] Bills and debts of all sorts became payable at the beginning
(Calends) and the middle (Ides) of the month. Catiline's financial
backers, seeing that his conspiracy had failed, would undoubtedly
demand their money on the approaching Ides (Nov. 13).

[3] *the highest interest of the state.*

[4] Used like a preposition governing the accusative: *the day before*
the Calends of January (*i.e.* Dec. 29; see **410**). This event took place
three years before, during Catiline's so-called "first conspiracy."

[5] An open place in front of the senate, in which meetings were held.

[6] *armed.*   [7] Object of **parāvisse,** whose subject is **tē.**

[8] Depends upon **obstitisse (314).**

[9] *thoughtfulness, consideration.* In thought **aliquam** and **tuum** belong
with both nouns.

[10] *the following.* What figure in **omittō?**

[11] With **nōn = pauca.** What figure?

[12] *your later crimes.*

[13] *thrusts.* The language is that of the gladiatorial arena.

vidērentur parvā quādam dēclīnātiōne et, ut aiunt,
corpore[1] effūgī! Nihil agis, nihil assequeris, neque
tamen cōnārī ac velle dēsistis. **16.** Quotiēns iam tibi[2]
extorta est ista sīca dē manibus, quotiēns excidit cāsū
5 aliquō et ēlāpsa est! Quae[3] quidem quibus[4] abs tē
initiāta sacrīs ac dēvōta sit nesciō, quod[5] eam necesse
putās esse in cōnsulis corpore dēfīgere.

Vocabulary Drill. — dēlectō, ōdī, dēdecus, haereō, facinus,
Īdūs, Kalendae, omittō, sīca, sacer.

*All Shun Catiline as a Traitor. Why Does
He Not Leave?*

VII. Nunc vērō quae tua est ista vīta? Sīc enim
iam tēcum loquar, nōn ut odiō permōtus esse videar,
10 quō dēbeō,[6] sed ut[7] misericordiā, quae tibi nūlla[8]
dēbētur. Vēnistī paulō ante in senātum. Quis tē ex
hāc tantā frequentiā, tot ex tuīs amīcīs ac necessāriīs
salūtāvit? Sī hoc post hominum memoriam contigit
nēminī, vōcis[9] exspectās[10] contumēliam, cum sīs gra-
15 vissimō iūdiciō taciturnitātis oppressus? Quid, quod[11]

---

[1] Translate as if genitive depending upon **dēclīnātiōne**: *with a sort
of little twist of the body, as they say.* What figure?

[2] = *your.* See **311.**

[3] *And this* (*dagger*)   See **293.**

[4] Interrogative adjective agreeing with **sacrīs**: *with what rites it*
(*i.e.* the **sīca**). It introduces an indirect question depending on **nesciō.**
It was customary for cutthroats to promise the dagger to some god if
the murder was successfully carried out.

[5] *that.*   [6] *as I ought.*   [7] Omit in translating.

[8] Emphatic for **nōn**: *not at all.*

[9] *an expressed rebuke.* Note the chiastic word order (**154**). At West
Point to-day " the silence " is said to be the strongest of all protests.

[10] The derivative will not do here in translating.

[11] *What* (*of the fact*) *that?*

adventū tuō ista¹ subsellia² vacuēfacta sunt, quod omnēs cōnsulārēs quī tibi³ persaepe ad caedem cōnstitūtī
fuērunt, simul atque⁴ assēdistī, partem istam subselli-
ōrum nūdam atque inānem relīquērunt, quō tandem
animō tibi ferendum putās? **17.** Servī mehercule meī ;
sī mē istō pactō metuerent⁵ ut tē metuunt omnēs cīvēs

FIG. 56. CATILINE SITS ALONE AS CICERO SPEAKS
From a painting by Maccari in the modern senate house of Rome.

tuī, domum meam relinquendam putārem; tū tibi
urbem⁶ nōn arbitrāris? Et sī mē meīs cīvibus iniū-
riā⁷ suspectum tam graviter atque offēnsum vidērem,
carēre mē aspectū⁸ cīvium quam īnfestīs omnium ocu- 10

---

¹ *those near you.*

² Maccari's painting (Fig. 56) unfortunately gives a wrong impression
of the scene, for the artist has pictured the interior of the curia, not the
temple of Jupiter Stator with its rows of temporary benches.

³ *by you* (**317**).

⁴ With **simul**: *as soon as.*   Translate this clause after **quod**.

⁵ *if they feared.*   For mood see **390, II.**

⁶ Supply **relinquendam esse.**   ⁷ *unjustly.*

⁸ For case see **327.**

līs cōnspicī māllem ; tū,[1] cum cōnscientiā scelerum tuōrum agnōscās odium omnium iūstum et iam diū tibi
dēbitum, dubitās quōrum[2] mentīs sēnsūsque vulnerās,
eōrum aspectum praesentiamque vītāre ? Sī tē paren-
5 tēs[3] timērent atque ōdissent[4] tuī neque eōs ratiōne
ūllā plācāre possēs, ut opīnor, ab eōrum oculīs aliquō[5]
concēderēs. Nunc tē patria, quae commūnis est parēns
omnium nostrum, ōdit ac metuit et iam diū nihil tē
iūdicat[6] nisi dē parricīdiō[7] suō cōgitāre ; huius tū
10 neque auctōritātem verēbere[8] nec iūdicium sequēre
nec vim pertimēscēs ?

His Country Pleads with Him to Go

18. Quae[9] tēcum, Catilīna, sīc agit et quōdam
modō tacita[10] loquitur : " Nūllum iam aliquot annīs
facinus exstitit nisi per tē, nūllum flāgitium sine tē ;
15 tibi ūnī multōrum cīvium necēs,[11] tibi vexātiō dīrep-

---

[1] With **dubitās**.

[2] Translate the antecedent **eōrum** first. How was Catiline wound-
ing their feelings?

[3] Juxtaposition for contrast. This is a common rhetorical device.
Watch for other examples.

[4] Remember that this verb has no present stem.

[5] *somewhere.*

[6] With **iam diū** the present is used where English uses the present
perfect.

[7] Why is this an apt word here?

[8] Future second singular.

[9] *She* (your country) *pleads with you.* The passage of personifica-
tion which follows is justly famous.

[10] *(though) silent speaks.* This violent contrast in ideas mutually
opposed is known as oxymoron. Cf. " foolish wisdom." The phrase
quōdam modō, *in a certain sense*, apologizes for the expression.

[11] From **nex**. Catiline had been a leader in the political murders of
Sulla.

tiōque sociōrum[1] impūnīta fuit ac lībera; tū nōn
sōlum ad neglegendās lēgēs et quaestiōnēs vērum etiam
ad ēvertendās perfringendāsque valuistī. Superiōra[2]
illa, quamquam ferenda nōn fuērunt, tamen ut[3] potuī
tulī; nunc vērō mē tōtam[4] esse in metū propter ūnum tē, 5
quicquid increpuerit,[5] Catilīnam timērī, nūllum vidērī
contrā mē cōnsilium inīrī posse[6] quod ā tuō scelere abhorreat[7] nōn est ferendum.[8] Quam ob rem discēde
atque hunc mihi[9] timōrem ēripe; sī est[10] vērus, nē oppri-
mar, sīn falsus, ut tandem aliquandō timēre dēsinam." 10

Vocabulary Drill. — misericordia, contingō, inānis, pactum,
cōnscientia, plācō, opīnor, aliquot, ēvertō, abhorreō.

Word Study. — Trace the development of meaning of the following words, derived from Latin words in sections 10–18: *exhaust,
accumulation, ignominious, calendar, extortion, parricide, impunity.*

What is the effect of prefix and suffix in **pertimēscō** (section 17)?
The difference between **timeō** and **vereor** in this sentence is made
clear by the English derivatives *timid* and *reverence.*

Catiline, Rebuffed by Decent Citizens, Is Condemned by the Senate's Silence

VIII.   **19.** Haec sī tēcum, ut dīxī, patria loquātur,[11]
nōnne impetrāre dēbeat, etiam sī vim adhibēre nōn

---

[1] While propraetor in Africa (67 B.C.) Catiline had been guilty of
extortion. When brought to trial later at Rome, he escaped punishment by bribing the jurors. Do you recall instances of political graft
in your city or state?

[2] *those former crimes.*   [3] *as (well as).*

[4] Adverbial: *wholly.* Translate: *for me to be,* etc. Note the chiasmus.

[5] *at the least sound.* What literally? For mood see **388.**

[6] Depends on **vidērī.**

[7] *is inconsistent with.* For mood see **380, 388.**

[8] What is the subject?   [9] *from me* (**315**).

[10] Supply **timor.** The conclusion to this condition is in **ēripe.**

[11] *should speak* (**390, III**).

possit? Quid, quod tū tē in custōdiam[1] dedistī, quod
vītandae suspīciōnis causā ad[2] M'.[3] Lepidum tē habitāre velle dīxistī? Ā quō nōn receptus etiam ad mē
venīre ausus es, atque ut domī meae tē asservārem
5 rogāstī. Cum ā mē quoque id respōnsum tulissēs,
mē nūllō modō posse īsdem parietibus[4] tūtō esse tēcum,
quia magnō in perīculō essem[5] quod īsdem moenibus
continērēmur, ad Q. Metellum praetōrem vēnistī. Ā
quō repudiātus ad sodālem tuum, virum optimum,[6]
10 M. Metellum dēmigrāstī, quem tū vidēlicet et ad cus-
tōdiendum tē dīligentissimum et ad suspicandum
sagācissimum et ad vindicandum fortissimum fore
putāstī. Sed quam longē vidētur[7] ā carcere atque ā
vinculīs abesse dēbēre quī sē ipse iam dignum custōdiā[8]
15 iūdicārit?[9]

20. Quae cum ita sint, Catilīna, dubitās, sī ēmorī
aequō animō nōn potes, abīre in aliquās terrās et vītam
istam multīs suppliciīs iūstīs dēbitīsque ēreptam fugae
sōlitūdinīque[10] mandāre?

---

[1] Instead of giving bail for his appearance at court or being impris-
oned while awaiting trial, a prominent Roman, if accused of some crime
against the state, voluntarily put himself under the surveillance of some
well-known public official or citizen, who thus became surety for his
appearance at court when wanted.

[2] = **apud.**

[3] = **Mānius.** What does **M.** stand for?

[4] *house walls*, as contrasted with **moenibus**, *city walls.* For case see
343.

[5] For mood see **387.**

[6] Irony, made clear by the use of **vidēlicet.**

[7] Translate as if impersonal: *does it seem that he.*

[8] For case see **349.**

[9] = **iūdicāverit.** For mood see **380.**

[10] Exile was political death.

No Vote Needed: "Go!"

"Refer,"[1] inquis, "ad senātum;" id enim postulās[2]
et, sī hic ōrdō[3] placēre[4] sibi dēcrēverit tē īre in exsilium, obtemperātūrum tē esse dīcis. Nōn referam, id
quod abhorret ā meīs mōribus,[5] et tamen faciam ut
intellegās quid hī dē tē sentiant. Ēgredere ex urbe, 5
Catilīna; līberā rem pūblicam metū; in exsilium, sī
hanc vōcem[6] exspectās, proficīscere.[7] Quid est?
Ecquid[8] attendis, ecquid animadvertis hōrum silentium? Patiuntur, tacent. Quid exspectās auctōritātem loquentium,[9] quōrum voluntātem tacitōrum 10
perspicis? **21.** At sī hoc idem huic adulēscentī optimō P. Sēstiō,[10] sī fortissimō virō M. Mārcellō dīxissem,
iam mihi cōnsulī hōc ipsō in templō senātus iūre optimō
vim[11] et manūs intulisset. Dē tē autem, Catilīna, cum
quiēscunt, probant, cum patiuntur, dēcernunt, cum 15
tacent, clāmant,[12] neque hī[13] sōlum quōrum tibi auc-

---

[1] Supply **rem,** *the matter.* For form see **286.**

[2] Cicero revised this speech for publication. In its original form it is
likely that Catiline interrupted at this point.

[3] *this body* (the senate).   [4] *that it is its pleasure.*

[5] The senate had no authority to banish Catiline. This Cicero well
knew. Yet in the very next sentence he cleverly elicits a silent vote
from the senate on the question.

[6] = **verbum.**   [7] We can imagine a rhetorical pause at this point.
[8] *at all.*

[9] Translate as if an adjective: *spoken command.* Opposed to
tacitōrum: *though silent.*

[10] Like Marcellus, an outstanding citizen and loyal to the government
at this crisis. Two speeches (**Prō Sēstiō** and **Prō Mārcellō**) show
Cicero's loyalty to these two friends later.

[11] Translate with **manūs** as if an adjective. What figure? What
type of conditional sentence?   [12] Note the oxymoron (**408**).

[13] The senators before him, in contrast with **illī equitēs,** who were
outside the temple.

tōritās est vidēlicet cāra, vīta vīlissima, sed etiam illī
equitēs Rōmānī, honestissimī atque optimī virī, cēterīque fortissimī cīvēs quī circumstant senātum, quōrum
tū et frequentiam vidēre et studia perspicere et vōcēs
5 paulō ante[1] exaudīre potuistī. Quōrum[2] ego vix
abs tē iam diū manūs ac tēla contineō,[3] eōsdem facile
addūcam ut tē haec[4] quae vāstāre iam prīdem studēs
relinquentem usque ad portās prōsequantur.[5]

Vocabulary Drill. — quia, praetor, vidēlicet, vindicō, carcer,
ecquis, honestus.

Catiline Is Bent on Civil War — Why
Speak of Exile?

IX. 22. Quamquam[6] quid loquor? Tē ut ūlla
10 rēs frangat,[7] tū ut umquam tē corrigās, tū ut ūllam
fugam meditēre, tū ut ūllum exsilium cōgitēs? Utinam
tibi istam mentem dī immortālēs duint![8] Tametsī[9]
videō, sī meā vōce perterritus īre in exsilium animum
indūxeris,[10] quanta tempestās invidiae nōbīs, sī minus[11]

---

[1] There was probably a hostile demonstration when Catiline entered
the temple.

[2] Translate this clause after eōsdem.

[3] For tense see **361**.   [4] *these precincts.*

[5] This sentence is a fitting climax to Cicero's preceding irony. All
will be so glad to see Catiline go that they will give him a great " send-
off." We often " speed the parting guest " to-day by seeing him off at
the station.

[6] *And yet.*

[7] The four verbs, arranged in two pairs, are used in an exclamatory
question (**375**) : *anything ever crush you!* Note the emphatic position
of tē and tū before the ut clause.

[8] An old form for dent. For mood see **376**.

[9] = quamquam as used above.

[10] *if you will make up your mind to.*   [11] *if not.*

in[1] praesēns tempus recentī memoriā[2] scelerum tuōrum,
at[3] in posteritātem impendeat. Sed est tantī,[4] dum
modo tua ista sit[5] prīvāta calamitās et ā reī pūblicae
perīculīs sēiungātur. Sed tū ut vitiīs tuīs commove-
āre,[6] ut lēgum poenās pertimēscās, ut temporibus[7] reī
pūblicae cēdās nōn est postulandum. Neque enim
is[8] es, Catilīna, ut tē aut pudor ā turpitūdine aut metus
ā perīculō aut ratiō ā furōre revocārit. 23. Quam ob
rem, ut saepe iam dīxī, proficīscere ac, sī mihi, inimīcō,
ut praedicās,[9] tuō, cōnflāre vīs[10] invidiam, rēctā perge
in exsilium; vix feram sermōnēs hominum, sī id fēceris,
vix mōlem istīus invidiae, sī in exsilium iussū cōnsulis
īveris, sustinēbō. Sīn autem servīre meae laudī[11] et
glōriae māvīs,[12] ēgredere[13] cum importūnā scelerātōrum
manū, cōnfer tē ad Mānlium, concitā perditōs cīvīs, sē-
cerne tē ā bonīs, īnfer patriae bellum, exsultā impiō
latrōciniō, ut ā mē nōn ēiectus ad aliēnōs, sed invītātus
ad tuōs īsse[14] videāris.[15] 24. Quamquam quid ego tē
invītem,[16] ā quō[17] iam sciam esse praemissōs quī tibi

---

[1] *for.*   [2] *while the memory . . . is fresh.*   [3] *at least.*

[4] *it is worth the price* (**308**).   [5] Why subjunctive? See **374**.

[6] This and the following **ut** clauses are subjects of **nōn est postulandum**. What figure is illustrated here?

[7] *needs.*

[8] = **tālis,** *such a one,* followed by a result clause.

[9] From **praedĭcō,** not **praedīcō.**   [10] From what verb?

[11] For case see **313**.

[12] From **mālō.**

[13] Note how the six imperatives are grouped in three pairs.

[14] = **īvisse.**

[15] *so that it may appear that you did not go to strangers by expulsion but
to your friends on invitation.*

[16] *why should I urge?* Deliberative subjunctive (**375**).

[17] Causal: *since I know that . . . by you.* The antecedent of **quō** is
tē. Supply **virōs** as subject of **esse praemissōs** and antecedent of **quī.**

ad Forum Aurēlium praestōlārentur armātī, cui [1] sciam
pactam et cōnstitūtam cum Mānliō diem,[2] ā quō etiam
aquilam [3] illam argenteam, quam tibi ac tuīs omnibus
cōnfīdō perniciōsam ac fūnestam futūram, cui domī

FIG. 57. A SHRINE IN A ROMAN HOUSE

Almost every Roman house had its shrine for the household deities. In this
Pompeian house the shrine is in the garden.

5 tuae sacrārium scelerum cōnstitūtum fuit, sciam esse
praemissam? Tū ut illā [4] carēre diūtius possīs [5] quam

---

[1] Dative of agent with **pactam** (from **pacīscor**) and **cōnstitūtam** (esse).

[2] October 27 (**158**).

[3] Note that **illam** follows and is therefore particularly emphatic:
that famous silver eagle. The eagle was the emblem of the Roman legion,
equivalent to our regimental colors. This one had belonged to Marius.
Since the eagle has already been sent to the front, Catiline is sure to
follow soon. See Figs. 11, 42.

[4] For case see **327**.

[5] An exclamatory question: *can you any longer do without.*

venerārī ad caedem proficīscēns solēbās, ā cuius altāri-
bus[1] saepe istam impiam dexteram ad necem cīvium
trānstulistī?

Vocabulary Drill. — quamquam, utinam, tametsī, serviō,
sēcernō, careō, soleō, nex.

Word Study. — In the Middle Ages the word **vidēlicet** was abbreviated **vi** with an abbreviation symbol after it.   When printing
was invented the letter *z* was chosen to represent this symbol —
hence our abbreviation *viz.* (cf. *oz.* for *ounce*).

Trace the meaning of the following words from the Latin originals found in sections 19–24: *incarcerate, abhorrent, equanimity,
aquiline, argentiferous.*

Nature Has Trained Catiline for a Criminal Career

X.   **25.**   Ībis[2] tandem aliquandō quō tē iam prīdem
tua ista cupiditās effrēnāta[3] ac furiōsa rapiēbat;[4] neque 5
enim tibi haec rēs[5] affert dolōrem, sed quandam incrēdibilem voluptātem.   Ad hanc tē āmentiam nātūra pepe-
rit,[6] voluntās exercuit, fortūna servāvit.   Numquam tū
nōn modo[7] ōtium sed nē bellum quidem nisi nefārium
concupīstī.   Nactus es ex perditīs atque[8] ab omnī 10
nōn modo fortūnā vērum etiam spē dērelīctīs[9] cōn-
flātam[10] improbōrum manum.   **26.**   Hīc[11] tū quā lae-

---

[1] To be translated as singular.   Catiline is pictured as an assassin
who prays to this eagle as to a fetish or god of good luck to bless the
bloody hand which he will lift against his fellow men.

[2] From **eō.**   [3] What figure?   See section 1.

[4] *had been hurrying you.*   [5] *i.e.* his actual entry upon civil war.

[6] From **pariō.**   Distinguish **parō, pāreō, pariō, parcō.**

[7] Combine with **Numquam :** *Not only have you never,* etc.

[8] Connects **perditīs** and **dērelīctīs.**

[9] *those deserted not only by fortune,* etc.   The use of **ab** with **Fortūnā**
shows that this word is personified.

[10] *composed,* agreeing with **manum,** the object of **nactus es.**

[11] *here, i.e.* with such companions.

titiā[1] perfruēre, quibus gaudiīs exsultābis, quantā in voluptāte bacchābere,[2] cum in tantō numerō tuōrum neque audiēs virum bonum quemquam neque vidēbis! Ad huius vītae studium meditātī[3] illī sunt quī ferun-
5 tur[4] labōrēs tuī, iacēre humī nōn sōlum ad obsidendum stuprum[5] vērum etiam ad facinus obeundum,[6] vigilāre nōn sōlum īnsidiantem[7] somnō marītōrum vērum etiam bonīs ōtiōsōrum. Habēs ubi[8] ostentēs tuam illam praeclāram patientiam famis, frīgoris, inopiae
10 rērum omnium quibus tē brevī tempore cōnfectum esse sentiēs. **27.** Tantum prōfēcī, cum tē ā cōnsulātū reppulī,[9] ut exsul potius temptāre quam cōnsul[10] vexāre rem pūblicam possēs, atque ut id quod esset[11] ā tē scelerātē susceptum latrōcinium potius quam
15 bellum nōminārētur.

Vocabulary Drill. — voluptās, iaceō, stuprum, obeō, somnus, praeclārus, frīgus, cōnsulātus.

Rome Charges Cicero with Inaction and Ingratitude

XI. Nunc, ut ā mē, patrēs cōnscrīptī, quandam prope iūstam patriae querimōniam dētester ac dēprecer,[12]

---

[1] *what joy will you experience.* For case see **337.**

[2] Climax and metaphor.

[3] *were practiced.* Here **meditor** has passive force. The subject is **labōrēs**, explained by the appositional infinitives, to be rendered as nouns: *your lying on the ground*, etc.

[4] *which are talked about.*   [5] *to look for a debauch.*   [6] *commit.*

[7] Modifies **tē**, to be supplied as subject of **iacēre.**

[8] *a chance to show.* The subjunctive is potential and descriptive.

[9] *kept you from.* He is referring to the election of 63 B.C

[10] Contrasted with **exsul.** Cicero is fond of such wordplay (**139**). Both words are in apposition with **tū**, to be supplied as subject of **possēs.**

[11] For mood see **388.**

[12] *that I may prevent by protest and plea.*

percipite, quaesō, dīligenter quae[1] dīcam, et ea penitus
animīs vestrīs mentibusque mandāte. Etenim sī mēcum patria, quae mihi vītā[2] meā multō est cārior, sī
cūncta Italia, sī omnis rēs pūblica loquātur:[3] " M.
Tullī, quid agis? Tūne[4] eum quem[5] esse hostem com- 5
peristī, quem ducem bellī futūrum vidēs, quem exspec-
tārī imperātōrem in castrīs hostium sentīs, auctōrem
sceleris, prīncipem coniūrātiōnis, ēvocātōrem servōrum[6]
et cīvium perditōrum, exīre patiēre, ut abs tē nōn
ēmissus ex urbe, sed immissus[7] in urbem esse videātur? 10
Nōnne hunc in vincula dūcī,[8] nōn ad mortem rapī,
nōn summō suppliciō mactārī imperābis? Quid tandem tē impedit? mōsne maiōrum? **28.** At[9] persaepe[10] etiam prīvātī in hāc rē pūblicā perniciōsōs
cīvīs morte multārunt.[11] An lēgēs[12] quae dē cīvium 15

---

[1] *what* (relative); hence **dīcam** is future indicative, not present
subjunctive.   [2] For case see **331.**

[3] *should say* (**390, III**). On account of the long quotation the conclusion of the condition was forgotten. Note the series of three in this
sentence. Find five other examples in this chapter.

[4] *Will you (of all men).* The separation from its verb (**patiēre,** four
lines below) makes **Tū** very emphatic.

[5] *who* or *whom* in English?

[6] To Catiline's credit it must be said that he did not recruit his army
from this source, although urged to do so. With the bloody revolt of
Spartacus (73–71 B.C.) still fresh in their minds, all classes of citizens
would have turned against Catiline, as he well knew, if he dared to incite
the slaves to another revolt.

[7] Cf. **exsul, cōnsul,** p. 188, line 12, and **139.**

[8] The infinitive with **imperō** is restricted to passive forms.

[9] Introduces Cicero's answer.

[10] An exaggeration. Cicero gives only one example in section 3.

[11] See **286.**

[12] No Roman citizen could be scourged or put to death by a magistrate without a chance to appeal to the people. The Apostle Paul
saved himself from a scourging in this way (Acts xxii, 25–29).

Rōmānōrum suppliciō rogātae sunt? At numquam in
hāc urbe quī ā rē pūblicā dēfēcērunt cīvium iūra tenu-
ērunt.[1] An invidiam posteritātis timēs? Praeclāram[2]
vērō populō Rōmānō refers grātiam quī tē, hominem
5 per tē cognitum, nūllā commendātiōne[3] maiōrum tam
mātūrē ad summum imperium[4] per omnīs honōrum
gradūs[5] extulit, sī propter invidiam aut alicuius perīculī
metum salūtem cīvium tuōrum neglegis. **29.** Sed sī
quis est invidiae metus, nōn est vehementius sevēritā-
10 tis[6] ac fortitūdinis invidia quam inertiae[7] ac nēquitiae
pertimēscenda. An, cum bellō vāstābitur Italia, vexā-
buntur urbēs, tēcta ārdēbunt, tum tē nōn exīstimās
invidiae incendiō cōnflagrātūrum? "

Vocabulary Drill. — **dēprecor, quaesō, cārus, cūnctus, gradus,
inertia, vexō.**

Cicero Defends His Course of Watchful Waiting

XII.   Hīs ego sānctissimīs reī pūblicae vōcibus et
15 eōrum hominum quī hoc idem sentiunt mentibus[8]
pauca respondēbō. Ego, sī hoc optimum factū[9] iūdi-
cārem,[10] patrēs cōnscrīptī, Catilīnam morte multārī,

---

[1] Cicero maintained that the **cōnsultum ultimum** passed by the senate
empowered him as consul to proceed against Catiline and his followers
as **hostēs** and no longer **cīvēs,** but this was then — as it still is — a moot
question.

[2] Ironical.

[3] Cicero was a **novus homō,** *i.e.* he was the first of his family line to
hold a curule office (**110, 3; 114**).

[4] The consulship, which Cicero reached at the age of forty-three,
the minimum age.   How old must the President of the United States be?

[5] For the *grades of office* see **114** ff.

[6] *arising from severity.*   [7] *that arising from,* etc.

[8] *thoughts,* as opposed to **vōcibus,** *words.*

[9] See **405** (*b*).   [10] For the condition see **390, II.**

ūnīus ūsūram hōrae gladiātōrī[1] istī ad vīvendum nōn dedissem. Etenim sī summī virī et clārissimī cīvēs Sāturnīnī[2] et Gracchōrum et Flaccī et superiōrum complūrium[3] sanguine nōn modo sē nōn contāminārunt[4] sed etiam honestārunt,[4] certē verendum mihi[5] nōn erat 5 nē quid,[6] hōc parricīdā[7] cīvium interfectō, invidiae mihi in posteritātem redundāret.[8] Quod sī ea[9] mihi maximē impendēret, tamen hōc animō[10] fuī semper ut invidiam virtūte partam[11] glōriam, nōn invidiam putārem.   10

30. Quamquam nōn nūllī sunt in hōc ōrdine quī aut ea quae imminent nōn videant[12] aut ea quae vident dissimulent; quī spem Catilīnae mollibus sententiīs aluērunt[13] coniūrātiōnemque nāscentem nōn crēdendō corrōborāvērunt; quōrum auctōritāte multī nōn sōlum 15 improbī vērum etiam imperītī, sī in hunc animadvertissem,[14] crūdēliter et rēgiē[15] factum esse dīcerent. Nunc intellegō, sī iste, quō[16] intendit, in Mānliāna castra pervēnerit,[17] nēminem tam stultum fore quī

---

[1] Scornful, like our "thug."

[2] Genitive, depending on **sanguine.** For these men see sections 3 and 4.

[3] *of many men of early days.*   [4] Explain the form.

[5] *I did not need to fear* (**317**).   [6] With **invidiae:** *any unpopularity.*

[7] Explain why this is an apt word here. The ablative absolute is conditional.

[8] Why subjunctive? See **373**.   [9] *i.e.* **invidia.**

[10] Ablative of description.

[11] From **pariō:** *gained;* **glōriam** is a second object.

[12] For mood see **380**.   [13] Indicative because **quī** = **et hī.**

[14] Distinguish carefully between this and the following tense.

[15] A word hated by Romans.   [16] *where.*

[17] Perfect subjunctive representing a future perfect indicative. Why subjunctive? Translate as if present. **Intendit** was not changed to the subjunctive because it is parenthetical.

nōn videat[1] coniūrātiōnem esse factam, nēminem tam
improbum quī nōn fateātur. Hōc[2] autem ūnō interfectō, intellegō hanc reī pūblicae pestem paulisper re-
primī, nōn in perpetuum comprimī[3] posse. Quod sī
5 sēsē ēiēcerit sēcumque suōs ēdūxerit et eōdem[4] cēterōs
undique collēctōs naufragōs[5] aggregārit, exstinguētur
atque dēlēbitur nōn modo haec tam adulta reī pūblicae
pestis vērum etiam stirps ac sēmen[6] malōrum omnium.

Vocabulary Drill. — sanguis, dissimulō, intendō. stultus,
fateor, exstinguō, sēmen.

Only Temporary Relief if Catiline Goes.
Let All Conspirators Depart!

XIII. 31. Etenim iam diū, patrēs cōnscrīptī, in hīs
10 perīculīs coniūrātiōnis īnsidiīsque versāmur, sed nesciō
quō pactō[7] omnium scelerum ac veteris furōris et
audāciae mātūritās[8] in nostrī cōnsulātūs tempus ērūpit.
Nunc sī ex tantō latrōciniō[9] iste ūnus tollētur, vidē-
bimur fortasse ad breve quoddam tempus cūrā et
15 metū esse relevātī, perīculum autem residēbit et erit
inclūsum penitus in vēnīs[10] atque in vīsceribus reī pūblicae. Ut saepe hominēs aegrī morbō gravī, cum[11]

---

[1] For mood see **380.**
[2] The ablative absolute is conditional.
[3] Keep the wordplay : *repressed, suppressed.*
[4] Adverb.   [5] Figurative : *stranded derelicts.*
[6] *root and seed*, carrying on the metaphor begun in **adulta.**
[7] With **nesciō quō** : *somehow.* What literally?
[8] This continues the metaphor of the preceding chapter. Cicero
compares Catiline's conspiracy to a harmful weed that has burst forth
in full bloom in the time of his consulship.
[9] Abstract for concrete : *from this band of brigands.*
[10] Explain the comparison.   [11] Conjunction.

aestū febrīque[1] iactantur, sī aquam gelidam bibērunt,[2]
prīmō relevārī videntur, deinde multō gravius vehe-
mentiusque afflīctantur, sīc hic morbus quī est in rē
pūblicā relevātus[3] istīus poenā vehementius, reliquīs
vīvīs, ingravēscet.[4] **32.** Quārē sēcēdant improbī, sē- 5
cernant sē ā bonīs, ūnum in locum congregentur, mūrō
dēnique, quod[5] saepe iam dīxī, sēcernantur ā nōbīs;
dēsinant īnsidiārī domī[6] suae cōnsulī, circumstāre tribūnal praetōris urbānī, obsidēre cum gladiīs cūriam,
malleolōs et facēs[7] ad īnflammandam urbem com- 10
parāre; sit dēnique īnscrīptum in fronte[8] ūnīus
cuiusque quid dē rē pūblicā sentiat. Polliceor hoc
vōbīs, patrēs cōnscrīptī, tantam in nōbīs cōnsulibus
fore dīligentiam, tantam in vōbīs auctōritātem, tantam
in equitibus Rōmānīs virtūtem, tantam in omnibus 15
bonīs cōnsēnsiōnem ut Catilīnae profectiōne omnia
patefacta, illūstrāta, oppressa, vindicāta[9] esse videātis.[10]

Jove Will Aid and Punish

33. Hīsce[11] ōminibus, Catilīna, cum summā reī
pūblicae salūte, cum tuā peste ac perniciē cumque 20
eōrum exitiō quī sē tēcum omnī scelere parricīdiōque

---

[1] Hendiadys: *burning heat of fever.*
[2] Translate by the present tense.
[3] Conditional, like the following ablative absolute.
[4] Note force of -sc-: *grow worse.*   [5] *as;* literally, *which.*
[6] Locative (**351**), while cōnsulī is the dative after īnsidiārī (**314**).
[7] From **fax.**
[8] The face has been called the " mirror of the mind."
[9] Note anaphora, climax, and asyndeton in this sentence, and the
use of four nouns and participles arranged in pairs.
[10] Translate with future force.
[11] = **Hīs.** The enclitic is intensive: *With such prospects as these.*

iūnxērunt, proficīscere ad impium bellum ac nefārium.
Tū,[1] Iuppiter, quī īsdem quibus haec urbs auspiciīs ā
Rōmulō es cōnstitū-
tus,[2] quem Statōrem[3]
5 huius urbis atque im-
perī vērē nōmināmus,
hunc et huius sociōs ā
tuīs cēterīsque templīs,
ā tēctīs urbis ac moe-
10 nibus, ā vītā fortūnīsque cīvium omnium
arcēbis[4] et hominēs
bonōrum inimīcōs,
hostīs patriae, latrōnēs
15 Italiae scelerum foe-
dere inter sē ac nefāriā
societāte coniūnctōs
aeternīs suppliciīs vī-
vōs mortuōsque mac-
20 tābis.

FIG. 58. JUPITER

Vocabulary Drill. — fortasse, cūria, fax, patefaciō, ōmen,
foedus (-eris), societās, auspicium, latrō.

Word Study. — Give the meanings and Latin originals of the
following words; *derelict, Letitia, ostentatious, deficiency, envy,
sanguinary.*

---

[1] *Thou* (use the solemn style throughout), subject of **arcēbis** and
mactābis below.   The speech closes naturally with this prayer to the god
in whose temple the senate was then meeting and whose statue was in full
view.   There are fourteen members in this periodic sentence (**132**, 4).

[2] *whose worship was founded under the same auspices as this city.*

[3] Cicero interprets the word here as *mainstay*, not *stayer in battle*.

[4] *thou wilt surely keep this man.*   We should expect the imperative,
but the future indicative has the force of a mild command.   What are
the rhetorical devices in this final sentence?

The word **exsultō** comes from **ex** and **saliō**, *jump up*; with **gaudiō** it means *jump up with joy*, and that is the meaning of the derivative *exult*. **Bacchor** is to *do the Bacchus stunt*, *i.e.* to act like the reveling followers of that god. **Corrōborō** is to *make like the oak*, *i.e.* strong as the oak (**rōbur**). Note the derivatives *robust, corroborate*.

Review Questions. — 1. Where was this meeting held? Why? 2. What was Cicero's purpose in making the speech? 3. Why did not Cicero have Catiline executed? 4. Why did not the senate vote to have him executed? 5. Who presided at this meeting? 6. Who killed C. Gracchus? 7. What was the Roman equivalent of martial law? 8. What happened on November 6? 9. How did Cicero know about Catiline's plans? 10. What was planned by Catiline for October 28? 11. Where was Manlius? 12. With what crimes does Cicero charge Catiline? 13. Did any of the senators sympathize with Catiline? 14. What are the good qualities of a government official, according to Cicero?

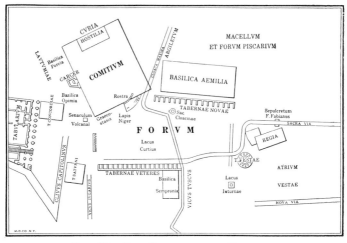

FIG. 59. THE FORUM OF THE REPUBLIC

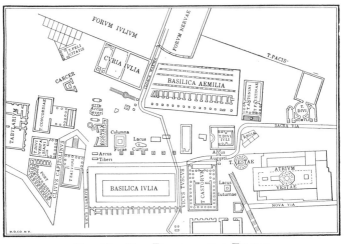

FIG. 60. THE FORUM OF THE EMPIRE

160.　　M. TULLI CICERONIS
IN L. CATILINAM ORATIO SECUNDA
HABITA AD POPULUM

Selections

The second speech was held in the Forum before the people
on the day after the first speech, on November 8 (or 9, according
to those who think the first speech was held November 8).
The only new development was that Catiline had left the city —
according to his friends to go into exile on account of Cicero's
threats, but really to join Manlius. Cicero's purpose is to ac-
quaint the people (generally sympathetic with Catiline) with the
facts and to win them over to his side. Many a jeer and hiss
must have been heard during the speech.

Rejoice, Fellow Citizens, Catiline Is Gone!

I. 1. Tandem aliquandō, Quirītēs, L. Catilīnam,
furentem audāciā, scelus anhēlantem,[1] pestem patriae
nefāriē mōlientem, vōbīs[2] atque huic urbī ferrō flam-
māque[3] minitantem ex urbe vel ēiēcimus vel ēmīsimus[4]
vel ipsum ēgredientem verbīs[5] prōsecūtī sumus.[6] 5
Abiit, excessit, ēvāsit, ērūpit.

First Class of Catiline's Followers: Land Owners
Deeply in Debt

VIII. 17. Sed cūr tam diū dē ūnō hoste loquimur,
et dē eō hoste quī iam fatētur[7] sē esse hostem, et

---

[1] *breathing forth crime.*　　　　[2] Depends upon **minitantem.**

[3] Use the English idiom, of course.

[4] *let go.*　　　　[5] *fond farewells;* ironical.

[6] Note the polysyndeton and anticlimax, in contrast with the asyndeton and climax of the following sentence. There are four participles
arranged in two pairs, followed by three verbs. In the next sentence
the four verbs are arranged in two pairs.

[7] *i.e.* by joining Manlius. Notice that **hostis** is used three times in

197

quem,[1] quia, quod [2] semper voluī, mūrus interest, nōn
timeō; dē hīs quī dissimulant, quī Rōmae remanent,
quī nōbīscum sunt, nihil dīcimus? Quōs quidem ego,
sī ūllō modō fierī possit, nōn tam ulcīscī studeō quam
5 sānāre sibi ipsōs, plācāre [3] reī pūblicae neque [4] id
quārē fierī nōn possit, sī iam mē audīre volent, intellegō. Expōnam enim vōbīs, Quirītēs, ex quibus ge-
neribus hominum istae cōpiae comparentur; deinde
singulīs medicīnam cōnsilī atque ōrātiōnis [5] meae, sī
10 quam [6] poterō, afferam.

   18. Ūnum genus est eōrum quī magnō in aere aliēnō [7]
maiōrēs etiam possessiōnēs habent, quārum amōre
adductī dissolvī [8] nūllō modō possunt. Hōrum hominum speciēs est honestissima,[9] sunt enim locuplētēs;
15 voluntās vērō et causa impudentissima. Tū [10] agrīs,
tū aedificiīs, tū argentō, tū familiā, tū rēbus omnibus
ōrnātus et cōpiōsus sīs, et dubitēs dē possessiōne dētra-

---

accordance with Cicero's purpose to impress on his hearers that Catiline
is to be treated as an enemy.

   [1] *one whom,* object of **timeō.**

   [2] *as.*   Note that one clause is within the other, that therefore the
three introductory words come first and the three verbs follow in inverse
order.   Cf. the arrangement of the petals of a rose, or, if you prefer, the
leaves of a cabbage.

   [3] *to win them over to the state.*   [4] = **et nōn.**

   [5] Genitives (by hendiadys) explaining **medicīnam:**   *the remedy (consisting) of my words of advice.*

   [6] *any (remedy).*

   [7] Adversative: *though heavily in debt.*

   [8] *free themselves from debt.*

   [9] Avoid the English derivative in translating this word and **familia**
below.

   [10] The orator fancies that he has before him one of these " land-poor "
gentry.   The question which he flings at him is purely rhetorical (**375**),
expecting no answer: *you equipped and provided with . . . and you
hesitate.*

here, acquīrere ad fidem? Quid enim exspectās?
Bellum? Quid ergō? in vāstātiōne omnium tuās
possessiōnēs sacrōsānctās futūrās putās? An tabulās
novās?[1] Errant quī istās ā Catilīnā exspectant; meō
beneficiō tabulae novae prōferuntur, vērum auctiōnā-5
riae;[2] neque enim istī quī possessiōnēs habent aliā
ratiōne ūllā salvī esse possunt. Quod[3] sī mātūrius
facere voluissent neque, id quod stultissimum est,
certāre cum ūsūrīs[4] frūctibus praediōrum, et locuplē-
tiōribus hīs et meliōribus cīvibus ūterēmur.[5]   Sed 10
hōsce hominēs minimē putō pertimēscendōs, quod aut
dēdūcī dē sententiā possunt aut, sī permanēbunt,
magis mihi videntur vōta factūrī[6] contrā rem pūblicam
quam arma lātūrī.

Vocabulary Drill. — furō, flamma; ulcīscor, sānō, locuplēs,
argentum, errō, certō, frūctus, voveō.

Second: Bankrupt but Ambitious Politicians

IX.   **19.** Alterum[7] genus est eōrum quī, quamquam 15
premuntur aere aliēnō, dominātiōnem tamen exspectant, rērum[8] potīrī volunt, honōrēs[9] quōs quiētā rē

---

[1] Catiline had promised, as a part of his revolutionary program,
that he would cancel all debts so that *new accounts* could then be opened
by his followers with their creditors.   This would amount to a general
declaration of bankruptcy.

[2] Cicero must have his little joke every now and then.   He intends
to sell their property at auction in order to pay their debts.

[3] Connecting relative.

[4] *to strive to meet the interest rates.*   The income from the farms was
not sufficient to pay interest on the mortgages.

[5] *we should find them.*   [6] *more likely to utter vows.*

[7] *second.*

[8] *to get political control.*   What case does **potior** usually take?

[9] *political offices.*

pūblicā dēspērant perturbātā[1] sē cōnsequī posse arbitrantur. Quibus[2] hoc praecipiendum vidētur, ūnum scīlicet et idem quod reliquīs omnibus, ut dēspērent id quod cōnantur sē cōnsequī posse : prīmum omnium mē 5 ipsum vigilāre,[3] adesse, prōvidēre reī pūblicae ; deinde

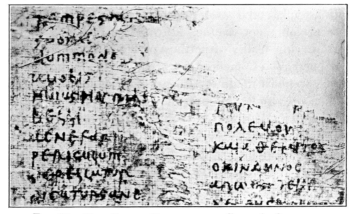

FIG. 61. THE OLDEST FRAGMENT OF CICERO'S ORATIONS

A bit of papyrus of the fifth century found in Egypt. In the first column: **tempestātem subīre dum modo ā vōbīs huius horribilis bellī ac nefāriī perīculum dēpellātur. Dīcātur sānē** (Cat. II, 15). In the second column is a Greek translation for the benefit of those who did not know Latin.

magnōs animōs esse in bonīs virīs, magnam concordiam ōrdinum, maximam multitūdinem,[4] magnās praetereā mīlitum cōpiās ; deōs dēnique immortālīs huic invictō populō, clārissimō imperiō, pulcherrimae[5] urbī contrā

---

[1] Supply **rē pūblicā.**

[2] *These, it seems, need a warning, one and the same warning which all the rest (need).*

[3] The infinitives explain **hoc.**

[4] Understand **adesse** with this and **cōpiās.**

[5] Note the style of the "Fourth of July" orator in these adjectives.

tantam vim sceleris praesentīs[1] auxilium esse lātūrōs.
Quod sī iam sint[2] id quod summō furōre cupiunt adeptī,
num[3] illī in cinere urbis et in sanguine cīvium, quae[4]
mente cōnscelerātā ac nefāriā concupīvērunt, cōnsulēs
sē aut dictātōrēs aut etiam rēgēs spērant futūrōs?[5]
Nōn[5] vident id sē cupere quod,[6] sī adeptī sint, fugitīvō
alicui aut gladiātōrī concēdī sit necesse?

Third: Sulla's Veterans, Dreaming of Fresh Spoils

20. Tertium genus est aetāte iam affectum, sed
tamen exercitātiōne rōbustum ; quō ex genere iste est
Mānlius[7] cui nunc Catilīna succēdit.   Hī sunt homi- 10
nēs ex eīs colōniīs quās Sulla cōnstituit ;[8] quās ego
ūniversās[9] cīvium esse optimōrum et fortissimōrum
virōrum sentiō, sed tamen eī sunt colōnī quī sē in
īnspērātīs ac repentīnīs pecūniīs sūmptuōsius īnsolen-
tiusque iactārunt.[10]   Hī dum aedificant tamquam be- 15
ātī,[11] dum praediīs lēctīs, familiīs magnīs, conviviīs
apparātīs dēlectantur, in tantum aes aliēnum incidērunt

---

[1] Agrees with **deōs**: *in person.*

[2] With **adeptī** (from **adipīscor**) : *But supposing they should attain.*
What kind of condition?

[3] With **spērant** below : *they don't hope, do they?*

[4] *things which,* referring to **cinere** and **sanguine.**

[5] = **Nōnne.**

[6] As a relative, **quod** introduces **sit** ; as a pronoun it is the object of
adeptī sint: *which, if obtained, must be,* etc.

[7] He had served under Sulla as a centurion twenty years before.

[8] Sulla gave land to 120,000 of his soldiers.   The United States, at
the close of the Revolution and at other times, made similar land grants
to veterans.

[9] *as a whole.*

[10] With **sē**: *have made a display,* " shown off."

[11] *rich.*

ut, sī salvī esse velint, Sulla sit eīs ab īnferīs excitandus.[1]
Quī etiam nōn nūllōs agrestīs hominēs tenuīs atque
egentīs in eandem illam spem rapīnārum veterum im-
pulērunt. Quōs ego utrōsque in eōdem genere prae-
5 dātōrum dīreptōrumque pōnō, sed eōs hoc[2] moneō,
dēsinant furere ac prōscrīptiōnēs et dictātūrās cōgitāre.
Tantus enim illōrum temporum dolor inustus est cīvitātī
ut iam ista nōn modo hominēs sed nē[3] pecudēs quidem
mihi passūrae esse videantur.

Vocabulary Drill. — colōnus, sūmptus, beātus, legō (-ere),
īnferī, agrestis, tenuis, dēsinō.

Fourth: Hopeless Bankrupts

10   X.   **21.** Quārtum genus est sānē varium et mixtum
et turbulentum ; quī iam prīdem premuntur, quī numquam ēmergunt,[4] quī partim inertiā, partim male gerendō negōtiō, partim etiam sūmptibus in vetere aere
aliēnō vacillant, quī vadimōniīs, iūdiciīs, prōscrīptiōne[5]
15 bonōrum dēfatīgātī permultī et ex urbe et ex agrīs
sē in illa castra cōnferre dīcuntur. Hōsce ego nōn tam
mīlitēs ācrīs quam īnfitiātōrēs[6] lentōs esse arbitror.
Quī hominēs quam prīmum, sī stāre nōn possunt, cor-

---

[1] To initiate further proscriptions and confiscations. Sulla had now
been dead fifteen years.

[2] Two accusatives with **moneō**: *I warn them of this*, explained by
dēsinant (**370**).

[3] The negative idea covers the preceding **nōn modo,** as if it were
nōn modo nōn: *not only not . . . but not even,* or *not only . . . but
even . . . do not seem likely to endure.*

[4] Cf. our expression " he never gets his head above water," in speak-
ιng of one who never gets out of debt.

[5] *forced sale of their property* — the last of the three steps in " selling
out " a debtor, preceded by the giving of bail and trial.

[6] With **lentōs**: *shirkers,* in war as in debt.

ruant,[1] sed ita ut nōn modo[2] cīvitās sed nē vīcinī quidem proximī sentiant. Nam illud nōn intellegō quam
ob rem, sī vīvere honestē[3] nōn possunt, perīre turpiter
velint, aut cūr minōre dolōre peritūrōs sē cum multīs
quam sī sōlī pereant arbitrentur.　　　　　　　　　　5

Fifth: Criminals of Every Class

22. Quīntum genus est parricīdārum, sīcāriōrum,
dēnique omnium facinorōsōrum. Quōs ego ā Catilīnā
nōn revocō ; nam neque ab eō dīvellī possunt et pereant[4]
sānē in latrōciniō, quoniam sunt ita multī ut eōs carcer
capere nōn possit.　　　　　　　　　　　　　　　10

Sixth: Effeminate and Dissolute Youths
after Catiline's Own Heart

Postrēmum autem genus est[5] nōn sōlum numerō
vērum etiam genere ipsō atque vītā, quod proprium[6]
Catilīnae est, dē eius dīlēctū, immō vērō dē complexū
eius ac sinū ; quōs pexō capillō, nitidōs, aut imberbīs[7]
aut bene barbātōs[8] vidētis, manicātīs et tālāribus 15
tunicīs,[9] vēlīs[10] amictōs, nōn togīs ; quōrum omnis

---

[1] For mood see **366.** The subject is **Quī** (= **Hī**) **hominēs.**

[2] As before for **nōn modo nōn:** *not only . . . but also . . . may not
know.*

[3] Avoid the derivative in translating.

[4] For mood see **366.**　　　　　[5] *is (such), i.e.* last.

[6] *which is Catiline's own.*　　　[7] *i.e.* very young.

[8] It was the latest style for the young bloods to grow beards. Most
Romans were smooth shaven.

[9] A mark of effeminacy, for the ordinary tunic of Roman men had
short sleeves and reached only to the knees.

[10] *i.e.* containing enough cloth to serve as *sails.* Cf. the " collegiate "
clothing (baggy trousers, plus fours, etc.) worn by smart young men of
to-day.

industria vītae et vigilandī labor in antelūcānīs cēnīs exprōmitur.[1] **23.** In hīs gregibus[2] omnēs āleātōrēs, omnēs adulterī, omnēs impūrī impudīcīque versantur. Hī puerī tam lepidī ac dēlicātī nōn sōlum amāre et
5 amārī neque[3] saltāre et cantāre[4] sed etiam sīcās vi-

Fig. 62. Snow in the Forum

brāre et spargere venēna didicērunt. Quī nisi exeunt, nisi pereunt, etiam sī Catilīna perierit, scītōte[5] hoc[6]

---

[1] *whose whole energy in life and effort to keep awake are displayed in banquets that last till morning.*

[2] *gangs* — contemptuous, applied to cattle.

[3] = et nōn sōlum.

[4] Evidently the refined young men of Cicero's day did not indulge in " petting," dancing, and singing.

[5] Future imperative with present force: *know,* or *let me tell you.*

[6] Translate as if hōs . . . futūrōs esse; sēminārium is predicate accusative.

in rē pūblicā sēminārium Catilīnārum futūrum.   Vērum tamen quid sibi istī miserī volunt?[1] num suās
sēcum mulierculās[2] sunt in castra ductūrī?   Quem ad
modum autem illīs carēre poterunt, hīs praesertim iam
noctibus?   Quō autem pactō illī Appennīnum atque 5
illās pruīnās ac nivīs[3] perferent?   nisi idcircō[4] sē facilius
hiemem tolerātūrōs putant, quod nūdī in convīviīs
saltāre didicērunt.[5]

Vocabulary Drill. — parricīda, sānē, proprius, dīlēctus, industria, grex, amō, venēnum.

[1] With sibi: *mean.*

[2] *sweethearts.*   The diminutive is contemptuous.

[3] Snow is rare at Rome.

[4] Explained by the following quod clause.   The whole passage is
ironical.

[5] The Romans, too, had their " wild parties."

161.   M. TULLI CICERONIS
IN L. CATILINAM ORATIO TERTIA
HABITA AD POPULUM

Between the time of the second and third speeches the situation changed entirely in a most dramatic fashion through the mistakes of Catiline's representatives. When Cicero made the first two speeches he was morally certain of Catiline's intentions, but had no direct proof. The citizens in general were inclined to look upon Cicero's attacks as political fulminations and many were sympathetic with Catiline.

After Catiline left Rome his subordinates opened negotiations with a committee of a Gallic tribe, the Allobroges, who happened to be in Rome. They wanted to get military aid from this foreign nation against their own government. The Allobroges consulted their Roman patron, who reported the whole matter to Cicero. On his advice they asked Catiline's negotiators to put the proposition in writing. This was done. At the same time Lentulus, one of Catiline's men, wrote a letter to his chief, urging the use of slaves. By arrangement with the Allobroges Cicero had a force of soldiers waiting when the Gauls and their Roman guides set out from Rome on the night of December 2. The incriminating documents were found. The ringleaders were arrested early the next morning and were brought to a meeting of the senate called by Cicero, where they confessed. At the end of the day Cicero made the speech that follows to explain to the people all that happened. It may be compared to a statement made to the press by the president on some important occasion. The mistake that the conspirators made in calling foreigners and slaves to their aid turned popular opinion against them. At the close of his speech, as Sallust tells us, Cicero was praised to the skies.

Rome Has Been Saved

I. 1. Rem pūblicam,[1] Quirītēs, vītamque[2] omnium vestrum, bona, fortūnās, coniugēs līberōsque vestrōs atque hoc domicilium clārissimī imperī, fortūnātissimam pulcherrimamque urbem, hodiernō diē deōrum immortālium summō ergā vōs amōre, labōribus, cōnsiliīs, 5 perīculīs meīs ē flammā atque ferrō ac paene ex faucibus[3] fātī ēreptam et vōbīs cōnservātam ac restitūtam vidētis. 2. Et sī nōn minus nōbīs iūcundī atque illūstrēs sunt eī diēs quibus cōnservāmur quam illī quibus nāscimur, quod salūtis certa laetitia est, nāscendī 10 incerta condiciō,[4] et quod sine sēnsū[5] nāscimur, cum voluptāte servāmur, profectō, quoniam illum[6] quī hanc urbem condidit ad deōs immortālīs benevolentiā fāmāque sustulimus,[7] esse apud vōs posterōsque vestrōs in honōre dēbēbit[8] is quī eandem hanc urbem conditam 15 amplificātamque servāvit. Nam tōtī urbī,[9] templīs, dēlūbrīs, tēctīs ac moenibus subiectōs prope iam ignīs circumdatōsque restīnximus, īdemque[10] gladiōs in rem

---

[1] This periodic sentence has twelve members of varying length, each presenting a successive step in the development of the thought. The position of the verb indicates that the thought is not fully revealed until the end. Read the sentence aloud several times, and the short thought units will then stand out clearly. Translate each thought unit as it stands and do not bother about the verb until you reach it. Then finally translate into good English.

[2] We use the plural in English.

[3] What figure?

[4] *our lot at birth.*   [5] *consciousness.*

[6] Romulus, who was deified by the Romans.

[7] From **tollō**: *we have exalted to the gods by our affectionate praise.* He is " first in the hearts of his countrymen."

[8] *he will deserve to be . . . who;* is refers to Cicero.

[9] The datives depend on the participles.   [10] *likewise.*

pūblicam dēstrictōs rettudimus mūcrōnēsque eōrum ā
iugulīs vestrīs dēiēcimus.

3. Quae quoniam in senātū illūstrāta, patefacta,
comperta[1] sunt per mē, vōbīs iam expōnam breviter ut[2]
5 et quanta et quam manifesta et quā ratiōne investīgāta
et comprehēnsa sint vōs quī et ignōrātis et exspectātis
scīre possītis.

Prīncipiō, ut[3] Catilīna paucīs ante diēbus[4] ērūpit
ex urbe, cum sceleris suī sociōs huiusce nefāriī bellī
10 acerrimōs ducēs[5] Rōmae relīquisset, semper vigilāvī et
prōvīdī, Quirītēs, quem ad modum in tantīs et tam
absconditīs īnsidiīs salvī esse possēmus.

Vocabulary Drill. — coniūnx, hodiernus, illūstris, condō,
benevolentia, dēlūbrum, manifestus.

Treasonable Letters Seized by a Clever Ruse

II. Nam tum cum ex urbe Catilīnam ēiciēbam[6]
(nōn enim iam vereor huius verbī invidiam,[7] cum illa[8]
15 magis sit timenda, quod vīvus exierit[9]) sed tum cum
illum extermināri[10] volēbam, aut reliquam coniūrātōrum
manum simul exitūram aut eōs quī restitissent[11] īnfirmōs
sine illō ac dēbilīs fore putābam.   **4.** Atque ego, ut[12]

---

[1] The order of the verbs is the reverse of chronological.

[2] Introducing a purpose clause.   [3] *ever since* (**364**).

[4] Actually almost a month before.   [5] Predicate : *as leaders.*

[6] *at the time when I was trying to drive out.* The verb is in the indicative because the clause indicates the exact time of the event.

[7] *the unpopularity produced by this word (i.e.* **ēiciēbam**).

[8] *i.e.* **invidia.**

[9] A quoted reason : *because (as my enemies will charge) he left alive* (**389**).

[10] *banished* (lit., *put outside the boundaries*).

[11] *who would remain.* What form would this be in direct discourse?

[12] There are four occurrences of **ut** in this sentence in four different uses.

vīdī, quōs maximō furōre et scelere esse īnflammātōs
sciēbam, eōs nōbīscum esse et Rōmae remānsisse, in
eō[1] omnīs diēs noctēsque cōnsūmpsī, ut quid agerent,
quid mōlīrentur sentīrem ac vidērem, ut, quoniam auribus vestrīs propter incrēdibilem magnitūdinem sceleris 5
minōrem fidem faceret ōrātiō[2] mea, rem ita compre-
henderem[3] ut tum dēmum animīs salūtī vestrae prōvi-
dērētis cum oculīs maleficium ipsum vidērētis. Itaque
ut comperī lēgātōs[4] Allobrogum bellī Trānsalpīnī et
tumultūs Gallicī excitandī causā ā P. Lentulō[5] esse 10
sollicitātōs, eōsque in Galliam ad suōs cīvīs eōdemque
itinere cum litterīs mandātīsque[6] ad Catilīnam esse
missōs, comitemque eīs adiūnctum esse T. Volturcium,
atque huic esse ad Catilīnam datās litterās, facultātem
mihi oblātam putāvī ut, quod[7] erat difficillimum quod- 15
que ego semper optābam ab dīs immortālibus, tōta rēs
nōn sōlum ā mē sed etiam ā senātū et ā vōbīs manifestō
dēprēnderētur.   **5.** Itaque hesternō diē L. Flaccum
et C. Pomptīnum praetōrēs,[8] fortissimōs atque amantissimōs reī pūblicae virōs, ad mē vocāvī, rem exposuī, 20
quid fierī placēret ostendī. Illī autem, quī omnia dē

---

[1] *in this work*, explained by **ut . . . sentīrem**.

[2] *my argument did not sound credible to your ears.* For mood see
388.

[3] *get hold of the situation.*

[4] Cf. the delegations sent to Washington by Indian tribes from time
to time to complain about the mismanagement of their affairs. The
Allobroges had been conquered in 121 B.C. but they were always ready
for revolt, as Caesar later learned.

[5] A praetor, one of the " higher-ups " of the conspiracy.

[6] *letters and oral instructions.*

[7] *a thing which*, explained by **ut . . . dēprēnderētur.**

[8] Next to the consuls in rank and, like them, possessing the **imperium**
or right to command troops.

rē pūblicā praeclāra atque ēgregia sentīrent,[1] sine
recūsātiōne ac sine ūllā morā negōtium suscēpērunt et,
cum advesperāsceret,[2] occultē ad pontem Mulvium[3]
pervēnērunt atque ibi in proximīs vīllīs ita bipertītō
5 fuērunt ut Tiberis inter eōs et pōns interesset. Eōdem
autem et ipsī sine cuiusquam suspīciōne multōs fortīs
virōs ēdūxerant, et ego ex praefectūrā Reātīnā complūrīs dēlēctōs adulēscentīs quōrum operā ūtor assiduē
in reī pūblicae praesidiō[4] cum gladiīs mīseram. **6.** In-
10 terim tertiā ferē vigiliā exāctā,[5] cum iam pontem
Mulvium magnō comitātū[6] lēgātī Allobrogēs ingredī
inciperent ūnāque Volturcius, fit in eōs impetus ; dūcun-
tur et ab illīs gladiī et ā nostrīs. Rēs[7] praetōribus
erat nōta sōlīs, ignōrābātur ā cēterīs.

Vocabulary Drill. — invidia, restō, auris, assiduus, exigō,
comitātus.

The Conspirators Arrested and a Meeting of the Senate Called

15 **III.** Tum interventū Pomptīnī atque Flaccī pugna
quae erat commissa[8] sēdātur. Litterae quaecumque
erant in eō comitātū integrīs signīs praetōribus trādun-

---

[1] *since they cherished only the most loyal sentiments.* What literally?

[2] Both tense and verbal ending -scō are inceptive: *it was getting dark* (**357**).

[3] A short distance north of Rome and still standing in part (see Fig. 63).

[4] Rome had no police force, and Cicero at this crisis was compelled to depend largely upon a sort of " governor's troop," recruited at the Sabine town Reate. They were bound to him by ties of loyalty as the town's patron or legal adviser at Rome.

[5] *i.e.* about 3 A.M.   [6] For construction see **332**, *b.*
[7] Meaning here?   [8] *had commenced.*

FIG. 63. THE MULVIAN BRIDGE

tur; ipsī[1] comprehēnsī ad mē, cum iam dīlūcēsceret,
dēdūcuntur. Atque hōrum omnium scelerum[2] im-
probissimum māchinātōrem, Cimbrum Gabīnium, statim ad mē nihildum suspicantem vocāvī; deinde item
arcessītus est L. Statilius et post eum Cethēgus; tar- 5
dissimē autem Lentulus[3] vēnit, crēdō quod in litterīs
dandīs[4] praeter cōnsuētūdinem proximā nocte vigilārat.
7. Cum summīs et clārissimīs huius cīvitātis virīs,[5] quī,
audītā rē, frequentēs ad mē māne convēnerant, litterās
ā mē prius aperīrī quam ad senātum dēferrī[6] placēret, 10
nē, sī nihil esset inventum, temere ā mē tantus tumultus
iniectus cīvitātī[7] vidērētur, negāvī[8] mē esse factūrum
ut dē perīculō pūblicō nōn ad cōnsilium pūblicum rem
integram dēferrem. Etenim, Quirītēs, sī ea quae erant
ad mē dēlāta reperta nōn essent, tamen ego nōn arbitrā- 15
bar in tantīs reī pūblicae perīculīs esse mihi nimiam dīligentiam pertimēscendam. Senātum frequentem celeriter, ut vīdistis, coēgī. 8. Atque intereā statim admonitū
Allobrogum C. Sulpicium praetōrem, fortem virum, mīsī
quī ex aedibus Cethēgī sī quid[9] tēlōrum esset efferret;[10] 20

---

[1] Volturcius and the Allobrogian envoys.

[2] *i.e.* this attempt to secure the alliance of the Allobroges.

[3] Lentulus was notoriously lazy.

[4] *in writing the letters.* The irony becomes all the more apparent
when you turn to one of the two letters (p. 216) and find that it is only
a few lines long.

[5] With **placēret**, whose subject is the infinitive phrase: *although the
most eminent men . . . thought it best that.*

[6] We should expect **dēferrētur** because it is here introduced by **priusquam**, but Cicero emphasizes the comparative idea here, which gives the
same construction to both **aperīrī** and **dēferrī**.

[7] Dependent upon **iniectus.**

[8] *I said that I would not fail to lay before the public council.*

[9] With **sī:** *whatever.*

[10] Relative clause of purpose (**368**).

ex quibus ille maximum sīcārum numerum et gladiō-
rum extulit.

Word Study. — Why is a *jugular* vein so called? Analyze the
words **patefacta, maleficium, invēstīgō.** Find two inceptive verbs
in sections 1–7.

The Statements of Volturcius and the Gauls

IV.   Intrōdūxī Volturcium sine Gallīs ; fidem pūblicam[1] iussū senātūs dedī ; hortātus sum ut ea quae scīret

FIG. 64.   THE SIBYL
From the painting by Vedder.

5 sine timōre indicāret.   Tum ille dīxit, cum vix sē ex
magnō timōre recreāsset, ā P. Lentulō sē habēre ad
Catilīnam mandāta et litterās[2] ut servōrum praesidiō
ūterētur, ut ad urbem quam prīmum cum exercitū

---

[1] *promise of pardon.*   This is called to-day "turning state's evidence."
[2] *a letter* (as seen later).   Supply *urging him,* to introduce the **ut**
clauses.

accēderet; id autem eō cōnsiliō ut, cum urbem ex omnibus partibus quem ad modum dīscrīptum distribūtum-
que erat incendissent caedemque īnfīnītam cīvium
fēcissent, praestō esset ille[1] quī et fugientīs exciperet[2]
et sē cum hīs urbānīs ducibus coniungeret.   **9.** Intrō-5
ductī autem Gallī iūs iūrandum sibi et litterās ā P.
Lentulō, Cethēgō, Statiliō ad suam gentem datās esse

Fɪɢ. 65.   Sᴀᴛᴜʀɴᴀʟɪᴀ
From a group by Biondo.

dīxērunt, atque ita sibi ab hīs et ā L. Cassiō[3] esse praescrīptum[4] ut equitātum in Italiam quam prīmum mit-
terent; pedestrīs sibi cōpiās nōn dēfutūrās.[5]   Lentulum 10
autem sibi cōnfirmāsse ex fātīs Sibyllīnīs haruspicumque
respōnsīs sē esse tertium illum Cornēlium[6] ad quem rēgnum[7] huius urbis atque imperium pervenīre esset

---

[1] *i.e.* Catiline.   [2] Purpose.

[3] Cassius was too wise to incriminate himself by writing a letter like
the others, but confined himself to oral instructions.

[4] *that they had been instructed to.*   What literally?

[5] Not a part of the command, although a part of the letter; supply
they stated that.

[6] His full name was Publius Cornelius Lentulus Sura.

[7] *throne* — an idea abhorrent to Romans ever since their sorry experience with the Tarquin kings.

necesse : Cinnam ante sē et Sullam¹ fuisse. Eundemque dīxisse fātālem² hunc annum esse ad interitum
huius urbis atque imperī, quī³ esset annus decimus post
virginum absolūtiōnem, post Capitōlī autem incēn-
5 siōnem vīcēsimus.   **10.** Hanc autem Cethēgō⁴ cum
cēterīs contrōversiam fuisse dīxērunt quod Lentulō et
aliīs Sāturnālibus⁵ caedem fierī atque urbem incendī
placēret, Cethēgō nimium id longum vidērētur.

Vocabulary Drill (7–10). — frequēns, aedēs; indicō (-āre),
virgō.

The Confessions

V. Ac nē longum sit,⁶ Quirītēs, tabellās prōferrī
10 iussimus quae ā quōque dīcēbantur datae.⁷ Prīmō
ostendimus Cethēgō ; signum cognōvit. Nōs līnum
incīdimus ; lēgimus. Erat scrīptum ipsīus⁸ manū
Allobrogum senātuī et populō sēsē quae eōrum lēgātīs
cōnfirmāsset factūrum esse ; ōrāre ut item illī facerent
15 quae sibi eōrum lēgātī recēpissent.⁹ Tum Cethēgus,
quī¹⁰ paulō ante aliquid tamen dē gladiīs ac sīcīs quae
apud ipsum¹¹ erant dēprehēnsa respondisset dīxissetque

---

¹ L. Cornelius Cinna and L. Cornelius Sulla.

² *appointed by fate for* (**ad**).   ³ *since it* (**380**).   ⁴ *Cethegus had* (**316**).

⁵ The Roman Saturnalia (Dec. 17) partook of the gift-giving spirit
of our Christmas and the license and merry-making of our Hallowe'en,
with all restrictions removed — an ideal time for revolutionists to strike
their blow.

⁶ *not to be too long.*

⁷ = **scrīptae esse.** The wax tablets were tied together, then sealed
with the writer's ring. Cethegus had to admit that the seal was his,
that the letter was genuine.

⁸ Letters were often dictated to slaves, but Cethegus intended to take
no chances with this one.

⁹ = **pollicitī essent.**   ¹⁰ Adversative : *though he* (**380**).

¹¹ *at his home.*

sē semper bonōrum[1] ferrāmentōrum studiōsum fuisse,
recitātīs litterīs, dēbilitātus atque abiectus cōnscientiā[2]
repente conticuit. Intrōductus Statilius cognōvit et
signum et manum suam. Recitātae sunt tabellae in
eandem ferē sen-[5]
tentiam;[3] cōnfes-
sus est. Tum os-
tendī tabellās
Lentulō et quae-
sīvī cognōsceretne[10]
signum. Annuit.
"Est vērō," in-
quam, "nōtum qui-
dem signum, imāgō
avī[4] tuī, clārissimī[15]
virī, quī amāvit
ūnicē patriam et

FIG. 66.   WAX TABLET AND PAPYRUS ROLLS
Note the **līnum**.   (From a model.)

cīvīs suōs; quae[5] quidem tē ā tantō scelere etiam
mūta revocāre[6] dēbuit." 11. Leguntur eādem ratiōne[7] ad senātum Allobrogum populumque litterae.[20]
Sī quid dē hīs rēbus dīcere vellet,[8] fēcī potestātem.
Atque ille prīmō quidem negāvit; post autem aliquantō,
tōtō iam indiciō expositō atque ēditō,[9] surrēxit, quaesīvit ā Gallīs quid sibi esset cum eīs,[10] quam ob rem

---

[1] Emphatic: *fine weapons.*   He asserted that he was a collector.
[2] What is our idiom?   [3] *with about the same content.*
[4] P. Cornelius Lentulus, a consul.   [5] *i.e.* **imāgō.**

[6] Juxtaposition of apparently contradictory ideas (called oxymoron):
even though mute it ought to have recalled you.   Because the English verb
" ought " is defective, we must express the time with the infinitive
instead of the main verb.   [7] *of the same tenor.*

[8] Subjunctive because of the implied indirect discourse.

[9] *had been arranged and put into form* (by the court clerks).

[10] *what he had to do with them.*

domum suam vēnissent, itemque ā Volturciō. Quī
cum illī breviter cōnstanterque respondissent per quem
ad eum quotiēnsque vēnissent, quaesīssentque ab eō
nihilne[1] sēcum esset dē fātīs Sibyllīnīs locūtus, tum ille
5 subitō scelere dēmēns quanta cōnscientiae vīs esset
ostendit.   Nam, cum id posset īnfitiārī, repente praeter
opīniōnem omnium cōnfessus est.   Ita eum nōn modo
ingenium illud et dīcendī exercitātiō quā semper valuit
sed etiam propter vim sceleris manifestī atque dēpre-
10 hēnsī impudentia quā superābat omnīs improbitāsque
dēfēcit.[2]   **12.** Volturcius vērō subitō litterās prōferrī
atque aperīrī iubet quās sibi ā Lentulō ad Catilīnam
datās esse dīcēbat.   Atque ibi vehementissimē pertur-
bātus Lentulus tamen et signum et manum suam cog-
15 nōvit.   Erant autem sine nōmine,[3] sed ita : " Quis
sim sciēs ex eō quem ad tē mīsī.   Cūrā ut vir sīs et
cōgitā quem in locum sīs prōgressus.[4]   Vidē ecquid[5]
tibi iam sit necesse et cūrā ut omnium tibi auxilia ad-
iungās, etiam īnfimōrum."[6]   Gabīnius deinde intrō-
20 ductus, cum prīmō impudenter respondēre coepisset,
ad extrēmum nihil ex eīs quae Gallī īnsimulābant negāvit.   **13.** Ac mihi quidem, Quirītēs, cum[7] illa certissima vīsa sunt argūmenta atque indicia sceleris, tabellae, signa, manūs, dēnique ūnīus cuiusque cōnfessiō,

---

[1] *whether he had said nothing to them.*

[2] Agrees with the nearer subject ; the object is **eum.**

[3] Cf. the usual heading of letters, *e.g.* **Cicerō Atticō Salūtem Dīcit.**

[4] *how far you have gone.*   [5] *whether anything.*

[6] = **servōrum.** Cicero's version of the letter differs in form but not
in thought from that of Sallust (p. 249).   The careful balancing of the
four clauses shows that Cicero has made changes to adapt it to his own
rhetorical style.

[7] With **tum** below : *not only . . . but also.*

tum multō certiōra illa, color,[1] oculī, vultūs, taciturnitās. Sīc enim obstupuerant, sīc terram intuēbantur, sīc
fūrtim nōn numquam[2] inter sēsē aspiciēbant ut nōn
iam ab aliīs indicārī sed indicāre sē ipsī vidērentur.

Vocabulary Drill. — tabella, recitō, dēbilitō, quotiēns, dēmēns,
ingenium, intueor.

The Action of the Senate

VI.   Indiciīs expositīs atque ēditīs,[3] Quirītēs, senātum cōnsuluī dē summā rē pūblicā[4] quid fierī placēret.[5]
Dictae sunt ā prīncipibus[6] ācerrimae ac fortissimae sententiae, quās senātus sine ūllā varietāte est secūtus.
Et quoniam nōndum est perscrīptum senātūs cōnsultum, ex memoriā vōbīs, Quirītēs, quid senātus cēnsuerit
expōnam.   **14.** Prīmum mihi grātiae verbīs amplissimīs aguntur, quod virtūte, cōnsiliō, prōvidentiā meā
rēs pūblica maximīs perīculīs sit līberāta.[7] Deinde
L. Flaccus et C. Pomptīnus praetōrēs, quod eōrum
operā fortī fidēlīque ūsus essem,[8] meritō ac iūre lau-
dantur. Atque etiam virō fortī, collēgae[9] meō, laus
impertītur, quod eōs quī huius coniūrātiōnis participēs
fuissent[10] ā suīs et ā reī pūblicae cōnsiliīs remōvisset.

---

[1] (change of) color.   [2] With nōn = interdum (**157**).
[3] As on p. 215, line 23.   [4] the highest interest of the state.
[5] should be done. What literally?

[6] the leading senators, who were called upon by Cicero, the presiding
consul, according to an established order, beginning with the consuls-
elect. Later a committee put the gist of the majority opinion into
written form.

[7] Quoted from the vote of thanks, hence the subjunctive.

[8] I had found their services effective and loyal.

[9] Antonius had been led to sever outward connections with the conspiracy by the promise of the governorship of the rich province of
Macedonia.   [10] Subjunctive by attraction (**388**).

Atque ita cēnsuērunt ut P. Lentulus, cum sē praetūrā
abdicāsset,[1] in custōdiam trāderētur; itemque utī
C. Cethēgus, L. Statilius, P. Gabīnius, quī omnēs praesentēs erant, in custōdiam trāderentur; atque idem hoc
5 dēcrētum est in L. Cassium,[2] quī sibi prōcūrātiōnem
incendendae urbis dēpoposcerat, in M. Cēpārium, cui
ad sollicitandōs pāstōrēs Āpūliam attribūtam esse erat
indicātum, in P. Fūrium, quī est ex eīs colōnīs quōs
Faesulās L. Sulla dēdūxit, in Q. Annium Chīlōnem, quī
10 ūnā cum hōc Fūriō semper erat in hāc Allobrogum sol-
licitātiōne versātus, in P. Umbrēnum, lībertīnum
hominem, ā quō prīmum Gallōs ad Gabīnium perductōs
esse cōnstābat. Atque eā[3] lēnitāte senātus est ūsus,
Quirītēs, ut ex tantā coniūrātiōne tantāque hāc mul-
15 titūdine domesticōrum hostium novem[4] hominum per-
ditissimōrum poenā rē pūblicā cōnservātā, reliquōrum
mentīs sānārī posse arbitrārētur. **15.** Atque etiam
supplicātiō dīs immortālibus prō singulārī eōrum meritō
meō nōmine dēcrēta est, quod mihi prīmum post hanc
20 urbem conditam togātō contigit,[5] et hīs dēcrēta verbīs
est: " quod urbem incendiīs, caede cīvīs, Italiam bellō
līberāssem."[6] Quae supplicātiō sī cum cēterīs sup-
plicātiōnibus cōnferātur,[7] hoc interest, quod cēterae

---

[1] A Roman official could not be brought to trial during his term of
office. The same is true of members of Congress and other officials
to-day.

[2] Evidently Cassius and the three others here mentioned had not yet
been arrested. Ceparius was the only one actually seized.

[3] = **tālī**, anticipating the result clause **ut . . . arbitrārētur.**

[4] Only five of these were actually punished, the rest having fled in time.

[5] *a thing which happened to a civilian (like) me for the first time since
the founding of this city.*

[6] What does the mood show? See **sit līberāta**, p. 217, line 13.

[7] For mood see **390, III.** Note that the conclusion is one of fact.

bene gestā,[1] haec ūna cōnservātā rē pūblicā cōnstitūta
est. Atque illud quod faciendum prīmum fuit factum
atque trānsāctum est. Nam P. Lentulus, quamquam
patefactīs indiciīs, cōnfessiōnibus suīs, iūdiciō senātūs
nōn modo praetōris iūs vērum etiam cīvis āmīserat, 5
tamen magistrātū sē abdicāvit,[2] ut quae religiō[3] C.
Mariō,[4] clārissimō virō, nōn fuerat quō minus[5] C.
Glauciam, dē quō nihil nōminātim erat dēcrētum, praetōrem occīderet, eā nōs religiōne[6] in prīvātō P. Lentulō pūniendō līberārēmur.[7]   10

Vocabulary Drill. — fidēlis, praetūra, perdō, togātus, pūniō.

Word Study. — The suffix -ātus indicates an office or an official
body : sen-ātus, a body of senēs (old men) ; magistr-ātus, the
office of a " higher-up " (magis-ter). In English this becomes
-ate. The suffix -ester (-estris) is used to form adjectives : pedester. Review the prefixes intrā-, intrō-, (411).

A *pastor* is the " shepherd " of his " flock " or *congregation* (from
con- and grex, *flock*).

The English abbreviation *cf.* is from cōnfer in the sense used in
section 15.

The Collapse of the Conspiracy

VII. 16. Nunc quoniam, Quirītēs, cōnscelerātissimī
perīculōsissimīque bellī nefāriōs ducēs captōs iam et
comprehēnsōs tenētis, exīstimāre dēbētis omnīs Catilīnae cōpiās, omnīs spēs atque opēs, hīs dēpulsīs urbis
perīculīs, concidisse.[8]   Quem quidem ego cum ex urbe 15

---

[1] Supply rē pūblicā ; also cōnstitūtae sunt with cēterae.
[2] He was doubtless forced to do so.   [3] *scruple.*
[4] Dative of possessor: *which Marius did not have.*
[5] *(to prevent him) from.* See **371.**   [6] Antecedent of quae.
[7] With ut.
[8] An optimism not warranted by the danger still confronting the
state.

peiiēbam,[1] hoc prōvidēbam animō, Quirītēs, remōtō
Catilīnā, nōn mihi esse P. Lentulī somnum nec L. Cassī
adipēs nec C. Cethēgī furiōsam temeritātem pertimēscendam.   Ille erat ūnus timendus ex istīs[2] omnibus,
5 sed tam diū dum urbis moenibus continēbātur.   Omnia
nōrat,[3] omnium aditūs tenēbat[4]; appellāre,[5] temptāre,
sollicitāre poterat, audēbat.   Erat eī cōnsilium[6] ad
facinus aptum, cōnsiliō autem neque lingua neque
manus deerat.   Iam ad certās rēs cōnficiendās certōs[7]
10 hominēs dēlēctōs ac dēscrīptōs habēbat.   Neque vērō,
cum aliquid mandārat,[8] cōnfectum putābat : nihil erat
quod nōn ipse obīret, occurreret, vigilāret, labōrāret;
frīgus, sitim, famem[9] ferre poterat.   **17.** Hunc[10] ego
hominem tam ācrem, tam audācem, tam parātum, tam
15 callidum, tam in scelere vigilantem, tam[11] in perditīs
rēbus dīligentem nisi ex domesticīs īnsidiīs in castrēnse
latrōcinium compulissem — dīcam id quod sentiō,
Quirītēs — nōn facile hanc tantam mōlem malī ā cervīcibus vestrīs dēpulissem.   Nōn ille nōbīs Sāturnālia
20 cōnstituisset,[12] neque tantō ante[13] exitī ac fātī diem reī

---

[1] *I was trying to drive.* Why indicative? See **382, Note.**

[2] Note the scornful **istīs** : *of all that gang.*

[3] = **nōverat** : *he knew.*

[4] *he had ways of reaching everybody.*

[5] He not only remembered names but knew whom to call " Bill "
and whom " Mr. Jones."

[6] *ability.*

[7] *particular* (not *certain*) *men for particular things, i.e.* the right man
for every task.

[8] What tense?   [9] What figure? See **136.**

[10] Keep the emphasis and order : *As for this man,* etc.

[11] Note the effective repetition. What figure? See **136.**   The six
phrases are in three pairs.

[12] *i.e.* Catiline would not have waited so long.

[13] *so long before.*

pūblicae dēnūntiāvisset neque commīsisset ut signum,
ut litterae suae testēs manifestī sceleris dēprehenderen-
tur. Quae nunc, illō absente, sīc gesta[1] sunt ut nūllum
in prīvātā domō fūrtum umquam sit tam palam inventum quam haec in tōtā rē pūblicā coniūrātiō manifestō[2] 5
comprehēnsa est. Quod sī Catilīna in urbe ad hanc
diem remānsisset, quamquam, quoad fuit, omnibus eius
cōnsiliīs occurrī atque obstitī, tamen, ut levissimē
dīcam,[3] dīmicandum nōbīs cum illō fuisset, neque nōs
umquam, cum ille in urbe hostis esset, tantīs perīculīs 10
rem pūblicam tantā pāce,[4] tantō ōtiō, tantō silentiō
līberāssēmus.

Vocabulary Drill. — temeritās, latrōcinium, cervīx, fātum,
dēnūntiō, fūrtum, palam, aptus.

Revelations of the Will of the Gods

VIII. **18.** Quamquam[5] haec omnia, Quirītēs, ita
sunt ā mē administrāta ut deōrum immortālium nūtū
atque cōnsiliō et gesta et prōvīsa esse videantur. Idque 15
cum[6] coniectūrā cōnsequī possumus, quod[7] vix vidētur
hūmānī cōnsilī[8] tantārum rērum gubernātiō esse potuisse, tum vērō ita praesentēs hīs temporibus opem et
auxilium nōbīs tulērunt ut eōs paene oculīs vidēre
possīmus. Nam ut illa omittam,[9] vīsās nocturnō tem- 20

---

[1] *mismanaged*, as the context shows.

[2] Balances **tam palam,** but unnecessary in translating.

[3] *to say the least.*

[4] Best rendered as adverbs (**333**).

[5] Transitional or concessive — which?

[6] *not only*, correlated with **tum,** *but also.*   [7] Causal.

[8] Predicate genitive (**298**): *scarcely could, it seems, have been within
the scope of human wisdom.*

[9] A parenthetical purpose clause.

pore ab occidente facēs[1] ārdōremque caelī, ut fulminum
iactūs, ut terrae mōtūs relinquam, ut omittam cētera

quae tam multa nōbīs
cōnsulibus facta sunt
5 ut haec quae nunc
fīunt canere dī immor-
tālēs vidērentur, hoc
certē, Quirītēs, quod
sum dictūrus neque
10 praetermittendum ne-
que relinquendum est.
19. Nam profectō me-
moriā tenētis, Cottā et
Torquātō cōnsulibus,[2]
15 complūrīs in Capitōliō
rēs dē caelō[3] esse per-
cussās, cum et simu-
lācra deōrum dēpulsa
sunt et statuae vete-
20 rum hominum dēiectae
et lēgum aera[4] lique-
facta et tāctus[5] etiam

FIG. 67.   THE ROMAN WOLF
Copy in New York City.

ille quī hanc urbem condidit Rōmulus, quem inau-
rātum in Capitōliō, parvum atque lactantem, ūbe-
25 ribus lupīnīs inhiantem fuisse meministis.[6]   Quō qui-

---

[1] *Meteors* seen *in* (**ab**) *the west* were supposed to be ominous of
approaching disaster, for the Romans considered the western quarter
of the sky unlucky.   The same was true of lightning out of a blue sky.
The ignorant regarded these phenomena as direct manifestations of God.
Cicero is " playing to the gallery."

[2] 65 B.C.   [3] *i.e.* by lightning.   [4] *bronze tablets.*   [5] *struck.*

[6] *whose gilded likeness as a suckling infant, clinging to the breasts of a
wolf.*   The bronze wolf preserved in Rome is the very one that Cicero

dem tempore cum haruspicēs ex tōtā Etrūriā[1] con-
vēnissent, caedīs atque incendia et lēgum interitum et
bellum cīvīle ac domesticum et tōtīus urbis atque
imperī occāsum appropinquāre dīxērunt, nisi dī immortālēs omnī ratiōne plācātī suō nūmine prope fāta

FIG. 68.   LŪDĪ   *From " Ben Hur "*

ipsa flexissent.[2]   **20.**   Itaque illōrum respōnsīs tum et[3]
lūdī[4] per decem diēs factī sunt neque rēs ūlla quae ad

here describes, although the present figures of Romulus and Remus are
an addition of the fifteenth century to replace the lost ones. The left
hind leg of the wolf shows the marks of lightning. Rome to-day looks
upon it as the symbol of its history. In 1919 a gold replica was given
to President Wilson, and in 1929 a copy was presented to the city
of New York by the mayor of Rome (Fig. 67).

[1] The original home and in Cicero's day still the chief center of most
forms of Roman divination.

[2] *unless the gods by their divine power should change almost fate itself.*

[3] *both*, balanced by **neque**, which = **et nōn.**

[4] Usually circus games, with chariot races. Ostensibly given to appease the gods, they served in actual fact as a political expedient to keep
the common people in line.

plācandōs deōs pertinēret praetermissa est. Īdemque iussērunt simulācrum Iovis facere maius et in excelsō collocāre et contrā atque[1] anteā fuerat ad orientem convertere; ac sē spērāre dīxērunt, sī illud signum quod 5 vidētis sōlis ortum et forum cūriamque cōnspiceret, fore ut[2] ea cōnsilia quae clam essent inita contrā salūtem urbis atque imperī illūstrārentur ut ā senātū populōque Rōmānō[3] perspicī possent. Atque illud signum collocandum cōnsulēs illī locāvērunt;[4] sed tanta 10 fuit operis tarditās ut neque superiōribus cōnsulibus neque nōbīs ante hodiernum diem collocārētur.

Vocabulary Drill. — nūtus, hūmānus, occĭdō, caelum, flectō, lūdus, excelsus, forum.

The Gods Have Saved the City

IX.   **21.**   Hīc[5] quis potest esse tam āversus[6] ā vērō, tam praeceps, tam mente captus[7] quī neget[8] haec omnia quae vidēmus praecipuēque hanc urbem deōrum im-15 mortālium nūtū ac potestāte administrārī? Etenim cum esset ita respōnsum, caedīs, incendia, interitum reī pūblicae comparārī, et ea[9] per cīvīs, quae[10] tum propter magnitūdinem scelerum nōn nūllīs incrēdibilia vidē-bantur, ea nōn modo cōgitāta ā nefāriīs cīvibus vērum

---

[1] *contrary to its previous position.*

[2] *the result would be.* This circumlocution is a substitute for the rare future passive infinitive (of **illūstrō**).

[3] This phrase sums up the authority of the Roman state, and its abbreviation S. P. Q. R. was and still is used symbolically to repɪesent the power of Rome (Fig. 69).

[4] With **collocandum,** *let the contract for the erection.*

[5] *Under these circumstances.*   [6] With **ā:** *opposed to.*

[7] *insane.*   Note the climax.

[8] *as to deny.*   For mood see **380, Note.**

[9] *and that too.*   [10] *(acts) which.*

etiam suscepta esse sēnsistis. Illud[1] vērō nōnne ita praesēns est ut nūtū Iovis Optimī Maximī factum esse videātur, ut, cum hodiernō diē māne per forum meō iussū et coniūrātī et eōrum indicēs in aedem Concordiae

dūcerentur, eō ipsō tempore signum 5 statuerētur? Quō collocātō atque ad vōs senātumque conversō, omnia

FIG. 69.   THE POWER
OF ROME

Used in Rome to-day
to indicate one-way
streets.

et senātus et vōs quae[2] erant contrā salūtem omnium cōgitāta illūstrāta et patefacta vīdistis.   22. Quō[3] 10 etiam maiōre sunt istī odiō[4] suppli-cioque dignī quī nōn sōlum vestrīs domiciliīs atque tēctīs sed etiam deōrum templīs atque dēlūbrīs sunt fūnestōs ac nefāriōs ignīs īnferre cōnātī.   Quibus ego sī mē resti-tisse dīcam,[5] nimium mihi sūmam et nōn sim ferendus : 15 ille, ille Iuppiter restitit ; ille[6] Capitōlium, ille haec templa, ille cūnctam urbem, ille vōs omnīs salvōs esse voluit.   Dīs ego immortālibus ducibus, hanc mentem voluntātemque suscēpī atque ad haec tanta indicia per-vēnī.   Iam vērō illa Allobrogum sollicitātiō,[7] iam ab 20 Lentulō cēterīsque domesticīs hostibus tam dēmenter tantae rēs crēditae et ignōtīs et barbarīs commissaeque litterae numquam essent profectō, nisi ab dīs immortā-libus huic tantae audāciae[8] cōnsilium esset ēreptum.

---

[1] *The following*, explained by **ut . . . statuerētur.**

[2] The antecedent is **omnia.**   [3] *Therefore.*

[4] For case see **349.**   [5] What kind of condition ? See **390, III.**

[6] In a series of gestures Cicero takes in the panoramic view before him, pointing first of all to the newly-erected statue of Jupiter.   In translating omit the last three repetitions of **ille.**   What is this figure called?

[7] Supply **facta esset** from the following verb.

[8] Make concrete : *from these bold men* (**315**).   What kind of condition ? See **390, II.**

Quid vērō ? ut hominēs Gallī ex cīvitāte male[1] pācātā, quae gēns ūna restat quae bellum populō Rōmānō facere posse et nōn nōlle videātur, spem imperī ac rērum maximārum ultrō sibi ā patriciīs hominibus oblātam 5 neglegerent vestramque salūtem suīs opibus antepōnerent, id[2] nōn dīvīnitus esse factum putātis, praesertim quī[3] nōs nōn pugnandō sed tacendō superāre potuērunt ?

Word Study. — Review the suffixes **-āx** and **-ēnsis** (**412**) and find one example of each in section 17. Review the prefix **ante-** (**411**).

Distinguish **fāma** and **famēs** and give English derivatives of each. Give derivatives of **fulmen** and **liquefacta**. From what is **liquefacta** derived?

No Victory over Civil Foes Has Ever Equaled This

X. **23.** Quam ob rem, Quirītēs, quoniam ad omnia 10 pulvīnāria supplicātiō dēcrēta est, celebrātōte[4] illōs diēs cum coniugibus ac līberīs vestrīs. Nam multī saepe honōrēs dīs immortālibus iūstī habitī sunt ac dēbitī,[5] sed profectō iūstiōrēs numquam. Ēreptī enim estis ex crūdēlissimō ac miserrimō interitū, ēreptī sine caede, 15 sine sanguine, sine exercitū, sine dīmicātiōne;[6] togātī. mē ūnō togātō duce et imperātōre, vīcistis. **24.** Etenim recordāminī, Quirītēs, omnīs cīvīlīs dissēnsiōnēs, nōn sōlum eās quās audīstis sed eās quās vōsmet ipsī meministis atque vīdistis. L. Sulla P. Sulpicium[7]

---

[1] *incompletely.*   [2] The preceding **ut** clause is in apposition.

[3] *especially since they.* The subjunctive is more common in such clauses.

[4] Imperative (**276**).   [5] *due*, connected by **ac** with **iūstī.**

[6] Note the anaphora. The four nouns are in two pairs.

[7] He had sponsored a bill transferring the command of the forces against Mithridates from Sulla to Marius.

oppressit: C. Marium, custōdem[1] huius urbis, multōsque fortīs virōs partim[2] ēiēcit ex cīvitāte, partim interēmit. Cn. Octāvius cōnsul armīs expulit ex urbe collēgam[3]: omnis hic locus acervīs corporum et cīvium

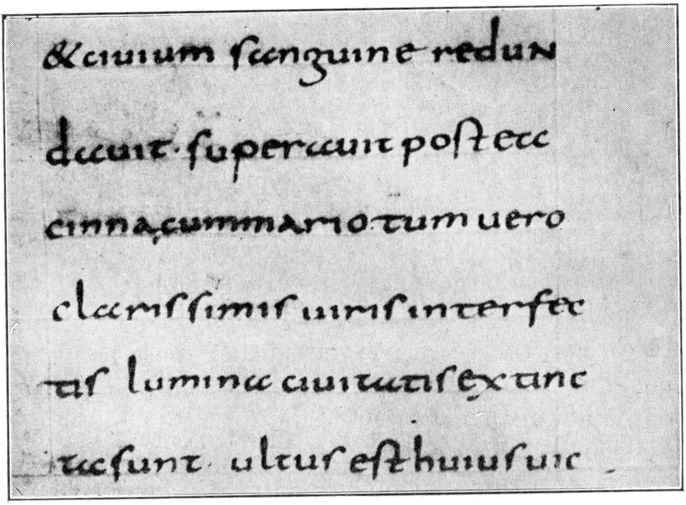
&ciuium ſanguine redun
dauit· ſuperauit poſtea
cinna cum mario· tum uero
clariſſimiſ uiriſ interfec
tiſ lumina ciuitatiſ extinc
ta ſunt· ultuſ eſt huiuſ uic

FIG. 70. THE OLDEST MANUSCRIPT OF THE SPEECHES AGAINST CATILINE

Except for the papyrus fragment (Fig. 61) this parchment manuscript of the ninth century is the oldest we have. The above reproduction gives part of Cat. III, 24.

sanguine redundāvit.[4] Superāvit posteā Cinna cum Mariō: tum vērō, clārissimīs virīs interfectīs, lūmina[5]

[1] He had saved Rome from the invading Cimbri and Teutons thirty-eight years before this.

[2] = **aliōs . . . aliōs.**

[3] Cinna, a partisan of Marius. Plutarch says that 10,000 were slain in the Forum during the rioting.

[4] A good case of zeugma (**409**). In translating select a neutral verb that will go equally well with both **sanguine** and **acervīs,** such as *covered.*

[5] *shining lights.* Note the metaphor, anticipated by **clārissimīs** (*most brilliant*).

cīvitātis exstīncta sunt. Ultus est huius victōriae
crūdēlitātem posteā Sulla : nē dīcī quidem opus est
quantā dēminūtiōne cīvium et quantā calamitāte reī
pūblicae. Dissēnsit M. Lepidus ā clārissimō et for-
5 tissimō virō Q. Catulō :[1] attulit nōn tam ipsīus interitus
reī pūblicae[2] lūctum quam cēterōrum.

25. Atque illae tamen omnēs dissēnsiōnēs erant eius
modī quae nōn ad dēlendam sed ad commūtandam rem
pūblicam pertinērent. Nōn illī nūllam esse rem pūbli-
10 cam sed in eā quae esset sē esse prīncipēs, neque hanc
urbem cōnflagrāre sed sē in hāc urbe flōrēre voluērunt.
Atque illae tamen omnēs dissēnsiōnēs, quārum nūlla
exitium reī pūblicae quaesīvit, eius modī fuērunt ut nōn
reconciliātiōne concordiae sed internecīōne cīvium
15 dīiūdicātae sint.[3] In hōc autem ūnō[4] post hominum
memoriam maximō crūdēlissimōque bellō, quāle[5] bellum nūlla umquam barbaria cum suā gente gessit, quō
in bellō lēx[6] haec fuit ā Lentulō, Catilīnā, Cethēgō,
Cassiō cōnstitūta, ut omnēs quī, salvā urbe, salvī[7] esse
20 possent in hostium numerō dūcerentur, ita mē gessī,
Quirītēs, ut salvī omnēs cōnservārēminī, et, cum hostēs
vestrī tantum cīvium[8] superfutūrum putāssent quantum īnfīnītae caedī restitisset, tantum autem urbis

---

[1] A leader of the aristocratic party. It is easy enough to discover to
what party Cicero himself belonged by a study of the adjectives used
here and elsewhere in referring to adherents of the senatorial party.

[2] Dative with **attulit**.

[3] For the tense see **378** (*b*).

[4] Emphasizing **maximō**: *the very greatest.*

[5] Supply **tāle**: *such a war as.*

[6] *rule.*

[7] " sound " (financially), therefore *solvent*, while below it has its
literal meaning.

[8] *only so many citizens as.*

quantum flamma obīre nōn potuisset, et urbem et cīvīs
integrōs incolumīsque servāvī.

Vocabulary Drill (21–25). — index, profectō ; recordor,
cīvīlis, lūmen, flōreō, concordia.

Gratitude Is the Only Reward I Ask

XI. 26. Quibus prō tantīs rēbus, Quirītēs, nūllum
ego ā vōbīs praemium virtūtis, nūllum īnsigne honōris,
nūllum monumentum laudis postulābō praeterquam 5
huius diēī memoriam sempiternam. In animīs[1] ego
vestrīs omnīs triumphōs meōs, omnia ōrnāmenta honōris, monumenta glōriae, laudis īnsignia condī et collocārī volō. Nihil mē mūtum[2] potest dēlectāre, nihil
tacitum, nihil dēnique eius modī quod etiam minus 10
dignī assequī possint. Memoriā vestrā, Quirītēs, nostrae rēs alentur,[3] sermōnibus crēscent, litterārum
monumentīs[4] inveterāscent et corrōborābuntur ; eandemque diem[5] intellegō, quam spērō aeternam fore,
prōpāgātam esse et ad salūtem urbis et ad memoriam 15
cōnsulātūs meī, ūnōque[6] tempore in hāc rē pūblicā duōs
cīvīs exstitisse, quōrum alter[7] fīnīs vestrī imperī nōn
terrae sed caelī regiōnibus termināret, alter[8] huius imperī domicilium sēdīsque servāret.

---

[1] Emphatic — why? Cf. **Memoriā vestrā** below.

[2] Applicable to a monument, as opposed to **tacitum,** which would
apply to a literary record.

[3] *my deeds will be kept alive.*

[4] *literary documents.*   Horace called his poetical works a " monument
more enduring than bronze."

[5] *length of time.*   [6] **intellegō** is carried over by **-que.**

[7] Pompey, fresh from his conquest of Sertorius in the west and of
Mithridates in the east.

[8] Cicero, of course.

I Have Saved You — You Must Protect Me

XII.   27.   Sed quoniam eārum rērum quās ego gessī
nōn eadem est fortūna atque condiciō quae[1] illōrum quī
externa bella gessērunt, quod mihi cum eīs vīvendum
est quōs vīcī ac subēgī, illī hostīs aut interfectōs aut
5 oppressōs relīquērunt, vestrum est,[2] Quirītēs, sī cēterīs
facta sua rēctē prōsunt,[3] mihi mea nē quandō[4] obsint
prōvidēre.   Mentēs[5] enim hominum audācissimōrum
scelerātae ac nefāriae nē vōbīs nocēre possent ego prōvīdī, nē mihi noceant[6] vestrum est prōvidēre.   Quam-
10 quam, Quirītēs, mihi quidem ipsī nihil ab istīs iam
nocērī[7] potest.   Magnum enim est in bonīs praesidium
quod mihi in perpetuum comparātum est, magna in
rē pūblicā dignitās quae mē semper tacita dēfendet,
magna vīs cōnscientiae quam[8] quī neglegunt, cum mē
15 violāre volent,[9] sē indicābunt.   28.   Est enim nōbīs[10]
is animus, Quirītēs, ut nōn modo nūllīus audāciae cēdā-
mus sed etiam omnīs improbōs ultrō semper lacessāmus.
Quod sī omnis impetus domesticōrum hostium[11] dēpul-
sus ā vōbīs sē in mē ūnum converterit,[12] vōbīs erit viden-

---

[1] *as,* following **eadem.**   [2] *your duty, it's up to you.*

[3] *if other men's deeds rightly benefit them.*

[4] *at some time;* like **quis,** indefinite after **nē.**

[5] *plans.*

[6] And yet five years later Cicero was banished as a result of the
hatred aroused at this time.

[7] In translating make personal: *I at any rate cannot be injured by
them* (**313,** *a*).

[8] *and those who neglect it.*   [9] *in wanting to.*   [10] = **mihi.**

[11] Cicero again emphasizes the claim he has made repeatedly, that the
conspirators should be treated as foreign foes and not as citizens who
have rebelled.

[12] Often a verb with a reflexive pronoun is best translated as here by
the passive.

dum, Quirītēs, quā condiciōne[1] posthāc eōs esse velītis
quī sē prō salūte vestrā obtulerint invidiae perīculīsque
omnibus : mihi quidem ipsī quid est quod iam ad vītae
frūctum possit acquīrī, cum praesertim neque in honōre
vestrō[2] neque in glōriā virtūtis[3] quicquam videam 5
altius quō mihi libeat ascendere?   **29.** Illud[4] perficiam
profectō, Quirītēs, ut ea quae gessī in cōnsulātū prīvātus
tuear atque ōrnem, ut, sī qua est invidia in cōnservandā
rē pūblicā suscepta, laedat invidōs, mihi valeat[5] ad
glōriam.   Dēnique ita mē in rē pūblicā trāctābō ut 10
meminerim semper quae gesserim, cūremque ut ea
virtūte nōn cāsū gesta esse videantur.   Vōs, Quirītēs,
quoniam iam est nox,[6] venerātī Iovem illum custōdem
huius urbis ac vestrum in vestra tēcta discēdite et ea,
quamquam iam est perīculum dēpulsum, tamen aequē 15
ac[7] priōre[8] nocte custōdiīs vigiliīsque dēfendite.   Id
nē vōbīs diūtius faciendum sit atque ut in perpetuā pāce
esse possītis prōvidēbō, Quirītēs.

Vocabulary Drill (26–29). — monumentum, assequor, exsistō; externus, rēctē, prōsum, quandō, invidia.

Word Study. — Give and explain meaning of English derivatives of **sanguis, lūmen, cōnflagrō.** Explain the formation of
sempiternus.

Review Questions. — 1. Before what body was this speech
made and why?   2. About how long after the first two speeches
was the third delivered?   3. What important developments had
taken place?   4. Who was Volturcius?   5. Who were the four
leading conspirators in Rome at this time?   6. What happened

---

[1] *in what condition.*   [2] *in the offices given by you.*
[3] *(gained by) good character.*
[4] Explained by the following **ut** clause.   [5] *redound.*
[6] The speech was made after the senate adjourned.
[7] With **aequē :** *just as.*   [8] *last.*

at the Mulvian Bridge? 7. What action did the senate take? 8. What mistakes did the conspirators make? 9. Does Cicero think that Catiline would have made these mistakes if he had been in the city? 10. Where was Catiline? 11. What happened to the statue of the wolf on the Capitoline Hill? 12. What reward does Cicero desire?

162. M. TULLI CICERONIS
IN L. CATILINAM ORATIO QUARTA
HABITA IN SENATU

Selection

On December 5 a special session of the senate was held in the
temple of Concord to decide the punishment of the five conspirators under arrest. Cicero as consul presided. After Silanus, the
consul-elect, had proposed the death penalty, Caesar in a speech
which created a profound impression proposed life imprisonment
and the confiscation of the conspirators' property. After some
discussion Cicero, as chairman, summarized the two proposals
then before the senate in the selection which follows. Though
forced as presiding officer to maintain at least an outward sem-
blance of neutrality, his hearers had no difficulty in perceiving
that he personally favored the death penalty.

After Caesar's proposal seemed likely to prevail, Cato arose
and by a fearless plea for a return to old-time severity in dealing
with their foes without and within, rallied the wavering resolu-
tion of the senators, who then condemned the conspirators to
death by a decisive vote. Cicero lost no time in having the
senate's decree carried out, and the five conspirators were immediately strangled to death (the official mode of execution) in
a dark underground dungeon called the Tullianum, cut in the
rock at the base of the Capitoline. Catiline died a month later
in Etruria while fighting bravely at the head of his troops, and
with his death the conspiracy came to an end.

What Punishment for the Conspirators?

IV. **7.** Videō duās adhūc esse sententiās, ūnam
D. Sīlānī,[1] quī cēnset eōs quī haec[2] dēlēre cōnātī sunt
morte esse multandōs, alteram C. Caesaris,[3] quī mortis

---

[1] As consul-elect he had spoken first.   [2] *this city.*

[3] Now praetor-elect. This is five years before the Gallic War, and
Caesar is already the recognized leader of the democratic party.

poenam removet, cēterōrum suppliciōrum omnīs acer-
bitātēs amplectitur.[1]   Uterque et prō suā dignitāte et
prō rērum magnitūdine in summā sevēritāte versātur.[2]
Alter[3] eōs quī nōs omnīs, quī populum Rōmānum vītā
5 prīvāre cōnātī sunt, quī dēlēre imperium, quī populī
Rōmānī nōmen exstinguere, pūnctum temporis[4] fruī
vītā et hōc commūnī spīritū nōn putat oportēre atque
hoc genus poenae saepe in[5] improbōs cīvīs in hāc rē
pūblicā esse ūsūrpātum recordātur.   Alter[6] intellegit
10 mortem ā dīs immortālibus nōn esse supplicī causā cōnstitūtam, sed aut necessitātem nātūrae aut labōrum[7]
ac miseriārum quiētem.   Itaque eam sapientēs numquam invītī, fortēs saepe etiam libenter oppetīvērunt.
Vincula vērō et ea sempiterna[8] certē ad singulārem
15 poenam nefāriī sceleris inventa sunt.   Mūnicipiīs dis-
pertīrī[9] iubet.   Habēre vidētur ista rēs[10] inīquitātem,
sī imperāre velīs, difficultātem, sī rogāre.[11]   Dēcernātur
tamen, sī placet.   **8.** Ego enim suscipiam et, ut
spērō, reperiam quī[12] id quod salūtis omnium causā
20 statuerītis nōn putent esse suae dignitātis[13] recūsāre.
Adiungit gravem poenam mūnicipiīs, sī quis eōrum[14]

---

[1] *but includes.*   [2] With **in**: *insists on.*

[3] *The one* (*i.e.* Silanus), the subject of **putat** three lines below.

[4] *for a single moment.*   For case see **319.**   [5] *against.*

[6] *The other* (*i.e.* Caesar).   [7] Objective genitive (**302**): *from toils.*

[8] *and those for life.*   Life imprisonment was very rare.   We know of
the case of a slacker who cut off some of his fingers so that he would not
have to serve in the army.

[9] Supply **eōs.**   Caesar suggested that the prisoners be turned over to
various towns for imprisonment.

[10] *that proposal seems to involve unfairness if . . . , difficulty if . . .*

[11] Supply **velīs.**   [12] Supply **eōs** as antecedent.

[13] Predicate genitive: *who will not think it in keeping with their rank*

[14] With **vincula; quis** refers to some one in the towns.

vincula rūperit; horribilīs custōdiās circumdat et dig-
nās scelere hominum perditōrum; sancit nē quis eōrum[1]
poenam quōs condemnat aut per senātum aut per
populum levāre possit; ēripit etiam spem, quae sōla
hominem in miseriīs cōnsōlārī solet. Bona praetereā 5
pūblicārī iubet; vītam sōlam relinquit nefāriīs hominibus; quam sī ēripuisset, multās ūnō dolōre animī
atque corporis miseriās et omnīs scelerum poenās adē-
misset. Itaque ut aliqua in vītā formīdō improbīs
esset prōposita, apud īnferōs eius modī quaedam illī 10
antīquī[2] supplicia impiīs cōnstitūta esse voluērunt,[3]
quod vidēlicet intellegēbant, hīs remōtīs, nōn esse
mortem ipsam pertimēscendam.

Vocabulary Drill (7–8). — prīvō, necessitūdō, libenter, mūnicipium; adimō, formīdō.

---

[1] With **poenam.** Caesar would have no board of pardons free the
conspirators, as is so often the case with criminals to-day.

[2] *those men of old (i.e. philosophers).*   [3] *wanted (us to understand).*

FIG. 71. THE PRISON IN WHICH THE CONSPIRATORS WERE KEPT

Fig. 72. The Roman Forum as It Was during the Empire

Looking toward the east from the Capitoline Hill.

FIG. 73. THE ROMAN FORUM AS IT IS

At the left, the arch of Septimius Severus; at the right, the temple of Saturn; beyond it, the remains of the Basilica Julia and then the Palatine Hill.

163.   SALLUST ON THE CONSPIRACY OF CATILINE

C. Sallustius Crispus was born in 86 B.C.   He started on a political career and obtained a position in the

senate through election to the quaestorship in 59 B.C.   He was expelled from the senate but was reinstated by Caesar after 49 B.C.   He remained loyal to Caesar and was promoted to the praetorship.   He died in 35 B.C.

Sallust was a writer of several historical works; but the only two which have survived in complete form

FIG. 74.   SALLUST

are monographs on the war with Jugurtha and the conspiracy of Catiline.   The latter he wrote some twenty years after the conspiracy.   In his account he relied not only on Cicero's speeches for authority, but also on his own recollections and other available records. Sallust was a radical in politics, but in spite of that fact he denounces Catiline and speaks respectfully of Cicero.   He tried to give a fair and impartial account of the conspiracy and to analyze its causes.

164. C. SALLUSTI CRISPI
CATILINAE CONIURATIO

The Character of Catiline

5. L. Catilīna, nōbilī genere[1] nātus, fuit magnā vī
et animī et corporis sed ingeniō malō prāvōque. Huic
ab adulēscentiā bella intestīna, caedēs, rapīnae, discordia cīvīlis grāta fuēre,[2] ibique[3] iuventūtem suam
exercuit. Corpus[4] patiēns[5] inediae, algōris,[6] vigiliae 5
suprā quam cuiquam crēdibile est. Animus audāx,
subdolus,[7] varius, cuius reī libet[8] simulātor ac dissimulātor, aliēnī appetēns, suī profūsus,[9] ārdēns in cupi-
ditātibus; satis ēloquentiae, sapientiae parum. Vāstus[10]
animus immoderāta, incrēdibilia, nimis alta semper 10
cupiēbat. Hunc post dominātiōnem L. Sullae libīdō
maxima invāserat reī pūblicae capiendae, neque id
quibus modīs assequerētur, dum[11] sibi rēgnum parāret,
quicquam pēnsī habēbat.[12] Agitābātur magis magisque
in diēs[13] animus ferōx inopiā reī familiāris et cōnscientiā 15
scelerum, quae utraque[14] eīs artibus auxerat quās
suprā memorāvī. Incitābant[15] praetereā corruptī
cīvitātis mōrēs, quōs pessima ac dīversa inter sē[16]
mala, lūxuria atque avāritia, vexābant.[17]

---

[1] For case see **329**.
[2] Sallust is fond of the perfect ending -ēre for -ērunt.
[3] *and in these things.*
[4] Supply **erat**. Forms of **sum** are frequently omitted in Sallust.
[5] *capable of enduring*, with the following objective genitives (**302**).
[6] *cold.*   [7] *crafty.*   [8] = cuiuslibet reī: *of everything.*
[9] *desiring other people's property, wasteful of his own.*
[10] *insatiable.*   [11] *provided that* (**374**).
[12] *nor did he consider it of any importance by what means.*
[13] *day by day.*   [14] *both of which* (object of **auxerat**).
[15] Supply **eum.**   [16] *mutually opposed.*   [17] *weakened.*

Catiline's Speech to His Followers in 64 B.C.

20. "Sed ego quae mente agitāvī, omnēs iam anteā
dīversī[1] audīstis. Cēterum[2] mihi in diēs[3] magis animus
accenditur, cum cōnsīderō quae condiciō vītae futūra
sit, nisi nōsmet ipsī vindicāmus in lībertātem. Nam
5 postquam rēs pūblica in paucōrum potentium iūs atque
diciōnem concessit, semper illīs rēgēs, tetrarchae[4]
vectīgālēs[5] esse,[6] populī, nātiōnēs stīpendia pendere;
cēterī omnēs, strēnuī, bonī, nōbilēs atque ignōbilēs,
vulgus fuimus, sine grātiā, sine auctōritāte, eīs obnoxiī[7]
10 quibus, sī rēs pūblica valēret, formīdinī essēmus.
Itaque omnis grātia, potentia, honōs, dīvitiae apud
illōs sunt aut ubi illī volunt; nōbīs relīquēre perīcula,
repulsās,[8] iūdicia,[9] egestātem. Quae quō usque tandem[10]
patiēminī, ō fortissimī virī? Nōnne ēmorī per virtūtem
15 praestat quam vītam miseram atque inhonestam, ubi
aliēnae superbiae lūdibriō[11] fuerīs, per dēdecus āmittere?
Vērum enim vērō, prō[12] deum atque hominum fidem,[13]
victōria in manū nōbīs est, viget aetās, animus valet;
contrā[14] illīs[15] annīs[16] atque dīvitiīs omnia cōnsenuērunt.[17]
20 Tantum modo inceptō[18] opus est, cētera rēs expediet.[19]
Etenim quis mortālium, cui virīle ingenium est, tolerāre

---

[1] *as individuals.* [2] *But.* [3] *day by day.*

[4] *princes.* [5] Predicate nominative : *tributary.*

[6] This infinitive and **pendere** are historical infinitives used for vividness instead of the perfect indicative. The subject is always nominative.

[7] *subject to.* [8] *political defeats.*

[9] *court trials; i.e.* as defendants.

[10] Where have you seen these words before?

[11] *the sport of other people's arrogance.*

[12] Interjection, not preposition : *Oh!* **deum** is genitive plural.

[13] Accusative of exclamation. [14] Adverb : *on the other hand.*

[15] Dative (**311**). [16] Ablative of cause. [17] *have wasted away.*

[18] Noun ; for case see **333**. [19] *events will decide the rest.*

potest illīs dīvitiās superāre,[1] quās profundant in exstruendō marī[2] et montibus coaequandīs,[3] nōbīs rem familiārem etiam ad necessāria deesse? Illōs bīnās aut amplius domōs continuāre,[4] nōbīs larem familiārem nusquam ūllum esse? Cum tabulās, signa, toreumata[5] 5 emunt, nova dīruunt, alia aedificant, postrēmō omnibus

FIG. 75. CALIGULA'S GALLEY

An artist's restoration of the luxurious floating palace on Lake Nemi (cf. Figs. 32, 34). Luxury increased, rather than diminished, after Catiline's day.

modīs pecūniam trahunt, vexant,[6] tamen summā libīdine dīvitiās suās vincere nequeunt. At nōbīs est domī inopia, forīs aes aliēnum; mala rēs, spēs multō asperior; dēnique quid reliquī habēmus praeter mise- 10 ram animam?

"Quīn igitur expergīsciminī?[7] Ēn[8] illa, illa quam

---

[1] *abound for them* (*i.e.* the patricians).

[2] At such places as Baiae wealthy Romans built concrete foundations out into the sea.

[3] *leveling.*   [4] *build next to each other.*   [5] *decorated ware.*

[6] *squander and waste.*   [7] *Why don't you wake up?*   [8] *Look!*

saepe optāstis lībertās, praetereā dīvitiae, decus, glōria
in oculīs sita sunt; fortūna omnia ea victōribus praemia posuit. Rēs, tempus, perīcula, egestās, bellī
spolia magnifica magis quam ōrātiō mea vōs hortantur.
5 Vel imperātōre vel mīlite[1] mē ūtiminī; neque animus
neque corpus ā vōbīs aberit. Haec ipsa, ut spērō,
vōbīscum ūnā cōnsul[2] agam, nisi forte mē animus
fallit et vōs servīre magis quam imperāre parātī estis."

How Cicero Learned about the Conspiracy

23. In eā coniūrātiōne fuit Q. Cūrius, nātus haud
10 obscūrō locō, flāgitiīs atque facinoribus coopertus,
quem cēnsōrēs[3] senātū probrī grātiā[4] mōverant. Huic
hominī nōn minor vānitās inerat quam audācia : neque
reticēre quae audierat, neque suamet ipse scelera occultāre, prōrsus[5] neque dīcere neque facere quicquam
15 pēnsī habēbat.[6] Erat eī cum Fulviā, muliere nōbilī,
vetus cōnsuētūdō.[7] Cui cum minus grātus esset, quia
inopiā minus largīrī poterat, repente glōriāns maria
montīsque[8] pollicērī coepit et minārī interdum ferrō,
nī sibi obnoxia[9] foret, postrēmō ferōcius agitāre quam
20 solitus erat. At Fulvia, īnsolentiae[10] Cūrī causā cognitā,
tāle perīculum reī pūblicae haud occultum habuit,[11]
sed, sublātō auctōre,[12] dē Catilīnae coniūrātiōne quae
quōque modō[13] audierat, complūribus nārrāvit.

Ea rēs in prīmīs studia hominum accendit ad cōn-

---

[1] In apposition with **mē:** *as,* etc.   [2] *when I am consul.*
[3] See **116.**   [4] *because of* rather than *for the sake of.*   [5] *in short.*
[6] *he considered it of no importance to* . . . *or (what) he said or did.*
[7] *intimacy.*   [8] A proverbial expression for huge wealth.
[9] *loyal;* foret = **esset.**   [10] *unusual conduct.*   [11] *keep.*
[12] *without mentioning her authority.* What literally?
[13] *what and how.*

ₛulātum mandandum M. Tulliō Cicerōnī. Namque
anteā plēraque nōbilitāₛ invidiā aestuābat, et quasi
polluī[1] cōnsulātum crēdēbant sī eum[2] quamvīs[3] ēgregius homō novus adeptus foret.[4] Sed ubi perīₒulum
advēnit, invidia atque superbia post fuēre.   5

Catiline's Reply to Cicero's Speech in the Senate

31. Postrēmō dissimulandī causā aut suī expūr-
gandī, sīcut iūrgiō lacessītus foret,[6] in senātum vēnit.
Tum M. Tullius cōnsul, sīve praesentiam eius timēns
sīve īrā commōtus, ōrātiōnem[7] habuit lūculentam
atque ūtilem reī pūblicae, quam posteā scrīptam ēdidit.[8] 10
Sed ubi ıle assēdit, Catilīna, ut erat parātus ad dissi-
mulanda omnia, dēmissō vultū, vōce supplicī postulāre
ā patribus coepit nē quid dē sē temere crēderent: eā[9]
familiā[10] ortum, ita sē ab adulēscentiā vītam īnstituisse
ut omnia bona in spē habēret. Nē exīstīmārent[11] sibi, 15
patriciō hominī, cuius ipsīus atque maiōrum plūrima
beneficia in plēbem Rōmānam essent, perditā rē pūblicā
opus esse,[12] cum eam servāret M. Tullius, inquilīnus[13]
cīvis urbis Rōmae. Ad hoc maledicta alia cum adderet,
obstrepere omnēs, hostem atque parricīdam vocāre.[14] 20

---

[1] *was defiled.*   [2] *i.e.* the consulship.

[3] With **ēgregius**: *however distinguished.*   [4] = **esset.**

[5] *(left) behind, i.e.* they were forgotten.

[6] *as if he had been attacked in a (personal) quarrel, i.e.* he (Catiline)
wore an air of injured innocence.

[7] Cicero's first speech against Catiline.

[8] The speeches against Catiline were polished up by Cicero and
published about three years later.

[9] = **tālī.**   [10] For case see **329.**

[11] Represents a command in indirect discourse: *they should not,* etc.

[12] *that he wanted the state ruined* (**338**).   [13] *foreign-born.*

[14] Historical infinitives (**404**). The subject is **omnēs** (*i.e.* the senators).

Tum ille furibundus, "quoniam quidem circumventus," inquit, "ab inimīcīs praeceps agor, incendium meum ruīnā restinguam."[1]

The Appeal of Manlius

32. Dum haec Rōmae geruntur, C. Mānlius ex 5 suō numerō lēgātōs ad Mārcium Rēgem[2] mittit cum mandātīs huiusce modī :

33. "Deōs hominēsque testāmur, imperātor, nōs arma neque contrā patriam cēpisse neque quō[3] perī-culum aliīs facerēmus, sed utī corpora nostra ab iniūriā 10 tūta forent,[4] quī[5] miserī, egentēs violentiā atque crūdē-litāte faenerātōrum[6] plērīque patriā, sed omnēs fāmā atque fortūnīs expertēs sumus.[7] Saepe maiōrēs ves-trum,[8] miseritī[9] plēbis Rōmānae, dēcrētīs suīs inopiae eius opitulātī[10] sunt, ac novissimē memoriā nostrā 15 propter magnitūdinem aeris aliēnī, volentibus omnibus bonīs, argentum aere solūtum est.[11] Saepe ipsa plēbs,

---

[1] Somewhat like our expression "to fight fire with fire." He will tear things down to prevent the fire from spreading (figuratively).

[2] Commander of the army sent by the government to destroy Manlius' forces.

[3] = **ut.**   [4] = **essent.**

[5] The antecedent is **nōs**, implied in **nostra**.

[6] *usurers.* Money was scarce and obtainable only at very high interest rates.

[7] *most of us are robbed of our country, and all of us of our reputations and property.* The ablative is used here with **expertēs.**

[8] From the pronoun **vōs** ; the adjective **vestrī** would be more usual.

[9] *pitying*, with genitive.   [10] *aided*, with dative.

[11] *silver was paid with bronze, i.e.* a debt of a certain number of silver coins could, by the law passed in 86 B.C., be paid in bronze. As the value of the two metals was about 4 to 1, the law provided for the pay-ment of 25 cents on the dollar in full satisfaction of debts. Somewhat similarly after the World War, debts incurred previously on the gold

aut dominandī studiō permōta aut superbiā magistrātuum, armāta ā patribus sēcessit.[1] At nōs nōn imperium neque dīvitiās petimus, quārum rērum causā
bella atque certāmina omnia inter mortālīs sunt, sed
lībertātem, quam nēmō bonus nisi cum animā simul [5]
āmittit. Tē atque senātum obtestāmur, cōnsulātis [2]
miserīs cīvibus, lēgis praesidium, quod inīquitās praetōris ēripuit, restituātis, nēve nōbīs eam necessitū-
dinem impōnātis, ut quaerāmus quōnam modō maximē
ultī sanguinem nostrum pereāmus."[3]   10

The Serious Illness of the Roman State Midst Wealth and Power

36. Eā tempestāte[4] mihi imperium populī Rōmānī
multō maximē miserābile vīsum est. Cui[5] cum ad occāsum ab ortū sōlis[6] omnia domita armīs pārērent, domī
ōtium atque dīvitiae, quae prīma mortālēs putant,
affluerent,[7] fuēre tamen cīvēs quī sēque remque pūblicam [15]
obstinātīs animīs perditum[8] īrent. Namque duōbus
senātī[9] dēcrētīs ex tantā multitūdine neque praemiō
inductus[10] coniūrātiōnem patefēcerat[11] neque ex castrīs

---

basis were paid off in the debased paper currency of various European
countries.

[1] There are three cases of secession on record : 494, 449, 287 B.C.

[2] Dependent on **obtestāmur ; ut** might have been used : *take counsel
for* (with dative).

[3] *how we may best avenge our blood (before) perishing.*

[4] = **tempore.**   [5] With **pārērent (313).**

[6] *from the far east to the far west.* What literally ?

[7] *abounded.*

[8] Supine (**405,** *a*) : *would go to destroy.*   [9] = **senātūs** (genitive).

[10] Agrees with **quisquam,** subject of both verbs.

[11] The senate had promised rewards for information about the conspiracy.

Catilīnae quisquam omnium discesserat; tanta vīs morbī, atque utī tābēs,[1] plērōsque[2] cīvium animōs invāserat.

Lentulus Approaches the Allobroges through Umbrenus

39. Īsdem temporibus Rōmae Lentulus, sīcutī Catilīna praecēperat, quōscumque mōribus aut fortūnā 5 novīs rēbus idōneōs crēdēbat, aut per sē aut per aliōs sollicitābat, neque sōlum cīvīs, sed cuiusque modī genus hominum,[3] quod modo[4] bellō ūsuī foret.[5]

40. Igitur P. Umbrēnō cuidam negōtium dat, utī lēgātōs Allobrogum requīrat eōsque, sī possit, impellat 10 ad societātem bellī, exīstimāns pūblicē prīvātimque aere aliēnō oppressōs,[6] praetereā quod nātūrā gēns Gallica bellicōsa esset, facile eōs ad tāle cōnsilium addūcī posse. Umbrēnus quod in Galliā negōtiātus erat,[7] plērīsque prīncipibus cīvitātum nōtus erat atque 15 eōs nōverat. Itaque sine morā, ubi prīmum lēgātōs in forō cōnspexit, percontātus pauca dē statū cīvitātis et quasi dolēns eius[8] cāsum, requīrere coepit quem exitum tantīs malīs[9] spērārent. Postquam illōs videt querī dē avāritiā magistrātuum, accūsāre senātum, quod in eō 20 auxilī nihil esset, miseriīs suīs remedium[10] mortem expectāre, "at ego," inquit, "vōbīs, sī modo virī esse vultis, ratiōnem ostendam quā tanta ista mala effugiātis."[11] Haec ubi dīxit, Allobrogēs in maximam spem

---

[1] *like a pestilence.*

[2] In thought belongs with **cīvium** rather than **animōs**.

[3] Sallust here confuses two types of expression, **cuiusque generis hominēs** and **omne genus hominum**. Translate *all sorts of men.*

[4] With **quod** = **dum modo**: *provided* (**374**).

[5] = **esset**.   [6] Modifies **eōs** below.   [7] Deponent: *had done business.*

[8] *i.e.* **cīvitātis**.   [9] Dative: *troubles.*

[10] *as a remedy for their misfortunes.*   [11] *you may escape* (**377, 380**).

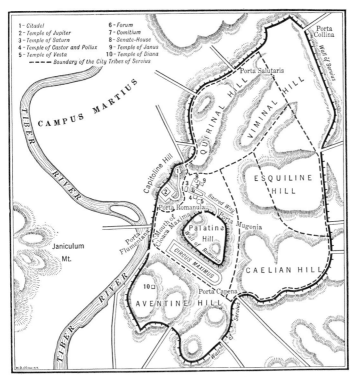

FIG. 76. PLAN OF ANCIENT ROME

adductī Umbrēnum ōrāre[1] ut suī miserērētur;[2] nihil
tam asperum neque tam difficile esse quod nōn cupi-
dissimē factūrī essent, dum ea rēs cīvitātem aere aliēnō
līberāret.[3] Coniūrātiōnem aperit, nōminat sociōs,
praetereā multōs cuiusque generis innoxiōs,[4] quō 5

---

[1] Historical infinitive (**404**).

[2] *that he should take pity on them.* This verb governs the genitive.

[3] For mood see **374**.

[4] *not involved* in the conspiracy. He mentions influential persons to
make an impression.

lēgātīs animus amplior esset.   Deinde eōs pollicitōs
operam suam domum dīmittit.

The Plot Is Revealed to Cicero

41.   Sed Allobrogēs diū in incertō habuēre[1] quidnam
cōnsilī caperent.   In alterā parte erat aes aliēnum,
5 studium bellī, magna mercēs in spē victōriae, at in
alterā maiōrēs opēs,[2] tūta cōnsilia, prō incertā spē certa
praemia.   Haec illīs volventibus, tandem vīcit fortūna
reī pūblicae.   Itaque Q. Fabiō Sangae, cuius patrōciniō[3] cīvitās plūrimum ūtēbātur, rem omnem utī
10 cognōverant, aperiunt.   Cicerō per Sangam cōnsiliō
cognitō lēgātīs praecēpit ut studium coniūrātiōnis
vehementer simulent, cēterōs adeant, bene polliceantur,
dentque operam utī eōs quam maximē manifestōs
habeant.[4]

The Seizure of the Incriminating Documents

15 **44.**   Sed Allobrogēs ex praeceptō Cicerōnis per
Gabīnium cēterōs conveniunt.   Ab Lentulō, Cethēgō,
Statiliō, item Cassiō postulant iūs iūrandum,[5] quod
signātum ad cīvīs perferant:[6] aliter haud facile eōs
ad tantum negōtium impellī posse.[7] Cēterī nihil suspi-
20 cantēs dant, Cassius sēmet eō brevī ventūrum pollicētur

---

[1] *were in uncertainty.*

[2] *resources* of the constitutional government of Rome.

[3] *patronage.*   He was their legal representative, almost like a consul
among us.

[4] *devote their efforts to catching them in the act as nearly as possible.*

[5] *i.e.* in writing.   [6] Purpose (**368**).

[7] Indirect statement depending on the idea of saying implied in
postulant.

ac paulō ante lēgātōs ex urbe proficīscitur.[1] Lentulus cum eīs T. Volturcium quendam Crotōniēnsem mittit, ut Allobrogēs, prius quam domum pergerent, cum Catilīnā, datā atque acceptā fidē, societātem cōnfirmārent. Ipse Volturciō litterās ad Catilīnam dat,[5] quārum exemplum īnfrā scrīptum est :[2]

"Quī sim, ex eō quem ad tē mīsī[3] cognōscēs. Fac cōgitēs[4] in quantā calamitāte[5] sīs, et meminerīs[6] tē virum esse. Cōnsīderēs quid tuae ratiōnēs postulent. Auxilium petās ab omnibus, etiam ab īnfimīs."[7] 10

Aftermaths of the Conspiracy — Sensational Charges against Crassus

48. Intereā plēbs, coniūrātiōne patefactā, quae[8] prīmō cupida rērum novārum nimis[9] bellō[10] favēbat, mūtātā mente, Catilīnae cōnsilia exsecrārī, Cicerōnem ad caelum tollere ;[11] velutī ex servitūte ērepta gaudium atque laetitiam agitābat. 15

Post eum diem quīdam L. Tarquinius ad senātum adductus erat, quem ad Catilīnam proficīscentem ex itinere retrāctum aiēbant. Is cum sē dīceret indicātūrum dē coniūrātiōne, sī fidēs pūblica[12] data esset, iussus ā cōnsule quae scīret ēdīcere, eadem[13] ferē quae[20]

---

[1] Cassius "smelled a rat."

[2] Cf. with Cicero's version in Cat. III. 12.

[3] We should say *I am sending*. He means Volturcius.

[4] *Be sure to reflect.* What literally?

[5] *in what a desperate situation.*

[6] This and the following independent subjunctives are used in place of imperatives.

[7] *i.e.* slaves.   [8] The antecedent is **plēbs.**   [9] Modifies **cupida.**

[10] Dative with **favēbat.**   [11] Historical infinitives (**404**).

[12] *if the state's assurance (of immunity).*

[13] Double accusative with **senātum** below after **docet.**

Volturcius dē parātīs incendiīs, dē caede bonōrum, dē
itinere hostium senātum docet; praetereā sē missum
ā M. Crassō, quī Catilīnae nūntiāret nē eum Lentulus
et Cethēgus aliīque ex coniūrātiōne dēprehēnsī terrē-
5 rent,[1] eōque[2] magis properāret ad urbem accēdere, quō[3]
et cēterōrum animōs reficeret et illī facilius ē perīculō
ēriperentur. Sed ubi Tarquinius Crassum nōmināvit,
hominem nōbilem, maximīs dīvitiīs, summā potentiā,
aliī rem incrēdibilem ratī,[4] pars tametsī vērum exīsti-
10 mābant,[5] tamen quia in tālī tempore tanta vīs hominis[6]
magis lēnienda quam exagitanda vidēbātur, plērīque
Crassō ex negōtiīs prīvātīs obnoxiī[7] conclāmant indicem falsum esse, dēque eā rē postulant utī referātur.[8]
Itaque cōnsulente Cicerōne, frequēns senātus dēcernit
15 Tarquinī indicium falsum vidērī eumque in vinculīs
retinendum neque amplius potestātem[9] faciendam,
nisi dē eō indicāret cuius cōnsiliō tantam rem esset
mentītus. Erant eō tempore quī exīstimārent indicium
illud ā P. Autrōniō[10] māchinātum,[11] quō facilius,
20 appellātō Crassō, per societātem perīculī reliquōs
illīus potentiā tegeret.[12] Aliī Tarquinium ā Cicerōne
immissum[13] aiēbant, nē Crassus mōre suō, susceptō

---

[1] *that the arrest of Lentulus . . . should not frighten him from.*
[2] *and for this reason.*   [3] = **ut.**   [4] *thinking* (from **reor**).
[5] With **pars** a plural verb is often used: *although some thought it true.*
[6] We should say *a man of such power.*
[7] *under obligations to Crassus.* He controlled "big business" and
could bankrupt many a senator.
[8] *a motion be made concerning this thing, i.e.* Tarquinius' testimony.
[9] *i.e.* of testifying.   [10] One of the conspirators.
[11] *was concocted.*
[12] On the theory that Crassus was too powerful to be convicted and
that the rest would be freed with him. See **369.**
[13] *egged on.*

malōrum patrōciniō, rem pūblicam conturbāret. Ipsum Crassum ego posteā praedicantem audīvī tantam illam contumēliam sibi ab Cicerōne impositam.

Caesar Implicated

49. Sed īsdem temporibus Q. Catulus et C. Pīsō neque precibus neque grātiā neque pretiō Cicerōnem[5] impellere potuēre utī per Allobrogēs aut alium indicem C. Caesar falsō nōminārētur. Nam uterque cum illō[1] gravīs inimīcitiās exercēbant.[2] Rēs autem opportūna vidēbātur, quod is prīvātim ēgregiā līberālitāte,[3] pūblicē maximīs mūneribus[4] grandem pecūniam dēbē-[10] bat. Sed ubi cōnsulem ad tantum facinus impellere nequeunt, ipsī singillātim circumeundō atque ēmentiendō[5] quae sē ex Volturciō aut Allobrogibus audīsse dīcerent, magnam illī invidiam cōnflāverant, usque eō[6] ut nōn nūllī equitēs Rōmānī, quī praesidī causā cum[15] tēlīs erant circum aedem Concordiae, seu perīculī magnitūdine seu animī mōbilitāte impulsī, quō[7] studium suum in rem pūblicam clārius esset, ēgredientī ex senātū Caesarī[8] gladiō minitārentur.

---

[1] Caesar.

[2] *maintained . . . toward.* The subject is **uterque,** which usually requires a singular verb.

[3] *personally on account of his generosity.*

[4] *games,* given while aedile.

[5] *telling falsely.*

[6] *to the point that.*   [7] = **ut (369).**

[8] For case see **313.**

165. The Speech for the Poet Archias

The Greek poet Archias was born at Antioch in Syria about 120 B.C. He early displayed a remarkable

FIG. 77. CICERO

A modern conception of the orator by J. S. Gelert.

talent for poetry; we may in fact call him a "boy wonder" in this field. At the age of seventeen he left home and wandered about in Asia Minor and Greece, composing and reciting poems. Everywhere he went he was received with great acclaim, much as our young pianists and violinists to-day, probably on account of his extraordinary ability to extemporize poetry in the presence of his audiences. From Greece he went to Magna Graecia, the southern or Greek part of Italy, thus completing what may be called the "world tour" of those days. Here he repeated his triumphs, and received many rewards, including honorary citizenship in various towns.

At this time Rome was a relatively new city as far as Greek culture was concerned. But a number of prominent families were interested in the new movement, and Greek philosophers, teachers, and poets had begun to come to Rome in rather large numbers. The bustling city of business, politics, and war was taking on a literary polish. It was not strange therefore that Archias should see possibilities for profit and glory in the chief city of Italy. In the year 102 B.C., when less than eighteen years old, he came to Rome and at once made friends with a number of leading men, particularly with the family of the Luculli, who remained his friends and patrons. He went on several trips with them, in the course of one of which he was made a citizen of Heraclea, in southern Italy.

In 90 B.C. the Social War broke out as a result of the dissatisfaction of some of the Italian communities with their treatment by the dominant Romans. Their chief demand was for Roman citizenship. This was granted by a law passed in 89 B.C. Under this law Archias was eligible for citizenship by reason of his being a citizen of Heraclea. Accordingly he registered before a praetor and thereafter considered himself a Roman. As a token thereof he took the family name (Licinius) of his patrons, the Luculli, and was henceforth called A. Licinius Archias. When L. Lucullus went to the East to take part in the war against Mithridates, Archias went with him. They were together for many years, in the course of which Archias wrote a poem on the exploits of his patron.

In the year 65 B.C. a law was passed for the deportation of undesirable aliens, of much the same nature as some of our own legislation. In 62 B.C. a certain Grattius, otherwise unknown, brought charges under this law against Archias, with the claim that Archias had never been legally made a citizen. It is obvious that the attack was aimed, not at Archias, but at his patron, and that Grattius was the tool of political enemies of Lucullus.

As lawyers received no fees in those days, some other motive than financial gain must have led Cicero to take up Archias' defense. It is true that he had studied under Archias, but a more important inducement than the affection of a student toward a teacher was Archias' promise to write a poem about Cicero's consulship and his suppression of the conspiracy of Catiline. Besides, Cicero may have wanted to please Lucullus. The case came up in a court in the Forum before the praetor Q. Cicero, brother of the defense attorney. Cicero devoted little time to the defense proper. Most of the speech is an enthusiastic eulogy of literature, and it is this which has made it one of Cicero's most delightful and popular works.

We are almost certain that Cicero not only won his case but lost his fee. It seems that the promised poem was never written. It is one of the ironies of fate that none of Archias' poems has survived, and that he owes his immortality to Cicero's speech in his defense rather than to any of his own writings.

166.   M. TULLI CICERONIS
PRO A. LICINIO ARCHIA POETA ORATIO
AD IUDICES

Cicero's Debt to Archias

I. 1. Sī quid est in mē ingenī,[1] iūdicēs,[2] quod[3] sentiō quam[4] sit exiguum, aut sī quā[5] exercitātiō dīcendī, in quā mē nōn īnfitior mediocriter esse versātum, aut sī huiusce reī ratiō[6] aliqua ab optimārum artium[7] studiīs ac disciplīnā profecta, ā quā[8] ego nūllum cōn-5 fiteor aetātis meae tempus abhorruisse, eārum rērum omnium vel in prīmīs hic A. Licinius[9] frūctum ā mē repetere prope suō iūre[10] dēbet. Nam quoad[11] longissimē potest mēns mea respicere spatium praeteritī temporis et pueritiae memoriam recordārī ultimam,[12] 10 inde usque repetēns[13] hunc videō mihi prīncipem et ad suscipiendam et ad ingrediendam ratiōnem hōrum studiōrum exstitisse. Quod sī haec vōx[14] huius hortātū

---

[1] *ability.*   [2] Not *judges.*

[3] Connecting relative, subject of **sit**. Translate as if it read **et sentiō quam exiguum hoc sit.**

[4] Interrogative adverb. What then is the construction of **sit**?

[5] = **aliqua.** Note the kinds of pronouns in this first sentence.

[6] *theoretical knowledge.* Note that **ingenium, exercitātiō,** and **ratiō** are the three qualifications of a good orator.

[7] With **optimārum**: *cultural arts.* These included grammar, rhetoric, poetry, philosophy. In Cicero's day the man most useful to society was one well versed in these subjects. Is this true of our own society to-day?

[8] With **abhorruisse**: *to which I have been averse.*

[9] Cicero uses Archias' Roman name as if the poet's citizenship were not in question. The same tactics are used in modern law courts.

[10] *by a right quite his own.*   [11] *as far back as.*

[12] *earliest.*   [13] *recalling from then on.*

[14] *Now if this voice of mine.* He exaggerates Archias' influence.

praeceptīsque cōnfōrmāta nōn nūllīs aliquandō salūtī
fuit, ā quō[1] id accēpimus quō cēterīs opitulārī et aliōs
servāre[2] possēmus huic profectō ipsī, quantum est
situm in nōbīs, et opem et salūtem ferre dēbēmus.

5 **2.** Ac nē quis ā nōbīs hoc ita dīcī[3] forte mīrētur,[4]
quod alia[5] quaedam in hōc[6] facultās sit ingenī neque
haec dīcendī ratiō aut disciplīna, nē nōs[7] quidem huic
ūnī studiō[8] penitus umquam dēditī fuimus. Etenim
omnēs artēs quae ad hūmānitātem[9] pertinent habent
10 quoddam commūne vinculum et quasi cognātiōne
quādam inter sē continentur.

Vocabulary Drill. — iūdex, repetō, quoad, penitus.

The Case Demands an Unusual Style of Speaking

II. **3.** Sed nē[10] cui vestrum mīrum esse videātur mē
in quaestiōne lēgitimā et in iūdiciō pūblicō,[11] cum rēs
agātur[12] apud praetōrem[13] populī Rōmānī, lēctissi-
15 mum virum, et apud sevērissimōs iūdicēs, tantō con-

---

[1] The antecedent is **huic,** line 3. The following **quō** has **id** for antecedent.

[2] *help all others and save some.*

[3] Make active : *that I am talking this way.*

[4] The clause is parenthetical. Supply *I will say this* before **nē nōs.**

[5] *i.e.* different from Cicero's, while **haec** refers to Cicero.

[6] *i.e.* Archias.   [7] = **ego.**   [8] *i.e.* **dīcendī ratiō.**

[9] *culture.* This is a fine sentence, and you might well memorize it.

[10] Gives the purpose of **quaesō** below. This long sentence becomes simple when it is analyzed into its component groups. Note the many pairs of words and phrases, some of which are inserted only for balance.

[11] *legal inquiry (i.e.* a trial in court) and *state trial (i.e.* a trial in which the state, not a private individual, is a party). Both phrases are much the same.

[12] *the case is being tried.*

[13] Thought to be Quintus, the brother of Cicero.

ventū[1] hominum ac frequentiā hōc ūtī[2] genere dīcendī
quod nōn modo ā cōnsuētūdine iūdiciōrum[3] vērum etiam
ā forēnsī sermōne abhorreat, quaesō ā vōbīs ut in hāc
causā mihi dētis hanc veniam accommodātam huic

FIG. 78. THE BASILICA JULIA AS IT WAS
A courthouse built by Julius Caesar. It faced the Forum.

reō,[4] vōbīs, quem ad modum[5] spērō, nōn molestam, 5
ut[6] mē[7] prō summō poētā atque ērudītissimō homine

---

[1] Ablative of attendant circumstances: *in the presence of such an
assemblage.* So **concursū, hūmānitāte, praetōre** below.

[2] The subject is **mē** above.

[3] *court room practice,* as opposed to **forēnsī sermōne**, *language of the
Forum.* Cicero's style in this speech is not that regularly used either by
lawyers in court or by public speakers in the Forum.

[4] From **reus.**

[5] As usual, this phrase is a substitute for **ut**, to avoid ambiguity with
the preceding and the following **ut.**

[6] With **patiāminī.** The clause is in apposition with **veniam.**

[7] Remember to find a construction for this word.

dīcentem hōc concursū hominum litterātissimōrum,[1]
hāc vestrā hūmānitāte, hōc dēnique praetōre exercente
iūdicium, patiāminī dē studiīs hūmānitātis ac litterārum
paulō loquī līberius et in eius modī persōnā,[2] quae
5 propter ōtium ac studium minimē in iūdiciīs perīculīsque[3] trāctāta est, ūtī prope novō quōdam et
inūsitātō genere dīcendī.

4. Quod[4] sī mihi ā vōbīs tribuī concēdīque sentiam,
perficiam[5] profectō ut hunc A. Licinium nōn modo
10 nōn sēgregandum, cum sit cīvis, ā numerō cīvium,
vērum etiam, sī nōn esset, putētis ascīscendum fuisse.

Vocabulary Drill. — quaestiō, sevērus, sermō, reus, molestus,
trāctō.

Archias' Early Years and Arrival in Rome

III. Nam, ut prīmum ex puerīs[6] excessit Archiās
atque ab eīs artibus quibus aetās puerīlis ad hūmānitātem īnfōrmārī solet, sē ad scrībendī studium contulit,
15 prīmum Antiochīae (nam ibi nātus est locō[7] nōbilī),
celebrī[8] quondam urbe[9] et cōpiōsā atque ērudītissimīs
hominibus līberālissimīsque studiīs affluentī, celeriter
antecellere omnibus[10] ingenī glōriā coepit. Post[11] in
cēterīs Asiae partibus cūnctāque Graeciā sīc eius
20 adventūs[12] celebrābantur ut fāmam ingenī exspectātiō

---

[1] *in the presence of such cultured gentlemen as you.*

[2] *in a character of the kind,* referring to Archias. The language is
that of the stage, for **persōna** means *mask,* then *character* (in a play).

[3] *the courts and their cases.*   [4] Connecting relative.

[5] *I will doubtless make you think* (**379**).

[6] *boyhood.*   [7] *rank.* For case see **329.**

[8] Do not use the derivative in translating.

[9] Ablative of place, in apposition with the locative **Antiochīae.** In
such cases the preposition **in** usually precedes.

[10] For case see **314.**   [11] = **posteā.**   [12] *appearances,* at various towns.

hominis, exspectātiōnem ipsīus adventus admīrātiōque
superāret. **5.** Erat Italia tum plēna Graecārum artium
ac disciplīnārum,[1] studiaque haec et in Latiō[2] vehementius tum colēbantur quam nunc īsdem in oppidīs et hīc
Rōmae propter tranquillitātem reī pūblicae nōn neglegē- 5
bantur.[3] Itaque hunc et Tarentīnī et Locrēnsēs et
Rēgīnī et Neāpolitānī[4] cīvitāte[5] cēterīsque praemiīs
dōnārunt,[6] et omnēs quī aliquid dē ingeniīs poterant
iūdicāre cognitiōne atque hospitiō[7] dignum[8] exīsti-
mārunt. Hāc tantā celebritāte fāmae cum esset iam 10
absentibus[9] nōtus, Rōmam vēnit,[10] Mariō cōnsule et
Catulō. Nactus est prīmum cōnsulēs eōs quōrum alter
rēs ad scrībendum maximās, alter cum[11] rēs gestās, tum
etiam studium atque aurīs[12] adhibēre posset.[13] Statim
Lūcullī,[14] cum praetextātus[15] etiam tum Archiās esset, 15

---

[1] *sciences.*

[2] Where Latin was spoken, in contrast to Italia (**Magna Graecia,** or
southern Italy) which was largely Greek in language and culture.

[3] Is it, or is it not, true in modern times that a period of peace is
most conducive to the development of the arts?

[4] *the inhabitants of Tarentum, Locri, Regium, and Naples.* See the
map of Italy (opposite p. 132).

[5] An honorary citizenship, like the presentation of the keys of the
city to a prominent visitor to-day.

[6] What is the full form?   [7] Ablative with **dignum** (**349**).

[8] Supply **eum.**   [9] *even to those far away.*

[10] 102 B.C., when Archias was only seventeen.

[11] With **tum:** *not only . . . but also.*

[12] With **studium:** *an appreciative audience.* Can you name other
ancient military leaders who also possessed an appreciation for literature?   Any modern leaders?

[13] Descriptive: Archias fell in with *the kind of* consuls who could
appreciate him.

[14] Lucius and Marcus.

[15] Not literally, but *quite young.* Being a Greek, he would not have
worn the **toga praetexta** at all.

eum domum suam recēpērunt. Est iam hoc nōn sōlum
ingenī ac litterārum,[1] vērum etiam nātūrae atque
virtūtis, ut domus quae huius adulēscentiae prīma
fāvit, eadem esset familiārissima senectūtī. **6.** Erat
5 temporibus illīs iūcundus[2] Q. Metellō illī Numidicō
et eius Piō fīliō, audiēbātur ā M. Aemiliō, vīvēbat cum
Q. Catulō et patre et fīliō, ā L. Crassō colēbātur,
Lūcullōs vērō et Drūsum et Octāviōs et Catōnem et
tōtam Hortēnsiōrum domum dēvīnctam cōnsuētūdine[3]
10 cum tenēret, afficiēbātur summō honōre, quod eum nōn
sōlum colēbant quī aliquid percipere atque audīre
studēbant vērum etiam sī quī forte simulābant.

Vocabulary Drill. — ars, celeber, plēnus, hīc, faveō, senectūs.

Archias Becomes a Roman Citizen

IV. Interim satis longō intervāllō,[4] cum esset cum
M. Lūcullō in Siciliam profectus et cum ex eā prōvinciā
15 cum eōdem Lūcullō dēcēderet, vēnit Hēraclēam. Quae
cum esset cīvitās aequissimō iūre ac foedere,[5] ascrībī
sē in eam cīvitātem voluit idque, cum[6] ipse per sē dignus
putārētur, tum[7] auctōritāte et grātiā Lūcullī ab Hēra-
cliēnsibus impetrāvit. **7.** Data est cīvitās[8] Silvānī

---

[1] Predicate genitives: (proof of) his talent, etc.

[2] he was a favorite with.   [3] bound by ties of friendship.

[4] Ablative absolute.

[5] with most favorable treaty rights, with Rome. So favorable in fact
that they hesitated to accept Roman citizenship in 90 B.C.

[6] although.   [7] besides.

[8] (Roman) citizenship. In 89 B.C. the tribunes M. Plautius Silvanus
and C. Papirius Carbo succeeded in having a bill passed which gave
Roman citizenship on the terms mentioned. The three provisions of
the law may be roughly compared to our qualifications for voting:
citizenship in the United States, residence in a locality for a certain
length of time, registration.

lēge et Carbōnis : *Sī quī foederātīs cīvitātibus ascrīptī*[1]
fuissent,[2] *sī tum cum lēx ferēbātur in Italiā domicilium*
habuissent, et sī sexāgintā diēbus apud praetōrem essent
professī.[3] Cum hic domicilium Rōmae multōs iam annōs
habēret, professus est apud praetōrem Q. Metellum, 5
familiārissimum suum. **8.** Sī nihil aliud nisi dē
cīvitāte ac lēge dīcimus,[4] nihil dīcō amplius ; causa dicta
est. Quid enim hōrum[5] īnfirmārī, Grattī,[6] potest?
Hēraclēaene esse tum ascrīptum negābis? Adest vir
summā auctōritāte et religiōne[7] et fidē, M. Lūcullus ; 10
quī sē nōn opīnārī sed scīre, nōn audīsse sed vīdisse,
nōn interfuisse sed ēgisse[8] dīcit. Adsunt Hēraclīēnsēs
lēgātī, nōbilissimī hominēs : huius iūdicī causā cum
mandātīs et cum pūblicō testimōniō vēnērunt ; quī
hunc ascrīptum Hēraclēae esse dīcunt. Hīc tū tabulās 15
dēsīderās Hēraclīēnsium pūblicās, quās Italicō bellō,[9]
incēnsō tabulāriō,[10] interīsse scīmus omnēs? Est rīdiculum ad ea[11] quae habēmus nihil dīcere, quaerere quae
habēre nōn possumus, et dē hominum memoriā tacēre,

---

[1] *i.e.* as citizens.   Our word is "naturalized."

[2] This and the following subjunctives would be future perfect indicative in direct discourse. **Ferēbātur** is indicative because parenthetical.
It was not included in the original statement of the law.

[3] *registered.*   Supply the conclusion **cīvēs Rōmānī essent.**

[4] *If we are to talk about nothing else but,* etc.

[5] Depending on **Quid** and referring to the arguments based on the
provisions of the law.

[6] The otherwise unknown prosecutor of Archias. It is supposed that
he was the tool of the enemies of Lucullus, patron of Archias.

[7] *scruples,* or *honesty.*   [8] *arranged.*   Note the climax.

[9] The Social War (90–88 B.C.).

[10] *record office.*

[11] *in answer to those proofs.*   Note the two kinds of evidence presented
in any court, ancient or modern : *oral* and *documentary.*   Is Cicero
building up a strong case?

litterārum memoriam flāgitāre et, cum habeās amplis-
simī virī religiōnem, integerrimī [1] mūnicipī iūs iūrandum fidemque, ea quae dēprāvārī nūllō modō possunt
repudiāre, tabulās quās īdem [2] dīcis solēre cor-
5 rumpī dēsīderāre. **9.** An domicilium Rōmae nōn habuit is quī tot annīs [3] ante cīvitātem datam sēdem
omnium rērum ac fortūnārum suārum Rōmae collo-
cāvit? An nōn est professus? Immō vērō eīs tabulīs [4] professus quae sōlae ex illā professiōne collē-
10 giōque praetōrum [5] obtinent pūblicārum tabulārum
auctōritātem.

Vocabulary Drill. — profiteor, flāgitō, corrumpō, immō.

Word Study. — The adjective suffix **-timus** (English -time)
means *belonging to;* **lēgi-timus.** From what is *maritime* derived?

The prefix **sē-** means *apart from:* **sē-gregō,** *put apart from
the flock.* Differentiate *segregate* and *congregate.*

Persōna has a long and interesting history. It comes from
the Greek word πρόσωπον, *mask* (lit., "before the face")
through Etruscan. Masks were worn by actors in plays to
represent various *characters.* Hence the English *dramatis
personae, "characters of a play."* Eventually **persōna** came to
mean *individual,* from which we get our word *person.*

---

[1] In ancient as in modern times some cities had better reputations
than others.

[2] *you yourself.* Grattius calls into question the registration list in
which Archias' name appears, as made clear in the next section.

[3] Ablative of measure of difference. Archias came to Rome in
102 B.C. and became a citizen in 89 B.C. In this sentence Cicero shows
that Archias had complied with the second provision of the law, and then
proceeds to take up the third.

[4] Means. Literally, *he declared his intentions* (i.e. *registered*) *by
means of the records.*

[5] Hendiadys: *which alone of the registration books of the board of
praetors in that year* (**illā**). Only the books of the praetor with whom
Archias registered were reliable.

Why Archias' Name Is Not on the Census Rolls

V.　Nam, cum Appī[1] tabulae neglegentius asservātae
dīcerentur, Gabīnī,[2] quam diū incolumis[3] fuit, levitās,
post damnātiōnem calamitās omnem tabulārum fidem
resignāsset,[4] Metellus, homō sānctissimus modestissi-
musque omnium, tantā dīligentiā fuit ut ad L. Lentu- 5
lum praetōrem et ad iūdicēs vēnerit[5] et ūnīus nōminis
litūrā sē commōtum esse dīxerit. Hīs igitur in tabulīs
nūllam litūram in nōmine A. Licinī vidētis.　**10.** Quae
cum ita sint, quid est quod[6] dē eius cīvitāte dubitētis,
praesertim cum aliīs quoque in cīvitātibus fuerit 10
ascrīptus? Etenim, cum mediocribus[7] multīs et aut
nūllā aut humilī aliquā arte praeditīs grātuītō cīvitātem in Graeciā[8] hominēs impertiēbant, Rēgīnōs crēdō[9]
aut Locrēnsīs aut Neāpolitānōs aut Tarentīnōs, quod[10]
scaenicīs[11] artificibus largīrī solēbant, id huic summā 15
ingenī praeditō glōriā nōluisse![12]　Quid? cum cēterī
nōn modo post cīvitātem datam sed etiam post lēgem

---

[1] Appius Claudius Pulcher, father of Cicero's bitter enemy, Clodius.
He and Gabinius were fellow-praetors of Metellus, with whom Archias
had registered.

[2] Depends on both **levitās** and **calamitās**. Supply **et** before it.

[3] *before his trial.* He was convicted of graft.

[4] *destroyed;* lit., *unsealed.* To break the seal of a document was to
destroy its value.

[5] For the irregular sequence see **378** (*b*). Metellus went before the
court to make certain that the erasure would not make trouble for the
person involved.

[6] *why is it that,* introducing a descriptive clause.

[7] Supply **virīs.** Dative, depending upon **impertiēbant.**

[8] *i.e.* Magna Graecia (southern Italy).

[9] Ironical.

[10] The antecedent is **id** below and refers to citizenship.

[11] At this period actors were not in good repute.

[12] Supply **largīrī.**

Pāpiam[1] aliquō modō in eōrum mūnicipiōrum tabulās irrēpsērunt, hic, quī nē ūtitur quidem illīs[2] in quibus est scrīptus, quod semper sē Hēracliēnsem esse voluit, reiciētur?

11. Cēnsūs[3] nostrōs requīris. Scīlicet;[4] est enim obscūrum[5] proximīs cēnsōribus[6] hunc cum clārissimō imperātōre, L. Lūcullō, apud[7] exercitum fuisse, superiōribus cum eōdem quaestōre[8] fuisse in Asiā, prīmīs,

[1] A law by which aliens might be ejected from the city. In spite of the laws people were still finding it easy to become citizens. What provisions have been made for deporting undesirable aliens from the United States? May a person live here indefinitely without taking out citizenship papers?

[2] Supply **tabulīs**.

[3] *census lists.*

[4] The irony involves the whole sentence.

[5] *it is not generally known.*

[6] *in the last censorship* (70 B.C.). The previous censorship (**superiōribus**) was in 86 B.C., the first after he became a citizen in 89 B.C.

[7] This shows that Archias was a guest in camp, not a soldier.

[8] In apposition with **eōdem**: *then quaestor.*

Fig. 79. The Forum Inscription

Because of its age (sixth century B.C.) and its fragmentary character the Latin has not been successfully interpreted. The letters read up one column and down the next. It is near the Rostra and not far from the tribunal of the praetor.

Iūliō et Crassō, nūllam populī partem esse cēnsam.
Sed, quoniam cēnsus nōn iūs cīvitātis cōnfirmat ac
tantum modo indicat eum quī sit cēnsus ita sē iam
tum gessisse prō cīve eīs temporibus,[1] is quem tū crī-
mināris nē ipsīus[2] quidem iūdiciō in cīvium Rōmānō- 5
rum iūre esse versātum, et testāmentum saepe fēcit
nostrīs lēgibus et adiit[3] hērēditātēs cīvium Rōmānōrum
et in beneficiīs[4] ad aerārium dēlātus est ā L. Lūcullō
prō cōnsule.

Vocabulary Drill. — praeditus, scīlicet, requīrō, cēnsor, tantum, testāmentum, aerārium.

Literature as Recreation and Education

VI. Quaere argūmenta, sī quae potes ; numquam 10
enim hic neque suō neque amīcōrum iūdiciō revincētur.

12. Quaerēs ā nōbīs, Grattī, cūr tantō opere hōc
homine dēlectēmur.[5] Quia suppeditat nōbīs ubi[6] et
animus ex hōc forēnsī[7] strepitū reficiātur et aurēs con-
vīciō dēfessae conquiēscant.[8] An tū exīstimās aut 15

---

[1] *merely shows that the man whose name was recorded had been acting
as a citizen at that time.* Following this supply some such expression as
I may say.

[2] Archias. The argument is that his failure to get his name on the
census lists shows that he did not consider himself a citizen.

[3] *had a share in.*

[4] *among the beneficiaries.* Only a Roman citizen could legally make
a will, receive an inheritance, or be cited to the treasury for a bonus in
return for distinguished services abroad.

[5] It is not likely that Grattius would ask any such thing. The sentence is a mere excuse for introducing what has been termed the most
convincing exposition of the value of literature ever presented.

[6] = **id quō**, *the means by which*, introducing a descriptive clause.

[7] *of the court room.*

[8] Do you know of business and professional men who refresh their
minds by reading good literature ?

suppetere nōbīs posse quod cotīdiē dīcāmus[1] in tantā
varietāte rērum, nisi animōs nostrōs doctrīnā excolā-
mus, aut ferre animōs tantam posse contentiōnem, nisi
eōs doctrīnā eādem relaxēmus? Ego vērō fateor mē
5 hīs studiīs esse dēditum. Cēterōs pudeat,[2] sī quī ita
sē litterīs[3] abdidērunt ut nihil possint ex eīs neque[4] ad
commūnem afferre frūctum neque in aspectum lūcem-
que prōferre;[5] mē autem quid pudeat[6] quī tot annōs
ita vīvō, iūdicēs, ut ā nūllīus umquam mē tempore aut
10 commodō[7] aut ōtium meum abstrāxerit aut voluptās
āvocārit aut dēnique somnus retardārit? **13.** Quārē
quis tandem mē reprehendat,[8] aut quis mihi iūre sus-
cēnseat, sī,[9] quantum cēterīs[10] ad suās rēs obeundās,
quantum ad fēstōs diēs lūdōrum celebrandōs, quantum
15 ad aliās voluptātēs et ad ipsam requiem animī et
corporis concēditur temporum, quantum aliī[11] tribuunt
tempestīvīs[12] convīviīs, quantum dēnique alveolō,[13]
quantum pilae, tantum mihi egomet ad haec studia

---

[1] *that we could be supplied with material for our daily speeches.*

[2] *let others feel ashamed.*   [3] Ablative: *in books* (lit., *with*).

[4] Translate *either . . . or.*

[5] *i.e.* they produce no literary works themselves.

[6] *why should I be ashamed* (**375**)?

[7] *(legal) need or advantage.*

[8] Potential subjunctive (**377**): *can criticize.*

[9] Do not forget to find the verb which this word introduces as well as
the word which completes the meaning of **quantum.**

[10] With **concēditur:** contrasts with **egomet** below.

[11] Contrasts with **cēterīs:** *everybody* does the things that precede,
only *some* do those which follow.

[12] *early,* therefore *protracted.* They lengthened their celebrations by
beginning early rather than staying late.

[13] *dice board.* Gambling was forbidden by law, as now, but enforce-
ment was difficult and lax. Cicero is thinking of dice playing rather as
a waste of time than as something wicked.

recolenda sūmpserō? Atque hoc ideō mihi concēden-
dum est magis, quod ex hīs studiīs haec quoque crēscit
ōrātiō et facultās,[1] quae quantacumque est in mē,[2]
numquam amīcōrum perīculīs dēfuit. Quae[3] sī cui
levior vidētur, illa[4] quidem certē quae summa sunt ex 5
quō fonte hauriam sentiō. **14.** Nam nisi multōrum
praeceptīs multīsque litterīs[5] mihi ab adulēscentiā
suāsissem nihil esse in vītā magnō opere expetendum
nisi laudem atque honestātem, in eā autem persequendā
omnīs cruciātūs corporis, omnia perīcula mortis atque 10
exsilī parvī[6] esse dūcenda, numquam mē prō salūte
vestrā in tot ac tantās dīmicātiōnēs atque in hōs
prōflīgātōrum[7] hominum cotīdiānōs impetūs obiēcis-
sem. Sed plēnī omnēs sunt librī, plēnae sapientium[8]
vōcēs, plēna exemplōrum vetustās; quae iacērent[9] in 15
tenebrīs omnia, nisi litterārum lūmen accēderet.[10]
Quam multās nōbīs imāginēs[11] nōn sōlum ad intuendum
vērum etiam ad imitandum fortissimōrum virōrum
expressās scrīptōrēs et Graecī et Latīnī relīquērunt!
Quās ego mihi semper in administrandā rē pūblicā 20

---

[1] Hendiadys with **ōrātiō**.

[2] Conventional, rather than real modesty.

[3] Refers to **facultās**.

[4] *those principles*, object of **hauriam**.

[5] *wide reading.*　　　　　　[6] *of small value* (**308**).

[7] Cicero so terms the members of the popular party who were
determined to make Cicero suffer for his execution of the ringleaders
in the conspiracy of Catiline.

[8] *philosophers.* The principle which Cicero follows is found in books
and is mentioned by philosophers, while history (**vetustās**) furnishes
many examples of men who practiced it.

[9] Conclusion to the condition (**390, II**).

[10] *were shed (upon them).*

[11] *(literary) portraits.*

prōpōnēns animum¹ et mentem meam ipsā cōgitātiōne
hominum excellentium² cōnfōrmābam.

Vocabulary Drill. — strepitus, doctrīna, pudet, convīvium,
suādeō, tenebrae.

*Talent and Training Both Necessary for the Greatest
Success*

VII. **15.** Quaeret quispiam : " Quid? illī ipsī
summī virī quōrum virtūtēs litterīs prōditae sunt,
5 istāne doctrīnā quam tū effers laudibus ērudītī fuērunt? " Difficile est hoc dē omnibus cōnfirmāre, sed
tamen est certum quid respondeam.³ Ego multōs
hominēs excellentī animō ac virtūte fuisse sine doctrīnā, et nātūrae ipsīus habitū⁴ prope dīvīnō per sē ipsōs
10 et moderātōs et gravīs⁵ exstitisse fateor ; etiam illud
adiungō, saepius ad laudem atque virtūtem nātūram sine
doctrīnā quam sine nātūrā valuisse⁶ doctrīnam. Atque⁷
īdem ego hoc contendō, cum ad nātūram eximiam
et illūstrem accesserit ratiō quaedam cōnfōrmātiōque
15 doctrīnae,⁸ tum illud nesciō quid praeclārum ac singu-
lāre⁹ solēre exsistere. **16.** Ex hōc esse¹⁰ hunc numerō

---

¹ *heart,* as opposed to **mentem,** *mind.*

² Can you name any great Greeks and Romans whom Cicero must
have had in mind?

³ *what reply I should make.*   ⁴ *quality of their natures, i.e.* genius.

⁵ *self-controlled and influential men.*   Can you name any men to-day
who have risen to prominence without much book-learning?

⁶ With **ad :** *has had the power to produce.*

⁷ *And yet.*

⁸ Hendiadys : *a sort of* (**quaedam**) *systematic development* (*produced
by*) *study.*

⁹ *something remarkable and unique.*   For **nesciō quid** cf. our "what
you may call it."

¹⁰ The indirect statement is continued from **contendō** above.

quem patrēs nostrī vīdērunt, dīvīnum hominem,
Āfricānum,[1] ex hōc C. Laelium, L. Fūrium, moderā-
tissimōs hominēs et continentissimōs, ex hōc fortissimum virum et illīs temporibus[2] doctissimum, M.
Catōnem illum senem; quī profectō sī nihil ad perci- 5
piendam colendamque virtūtem litterīs adiuvārentur,

FIG. 80. THE PALATINE HILL SEEN FROM THE AVENTINE

In the year 62, when the speech for Archias was delivered, Cicero acquired
a fine house on the Palatine. In this picture we see ruins of the buildings
of the Empire.

numquam sē ad eārum studium contulissent. Quod
sī[3] nōn hic tantus frūctus ostenderētur, et sī ex hīs

[1] The younger Scipio (185–129 B.C.). He, with Laelius and Furius,
did much to improve Roman literature and manners by the introduction
of Greek culture. Cato, on the other hand, who belonged to a preceding
generation, hated everything Greek and was as conspicuously conservative as the others were liberal, though he began the study of Greek when
an old man. Do you know whether such a condition exists in this
country to-day? Should an American be conservative or liberal with
regard to the literature and culture of foreign nations?

[2] Ablative, but we would say *for those times.*

[3] *But if.* The rest of the section may well be memorized. Note the
pleasant rhythm of the words and the groups of twos and threes.

studiīs dēlectātiō sōla peterētur, tamen, ut opīnor, hanc animī remissiōnem hūmānissimam ac līberālissimam iūdicārētis. Nam cēterae[1] neque temporum[2] sunt neque aetātum omnium neque locōrum; at haec 5 studia adulēscentiam acuunt, senectūtem oblectant, secundās rēs ōrnant, adversīs[3] perfugium ac sōlācium praebent, dēlectant domī, nōn impediunt forīs, pernoctant nōbīscum, peregrīnantur, rūsticantur.

17. Quod sī ipsī haec[4] neque attingere neque sēnsū 10 nostrō gustāre[5] possēmus, tamen ea mīrārī dēbērēmus, etiam cum in aliīs vidērēmus.

Vocabulary Drill. — ērudiō, nesciō, senex.

The Divine Inspiration of Poets

VIII. Quis nostrum tam animō agrestī ac dūrō fuit ut Rōscī[6] morte nūper nōn commovērētur? Quī cum esset senex mortuus, tamen propter excellentem artem 15 ac venustātem vidēbātur[7] omnīnō morī nōn dēbuisse. Ergō ille corporis mōtū tantum amōrem sibi conciliārat ā nōbīs omnibus; nōs animōrum incrēdibilīs mōtūs celeritātemque ingeniōrum[8] neglegēmus? **18.** Quotiēns ego hunc Archiam vīdī, iūdicēs (ūtar enim vestrā 20 benignitāte,[9] quoniam mē in hōc novō genere dīcendī

---

[1] Supply **remissiōnēs**.   [2] *suited to*, etc.

[3] *adversity*, as opposed to **secundās rēs**, *prosperity*.

[4] Supply **studia**.   [5] *take part in*.

[6] A Roman actor, friend of Cicero.

[7] Translate as if impersonal: *who, it seemed*.

[8] *mental activity* (in contrast to **corporis**) and *intellectual quickness*.

[9] By apologizing again for the unusual style of his defense Cicero artfully stirs up interest in his next remark. One can imagine the jurors leaning forward to catch his remarks.

tam dīligenter attenditis), quotiēns ego hunc vīdī, cum
litteram scrīpsisset nūllam,[1] magnum numerum optimōrum versuum dē eīs ipsīs rēbus quae tum agerentur
dīcere ex tempore, quotiēns revocātum[2] eandem rem
dīcere commūtātīs verbīs atque sententiīs! Quae vērō 5
accūrātē cōgitātēque scrīpsisset,[3] ea sīc vīdī probārī ut
ad veterum scrīptōrum[4] laudem pervenīret. Hunc ego
nōn dīligam, nōn admīrer, nōn omnī ratiōne dēfendendum putem?[5] Atque sīc[6] ā summīs hominibus ērudī-
tissimīsque accēpimus, cēterārum rērum studia ex 10
doctrīnā et praeceptīs et arte cōnstāre,[7] poētam[8]
nātūrā ipsā valēre et mentis vīribus excitārī et quasi
dīvīnō quōdam spīritū īnflārī.[9] Quārē suō iūre noster
ille Ennius[10] "sānctōs" appellat poētās, quod quasi
deōrum aliquō dōnō atque mūnere commendātī nōbīs 15

---

[1] *without having written a letter.* The "circus stunt" of writing
extemporaneous (**ex tempore**) verse on current affairs (**quae tum
agerentur**) or perhaps on subjects suggested by a bystander must have
excited the admiration of the jurors, some of whom no doubt were
indifferent to literature. One need not assume that Cicero himself
considered this a very great accomplishment.

[2] As if *called back* to the stage to do his trick again.

[3] The indirect discourse idea after **vīdī** carries over.

[4] The famous Greek writers of antiquity. Objective genitive: *praise
accorded the writers of old.*

[5] Why subjunctive? See **375.**

[6] *as follows,* explained by the infinitives.	[7] *depend upon.*

[8] The contrast makes a conjunction unnecessary in Latin, but we
would say *but the poet,* etc.

[9] There are three infinitives to balance the three nouns of the preceding clause.

[10] *our own famous Ennius.* Romans looked with pride upon Quintus
Ennius (239–169 B.C.) as the father of Roman poetry. He first introduced the hexameter (the favorite line of six feet in Greek poetry) in his
Latin national epic, the **Annālēs.** This remained the standard Latin
epic until Virgil wrote the Aeneid.

esse videantur.[1] **19.** Sit igitur, iūdicēs, sānctum apud
vōs, hūmānissimōs hominēs, hoc poētae nōmen, quod
nūlla umquam barbaria violāvit. Saxa atque sōli-
tūdinēs vōcī respondent, bēstiae saepe immānēs
5 cantū flectuntur atque cōnsistunt;[2] nōs īnstitūtī rēbus
optimīs nōn poētārum vōce moveāmur?[3] Homērum
Colophōniī[4] cīvem esse dīcunt suum, Chiī suum vindi-
cant, Salamīniī repetunt, Smyrnaeī vērō suum esse
cōnfirmant itaque etiam dēlūbrum eius[5] in oppidō
10 dēdicāvērunt, permultī[6] aliī praetereā pugnant inter
sē atque contendunt.[7]

Word Study. — Explain the derivation of *reptile, largess,
extemporaneous, inflation.*

Great Men Look with Favor upon Poets

IX. Ergō illī aliēnum,[8] quia poēta fuit, post mortem etiam expetunt; nōs hunc vīvum, quī et voluntāte
et lēgibus noster est, repudiāmus, praesertim cum
15 omne ōlim studium atque omne ingenium contulerit

---

[1] For mood see **389.**

[2] Amphion, king of Thebes, played the lyre so well that the stones of
their own accord fell into place to form a wall. Orpheus charmed the
trees and wild beasts by his playing (cf. Gayley, *Classic Myths*, pp. 102–
104, 185–188; Sabin, *Classical Myths That Live Today*, pp. 243–249,
etc.). What likeness to the story of the Pied Piper?

[3] *should we not be moved* (**375**).

[4] *the inhabitants of Colophon*, etc.   [5] *to him.*

[6] Three others — Athens, Rhodes, and Argos. The four he chose to
mention form an alliterative pair.

        " Seven cities claimed great Homer dead
        Through which the living Homer begged his bread."

[7] Note the skillful use of nearly synonymous verbs in this sentence.

[8] *foreigner.* Not quite accurate, for he probably was a native of one
of the seven cities.

Archiās ad populī Rōmānī glōriam laudemque celebran-
dam?[1] Nam et Cimbricās rēs[2] adulēscēns attigit et
ipsī illī C. Mariō, quī dūrior[3] ad haec studia vidēbātur,

FIG. 81. THE MUSE CLIO

iūcundus fuit. 20. Ne-
que enim quisquam est 5
tam āversus ā Mūsīs[4] quī
nōn mandārī versibus
aeternum suōrum labō-
rum praecōnium facile
patiātur.[5] Themisto- 10
clem[6] illum, summum
Athēnīs virum, dīxisse
aiunt, cum ex eō quaere-
rētur[7] quod acroāma[8] aut
cuius vōcem libentissimē 15
audīret: "eius ā quō sua
virtūs[9] optimē praedicā-
rētur." Itaque ille Ma-
rius item eximiē L. Plō-
tium dīlēxit, cuius ingeniō 20
putābat ea quae gesserat

[1] In the absence of definite
proof of Archias' citizenship, this
is well calculated to impress the
jury favorably.

[2] *the Cimbrian affair.* Marius' repulse of the Cimbri in 101 B.C.

[3] *too rough for.*   [4] *hostile to literature.*

[5] A descriptive clause of result.

[6] A famous Athenian general of the fifth century B.C. What word
here indicates that he was well-known?

[7] The **quod** clause is subject, but translate *when he was asked,* etc.

[8] A Greek word (neuter acc. sing.) meaning "something to hear,"
hence *entertainment.*

[9] *valorous deeds.* The clause is really indirectly quoted, hence the
subjunctive and **sua** for **mea**

posse celebrārī. **21.** Mithridāticum vērō bellum, magnum atque difficile et in multā varietāte[1] terrā marīque
versātum, tōtum[2] ab hōc expressum est; quī librī nōn
modo L. Lūcullum, fortissimum et clārissimum virum,
5 vērum etiam populī Rōmānī nōmen illūstrant. Populus
enim Rōmānus aperuit, Lūcullō imperante, Pontum
et rēgiīs quondam opibus et ipsā nātūrā et regiōne
vāllātum, populī Rōmānī exercitus, eōdem dūce, nōn
maximā[3] manū innumerābilīs Armeniōrum cōpiās fūdit,
10 populī Rōmānī laus est urbem amīcissimam Cyzicēnōrum[4] eiusdem cōnsiliō ex omnī impetū rēgiō atque tōtīus
bellī ōre ac faucibus[5] ēreptam esse atque servātam; nostra[6] semper ferētur[7] et praedicābitur, L. Lūcullō dīmi-
cante, cum, interfectīs ducibus, dēpressa hostium classis
15 est, incrēdibilis apud Tenedum[8] pugna illa nāvālis, nostra sunt tropaea, nostra monumenta, nostrī triumphī.[9]

---

[1] *involving many changes of fortune, i.e.* it had its "ups and downs."
To describe these versatility was required.

[2] Probably, as the following shows, only that part which dealt with
Lucullus' successes.

[3] With **maximā**. What figure? See **157.** Lucullus had 10,000 men,
Tigranes 200,000 at the battle of Tigranocerta (69 B.C.).

[4] *the people of Cyzicus.*

[5] What rhetorical figure? See **142.**

[6] *as ours;* predicate adjective agreeing with **pugna.** Note the
anaphora.

[7] *will be talked about.*

[8] The scene of other exciting naval operations besides this one of
73 B.C. Virgil in the Aeneid (Book II) speaks of it as the island behind
which the Greeks hid their vessels just before capturing Troy. The
British used it as a naval base for operations against Gallipoli and the
Turks in 1915.

[9] This passage illustrates Rome's policy of expansion. By consult-
ing the map **Imperium Rōmānum** (opposite p. 132), you will note
how rapidly Rome was bringing the countries of the Mediterranean
under her power as provinces. All great men like Cicero justified this

Quae[1] quōrum ingeniīs efferuntur, ab eīs populī Rōmānī fāma celebrātur. **22.** Cārus fuit Āfricānō supe-
riōrī[2] noster Ennius, itaque etiam in sepulcrō Scīpi-
ōnum putātur is esse cōnstitūtus ex marmore;[3] at
eīs laudibus[4] certē nōn sōlum ipse quī laudātur sed 5
etiam populī Rōmānī nōmen ōrnātur. In caelum
huius[5] proavus Catō tollitur; magnus honōs populī
Rōmānī rēbus adiungitur. Omnēs dēnique illī Maximī,
Mārcellī, Fulviī[6] nōn sine commūnī omnium nostrum[7]
laude decorantur.   10

Vocabulary Drill (17-20). — **morior, conciliō, attendō, versus
(-ūs)**; **iūcundus, aiō.**

Poets Are Needed to Give Immortality to Great Achievements

X. Ergō illum quī haec fēcerat,[8] Rudīnum[9] hominem, maiōrēs nostrī in cīvitātem recēpērunt; nōs hunc

policy. What is the policy of the United States? Can our country
rightly be called imperialistic?

[1] Connecting relative, subject of **efferuntur.** The antecedent of **quōrum** is **eīs.** Translate in this order: **fāma populī Rōmānī celebrātur
ab eīs quōrum ingeniīs quae** (these deeds) **efferuntur.**

[2] The older Scipio, conqueror of Hannibal.

[3] *i.e.* a marble bust. Two busts were discovered in this tomb, which
was opened in 1780, but it is not known whether either represents
Ennius. The tomb was on the Appian Way, just inside the later wall of
Aurelian. The sarcophagi of various Scipios found there were moved
to the Vatican. The tombs were reopened to the public on the birthday
of Rome, April 21, 1929. Nearby are ancient Etruscan tombs, tombs of
the Empire, and Christian catacombs.

[4] Contained in Ennius' **Annālēs.**   [5] *the present (Cato).*

[6] *famous men like Maximus,* etc.

[7] Objective genitive with **laude.** *of us all.*

[8] *wrote these poems, i.e.* Ennius.

[9] *of Rudiae,* in Calabria, Ennius' birthplace.

Hēraclīēnsem multīs cīvitātibus[1] expetītum, in hāc autem lēgibus cōnstitūtum, dē nostrā cīvitāte ēiciēmus?

23. Nam sī quis minōrem glōriae frūctum putat ex Graecīs versibus percipī quam ex Latīnīs, vehementer 5 errat, proptereā quod Graeca[2] leguntur in omnibus ferē gentibus, Latīna suīs fīnibus exiguīs sānē[3] continentur.[4] Quārē sī rēs eae quās gessimus 10 orbis terrae regiōnibus dēfīniuntur, cupere dēbēmus quō[5] manuum nostrārum tēla pervēnerint, eōdem glōriam fāmamque penetrāre, quod cum[6] 15 ipsīs populīs dē quōrum rēbus scrībitur[7] haec ampla[8] sunt, tum eīs certē quī dē[9] vītā glōriae causā dīmicant, hoc maximum et perīculōrum 20 incitāmentum est et labōrum.[10] **24.** Quam multōs

Fig. 82. The Dying Alexander

---

[1] Dative of agent with **expetītum** (**317**).

[2] Supply **scrīpta**, *literature*.   [3] *as you know.*

[4] In Cicero's time Latin was just becoming the dominant language in Italy. Its rivals were other related languages (such as Oscan), Greek, Celtic, etc. During the Empire Latin spread to the whole western Mediterranean where the Romance languages are now spoken. Greek remained the chief language of the eastern Mediterranean. Besides, every educated Roman could speak and read it.

[5] Relative adverb, correlating with **eōdem**: *wherever . . . to that point.*

[6] With **tum**: *not only . . . but also.*

[7] Impersonal: *whose deeds are described.*

[8] *these poems are a source of honor.*   [9] *at the risk of.*

[10] Objective genitives (**302**): *the greatest inducement for undergoing dangers and toil.*

scrīptōrēs rērum suārum magnus ille Alexander sēcum
habuisse dīcitur! Atque is[1] tamen, cum in Sīgēō[2] ad
Achillis tumulum astitisset: "Ō fortūnāte," inquit,
"adulēscēns, quī[3] tuae virtūtis Homērum praecōnem
invēnerīs!" Et vērē. Nam, nisi Īlias illa exstitisset,[5]
īdem tumulus quī corpus eius contēxerat nōmen etiam
obruisset. Quid? noster hic Magnus[4] quī cum virtūte
fortūnam adaequāvit, nōnne Theophanem[5] Mytilē-
naeum, scrīptōrem rērum suārum, in cōntiōne mīlitum
cīvitāte dōnāvit, et nostrī illī fortēs virī, sed[6] rūsticī[10]
ac mīlitēs, dulcēdine quādam glōriae commōtī quasi
participēs eiusdem laudis[7] magnō illud clāmōre appro-
bāvērunt?[8] **25.** Itaque, crēdō,[9] sī cīvis Rōmānus
Archiās lēgibus nōn esset, ut ab aliquō imperātōre
cīvitāte dōnārētur perficere nōn potuit.[10] Sulla cum[15]
Hispānōs et Gallōs dōnāret,[11] crēdō, hunc petentem
repudiāsset; quem[12] nōs in cōntiōne vīdimus, cum eī
libellum malus poēta dē populō[13] subiēcisset,[14] quod

---

[1] Translate **cum** first.

[2] A promontory at the entrance of the Hellespont, near Troy.

[3] *since you.*

[4] *our own Pompey the Great,* in contrast to **magnus ille Alexander**
above.

[5] Object of **dōnāvit.**   [6] *though.*

[7] Objective genitive (**302**).

[8] Similar approval, attended with appropriate ceremonies, has been
accorded worthy foreigners in America when they have attained to full
citizenship.

[9] Ironical, as usual.

[10] For indicative see **390, II, Note.**   The ut clause is object of **perficere:**
could not have succeeded in being presented, etc.

[11] Supply **cīvitāte.**   [12] *i.e.* Sulla.

[13] *an inferior poet of the common people.*

[14] *handed up* to Sulla, who was on a platform in the Forum, conducting
an auction sale of confiscated property.

epigramma[1] in eum fēcisset, tantum modo alternīs
versibus longiusculīs,[2] statim ex eīs rēbus quās tum
vēndēbat iubēre eī praemium tribuī, sed eā condiciōne, nē quid posteā scrīberet.[3]   Quī[4] sēdulitātem malī
5 poētae dūxerit aliquō tamen praemiō dignam, huius[5]
ingenium et virtūtem in scrībendō et cōpiam nōn
expetīsset?   **26.** Quid?   ā Q. Metellō Piō, familiāris-
simō suō, quī cīvitāte multōs dōnāvit, neque per sē
neque per Lūcullōs[6] impetrāvisset?   Quī praesertim
10 usque eō[7] dē suīs rēbus scrībī[8] cuperet ut etiam
Cordubae[9] nātīs poētīs pingue quiddam sonantibus
atque peregrīnum[10] tamen aurīs suās dēderet.

Immortality in Literature the Only Reward of Statesmanship

XI.   Neque enim est hoc dissimulandum, quod
obscūrārī nōn potest sed prae nōbīs ferendum:[11] tra-
15 himur omnēs studiō laudis, et optimus quisque[12] maximē

---

[1] *an epigram which;* in apposition with **libellum.**

[2] Ablative absolute: *(in which) every other line was a bit longer.* It had
the form of verse but was not poetry. Reference is made to the elegiac
meter, commonly used in epigrams and short poems, in which the odd
lines were longer than the even.

[3] Like giving money to a street musician to get rid of him.

[4] *Since he* (Sulla).   [5] *i.e.* Archias.

[6] They were related to Metellus.   [7] *so much.*

[8] Impersonal: *something written.*

[9] An important city in Spain (now Cordova) which had been a
Roman colony since 152 B.C.   What case?

[10] *having a certain sort of heavy, foreign sound.* Unfortunately for the
Cordovans, Cicero did not live long enough to take back his sneer: three
leading writers, the two Senecas and Lucan, came from this "small
town" to the "big city."

[11] *we must show openly,* i.e. *admit frankly.*

[12] *all the best men.* Remember this as the "optimus quisque" idiom.

glōriā dūcitur. Ipsī illī philosophī etiam in eīs libellīs quōs dē contemnendā glōriā scrībunt nōmen suum

FIG. 83.   THE MUSE EUTERPE

īnscrībunt; in eō ipsō[1] in quō praedicātiōnem nōbilitātemque dēspiciunt[5] praedicārī dē sē ac nōminārī[2] volunt.

27. Decimus quidem Brūtus, summus vir et imperātor, Accī, amīcissimī[10] suī, carminibus templōrum ac monumentōrum aditūs exōrnāvit suōrum.[3] Iam vērō ille quī cum Aetōlīs, Enniō comite, bellāvit Fulvius[15] nōn dubitāvit Mārtis[4] manubiās[5] Mūsīs cōnsecrāre. Quārē in quā urbe[6] imperātōrēs prope armātī[7] poētārum nōmen et Mūsārum[20] dēlūbra coluērunt, in eā nōn dēbent togātī iūdicēs ā Mūsārum honōre et ā poētārum salūte abhorrēre.

28. Atque ut id[8] libentius faciātis, iam mē vōbīs,[25]

---

[1] *by that very act.*

[2] Translate as if **sē** were the subject of both verbs.

[3] *which he built.* The order is perhaps due to the desire to avoid three genitive plural endings in a row.

[4] For **bellī**. Note the alliteration.   [5] *spoils.*

[6] Translate as if **in eā urbe in quā.**

[7] *i.e.* immediately after their return from war.

[8] *i.e.* protect poets.

iūdicēs, indicābō[1] et dē meō quōdam amōre glōriae
nimis ācrī fortasse,[2] vērum tamen honestō vōbīs cōnfitēbor. Nam quās rēs nōs[3] in cōnsulātū nostrō
vōbīscum simul prō salūte huius urbis atque imperī et
5 prō vītā cīvium prōque ūniversā rē pūblicā gessimus,
attigit hic[4] versibus atque inchoāvit.[5] Quibus audītīs,
quod mihi magna rēs et iūcunda vīsa est, hunc ad
perficiendum adōrnāvī.[6] Nūllam enim virtūs aliam
mercēdem labōrum perīculōrumque dēsīderat praeter
10 hanc laudis et glōriae; quā quidem dētrāctā,[7] iūdicēs,
quid est quod[8] in hōc tam exiguō vītae curriculō et
tam brevī tantīs nōs[9] in labōribus exerceāmus? **29.**
Certē, sī nihil animus praesentīret[10] in posterum, et sī
quibus regiōnibus vītae spatium circumscrīptum est,
15 īsdem[11] omnīs cōgitātiōnēs termināret suās, nec tantīs
sē labōribus frangeret neque tot cūrīs vigiliīsque
angerētur nec totiēns dē ipsā vītā dīmicāret. Nunc[12]

---

[1] *I will disclose myself to you*, i.e. *I will take you into my confidence.*

[2] *perhaps too keen;* with **amōre.**

[3] = **ego** (plural of modesty).

[4] Archias.

[5] Supply the object from **quās rēs.** The poem was apparently not
finished. So Cicero wrote one himself (in both Greek and Latin). It
was much ridiculed, especially for the conceit shown in such lines as
Ō fortūnātam nātam mē cōnsule Rōmam.

[6] *I furnished him with the data.*

[7] Conditional. Is Cicero's philosophy here sound? What reward
may he have omitted?

[8] *for which.*

[9] Object of **exerceāmus.** What comparison is involved in this
sentence?

[10] What kind of condition?

[11] With **regiōnibus:** *by the same boundaries by which.*

[12] *As a matter of fact*, in contrast to the contrary to fact condition of
the preceding sentence.

īnsidet quaedam in optimō quōque virtūs,[1] quae noctīs
ac diēs animum glōriae stimulīs concitat atque admonet
nōn cum[2] vītae tempore esse dīmittendam comme-
morātiōnem nōminis nostrī, sed cum omnī posteritāte
adaequandam.   5

**Vocabulary Drill (22–29). — ergō, cōntiō, dōnō, vēndō;
prae, templum, colō, admoneō.**

Archias Deserves to Be Acquitted

XII.   **30.**   An vērō tam parvī animī videāmur[3] esse
omnēs quī in rē pūblicā atque in hīs vītae perīculīs
labōribusque versāmur ut, cum usque ad extrēmum
spatium[4] nūllum tranquillum atque ōtiōsum spīritum
dūxerīmus, nōbīscum simul moritūra omnia arbitrēmur? 10
An[5] statuās et imāginēs, nōn animōrum simulācra sed
corporum, studiōsē multī summī hominēs relīquērunt;
cōnsiliōrum relinquere ac virtūtum nostrārum effigiem
nōnne multō mālle dēbēmus summīs ingeniīs[6] expressam
et polītam? Ego vērō omnia quae gerēbam iam tum 15
in gerendō[7] spargere[8] mē ac dissēmināre arbitrābar[9]
in orbis terrae memoriam sempiternam. Haec vērō

---

[1] *noble impulse.*

[2] Preposition. Fame should not end at death but should last
forever.

[3] Deliberative subjunctive (**375**) : *are all of us to seem so shortsighted*
(lit., "small-minded ") ; **animī** is predicate genitive.

[4] *moment;* lit., *lap,* with a return to the comparison of life to a
race.

[5] As in Cat. I. 3, it is best to omit this word in translating and to
make the first clause a statement.

[6] *by the greatest geniuses.*

[7] *even while so employed.* What literally?

[8] What is the metaphor?

[9] *I used to think:* imperfect of customary act.

sīve ā meō sēnsū post mortem āfutūra est sīve, ut
sapientissimī hominēs[1] putāvērunt, ad aliquam animī
meī partem pertinēbit,[2] nunc quidem certē cōgitātiōne
quādam spēque dēlector.

5   31. Quārē cōnservāte, iūdicēs, hominem pudōre eō
quem amīcōrum[3] vidētis comprobārī cum dignitāte,
tum etiam vetustāte, ingeniō[4] autem tantō quantum
id convenit exīstimārī, quod summōrum hominum
ingeniīs expetītum esse videātis,[5] causā vērō eius modī
10 quae beneficiō lēgis,[6] auctōritāte mūnicipī, testimōniō
Lūcullī, tabulīs Metellī comprobētur. Quae cum ita
sint, petimus[7] ā vōbīs, iūdicēs, sī qua nōn modo
hūmāna vērum etiam dīvīna in tantīs ingeniīs commendātiō dēbet esse, ut eum[8] quī vōs, quī vestrōs
15 imperātōrēs, quī populī Rōmānī rēs gestās semper
ōrnāvit, quī etiam hīs recentibus nostrīs vestrīsque
domesticīs perīculīs[9] aeternum sē testimōnium laudis
datūrum esse profitētur estque ex eō numerō quī semper
apud omnēs sānctī sunt habitī itaque[10] dictī, sīc in

---

[1] Cicero, in common with many Greeks, such as Plato and Socrates,
believed in an after life.

[2] *shall belong to*, i.e. *shall be known to.*

[3] Modifies **dignitāte**. Both the high position of his friends and the
length of the friendship are proofs of Archias' good character.

[4] Another ablative of description like **pudōre** ; so too **causā** (*with a
case*) below.

[5] *A man of genius, the greatness of which should be estimated from the
fact that, as you see, it is much sought after by men of genius.* The subject
of **exīstimārī** is **id** (ingenium), and the subject of **convenit** is **exīstimārī**.
We might have expected **ab hominibus summī ingenī** for **summōrum
hominum ingeniīs** ; the latter form puts the emphasis on **ingeniīs.**

[6] The law of 89 B.C., discussed in section 7.

[7] Remember to look for an object.

[8] Do not forget to find a construction for **eum.**

[9] *i.e.* the Catilinarian conspiracy.   [10] = **et ita.**

vestram accipiātis fidem ut hūmānitāte vestrā levātus
potius quam acerbitāte violātus esse videātur.[1]

32. Quae[2] dē causā prō meā cōnsuētūdine breviter
simpliciterque dīxī, iūdicēs, ea cōnfīdō probāta esse
omnibus; quae ā forēnsī aliēna iūdiciālīque cōnsuētū- 5
dine et dē hominis ingeniō et commūniter dē ipsō
studiō locūtus sum, ea, iūdicēs, ā vōbīs spērō esse in
bonam partem accepta, ab eō[3] quī iūdicium exercet
certō sciō.

Vocabulary Drill. — spīritus, imāgō, aeternus, levō.

Word Study. — Explain the derivation of *inchoate, presenti-
ment, sparse, disseminate.*

The suffix **-culum** is a diminutive: **curri-culum,** *little run.*
Do you consider the high school curriculum to be well named?

In English this suffix has the forms *-culum, -cule, -cle: ridicule, parti-cle.* What other examples can you give?

Review Questions. — 1. What reason does Cicero give for
defending Archias? 2. What other reasons were there? 3. For
what does Cicero apologize? 4. How and when did Archias
become eligible for Roman citizenship? 5. What three qualifications did he meet? 6. How does a foreigner qualify for
citizenship in this country? 7. What advantage was it to
Archias to become a Roman citizen? 8. What advantage is it
to a foreigner in the United States to become a citizen? 9. On
what did the prosecution base its claim that Archias was not
a citizen? 10. What provision was there for deporting aliens
from Rome? 11. What provision is there in this country
to-day? 12. Why were the charges brought against Archias?
13. What were Cicero's two chief aims in life? 14. What are
the values of literature according to Cicero?

---

[1] The assonance of **levātus** with **violātus** and **hūmānitāte** with
acerbitāte, as well as the rhetorical balance of the clause, makes a conspicuous ending to the sentence. **Esse videātur** was a favorite ending of
Cicero's on account of its rhythm.

[2] The antecedent is **ea.**   [3] Who was presiding?

FIG. 84. THE ROMAN FORUM DURING THE EMPIRE

Looking toward the north. At the left, in the foreground, the Rostra; in the background, the senate house; to the right, the Basilica Aemilia. The Rostra of Cicero's day was near the one shown here.

167. THE SPEECH IN FAVOR OF THE MANILIAN LAW

In 88 B.C. Mithridates, King of Pontus in Asia Minor, invaded the Roman provinces there with the intention of driving the hated Romans from the East. His slogan was "Asia for the Asiatics." In a single day he massacred eighty thousand Roman provincials, including helpless women and children. Rome waged three wars against Mithridates, sending against him one general after another with varying success. In the Third Mithridatic War, the king was finally defeated and fled to Armenia, where his son-in-law, Tigranes, ruled.

FIG. 85. CICERO

The latter granted him protection and refused to surrender him upon the demand of the Roman commander Lucullus. With a small and mutinous army Lucullus captured Tigranes' capital; but his troops, clamoring for discharge, refused to press the campaign further. Mithridates at once resumed hostilities and recaptured Pontus, while Tigranes advanced from the east. Lucullus had to retreat. Glabrio was appointed to succeed him, but he could do nothing to restore the morale of the troops. Such was the situation in 66 B.C. — one which clearly demanded a general of outstanding ability who could turn defeat into victory and insure peace in the East.

Pompey, in the popular mind, was the greatest soldier of his day, and the tribune Manilius, in sponsoring before the Comitia Tributa in the Forum the bill which aimed to make Pompey supreme dictator of Roman affairs in the East, was merely voicing a widespread public demand. Although such prominent statesmen as Catulus and Hortensius opposed the Manilian bill as unconstitutional and dangerous, yet Cicero, who was already aspiring to the consulship, saw here an opportunity to ingratiate himself with the masses and win Pompey's political support. Never did an orator throw himself more unreservedly into any cause. As a result, the bill of Manilius became law, and Pompey not only brought the Mithridatic War to a successful close, but restored Roman power in the East, including Syria and Palestine.

How to Outline This Speech. — As you advance, you will observe that the orator follows a definite outline, consisting of six main divisions, with subpoints under each — an outline which you will do well to follow whenever called upon to prepare a debate or a formal address of any length. The first chapter constitutes the **exordium** or *introduction*. As you proceed, assign Roman numerals to the main divisions (which will be mentioned in the notes) and see if you can fill in the subpoints under each, using arabic numerals. For further divisions under the latter, you may use the letters, *a, b, c,* etc.

Note. — Those portions of the text which are printed in smaller type may be omitted or read rapidly.

168.

M. TULLI CICERONIS
DE IMPERIO CN. POMPEI
AD QUIRITES ORATIO

Why Cicero Has Not Previously Spoken from the Rostra

I. 1. Quamquam mihi semper frequēns cōnspectus vester[1] multō iūcundissimus, hic autem locus[2] ad agendum[3] amplissimus,[4] ad dīcendum ōrnātissimus est vīsus, Quirītēs, tamen hōc aditū laudis[5] quī semper optimō cuique[6] maximē patuit nōn mea mē voluntās[5] adhūc sed vītae meae ratiōnēs ab ineunte aetāte[7] susceptae prohibuērunt. Nam cum[8] anteā nōndum 'huius auctōritātem[9] locī attingere audērem statueremque nihil hūc nisi perfectum ingeniō, ēlabōrātum industriā afferrī oportēre, omne meum tempus amīcō-[10] rum temporibus[10] trānsmittendum putāvī.

2. Ita neque[11] hic locus vacuus fuit umquam ab eīs quī vestram causam dēfenderent[12] et meus labor in prīvātōrum

---

[1] *the sight of your assembled presence.*

[2] The Rostra, or speakers' platform in the Forum.

[3] *for discussion* by a magistrate, as contrasted with **ad dīcendum,** which refers to a speech by a private individual.

[4] *most dignified.* Cicero regularly uses **amplissimus** in speaking of magistrates.

[5] *from this pathway to fame* (with **prohibuērunt**).

[6] *all the best men.*

[7] *from earliest manhood.* Cicero was now forty.

[8] *since.*

[9] The abstract noun used (as often) for the concrete adjective: *this influential place.*

[10] *(legal) difficulties.*

[11] = **et nōn,** with et below: *on the one hand . . . on the other.*

[12] For mood see **380.**

perīculīs[1] castē integrēque versātus ex vestrō iūdiciō frūctum[2] est amplissimum cōnsecūtus. Nam cum propter dīlātiōnem[3] comitiōrum ter praetor prīmus[4] centuriīs cūnc-5 tīs[5] renūntiātus sum, facile intellēxī, Quirītēs, et quid dē mē iūdicārētis et quid aliīs praescrībe- rētis. Nunc cum et 10 auctōritātis in mē tan- tum sit quantum vōs ho- nōribus mandandīs[6] esse voluistis, et ad agendum facultātis tantum quan- 15 tum hominī vigilantī ex forēnsī ūsū[7] prope cotī- diāna dīcendī exercitātiō potuit afferre, certē et, sī quid auctōritātis in mē 20 est, apud eōs ūtar[8] quī eam mihi dedērunt et, sī quid in dīcendō cōnsequī possum, eīs ostendam potissimum[9] quī eī quoque reī[10] frūctum suō iūdiciō tribuendum esse dūxērunt.

FIG. 86.　CŪRIA

This building was built after Cicero's time. In front of it was the Comitium.

---

[1] "trials" in the sense of *lawsuits*.

[2] They had recently elected him praetor.

[3] Such delays could be caused by rioting at the polls or by a bad omen, such as a sudden thunderstorm, etc.

[4] To be taken adverbially with **renūntiātus sum**: *first to be declared elected praetor*. The first two elections had been stopped before all eight praetors had been elected, and the whole election had to be repeated. Cicero was elected first.

[5] See **112**, 1.

[6] *by intrusting me with public office*.

[7] *from a law practice* (the law courts surrounded the Forum).

[8] Supply **eā** (**auctōritāte**).

[9] *preferably*.

[10] *for this (oratorical) gift*.

3. Atque illud in prīmīs mihi laetandum[1] iūre esse
videō, quod[2] in hāc īnsolitā mihi ex hōc locō ratiōne[3]
dīcendī causa tālis oblāta est in quā ōrātiō[4] deesse
nēminī possit. Dīcendum est enim dē Cn. Pompeī
singulārī eximiāque virtūte ; huius autem ōrātiōnis diffi- 5
cilius est exitum quam prīncipium invenīre. Ita mihi
nōn tam cōpia quam modus in dīcendō quaerendus est.

A Crisis in the East.   Character of the War

II.   **4.**[5] Atque ut inde[6] ōrātiō mea proficīscātur unde
haec omnis causa dūcitur, bellum grave et perīculōsum
vestrīs vectīgālibus[7] atque sociīs ā duōbus potentissimīs 10
īnfertur rēgibus, Mithridāte et Tigrāne, quōrum alter
relīctus,[8] alter lacessītus occāsiōnem sibi ad occupan-
dam Asiam[9] oblātam esse arbitrātur. Equitibus
Rōmānīs, honestissimīs virīs, afferuntur ex Asiā cotīdiē
litterae, quōrum magnae rēs aguntur in vestrīs vectī- 15
gālibus exercendīs occupātae ;[10] quī ad mē prō necessitūdine[11] quae mihi est cum illō ōrdine causam

---

[1] *I have this to rejoice over.*

[2] *that.*   The clause explains **illud.**   [3] *situation.*   [4] *words.*

[5] Sections 4–5 comprise the **nārrātiō** or *statement.*

[6] With **unde:** *at that point from which . . . starts.*

[7] Masculine: *tributaries,* with **īnfertur.**

[8] *let go.*   He had escaped into Armenia.

[9] That part of western Asia Minor which formed the Roman province.

[10] *vast interests invested in collecting your revenues are at stake.*   The
knights were the capitalistic class.   They formed tax-collecting agencies,
employing large numbers of **pūblicānī** (*taxgatherers*) to collect the
government revenues from the provinces, with the right to levy as
high a surtax as they could extort from the helpless provinciais.   No
wonder that " publican " became a synonym for " sinner " in the populai
mind !

[11] Cicero, a senator since his quaestorship, belonged by birth to the
equestrian order.

reī pūblicae perīculaque rērum suārum dētulērunt :

5. Bīthȳniae, quae nunc vestra prōvincia est,[1] vīcōs exustōs esse[2] complūrīs, rēgnum Ariobarzānis, quod fīnitimum est vestrīs vectīgālibus, tōtum esse in hostium 5 potestāte ; L. Lūcullum, magnīs rēbus gestīs,[3] ab eō bellō discēdere ; huic quī[4] successerit[5] nōn satis esse parātum ad tantum bellum administrandum ; ūnum ab omnibus sociīs et cīvibus ad id bellum imperātōrem[6] dēposcī atque expetī, eundem hunc ūnum ab hostibus 10 metuī, praetereā nēminem.

6.[7] Causa quae sit vidētis ; nunc quid agendum sit ipsī cōnsīderāte. Prīmum mihi vidētur dē genere bellī, deinde dē magnitūdine, tum dē imperātōre dēligendō esse dīcendum.

15 Genus[8] est eius bellī quod maximē vestrōs animōs excitāre atque īnflammāre ad persequendī studium dēbeat. In quō agitur[9] populī Rōmānī glōria quae vōbīs ā maiōribus cum magna in omnibus rēbus tum summa in rē mīlitārī trādita est ; agitur salūs sociōrum 20 atque amīcōrum, prō quā multa maiōrēs vestrī magna et gravia bella gessērunt ; aguntur certissima populī Rōmānī vectīgālia et maxima, quibus āmissīs,[10] et pācis ōrnāmenta et subsidia bellī requīrētis ; aguntur bona

---

[1] King Nicomedes III, being without an heir, bequeathed his kingdom to Rome in 75 B.C.

[2] Why infinitive?   [3] Concessive.

[4] Supply **eum** as antecedent and as subject of **esse parātum.** The reference is to the notoriously incompetent Glabrio.

[5] Why subjunctive?   [6] *as commander.* Who is meant?

[7] Section 6, first paragraph, constitutes the **partītiō** or *division* of the argument. Note the three main heads and add them to your outline.

[8] *The character of the war* is the first topic under the **cōnfirmātiō** or *affirmative argument.*

[9] *there is at stake.*   [10] Conditional : *and if these are lost.*

multōrum cīvium quibus[1] est ā vōbīs[2] et ipsōrum causā
et reī pūblicae cōnsulendum.

Vocabulary Drill (1–6). — adhūc, comitia, potissimum, laetor;
vectīgal, cōnsīderō.

The Unconquered Mithridates

III. **7.** Et quoniam semper appetentēs glōriae[3] praeter cēterās gentīs atque avidī laudis fuistis, dēlenda
vōbīs est illa macula[4] Mithridāticō bellō superiōre[5] 5
concepta quae penitus iam īnsēdit ac nimis inveterāvit
in populī Rōmānī nōmine, quod is quī ūnō diē tōtā in
Asiā tot in cīvitātibus ūnō nūntiō atque ūnā significātiōne litterārum[6] cīvīs Rōmānōs necandōs trucīdandōs-
que[7] cūrāvit, nōn modo adhūc poenam nūllam suō 10
dignam scelere suscēpit sed ab illō tempore annum
iam tertium et vīcēsimum rēgnat, et ita rēgnat ut sē
nōn Pontī neque Cappadociae latebrīs[8] occultāre velit
sed ēmergere ex patriō rēgnō atque in vestrīs vectīgālibus, hoc est[9] in Asiae[10] lūce, versārī. **8.** Etenim adhūc 15

---

[1] Dative depending upon **cōnsulendum**: *for whom you ought to take
counsel.*

[2] The ablative of agent is used instead of the more usual dative
because two different datives here would be confusing.

[3] Objective genitive with **appetentēs (302).** So too laudis with avidī.

[4] *stain.* The massacre of 80,000 Romans by Mithridates, as explained by **quod** (*the fact that*).

[5] First Mithridatic War (88–83 B.C.)

[6] *with a single stroke of the pen.*

[7] With **cūrō**: *had   .   .   .   butchered* **(398, II, b).**

[8] Ablative of means, but translate as place. The language which
Cicero here employs would apply equally well to a skulking beast of the
jungle.

[9] = the more familiar **id est** (*i.e.*).

[10] The western part of Asia Minor. Mithridates **wanted his** place
in the sun."

ita nostrī cum illō rēge contendērunt imperātōrēs ut ab illō īnsignia [1] victōriae, nōn victōriam reportārent. Triumphāvit [2] L. Sulla, triumphāvit L. Mūrēna dē Mithridāte, duo fortissimī virī et summī imperātōrēs, 5 sed ita triumphārunt ut ille pulsus superātusque rēgnā-

FIG. 87. ARCH OF CONSTANTINE, ROME

Like most Roman arches, this one was set up in honor of a triumph. This picture was taken while snow was on the ground.

ret.[3] Vērum tamen illīs imperātōribus laus est tri- buenda quod ēgērunt,[4] venia danda quod relīquērunt,[5] proptereā quod ab eō bellō Sullam in Italiam rēs pūblica,[6] Mūrēnam Sulla revocāvit.

---

[1] *the (outward) symbols.* In the triumphal processions at Rome there were always lavish displays of trophies and captives.

[2] *celebrated a triumph over* — not to be taken in the sense of **vīcit**.

[3] *kept on reigning.*   [4] *for what they did.*

[5] *for what they left undone.* Here as above **quod** is the conjunction. and the verb is used without an expressed object.

[6] Not "the republic" so much as *the political situation* at Rome. caused by his enemies of the Marian faction.

Word Study. — Explain the derivation of *indelible, immaculate, inveterate.* Note that *insignia* is a plural form in English as in Latin, and that we must therefore say *these insignia.*

Mithridates Renews His Activities

IV. **9.** Mithridātēs autem omne reliquum tempus nōn ad oblīviōnem veteris bellī sed ad comparātiōnem novī contulit. Quī[1] posteā, cum maximās aedificāsset ōrnāssetque classīs exercitūsque permagnōs quibuscumque ex gentibus potuisset[2] comparāsset et sē[5] Bosporānīs, fīnitimīs suīs, bellum īnferre simulāret, usque in Hispāniam lēgātōs ac litterās mīsit ad eōs ducēs[3] quibuscum tum bellum gerēbāmus, ut,[4] cum duōbus in locīs disiūnctissimīs maximēque dīversīs[5] ūnō cōnsiliō ā bīnīs[6] hostium cōpiīs bellum terrā[10] marīque gererētur, vōs ancipitī contentiōne districtī[7] dē imperiō[8] dīmicārētis. **10.** Sed tamen alterius partis[9] perīculum, Sertōriānae atque Hispāniēnsis,[10] quae multō plūs firmāmentī ac rōboris habēbat, Cn. Pompeī dīvīnō cōnsiliō ac singulārī virtūte dēpulsum[15]

---

[1] Start with **posteā** and make **quī** (*he*) the subject of the subordinate verbs instead of **mīsit.**

[2] Subjunctive by attraction.

[3] The Roman general Sertorius and his staff. As a follower of Marius, he organized the native Spanish tribes into a sort of rebel Roman state and continued to defy Rome until murdered a year later. In return for the promise of a fleet, Sertorius sent officers to train Mithridates' troops to fight in the Roman fashion.

[4] Introduces **dīmicārētis.**

[5] *in two very widely separated and totally different places.*

[6] Used instead of **duōbus** with a noun which is plural in form but singular in meaning; **cōpiae** = **exercitus.**

[7] *distracted by an attack on a double front.*　　　　[8] *for supremacy.*

[9] *on the one front.*

[10] *(threatening) from Sertorius and Spain.*

est; in alterā parte ita rēs ab L. Lūcullō, summō virō,
est administrāta ut initia illa rērum gestārum[1] magna
atque praeclāra nōn fēlīcitātī eius sed virtūtī, haec
autem extrēma[2] quae nūper accidērunt nōn culpae sed
5 fortūnae tribuenda esse videantur. Sed dē Lūcullō
dīcam aliō locō,[3] et ita dīcam, Quirītēs, ut neque vēra
laus eī[4] dētrācta ōrātiōne meā neque falsa afficta esse
videātur; 11. dē vestrī imperī dignitāte atque glōriā,
quoniam is est exōrsus[5] ōrātiōnis meae, vidēte quem
10 vōbīs animum suscipiendum putētis.[6]

Vocabulary Drill (7–11). — appetō, avidus, rēgnō, venia;
rōbur, culpa.

Rome Guarded Its National Honor in the Past

V.   Maiōrēs nostrī saepe prō mercātōribus aut nāviculā-
riīs nostrīs iniūriōsius[7] trāctātīs bella gessērunt; vōs, tot
mīlibus[8] cīvium Rōmānōrum ūnō nūntiō atque ūnō tempore
necātīs, quō tandem animō esse dēbētis? Lēgātī quod erant
15 appellātī superbius,[9] Corinthum patrēs vestrī tōtīus Graeciae
lūmen exstīnctum[10] esse voluērunt; vōs eum rēgem inultum
esse patiēminī quī lēgātum populī Rōmānī cōnsulārem vinculīs ac verberibus atque omnī suppliciō excruciātum[11] necāvit?

---

[1] *his early successes*, subject of **videantur**; but render the latter
impersonally: *it seems.*

[2] *these latest disasters.*   [3] In chapter VIII.

[4] For case see **315.**   [5] *the first topic.*   [6] *in your opinion.*

[7] *rather unjustly.*   [8] 80,000.

[9] *because their ambassadors had been somewhat arrogantly addressed.*
Other authorities indicate that the mistreatment of the ambassadors
was much more serious. What would be the result of similar incidents
to-day?

[10] Agrees in gender with **lūmen,** which is in apposition with **Corinthum.**
The destruction of Corinth took place in 146 B.C.

[11] As often, the perfect participle where we use a verb: *tortured and
slew.* The reference is to a certain Aquilius.

Illī lībertātem imminūtam[1] cīvium Rōmānōrum nōn tulērunt; vōs ēreptam vītam neglegētis? Iūs lēgātiōnis verbō
violātum illī persecūtī sunt;[2] vōs lēgātum omnī suppliciō
interfectum relinquētis?[3] **12.** Vidēte nē, ut illīs pulcherri-
mum fuit[4] tantam vōbīs imperī glōriam trādere, sīc vōbīs 5
turpissimum sit id quod accēpistis tuērī et cōnservāre nōn
posse.

The Safety of the Allies at Stake

Quid? quod salūs sociōrum summum in perīculum ac
discrīmen[5] vocātur, quō id tandem animō[6] ferre dēbētis?
Rēgnō est expulsus Ariobarzānēs rēx, socius populī Rōmānī 10
atque amīcus; imminent duo rēgēs tōtī Asiae nōn sōlum
vōbīs inimīcissimī sed etiam vestrīs sociīs atque amīcīs;
cīvitātēs autem omnēs cūnctā Asiā[7] atque Graeciā vestrum
auxilium exspectāre propter perīculī magnitūdinem cōguntur;
imperātōrem ā vōbīs certum[8] dēposcere, cum praesertim 15
vōs alium[9] mīserītis, neque audent neque id sē facere sine
summō perīculō posse arbitrantur. **13.** Vident enim et
sentiunt hoc[10] idem quod vōs, ūnum virum esse in quō
summa sint omnia,[11] et eum propter[12] esse, quō etiam carent
aegrius;[13] cuius adventū ipsō atque nōmine, tametsī ille ad 20
maritimum bellum vēnerit, tamen impetūs hostium repressōs
esse intellegunt ac retardātōs. Hī vōs, quoniam līberē loquī
nōn licet, tacitī rogant[14] ut sē quoque dignōs exīstimētis
quōrum salūtem tālī virō commendētis,[15] atque hōc etiam

---

[1] The participle carries the burden of the thought: *the infringement of the liberty.* Similarly the following participles.

[2] *avenged.*   [3] *disregard.*

[4] *Beware lest, just as for them it was a most glorious thing.*

[5] Hendiadys: *most dangerous crisis.*   [6] *with what feelings.*

[7] Supply **in.**   [8] *particular.*   [9] Glabrio.

[10] Explained by the following infinitives.

[11] *all qualifications exist in the highest degree.*

[12] Adverb: *near by.* Pompey was still in the East after conquering the pirates.

[13] *and for this reason they miss him the more sorely.*

[14] Note the oxymoron (**408**).

[15] *worthy to intrust their* (**quōrum**) *safety* (**381**).

magis, quod cēterās in prōvinciās eius modī hominēs cum
imperiō mittimus ut, etiam sī ab hoste dēfendant,[1] tamen
ipsōrum adventūs in urbīs[2] sociōrum nōn multum ab hostīlī
expugnātiōne differant; hunc audiēbant anteā, nunc prae-
5 sentem vident tantā temperantiā,[3] tantā mānsuētūdine,
tantā hūmānitāte ut eī beātissimī esse videantur apud quōs
ille diūtissimē commorētur.

Important Revenues at Stake

VI. **14.** Quārē sī propter sociōs[4] nūllā ipsī iniūriā
lacessītī[5] maiōrēs nostrī cum Antiochō, cum Philippō,
10 cum Aetōlīs, cum Poenīs bella gessērunt, quantō vōs
studiōsius convenit[6] iniūriīs prōvocātōs sociōrum salūtem ūnā cum imperī vestrī dignitāte dēfendere, praesertim cum dē maximīs vestrīs vectīgālibus agātur?[7]
Nam cēterārum prōvinciārum vectīgālia, Quirītēs,
15 tanta[8] sunt ut eīs ad ipsās prōvinciās tuendās vix con-
tentī esse possīmus, Asia vērō tam opīma est ac fertilis
ut et ūbertāte agrōrum et varietāte frūctuum et
magnitūdine pāstiōnis et multitūdine eārum rērum
quae exportentur facile omnibus terrīs[9] antecellat.
20 Itaque haec vōbīs[10] prōvincia, Quirītēs, sī et bellī ūtilitātem et pācis dignitātem retinēre vultis, nōn modo ā

---

[1] For mood see **308.**
[2] The prepositional phrase depends on **adventūs.**
[3] Ablative of description : (*a man of*), etc.
[4] A mere pretext, of course, for territorial expansion. King Antiochus
of Syria and his Aetolian allies were defeated in 190 B.C., Philip V of
Macedon in 197 B.C. The three Punic wars took place 264–241, 218–
201, 149–146 B.C.
[5] Concessive.　　　　　　　[6] *how much the more zealously is it fitting.*
[7] *it is a question of.*　　　　[8] *only so great,* as the context shows.
[9] For case see **314.**
[10] Do not forget to find a construction for this word.

calamitāte sed etiam ā metū calamitātis est dēfendenda. **15.** Nam in cēterīs rēbus cum vēnit[1] calamitās,
tum dētrīmentum accipitur; at in vectīgālibus nōn
sōlum adventus malī sed etiam metus ipse affert calamitātem.[2] Nam cum hostium cōpiae nōn longē absunt, 5
etiam sī irruptiō nūlla facta est, tamen pecua[3] relin-
quuntur, agrī cultūra dēseritur, mercātōrum nāvigātiō conquiēscit. Ita neque ex portū[4] neque ex decu-
mīs[5] neque ex scrīptūrā[6] vectīgal cōnservārī potest;
quārē saepe tōtīus annī frūctus ūnō rūmōre perīculī 10
atque ūnō bellī terrōre āmittitur. **16.** Quō tandem
igitur animō esse exīstimātis aut eōs quī vectīgālia
nōbīs pēnsitant, aut eōs quī exercent atque exigunt,[7]
cum duo rēgēs cum maximīs cōpiīs propter[8] adsint,
cum ūna excursiō equitātūs perbrevī tempore tōtīus 15
annī vectīgal auferre possit, cum pūblicānī familiās[9]
maximās quās in salīnīs[10] habent, quās in agrīs, quās in
portibus atque in custōdiīs[11] magnō perīculō sē habēre
arbitrentur? Putātisne vōs illīs rēbus[12] fruī posse, nisi
eōs quī vōbīs frūctuī sunt cōnservāveritis nōn sōlum, ut 20

---

[1] When **cum** means *whenever*, we use the present tense in English.

[2] A panic will bring on hard times, even if there is no good reason
for the panic. Confidence is a basic factor in prosperity. Even the
uncertainty before important elections to-day causes a let-down in in-
dustry.

[3] *cattle-raising* (lit., "herds").   [4] *from customs*, levied on exports.

[5] *from tithes*, levied on agricultural products.

[6] *from the pasture tax*, levied on herders and shepherds who used
state lands for grazing purposes.   To which of the occupations of the
preceding sentence does each of these taxes refer?

[7] *contract for and collect.*   [8] Adverb: *near by.*

[9] *companies of slaves.*   [10] *salt works.*

[11] *coast-guard stations*, to prevent goods from being smuggled — out
not in.

[12] *i.e.* the revenues.   For case see **337.**

ante dīxī, calamitāte sed etiam calamitātis formīdine
līberātōs?

Vocabulary Drill (11–16). — violō, tālis, temperantia, mānsuētūdō; auferō, fruor.

The Investments of Citizens Are in Danger

VII. **17.** Ac nē illud quidem[1] vōbīs neglegendum
est quod mihi ego extrēmum[2] prōposueram, cum essem
5 dē bellī genere dictūrus, quod[3] ad multōrum bona
cīvium Rōmānōrum pertinet; quōrum vōbīs prō vestrā
sapientiā, Quirītēs, habenda est ratiō[4] dīligenter. Nam
et[5] pūblicānī, hominēs honestissimī atque ōrnātissimī,
suās ratiōnēs et cōpiās in illam prōvinciam contulērunt,[6]
10 quōrum ipsōrum per sē[7] rēs et fortūnae vōbīs cūrae esse
dēbent. Etenim, sī vectīgālia nervōs[8] esse reī pūblicae
semper dūximus,[9] eum certē ōrdinem[10] quī exercet illa
firmāmentum cēterōrum ōrdinum rēctē esse dīcēmus.
18. Deinde[11] ex cēterīs ōrdinibus hominēs gnāvī atque
15 industriī partim ipsī[12] in Asiā negōtiantur, quibus vōs

---

[1] *and the following fact too must not,* etc.

[2] *as my last (point).*

[3] The clause is in apposition with **illud**: *that it (i.e. the war) affects.*

[4] *account must be taken.* Do modern governments concern themselves about the investments of their citizens in foreign countries?
What has been the attitude of our government about the investments
of its citizens in Mexico, Nicaragua, etc.?

[5] Omit or else translate *in the first place,* since it is balanced by
Deinde below instead of a second **et.**

[6] *transferred their interests and funds.*   [7] *for their own sake.*

[8] *sinews,* i.e. *strength.* Cf. our expression "sinews of war."

[9] What does this word mean when it has a dependent infinitive as
here?

[10] The knights, as contrasted with the senators and plebs.

[11] *In the next place.*

[12] *some in person,* in apposition with **hominēs.**

absentibus cōnsulere dēbētis,[1] partim eōrum[2] in eā
prōvinciā pecūniās magnās collocātās[3] habent. Est
igitur hūmānitātis[4] vestrae magnum numerum cīvium
calamitāte prohibēre, sapientiae vidēre multōrum cīvium
calamitātem ā rē pūblicā[5] sēiūnctam esse nōn posse. 5
Etenim illud prīmum parvī rēfert,[6] vōs pūblicānīs[7]
āmissa vectīgālia posteā victōriā recuperāre ; neque
enim īsdem[8] redimendī[9] facultās erit propter calamitātem neque aliīs voluntās propter timōrem.　**19.** Deinde[10] quod nōs eadem Asia atque īdem iste Mithridātēs 10
initiō bellī Asiāticī docuit, id quidem certē calamitāte
doctī memoriā retinēre dēbēmus.　Nam tum cum in
Asiā magnās permultī rēs āmīsērunt, scīmus Rōmae,
solūtiōne impedītā, fidem concidisse.[11]　Nōn enim
possunt ūnā in cīvitāte multī rem ac fortūnās āmittere 15
ut[12] nōn plūrīs sēcum in eandem trahant calamitātem ;
ā quō perīculō prohibēte rem pūblicam.　Etenim (mihi
crēdite id quod ipsī vidētis) haec fidēs atque haec ratiō
pecūniārum[13] quae Rōmae, quae in forō versātur,
implicāta est cum illīs pecūniīs Asiāticīs et cohaeret ; 20

---

[1] *whose interests you ought to safeguard in their absence.*

[2] *(while) others of them.*

[3] *sums invested.*　Many of these would be senators who could not
legally engage in active business.

[4] *it is kindness on your part;* so also **sapientiae.** See **298.**

[5] *from (that of) the republic.*　　　[6] *it* (**illud**) *matters little* (**308**).

[7] *for the tax collectors* (**311**).

[8] Like **aliīs** below, the dative of possession.

[9] *buying up (contracts),* for collecting taxes.　The present contrac-
tors will have been ruined and will be unable to bid on future contracts.

[10] *Then again.*

[11] *when payments were stopped, credit collapsed.*

[12] Result clause : *without dragging.*　What literally?

[13] *this system of credit and finance.*

ruere illa¹ nōn possunt ut haec nōn eōdem labefacta
mōtū² concidant. Quārē vidēte num³ dubitandum⁴
vōbīs sit omnī studiō ad id bellum incumbere in
quō glōria nōminis vestrī, salūs sociōrum, vectīgālia
5 maxima, fortūnae plūrimōrum cīvium coniūnctae
cum rē pūblicā⁵ dēfendantur.

Word Study. — Give English derivatives of **vetus, immineō,
haereō, (in)cumbō.** What is the original meaning of *temperance?*

Lucullus Has Accomplished Much

VIII. **20.** Quoniam dē genere bellī dīxī, nunc dē
magnitūdine pauca dīcam. Potest enim hoc dīcī, bellī
genus esse ita necessārium ut sit gerendum, nōn esse ita
10 magnum ut sit pertimēscendum. In quō maximē
labōrandum est⁶ nē forte ea vōbīs quae dīligentissimē
prōvidenda sunt contemnenda esse videantur.

Atque ut omnēs intellegant mē L. Lūcullō tantum impertīre laudis quantum fortī virō et sapientī hominī et magnō
15 imperātōrī dēbeātur, dīcō eius adventū maximās Mithridātī⁷
cōpiās omnibus rēbus ōrnātās atque īnstrūctās fuisse, urbem-
que Asiae clārissimam nōbīsque amīcissimam Cyzicēnōrum
oppressam esse ab ipsō rēge maximā multitūdine et oppug-

---

¹ *that (i.e.* the financial situation in Asia), as opposed to **haec :** *this
(i.e.* at Rome).

² *shock.* This is still true to-day. Cf. the effect of a stock market
crash. Panics were much more numerous before the organization of
Federal reserve banks. Any serious disturbance in the business of one
part of the world affects other parts.

³ *whether.*

⁴ **Dubitō** in the sense of *hesitate* (as here) takes the infinitive.

⁵ *public welfare.* Cicero here re-states the four points under which
he has just discussed the " character of the war."

⁶ *In this connection I must take the greatest care.*

⁷ Dative of possession.

Fig. 88.   Medea and Her Children

From the painting by Feuerbach.

nātam vehementissimē ; quam L. Lūcullus virtūte, assidui-
tāte, cōnsiliō summīs obsidiōnis perīculīs¹ līberāvit. **21.** Ab
eōdem imperātōre classem magnam et ōrnātam quae, ducibus
Sertōriānīs,² ad Italiam studiō atque odiō īnflammāta raperē-
tur³ superātam esse atque dēpressam ; magnās hostium prae- 5
tereā cōpiās multīs proeliīs esse dēlētās patefactumque nostrīs
legiōnibus⁴ esse Pontum, quī anteā populō Rōmānō ex omnī
aditū clausus fuisset ; Sinōpēn⁵ atque Amīsum, quibus in
oppidīs erant domicilia rēgis omnibus rēbus ōrnāta ac
referta, cēterāsque urbīs Pontī et Cappadociae permultās 10
ūnō aditū adventūque esse captās ; rēgem spoliātum rēgnō
patriō atque avītō ad aliōs sē rēgēs atque ad aliās gentīs
supplicem contulisse ; atque haec omnia, salvīs populī
Rōmānī sociīs atque integrīs vectīgālibus,⁶ esse gesta. Satis
opīnor hoc esse laudis atque ita,⁷ Quirītēs, ut hoc vōs intelle- 15
gātis, ā nūllō istōrum quī huic obtrectant lēgī⁸ atque causae
L. Lūcullum similiter ex hōc locō⁹ esse laudātum.

Vocabulary Drill (19–21). — ruō ; spoliō, supplex, salvus.

The Escape of Mithridates and His Later Successes

IX. **22.** Requīrētur fortasse nunc quem ad modum,
cum haec ita sint, reliquum¹⁰ possit magnum esse bellum.
Cognōscite, Quirītēs ; nōn enim hoc sine causā quaerī 20
vidētur. Prīmum ex suō rēgnō sīc Mithridātēs pro-
fūgit ut ex eōdem Pontō Mēdēa illa¹¹ quondam fūgisse

---

¹ For case see **327**.   ² *under officers furnished by Sertorius.*
³ *was being rushed to.*   ⁴ Dative.
⁵ Greek form of accusative.
⁶ *without harming the allies or touching the revenues.* He paid for his
campaigns out of the booty.
⁷ *of such a sort.*   ⁸ What law ?   ⁹ What place ?
¹⁰ *rest of;* **magnum** is predicate adjective.
¹¹ *that famous.* Jason came to Colchis in search of the Golden Fleece.
This he secured with the aid of Medea, the king's daughter, who had
fallen in love with him. They then fled, taking Medea's younger
brother with them. When her father pursued them, Medea killed her

dīcitur, quam praedicant in fugā frātris suī membra in
eīs locīs quā sē[1] parēns persequerētur dissipāvisse, ut
eōrum collēctiō dispersa[2] maerorque patrius celeritātem
cōnsequendī retardāret. Sīc Mithridātēs fugiēns maxi-
5 mam vim aurī atque argentī pulcherrimārumque
rērum omnium quās et ā maiōribus accēperat et ipse
bellō superiōre ex tōtā Asiā dīreptās[3] in suum rēgnum
congesserat in Pontō omnem[4] relīquit. Haec dum
nostrī colligunt omnia dīligentius, rēx ipse ē manibus
10 effūgit.[5] Ita illum[6] in persequendī studiō maeror, hōs[7]
laetitia tardāvit.

23. Hunc in illō timōre et fugā Tigrānēs,[8] rēx Armēnius,
excēpit diffīdentemque rēbus suīs[9] cōnfirmāvit et afflīctum
ērēxit perditumque recreāvit. Cuius[10] in rēgnum posteā
15 quam[11] L. Lūcullus cum exercitū vēnit, plūrēs etiam gentēs
contrā imperātōrem nostrum concitātae sunt. Erat enim
metus iniectus eīs nātiōnibus quās numquam populus Rōmānus neque lacessendās bellō neque temptandās putāvit;
erat etiam alia gravis atque vehemēns opīniō quae per
20 animōs gentium barbarārum pervāserat, fāni locuplētissimī
et religiōsissimī dīripiendī causā in eās ōrās nostrum esse

---

brother, cut him up into small pieces, and threw them into the sea to
delay the pursuit. In this way they escaped.

[1] *her.* Reflexive because it refers to the subject of the main verb.

[2] *the collecting of these scattered (remains).*

[3] Make a main verb in English.

[4] Agrees with **vim:** *a vast amount . . . all together.* For **vim**
cf. our colloquial expression "power of money."

[5] Plutarch tells us that the sight of the money bags on a pack mule
belonging to Mithridates proved to be too much for the pursuing
Roman soldiers, who, like Atalanta in the race, stopped to get the
gold and lost the chief prize, for Mithridates escaped in the excite-
ment.

[6] *the former* (Medea's father).   [7] *the latter* (the Roman soldiers).

[8] Mithridates' son-in-law.   [9] *despairing of his situation* (**346**).

[10] *i.e.* Tigranes.   [11] With **posteā = postquam.**

exercitum adductum.[1] Ita nātiōnēs multae atque[2] magnae
novō quōdam terrōre ac metū concitābantur. Noster autem
exercitus, tametsī urbem[3] ex Tigrānis rēgnō cēperat et proeliīs ūsus erat[4] secundīs, tamen nimiā longinquitāte locōrum
ac dēsīderiō suōrum[5] commovēbātur. **24.** Hīc iam plūra 5
nōn dīcam ; fuit enim illud extrēmum, ut ex eīs locīs ā mīlitibus nostrīs reditus magis mātūrus quam prōgressiō longior
quaererētur. Mithridātēs autem sē et suam manum iam
cōnfirmārat eōrum operā quī ad eum ex ipsīus rēgnō con-
cesserant et magnīs adventīciīs auxiliīs multōrum rēgum et 10
nātiōnum iuvābātur. Iam hoc ferē sīc fierī solēre accēpimus,[6] ut rēgum afflīctae fortūnae facile multōrum opēs
alliciant ad misericordiam, maximēque eōrum quī aut rēgēs
sunt aut vīvunt in rēgnō, ut[7] eīs nōmen rēgāle[8] magnum et
sānctum esse videātur.   15

The Roman Disaster

25. Itaque tantum victus efficere potuit quantum
incolumis numquam[9] est ausus optāre. Nam cum sē
in rēgnum suum recēpisset, nōn fuit eō[10] contentus quod
eī praeter spem acciderat, ut illam posteā quam pulsus
erat terram umquam attingeret, sed in exercitum nos- 20
trum clārum atque victōrem impetum fēcit. Sinite hōc

---

[1] Religious fanaticism thus turned this into a sort of holy war.

[2] May be omitted in translation. Its use gives emphasis to both
adjectives.

[3] His capital, Tigranocerta.   [4] *had enjoyed success in battle.*

[5] Objective genitive (**302**) : *longing for their families,* or *homesickness.*
This led to mutiny.

[6] *this we have learned almost invariably happens.* What literally?
Hoc is explained by the **ut** clause.

[7] *so that.*

[8] = **nōmen rēgis.** The World War did much to destroy the power
and influence of kings.

[9] With **tantum quantum**: *more than he ever.* What literally?

[10] Antecedent of **quod ;** the **ut** clause is in apposition.

locō, Quirītēs, sīcut poētae[1] solent quī rēs Rōmānās
scrībunt, praeterīre[2] mē nostram calamitātem, quae
tanta fuit ut eam ad aurīs imperātōris nōn ex proeliō
nūntius sed ex sermōne rūmor[3] afferret.

5   **26.** Hīc in illō ipsō malō gravissimāque bellī offēnsiōne
L. Lūcullus, quī tamen aliquā ex parte[4] eīs incommodīs
medērī fortasse potuisset,[5] vestrō iussū coāctus, quī imperī
diūturnitātī modum[6] statuendum vetere exemplō putāvistis,
partim[7] mīlitum quī iam stīpendiīs cōnfectīs[8] erant dīmīsit,
10 partim M'. Glabriōnī trādidit. Multa prantereō cōnsultō ;
sed ea[9] vōs coniectūrā perspicite quantum illud bellum
factum putētis quod coniungant[10] rēgēs potentissimī, renovent
agitātae nātiōnēs, suscipiant integrae gentēs, nevus imperātor
noster accipiat,[11] vetere exercitū pulsō.[12]

Vocabulary Drill. — parēns, maeror, pulcher, afflīgō, fānum,
ōra, agitō.

Pompey Alone Has the Four Necessary Qualifications

15 **X. 27.** Satis multa mihi verba fēcisse videor quārē[13]
esset[14] hoc bellum genere ipsō necessārium, magnitūdine

---

[1] *e.g.* Naevius, who wrote an epic on the First Punic War, and
Ennius, who wrote a history of Rome in verse.

[2] What figure is here introduced, named from this verb? See **154.**

[3] *talk (among the natives).* Cicero here alludes to the overwhelming
defeat of Triarius, a general of Lucullus, whose force was almost annihi-
lated by Mithridates (67 B.C.).

[4] *in some measure.*   [5] *might have been able.*   [6] *limit.*   [7] *part of.*

[8] Ablative of description : *had now finished their terms of service.*

[9] Explained by the **quantum** clause and the four points it contains.

[10] *wage jointly* (Mithridates and Tigranes).

[11] *a new general is to take over.*

[12] Observe that the last sentence neatly sums up the points discussed
under " Greatness of the war."

[13] *(to show) why.* This sentence very appropriately summarizes the
two main points of the **cōnfirmātiō** already discussed. The next question
is " Choice of a commander."

[14] Translate by the present.

perīculōsum. Restat¹ ut dē imperātōre ad id bellum
dēligendō ac tantīs rēbus praeficiendō dīcendum esse
vīdeātur. Utinam, Quirītēs, virōrum fortium atque
innocentium² cōpiam tantam habērētis³ ut haec vōbīs
dēlīberātiō difficilis esset quemnam⁴ potissimum tantīs 5
rēbus ac tantō bellō praeficiendum putārētis! Nunc
vērō cum sit ūnus Cn. Pompeius quī nōn modo eōrum
hominum quī nunc sunt glōriam sed etiam antīquitātis
memoriam⁵ virtūte⁶ superārit,⁷ quae rēs est quae
cuiusquam animum in hāc causā dubium facere possit? 10
28.　Ego enim sīc exīstimō, in summō imperātōre
quattuor hās rēs inesse oportēre, scientiam reī mīlitāris,
virtūtem, auctōritātem, fēlīcitātem. Quis igitur hōc
homine scientior⁸ umquam aut fuit aut esse dēbuit?⁹
Quī ē lūdō atque ē puerītiae disciplīnīs bellō maximō 15
atque ācerrimīs hostibus¹⁰ ad patris¹¹ exercitum atque
in mīlitiae disciplīnam profectus est, quī extrēmā
puerītiā¹² mīles in exercitū summī fuit imperātōris,¹³
ineunte adulēscentiā maximī ipse exercitūs imperā-

---

¹ The **ut** clause is the subject : *it remains (for me) to speak, as it seems.*

² Do not use the English derivative.

³ The imperfect shows the hopelessness of the wish (**376**).

⁴ *who* (not " whom ") *in the world you think.*

⁵ This is exaggeration, for *the records of the past* included some famous names. Can you name any?

⁶ *ability* (as elsewhere in this speech).

⁷ Explain form and construction.

⁸ *i.e.* in military science, alluding to **scientiam** above.

⁹ *could have been;* explained in the next sentence.

¹⁰ Ablative of attendant circumstances : *when the enemy were*, etc.

¹¹ Pompey's father, Cn. Pompeius Strabo, was a prominent general in the Social War (90–88 B.C.).

¹² Pompey (who was the same age as Cicero) was then 19.

¹³ His father, fighting against Cinna in the Civil War (87 B.C.).

tor,[1] quī saepius cum hoste cōnflīxit quam quisquam
cum inimīcō concertāvit,[2] plūra bella gessit quam
cēterī lēgērunt, plūrīs prōvinciās cōnfēcit[3] quam aliī
concupīvērunt, cuius adulēscentia ad scientiam[4] reī
5 mīlitāris nōn aliēnīs praeceptīs sed suīs imperiīs, nōn
offēnsiōnibus[5] bellī sed victōriīs, nōn stīpendiīs sed
triumphīs est ērudīta. Quod dēnique genus esse bellī
potest in quō illum nōn exercuerit fortūna reī pūblicae?
Cīvīle,[6] Āfricānum, Trānsalpīnum, Hispāniēnse mix-
10 tum ex[7] cīvibus atque ex bellicōsissimīs nātiōnibus,
servīle, nāvāle bellum, varia et dīversa genera et
bellōrum et hostium nōn sōlum gesta[8] ab hōc ūnō
sed etiam cōnfecta nūllam rem esse dēclārant in ūsū
positam mīlitārī quae huius virī scientiam fugere
15 possit.

Word Study. — Show the development of meaning of *science,
virtue, authority, felicity* from the Latin originals as used in
section 28.

---

[1] Pompey, now 23 years old, recruited three legions and joined Sulla,
who honored the dashing enterprise of the gallant youth by saluting
him as **imperātor**.

[2] *has contested* (in court). Bring out the contrast between **hoste** and
inimīcō.

[3] *conquered*, with emphasis on the intensive prefix.

[4] With **est ērudīta:** *was trained to a mastery of.*

[5] *disasters.*

[6] With **bellum** below. This sentence runs the gamut of Pompey's
military experience, extending over a quarter of a century. The wars
are those against Cinna and other followers of Marius, against the king
of Numidia and his Roman supporters, against the Gauls who attacked
him on his way to Spain, against Sertorius in Spain, against Spartacus'
slaves, and against the pirates.

[7] *involving.*

[8] *faced*, a word neutral enough to go in thought with **bellōrum** and
hostium.

Pompey's Conquests on Land and Sea

XI. 29. Iam vērō virtūtī Cn. Pompeī quae potest
ōrātiō[1] pār invenīrī? Quid est quod quisquam aut illō

FIG 89. SICILIA
The temple of Concord at Agrigentum.

dignum aut vōbīs no-
vum aut cuiquam inau-
dītum possit afferre?5
Neque enim sōlae sunt
virtūtēs imperātōriae[2]
quae vulgō exīstiman-
tur, labor in negōtiīs,
fortitūdō in perīculīs, 10
industria in agendō,
celeritās in cōnficiendō,
cōnsilium in prōvi-
dendō, quae tanta sunt
in hōc ūnō quanta in 15
omnibus reliquīs impe-
rātōribus quōs aut vī-
dimus aut audīvimus
nōn fuērunt. **30.** Tes-
tis[3] est Italia, quam ille ipse victor L. Sulla huius virtūte 20
et subsidiō cōnfessus est līberātam ; testis Sicilia,[4] quam
multīs undique cīnctam perīculīs nōn terrōre bellī sed
cōnsilī celeritāte explicāvit ; testis Āfrica, quae magnīs
oppressa hostium cōpiīs eōrum ipsōrum sanguine
redundāvit ; testis Gallia, per quam legiōnibus nostrīs 25

---

[1] *words.*   [2] *of a (successful) commander.*

[3] Used seven times for effect — what figure? Find an instance of
chiasmus in this sentence. This passage gives a detailed account of
Pompey's war record which was briefly mentioned in the last sentence
of the preceding chapter.

[4] In 82 B.C., before going to Africa.

iter in Hispāniam Gallōrum interneciōne patefactum
est; testis Hispānia, quae saepissimē[1] plūrimōs hostīs ab
hōc superātōs prōstrātōsque cōnspexit; testis iterum et
saepius[2] Italia, quae, cum servīlī bellō taetrō perīculō-
5 sōque premerētur, ab hōc auxilium absente expetīvit,
quod bellum exspectātiōne eius attenuātum atque
imminūtum est, adventū sublātum ac sepultum.[3]
31.   Testēs nunc vērō iam[4] omnēs ōrae atque omnēs
terrae, gentēs, nātiōnēs, maria dēnique omnia cum ūni-
10 versa tum in singulīs ōrīs omnēs sinūs atque portūs.
Quis enim tōtō marī locus per hōs annōs aut tam firmum habuit praesidium ut tūtus esset, aut tam fuit
abditus ut latēret? Quis nāvigāvit quī nōn sē aut
mortis aut servitūtis perīculō committeret, cum aut
15 hieme aut refertō praedōnum[5] marī nāvigāret? Hoc
tantum bellum, tam turpe, tam vetus, tam lātē dīvīsum
atque dispersum quis umquam arbitrārētur[6] aut ab
omnibus imperātōribus ūnō annō aut omnibus annīs[7]
ab ūnō imperātōre cōnficī posse?   **32.**   Quam prōvin-
20 ciam tenuistis ā praedōnibus līberam per hōsce annōs?
quod vectīgal vōbīs tūtum fuit? quem socium dēfen-
distis? cui[8] praesidiō classibus[9] vestrīs fuistis? quam
multās exīstimātis īnsulās esse dēsertās, quam multās

---

[1] Only after the assassination of Sertorius, who had out-generaled
Pompey before this.

[2] *again and again.*

[3] *buried in oblivion.*   Cicero here gives Pompey too much credit, for
the latter had merely wiped out the fleeing remnant of Spartacus' army,
which had already been defeated by Crassus.

[4] Transitional and emphatic : *in fact.*

[5] *swarming with pirates* (**304**). The pirates were active in the summer
only.

[6] *would have thought.*   [7] *i.e.* of his life.

[8] Does not modify **praesidiō**.   [9] Ablative of means.

aut metū relīctās aut ā praedōnibus captās urbīs esse
suciōrum?

Vocabulary Drill (27–31). — innocēns, quisnam, mīlitia,
misceō; sepeliō, lateō, praedō.

Pompey Has Swept Piracy from the Seas

XII. Sed quid ego longinqua commemorō? Fuit[1]
hoc quondam, fuit proprium populī Rōmānī longē ā
domō bellāre et prōpugnāculīs[2] imperī sociōrum for- 5
tūnās, nōn sua tēcta dēfendere. Sociīs ego vestrīs
mare per hōsce[3] annōs clausum fuisse dīcam,[4] cum
exercitūs vestrī numquam Brundisiō nisi hieme summā[5]
trānsmīserint? Quī ad vōs ab exterīs nātiōnibus
venīrent, captōs[6] querar, cum lēgātī populī Rōmānī 10
redēmptī sint? Mercātōribus mare tūtum nōn fuisse
dīcam, cum duodecim secūrēs[7] in praedōnum potestātem pervēnerint? 33. Cnidum aut Colophōnem aut
Samum, nōbilissimās urbīs, innumerābilīsque aliās
captās esse commemorem, cum vestrōs portūs atque 15
eōs portūs quibus vītam ac spīritum[8] dūcitis, in prae-

---

[1] Tense, position, and repetition are alike expressive — why?

[2] The *bulwarks of power* were of course the Roman fleets and armies.

[3] *recent.* The point is that the seas were unsafe even for Roman
armies, not merely for distant allies.

[4] For mood see **375.**

[5] *in midwinter,* when the pirates did not venture out on account of
the weather. The Adriatic Sea is still notoriously uncertain.

[6] Supply eōs as subject and as antecedent of Quī.

[7] *i.e.* two praetors. Each praetor was attended by six lictors bearing
the fasces (a bundle of rods inclosing an ax; see Fig. 41) as a symbol of
his authority.

[8] He refers to the imports of grain, without which Rome would
starve. For dependence on a merchant marine we may compare Rome
with England.

dōnum fuisse potestāte sciātis? An vērō ignōrātis
portum Caiētae celeberrimum et plēnissimum nāvium,
īnspectante praetōre, ā praedōnibus esse dīreptum, ex
Mīsēnō autem eius ipsīus līberōs[1] quī cum praedōnibus

Fig. 90. A Street in Ostia

5 anteā bellum gesserat ā praedōnibus esse sublātōs?
Nam quid ego Ōstiēnse incommodum[2] atque illam
lābem atque ignōminiam reī pūblicae querar, cum,
prope īnspectantibus vōbīs, classis ea cui cōnsul populī
Rōmānī praepositus esset ā praedōnibus capta atque

[1] An exaggeration, for Cicero probably is alluding to the capture and
ransom of the daughter of M. Antonius, who defeated the pirates in
103 B.C.

[2] *Inconvenience* is an understatement for *disaster*. Ostia, the seaport
of Rome at the mouth of the Tiber, has recently been excavated from the
deep deposits of river sand and mud under which it lay buried for cen

dēpressa est? Prō[1] dī immortālēs! tantamne ūnīus
hominis incrēdibilis ac dīvīna virtūs tam brevī tempore
lūcem afferre[2] reī pūblicae potuit ut vōs, quī modo[3]
ante ōstium Tiberīnum classem hostium vidēbātis, eī[4]
nunc nūllam intrā Ōceanī ōstium[5] praedōnum nāvem 5
esse audiātis? **34.** Atque haec quā celeritāte gesta
sint, quamquam vidētis, tamen ā mē[6] in dīcendō
praetereunda nōn sunt. Quis enim umquam aut
obeundī negōtī aut cōnsequendī quaestūs studiō tam
brevī tempore tot loca adīre, tantōs cursūs cōnficere 10
potuit, quam celeriter, Cn. Pompeiō duce, tantī bellī
impetus nāvigāvit?[7] Quī[8] nōndum tempestīvō ad
nāvigandum marī[9] Siciliam adiit, Āfricam explōrāvit,
inde Sardiniam cum classe vēnit atque haec tria
frūmentāria subsidia reī pūblicae firmissimīs prae- 15
sidiīs classibusque mūnīvit. **35.** Inde cum sē in
Italiam recēpisset, duābus Hispāniīs[10] et Galliā Trāns-

---

turies. How did it get its name? See below and compare " Ports-
mouth," " Yarmouth," etc.

[1] Interjection, not preposition.　　　　[2] *shed such glory.*

[3] *recently*, contrasted with **nunc.** Beginning here, copy the rest of
the sentence on one line of a wide sheet of paper and assign identical
numbers to the words which are paired off with each other and see
whether you can find six sets of these contrasted words; then connect
with curves the words bearing the same numbers, to show the interlocking word order.

[4] Points back to **vōs** as the subject of the verb at the end. It may be
translated *you, I repeat.*

[5] The Straits of Gibraltar.

[6] Why would you expect to find **mihi?** The unexpected form
attracts attention and gives emphasis.

[7] *so swiftly as the fury of this mighty war swept the sea under Gnaeus
Pompey.* **Celeriter** is unnecessary but is used to parallel the synonymous **brevī tempore.**

[8] *For he.*　　　　[9] Ablative absolute, expressing concession.

[10] Spain was divided into two provinces by the river Ebro.

alpīnā praesidiīs ac nāvibus cōnfirmātā,[1] missīs item
in ōram Īllyricī maris et in Achaiam omnemque Graeciam nāvibus, Italiae duo maria[2] maximīs classibus
firmissimīsque praesidiīs adōrnāvit, ipse autem ut[3]
5 Brundisiō profectus est, ūndēquīnquāgēsimō diē tōtam ad imperium populī Rōmānī Ciliciam[4] adiūnxit;
omnēs quī ubīque praedōnēs fuērunt partim[5] captī
interfectīque sunt, partim ūnīus huius sē imperiō ac
potestātī dēdidērunt. Īdem Crētēnsibus,[6] cum ad eum
10 usque[7] in Pamphȳliam lēgātōs dēprecātōrēsque mīsis-
sent, spem dēditiōnis nōn adēmit obsidēsque imperāvit.
Ita tantum bellum, tam diūturnum, tam longē lātēque
dispersum, quō bellō omnēs gentēs ac nātiōnēs premē-
bantur, Cn. Pompeius extrēmā hieme apparāvit,[8]
15 ineunte vēre suscēpit, mediā aestāte cōnfēcit.

Pompey's Honesty

XIII.   **36.** Est haec[9] dīvīna atque incrēdibilis virtūs
imperātōris.   Quid? cēterae quās paulō ante com-

---

[1] Agrees with **Galliā**, but is to be taken with **Hispāniīs** also. Can you
see the reason why Cicero did not write **cōnfirmātīs**?

[2] What seas?

[3] *from the time when*, to be taken after **diē**.

[4] The stronghold of the organized pirates in the eastern Mediterranean — reminding one of the Barbary pirates of modern times, who
menaced shipping in the western Mediterranean until crushed by the
United States Navy at the beginning of the nineteenth century.

[5] = **aut . . . aut**.

[6] Dative of separation (**315**) with **adēmit**: *from the Cretans*. They
had aided the pirates.

[7] Pamphylia was not " way off " from Crete, but for impressiveness
Cicero chooses to think of its distance from Rome. See map of **Imperium
Rōmānum** (p. 132).

[8] *prepared for at the close of winter.*

[9] *Such is (his).*

memorāre coeperam, quantae atque quam multae sunt !
Nōn enim bellandī virtūs sōlum in summō ac perfectō imperātōre quaerenda est, sed multae sunt artēs[1]
eximiae huius[2] administrae comitēsque virtūtis. Ac
prīmum quantā innocentiā[3] dēbent esse imperātōrēs, 5
quantā deinde in omnibus rēbus temperantiā, quantā
fidē, quantā facilitāte,[4] quantō ingeniō, quantā hūmānitāte ! Quae breviter quālia sint in Cn. Pompeiō cōn-
sīderēmus. Summa enim sunt omnia, Quirītēs, sed ea
magis ex aliōrum contentiōne[5] quam ipsa per sēsē 10
cognōscī atque intellegī possunt. **37.** Quem enim
possumus imperātōrem ūllō in numerō putāre[6] cuius in
exercitū centuriātūs[7] vēneant[8] atque vēnierint? Quid
hunc hominem magnum aut amplum dē rē pūblicā
cōgitāre[9] quī pecūniam ex aerāriō dēprōmptam ad 15
bellum administrandum aut propter cupiditātem prōvinciae magistrātibus dīvīserit[10] aut propter avāritiam
Rōmae in quaestū[11] relīquerit? Vestra admurmurātiō

---

[1] *qualities.*

[2] With **virtūtis,** which depends on **administrae comitēsque.**   By
putting **huius** with one noun and **virtūtis** with the other Cicero achieves
a neat symmetry and a sort of chiasmus.

[3] This and the following descriptive ablatives are best rendered as
adjectives : *how incorruptible,* etc.

[4] *how easy (to approach).*

[5] *from comparison with others.*

[6] *Whom can we consider a general of any standing.*

[7] *Centurionships* ordinarily were bestowed only upon men who had
fought their way up from the ranks.

[8] From **vēneō,** not from **veniō.**

[9] Supply **possumus putāre** from the preceding sentence : *What great
and lofty patriotism can we imagine that man feels.*

[10] *i.e.* bribery of the magistrates at Rome to secure their support for
continuance in military power.

[11] *at interest.* Such misuse of public funds is not unknown to-day.

facit, Quirītēs, ut agnōscere videāminī[1] quī haec fēcerint; ego autem nōminō nēminem; quārē īrāscī mihi nēmō poterit nisi quī ante dē sē voluerit[2] cōnfitērī. Itaque propter hanc avāritiam imperātōrum quantās

FIG. 91. THE TEMPLE OF JUPITER AT OSTIA

5 calamitātēs, quōcumque ventum sit,[3] nostrī exercitūs afferant quis ignōrat? **38.** Itinera quae per hōsce annōs in Italiā per agrōs atque oppida cīvium Rōmānōrum nostrī imperātōrēs fēcerint recordāminī;[4] tum facilius statuētis quid apud exterās nātiōnēs fierī exīs-

---

[1] *shows that you recognize.* Denunciation of graft always wins an audience.

[2] We use the present in English.

[3] Make personal: *they have come.* The verb is subjunctive because it is in a subordinate clause in indirect discourse.

[4] Imperative.

timētis.   Utrum plūrīs[1] arbitrāminī per hōsce annōs
mīlitum vestrōrum armīs hostium urbīs an hībernīs[2]
sociōrum[3] cīvitātēs esse dēlētās?   Neque enim potest
exercitum is continēre imperātor quī sē ipse nōn con-
tinet, neque sevērus esse in iūdicandō quī aliōs in sē 5
sevērōs esse iūdicēs nōn vult.[4]

39.   Hīc mīrāmur hunc hominem tantum excellere cēterīs,[5]
cuius legiōnēs sīc in Asiam pervēnerint ut nōn modo[6] manus
tantī exercitūs sed nē vēstīgium quidem cuiquam pācātō
nocuisse dīcātur?   Iam vērō quem ad modum mīlitēs hīber- 10
nent cotīdiē sermōnēs ac litterae perferuntur; nōn modo ut
sūmptum faciat[7] in mīlitem nēminī vīs affertur[8] sed nē
cupientī quidem quicquam permittitur.   Hiemis enim, nōn
avāritiae perfugium[9] maiōrēs nostrī in sociōrum atque
amīcōrum tēctīs esse voluērunt.   15

Vocabulary Drill (32–37). — **exterus, ignōminia, praetereō,
diūturnus; quālis, avāritia, quaestus, īrāscor.**

Word Study. — Explain the derivation of *attenuate, redemption,
innocence, irascible.*

---

[1] With **cīvitātēs** as well as with **urbīs.** The word order brings the
contrasted words into close relation to each other.

[2] It was the duty of the allies to feed the Roman troops over winter.
Naturally much damage was done to the towns and villages where
soldiers were billeted, and often large sums were paid by the provincials
in order to be spared this form of oppression.

[3] Modifies **cīvitātēs.**

[4] A famous sentence, true to-day and worth memorizing.

[5] For case see **313.**

[6] Supply **nōn** from the following **nē.** Not a hand, not a foot of that
great army, Cicero says, did any harm to a peaceful civilian, in contrast
with the looting of wealth and the trampling of crops that so often blazed
the trail of a "friendly" Roman army sent to "protect" the provincials.

[7] *to spend money on.*   [8] *pressure is applied.*

[9] *a refuge from the winter, not for greed* — evidently two different uses
of the genitive, the former objective (**302**), the latter subjective (**301**).

Pompey's Self-Control and Other Good Qualities

XIV. **40.** Age vērō,[1] cēterīs in rēbus quae sit temperantia
cōnsīderāte. Unde illam tantam celeritātem et tam incrēdibilem cursum inventum[2] putātis? Nōn enim illum eximia
vīs rēmigum aut ars inaudīta quaedam gubernandī aut ventī
5 aliquī novī tam celeriter in ultimās terrās pertulērunt, sed
eae rēs quae cēterōs remorārī solent nōn retardārunt. Nōn
avāritia ab īnstitūtō cursū ad praedam aliquam dēvocāvit,
nōn libīdō ad voluptātem, nōn amoenitās[3] ad dēlectātiōnem,
nōn nōbilitās urbis ad cognitiōnem, nōn dēnique labor ipse ad
10 quiētem; postrēmō signa et tabulās cēteraque ōrnāmenta
Graecōrum oppidōrum quae cēterī tollenda[4] esse arbitrantur,
ea sibi ille nē vīsenda[5] quidem exīstimāvit. **41.** Itaque
omnēs nunc in eīs locīs Cn. Pompeium sīcut aliquem nōn ex
hāc urbe missum sed dē caelō dēlāpsum intuentur; nunc
15 dēnique incipiunt crēdere fuisse[6] hominēs Rōmānōs hāc
quondam continentiā, quod iam nātiōnibus exterīs incrēdibile ac falsō memoriae prōditum vidēbātur;[7] nunc imperī
vestrī splendor illīs gentibus lūcem afferre coepit; nunc
intellegunt nōn sine causā maiōrēs suōs tum cum eā tempe-
20 rantiā magistrātūs habēbāmus servīre populō Rōmānō[8] quam
imperāre aliīs māluisse. Iam vērō ita facilēs aditūs[9] ad eum
prīvātōrum, ita līberae querimōniae dē aliōrum[10] iniūriīs esse
dīcuntur, ut is quī dignitāte prīncipibus excellit facilitāte
īnfimīs pār esse videātur. **42.** Iam quantum cōnsiliō, quan-
25 tum dīcendī gravitāte et cōpiā valeat, in quō ipsō inest quaedam dignitās imperātōria, vōs, Quirītēs, hōc ipsō ex locō[11]
saepe cognōstis.[12] Fidem vērō eius quantam inter sociōs

---

[1] See **133**.   [2] *have been made possible.*

[3] Supply **locōrum**: *beautiful scenery.*

[4] *to be carried off,* i.e. as spoils of war—a reference to the priceless
art treasures of Greece.

[5] *go to see* (from **vīsō**).   [6] *that there really were.*

[7] *(a fact) which was beginning to appear . . . a false tradition.*

[8] For case see **313**.   [9] *access.*

[10] Subjective genitive (**301**): *done by others.*

[11] *i.e.* the Rostra.   [12] = **cognō(vi)stis.**

exīstimārī putātis quam hostēs omnēs omnium generum
sānctissimam iūdicārint? Hūmānitāte iam tantā est ut
difficile dictū[1] sit utrum hostēs magis virtūtem eius pug-
nantēs timuerint an mānsuētūdinem victī dīlēxerint. Et
quisquam dubitābit quīn[2] huic hoc tantum bellum permitten- 5
dum sit quī ad omnia nostrae memoriae bella cōnficienda
dīvīnō quōdam cōnsiliō nātus esse videātur?

Pompey's Prestige

XV. 43. Et quoniām auctōritās[3] quoque in bellīs
administrandīs multum atque[4] in imperiō mīlitārī valet,
certē nēminī dubium est quīn eā rē īdem ille imperātor 10
plūrimum possit.[5] Vehementer autem pertinēre[6] ad
bella administranda quid hostēs, quid sociī dē imperātōribus nostrīs exīstiment quis ignōrat, cum sciāmus
hominēs in tantīs rēbus ut aut metuant aut contemnant
aut ōderint aut ament[7] opīniōne nōn minus[8] et fāmā 15
quam aliquā ratiōne certā commovērī? Quod igitur
nōmen umquam in orbe terrārum clārius fuit, cuius rēs
gestae parēs? Dē quō homine vōs, id quod[9] maximē
facit auctōritātem, tanta et tam praeclāra iūdicia[10]
fēcistis? **44.** An vērō ūllam usquam esse ōram tam 20
dēsertam putātis quō[11] nōn illīus diēī[12] fāma pervāserit
cum ūniversus populus Rōmānus, refertō forō com-

---

[1] See **405** (b).   [2] For construction see **372**.

[3] *prestige.*   [4] *and particularly.*   [5] *excels* (**372**).

[6] *has strong bearing upon* (**ad**). The subject is **quid . . . exīsti-**
ment, which depends on **ignōrat**.

[7] The **ut** clause of result depends upon **commovērī**.

[8] Translate before **opīniōne**.   [9] *a thing which.*

[10] *acknowledgments* (of service), in the form of honors.

[11] = **ut ad eam** (result).

[12] The day that the revolutionary **Lēx Gabīnia** was passed, placing
Pompey in sole command against the pirates.

plētīsque omnibus templīs[1] ex quibus hic locus cōnspicī potest, ūnum sibi ad commūne omnium gentium
bellum Cn. Pompeium imperātōrem dēpoposcit? Itaque ut plūra nōn dīcam[2] neque aliōrum exemplīs cōn-
5 firmem quantum auctōritās valeat in bellō, ab eōdem
Cn. Pompeiō omnium rērum ēgregiārum exempla
sūmantur. Quī quō diē[3] ā vōbīs maritimō bellō praepositus est imperātor, tanta repente vīlitās ex[4] summā
inopiā et cāritāte reī frūmentāriae cōnsecūta est ūnīus
10 hominis[5] spē ac nōmine quantam vix in summā ūbertāte agrōrum diūturna pāx efficere potuisset.[6]

45. Iam acceptā in Pontō calamitāte ex eō proeliō dē quō
vōs paulō ante invītus admonuī, cum sociī pertimuissent,
hostium opēs animīque crēvissent, satis firmum praesidium
15 prōvincia nōn habēret, āmīsissētis Asiam, Quirītēs, nisi ad
ipsum discrīmen eius temporis dīvīnitus Cn. Pompeium ad
eās regiōnēs Fortūna populī Rōmānī attulisset.[7] Huius
adventus et Mithridātem īnsolitā īnflātum victōriā continuit
et Tigrānem magnīs cōpiīs minitantem Asiae[8] retardāvit.
20 Et quisquam dubitābit quid virtūte perfectūrus sit quī
tantum auctōritāte perfēcerit, aut quam facile imperiō atque
exercitū sociōs et vectīgālia cōnservātūrus sit quī ipsō nōmine
ac rūmōre dēfenderit?

Vocabulary Drill (40–45). — libīdō, splendor; usquam, discrīmen.

---

[1] What temples? See Figs. 50, 59, 72, 73.

[2] **nōn** goes closely with **dīcam**: *to refrain from saying more and not to*
(**neque**), introducing subjunctives of purpose.

[3] *For on the day that he.*

[4] *after.*

[5] Objective genitive with **spē** *(hope in)* and possessive with
minis.

[6] *would have been able* (**390, II**).

[7] What kind of condition? See **390, II.**

[8] Dative with **minitantem.**

FIG. 92.   TEMPLUM

One of four temples discovered in widening a busy street in Rome.   The
excavation was completed in 1929.   It is not far from the site of the portico
and theater built by Pompey.

XVI.   **46.** Age vērō illa rēs¹ quantam dēclārat eiusdem
hominis apud hostīs populī Rōmānī auctōritātem, quod ex
locīs tam longinquīs tamque dīversīs tam brevī tempore
omnēs huic sē ūnī dēdidērunt ! quod ā commūnī² Crētēnsium
lēgātī, cum³ in eōrum īnsulā noster imperātor⁴ exercitusque 5
esset, ad Cn. Pompeium in ultimās prope terrās vēnērunt
eīque sē omnīs Crētēnsium cīvitātēs dēdere velle dīxērunt !
Quid? īdem iste Mithridātēs nōnne ad eundem Cn. Pompeium lēgātum usque in Hispāniam mīsit ? Eum⁵ quem Pom-

---

¹ *this fact . . . that* (**quod**).   ² *from the commonwealth.*

³ Concessive.

⁴ Metellus, who had practically subdued the Cretans after two years
of fighting, and was thus deprived of the fruits of his victory.

⁵ *one*, in apposition with the preceding **lēgātum.** Supply *while* before
the following **eī** (Pompey's critics).

peius lēgātum semper iūdicāvit, eī quibus erat molestum
ad eum[1] potissimum esse missum, speculātōrem quam lēgātum iūdicārī māluērunt. Potestis igitur iam cōnstituere,
Quirītēs, hanc auctōritātem[2] multīs posteā rēbus gestīs mag-
5 nīsque vestrīs iūdiciīs amplificātam quantum apud illōs
rēgēs, quantum apud exterās nātiōnēs valitūram esse exīstimētis.

Pompey's Good Luck

47. Reliquum est ut dē fēlīcitāte[3] (quam praestāre
dē sē ipsō nēmō potest, meminisse[4] et commemorāre
10 dē alterō[5] possumus), sīcut aequum est hominēs dē
potestāte deōrum,[6] timidē et pauca dīcāmus. Ego
enim sīc exīstimō, Maximō, Mārcellō, Scīpiōnī, Mariō
cēterīsque magnīs imperātōribus nōn sōlum propter
virtūtem sed etiam propter fortūnam saepius[7] imperia
15 mandāta atque exercitūs esse commissōs. Fuit enim
profectō quibusdam summīs virīs quaedam[8] ad ampli-
tūdinem et ad glōriam et ad rēs magnās bene gerendās
dīvīnitus adiūncta fortūna. Dē huius autem hominis
fēlīcitāte quō dē[9] nunc agimus hāc[10] ūtar moderātiōne
20 dīcendī, nōn ut in illīus potestāte fortūnam positam esse
dīcam sed ut praeterita meminisse, reliqua spērāre

---

[1] Pompey. The subject of **esse missum** is **lēgātum**.

[2] Emphatic: *as to this prestige;* modified by **amplificātam** and subject of **valitūram esse**.

[3] The last of the four requirements for good leadership.

[4] Supply **sed quam** before this.

[5] *some one else.*

[6] Supply **dīcere**.

[7] *on more than one occasion.*

[8] Agrees with the emphatic subject **fortūna**: *a sort of good luck.*
Notice also the emphatic separation of **Fuit . . . adiūncta:** *in the past there was,* etc.

[9] For the more usual **dē quō.**

[10] = **tālī.**

videāmur,[1] nē aut invīsa[2] dīs immortālibus ōrātiō nostra aut ingrāta esse videātur. **48.** Itaque nōn sum praedicātūrus[3] quantās ille rēs domī mīlitiae,[4] terrā marīque quantāque fēlicitāte gesserit, ut[5] eius semper voluntātibus nōn modo cīvēs assēnserint, sociī obtem-5 perārint, hostēs oboedierint, sed etiam ventī tempestātēsque obsecundārint; hoc brevissimē dīcam, nēminem umquam tam impudentem fuisse quī[6] ab dīs immortālibus tot et tantās rēs tacitus audēret optāre quot et quantās dī immortālēs ad Cn. Pompeium 10 dētulērunt. Quod ut illī proprium ac perpetuum sit,[7] Quirītēs, cum commūnis salūtis atque imperī tum ipsīus hominis causā, sīcutī facitis, et velle et optāre dēbētis.

49. Quārē cum et bellum sit ita necessārium ut neglegī nōn possit, ita magnum ut accūrātissimē sit 15 administrandum, et cum eī imperātōrem praeficere possītis in quō sit eximia bellī scientia, singulāris virtūs, clārissima auctōritās, ēgregia fortūna,[8] dubitātis,[9] Quirītēs, quīn hoc tantum bonī quod vōbīs ab dīs immortālibus oblātum et datum est in rem pūblicam 20 cōnservandam atque amplificandam cōnferātis?

---

[1] *it will be seen that I recall the past and hope for the future.* Luck is not in Pompey's control, but we can judge his future luck by the past.

[2] Refers to the **dīcam** clause, as **ingrāta** refers to the **videāmur** clause. Note throughout this passage the superstitious fear of changing good luck. Cf. our practice of "knocking on wood."

[3] What figure?   [4] Supply **et** between these two locatives (**351**).

[5] *how*, introducing indirect questions.   [6] Result: *as to*.

[7] This substantive clause depends upon **velle et optāre**: *that it may be his own forever.*

[8] This sentence summarizes the various heads and subheads in the **cōnfirmātiō.** If you have made an outline as suggested, see whether you have included every point here given.

[9] Although followed by **quīn . . . cōnferātis,** translate *hesitate.* The usual construction is the infinitive.

Pompey Is on the Spot

XVII. **50.** Quod sī Rōmae Cn. Pompeius prīvātus esset hōc tempore, tamen ad tantum bellum is erat
dēligendus[1] atque mittendus; nunc cum ad cēterās
summās ūtilitātēs haec quoque opportūnitās[2] adiungā-
5 tur, ut in eīs ipsīs locīs adsit, ut habeat exercitum, ut
ab eīs quī habent accipere[3] statim possit, quid exspec-
tāmus?   Aut cūr nōn, ducibus[4] dīs immortālibus,
eīdem cui cētera[5] summā cum salūte reī pūblicae commissa sunt hoc quoque bellum rēgium commendāmus?[6]

If One-Man Power Succeeded Once, Why not Try It Again?

10 **51.** At[7] enim vir clārissimus, amantissimus reī pūblicae,[8]
vestrīs beneficiīs amplissimīs affectus, Q. Catulus, itemque
summīs ōrnāmentīs honōris, fortūnae, virtūtis, ingenī praeditus, Q. Hortēnsius, ab hāc ratiōne dissentiunt.   Quōrum
ego auctōritātem apud vōs multīs locīs[9] plūrimum valuisse et
15 valēre oportēre cōnfiteor; sed in hāc causā, tametsī cognōs-
cētis auctōritātēs[10] contrāriās virōrum fortissimōrum et clārissimōrum, tamen, omissīs auctōritātibus, ipsā rē ac ratiōne[11]
exquīrere possumus vēritātem, atque hōc[12] facilius, quod ea
omnia quae ā mē adhūc dicta sunt īdem istī[13] vēra esse con-
20 cēdunt, et necessārium bellum esse et magnum et in ūnō

---

[1] *would be the one to be chosen.* For indicative see **390, II, Note.**

[2] Explained by the three **ut** clauses.

[3] Supply **exercitūs.** The forces of Glabrio and Lucullus are meant.

[4] *under the guidance of.* What literally?   [5] Supply **bella.**

[6] *should we not intrust* (**375**).

[7] The **refūtātiō** (*rebuttal*) begins here.

[8] What one English word for the three?   [9] *occasions.*

[10] *Opinions* opposed to those of Catulus and Hortensius are given
later (section 68).

[11] Hendiadys: *by consideration of the actual situation.*

[12] *for this reason,* explained by **quod.**

[13] Catulus and Hortensius.

Cn. Pompeiō summa esse omnia. **52.** Quid igitur ait Hortēnsius? Sī ūnī omnia tribuenda sint, dignissimum esse
Pompeium, sed ad ūnum tamen omnia dēferrī nōn oportēre. Obsolēvit iam ista[1] ōrātiō rē[2] multō magis quam verbīs refūtāta. Nam tū īdem, Q. Hortēnsī, multa prō[3] tuā 5
summā cōpiā ac singulārī facultāte dīcendī et in senātū
contrā virum fortem, A. Gabīnium, graviter ōrnātēque
dīxistī, cum is dē ūnō imperātōre contrā praedōnēs cōnstitu-
endō lēgem prōmulgāsset,[4] et ex hōc ipsō locō[5] permulta
item contrā eam lēgem verba fēcistī. **53.** Quid? tum,[6] per 10
deōs immortālīs, sī plūs apud populum Rōmānum auctōritās tua quam ipsīus populī Rōmānī salūs et vēra causa
valuisset, hodiē hanc glōriam atque hoc orbis terrae imperium tenērēmus? An tibi tum imperium hoc esse vidēbātur cum populī Rōmānī lēgātī, quaestōrēs, praetōrēsque 15
capiēbantur, cum ex omnibus prōvinciīs commeātū[7] et prīvātō et pūblicō prohibēbāmur, cum ita clausa nōbīs erant
maria omnia ut neque prīvātam rem trānsmarīnam neque
pūblicam iam obīre possēmus?

Vocabulary Drill (46–53). — **dēclārō, longinquus, optō ; igitur,
aiō, verbum, hodiē.**

Conditions before the Passing of the Gabinian Law

XVIII. **54.** Quae cīvitās umquam fuit anteā, nōn dīcō[8] 20
Athēniēnsium, quae satis lātē quondam mare tenuisse dīcitur,

---

[1] = **tua.**   [2] *experience.*   [3] *in accordance with.*

[4] A bill had to be "advertised" or announced at least 17 days before
it could be passed, in order to allow full discussion.

[5] What place?

[6] Translate with **valuisset.** What kind of condition? Cicero ignores
the danger of placing absolute power in the hands of one man (the constitutional objection which his opponents had rightly raised) and
reasons, after the fashion of the crowd whom he is addressing, that if it
worked once, why not try it again?

[7] Ablative of separation : *kept from intercourse with* (**ex**).

[8] What figure?

FIG. 93. AN ANCIENT MARBLE PLAN OF ROME

The dark bits are ancient; the rest is modern restoration. In Roman maps
the top is south, not north. Cf. Fig. 76.

nōn Carthāginiēnsium,[1] quī permultum classe ac maritimīs
rēbus valuērunt, nōn Rhodiōrum, quōrum usque ad nostram
memoriam disciplīna nāvālis et glōria permānsit, quae cīvitās, inquam, anteā tam tenuis aut tam parvula fuit quae nōn
5 portūs suōs et agrōs et aliquam partem regiōnis atque ōrae

---

[1] Supply **eam.** The Athenians controlled the Aegean as a result of
the Persian Wars. Rhodes later became the dominant sea power in the
east and Carthage in the west, until the latter was conquered in the
Second Punic War by the Romans.

maritimae per sē ipsa dēfenderet? At herculēs[1] aliquot
annōs continuōs ante lēgem Gabīniam ille populus Rōmānus,
cuius usque ad nostram memoriam nōmen invictum in
nāvālibus pugnīs permānserit, magnā ac multō maximā[2]
parte nōn modo ūtilitātis sed etiam dignitātis atque imperī 5
caruit. **55.** Nōs, quōrum maiōrēs Antiochum[3] rēgem classe
Persemque superārunt omnibusque nāvālibus pugnīs Carthā-
giniēnsīs, hominēs in maritimīs rēbus exercitātissimōs parā-
tissimōsque, vīcērunt, eī[4] nūllō in locō iam praedōnibus parēs
esse poterāmus. Nōs quī anteā nōn modo Italiam tūtam 10
habēbāmus sed omnīs sociōs in ultimīs ōrīs auctōritāte nostrī imperī salvōs praestāre poterāmus, tum cum īnsula Dēlos
tam procul ā nōbīs in Aegaeō marī posita, quō omnēs undique cum mercibus atque oneribus commeābant, referta
dīvitiīs, parva, sine mūrō nihil timēbat,[5] īdem nōn modo 15
prōvinciīs atque ōrīs Italiae maritimīs ac portibus nostrīs
sed etiam Appiā iam viā[6] carēbāmus. Et eīs temporibus[7]
nōnne pudēbat magistrātūs populī Rōmānī in hunc ipsum
locum[8] ēscendere, cum eum nōbīs maiōrēs nostrī exuviīs
nauticīs et classium spoliīs ōrnātum relīquissent?   20

Gabinius Should Be Appointed to Assist Pompey

XIX. **56.** Bonō tē animō[9] tum, Q. Hortēnsī, populus
Rōmānus et cēterōs quī erant in eādem sententiā dīcere

---

[1] *by Hercules.*   [2] Note alliteration of *m*.

[3] King of Syria.   Perse(u)s, king of Macedonia, was defeated by
Aemilius Paulus in 168 B.C.

[4] Repeats **nōs** emphatically: *we, I say.*   So also **īdem** below.

[5] Delos, revered by the ancients as the birthplace of Apollo and
Diana, was not molested by the pirates.   The **cum** clause contrasts
with the following statement.

[6] Rome's chief highway to the south, paralleling the coast at several
places and thus exposed to pirate raids.   Cicero is no doubt exaggerating.

[7] When the pirates were most active.

[8] The speakers' platform in the Forum had received its name Rostra
from the fact that it was adorned with the " beaks " of ships captured in
war.

[9] *with honest convictions*, modifying **dīcere**.

exīstimāvit et[1] ea quae sentiēbātis; sed tamen in salūte
commūnī īdem populus Rōmānus dolōrī[2] suō māluit quam
auctōritātī vestrae obtemperāre. Itaque ūna lēx, ūnus vir,
ūnus annus nōn modo vōs illā miseriā ac turpitūdine līberāvit
5 sed etiam effēcit ut aliquandō vērē vidērēminī omnibus
gentibus ac nātiōnibus terrā marīque imperāre. **57.** Quō[3]
mihi etiam indignius vidētur obtrectātum esse[4] adhūc
(Gabīniō dīcam anne Pompeiō an utrīque, id quod est vērius)[5]
nē lēgārētur A. Gabīnius Cn. Pompeiō expetentī ac postu-
10 lantī. Utrum[6] ille quī postulat ad tantum bellum lēgātum
quem velit idōneus nōn est quī impetret,[7] cum cēterī ad
expīlandōs sociōs dīripiendāsque prōvinciās quōs voluērunt
lēgātōs ēdūxerint, an ipse cuius lēge salūs ac dignitās populō
Rōmānō atque omnibus gentibus cōnstitūta est expers esse
15 dēbet victōriae[8] eius imperātōris atque eius exercitūs quī
cōnsiliō ac perīculō[9] illīus est cōnstitūtus? **58.** An[10] C.
Falcidius, Q. Metellus, Q. Caelius Latīniēnsis, Cn. Lentulus,
quōs omnīs honōris causā nōminō, cum tribūnī plēbī[11] fuissent,
annō proximō lēgātī esse potuērunt; in ūnō Gabīniō sunt
20 tam dīligentēs, quī in hōc bellō quod lēge Gabīniā geritur,
in[12] hōc imperātōre atque exercitū quem per vōs ipse cōnstituit, etiam praecipuō iūre[13] esse dēbēbat? Dē quō lēgandō
cōnsulēs spērō ad senātum relātūrōs. Quī sī dubitābunt
aut gravābuntur, ego mē profiteor relātūrum; neque mē

---

[1] Connects **bonō animō** and **ea**, etc.

[2] *sorrowful experience* with the pirates.   [3] *For this reason.*

[4] *that objection has been raised*, explained by the **nē** clause (*so that
. . . should not be appointed a general for*). The rest of this chapter
is a digression. The objection to Gabinius was that the proposer of a
law could not legally hold a position created by that law.

[5] *should I say to . . . as is nearer the truth.*

[6] Omit in translating.

[7] *to obtain his request* (**381**).   [8] See **304.**

[9] Sometimes the sponsor of an unpopular bill was mobbed.

[10] Omit in translating and make the first part of the sentence a
statement.

[11] Genitive.   [12] *in the case of.*

[13] Ablative of description : *ought to have special privileges.*

impediet cuiusquam inīquitās quō minus vōbīs[1] frētus vestrum iūs beneficiumque dēfendam,[2] neque praeter interces-
siōnem quicquam audiam, dē quā, ut ego arbitror, istī ipsī
quī minitantur etiam atque etiam quid liceat[3] cōnsīderābunt.
Meā quidem sententiā, Quirītēs, ūnus A. Gabīnius bellī 5
maritimī rērumque gestārum Cn. Pompeiō socius ascrībitur,[4]
proptereā quod alter ūnī illud bellum suscipiendum vestrīs
suffrāgiīs dētulit, alter dēlātum susceptumque cōnfēcit.

Vocabulary Drill (54–58). — **quondam, dīvitiae, spolium;
lēgō** (-āre), **praecipuus, frētus, suffrāgium.**

The Objections Raised by Catulus

XX. 59. Reliquum est ut dē Q. Catulī auctōritāte et
sententiā[5] dīcendum esse videātur. Quī cum ex vōbīs quaere- 10
ret,[6] sī in ūnō Cn. Pompeiō omnia pōnerētis, sī quid eō
factum esset,[7] in quō spem essētis habitūrī, cēpit magnum
suae virtūtis frūctum[8] ac dignitātis, cum omnēs ūnā prope
vōce in eō ipsō[9] vōs spem habitūrōs esse dīxistis. Etenim
tālis est vir ut nūlla rēs tanta sit ac tam difficilis quam ille 15
nōn et cōnsiliō regere et integritāte tuērī et virtūte cōnficere possit. Sed in hōc ipsō[10] ab eō vehementissimē dissentiō, quod quō[11] minus certa est hominum ac minus diūturna
vīta, hōc magis rēs pūblica, dum per deōs immortālīs licet,

---

[1] See **339.**   [2] Depends upon **quō minus** (**371**).

[3] *how far they may go.* While a tribune could stop Cicero with a
veto, yet the people would probably make such a tribune suffer for it
later, for he was dependent upon their votes. It might be added that
Gabinius was commissioned to serve on Pompey's staff and, like many
another political appointee, used his office to get rich.

[4] *is regarded as a partner to.*   [5] Hendiadys.

[6] The object is the **in quō** clause (indirect question).

[7] *if anything should happen to him.* We use this and other euphe-
misms so as to avoid the disagreeable reference to death.

[8] *tribute (to).* Note how the dependent words are interlocked.

[9] *i.e.* Catulus.   [10] *on this point,* explained by the **quod** clause.

[11] With the following **hōc**: *the less . . . the more.* See **341.**

fruī dēbet summī virī vītā atque virtūte.[1] **60.** At enim nē
quid novī fīat[2] contrā exempla atque īnstitūta maiōrum.
Nōn dīcam[3] hōc locō maiōrēs nostrōs semper in pāce cōn-
suētūdinī, in bellō ūtilitātī pāruisse, semper ad novōs cāsūs
5 temporum novōrum[4] cōnsiliōrum ratiōnēs accommodāsse,
nōn dīcam duo bella maxima, Pūnicum atque Hispāniēnse,
ab ūnō imperātōre[5] esse cōnfecta duāsque urbīs potentissi-
mās quae huic imperiō maximē minitābantur, Carthāginem
atque Numantiam, ab eōdem Scīpiōne esse dēlētās, nōn
10 commemorābō nūper ita vōbīs patribusque vestrīs esse
vīsum ut in ūnō C. Mariō spēs imperī pōnerētur,[6] ut īdem
cum Iugurthā, īdem cum Cimbrīs, īdem cum Teutonīs
bellum administrāret; in ipsō Cn. Pompeiō, in quō novī
cōnstituī nihil vult Q. Catulus, quam multa sint nova summā
15 Q. Catulī voluntāte cōnstitūta recordāminī.

Pompey Has Already Broken Many Precedents

XXI. 61. Quid tam novum[7] quam adulēscentulum
prīvātum exercitum difficilī reī pūblicae tempore cōnficere? Cōnfēcit. Huic praeesse?[8] Praefuit. Rem[9]
optimē ductū suō gerere?[8] Gessit. Quid tam praeter
20 cōnsuētūdinem quam hominī peradulēscentī, cuius

---

[1] Note the alliteration.

[2] Cicero is quoting Catulus' objection. For mood see **366.** This is
the favorite dogma of all conservatives. What is the term applied to
the conservatives in the senate of the United States?

[3] What figure?

[4] With **cōnsiliōrum,** which modifies **ratiōnēs.**

[5] Scipio the Younger, twice elected consul illegally, for military
reasons, during the Third Punic War (146 B.C.) and the Spanish War
(133 B.C.).

[6] Elected consul five years in succession (104–100 B.C.). According
to law ten years were supposed to intervene between consulships.

[7] Supply **fuit.** Pompey, at the age of 23, raised troops for Sulla.
Cf. sections 28–30 and notes.

[8] Depends upon **Quid . . . prīvātum** above.   [9] *campaign.*

aetās ā senātōriō gradū[1] longē abesset, imperium atque
exercitum darī, Siciliam permittī atque Āfricam bellum-
que in eā prōvinciā administrandum? Fuit in hīs prōvinciīs singulārī innocentiā, gravitāte, virtūte,[2] bellum in
Āfricā maximum cōnfēcit, victōrem exercitum dēportā-5

FIG. 94.   SICILIA
Mt. Etna seen from Taormina.

vit.   Quid vērō tam inaudītum quam equitem Rōmānum triumphāre?[3]   At eam quoque rem populus Rōmānus nōn modo vīdit sed omnium etiam studiō vīsendam[4]

---

[1] Pompey at that time was six years under the minimum age required
for a seat in the senate.

[2] Do not translate the Latin nouns by their English derivatives.

[3] Only consuls and praetors had that right.

[4] A frequentative of **videō** (**77**) : *go to see.* The modern circus
parade presents many of the thrills and features of the old Roman
triumphal processions.

et concelebrandam putāvit. **62.** Quid tam inūsitā-
tum quam ut, cum duo cōnsulēs clārissimī fortissi-
mīque essent, eques Rōmānus ad bellum maximum
formīdolōsissimumque prō cōnsule[1] mitterētur? Mis-
5 sus est. Quō quidem[2] tempore, cum esset nōn nēmō[3]
in senātū quī dīceret nōn oportēre mittī hominem
prīvātum prō cōnsule,[1] L. Philippus[4] dīxisse dīcitur
nōn sē illum suā sententiā prō[5] cōnsule sed prō cōnsulibus mittere.[6] Tanta in eō reī pūblicae bene geren-
10 dae spēs cōnstituēbātur ut duōrum cōnsulum mūnus
ūnīus adulēscentis virtūtī committerētur. Quid tam
singulāre quam ut ex senātūs cōnsultō lēgibus solūtus[7]
cōnsul ante[8] fieret quam ūllum alium magistrātum per
lēgēs capere licuisset?[9] Quid tam incrēdibile quam ut
15 iterum eques Rōmānus ex senātūs cōnsultō trium-
phāret? Quae[10] in omnibus hominibus nova post
hominum memoriam cōnstitūta sunt, ea tam multa
nōn sunt quam haec quae in hōc ūnō homine vīdimus.
63. Atque haec tot exempla tanta ac tam nova prō-
20 fecta[11] sunt in eōdem homine ā Q. Catulī atque ā

---

[1] (as) proconsul.   [2] by the way.   [3] With **nōn** = some one.

[4] Noted for his wit. Cicero had a similar reputation (cf. **106**).

[5] Translate as the preposition: in place of (one) consul but of (two).
The pun on "proconsul" is obvious but hard to translate. This retort
is a fling at the consuls of that year, who were neither able nor willing
to fight against Sertorius in Spain.

[6] i.e. by his vote.

[7] Pompey, then only 36, had been freed from (the operation of) the
laws and elected consul before attaining the legal age (43) or holding
the office of praetor.

[8] With **quam**.

[9] The legal age for the quaestorship — the first rung in the political
ladder — was 36.

[10] The antecedent of **nova**: The precedents which.

[11] From **proficīscor**: arose out of the influence of Catulus.

cēterōrum eiusdem dignitātis amplissimōrum hominum
auctōritāte.

Vocabulary Drill (60–62). — exemplum, nūper; antequam, iterum.

The People Were Right Before — Why Not Trust Them Now?

XXII.   Quārē videant nē sit perinīquum et nōn ferendum
illōrum[1] auctōritātem dē Cn. Pompeī dignitāte ā vōbīs com-
probātam semper esse, vestrum ab illīs dē eōdem homine 5
iūdicium populīque Rōmānī auctōritātem improbārī, praesertim cum iam suō iūre populus Rōmānus in hōc homine
suam auctōritātem vel[2] contrā omnīs quī dissentiunt possit
dēfendere, proptereā quod, īsdem istīs reclāmantibus, vōs
ūnum illum ex omnibus dēlēgistis quem bellō praedōnum 10
praepōnerētis.[3]   **64.**   Hoc sī vōs temere fēcistis et reī pūblicae parum cōnsuluistis, rēctē istī studia vestra suīs cōnsiliīs regere cōnantur.   Sīn autem vōs plūs tum in rē pūblicā
vīdistis,[4] vōs, eīs repugnantibus, per vōsmet ipsōs dignitātem
huic imperiō, salūtem orbī terrārum attulistis,[5] aliquandō 15
istī prīncipēs et sibi et cēterīs populī Rōmānī ūniversī auctōritātī pārendum esse[6] fateantur.[7]   Atque in hōc bellō
Asiāticō et rēgiō, Quirītēs, nōn sōlum mīlitāris illa virtūs
quae est in Cn. Pompeiō singulāris sed aliae quoque animī
virtūtēs magnae et multae requīruntur.   Difficile est in 20
Asiā, Ciliciā, Syriā rēgnīsque interiōrum nātiōnum ita versārī nostrum imperātōrem[8] ut nihil aliud nisi dē hoste ac
dē laude cōgitet.   Deinde, etiam sī quī[9] sunt pudōre ac
temperantiā[10] moderātiōrēs, tamen eōs esse tālīs propter multitūdinem cupidōrum[11] hominum nēmō arbitrātur.   **65.**   Dif- 25

---

[1] The optimates.   [2] *even.*   [3] For mood see **368**.

[4] *showed more political insight.*   [5] Also introduced by **sīn**.

[6] See **313**, *a*.   Translate personally by making the datives of agent
(et sibi et cēterīs) the subject.

[7] *let . . . admit* (**366**).   [8] *one of our generals.*

[9] = aliquī.   Why?   [10] *because of their decency and restraint.*

[11] *greedy.*   In the midst of so much grafting even the honest man was
thought corrupt.

ficile est dictū,[1] Quirītēs, quantō in odiō sīmus apud exterās
nātiōnēs propter eōrum quōs ad eās per hōs annōs cum
imperiō mīsimus libīdin s et iniūriās.[2] Quod enim fānum
putātis in illīs terrīs nostrīs magistrātibus religiōsum, quam
5 cīvitātem sānctam, quam domum satis clausam ac mūnītam
fuisse? Urbēs iam locuplētēs et cōpiōsae requīruntur quibus[3] causa bellī propter dīripiendī facultātem īnferātur.
66. Libenter haec cōram cum Q. Catulō et Q. Hortēnsiō,
summīs et clārissimīs virīs, disputārem; nōrunt enim
10 sociōrum vulnera, vident eōrum calamitātēs, querimōniās
audiunt. Prō sociīs vōs contrā hostīs exercitūs mittere
putātis an hostium simulātiōne[4] contrā sociōs atque amīcōs? Quae cīvitās est in Asiā quae nōn modo imperātōris
aut lēgātī sed ūnīus tribūnī mīlitum animōs ac spīritūs
15 capere[5] possit?

Provincials and Experts Agree on Pompey

XXIII. Quārē, etiam sī quem habētis quī, collātīs signīs,[6]
exercitūs rēgiōs superāre posse videātur, tamen, nisi erit
īdem quī ā pecūniīs sociōrum, quī ab eōrum coniugibus ac
līberīs, quī ab ōrnāmentīs fānōrum atque oppidōrum, quī ab
20 aurō gazāque rēgiā manūs, oculōs, animum cohibēre possit,
nōn erit idōneus quī ad bellum Asiāticum rēgiumque mittā-
tur.[7] **67.** Ecquam putātis cīvitātem pācātam fuisse[8] quae
locuplēs sit, ecquam esse locuplētem quae istīs pācāta esse
videātur? Ōra maritima, Quirītēs, Cn. Pompeium nōn
25 sōlum propter reī mīlitāris glōriam sed etiam propter animī
continentiam requīsīvit. Vidēbat[9] enim praetōrēs locuplē-

---

[1] See **405** (b).

[2] With **propter**: *because of the wanton and unjust acts.*

[3] = ut eīs (**368**).

[4] *using the enemy merely as a pretext.*   [b] *satisfy.*

[6] *by fighting battles.* What literally?   [7] See **381.**

[8] *has been (considered) subdued.* These rapacious commanders never
considered any district subjugated which still offered a chance for
looting.

[9] The subject is **ōra maritima.**

tārī quotannīs pecūniā pūblicā praeter paucōs, neque nōs
quicquam aliud assequī classium nōmine[1] nisi ut dētrīmentīs
accipiendīs maiōre afficī turpitūdine vidērēmur.[2]   Nunc
quā cupiditāte hominēs in prōvinciās, quibus iactūrīs qui-
busque condiciōnibus[3] proficīscantur ignōrant vidēlicet[4] istī[5]
quī ad ūnum dēferenda omnia esse nōn arbitrantur.   Quasi[5]
vērō Cn. Pompeium nōn cum suīs virtūtibus tum etiam
aliēnīs vitiīs[6] magnum esse videāmus.   **68.**   Quārē nōlīte[7]
dubitāre[8] quīn huic ūnī crēdātis omnia quī inter tot annōs
ūnus inventus est quem sociī in urbīs suās cum exercitū
vēnisse gaudērent.

Quod sī auctōritātibus hanc causam, Quirītēs, cōnfirmandam putātis, est vōbīs auctor vir bellōrum omnium maxi-
mārumque rērum perītissimus, P. Servīlius, cuius tantae
rēs gestae terrā marīque exstitērunt[9] ut, cum dē bellō dē-
līberētis, auctor vōbīs gravior esse nēmō dēbeat; est C.
Cūriō, summīs vestrīs beneficiīs maximīsque rēbus gestīs,
summō ingeniō et prūdentiā praeditus,[10] est Cn. Lentulus,
in quō omnēs prō amplissimīs vestrīs honōribus[11] summum
cōnsilium, summam gravitātem esse cognōstis, est C. Cassius, integritāte, vēritāte, cōnstantiā singulārī.[12]   Quārē
vidēte ut[13] hōrum auctōritātibus illōrum ōrātiōnī quī dissentiunt respondēre posse videāmur.

---

[1] *so-called fleets.* They kept most of the money appropriated for the
navy.

[2] *it was seen that our disgrace was even greater* (than if we had not
fought at all).

[3] *with what expenses,* incurred in obtaining their provinces, and
terms made with creditors.

[4] Ironical.   [5] *As if we did not see.*

[6] *by* (*contrast with*) *other men's vices.*   [7] See **393.**

[8] See **372.**

[9] With **tantae:** *have been so outstanding.*

[10] Zeugma (**409**).

[11] *as shown by your most generous gifts of office.*

[12] All four of these "expert authorities" had been consuls and eminent
commanders.

[13] *how.*

Cicero's Pledge of Support to Manilius Not Due to Selfish Reasons

XXIV. **69.**[1] Quae cum ita sint, C. Mānīlī, prīmum istam tuam et lēgem et voluntātem et sententiam laudō vehementissimēque comprobō; deinde tē hortor ut, auctōre populō Rōmānō,[2] maneās in sententiā nēve[3] 5 cuiusquam vim aut minās pertimēscās.[4] Prīmum in tē satis esse animī persevērantiaeque arbitror; deinde, cum tantam multitūdinem tantō cum studiō adesse videāmus quantam iterum nunc in eōdem homine praeficiendō vidēmus, quid est quod aut dē rē aut dē 10 perficiendī facultāte dubitēmus?[5]   Ego[6] autem, quicquid est in mē studī, cōnsilī, labōris, ingenī, quicquid hōc beneficiō populī Rōmānī atque hāc potestāte praetōriā, quicquid auctōritāte, fidē, cōnstantiā possum,[7] id omne ad hanc rem cōnficiendam tibi et populō 15 Rōmānō polliceor ac dēferō (**70.**) testorque omnīs deōs, et eōs maximē quī huic locō templōque[8] praesident, quī omnium mentīs eōrum quī ad rem pūblicam adeunt[9] maximē perspiciunt, mē hoc neque rogātū facere cuiusquam, neque quō[10] Cn. Pompeī grātiam mihi per

---

[1] This chapter forms the **perōrātiō** (*conclusion*).

[2] *with the Roman people back of you.*   What literally?

[3] *and not to.*

[4] Gabinius had been mobbed and almost killed for sponsoring the bill which placed Pompey in charge of the pirate war just a year before this.

[5] See **380.**   [6] Emphatic by position: *As for me.*

[7] *whatever I can (accomplish).*

[8] *this sacred place.*   What figure?   In the Roman view any place that had been consecrated by the augurs while taking the auspices was a **templum.**   Cicero was speaking from the Rostra in the Forum.

[9] *who enter public life.*

[10] *nor because.*   A rejected reason is in the subjunctive.

hanc causam conciliārī putem, neque quō mihi ex
cuiusquam amplitūdine aut praesidia perīculīs aut
adiūmenta honōribus[1] quaeram, proptereā quod perīcula facile, ut hominem praestāre oportet,[2] innocentiā
tēctī repellēmus, honōrem autem neque ab ūnō neque ex 5
hōc locō sed eādem illā nostrā labōriōsissimā ratiōne vītae, sī vestra voluntās feret,[3] cōnsequēmur. **71.** Quam
ob rem, sī quid in hāc causā mihi[4] susceptum est,
Quirītēs, id ego omne mē reī pūblicae causā suscēpisse
cōnfirmō, tantumque abest[5] ut aliquam mihi bonam 10
grātiam quaesīsse videar, ut multās mē etiam simultātēs
partim obscūrās, partim apertās intellegam mihi nōn
necessāriās, vōbīs nōn inūtilīs suscēpisse. Sed ego mē[6]
hōc honōre[7] praeditum, tantīs vestrīs beneficiīs affectum statuī, Quirītēs, vestram voluntātem et reī pū- 15
blicae dignitātem et salūtem prōvinciārum atque sociōrum meīs omnibus commodīs et ratiōnibus praeferre
oportēre.

Vocabulary Drill (64–69). — parum, pudor; quasi, vitium,
gaudeō; minae, quisquis, testor.

Review Questions. — 1. What was Cicero's official position
when he made this speech? 2. What motives probably led Cicero
to speak in support of the Manilian Law? 3. What danger to the
republican form of government did the bill involve? 4. Who was
Tigranes? 5. What was at stake in the war with Mithridates?
6. Of what country was Mithridates king? 7. What Roman generals
fought against him? 8. How did the Romans collect taxes?
9. What sort of taxes were imposed in the provinces? 10. Why

---

[1] For case see **310.** What particular office has Cicero in mind?

[2] *so far as a human being should guarantee.*

[3] *will permit.*   [4] See **317.**   [5] *so far am I from seeming.*

[6] Do not forget to find a construction for **mē.**

[7] The praetorship, while **beneficiīs** refers to his earlier offices.

did Lucullus fail in the war against Mithridates? 11. What, according to Cicero, are the four qualities necessary for a successful commander? 12. In what wars had Pompey taken part? 13. What was the nature of Rome's policy toward foreign nations? 14. What was the Gabinian Law? 15. Who spoke in opposition to the bill of Manilius?

Fig. 95. Syracuse, Sicily

In the foreground is the Greek theater of the fifth century B.C.

169. M. TULLI CICERONIS
ACTIONIS IN C. VERREM SECUNDAE
LIBER QUINTUS

(Selections)

In the last of his speeches against Verres (cf. **107**) Cicero
deals with the severe and illegal penalties imposed by Verres on
the Sicilians.   Particularly offensive was his flogging and execution of a Roman citizen contrary to law.

The Crucifixion of a Roman Citizen

Caedēbātur virgīs[1] in mediō forō Messānae[2] cīvis
Rōmānus, iūdicēs; cum intereā nūllus gemitus, nūlla
vōx alia illīus miserī inter dolōrem crepitumque plāgā-
rum audiēbātur, nisi haec, "Cīvis Rōmānus sum!"
Hāc sē commemorātiōne cīvitātis omnia verbera dēpul- 5
sūrum cruciātumque ā corpore dēiectūrum arbitrābātur.
Is nōn modo hoc nōn perfēcit, ut virgārum vim dēpre-
cārētur; sed, cum implōrāret saepius, ūsūrpāretque
nōmen cīvitātis, crux[3] — crux, inquam — īnfēlīcī et
aerumnōsō,[4] quī numquam istam pestem[5] vīderat, 10
comparābātur.

Ō nōmen dulce lībertātis! Ō iūs eximium nostrae
cīvitātis! Ō lēx Porcia, lēgēsque Semprōniae![6]   Ō

---

[1] *was flogged with rods*. The rods used were those carried in fasces
by the lictors. Note the order of words, with the subject at the end
as a climax.

[2] Now Messina.

[3] The *cross* was used only in the punishment of slaves. Cicero's
tone in using the word was full of horror.

[4] Supply **hominī**; with **comparābātur**.

[5] *i.e.* the cross, or possibly Verres: *a curse such as this*.

[6] These laws forbade the flogging or execution of a citizen by a magistrate without a trial by the people.

337

graviter dēsīderāta et aliquandō reddita[1] plēbī Rōmānae tribūnīcia potestās ! Hūcine[2] tandem omnia
recidērunt, ut cīvis Rōmānus, in prōvinciā populī
Rōmānī, in oppidō foederātōrum, ab eō quī beneficiō
5 populī Rōmānī fascīs et secūrīs habēret dēligātus in
forō virgīs caederētur? Quid? cum ignēs ārdentēsque
lāminae[3] cēterīque cruciātūs admovēbantur, sī tē[4]
illīus acerba implōrātiō et vōx miserābilis nōn inhibē-
bat, nē cīvium[5] quidem Rōmānōrum quī tum aderant
10 flētū et gemitū maximō commovēbāre? In crucem tū
agere ausus es quemquam quī sē cīvem Rōmānum esse
dīceret?

Hominēs tenuēs, obscūrō locō[6] nātī, nāvigant; adeunt
ad ea loca quae numquam anteā vīdērunt, ubi neque nōtī
15 esse eīs quō vēnērunt, neque semper cum cognitōribus[7]
esse possunt. Hāc ūnā tamen fīdūciā cīvitātis, nōn
modo apud nostrōs magistrātūs, quī et lēgum et ex-
īstimātiōnis[8] perīculō[9] continentur, neque apud cīvīs
sōlum Rōmānōs, quī et sermōnis et iūris et multārum
20 rērum societāte iūnctī sunt, fore sē tūtōs arbitrantur;
sed, quōcumque vēnerint, hanc sibi rem [10] praesidiō
spērant futūram. (II. 5. 162, 163, 167)

---

[1] The participles modify **tribūnīcia potestās**. The power of tribunes
to protect citizens, curtailed by Sulla, had just been restored.

[2] = **Hūc + ne**; with **recidērunt**: *Have things come to this.*

[3] *hot plates*, of metal, used in torture.   [4] Verres.

[5] Modifies **flētū**.   [6] *rank* (**323**).

[7] *witnesses*, to testify to their citizenship.

[8] *public opinion.*   [9] *threat.*   [10] *i.e.* citizenship.

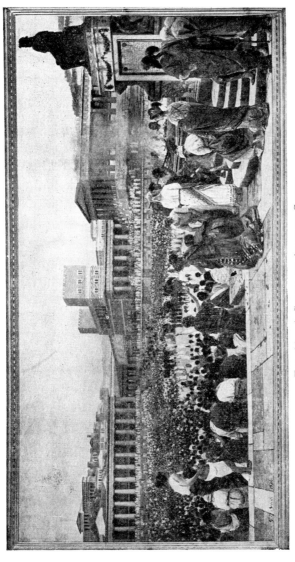

Fig. 96. A Scene in Ancient Sicily

"The Funeral of Timoleon," a painting by Sciuti.

170. M. TULLI CICERONIS
IN M. ANTONIUM
ORATIO PHILIPPICA SECUNDA

(Selections)

After the death of Caesar Cicero again took an active interest
in politics. When Antony seized the reins of power, Cicero
attacked him vigorously and fearlessly in fourteen speeches
called Philippics because they were comparable to Demosthenes'
attacks on Philip of Macedon. The second is considered the
greatest, though it was
never actually delivered,
for Antony had left Rome.
In the following selection
Cicero contrasts Caesar
and Antony.

Caesar and Antony

Fuit in illō[1] inge-
nium, ratiō, memoria,
litterae, cūra, cōgitātiō,
dīligentia; rēs bellō
5 gesserat, quamvīs reī
pūblicae calamitōsās,
at tamen magnās; mul-
tōs annōs rēgnāre medi-
tātus magnō labōre,
10 magnīs perīculīs quod

Fig. 97. Antony

cōgitārat effēcerat; mūneribus,[2] monumentīs, congiā-
riīs,[3] epulīs multitūdinem imperītam dēlēnierat; suōs
praemiīs, adversāriōs clēmentiae speciē dēvīnxerat.
Quid multa?[4] Attulerat iam līberae cīvitātī partim

---

[1] *i.e.* Caesar.   [2] *gladiatorial shows.*
[3] *gifts.*   [4] *In a word.* What literally?

metū, partim patientiā cōnsuētūdinem serviendī. Cum illō ego tē dominandī cupiditāte cōnferre possum, cēterīs vērō rēbus nūllō modō comparandus es.

Cicero Is Unafraid

Respice, quaesō, aliquandō rem pūblicam, M. Antōnī; quibus ortus sīs, nōn quibuscum vīvās, cōn-5 sīderā;[1] mēcum, ut volēs,[2] redī cum rē pūblicā in grātiam. Sed dē tē tū vīderis;[3] ego dē mē ipse profitēbor. Dēfendī rem pūblicam adulēscēns, nōn dēseram senex; contempsī Catilīnae gladiōs, nōn pertimēscam tuōs. Quīn etiam[4] corpus libenter obtulerim,[5] sī repraesentārī[6]10 morte meā lībertās cīvitātis potest. Etenim sī abhinc annōs prope vīgintī[7] hōc ipsō in templō[8] negāvī posse mortem immātūram esse cōnsulārī, quantō vērius nunc negābō senī![9] Mihi vērō, patrēs cōnscrīptī, iam etiam optanda mors est perfūnctō[10] rēbus eīs quās adeptus 15 sum quāsque gessī. Duo modo haec optō, ūnum ut moriēns populum Rōmānum līberum relinquam (hōc[11] mihi maius ab dīs immortālibus darī nihil potest), alterum ut ita cuique[12] ēveniat ut[13] dē rē pūblicā quisque mereātur.   (II. 116, 118, 119)   20

---

[1] *i.e.* Antony should consider his noble ancestry rather than the rabble with whom he associates.

[2] Supply **redī in grātiam**: *Become reconciled with me* (*or not*), *as you wish*, (*but*).

[3] *you will decide about your own plans.*   [4] *In fact.*

[5] *I would offer.*   [6] *be brought about quickly.*   [7] *almost twenty years ago.*

[8] The temple of Concord, where the senate met when Cicero made his fourth speech against Catiline, to which he here refers.

[9] Supply **mortem immātūram esse.**

[10] Modifies **Mihi.** It governs the ablative (**rēbus**): *I ought even to wish for death, now that I have finished.*

[11] See **331.**   [12] *everyone.*   [13] *as.*

FIG. 98. THE ROMAN FORUM DURING THE EMPIRE

Looking toward the south. At the extreme left, the temple of Julius Caesar; then the temple of Castor and Pollux and the Basilica Julia.

171. CICERO'S LETTERS

Unlike Pliny's letters, those of Cicero were not intended for publication. They were published after his death in several collections; of these the two largest which have come down to us are those to his closest friend, Atticus, and those to various friends and members of his family which go under the title **Ad Familiārēs**. Many of them are much less formal than the orations and give a good idea of the everyday Latin of a cultured Roman. In these letters we see Cicero at his best and at his worst — as is natural in communications intended only for a very intimate friend or a member of the family.

172.   1. CAMPAIGN PLANS[1]

Petītiōnis[2] nostrae, quam tibi summae cūrae esse sciō, huius modī ratiō est, quod[3] adhūc coniectūrā prōvidērī possit. Prēnsat[4] ūnus P. Galba; sine fūcō ac fallāciīs mōre maiōrum negātur.[5] Competītōrēs quī certī esse videantur Galba et Antōnius et Q. Cornificius. 5 Catilīna, sī iūdicātum erit merīdiē nōn lūcēre,[6] certus

---

[1] Written to Atticus in July, 65 B.C., a full year before the elections in which Cicero was chosen consul.

[2] *canvass,* for a political office.   [3] *as far as,* with subjunctive.

[4] *is canvassing openly;* lit., *is catching hold of, i.e.* "button-holing" people, or shaking hands to get supporters.

[5] *he is being refused in the good old fashion without camouflage;* lit. *without paint and pretext.*

[6] Catiline was under indictment for graft in his province and could not run for office unless acquitted. Cicero means that Catiline was guilty as surely as the sun shines at midday, but that the jurors might acquit him just the same.

343

erit competītor ; dē Aufidiō et dē Palicānō nōn putō tē exspectāre dum scrībam.[1]

Nōs[2] in omnī mūnere candidātōriō fungendō summam adhibēbimus dīligentiam et fortasse, quoniam
5 vidētur in suffrāgiīs multum posse[3] Gallia,[4] cum Rōmae ā iūdiciīs forum refrīxerit,[5] excurrēmus mēnse Septembrī lēgātī[6] ad Pīsōnem, ut Iānuāriō revertāmur. Cum perspexerō voluntātēs nōbilium, scrībam ad tē.

(A. I. 1. 1–2)

173. 2. Mother and Child Are Doing Well[7]

L. Iūliō Caesare C. Mārciō Figulō cōnsulibus,[8]
10 fīliolō mē auctum[9] scītō,[10] salvā Terentiā. Abs tē tam diū nihil litterārum![11] Ego dē meīs ad tē ratiōnibus scrīpsī anteā dīligenter. Hōc tempore Catilīnam, competītōrem nostrum, dēfendere cōgitāmus.[12] Iūdicēs habēmus quōs voluimus, summā accūsātōris voluntāte.[13]

---

[1] See **385**. The actual candidates were Galba, Antonius, Cornificius, Catiline, and two others. Antonius and Cicero were elected.

[2] = **ego**. [3] *have great influence.*

[4] *i.e.* Cisalpine Gaul, where there were many Roman citizens.

[5] *has cooled off in the matter of trials.* The courts were closed during most of September on account of the games (**lūdī Rōmānī**), and there were many interruptions during the rest of the autumn, culminating in the Saturnalia in December.

[6] *as a commissioner;* cf. the junketing trips of our congressmen.

[7] Written to Atticus in July, 65 B.C.

[8] As these were the consuls for 64 B.C., and as we know that this letter was written in 65, he must mean *consuls-elect.* Probably the elections had just been held, and this letter serves as a report of the result.

[9] *blessed.* [10] *know, let me inform you.*

[11] Depends on **nihil** (**300**). Supply **accēpī.**

[12] For **cōgitō** ; similarly **ferēmus** below.

[13] *with*, etc. The charges against Catiline were brought by a friend of his to secure an acquittal before his enemies could have him tried on these charges.

Spērō, sī absolūtus erit, coniūnctiōrem illum nōbīs fore in ratiōne[1] petītiōnis; sīn aliter acciderit, hūmāniter ferēmus.

Tuō adventū[2] nōbīs opus est mātūrō; nam prōrsus summa[3] hominum est opīniō tuōs familiārēs,[4] nōbilēs 5 hominēs, adversāriōs honōrī[5] nostrō fore. Ad eōrum voluntātem mihi conciliandam maximō tē mihi ūsuī fore videō. Quārē Iānuāriō mēnse, ut cōnstituistī, cūrā ut Rōmae sīs.[6]   (A. I. 2)

174.   3. THE TRIAL OF CLODIUS[7]

Quaeris ex mē quid acciderit dē iūdiciō, quod tam 10 praeter opīniōnem omnium factum sit, et simul vīs scīre quō modō ego minus quam soleam proeliātus sim. Respondēbō tibi ὕστερον πρότερον Ὁμηρικῶς.[8] Ego enim, quam diū senātūs auctōritās mihi dēfendenda fuit, sīc ācriter et vehementer proeliātus sum ut clāmor 15 concursusque maximā cum meā laude fierent. Quod sī tibi umquam sum vīsus in rē pūblicā fortis, certē mē in illā causā admīrātus essēs.

---

[1] in the matter of.   [2] For case see **338.**

[3] With **opīniō**: settled opinion.

[4] While Atticus was not a noble, he had close relations with them and had a good deal of influence through his wealth.

[5] my election.

[6] Since the next letter to Atticus was not written until 61 B.C., it seems that Atticus came to Rome as requested and probably helped Cicero very much in his candidacy.

[7] Written to Atticus in July, 61 B.C. Clodius had been tried for sacrilege, and Cicero had been a witness against him. Clodius was acquitted through bribery of the jurors, but he never forgave Cicero and eventually brought about his banishment.

[8] **hysteron proteron Homērikōs;** the second (point) first à la Homer. In the Odyssey of Homer, Odysseus' early adventures are told after some of the later ones.

Summō discessū[1] bonōrum, plēnō forō servōrum,[2]
xxv iūdicēs ita fortēs tamen fuērunt ut, summō prōpositō perīculō, vel perīre māluerint quam perdere
omnia;[3] xxxi fuērunt quōs famēs magis quam fāma

FIG. 99. A CORNER OF THE PALATINE HILL

In the foreground, remains of early walls; in the background at the right,
the house of Augustus. Many rich men had their homes on this hill.

5 commōverit;[4] quōrum Catulus cum vīdisset quendam,
" Quid vōs," inquit, " praesidium ā nōbīs postulābātis?[5]
An nē nummī vōbīs ēriperentur timēbātis?"

---

[1] *despite the withdrawal* (ablative of attendant circumstances). In
the omitted portion Cicero tells about the bribing.

[2] Sent by Clodius to intimidate honest citizens.

[3] *i.e.* twenty-five jurors voted for conviction.

[4] *i.e.* the jurors thought rather of their financial needs than their
reputations, when tempted by bribes. Note the pun.

[5] The jurors had asked police protection, presumably against Clodius'
thugs.

Surgit pulchellus puer.[1] " Quō usque," inquit, " hunc rēgem ferēmus ? " " Rēgem appellās," inquam, " cum Rēx tuī mentiōnem nūllam fēcerit ? "[2] Ille autem Rēgis hērēditātem spē dēvorārat. — " Domum,"[3] inquit, " ēmistī." " Putēs,"[4] inquam, " dīcere : iūdicēs ēmistī."[5] — " Iūrantī," inquit, " tibi nōn crēdidērunt." " Mihi vērō," inquam, " xxv iūdicēs crēdidērunt, xxxi, quoniam nummōs ante accēpērunt, tibi nihil crēdidērunt."[5] Magnīs clāmōribus afflīctus conticuit et concidit.

Nunc est exspectātiō comitiōrum, in quae, omnibus [10] invītīs, trūdit noster Magnus[6] Aulī fīlium,[7] atque in eō neque auctōritāte neque grātiā pugnat, sed quibus[8] Philippus[9] omnia castella expugnārī posse dīcēbat in quae modo[10] asellus onustus aurō posset ascendere.

(A. I. 16. 1, 5, 10, 12)

175. 4. THE THREATS OF CLODIUS[11]

Noster Pūblius[12] mihi minitātur, inimīcus est ; impen- [15] det negōtium,[13] ad quod tū scīlicet advolābis. Videor

---

[1] The scene is now in the senate, some time after the trial. Clodius rises to defend himself against a speech made by Cicero. His cognomen was Pulcher, on which Cicero puns in contemptuously calling him **pulchellus,** *handsome little fellow.*

[2] Another pun ; **Rēx** was the name of a man (cf. King) who had not left Clodius an expected legacy.

[3] Cicero had paid $175,000 for a house on the Palatine, and Clodius hints that he must have obtained the money through graft.

[4] *One would think that you.*

[5] A pun on the two meanings of **crēdō,** *believe* and *trust.*

[6] Pompey.   [7] *i.e.* a "nobody." The reference is to L. Afranius.

[8] *with those (weapons) with which.*

[9] Of Macedon, father of Alexander the Great.

[10] *provided that . . . to them,* a relative proviso clause. How could a donkey laden with gold capture a fort ?

[11] Written to Atticus in July, 59 B.C.

[12] Clodius. For the cause see the preceding letter.   [13] *trouble.*

mihi nostrum illum cōnsulārem exercitum[1] bonōrum
omnium, etiam satis bonōrum[2] habēre firmissimum.
Pompeius significat studium ergā mē nōn mediocre.
Īdem affirmat verbum dē mē illum[3] nōn esse factūrum ;
5 in quō nōn mē ille fallit, sed ipse fallitur.

FIG. 100. A VIEW OF MODERN ROME

A striking view from under the colossal horses on top of the monument
to Victor Emmanuel. In the foreground, the shops of the Forum of Trajan,
excavated in 1929.

Caesar mē sibi vult esse lēgātum. Honestior[4] haec
dēclīnātiō perīculī ; sed ego hoc nōn repudiō. Quid
ergō est ? Pugnāre mālō. Nihil tamen certī. Iterum

---

[1] *i.e.* the group of conservatives who supported him during his
consulship.

[2] With **satis**: *fairly conservative.*   [3] *i.e.* Clodius.

[4] *more honorable* than another appointment offered him. By accept-
ing such an appointment and leaving Rome Cicero would be safe from
Clodius' threats. Note the changes of attitude, which reveal Cicero's
nervousness.

dīcō : utinam adessēs! Sed tamen, sī erit necesse, arcessēmus. Quid aliud? quid? Hoc opīnor : certī sumus perīsse omnia. (A. II. 19. 4–5)

176. 5. DICTATED BUT NOT READ[1]

Numquam ante arbitror tē epistulam meam[2] lēgisse, nisi meā manū scrīptam. Ex eō colligere poteris 5 quantā occupātiōne distinear. Nam cum vacuī temporis nihil habērem,[3] et cum recreandae vōculae[4] causā necesse esset[3] mihi ambulāre, haec dictāvī[3] ambulāns.

Prīmum igitur illud tē scīre volō, Sampsicerāmum,[5] nostrum amīcum, vehementer suī statūs paenitēre[6] 10 restituīque in eum locum cupere ex quō dēcidit,[7] dolōremque suum impertīre nōbīs et medicīnam interdum apertē quaerere, quam[8] ego posse invenīrī nūllam putō. (A. II. 23. 1–2)

177. 6. TEARS, IDLE TEARS[9]

Nōlī putāre mē ad quemquam longiōrēs epistulās 15 scrībere, nisi sī[10] quis ad mē plūra scrīpsit cui putō rescrībī[11] oportēre; nec enim habeō quid scrībam, nec

---

[1] Written to Atticus in 59 B.C.   [2] *of mine.*   [3] Epistolary tense (**360**).

[4] Diminutive of **vōx**: *my poor little voice.* He had been making too many speeches in court.

[5] A nickname for Pompey, from the name of the Oriental potentates whom Pompey had conquered. The word is object of **paenitēre** and subject of **cupere.**

[6] Impersonal, with direct object and genitive of the cause. Make personal: *regrets his situation.* The reference is to the formation of the First Triumvirate by Caesar, Pompey, and Crassus.

[7] Pompey's popularity had waned.

[8] With **nūllam:** *but I don't think any.*

[9] Written to his wife and children October 5, 58 B.C., after being exiled.

[10] Omit.   [11] Impersonal: *a reply should be sent.*

hōc tempore quicquam difficilius faciō. Ad tē vērō et
ad nostram Tulliolam[1] nōn queō sine plūrimīs lacrimīs
scrībere; vōs enim videō esse miserrimās, quās ego
beātissimās semper esse voluī, idque praestāre dēbuī et,
5 nisi tam timidī[2] fuissēmus, praestitissem. (F. XIV. 2. 1)

178.　　　7. The Exile's Return[3]

Ad urbem ita vēnī ut nēmō ūllīus ōrdinis homō[4]
nōmenclātōrī[5] nōtus fuerit quī mihi obviam nōn

Fig. 101.　The Circus and the Palatine Hill

A restored view from the neighborhood of the Porta Capena.　The curious
building at the right was put up by the emperor Septimius Severus.

---

[1] Diminutive of affection: *my dear Tullia* (his daughter).

[2] *i.e.* in running off to exile instead of staying in Rome and fighting
the matter out with Clodius.

[3] Written to Atticus in September, 57 b.c., after his return to Rome.

[4] Omit, as superfluous with **nēmō**.

[5] Lit., "name caller," a slave who told his master the names of persons
met on the street.

vēnerit,[1] praeter eōs inimīcōs quibus id ipsum,[2] sē
inimīcōs esse, nōn licēret aut dissimulāre aut negāre.
Cum vēnissem ad portam Capēnam,[3] gradūs templōrum ab īnfimā plēbe complētī erant, ā quā[4] plausū
maximō cum esset mihi grātulātiō significāta, similis et 5
frequentia et plausus mē usque ad Capitōlium cele-
brāvit, in forōque et in ipsō Capitōliō mīranda multitūdō fuit. Postrīdiē in senātū, quī fuit diēs Nōn. Sept.,[5]
senātuī grātiās ēgimus. (A. IV. 1. 5)

179.   8. You Didn't Miss Much[6]

Omnīnō, sī quaeris, lūdī apparātissimī, sed nōn tuī 10
stomachī ;[7] coniectūram enim faciō dē meō. Nam
prīmum honōris causā in scaenam redierant iī quōs ego
honōris causā[8] dē scaenā dēcesse[9] arbitrābar. Dēliciae[10]
vērō tuae, noster Aesōpus,[11] eius modī fuit ut eī dēsinere
per[12] omnīs hominēs licēret. Is iūrāre cum coepisset, vōx 15
eum dēfēcit in illō locō : " Sī sciēns fallō."[13] Quid tibi
ego alia nārrem ?[14] Nōstī enim reliquōs lūdōs ; quī nē id

---

[1] *no one . . . was known . . . who did not come to meet me.*

[2] Object of **dissimulāre** and **negāre** and explained by **esse**.

[3] The gate in the wall of Rome which led to the Appian Way.

[4] *and . . . by them,* belongs in the **cum** clause.

[5] = **Nōnārum Septembrium.**

[6] Written to M. Marius in 55 B.C., to tell him that the plays given at the dedication of Pompey's theater were elaborate but uninteresting.

[7] Genitive : *to your taste.*

[8] A play on the meaning of the phrase : *in honor of the occasion . . . to save their honor.*

[9] = **dēcessisse.**   [10] *favorite.*

[11] A famous actor in his younger days.   [12] *by.*

[13] *i.e.* his voice happened to fail him just as he was saying these words while taking an oath.

[14] *should I tell* (**375**).

quidem lepōris[1] habuērunt quod solent mediocrēs lūdī. Apparātūs enim spectātiō tollēbat omnem hilaritātem, quō quidem apparātū[2] nōn dubitō quīn animō aequissimō caruerīs.   Quid enim dēlectātiōnis habent sescentī[3] 5 mūlī in Clytaemestrā,[4] aut in Equō Trōiānō[4] crēterrā-

Fig. 102. The Roman Theater at Orange, France

rum[5] tria mīlia, aut armātūra varia peditātūs et equitā-tūs in aliquā pugnā?   Quae populārem admīrātiōnem habuērunt, dēlectātiōnem tibi nūllam attulissent.

(F. VII. 1. 2)

---

[1] With id: *that charm.*

[2] With caruerīs (327).

[3] Merely an indefinitely large number, like our thousand.   Realism was rampant.

[4] *i.e.* the play by that name.   [5] *bowls,* of gold, representing booty.

180.   9. CICERO TURNS TUTOR[1]

Tua mandāta persequar dīligenter et adiungendīs[2] hominibus et in quibusdam nōn aliēnandīs.[3] Maximae vērō mihi cūrae erit ut Cicerōnem tuum nostrumque[4] videam scīlicet cotīdiē, sed īnspiciam quid discat quam saepissimē; et nisi ille contemnet, etiam magistrum[5] mē eī profitēbor, cuius reī nōn nūllam cōnsuētūdinem[5] nactus sum in hōc hōrum diērum ōtiō Cicerōne[6] nostrō minōre prōdūcendō.[7]   (Q. F. II. 13. 2)

181.   10. A FINE OPPORTUNITY[8]

Ego tē commendāre nōn dēsistō, sed quid prōficiam ex tē scīre cupiō. Spem maximam habeō in Balbō,[9] ad quem dē tē dīligentissimē et saepissimē scrībō. Illud soleō mīrārī, nōn mē totiēns accipere tuās litterās quotiēns ā Q. mihi frātre[10] afferantur. In Britanniä nihil esse audiō neque aurī neque argentī.[11] Id sī ita est, essedum aliquod capiās[12] suādeō et ad nōs quam prīmum recurrās. Sīn autem sine Britanniä tamen assequī quod volumus[13]

---

[1] Written to his brother Quintus in May, 54 B.C.

[2] Caesar's party.   [3] Pompey's party.

[4] Only one person is meant, the son of Quintus.

[5] *some experience.*   [6] Cicero's own son, M. Cicero, Jr.

[7] *by tutoring.* What literally?

[8] Written in June, 54 B.C., to Trebatius, a young friend who had become a member of Caesar's staff in Gaul on Cicero's recommendation. Most of Cicero's letters to him are full of banter.

[9] One of Caesar's officers.

[10] Quintus Cicero was one of Caesar's generals.

[11] Rumors about these no doubt had a share in attracting Caesar to Britain. Such rumors were probably based on the presence of tin in the island.

[12] *capture a war-chariot.* Supply **ut.**

[13] *i.e.* Trebatius' advancement by Caesar.

possumus, perfice ut sīs in familiāribus Caesaris.[1]
Multum tē in eō frāter adiuvābit meus, multum Balbus,
sed, mihi crēde, tuus pudor et labor plūrimum. Nactus
es imperātōrem līberālissimum, aetātem opportūnissi-
5 mam, commendātiōnem certē singulārem, ut tibi ūnum
timendum sit, nē ipse tibi dēfuisse videāre. (F. VII. 7)

182.   11. To the Greatest Lawyer
in — Samarobriva[2]

Ego sī forīs cēnitārem,[3] Cn. Octāviō, familiārī tuō,
nōn dēfuissem; cui tamen dīxī, cum mē aliquotiēns[4]
invītāret : " Ōrō tē, quis tū es? " Sed mercules, extrā
10 iocum, homō bellus[5] est ; vellem[6] eum tēcum abdūxis-
sēs. Quid agātis et ecquid[7] in Italiam ventūrī sītis hāc
hieme fac plānē sciam.[8] Balbus mihi cōnfirmāvit tē
dīvitem futūrum. Id utrum Rōmānō mōre[9] locūtus sit,
bene nummātum[10] tē futūrum, an quō modō Stōicī
15 dīcunt, omnēs esse dīvitēs quī caelō et terrā fruī possint,
posteā vidēbō. Quī istinc veniunt superbiam tuam
accūsant, quod negent tē percontantibus respondēre.[11]

---

[1] *see that you become one of Caesar's intimate friends.*

[2] Written to Trebatius, in November, 54 B.C.

[3] With **forīs**: *dining out.*

[4] *several times.* After the young Octavius repeatedly invited Cicero
to dinner, Cicero pretended jokingly not to know him.

[5] A colloquial word : *fine.*

[6] *I could wish.*

[7] *whether.*

[8] *let me know definitely.*

[9] *i.e.* literally.

[10] Colloquial : *loaded down with " coin."*

[11] With a double meaning, literally and in the legal sense of *give advice
to.* Trebatius was a legal expert.

Sed tamen est quod[1] gaudeās; cōnstat enim inter omnīs nēminem tē[2] ūnō Samarobrīvae[3] iūris perītiōrem esse. (F. VII. 16, 2–3)

FIG. 103. THE PALATINE HILL AT ROME

The building put up by Septimius Severus to enlarge the hill, as it was in the seventeenth century (cf. Fig. 101).

183. 12. As a Soldier, Trebatius Is a Fine Lawyer[4]

Lēgī tuās litterās, ex quibus intellēxī tē Caesarī nostrō valdē iūre cōnsultum[5] vidērī. Est quod[6] gaudeās tē in ista loca vēnisse ubi aliquid sapere vidērēre.[7]

---

[1] (something for) which io.   [2] Ablative of comparison.

[3] Locative. Now Amiens, where Caesar was in winter quarters. As the only lawyer there Trebatius was naturally the best.

[4] Written to Trebatius in December, 54 B.C.

[5] an expert in the law.

[6] (something for) which to.   [7] where you seem to know something.

Quod sī in Britanniam quoque profectus essēs,[1] profectō nēmō in illā tantā īnsulā perītior tē fuisset. Vērum tamen (rīdeāmus licet; sum enim ā tē invītātus) sub-invideō[2] tibi ultrō etiam arcessītum ab eō ad quem cēterī 5 nōn propter superbiam eius sed propter occupātiōnem aspīrāre nōn possunt. Sed tū in istā epistulā nihil mihi scrīpsistī dē tuīs rēbus, quae mercule mihi nōn minōrī cūrae sunt quam meae. Valdē metuō nē frīgeās in hībernīs. Quam ob rem camīnō lūculentō[3] ūtendum 10 cēnseō (idem Mūciō[4] et Mānīliō[4] placēbat), praesertim quī sagīs nōn abundārēs.[5] Quamquam vōs nunc istīc satis calēre[6] audiō; quō quidem nūntiō valdē mercule dē tē timueram. Sed tū in rē mīlitārī multō es cautior quam in advocātiōnibus,[7] quī neque in Ōceanō natāre[8] 15 volueris, studiōsissimus homō natandī, neque spectāre essedāriōs,[9] quem anteā nē andābatā[10] quidem dēfrau-dāre poterāmus. Sed iam satis iocātī sumus.

(F. VII. 10. 1–2)

---

[1] Trebatius had refused Caesar's invitation to take part in the second expedition to Britain. Note the pun.

[2] *I envy you a tiny bit.*

[3] *blazing fire.*

[4] Famous lawyers.

[5] *you are not oversupplied with.* Trebatius does not put on his uniform very often, *i.e.* he keeps out of battles.

[6] *i.e.* the enemy is " making it hot " for them.

[7] *legal matters.*

[8] Refers to Trebatius' refusal to go to Britain. What would Cicero have said on hearing that people actually could swim across the Channel!

[9] *chariot fighters.* The British chariots had knives attached. The Romans used them in their gladiatorial exhibitions, as they did the military equipment of many nations.

[10] *blindfolded gladiator*; ablative with **dēfraudāre.** At Rome Trebatius never missed the shows.

184.   13.   A Miracle : An Honest Governor[1]

Etsī in ipsō itinere et viā discēdēbant[2] pūblicānōrum tabellāriī,[3] et erāmus[2] in cursū, tamen surripiendum aliquid putāvī spatiī, nē mē immemorem mandātī tuī putārēs. Itaque subsēdī in ipsā viā, dum haec, quae longiōrem dēsīderant ōrātiōnem, summātim tibi per- 5 scrīberem.

Maximā exspectātiōne[4] in perditam et plānē ēversam in perpetuum[5] prōvinciam nōs vēnisse scītō prīdiē Kal. Sext. Audīvimus nihil aliud nisi cīvitātum gemitūs. Levantur tamen miserae cīvitātēs, quod nūllus fit 10 sūmptus in nōs[6] neque in lēgātōs neque in quaestōrem neque in quemquam. Scītō nōn modo nōs faenum,[7] aut quod ē lēge Iūliā[8] darī solet, nōn accipere, sed nē ligna quidem, nec praeter quattuor lectōs et tēctum[9] quemquam accipere quicquam, multīs locīs nē tēctum 15 quidem, et in tabernāculō manēre plērumque. Itaque incrēdibilem in modum concursūs[10] fīunt ex agrīs, ex vīcīs, ex domibus omnibus. Mehercule etiam adventū nostrō revīvīscunt. Iūstitia, abstinentia, clēmentia tuī Cicerōnis opīniōnēs omnium superāvit. (A. V. 16. 1–3) 20

---

[1] Written to Atticus in August, 51 B.C. Cicero was governor of the province of Cilicia at the time.

[2] Epistolary tense (**360**).

[3] *letter carriers of the tax collectors,* who maintained a postal system of their own.

[4] *i.e.* on the part of the natives.

[5] With **in** modifies **ēversam:** *for all time.*   [6] *for me.*

[7] *Hay* for the horses was bought, not obtained through levy by Cicero.

[8] A law introduced by Caesar, limiting the materials which might be levied upon by governors.

[9] *roof,* then *living quarters.*

[10] Out of curiosity to see this model governor.

185.   14. The Protest of the Panthers[1]

Dē panthērīs, per eōs quī vēnārī solent agitur man-
dātū meō dīligenter; sed mīra paucitās est, et eās quae
sunt valdē aiunt querī quod nihil cuiquam īnsidiārum[2]
in meā prōvinciā nisi sibi fīat; itaque cōnstituisse
5 dīcuntur in Cāriam ex nostrā prōvinciā dēcēdere. Sed
tamen[3] sēdulō fit, et in prīmīs ā Patiscō.[4]   Quicquid[5]
erit, tibi erit, sed quid esset plānē nesciēbāmus.[6]   Mihi
mercule magnae cūrae est aedīlitās tua.   Ipse diēs mē
admonēbat;[6] scrīpsī[6] enim haec ipsīs Megalēnsibus.[7]

(F. II. 11. 2)

186.   15. Storm-Bound[8]

10 Septimum iam diem Corcȳrae tenēbāmur,[9] Q. autem
pater et fīlius Būthrōtī.   Sollicitī erāmus[9] dē tuā
valētūdine mīrum in modum nec mīrābāmur[9] nihil ā
tē litterārum;[10] iīs enim ventīs istim[11] nāvigātur[12] quī sī

---

[1] Written to Caelius from Cilicia in April, 50 B.C.   Caelius wanted
Cicero to ship him some live panthers for the games he had to give at
Rome as curule aedile.   Cicero playfully couches his remarks in the
form of an official report and implies that this request is an imposition
on the province.

[2] *no trap*, both literally and figuratively of the plots of officials to rob
the provincials.

[3] In effect means *joking aside.*   [4] An official sent to look for panthers.

[5] Supply **panthērārum:** *You shall have all we get.*

[6] Epistolary tense (**360**).

[7] The festival of the goddess Cybele, celebrated by games conducted
by the aediles.

[8] Written from Corcyra (Corfu) in 50 B.C. to Tiro, Cicero's faithful
secretary, who was left behind at Patrae (Patras) in Greece on account of
illness.   Cicero was on his way home from his province.

[9] Epistolary tense (**360**).   [10] Supply **vēnisse** or **esse.**

[11] *from the place where you are* (Patrae).

[12] Impersonal: *one sails.*   If the wind permitted ships to sail from
Patrae to Corcyra, it would also permit Cicero to leave Corcyra.

essent,[1] nōs Corcȳrae nōn sedērēmus. Cūrā igitur tē et cōnfirmā et, cum commodē et per valētūdinem et per

Wide World

FIG. 104. GREEK STATUE

Found at Buthrotum (Butrinto) and presented to Italy by the king of Albania in 1929.

annī tempus nāvigāre poteris, ad nōs amantissimōs tuī[2] venī. Nēmō nōs amat quī tē nōn[5] dīligat; cārus omnibus exspectātusque veniēs. Cūrā ut valeās. Etiam atque etiam, Tīrō noster, valē. XV Kal. Dec. Corcȳrā.[3]   (F. XVI. 7) [10]

187. 16. MAKE HASTE SLOWLY[4]

A. d. V Kal. Dec. servus Cn. Plancī Brundisī tandem aliquandō mihi ā tē exspectātissimās litterās reddidit, datās[5] Īdibus Nov., quae mē molestiā [15] valdē levārunt; utinam omnīnō līberāssent! Sed tamen Asclāpō[6] medicus plānē cōnfirmat propediem[7] tē valentem fore. Nunc quid ego tē horter [20] ut omnem dīligentiam adhibeās ad convalēscendum? Tuam prūdentiam, temperantiam,

---

[1] *that if they were (blowing).*   [2] Pronoun, not adjective.

[3] *from Corcyra.* At other times the locative is used. For the date see **410.**

[4] Written to Tiro from Brundisium ten days after the preceding letter.

[5] *written.* Cf. the derivative *date.*   [6] Nominative: *Dr. Asclapo.*

[7] *shortly.*

amōrem ergā mē nōvī; sciō tē omnia factūrum ut nōbīscum quam prīmum sīs; sed tamen ita velim,[1] ut nē quid properēs. Symphōniam[2] Lȳsōnis vellem

Keystone View Co.

FIG. 105. THE HARBOR AT BRUNDISIUM

vītāssēs,[3] nē in quārtam hebdomada[4] incidereś; sed
5 quoniam pudōrī tuō māluistī obsequī[5] quam valētūdinī, reliqua[6] cūrā. Curiō mīsī[7] ut medicō honōs[8] habērētur

---

[1] *I should like.*

[2] *concert.* Lyso, at whose house Tiro was staying, invited him to a dinner concert. Tiro, although not feeling well, went out of politeness.

[3] *I could wish you had avoided.*

[4] Accusative singular (Greek form) of **hebdomas,** *crisis* (lit., *seventh day*). It was thought that a crisis came every seventh day, and a fourth such crisis would be dangerous.

[5] *yield to your politeness.*   [6] *in other respects.*

[7] *I am writing to Curius* (a banker at Patrae).

[8] *fee.* What derivative with this meaning?

et tibi daret quod opus esset; mē cui iussisset cūrātū-
rum.[1] Equum et mūlum Brundisī tibi relīquī.[2]
Rōmae vereor nē ex Kal. Iān. magnī tumultūs sint.[3]
Nōs agēmus omnia modicē.

Reliquum est ut tē hoc rogem et ā tē petam, nē temere[5]
nāvigēs. Solent nautae festīnāre quaestūs suī causā.
Cautus sīs, mī Tīrō; mare magnum et difficile tibi
restat. Sī poteris, cum Mesciniō[4] (cautē is solet
nāvigāre); sī minus, cum honestō[5] aliquō homine
cuius auctōritāte nāviculārius moveātur. In hōc[10]
omnem dīligentiam sī adhibueris tēque nōbīs incolu-
mem steteris,[6] omnia ā tē habēbō. Etiam atque
etiam,[7] noster Tīrō, valē. Medicō, Curiō, Lȳsōnī dē
tē scrīpsī dīligentissimē. Valē, salvē.[8] (F. XVI. 9. 2–4)

188. 17. USE YOUR OWN JUDGMENT[9]

Cōnsīderandum vōbīs etiam atque etiam, animae[15]
meae,[10] dīligenter putō quid faciātis, Rōmaene[11] sītis an
mēcum an aliquō tūtō locō. Id nōn sōlum meum

---

[1] Depends on **mīsī**: *I am writing that I will take care (of its repayment) to whomsoever he says.* Cicero will pay the money to Curius' agent
at Rome. Note what complete credit facilities the Romans had. How
would Cicero arrange matters to-day?

[2] Epistolary tense (**360**). Note how Cicero thinks of every detail:
the horse for Tiro, the mule for his baggage.

[3] Because of the approaching conflict between Caesar and Pompey.

[4] Supply **nāvigā**. He was a Roman official, whose wishes would be
respected by the shipowners.

[5] *of standing.*   [6] *bring yourself.*

[7] *Again and again.*   [8] *Farewell and be well.*

[9] Written to Terentia and Tullia in January, 49 B.C. They asked
Cicero whether they should stay in Rome in view of the threatened
arrival of Caesar and his army.

[10] *my dears.*   [11] *whether at Rome.*

cōnsilium est sed etiam vestrum. Mihi veniunt in
mentem haec, Rōmae vōs esse tūtō posse per Dolābellam,[1] eamque rem posse nōbīs adiūmentō esse, sī quae
vīs aut sī quae rapīnae fierī coeperint. Sed rūrsus illud
5 mē movet, quod videō omnīs bonōs[2] abesse Rōmā et eōs

FIG. 106. INTERIOR OF A ROMAN HOUSE AT POMPEII

mulierēs suās sēcum habēre. Haec autem regiō in quā
ego sum, nostrōrum est cum oppidōrum tum etiam
praediōrum,[3] ut et multum esse mēcum et, cum abierī-
tis, commodē et in nostrīs[4] esse possītis. Mihi plānē
10 nōn satis cōnstat adhūc, utrum[5] sit melius. Vōs

---

[1] Tullia's husband. He was with Caesar.

[2] *conservatives*, followers of Pompey.

[3] *consists not only of my towns but also of my estates.* The towns were
in the district assigned to him for defense.

[4] Supply **praediīs.**   [5] *which of the two.*

vidēte quid aliae faciant istō locō[1] fēminae, et nē,[2]
cum velītis, exīre nōn liceat. Id velim[3] dīligenter
etiam atque etiam vōbīscum et cum amīcīs cōnsīderētis.
Domus ut prōpugnācula[4] et praesidium habeat, Philo-
tīmō[5] dīcētis. Et velim tabellāriōs īnstituātis[6] certōs,[7] 5
ut cotīdiē aliquās ā vōbīs litterās accipiam. Maximē
autem date operam ut valeātis, sī nōs vultis valēre.
VIIII Kal. Formiīs.   (F. XIV. 18)

189.   18. CAESAR AND POMPEY[8]

Lippitūdinis[9] meae signum tibi sit librārī manus[10] et
eadem causa brevitātis, etsī nunc quidem quod scrībe- 10
rem nihil erat.[11] Omnis exspectātiō nostra erat[11] in
nūntiīs Brundisīnīs.[12] Sī nactus hic[13] esset Gnaeum
nostrum, spēs dubia pācis; sīn ille[14] ante trāmīsisset,[15]
exitiōsī bellī metus. Sed vidēsne in quem hominem
inciderit rēs pūblica? quam acūtum, quam vigilantem, 15
quam parātum?[16] Sī mehercule nēminem occīderit nec
cuiquam[17] quicquam adēmerit, ab iīs quī eum maximē
timuerant maximē dīligētur. Multum mēcum mūnici-
pālēs hominēs loquuntur, multum rūsticānī. Nihil
prōrsus aliud cūrant nisi agrōs, nisi vīllulās, nisi num- 20

---

[1] *of your position.*   [2] With **vidēte**: *be careful lest.*

[3] *I should like.*   [4] *barricades.* **Domus** is subject of **habeat.**

[5] A freedman in charge of the house.

[6] Supply **ut**: *I should like you to appoint.*

[7] *regular, i.e.* slaves whose one duty is to carry letters.

[8] Written to Atticus March 1, 49 B.C.   [9] *sore eyes.*

[10] *handwriting;* subject of **sit.**   [11] Epistolary tense (**360**).

[12] *messages from Brundisium*, where Pompey was.

[13] Caesar.   [14] Pompey.   [15] *crossed (the Adriatic).*

[16] *i.e.* Caesar.

[17] Dative of separation (**315**). Caesar was pursuing his usual policy
of mildness.

mulōs[1] suōs. Et vidē quam conversa rēs est :[2] illum[3] quō anteā cōnfīdēbant metuunt, hunc amant quem timēbant. Id quantīs nostrīs peccātīs vitiīsque ēvēnerit nōn possum sine molestiā cōgitāre. Quae autem 5 impendēre putārem,[4] scrīpseram[4] ad tē et iam tuās litterās exspectābam.[4]   (A. VIII. 13)

190.   19. THE DARKNESS OF DESPAIR[5]

Nihil habēbam[6] quod scrīberem. Neque enim novī quicquam audieram[6] et ad tuās omnīs rescrīpseram[6] prīdiē. Sed cum mē aegritūdō nōn sōlum somnō 10 prīvāret, vērum nē vigilāre quidem sine summō dolōre paterētur, tēcum[7] ut quasi loquerer, in quō ūnō acquiēscō, hoc nesciō quid,[8] nūllō argūmentō prōpositō, scrībere īnstituī.

Āmēns mihi fuisse videor ā prīncipiō, et mē ūna haec 15 rēs torquet, quod nōn omnibus in rēbus lābentem vel potius ruentem Pompeium tamquam ūnus manipulāris[9] secūtus sim. Vīdī hominem[10] XIIII K. Febr. plēnum formīdinis. Illō ipsō diē sēnsī quid ageret.[11] Num-

---

[1] The diminutives express contempt : *their worthless farm houses and their dirty dollars.* What part does self-interest play in such matters to-day?

[2] The indicative indirect question after **vidē** is a survival of an old construction.

[3] Pompey. Who therefore is meant by **hunc?**

[4] Epistolary tense (**360**).

[5] Written to Atticus March 18, 49 B.C.

[6] Epistolary tense (**360**).

[7] Belongs in the **ut** clause. It is the antecedent of **quō.**

[8] With **nesciō**: *trifle.*

[9] *a common private, i.e.* obeying implicitly without questioning.

[10] Pompey.

[11] *i.e.* Pompey's plan to leave Italy.

quam mihi posteā placuit[1] nec umquam aliud in aliō
peccāre[2] dēstitit.

Huius bellī genus fūgī et eō magis, quod crūdēliōra
etiam cōgitārī et parārī vidēbam. Mē, quem nōn
nūllī cōnservātōrem istīus urbis, quem parentem esse 5

FIG. 107. A ROMAN VILLA NEAR POMPEII

dīxērunt, Getārum et Armeniōrum et Colchōrum cōpiās
ad eam addūcere?[3] mē meīs cīvibus famem, vāstitātem
īnferre Italiae? Hunc prīmum mortālem esse,[4] deinde

---

[1] The subject is Pompey.

[2] *make one mistake after the other.*

[3] Infinitive of exclamation with **mē** as subject: *I lead an army of
Getans, Armenians, and Colchians against it!* Pompey's plan was to
recruit an army in the East, the scene of his great conquests.

[4] *I used to think that in the first place he* (Caesar) *was* (*only*) *a human
being.*

etiam multīs modīs posse exstinguī[1] cōgitābam, urbem autem et populum nostrum servandum ad immortālitātem, quantum in nōbīs esset,[2] putābam, et tamen spēs quaedam mē sustentābat fore ut aliquid convenī
5 ret[3] potius quam aut hic[4] tantum sceleris aut ille tantum flāgitī admitteret.[5] Alia rēs nunc tōta est, alia mēns mea. Sōl, ut est in tuā quādam epistulā, excidisse mihi ē mundō vidētur. Ut aegrōtō, dum anima est, spēs esse dīcitur, sīc ego, quoad Pompeius in Italiā
10 fuit, spērāre nōn dēstitī.   (A. IX. 10. 1–3)

191.   20. DON'T COME[6]

Quod[7] nōs in Italiam salvōs vēnisse gaudēs, perpetuō gaudeās velim ; sed perturbātī dolōre animī[8] magnīsque iniūriīs metuō nē id consilī cēperīmus quod nōn facile explicāre[9] possīmus. Quārē quantum potes adiuvā ;
15 quid autem possīs mihi in mentem nōn venit. In viam quod tē dēs hōc tempore, nihil est.[10] Et longum est iter et nōn tūtum, et nōn videō quid prōdesse possīs, sī vēnerīs. Valē. D.[11] pr. Nōn. Nov. Brundisiō. (F. XIV. 12)

---

[1] *put out of the way* (Caesar).   [2] *as far as it lay in our power.*

[3] *that some agreement would be made (between them).*

[4] Caesar.   Who then is **ille**?   [5] *commit.*

[6] Written to his wife Terentia in 48 B.C. on his return from Greece after the flight of Pompey. This and the following short, formal notes are among his last letters to Terentia before their divorce. Their differences began during Cicero's exile over the way she managed affairs at Rome.

[7] *As to the fact that.*

[8] *agitated by mental anguish;* **perturbātī** modifies the subject of **cēperīmus** (Cicero).

[9] *get out of.* If the Pompeians were to win, they would not pardon his return to Italy.

[10] *there is no reason why* (**quod**).   [11] For **Datum.**

192. 21. With Best Regards, Yours Truly[1]

Sī valēs, bene est. Ego valeō.[2] Valētūdinem tuam velim cūrēs[3] dīligentissimē ; nam mihi et scrīptum et nūntiātum est tē in febrim subitō incidisse. Quod celeriter mē fēcistī dē Caesaris litterīs certiōrem, fēcistī mihi grātum. Item posthāc, sī quid opus erit, sī quid acciderit novī, faciēs ut sciam. Cūrā ut valeās. Valē. D. iiii Nōn. Iūn. 5

(F. XIV. 8)

193. 22. The Blame for Tullia's Unhappiness[4]

S. v. b. E. v.[5] Tullia nostra vēnit ad mē pr.[6] Īdūs Iūn. Cuius summā virtūte et singulārī hūmānitāte graviōre etiam sum dolōre affectus nostrā[7] factum esse neglegentiā, ut longē aliā in fortūnā esset atque[8] eius pietās[9] ac dignitās postulābat. Nōbīs erat[10] in animō Cicerōnem[11] ad Caesarem mittere, et cum eō Cn. Sallustium.[12] Sī profectus erit, faciam tē certiōrem. Valētūdinem tuam cūrā dīligenter. Valē. xvii Kal. Quīnctīlīs. 10 15

(F. XIV. 11)

194.   23. Changed My Mind[13]

Sī valēs, bene est. Cōnstituerāmus, ut ad tē anteā scrīpseram, obviam Cicerōnem Caesarī[14] mittere, sed

---

[1] Written to Terentia in 47 B.C.

[2] A formal expression, already rare in Cicero's day (cf. p. 35, n. 3).

[3] *I should like you to take care of.*   [4] Written to Terentia in 47 B.C.

[5] = Sī valēs bene (est). Ego valeō.   [6] = prīdiē.

[7] The emphatic position of **nostrā** shows that the blame was really Terentia's. Dolabella, Tullia's husband, turned out to be a worthless fellow. The marriage had been arranged by Terentia against Cicero's wishes while he was in Cilicia.

[8] With aliā : *far different than.*   [9] *devotion* to her parents.

[10] Epistolary tense (**360**).   [11] Cicero, Jr.   [12] Not the historian.

[13] Written to Terentia in 47 B.C.   [14] With **obviam** : *to meet Caesar.*

mūtāvimus cōnsilium, quia dē illīus adventū nihil audiēbāmus. Dē cēterīs rēbus, etsī nihil erat novī, tamen quid velīmus et quid hōc tempore putēmus opus esse ex Siccā[1] poteris cognōscere. Tulliam adhūc

FIG. 108. TUSCULUM IN ANCIENT TIMES

Cicero had a villa near here. It was close enough to Rome so that he could come here for short vacations.

5 mēcum teneō. Valētūdinem tuam cūrā dīligenter. Valē. XII Kal. Quīnctīlīs. (F. XIV. 15)

195. 24. PREPARE FOR COMPANY[2]

In Tusculānum[3] nōs ventūrōs putāmus aut Nōnīs aut postrīdiē. Ibi ut[4] sint omnia parāta. Plūrēs enim fortasse nōbīscum erunt et, ut arbitror, diūtius ibi

---

[1] The bearer of the letter.

[2] Written to Terentia in 47 B.C. This is the last letter to Terentia, written shortly before seeing her after an absence of nearly two years.

[3] His villa at Tusculum.   [4] Supply cūrā before ut.

commorābimur.¹ Lābrum² sī in balineō nōn est, ut³ sit ;
item cētera quae sunt ad vīctum et ad valētūdinem
necessāria. Valē. Kal. Oct. dē Venusīnō.⁴ (F. XIV. 20)

196. 25. CICERO DEVELOPS AN APPETITE⁵

Dupliciter dēlectātus sum tuīs litterīs, et quod ipse
rīsī et quod tē intellēxī iam posse rīdēre ; mē autem ā 5
tē, ut scurram vēlitem,⁶ mālīs⁷ onerātum esse nōn mo-
lestē tulī ;⁸ illud doleō, in ista loca venīre mē, ut cōn-
stitueram, nōn potuisse ; habuissēs enim nōn hospitem,
sed contubernālem.⁹

Nōs iam ex arte istā¹⁰ tantum habēmus ut Verrium 10
tuum et Camillum¹¹ (quā munditiā¹² hominēs, quā
ēlegantiā !) vocāre¹³ saepius audeāmus. Sed vidē audāciam : etiam Hirtiō cēnam dedī, sine pāvōne¹⁴ tamen.
In eā cēnā coquus meus praeter iūs¹⁵ fervēns nihil nōn
potuit imitārī.¹⁶   15

---

¹ This must have made Terentia furious : no indication of the number of guests nor of the length of their stay.

² *wash-basin.*   ³ Supply **cūrā** before **ut**.   ⁴ His estate at Venusia.

⁵ Written to a young friend, Paetus, in August, 46 B.C.

⁶ With **mē**: *like a skirmishing jester.* The **scurrae** were professional
entertainers used at dinner parties. They aimed their jokes at the guests.

⁷ *apples.* They made fine missiles to throw at the jesters when the
latter became too personal. But in Cicero's case the apples are verbal —
there is a pun on **malīs,** *imprecations.*

⁸ *I did not mind.*

⁹ *boarder;* lit., *tent companion.* Cicero jokingly says that if he had
visited Paetus, he would have made a stay of indefinite length.

¹⁰ *i.e.* the fine art of eating, in which Paetus was an expert.

¹¹ Well-known epicures.   ¹² *exacting taste.*

¹³ *invite* to dinner.

¹⁴ *peacock,* a favorite but expensive dish of the epicures.

¹⁵ *sauce.* Evidently Hirtius' cook had a secret recipe for this.

¹⁶ *there was nothing that he could not imitate.*

Haec igitur est nunc vīta nostra : māne salūtāmus[1] domī et bonōs[2] virōs multōs, sed trīstīs, et hōs laetōs victōrēs, quī mē quidem perofficiōsē et peramanter observant.   Ubi salūtātiō dēflūxit,[3] litterīs mē involvō ; 5 aut scrībō aut legō.   Veniunt etiam quī mē audiunt

FIG. 109.   BATHS AT POMPEII

The niches in the wall were "lockers" for clothes — but without locks.   In spite of the slaves who watched the clothes, there was much stealing.

quasi doctum hominem, quia paulō sum quam ipsī doctior.   Inde corporī[4] omne tempus datur.   Patriam ēlūxī[5] iam et gravius et diūtius quam ūlla māter

---

[1] The morning reception (salūtātiō).

[2] *conservatives*, sad because Caesar was in the saddle.

[3] *is over;* the visitors *pour* out.   [4] *e.g.* to naps, exercise, baths, etc.

[5] From ēlūgeō: *I have mourned over.*

ūnicum fīlium. Sed cūrā, sī mē amās, ut valeās, nē ego, tē iacente,[1] bona tua comedim;[2] statuī enim tibi nē aegrōtō quidem parcere. (F. IX. 20)

197. 26. A FINE REPORT CARD[3]

Athēnās vēnī a. d. xɪ Kal. Iūn. atque ibi, quod maximē optābam, vīdī fīlium tuum dēditum optimīs studiīs[5] summāque modestiae fāmā.[4] Quā ex rē quantam voluptātem cēperim scīre poteris, etiam mē tacente; nōn enim nescīs quantī[5] tē faciam et quam prō[6] nostrō veterrimō vērissimōque amōre omnibus tuīs etiam minimīs commodīs, nōn modo tantō bonō[7] gaudeam. 10 Nōlī putāre, mī Cicerō, mē hoc auribus †tuīs dare;[8] nihil[9] adulēscente[10] tuō atque adeō[11] nostrō (nihil enim mihi ā tē potest esse sēiūnctum) aut amābilius omnibus iīs[12] quī Athēnīs sunt est aut studiōsius eārum artium quās tū maximē amās, hoc est optimārum. Itaque tibi, 15 quod vērē facere possum, libenter quoque grātulor nec minus etiam nōbīs, quod eum, quem necesse erat dīligere quāliscumque esset, tālem habēmus ut libenter quoque dīligāmus.

Quī cum mihi in sermōne iniēcisset[13] sē velle Asiam 20

---

[1] *lying ill.*   [2] Old form for **comedam:** *eat up.*

[3] Written to Cicero by Trebonius May 25, 44 B.C. Cicero, Jr., was studying at what might be called the University of Athens. Not all the reports about him were as favorable as this. His college education cost his father a good deal of money.

[4] *and with an excellent reputation for good conduct.*

[5] *how much I esteem you* (**308**).   [6] *in view of.*

[7] *so great a blessing* (*i.e.* of being the father of such a son).

[8] *flatter you.*   [9] Stronger than **nēmō.**

[10] Ablative of comparison.   [11] *or I should say.*   [12] Dative.

[13] *mentioned casually,* perhaps *hinted.*

vīsere, nōn modo invītātus, sed etiam rogātus est ā mē
ut id, potissimum nōbīs obtinentibus prōvinciam,[1]
faceret; cui nōs et cāritāte et amōre tuum officium
praestātūrōs[2] nōn dēbēs dubitāre. Illud quoque erit
5 nōbīs cūrae, ut Cratippus[3] ūnā cum eō sit, nē putēs in
Asiā fēriātum[4] illum ab iīs studiīs in quae tuā cohortā-
tiōne incitātur futūrum; nam illum parātum, ut videō,
et ingressum plēnō gradū[5] cohortārī nōn intermittēmus,
quō[6] in diēs[7] longius discendō exercendōque sē prō-
10 cēdat.   (F. XII. 16. 1–2)

---

[1] *preferably while I*, etc.   Trebonius was on his way to take up the
governorship of the province of Asia.

[2] *that I will perform your function* (as a father).

[3] The philosophy teacher of Cicero, Jr.

[4] *on a vacation from*, modifying **illum** (Cicero, Jr.).

[5] *starting ahead at full speed* (in his studies).

[6] = **ut.**   [7] *day by day.*

FIG. 110. THE CATTLE MARKET OF ANCIENT ROME
A restoration showing the **Forum Boārium** near the Tiber.

PART IV

198. PUBLIUS OVIDIUS NASO

Ovid was born in 43 B.C., the year in which Cicero was murdered, at Sulmo, about ninety miles east of Rome. He speaks proudly of his noble ancestry and states that his father was a man of considerable wealth.

With a brother exactly one year his senior, Ovid went to Rome for the best education to be had at that time, in rhetoric and law At his father's urging and against his own inclination, he began a public career by holding some minor offices, but his passion for poetry finally prevailed, and for the rest of his life he devoted himself to its cultivation.

FIG. 111. THE IMPERIAL PALACE

Augustus established the residence of the emperors on the Palatine Hill, though this portion was built later.

When Ovid was 50 years of age, in 8 A.D., he was notified by the emperor Augustus that he was *persona non grata* in court circles and must leave Rome for a place

called Tomi on the Black Sea (in what is now Bulgaria).
It is impossible to discover the exact reason for this
decree of banishment. Ovid says that it was due to a
" poem " and a " mistake." It is supposed that the
poem was his *Art of Love*, though this was written ten
years before. He lived in exile the rest of his life, in
spite of numerous pleas to the emperor. His death
occurred in 17 A.D.

Ovid gained his fame by the love poems of his earlier
years, but his greatest work was the *Metamor'phoses*, a
story of the transformation of animals, human beings,
and inanimate objects into other forms. These are
contained in fifteen books, thirteen of which deal with
Grecian myths and two with Roman. They follow a
certain chronological order from the creation down to
the poet's own day, and the two hundred or more
stories of change are told with a charm of style that
easily ranks the work as a masterpiece. Its subject
was best suited to Ovid's two particular gifts — his
power to write smoothly flowing verse and his ability
to tell stories. As the chief source book of Greek and
Roman mythology the poem has had an immense influence on modern literature and art.

The *Metamorphoses* was nearly complete when Ovid
received word of his banishment. In the first dark
hours of utter despondency he threw his copy of the
poem into the fire. But fortunately for us some copies
had already got into the hands of friends, and in this
way the work was preserved for posterity.

Ovid wrote another mythological work called the
Fasti, or " Calendar." This was in six books, one for
each month, from January to June, and dealt with

Roman holidays and the myths and legends connected with them. He was banished when he had completed his sixth book, or he would probably have carried the work through the remainder of the year.

199. Word Order in Latin Poetry

The order of words in Latin poetry is even freer than in prose. Words that belong together are often widely separated. This is especially true of adjectives and their nouns. Note particularly the following points, illustrated by references to lines in the first selection (Daedalus and Icarus):

1. The order, adjective — preposition — noun, is common. Often a number of other words come between the adjective and the preposition. In such cases preposition and noun are likely to be at the end of the line. Cf. 188, 201, 202.

2. An interlocking order, in which two or more phrases are involved, occurs frequently. A particular favorite is the use of two nouns and two adjectives in all possible combinations. Cf. 229–230.

3. A verb or participle is particularly likely to come between adjective and noun. Cf. 183, 192, 195, 196, 197, 200.

4. Subjects and other words often precede the introductory word of the subordinate clauses to which they belong. Cf. 203, 213–214, 217.

5. Coördinate conjunctions (**et, sed,** etc.) sometimes come second instead of first in their clauses.

6. Other remarkable characteristics are illustrated in the following lines: 211–212 (**nātō . . . suō**); 226 (appositive between adjective and noun).

200. DIRECTIONS FOR READING VERSE

English poetry depends for its rhythm upon the regular succession of word accents.[1] In Latin, however, the rhythm depends upon the regular recurrence of long and short syllables in groups, and the word accent is ignored. In both languages the unit is the syllable, corresponding to notes in music, grouped in feet, called bars in music.

Syllables are classed as long or short with reference to the time it takes to pronounce them. The rules for determining length are as follows:

1. A syllable is *naturally* long if it contains a long vowel or a diphthong.

2. A syllable is long *by position* if it contains a short vowel followed by two or more consonants or the double consonant **x** (= **cs**).

A mute (**p, b, c, g, t, d**) followed by a liquid (**l, r**) does not make a syllable long. There are occasional exceptions.

H is disregarded entirely. The combinations **qu** and **gu** (before a vowel) constitute one consonant; the **u** is disregarded.

In poetry a long syllable is treated as twice the length of a short syllable. Since a line of poetry is considered one long word, in a case like **in mē** the first word is a long syllable because the (short) vowel is followed by two consonants (**n, m**).

The following selections from Ovid's *Metamorphoses* are all written in the dactylic hexameter verse. A hexameter line is one containing six feet. A dactyl is a foot consisting of a long followed by two short syl-

---

[1] Observe that this is true in this opening line of Longfellow's *Evangeline*, which is written in dactylic hexameter:

"This' is the for'est prime'val, the mur'muring pines' and the hem'locks."

lables, written —∪∪.[1] A substitute for this is the spondee, consisting of two long syllables, ––. These two feet correspond to the musical notations ♩ ♪ ♪ and ♩ ♩. In the first four feet of the line either dactyl or spondee may be used; the fifth foot is almost always a dactyl; the sixth is always a spondee.[2]

If a word ends in a vowel or a vowel plus **m** and the next word begins with a vowel (or **h**) the first vowel disappears entirely (called " elision "; the vowel is said to be " elided ") : **atqu**(e) **ita,** pronounced **atquita, di**(em) **ālipedum,** pronounced **diālipedum.**

In reading, a beat (ictus) should be placed on the first syllable of every foot. The normal word accent should be ignored, though it will be found to agree regularly with the ictus in the last two feet and occasionally elsewhere.

Appreciation of the rhythm may be obtained in two ways :

1. By reading a number of lines aloud with careful attention to giving longer time to the long than to the short syllables and thus gradually getting into the swing of the rhythm.

2. By analyzing lines into their feet (" scanning ") before attempting to read, as follows :

Daédalus | íntere|ā, Crē|tēn lōn|gumque per|ōsus |

exsili|um, tāc|tusque lo|cī nā|tālis a|mōre,|

---

[1] Do not confuse this marking of syllables with the identical signs used in marking vowels.

[2] The last syllable is often short but the " rest " at the end of the line fills out the foot.

Fig. 112. The Death of Icarus
From a Pompeian wall painting.

201. THE FIRST AVIATORS — DAEDALUS AND ICARUS

Minos, king of Crete, to avenge the death of his son Androgeos, exacted as tribute from the Athenians each year seven boys and seven girls whom he fed to a huge monster called the Minotaur, kept in a remote part of his large palace, which was called the "labyrinth." This monster, half man and half bull, was slain by the hero Theseus with the aid of Ariadne, daughter of Minos, who furnished Theseus with a sword and with thread by which to retrace his steps from the labyrinth. Because Daedalus, the builder of the labyrinth, provided Ariadne with the clue to the maze of passage-ways, he was prevented from leaving the island.

Daedalus Decides to Leave Crete

Daedalus intereā, Crētēn[1] longumque perōsus
exsilium, tāctusque locī nātālis[2] amōre,
clausus erat pelagō. " Terrās licet," inquit, " et undās 185
obstruat,[3] at caelum certē patet ; ībimus illāc.
Omnia possideat,[4] nōn possidet āera Mīnōs."

Dīxit, et ignōtās animum dīmittit[5] in artīs,
nātūramque novat.[6] Nam pōnit in ōrdine pennās,
ā minimā coeptās,[7] longam breviōre sequente,[8]   190
ut clīvō crēvisse putēs.[9] Sīc rūstica quondam[10]
fistula[11] disparibus paulātim surgit avēnīs.

---

[1] A Greek form of the accusative.   [2] Athens.

[3] Supply **Mīnōs** : *Granted that Minos blocks.*

[4] *Granted that Minos owns everything.*

[5] *turns his attention.*   [6] *makes over nature's laws.*

[7] *beginning at the smallest (feather).*

[8] One would expect just the opposite : *a longer one following a short.*

[9] *so that one would think.* Note omission of **in** before **clīvō** (poetic). The row of feathers looked like trees on a hillside.

[10] *at times.*

[11] Associated with shepherds and the god Pan. What modern wind instrument is arranged in this manner?

Tum līnō mediās et cērīs alligat īmās,[1]
atque ita compositās parvō curvāmine flectit
195 ut vērās imitētur avīs. Puer Īcarus ūnā
stābat et, ignārus sua sē trāctāre perīcla,[2]
ōre renīdentī modo quās vaga mōverat aura
captābat plūmās, flāvam modo pollice cēram
mollībat,[3] lūsūque suō mīrābile patris
200 impediēbat[4] opus. Postquam manus uitima[5] coeptō[6].
imposita est, geminās opifex lībrāvit in[7] ālās
ipse suum corpus, mōtāque[8] pependit in aurā.

Daedalus Instructs His Son How to Fly

Īnstruit et[9] nātum, " Mediō "que[10] " ut līmite currās,[11]
Īcare," ait, " moneō, nē, sī dēmissior[12] ībis,
205 unda gravet pennās, sī celsior, ignis adūrat.
Inter utrumque volā ! Nec tē spectāre Boōtēn[13]
aut Helicēn[13] iubeō strictumque Ōrīonis ēnsem :
mē duce, carpe viam." Pariter praecepta volandī
trādit, et ignōtās umerīs accommodat ālās.
210 Inter opus monitūsque genae[14] maduēre senīlēs,

---

[1] Supply pennās.

[2] = perīcula: *unaware that he was handling things that meant his own destruction.*

[3] = molliēbat.

[4] Ovid had a little daughter who perchance bothered him at work.

[5] *the finishing touch.* How literally?

[6] Dative of the noun.   [7] *upon.*

[8] *put in motion (by his wings).*

[9] = etiam.   [10] Connects Īnstruit and ait.

[11] Not purpose, but object of moneō.

[12] *too low.*

[13] Accusative. This constellation and Helice are conspicuous in the northern skies; Orion rises in the south-east. Daedalus will do the piloting (by the stars) himself.

[14] Do not confuse with gēns, genus, or genū.

et patriae tremuēre manūs; dedit ōscula nātō —·
nōn iterum repetenda! — suō, pennīsque levātus
ante volat comitīque[1] timet, velut āles, ab altō[2]
quae teneram prōlem prōdūxit in āera nīdō,
hortāturque sequī[3] damnōsāsque ērudit artīs,   215
et movet ipse suās et nātī respicit ālās.

Icarus Flies Too Near the Sun

Hōs aliquis,[4] tremulā dum captat harundine piscīs,
aut pāstor baculō,[5] stīvāve[5] innīxus arātor,
vīdit et obstipuit, quīque[6] aethera carpere possent[7]
crēdidit esse deōs.   Et iam Iūnōnia laevā   220
parte Samos (fuerant Dēlosque Parosque relīctae),
dextra Lebinthus erat fēcundaque melle Calymnē,
cum puer audācī coepit gaudēre volātū[8]
dēseruitque ducem caelīque cupīdine tāctus
altius ēgit iter; rapidī vīcīnia sōlis   225
mollit odōrātās,[9] pennārum vincula, cērās;
tābuerant cērae: nūdōs quatit ille lacertōs,
rēmigiōque[10] carēns nōn ūllās percipit aurās,[11]

---

[1] *for his companion* (**311**).   [2] With **nīdō**.

[3] Supply **eum** or **fīlium** as subject.   Poets frequently use the infinitive where Cicero employs the volitive substantive clause.

[4] With **piscātor** (*fisherman*) understood, and with **pāstor** and **arātor**.

[5] Ablative with **innīxus**.

[6] The antecedent is **eōs** understood; **-que** connects **obstipuit** and **crēdidit**.

[7] For mood see **387**.

[8] Perhaps his father flew too slowly for him.

[9] Perhaps due to the melting wax, but probably Ovid is thinking of the fragrant flowers from which the honey was gathered.   Note the order: **vincula** is in apposition with **cērās**.

[10] *wings*, lit., *oarage*.   [11] *grips no air.*

ōraque[1] caeruleā patrium clāmantia nōmen
230 excipiuntur aquā, quae nōmen trāxit ab illō.[2]
 At pater īnfēlīx, nec iam[3] pater, " Īcare, " dīxit,
" Īcare," dīxit, " ubi es? quā tē regiōne requīram? "
" Īcare, " dīcēbat : pennās aspexit in undīs,
dēvōvitque suās artīs, corpusque sepulchrō
235 condidit. Et tellūs[4] ā nōmine dicta sepultī.

(Met. VIII. 183–235)

Read Bulfinch, pp. 192–194; Gayley, pp. 246–248; Guerber, pp. 253–255; Sabin, pp. 260–261.

Word Study. — What English words are derived from **nātālis** (184), **clīvō** (191), **flectit** (194), **plūmās** (198), **mollībat** (199), **senīlēs** (210), **ōscula** (211), **ērudit** (215), **piscīs** (217), **caeruleā** (229).

A *bacillus* is a " little staff," so called from its shape; the word is derived from **baculum**.

---

[1] It is better English to make *he* the subject: *as his lips call his father's name, he,* etc.

[2] The Icarian Sea.   [3] *and (yet) no longer.*

[4] The island Icaria west of Samos.

202.   MIDAS THE FOOL

While Bacchus was on his way into Phrygia from Thrace, Sile-
nus, his satyr companion, deserted him. Midas, king of Phrygia,
restored him to Bacchus, and the grateful god offered him any boon
he might choose.

A Foolish Choice

Ille[1] male ūsūrus[2] dōnīs, ait, " effice,[3] quicquid
corpore contigerō, fulvum vertātur in aurum."
Annuit optātīs[4] nocitūraque mūnera solvit
Līber[5] et indoluit quod nōn meliōra petīsset.[6]   105

Laetus abit gaudetque malō[7] Berecyntius[8] hērōs
pollicitīque[9] fidem tangendō singula temptat
vixque sibī crēdēns nōn altā[10] fronde[11] virentem
īlice dētrāxit virgam : virga[12] aurea facta est.
Tollit humō saxum : saxum quoque palluit aurō.   110

Contigit et[13] glaebam : contāctū glaeba potentī
māssa fit.   Ārentis Cereris[14] dēcerpsit aristās :
aurea messis erat.   Dēmptum[15] tenet arbore pōmum :
Hesperidas[16] dōnāsse putēs.[17]   Sī postibus altīs
admōvit digitōs, postēs radiāre videntur.   115

---

[1] Midas.   [2] destined to make a bad use of.

[3] Supply ut after **effice**.   [4] Supply **rēbus**: his prayer.

[5] Bacchus.   [6] For mood see **389**.

[7] Note how Ovid by using this word, with **male** (102), **nocitūraque**
(104), **nōn meliōra** (105), emphasizes the baneful effect of this choice.

[8] Midas was son of Cybele, worshiped on Mt. Berecyntus in Phrygia.

[9] Noun, with **fidem**: the truth of the promise.

[10] Litotes (**157**) ; modifies **īlice**.

[11] Ablative of respect with **virentem**.

[12] Juxtaposition of words for effect.   So also in next line.

[13] = **etiam**.   [14] By metonymy for **frūmentī** (**407**).

[15] plucked from.

[16] Daughters of Atlas and guardians of the tree which bore golden
apples.   Greek accusative form.

[17] one might think.

118 Vix spēs ipse suās animō capit,[1] aurea fingēns
omnia. Gaudentī[2] mēnsās posuēre ministrī
120 exstrūctās dapibus nec tostae frūgis egentēs.[3]
Tum vērō, sīve ille suā Cereālia dextrā
mūnera contigerat, Cereālia dōna rigēbant;
sīve dapēs avidō convellere dente parābat,
lāmina fulva dapēs, admōtō dente, premēbat.[4]
125 Miscuerat pūrīs auctōrem[5] mūneris undīs:
fūsile per rictūs aurum fluitāre vidērēs.[6]

Midas Freed from the Golden Touch by Bacchus

Attonitus novitāte malī, dīvesque miserque.
effugere optat opēs, et quae modo vōverat ōdit.
Cōpia nūlla famem relevat; sitis ārida guttur
130 ūrit, et invīsō meritus torquētur ab aurō,
ad caelumque manūs et splendida bracchia tollēns,
" dā veniam, Lēnaee[7] pater! peccāvimus," inquit,
" sed miserēre, precor, speciōsōque ēripe damnō."[8]
Mīte[9] deum[10] nūmen: Bacchus peccāsse fatentem[11]
135 restituit factīque fidē[12] data mūnera solvit.[13]
" Nēve male optātō maneās circumlitus[14] aurō,
vade, " ait, " ad magnīs vīcīnum Sardibus amnem[15]

---

[1] *realizes.*   [2] Supply **eī.**

[3] *not lacking bread* (lit., *roasted grain*).

[4] *covered.* The object is **dapēs**.

[5] Bacchus, *i.e.* wine. A daring figure (**407**).

[6] *one might have seen.*   [7] Epithet of Bacchus (vocative).

[8] Oxymoron or contradictory statement. **Damnum** could never be
really **speciōsum.** What does Midas mean?

[9] Supply **est.**   [10] For **deōrum.**   [11] Supply **eum.**

[12] *in proof of the act* (of restoration).

[13] *took away the boon.*

[14] From **circumlinō,** *incased;* lit., *smeared.*

[15] The Pactolus.

perque iugum rīpae lābentibus obvius[1] undīs
carpe viam, dōnec veniās ad flūminis ortūs,
spūmigerōque tuum fontī,[2] quā plūrimus exit,[3]   140
subde caput, corpusque simul, simul ēlue[4] crīmen."
Rēx iussae succēdit aquae.[5]   Vīs aurea tīnxit
flūmen et hūmānō dē corpore cessit in amnem.
Nunc quoque iam veteris perceptō sēmine vēnae
arva rigent[6] aurō[7] madidīs pallentia glaebīs.   145

The Musical Contest between Apollo and Pan

Ille perōsus opēs silvās et rūra colēbat
Pānaque[8] montānīs habitantem semper in antrīs.
Pingue[9] sed ingenium mānsit, nocitūraque, ut ante,
rūrsus erant dominō[10] stultae praecordia mentis.[11]
Nam freta prōspiciēns lātē riget arduus altō   150.
Tmōlus in ascēnsū clīvōque extēnsus utrōque
Sardibus hinc, illinc parvīs fīnītur Hypaepīs.[12]
Pān ibi dum tenerīs iactat sua carmina nymphīs
et leve cērātā modulātur harundine[13] carmen,

---

[1] *meeting the waters, i.e.* going upstream.

[2] Depends upon **subde**.   [3] *gushes forth most abundantly.*

[4] By zeugma it has two objects.   Translate *cleanse your body and wash away your guilt.*

[5] Dative.

[6] *the fields, after receiving that seed of ancient vein, are stiff,* etc.

[7] With **madidīs**.

[8] Accusative.

[9] *stupid.*   The prose order is **Sed pingue.**

[10] For case see **313**.   [11] **praecordia mentis = mēns.**

[12] *i.e.* the cities of Sardis and Hypaepa are located opposite to each other at the base of Mt. Tmolus.

[13] Pan's pipes were made of reeds fastened together with wax.   For the origin of these pipes, read the story of Pan and Syrinx, Bulfinch, pp. 42–43; Gayley, pp. 66–67: Guerber, pp. 300–301; Sabin, pp. 153–155.

155 ausus Apollineōs prae[1] sē contemnere cantūs,
iūdice sub Tmōlō[2] certāmen vēnit ad impār.[3]

Monte suō senior iūdex[4] cōnsēdit et aurēs
līberat arboribus;[5] quercū coma caerula tantum
cingitur, et pendent circum cava tempora glandēs.
160 Isque deum pecoris[6] spectāns, " in iūdice, " dīxit,
" nūlla mora est." [7]　Calamīs agrestibus īnsonat ille
barbaricōque Midān[8] (aderat nam forte canentī)
carmine[9] dēlēnit.　Post hunc sacer ōra retorsit
Tmōlus ad ōs Phoebī; vultum sua silva secūta est.
165　Ille caput[10] flāvum laurō Parnāside vīnctus[11]
verrit humum[12] Tyriō saturātā mūrice pallā,
īnstrictamque fidem[13] gemmīs et dentibus Indīs
sustinet ā laevā,[14] tenuit manus altera plēctrum.
Artificis[15] status ipse fuit.　Tum stāmina doctō
170 pollice sollicitat, quōrum dulcēdine captus
Pāna iubet Tmōlus citharae[16] summittere cannās.

Midas' Folly Punished by Apollo

Iūdicium sānctīque placet sententia montis
omnibus; arguitur[17] tamen atque iniūsta vocātur

---

[1] *in comparison with his own.*　　[2] *i.e.* the god of the mountain.
[3] As shown by the results of the contest.
[4] *the elderly judge* (Tmolus) *sat on his mountain.*
[5] Separation.　Trees grew on the top of the mountain like hair on a head.
[6] Pan was god of flocks.　　　　[7] *the court is ready.*
[8] Greek accusative ending.
[9] We might almost say " jazz."
[10] For case see **325.**　　　[11] From **vinciō.**
[12] A majestic movement.　See Fig. 19.
[13] From **fidēs, -is,** *lyre.*　　[14] *on the left side.*
[15] *was that of an artist.*　　　[16] Dative.
[17] *is criticized;* **sententia** is subject.

ūnīus sermōne Midae.   Nec Dēlius[1] aurēs
hūmānam stolidās patitur retinēre figūram,   175
sed trahit in spatium[2] villīsque albentibus implet
īnstabilēsque īmās[3] facit et dat[4] posse movērī.
Cētera sunt hominis;[5] partem damnātur in[6] ūnam
induiturque[7] aurēs lentē gradientis asellī.

   Ille quidem cēlāre cupit turpīque pudōre[8]   180
tempora purpureīs temptat vēlāre tiārīs;[9]
sed solitus[10] longōs ferrō[11] resecāre capillōs
vīderat hoc famulus.[12]   Quī, cum nec prōdere vīsum
dēdecus audēret, cupiēns efferre sub aurās,[13]
nec posset reticēre tamen, sēcēdit humumque   185
effodit et, dominī quālēs aspexerit aurēs,
vōce refert parvā terraeque immurmurat haustae[14]
indiciumque suae vōcis tellūre regestā
obruit[15] et scrobibus[16] tacitus discēdit opertīs.[17]
Crēber harundinibus tremulīs ibi surgere lūcus[18]   190
coepit et, ut prīmum plēnō mātūruit annō,[19]
prōdidit agricolam:[20] lēnī nam mōtus ab austrō
obruta verba refert dominīque coarguit aurēs.

                                                (Met. XI. 102–193)

---

[1] Apollo, born on the island of Delos.
[2] Humorously: *draws them out into space*, i.e. *lengthens them.*
[3] *loose at the bottom.*   [4] *makes them.*   [5] Predicate genitive.
[6] *in respect to;* governs **partem.**
[7] Active ("middle" voice): *puts on.*
[8] *because of the disgrace.*   [9] *turbans.*   [10] With **famulus.**
[11] By metonymy (**407**), the material for the instrument.
[12] = **servus;** *i.e.* his barber.
[13] *to broadcast (it).*   What literally?
[14] *into the place which he had scooped out.*
[15] *covered up the testimony of his words.*   [16] *hole.*
[17] Distinguish between **operiō** and **aperiō.**
[18] Distinguish from **locus, luctus,** and **lūx.**
[19] *in the course of a year.*   [20] *i.e.* the barber.

Read Bulfinch, pp. 46–48; Gayley, pp. 110–111, 157–158; Guerber, pp. 74–75; 177–179; Sabin, pp. 19–21.

Word Study. — What English words are derived from **digitōs** (115), **lāmina** (124), **tīnxit** (142), **stultae** (149), **contemnere** (155), **glandēs** (159), **stāmina** (169), **stolidās** (175), **capillōs** (182), **reticēre** (185).

Fig. 113.   Ceres

FIG. 114. AURORA AND THE SUN

Apollo in his chariot is surrounded by the Hours. Above the horses is Lucifer, with a torch. Aurora leads the way. From the painting by Guido Reni.

203. The Reckless Driving of Phaëthon

Phaëthon, son of Apollo, the sun-god, quarreled with a playmate who, tiring of Phaëthon's boasting about his parentage, said in effect, " You believe everything your foolish mother says and are all puffed up in thinking that Apollo is your father." Phaëthon then decided to go to Apollo to find out the truth.

Phaëthon Arrives at the Palace of the Sun

Quō simul[1] acclīvō Clymenēia[2] līmite prōlēs
vēnit et intrāvit dubitātī tēcta parentis,   20
prōtinus ad patriōs sua fert vēstīgia vultūs,
cōnsistitque procul ; neque enim propiōra ferēbat[3]
lūmina. Purpureā vēlātus veste sedēbat
in soliō Phoebus clārīs lucente smaragdīs.
Ā[4] dextrā laevāque Diēs et Mēnsis et Annus   25
Saeculaque et positae spatiīs aequālibus Hōrae[5]
Vērque novum[6] stābat cīnctum flōrente corōnā.
Stābat nūda[7] Aestās et spīcea serta[8] gerēbat,
stābat et Autumnus, calcātīs sordidus ūvīs,
et glaciālis Hiems, cānōs hirsūta capillōs.[9]   30

Apollo Offers Phaëthon Any Gift He May Ask

Inde locō medius[10] rērum novitāte paventem
Sōl oculīs iuvenem, quibus aspicit omnia, vīdit,[11]

---

[1] *as soon as . . . to this place.*

[2] Adjective from **Clymenē** (mother of Phaëthon).

[3] *did not* (i.e. *could not*) *bear.*   [4] *On.*   [5] See Fig. 114.

[6] Because everything is new and fresh.

[7] *in light garments.* Note how each season has its appropriate characteristics.

[8] *garlands of grain.*   [9] Accusative of respect (**325**).

[10] Lit., *middle in position,* i.e. *in the middle of the room.*

[11] The prose order = **Sōl oculīs . . . iuvenem rērum novitāte paventem vīdit.**

" quae " que[1] " viae tibi causa? Quid hāc," ait, "arce[2]
    petīstī,
prōgeniēs, Phaethōn, haud īnfitianda parentī? "[3]
35 Ille refert : " Ō lūx immēnsī pūblica mundī,
Phoebe pater, sī dās ūsum mihi nōminis huius,
nec falsā Clymenē culpam sub imāgine cēlat,
pignora[4] dā, genitor, per quae tua vēra propāgō
crēdar, et hunc animīs errōrem[5] dētrahe nostrīs."
40   Dīxerat, at genitor circum caput omne micantēs
dēposuit radiōs[6] propiusque accēdere iussit,
amplexūque datō, " nec[7] tū meus esse negārī[8]
dignus es, et Clymenē vērōs," ait, " ēdidit ortūs.[9]
Quŏque[10] minus dubitēs, quodvīs pete mūnus, ut
    illud,
45 mē tribuente, ferās.   Prōmissīs testis adestō
dīs iūranda palūs,[11] oculīs incognita nostrīs!"[12]
    Vix bene dēsierat,[13] currūs rogat ille paternōs
inque diem[14] ālipedum iūs et moderāmen equōrum.[15]

---

[1] Connects vīdit and ait.
[2] Ablative of place; used frequently in poetry without preposition.
[3] The all-seeing Phoebus anticipates his son's query.
[4] For singular; very common in poetry. So too animīs in next line.
[5] *uncertainty.*
[6] The dazzling rays were like a crown which Phoebus took off.
[7] = et nōn; with et in the next line : *not only . . . not . . . but also.*
[8] The infinitive with dignus is poetical.
[9] *told your true origin.*
[10] = utque (369).
[11] *let the swamp* (the River Styx in the lower world) *by which the gods swear be a witness.* A binding oath for a god.
[12] Naturally the sun could not penetrate to the lower world.
[13] From dēsinō.
[14] *for a day.*
[15] What genitive? Note the chiasmus (154).

Apollo Regrets His Promise

Paenituit iūrāsse patrem.[1] Quī terque quaterque
concutiēns illūstre caput, " temerāria," dīxit,   50
" vōx mea facta tuā[2] est. Utinam prōmissa licēret[3]
nōn dare! Cōnfiteor, sōlum hoc tibi, nāte, negārem.[4]
Dissuādēre licet : nōn est tua tūta voluntās.
Magna[5] petis, Phaethōn, et quae nec vīribus istīs
mūnera conveniant nec tam puerīlibus annīs.   55
Sors tua mortālis, nōn est mortāle quod optās.
Plūs etiam quam quod superīs contingere possit,
nescius affectās.[6] Placeat sibi quisque licēbit,[7]
nōn tamen igniferō quisquam cōnsistere in axe
mē valet exceptō. Vāstī quoque rēctor Olympī,   60
quī fera terribilī iaculātur[8] fulmina dextrā,
nōn aget hōs currūs ; et quid Iove maius habēmus?

Only a Skilled Aviator Can Fly Apollo's Course

" Ardua prīma via[9] est et quā[10] vix māne recentēs[11]
ēnītuntur equī ; media[12] est altissima caelō,[13]
unde[14] mare et terrās ipsī mihi saepe vidēre   65
sit timor,[15] et pavidā trepidet formīdine pectus.
Ultima prōna via est et eget moderāmine certō ;
tunc etiam quae[16] mē subiectīs excipit undīs,

---

[1] *The father was sorry he had sworn.* How literally?
[2] Supply **vōce**.   [3] For mood and tense see **376**, *b*.
[4] A contrary to fact conclusion ; the condition is implied in **licēret**.
[5] With **mūnera**.   [6] *you unwittingly aspire to.*
[7] *although each (of the gods) may be well satisfied with himself.*
[8] *hurls.*   [9] *the first part of the way.*   [10] *and one along which.*
[11] *(though) fresh.*   [12] Supply *via*.
[13] For **in caelō**.   [14] = **dē quā**.
[15] *I am afraid to look at* — because so far away.
[16] The prose order = **Tēthys ipsa quae . . . excipit solet verērī nē**,

nē ferar in praeceps, Tēthys solet ipsa verērī.
70 Adde quod[1] assiduā rapitur vertīgine caelum[2]
sīderaque alta trahit celerīque volūmine torquet.
Nītor in adversum,[3] nec mē, quī cētera, vincit
impetus, et rapidō contrārius ēvehor orbī.[4]

" *I Prove Myself Your Father by a Father's Fear!* "

" Finge datōs currūs : quid agēs?   Poterisne rotātīs
75 obvius īre polīs,[5] nē tē citus auferat axis?[6]
Forsitan et lūcōs illīc urbēsque deōrum
concipiās animō[7] dēlūbraque dītia dōnīs
esse?   Per īnsidiās iter est fōrmāsque ferārum.[8]
84 Nec tibi quadrupedēs[9] animōsōs ignibus illīs
85 quōs in pectore habent, quōs ōre et nāribus[10] efflant,
in prōmptū[11] regere est ; vix mē patiuntur, ubi ācrēs
incaluēre animī cervīxque repugnat habēnīs.[12]

" At tū, fūnestī nē sim tibi mūneris auctor,
nāte, cavē, dum rēsque[13] sinit, tua corrige vōta.

---

etc.   Tethys was wife of Oceanus and mother of Clymene.   Thus it is her son-in-law that she receives as he plunges into the western sea.

[1] *the fact that.*

[2] The sky was conceived as a firmament to which the stars were attached and by which their fires were fed.   This wheeled about in a direction contrary to that of the sun and the planets.   We know, of course, that the rotation of the earth explains the phenomenon.

[3] *against it,* referring to the apparent course of the sun.

[4] *contrary to the swiftly moving heavens.*

[5] *go against the whirling heavens.*   [6] = **caelum.**

[7] *perhaps you may imagine.*

[8] The signs of the zodiac (Lion, Scorpion, etc.), through which the sun passes in his apparent annual course.   But Phoebus forgets that Phaëthon wanted to try his luck for one day only.

[9] Object of **regere** (86).

[10] *from their nostrils.*   [11] With **in** = **facile.**   [12] For case see **313.**

[13] ⁓que connects **cavē** and **corrige.**

Scīlicet ut nostrō genitum tē sanguine[1] crēdās,   **90**
pignora certa petis? Dō pignora certa timendō,
et patriō pater[2] esse metū probor. Aspice vultūs
ecce meōs; utinamque oculōs in pectora possēs
īnserere et patriās intus dēprēndere cūrās!
Dēnique quicquid habet[3] dīves, circumspice, mundus,   **95**
ēque[4] tot ac tantīs caelī terraeque marisque
posce bonīs aliquid; nūllam patiēre[5] repulsam.[6]
Dēprecor[7] hoc ūnum, quod vērō nōmine poena,
nōn honor est; poenam, Phaethōn, prō mūnere poscis.
Quid mea colla tenēs blandīs, ignāre, lacertīs?   **100**
Nē dubitā,[8] dabitur (Stygiās iūrāvimus[9] undās)
quodcumque optāris;[10] sed tū sapientius optā."

A Description of the Sun-Chariot

Fīnierat monitūs; dictīs tamen ille repugnat
prōpositumque premit flagratque cupīdine currūs.[11]
Ergō quā licuit[12] genitor cūnctātus ad altōs   **105**
dēdūcit iuvenem, Vulcānia mūnera, currūs.[13]
Aureus axis erat, tēmō[14] aureus, aurea summae
curvātūra[15] rotae, radiōrum argenteus ōrdō;[16]
per iuga chrȳsolithī[17] positaeque ex ōrdine gemmae

---

[1] Ablative of origin (**329**).   [2] Juxtaposition of like words.
[3] The clause is object of **circumspice** (*observe*).
[4] *and from;* **ē** governs **bonīs**.   [5] Future second person singular.
[6] Noun.   [7] *plead against.*
[8] **Nē** with the imperative is not favored in prose.
[9] *I have sworn by.*   [10] What is the full form?
[11] Objective genitive depending upon **cupīdine**.
[12] *as long as he could;* with **cūnctātus**.
[13] Poetic plural, object of **ad**; **mūnera** is in apposition.
[14] *pole.*   [15] *rim.*
[16] *the spokes, arranged in order, were of silver.*
[17] *topaz.*

110 clāra repercussō reddēbant lūmina Phoebō.[1]
    Ḷumque ea magnanimus[2] Phaethōn mīrātur opusque
    perspicit, ecce vigil[3] nitidō patefēcit ab ortū
    purpureās Aurōra forēs et plēna rosārum[4]
    ātria. Diffugiunt stellae, quārum agmina cōgit[5]
115 Lūcifer et caelī statiōne novissimus exit.
    Quem[6] petere ut terrās mundumque rubēscere vīdit
    cornuaque extrēmae[7] velut ēvānēscere lūnae,
    iungere[8] equōs Tītān vēlōcibus imperat Hōrīs.
    Iussa deae celerēs[9] peragunt ignemque vomentēs,[10]
120 ambrosiae sūcō saturōs, praesēpibus[11] altīs
    quadrupedēs dūcunt adduntque sonantia frēna.
    Tum pater ōra suī sacrō medicāmine nātī
    contigit et rapidae fēcit patientia[12] flammae,
    imposuitque comae[13] radiōs, praesāgaque lūctūs[14]
125 pectore sollicitō repetēns suspīria dīxit :

Apollo Instructs His Son How to Drive

" Sī potes hīs saltem monitīs[15] pārēre parentis,
parce, puer, stimulīs et fortius[16] ūtere[17] lōrīs.

---

[1] Lit., *gave back the light to the reflected sun.*

[2] *high-spirited.*   [3] With **Aurōra.**

[4] *i.e.* rosy light.

[5] *whose marshaled hosts Lucifer drives along; i.e.* the Morning Star
fades last from sight.

[6] *i.e.* Lucifer. Subject of **petere.** Ovid thinks of the star as setting
rather than fading. The subject of **vīdit** is **Tītān** (the sun).

[7] *i.e.* in its last quarter.

[8] What is the prose construction? See **370.**

[9] We use an adverb: *quickly.*   [10] With **quadrupedēs.**

[11] For **ex praesēpibus.** In poetry prepositions are often omitted.

[12] Lit., *made his face* (**ōra**) *enduring of.*

[13] Dative. Why?   [14] For case see **302.**

[15] For case see **313.**   [16] *firmly.*   [17] What form ?

Sponte suā properant; labor est inhibēre volentēs.[1]
Utque ferant aequōs et caelum et terra calōrēs, 134
nec preme nec summum mōlīre per aethera currum.[2] 135
Altius ēgressus[3] caelestia tēcta[4] cremābis,
īnferius terrās; mediō tūtissimus ībis.
Neu tē dexterior[5] tortum dēclīnet ad Anguem,[6]
nēve sinisterior pressam rota dūcat ad Āram;[7]
inter utrumque tenē. Fortūnae cētera mandō, 140
quae iuvet[8] et melius quam tū tibi cōnsulat optō.
Dum loquor, Hesperiō[9] positās in lītore mētās[10]
ūmida[11] nox tetigit. Nōn est mora lībera nōbīs;
poscimur, et fulget tenebrīs aurōra fugātīs.
Corripe lōra manū; vel, sī mūtābile pectus 145
est tibi, cōnsiliīs, nōn curribus ūtere[12] nostrīs!
Dum potes et solidīs etiam nunc sēdibus[13] astās,
dumque male optātōs nōndum premis īnscius axēs,[14]
quae[15] tūtus spectēs, sine[16] mē dare lūmina terrīs."

---

[1] Supply **equōs**.

[2] *do not dip the chariot down nor make it soar through the upper air.*

[3] Conditional. [4] *the homes of the gods.*

[5] With **rota,** which is used by metonymy (**407**) for **currus.**

[6] *writhing Dragon,* a constellation.

[7] *low-lying Altar,* a constellation.

[8] Depends upon **optō**: *who, I hope, may aid.*

[9] *western.* Night, rising from the east, has reached the western shores.

[10] *goals,* as if night were running a race.

[11] Stock epithet. Give an example of similar usage in English. Note how Ovid makes daybreak and the passing of the shadows of night occur independently of the sun.

[12] Zeugma (**409**).

[13] Ablative of place (**343**).

[14] Poetic plural and metonymy for **currum.**

[15] The antecedent is **lūmina**: *which you may behold.*

[16] Imperative.

As Phaëthon Loses Control, the Chariot Swerves
from Its Course

150 Occupat ille levem iuvenālī corpore currum,
statque super manibusque levēs contingere habēnās
gaudet, et invītō grātēs agit inde parentī.
Intereā volucrēs Pyroīs et Eōus et Aethōn,
Sōlis equī, quārtusque Phlegōn,[1] hinnītibus[2] aurās
155 flammiferīs implent, pedibusque repāgula pulsant.[3]
Quae[4] postquam Tēthys, fātōrum ignāra nepōtis,[5]
reppulit, et facta est immēnsī cōpia[6] caelī,
corripuēre viam,[7] pedibusque per āera mōtīs,
obstantēs scindunt nebulās, pennīsque levātī
160 praetereunt ortōs īsdem dē partibus Eurōs.
Sed leve pondus erat, nec quod[8] cognōscere possent[9]
Sōlis equī, solitāque iugum gravitāte carēbat.[10]
Utque labant curvae iūstō sine pondere[11] nāvēs
perque mare īnstabilēs nimiā levitāte feruntur,
165 sīc onere assuētō vacuus[12] dat in āere saltūs
succutiturque altē similisque est currus inānī.[13]
Quod simul ac sēnsēre, ruunt, trītumque relinquunt

---

[1] The names of the horses are Greek and mean *fiery, of the dawn, burning, blazing.*

[2] *neighing.* An onomatopoetic word, *i.e.* one which reproduces the sound; cf. *whinny.*

[3] Note the effect of these three words (**136**). Note also throughout Phaëthon's mad course the frequent use of dactyls, which the poets regularly employ to represent speed.

[4] The antecedent is **repāgula.**   [5] Explain the relationship.

[6] *chance at the sky.*   [7] *dashed along the way.*

[8] *nor one* (*i.e.* weight) *which.*   [9] For mood see **380.**

[10] Phaëthon was a " lightweight " in more senses than one.

[11] *proper ballast.*

[12] Modifies **currus,** which is subject of **dat** and **est.**

[13] Supply **curruī.**

quadriiugī spatium nec quō prius ōrdine[1] currunt.
Ipse pavet, nec quā[2] commissās[3] flectat habēnās,
nec scit quā sit iter, nec, sī sciat, imperet illīs.[4]   170

He Almost Bumps into a Constellation

Ut vērō summō dēspexit ab aethere terrās   178
īnfēlīx Phaethōn penitus penitusque[5] patentēs,
palluit, et subitō genua intremuēre timōre,   180
suntque oculīs tenebrae per tantum lūmen[6] obortae.[7]
Et iam māllet[8] equōs numquam tetigisse paternōs,
iam cognōsse genus[9] piget et valuisse rogandō,[10]
iam Meropis[11] dīcī cupiēns ita fertur ut ācta
praecipitī pīnus[12] Boreā, cui victa remīsit   185
frēna suus rēctor,[13] quam dīs vōtīsque relīquit.

Quid faciat?[14] multum caelī post terga relīctum,
ante oculōs plūs est.   Animō mētītur utrumque,
et modo,[15] quōs[16] illī fātum contingere nōn est,
prōspicit occāsūs,[17] interdum respicit ortūs.   190

---

[1] *nor do they run in the same path as before.*

[2] *he knows neither where he should . . . nor.*

[3] *intrusted* (*to him*).

[4] *nor if he did know, would he (be able to) control them.*

[5] *far, far below.*   Note alliteration.

[6] *in spite of the intense light.*   [7] *arose before.*

[8] *he would prefer.*   [9] *descent* (from Phoebus).

[10] *to have prevailed in his request.*

[11] *Merops'* (*son*).   Merops was Clymene's earthly husband.

[12] By metonymy, *ship.*

[13] *which the driver has let have the rein* (*i.e.* let go as it pleases), a curiously mixed comparison: the driver is compared to a helpless ship, which in turn is compared to a runaway horse.

[14] Deliberative subjunctive (**375**).

[15] With **interdum** : *now . . . now.*

[16] The antecedent is **occāsūs.**

[17] Supply **sōlis.**

Quidque agat¹ ignārus stupet, et nec frēna remittit
nec retinēre valet nec nōmina nōvit equōrum.
Sparsa quoque in variō passim mīrācula caelō
vāstārumque videt trepidus simulācra ferārum.
195 Est locus, in geminōs ubi bracchia concavat arcūs
Scorpius, et caudā flexīsque utrimque lacertīs

Fig. 115. The Temple of Apollo at Pompeii

porrigit in spatium signōrum membra duōrum.²
Hunc puer ut³ nigrī⁴ madidum sūdōre venēnī
vulnera curvātā minitantem⁵ cuspide vīdit,
200 mentis inops⁶ gelidā formīdine lōra remīsit.

---

¹ Indirect deliberative question: *not knowing what he should do.*
² The Scorpion sprawled out so that he took up the *space of two signs*
of the zodiac.
³ *when.*   ⁴ A stock epithet for poison.
⁵ With **hunc.**   ⁶ *losing his head.*

The Chariot Swoops Down and the Earth Catches Fire.

Quae[1] postquam summō tetigēre iacentia tergō,[2]
exspatiantur[3] equī, nūllōque inhibente, per aurās
ignōtae regiōnis eunt, quāque impetus ēgit,
hāc[4] sine lēge[5] ruunt altōque sub aethere fīxīs
incursant stellīs rapiuntque per āvia currum.   205
Et modo summa[6] petunt, modo per dēclīve viāsque
praecipitēs spatiō terrae[7] propiōre feruntur.
Īnferiusque[8] suīs frāternōs currere Lūna[9]
admīrātur equōs, ambustaque nūbila fūmant.
Corripitur flammīs, ut quaeque altissima, tellūs,[10]   210
fissaque agit rīmās[11] et sūcīs āret adēmptīs.
Pābula cānēscunt, cum frondibus ūritur arbor,
māteriamque[12] suō praebet seges ārida damnō.
Parva queror : magnae pereunt cum moenibus urbēs,
cumque suīs tōtās populīs incendia gentēs   215
in cinerem vertunt. Silvae cum montibus ārdent.

Sanguine tunc crēdunt[13] in corpora summa[14] vocātō[15] 235
Aethiopum populōs nigrum trāxisse[16] colōrem ;
tum facta est Libyē, raptīs ūmōribus aestū,
ārida.[17]
Nīlus in extrēmum fūgit perterritus orbem   254

---

[1] *these (reins).*   [2] *lying on the tops of their backs.*
[3] *dash from the course.*   [4] With **quā :** *wherever . . . there.*
[5] *restraint.*   [6] Substantive, neuter plural.   [7] Dative with **propiōre.**
[8] *i.e.* the sun-chariot is nearer the earth than the moon is.
[9] Diana, the moon-goddess, sister of Apollo.
[10] *The earth catches fire, the highest parts first;* lit., *(according) as each (part) is highest.*
[11] *develops cracks.*   [12] *fuel.*
[13] *people believe.*   [14] *surface of.*
[15] With **sanguine ;** ablative absolute.
[16] *took on.*   [17] Predicate adjective.

255 occuluitque caput, quod adhūc latet.¹ Ōstia septem
pulverulenta vacant, septem sine flūmine vallēs.

The Seas Begin to Dry Up

260   Dissilit² omne solum, penetratque in Tartara rīmīs³
lūmen et īnfernum terret cum coniuge rēgem ;⁴
et mare contrahitur, siccaeque est⁵ campus harēnae
quod modo pontus erat ; quōsque⁶ altum tēxerat aequor,
exsistunt montēs et sparsās Cycladas augent.⁷
265 Īma petunt piscēs, nec sē super aequora curvī⁸
tollere cōnsuētās⁹ audent delphīnes in aurās.
Corpora phōcārum¹⁰ summō¹¹ resupīna profundō¹²
exanimāta natant. Ipsum quoque Nērea¹³ fāma est
Dōridaque¹⁴ et nātās tepidīs¹⁵ latuisse sub antrīs.
270 Ter Neptūnus aquīs cum torvō bracchia vultū
exserere ausus erat, ter nōn tulit āeris ignēs.

Jupiter Smites Phaëthon and Shatters the Chariot¹⁶

304 At pater omnipotēns, superōs testātus et ipsum¹⁷
305 quī dederat currūs, nisi opem ferat, omnia fātō

---

¹ Great masses of vegetation made it seem that the river disappeared.

² *yawns open.* ³ *through the cracks.* ⁴ Pluto and Proserpina.

⁵ The subject is (id) **quod**, etc. ⁶ The antecedent is **montēs.**

⁷ *increase (the number of) the Cyclades* (islands in the Aegean Sea).

⁸ Referring to the form of their bodies as they plunge through the waters.

⁹ Modifies **aurās :** *as usual.* ¹⁰ *seals.* ¹¹ As in line 235.

¹² *sea.* Note the different words which Ovid uses for " sea."

¹³ Accusative (Greek ending) of **Nēreus,** a sea-god.

¹⁴ Accusative of **Dōris,** wife of Nereus.

¹⁵ The heat had penetrated even here.

¹⁶ In the omitted lines Earth appeals to Jupiter.

¹⁷ Apollo.

interitūra gravī, summam petit arduus[1] arcem,
unde solet nūbēs lātīs indūcere terrīs,[2]
unde movet tonitrūs vibrātaque fulmina iactat,
Sed neque quās[3] posset terrīs indūcere nūbēs
tunc habuit, nec quōs caelō dīmitteret imbrēs.   310
Intonat et dextrā lībrātum fulmen ab aure[4]
mīsit in aurīgam[5] pariterque animāque rotīsque
expulit[6] et saevīs compescuit ignibus ignēs.
Cōnsternantur equī et, saltū in contrāria[7] factō,
colla iugō ēripiunt, abruptaque lōra relinquunt.   315
Illīc frēna iacent, illīc tēmōne revulsus
axis, in hāc radiī frāctārum parte rotārum,
sparsaque sunt lātē lacerī vēstīgia currūs.

Phaëthon Falls to His Death

At Phaethōn, rutilōs[8] flammā populante capillōs,
volvitur in praeceps longōque per āera trāctū   320
fertur, ut interdum dē caelō stella[9] serēnō,
etsī nōn cecidit, potuit cecidisse vidērī.
Quem procul ā patriā dīversō maximus orbe[10]
excipit Ēridanus fūmantiaque abluit ōra.
Nāides Hesperiae trifidā[11] fūmantia flammā   325
corpora dant tumulō, signant quoque carmine[12] saxum :

---

[1] *mounting upward.*

[2] Dative or ablative? See **314.**   [3] With **nūbēs.**

[4] With **lībrātum**: *poised at the right ear,* as in throwing a javelin or a baseball.

[5] Who is meant?

[6] What figure? See **409.**   [7] *in opposite directions.*

[8] *ruddy.* A proleptic epithet, *i.e.* it anticipates the action of the flames.

[9] *i.e.* a falling star.   [10] *in a remote part of the globe.*

[11] *three-forked.*   [12] *epitaph.*

HIC SITUS EST PHAETHON CURRUS AURIGA PATERNI
QUEM SI NON TENUIT[1] MAGNIS TAMEN EXCIDIT[2] AUSIS.[3]

(Met. II. 19–328)

Read Bulfinch, pp. 49–57; Gayley, pp. 121–125; Guerber, pp. 83–88, 388; Sabin, pp. 21–24.

Word Study. — What English words are derived from **glaciālis** (30), **hirsūta** (30), **propāgō** (38), **trepidet** (66), **repercussō** (110), **ēvānēscere** (117), **calōrēs** (134), **latet** (255), **vibrāta** (308), **lacerī** (318), **abluit** (324)?

---

[1] *manage, hold on to.*

[2] *failed in;* lit., *fell out of.* Not a bad pun.

[3] *venture;* **magnīs** is emphatic. On a scorching hot day followed by a thunderstorm you may recall this story.

204. PYRAMUS AND THISBE

Two Babylonian lovers have been forbidden by their parents to see each other. They arrange a secret meeting by night under a mulberry tree outside the city walls. Misfortune attends the meeting, and what happens explains how the mulberry came to be red instead of white.

Love Suppressed Grows More Intense

Pȳramus et Thisbē, iuvenum pulcherrimus alter,   55
altera, quās[1] Oriēns habuit, praelāta[2] puellīs,
contiguās tenuēre[3] domōs, ubi dīcitur altam
coctilibus[4] mūrīs cīnxisse Semīramis[5] urbem.
Nōtitiam prīmōsque gradūs[6] vīcīnia fēcit ;
tempore crēvit amor. Taedae quoque iūre[7] coïssent,[8]   60
sed vetuēre patrēs. Quod[9] nōn potuēre vetāre,
ex aequō captīs ārdēbant mentibus ambō.
Cōnscius omnis abest ; nūtū signīsque loquuntur,
quōque magis[10] tegitur, tēctus[11] magis aestuat ignis.[12]

Fissus[13] erat tenuī rīmā, quam dūxerat[14] ōlim   65
cum fieret, pariēs domuī commūnis utrīque.
Id vitium nūllī[15] per saecula longa notātum

---

[1] The antecedent is **puellīs.**   [2] *excelling;* lit., *preferred to.*
[3] Third plural perfect.   [4] *made of brick;* lit., *baked.*
[5] Queen Semir′amis was the fabled founder of Babylon.
[6] *the first steps (of love).*
[7] *the bonds of marriage;* lit., *the law of the torch,* referring to the torch used in the marriage procession.
[8] Conclusion of a condition contrary to fact.
[9] *a thing which,* explained by the next line.
[10] With **quō:** *the more.*
[11] Juxtaposition of like words for emphasis.
[12] Just the opposite is true of a real fire.
[13] From **findō.** The subject is **pariēs.**
[14] *had developed.*   [15] For case see **317.**

(quid nōn sentit amor?)[1] prīmī vīdistis amantēs,
et vōcis fēcistis iter;[2] tūtaeque per illud
70 murmure blanditiae minimō trānsīre solēbant.
Saepe, ubi cōnstiterant, hinc Thisbē, Pȳramus illinc,
inque vicēs fuerat captātus anhēlitus ōris,[3]

FIG. 116. THISBE
By Burne-Jones.

" Invide, " dīcēbant, " pariēs, quid amantibus obstās?
Quantum erat,[4] ut sinerēs tōtō nōs corpore[5] iungī,
75 aut, hoc sī nimium est, vel ad ōscula danda patērēs![6]

---

[1] Yet love is said to be blind!
[2] *you made it (i.e. the crack) a pathway for your voices.*
[3] *and each had caught the other's breathing.*
[4] *how slight a matter it would be.*   [5] *in full embrace.*
[6] From **pateō**, not **patior**.

Nec sumus ingrātī ;[1] tibi nōs dēbēre fatēmur,
quod[2] datus est verbīs[3] ad amīcās trānsitus aurēs."
Tālia dīversā nēquīquam sēde locūtī
sub noctem[4] dīxēre " valē," partīque dedēre
ōscula quisque[5] suae nōn pervenientia contrā.   80

Fig. 117. Pyramus
By Burne-Jones.

The Lovers' Tryst

Postera nocturnōs aurōra remōverat ignēs,
sōlque pruīnōsās radiīs siccāverat herbās ;

---

[1] What figure? See **157**.   [2] *the fact that.*
[3] Dative.   [4] *at sun-down.*
[5] In apposition with the subject : *they, each to his own side (of the wall).*

ad solitum coiēre locum. Tum murmure parvō
multa prius[1] questī,[2] statuunt ut nocte silentī
85 fallere custōdēs foribusque excēdere temptent,[3]
cumque domō exierint, urbis quoque tēcta relinquant ;
nēve[4] sit errandum[5] lātō spatiantibus[6] arvō,
conveniant ad busta Ninī[7] lateantque sub umbrā
arboris : arbor ibī[8] nivēis ūberrima pōmīs,
90 ardua mōrus, erat, gelidō contermina[9] fontī.

A Lioness Puts Thisbe to Flight

Pacta placent ; et lūx[10] tardē discēdere vīsa
praecipitātur aquīs,[11] et aquīs nox exit ab īsdem.
Callida per tenebrās versātō cardine[12] Thisbē
ēgreditur fallitque suōs[13] adopertaque vultum[14]
95 pervenit ad tumulum dictāque sub arbore sēdit.
Audācem[15] faciēbat amor. Venit ecce recentī
caede leaena[16] boum[17] spūmantēs oblita[18] rictūs,[19]
dēpositūra[20] sitim vīcīnī fontis in undā.

---

[1] *first.*   [2] From **queror,** not **quaerō.**

[3] Volitive substantive clause, object of **statuunt.** So too **relinquant,
conveniant, lateant.**

[4] = **et nē.**

[5] *may not have to wander aimlessly.*

[6] Supply **eīs.** Why dative? See **317.**

[7] Ninus was the husband of Semiramis.

[8] Poetry sometimes preserves old forms, as the long **i** here.

[9] *next to.*   [10] *day.*

[11] The sun was thought to set in the ocean.

[12] *opening the door.*   [13] *her family.*

[14] *with face veiled.* For case see **325.**

[15] Supply **eam.**   [16] *lioness.*

[17] From **bōs.** Objective genitive with **caede.**

[18] From **oblinō.** How does it differ from the participle of **oblivīs-
cor ?**

[19] *jaws.* For case see **325.**   [20] Purpose : *to slake.*

Quam[1] procul ad[2] lūnae radiōs Babylōnia Thisbē
vīdit et obscūrum timidō pede fūgit in antrum,   100
dumque fugit, tergō[3] vēlāmina lāpsa relīquit.
Ut lea[4] saeva sitim multā compescuit undā,
dum redit in silvās, inventōs forte sine ipsā[5]
ōre cruentātō tenuēs laniāvit amictūs.

Pyramus, Believing that Thisbe Is Dead, Kills Himself

Sērius ēgressus vēstīgia vīdit in altō   105
pulvere certa[6] ferae, tōtōque expalluit ōre
Pȳramus. Ut vērō vestem quoque sanguine tīnctam
repperit, " ūna duōs, " inquit, " nox perdet amantēs.
Ē quibus[7] illa fuit longā dignissima vītā,[8]
nostra nocēns anima est : ego tē, miseranda,[9] perēmī,   110
in loca plēna metūs quī iussī nocte venīrēs[10]
nec prior hūc vēnī. Nostrum dīvellite corpus
et scelerāta ferō cōnsūmite vīscera morsū,
Ō quīcumque sub hāc habitātis rūpe, leōnēs ![11]
Sed timidī[12] est optāre necem." Vēlāmina Thisbēs[13]   115
tollit et ad pactae sēcum fert arboris umbram,
utque dedit nōtae[14] lacrimās, dedit ōscula vestī,
" accipe nunc," inquit, " nostrī quoque sanguinis
    haustūs."
Quōque[15] erat accīnctus, dēmīsit in īlia ferrum,
nec mora,[16] ferventī moriēns ē vulnere trāxit[17]   120

---

[1] *i.e.* leaenam.   [2] *by.*   [3] With lāpsa: *from her back.*
[4] = leaena (97).   [5] *i.e.* Thisbe.   [6] *clear* (with vēstīgia).
[7] *of these* (*i.e.* the lovers).   [8] For case see **349.**   [9] *poor girl.*
[10] See **370.** The infinitive is much more common.
[11] Vocative.
[12] Predicate genitive: *it is* (*the part*) *of a coward* (*merely*) *to wish for.*
[13] Genitive.   [14] With vestī.   [15] The antecedent is **ferrum.**
[16] With nec = et sine morā.   [17] Supply **ferrum.**

et iacuit resupīnus humō.[1]   Cruor ēmicat altē,
nōn aliter quam[2] cum vitiātō fistula plumbō
scinditur[3] et tenuī strīdente forāmine[4] longās[5]
ēiaculātur aquās atque ictibus[6] āera rumpit.
125 Arboreī fētūs[7] aspergine[8] caedis in ātram
vertuntur faciem, madefactaque sanguine rādīx
purpureō tingit pendentia mōra colōre.

Thisbe, Returning, Finds Pyramus in the Throes of Death

Ecce metū nōndum positō,[9] nē fallat[10] amantem,
illa redit iuvenemque oculīs animōque[11] requīrit,
130 quantaque vītārit nārrāre perīcula gestit;[12]
utque[13] locum et vīsā[14] cognōscit in arbore fōrmam,
sīc facit incertam pōmī color.   Haeret[15] an haec sit.
Dum dubitat, tremebunda videt pulsāre cruentum
membra solum,[16] retrōque pedem tulit ōraque buxō
135 pallidiōra gerēns exhorruit aequoris īnstar,[17]
quod tremit, exiguā cum summum[18] stringitur aurā.

---

[1] on the ground; humī (locative) might have been used.

[2] nōn aliter quam = sīcut (157).

[3] when a water-pipe has cracked because of a flaw in the lead.   The Romans had an elaborate water system, in which lead pipes brought water from the aqueducts to the houses.

[4] through a tiny, hissing hole.

[5] With aquās: long (streams of) water.

[6] jets.   [7] fruit.   [8] spray.

[9] For dēpositō: laid aside.

[10] i.e. by failing to keep the appointment.   The clause gives the purpose of redit.

[11] thought.   [12] longs.

[13] With sīc: and although . . . still.   [14] which she had seen (before).

[15] she is doubtful whether.   [16] ground.

[17] and with countenance paler than boxwood, she shivers like the sea.

[18] surface.

Sed postquam remorāta suōs cognōvit amōrēs,[1]
percutit indignōs[2] clārō plangōre lacertōs
et laniāta comās[3] amplexaque corpus amātum
vulnera supplēvit lacrimīs flētumque cruōrī[4]   140
miscuit et gelidīs in vultibus ōscula fīgēns
" Pȳrame," clāmāvit, " quis[5] tē mihi[6] cāsus adēmit?
Pȳrame, respondē! tua tē cārissima Thisbē
nōminat. Exaudī vultūsque attolle iacentēs! "

Thisbe Joins Her Lover in Death

Ad nōmen Thisbēs[7] oculōs iam morte gravātōs   145
Pȳramus ērēxit vīsāque recondidit illā.
Quae[8] postquam vestemque suam cognōvit et ēnse[9]
vīdit ebur[10] vacuum, "tua tē manus," inquit, "amorque
perdidit, īnfēlīx. Est et mihi[11] fortis in ūnum
hoc[12] manus, est et amor; dabit hic[13] in vulnera vīrēs. 150
Persequar exstīnctum[14] lētīque miserrima dīcar
causa comesque tuī; quīque[15] ā mē morte revellī
heu sōlā poterās, poteris nec[16] morte revellī.
Hoc[17] tamen ambōrum verbīs estōte[18] rogātī,

---

[1] *lover.*   [2] *not deserving, i.e.* they had done no wrong.

[3] *tearing her hair.* For case see **325.**   [4] Dative with **miscuit.**

[5] For **quī.**   [6] For case see **315.**

[7] Genitive.   [8] *i.e.* Thisbe.

[9] Ablative of separation with **vacuum.**

[10] Lit., *ivory,* but by metonymy (**407**) *sheath.*

[11] *I too have.* Why dative? See **316.**   [12] *for this one deed.*

[13] Though the vowel is short, the syllable is sometimes long in this word because it was at one time spelled **hicc.**

[14] Supply **tē:** *I shall follow thee in death.*

[15] Supply **tū** as antecedent of **quī** and as subject of **poteris.**

[16] *not even.*

[17] Object of **rogātī,** explained by the **ut** clause (156).

[18] Imperative second plural: *be asked,* i.e. *let me ask.*

155 Ō multum miserī, meus illīusque parentēs,
ut quōs[1] certus amor, quōs hōra novissima iūnxit,
compōnī tumulō nōn invideātis[2] eōdem.
At tū, quae rāmīs arbor[3] miserābile corpus
nunc tegis ūnīus, mox es tēctūra duōrum,
160 signa tenē caedis pullōsque et lūctibus aptōs
semper habē fētūs, geminī monumenta cruōris."
Dīxit et aptātō pectus mūcrōne sub īmum
incubuit ferrō,[4] quod adhūc ā caede tepēbat.
Vōta tamen tetigēre deōs, tetigēre parentēs;
165 nam color in pōmō est, ubi permātūruit, āter,
quodque rogīs superest,[5] ūnā requiēscit in urnā.

(Met. IV. 55–166)

Read Bulfinch, pp. 23–26; Gayley, pp. 147–149; Guerber, pp. 117–118; Sabin, pp. 181–183; Shakespeare, *Midsummer Night's Dream*, Act V, Scene 1.

Word Study. — What English words are derived from **contiguās** (57), **fissus** (65), **lateant** (88), **umbrā** (88), **cardine** (93), **boum** (97), **pulvere** (106), **vīscera** (113), **plumbō** (122), **strīdente** (123), **tepēbat** (163).

[1] Supply **nōs** as antecedent of **quōs** and as subject of **compōnī**.
[2] *begrudge.*
[3] Attracted into the clause; for **tū, arbor, quae.**
[4] Dative: *fell upon the sword.*
[5] *and all that remains from the funeral pyres, i.e.* the ashes.

205. The Pride and Fall of Niobe

Niobe, queen of Thebes, resents the preparations which her people make for a festival in honor of the goddess Latona and her two children, Apollo and Diana. She believes that she herself is more deserving of worship.

" Behold My Lineage, My Beauty, and My Children!"

Ecce venit comitum Niobē crēberrima[1] turbā,   165
vestibus intextō Phrygiīs spectābilis aurō,[2]
et, quantum īra sinit, fōrmōsa movēnsque decōrō
cum capite[3] immissōs umerum per[4] utrumque capillōs
cōnstitit ; utque oculōs circumtulit alta[5] superbōs,
" quis[6] furor[7] audītōs,[8] " inquit, " praepōnere vīsīs   170
caelestēs? Aut cūr colitur Lātōna per ārās,
nūmen adhūc sine tūre[9] meum est? Mihi Tantalus auctor,[10]
cui licuit sōlī superōrum tangere mēnsās.[11]
Plēiadum soror est genetrīx[12] mea, maximus Atlās
est avus, aetherium quī fert cervīcibus axem ;   175
Iuppiter alter avus. Socerō quoque glōrior illō.[13]
Mē gentēs metuunt Phrygiae, mē rēgia[14] Cadmī

---

[1] attended by.

[2] Ablative of description with **vestibus**: with gold woven in.

[3] scattering, with (a toss of) her head.   [4] over.

[5] with lofty mien, i.e. drawn up to her full height.

[6] For **quī**.   [7] Supply **est**.   [8] (merely) heard of (by you).

[9] i.e. worship.   [10] father.

[11] Tantalus, son of Jupiter, was invited to Jupiter's dinner parties, but because he betrayed secrets he was sent to Hades for eternal punishment.

[12] mother (Dione). The Pleiades, daughters of Atlas, were changed into stars.

[13] in him as father-in-law. Her husband, Amphion, was son of Jupiter.

[14] palace. Cadmus was the founder of Thebes.

sub dominā[1] est, fidibusque meī commissa[2] marītī
moenia cum populīs ā mēque virōque reguntur.
180 In quamcumque domūs advertī lūmina[3] partem,
immēnsae spectantur opēs. Accēdit eōdem[4]
digna deā faciēs.[5] Hūc nātās adice septem
et totidem iuvenēs, et mox generōsque nurūsque.

" Compared with Me, Latona Is Almost a Childless Woman! "

Quaerite nunc, habeat quam nostra superbia causam ;
185 nesciō quōque[6] audēte satam Titānida[7] Coeō
Lātōnam praeferre mihī, cui[8] maxima quondam
exiguam sēdem paritūrae[9] terra negāvit.[10]
Nec caelō nec humō nec aquīs dea vestra recepta est ;
exsul erat mundī, dōnec miserāta[11] vagantem,
190 " hospita tū terrīs errās, ego," dīxit, " in undīs "[12]
īnstabilemque locum Dēlos dedit. Illa duōrum
facta parēns ; uterī[13] pars haec est septima nostrī.
Sum fēlīx (quis enim neget[14] hoc ?) fēlīxque manēbō
(hoc quoque quis dubitet ?) ; tūtam mē cōpia fēcit.
195 Maior sum quam cui possit Fortūna nocēre,[15]

---

[1] With mē : *under me as its mistress.*

[2] *put together by the lyre* (from **fidēs, -is,** *string,* pl. *lyre*). Amphion, Niobe's husband, played so well that the stones fell into place to form the city wall.

[3] *eyes.*   [4] *there is added to this.*   [5] Refers to herself.

[6] **nesciō quō** = **aliquō** ; modifies **Coeō.** Note the scorn : *some Coeus or other.* Scan **nesciō** as two long syllables.

[7] Accusative : *daughter of a Titan, descended from;* **satam** is from **serō.**
[8] The antecedent is **Lātōnam.**   [9] With **cui.**
[10] As a result of Juno's jealousy Latona could not find a home.
[11] With **Dēlos.**   [12] Delos was a floating island at that time.
[13] *offspring.*   [14] Potential (**377**).
[15] *I am too great for Fortune to harm.* What literally ?

multaque ut[1] ēripiat, multō mihi plūra relinquet.
Excessēre metum mea iam bona.[2] Fingite dēmī
huic aliquid populō[3] nātōrum posse meōrum :
nōn tamen ad numerum redigar spoliāta[4] duōrum,
Lātōnae turbae[5] : quae quantum distat ab orbā?[6]   200
Īte satis properē sacrīs[7] laurumque capillīs
pōnite."[8] Dēpōnunt et sacra īnfecta[9] relinquunt,
quodque licet,[10] tacitō venerantur murmure nūmen.

Latona's Anger Stirs Apollo and Diana to Action

Indignāta dea est summōque in vertice Cynthī
tālibus est dictīs geminā cum prōle locūta :   205
" Ēn[11] ego vestra parēns, vōbīs animōsa creātīs,[12]
et nisi Iūnōnī nūllī cessūra[13] deārum,
an dea sim dubitor,[14] perque omnia saecula cultīs[15]
arceor, Ō nātī, nisi vōs succurritis, ārīs.
Nec dolor hic sōlus : dīrō convīcia factō   210
Tantalis[16] adiēcit vōsque est postpōnere nātīs
ausa suīs et mē (quod in ipsam reccidat[17]) orbam

---

[1] *although.*   [2] *blessings* (subject).

[3] Dative of separation with **dēmī**: *from this nation of.*   Her children
are so numerous that they are a nation by themselves.

[4] *although even thus robbed.*

[5] In apposition with **duōrum** (**nātōrum**) : *a crowd for Latona.*   Two is
a crowd in this case.

[6] *a childless woman.*

[7] *Away from the rites, and quickly too;* satis emphasizes **properē.**

[8] For **dēpōnite.**   [9] *the sacred rites unfinished.*

[10] *(the one thing) which is permitted them.*   [11] *Lo !*

[12] *proud of having given you birth.*   [13] *willing to yield.*

[14] *doubt is raised whether.*

[15] With **ārīs**: *from worship at the altar.*

[16] *The daughter of Tantalus added insult to injury.*

[17] *and may this fall upon her own head.*

dīxit et exhibuit linguam scelerāta paternam."[1]

Adiectūra precēs erat hīs Lātōna relātīs :

₁₅" Dēsine," Phoebus ait ; " poenae mora[2] longa querēla est."

Dīxit idem Phoebē, celerīque per āera lāpsū contigerant tēctī[3] Cadmēida[4] nūbibus arcem.

Fɪɢ. 118. Jᴜɴᴏ

One by One the Sons Are Cruelly Slain

Plānus erat lātēque patēns prope moenia campus, assiduīs[5] pulsātus equīs, ubi turba rotārum

---

[1] Tantalus could not control his tongue when intrusted with the secrets of Jove; Niobe has the same unruly tongue.

[2] Predicate nominative.

[3] *concealed by clouds*, referring to Apollo and Diana.

[4] Accusative (Greek form): *Cadmean.*   [5] *constant (tread of) horses.*

dūraque mollierat subiectās ungula[1] glaebās.   220
Pars ibi dē septem genitīs Amphīone[2] fortēs[3]
cōnscendunt in equōs Tyriōque rubentia sūcō[4]
terga premunt, aurō gravidīs moderantur[5] habēnīs.
Ē quibus Ismēnus, quī mātrī sarcina[6] quondam
prīma suae fuerat, dum certum flectit in orbem[7]   225
quadrupedis cursūs spūmantiaque ōra coercet,
" Ei[8] mihi ! " conclāmat mediōque in pectore fīxa
tēla gerit, frēnīsque manū moriente remissīs,
in latus[9] ā dextrō paulātim dēfluit armō.[10]

Proximus, audītō sonitū per ināne[11] pharetrae,   230
frēna dabat Sipylus, velutī cum praescius[12] imbris
nūbe fugit vīsā, pendentiaque undique rēctor
carbasa dēdūcit,[13] nē quā[14] levis effluat aura ;
frēna tamen dantem[15] nōn ēvītābile tēlum
cōnsequitur, summāque tremēns cervīce sagitta   235
haesit, et exstābat nūdum dē gutture ferrum.
Ille, ut erat prōnus,[16] per crūra admissa iubāsque[17]
volvitur, et calidō tellūrem sanguine foedat.

Phaedimus īnfēlīx et, avītī nōminis hērēs,
Tantalus, ut solitō fīnem imposuēre labōrī,   240
trānsierant ad opus nitidae[18] iuvenāle palaestrae,

---

[1] hoof.   [2] For case see **329**.
[3] Modifies **equōs** : spirited.
[4] Tyrian dye, by metonymy for saddle-cloths.
[5] Supply **equōs**.   [6] burden, i.e. firstborn child.   [7] in a perfect circle.
[8] oh! **Mihi** is dative of reference, better omitted in translation.
[9] sidewise.   [10] shoulder (of the horse).
[11] air.   [12] With **rēctor**.   [13] spreads.
[14] Supply **parte**. He makes use of every bit of wind.
[15] Supply **eum**: as he gives rein.   [16] just as he was, leaning forward.
[17] between the flying legs (of his horse) and over its mane. The order
should be reversed.
[18] Transferred epithet ; the bodies of the wrestlers were shiny with oil.

et iam contulerant artō luctantia nexū
pectora pectoribus : contentō concita nervō,[1]
sīcut erant iūnctī, trāiēcit utrumque sagitta.
245 Ingemuēre simul, simul incurvāta dolōre
membra solō[2] posuēre, simul suprēma iacentēs
lūmina[3] versārunt, animam simul exhālārunt.[4]

Apollo Is Moved by the Prayer of the Last Son

Aspicit Alphēnor laniātaque[5] pectora plangēns
ēvolat, ut gelidōs complexibus allevet artūs,
250 inque piō cadit officiō ; nam Dēlius illī[6]
intima fātiferō rūpit praecordia ferrō.
Quod simul[7] ēductum est, pars est pulmōnis in hāmīs[8]
ēruta, cumque animā cruor est effūsus in aurās.
At nōn[9] intōnsum[10] simplex Damasichthona[11] vulnus
255 afficit : ictus erat quā crūs esse incipit et quā
mollia nervōsus facit internōdia poples.
Dumque manū temptat trahere exitiābile tēlum,
altera per iugulum pennīs tenus[12] ācta sagitta est.
Expulit hanc sanguis sēque ēiaculātus[13] in altum
260 ēmicat et longē terebrātā prōsilit aurā.
Ultimus Īlioneus nōn prōfectūra[14] precandō
bracchia sustulerat " dī " que " Ō commūniter omnēs,"

---

[1] *sent from the taut string (of the bow).*   [2] *on the ground.*

[3] *eyes (for the) last (time).*

[4] The spondee in the fifth foot expresses the labored effort of the dying youths.

[5] Anticipates the action of **plangēns**.   [6] = eius (311).

[7] For **simul ac**.   [8] *barbs*, of the arrow.   [9] With **simplex**.

[10] Young Greek boys wore the hair long.

[11] Accusative (Greek form).

[12] Governs **pennīs**.   [13] With **sē**: *gushing forth.*

[14] From **prōficiō**: *which were to gain nothing by prayer.*

dīxerat, ignārus nōn omnēs[1] esse rogandōs,
" parcite ! " Mōtus erat, cum iam revocābile tēlum
nōn fuit, Arcitenēns. Minimō tamen occidit ille   265
vulnere, nōn altē percussō corde sagittā.

Niobe Remains Defiant in the Midst of Her Dead

Fāma malī populīque dolor lacrimaeque suōrum[2]
tam subitae mātrem certam fēcēre ruīnae,[3]
mīrantem potuisse,[4] īrāscentemque quod ausī
hoc[5] essent superī, quod tantum iūris habērent.   270
Nam pater Amphīōn, ferrō per pectus adāctō,
fīnierat moriēns pariter cum lūce dolōrem.

Heu quantum haec Niobē Niobē distābat ab illā
quae modo Lātōīs populum summōverat ārīs,
et mediam tulerat gressūs resupīna[6] per urbem,   275
invidiōsa suīs, at nunc miseranda vel hostī !
Corporibus gelidīs incumbit et ōrdine nūllō
ōscula dispēnsat nātōs suprēma per omnēs.
Ā quibus ad caelum līventia[7] bracchia tollēns,
" pāscere,[8] crūdēlis, nostrō, Lātōna, dolōre ;   280
pāscere," ait, " satiāque meō tua pectora lūctū :
corque ferum satiā," dīxit ; " per fūnera septem
efferor.[9] Exsultā victrīxque inimīca triumphā !
Cūr autem victrīx? Miserae mihi plūra supersunt[10]
quam tibi fēlīcī. Post tot quoque fūnera vincō."   285

---

[1] Here Apollo alone was concerned.
[2] Niobe's household and friends.
[3] *informed the mother of the disaster.*   [4] *(that the gods) could (do this).*
[5] A long syllable (originally **hocc**).
[6] *proudly;* lit., *head thrown back.*
[7] From beating herself in mourning.   [8] Imperative.
[9] *i.e.* she is *borne out,* as it were, to her own grave seven times ; her
grief makes each son's death her own.
[10] *I still have more in my woe.*

The Daughters Meet Their Fate. Niobe Is Changed into Marble

Dīxerat et sonuit contentō nervus ab arcū,[1]
quī praeter Niobēn[2] ūnam conterruit omnēs;

Fig. 119. A Daughter of Niobe

illa malō est audāx.[3] Stābant cum vestibus ātrīs
ante torōs[4] frātrum dēmissō crīne[5] sorōrēs.
290 Ē quibus ūna trahēns haerentia vīscere tēla[6]

---

[1] We are left to infer that it is Diana's task to dispose of the daughters.
[2] Accusative. [3] *made reckless by misfortune.* [4] *biers.*
[5] A sign of mourning. [6] *the arrow fixed in (her brother's) heart*

impositō frātrī moribunda relanguit[1] ōre ;[2]
altera sōlārī miseram cōnāta parentem
conticuit subitō duplicātaque[3] vulnere caecō est,
ōraque compressit, nisi postquam spīritus ībat ;[4]
haec frūstrā fugiēns collābitur ; illa sorōrī   295
immoritur ; latet haec ; illam trepidāre vidērēs.[5]
   Sexque datīs lētō dīversaque vulnera passīs,
ultima restābat.   Quam tōtō corpore māter,
tōtā veste tegēns, " ūnam minimamque relinque!
Dē multīs minimam poscō," clāmāvit, " et ūnam."[6]   300
Dumque rogat, prō quā rogat occidit.[7]   Orba resēdit
exanimēs inter nātōs nātāsque virumque,
dēriguitque malīs ; nūllōs movet aura capillōs,
in vultū color est sine sanguine, lūmina maestīs
stant immōta genīs, nihil est in imāgine vīvum.   305
Ipsa quoque interius cum dūrō lingua palātō
congelat, et vēnae dēsistunt posse movērī ;
nec flectī cervīx nec bracchia reddere mōtūs
nec pēs īre potest ; intrā quoque vīscera saxum est.
Flet tamen et validī circumdata turbine ventī[8]   310
in patriam[9] rapta est.   Ibi fīxa cacūmine montis
līquitur, et lacrimās etiam nunc marmora mānant.[10]

                              (Met. VI. 165–312)

---

[1] Scan as four syllables.

[2] *with her face upon her brother.*   [3] *was bent double.*

[4] *except after she expired;* then her mouth opened.

[5] *one might have seen.*

[6] The pathos is only too evident.   One wonders why Latona's heart
was not touched by this evidence of broken pride.

[7] The subject is the unexpressed antecedent of **quā.**

[8] *enwrapped in a mighty gust of wind.*

[9] Phrygia.

[10] This figure, partly natural, partly artificial, is still visible on Mt.
Sipylus.   The tears are explained by the spring which trickles down

Read Bulfinch, pp. 111–115; Gayley, pp. 126-129; Guerber, pp. 93–96, 167; Sabin, pp. 13–15.

Word Study. — What English words are derived from **capillōs** (168), **rubentia** (222), **gutture** (236), **allevet** (249), **pulmōnis** (252), **ēiaculātus** (259), **percussō** (266), **collābitur** (295), **sanguine** (304).

Fig. 120. A Daughter of
Niobe

the face of the figure. Cf. Hawthorne's "Great Stone Face" and the figures being carved on Stone Mountain, Georgia, and in the Black Hills.

206. PHILEMON AND BAUCIS

It pays to treat with hospitality all who come to our doors, for we may be "entertaining angels unawares." Jupiter and Mercury, disguised as wanderers, after being denied entrance into one home after another, are at last admitted by an aged couple. The hosts make the strangers comfortable and later receive their reward.

The Strangers Are Welcomed

Iuppiter hūc [1] speciē mortālī, cumque parente
vēnit Atlantiadēs [2] positīs cādūcifer [3] ālīs.
Mīlle domōs adiēre locum requiemque [4] petentēs,
mīlle domōs clausēre serae. [5] Tamen ūna [6] recēpit,
parva quidem, stipulīs [7] et cannā tēcta palūstrī; [8] 630
sed pia Baucis anus [9] parilīque aetāte Philēmōn
illā [10] sunt annīs iūnctī iuvenālibus, illā
cōnsenuēre casā paupertātemque [11] fatendō
effēcēre levem nec inīquā mente ferendō.
Nec rēfert [12] dominōs illīc famulōsne requīrās; 635
tōta domus duo sunt, īdem pārentque iubentque.
    Ergō ubi caelicolae parvōs tetigēre penātēs, [13]
summissōque humilēs intrārunt vertice postēs,
membra senex positō iussit relevāre sedīlī,

---

[1] The humble home of Philemon and Baucis, in Phrygia.

[2] (grand)son of Atlas, i.e. Mercury, who was the son of Jupiter and Maia, a daughter of Atlas.

[3] staff-bearing, a stock epithet of Mercury, from the emblem, the caduceus (see Figs. 121, 123).

[4] Hendiadys (406).   [5] bolts.   [6] Supply domus.
[7] straw.   [8] marsh reeds.   [9] old woman.
[10] With casā.
[11] Object of the gerunds and the verb.
[12] it makes no difference whether (-ne).
[13] house.

FIG. 121. MERCURY

As conceived by the modern artist Bologna.

quō superiniēcit[1] textum[2] rude sēdula Baucis, 640
inque focō tepidum cinerem dīmōvit, et ignēs
suscitat hesternōs, foliīsque et cortice[3] siccō
nūtrit et ad flammās animā prōdūcit anīlī,
multifidāsque facēs[4] rāmāliaque[5] ārida tēctō[6]
dētulit et minuit parvōque admōvit aēnō.[7] 645
Quodque suus coniūnx riguō collēgerat hortō,
truncat holus foliīs.   Furcā levat illa bicornī
sordida[8] terga suis[9] nigrō pendentia tignō ;
servātōque diū resecat dē tergore partem
exiguam sectamque domat[10] ferventibus undīs. 650
   Intereā mediās fallunt sermōnibus hōrās,[11] 654
concutiuntque torum[12] dē mollī flūminis ulvā[13] 655
impositum lectō spondā[14] pedibusque salignīs.[15]
Vestibus hunc vēlant, quās nōn nisi tempore fēstō
sternere cōnsuerant ; sed et[16] haec vīlisque vetusque
vestis erat, lectō nōn indignanda salignō.

The Dinner — Such as It Is — Is Served

   Accubuēre[17] deī.   Mēnsam succīncta[18] tremēnsque 660
pōnit anus.   Mēnsae sed erat pēs tertius[19] impār :
testa parem fēcit.   Quae[20] postquam subdita clīvum

---

[1] *over which he threw.*   [2] *coverlet* (from **texō,** *weave*).   [3] *bark.*
[4] *kindling.*   [5] *branches.*   [6] *from (under) the roof.*
[7] *kettle.*   [8] *darkened* by the smoke.
[9] Genitive of **sūs,** *hog, pork.*   [10] *makes tender* (by cooking).
[11] *they while away the intervening time.*
[12] *mattress.*
[13] *sedge-grass;* the prepositional phrase modifies **torum.**
[14] Ablative of description modifying **lectō:** *with a frame.*
[15] *of willow* (with both nouns).   [16] = **etiam.**   [17] *reclined* at the table.
[18] *with skirts tucked up,* so that she might hobble about as freely as possible.
[19] *i.e.* it was three-legged.   [20] The antecedent is **testa.**

sustulit, aequātam[1] mentae tersēre virentēs.
Pōnitur hīc bicolor sincērae bāca Minervae,[2]
665 conditaque in liquidā corna[3] autumnālia faece,[4]
intibaque[5] et rādīx et lactis māssa coāctī,[6]

FIG. 122. CRĀTĒR CAELĀTUS

ōvaque nōn ācrī[7] leviter versāta favīllā,
omnia fictilibus.[8]   Post haec caelātus eōdem
sistitur argentō[9] crātēr, fabricātaque fāgō
670 pōcula, quā cava sunt,[10] flāventibus illita cērīs.

---

[1] Supply **mēnsam.**

[2] The *berry of Minerva* is the olive.   Both green and ripe (black)
olives were served.

[3] *cornel berries.*   [4] From **faex:** *dregs (of wine).*   [5] *endive.*

[6] **lactis māssa coāctī** = *cheese.*   What literally?

[7] *not hot,* therefore *merely warm.*

[8] *all (are placed) in earthern dishes*

[9] Ovid, of course, is jesting, for this refers to **fictilibus.**

[10] *where they are hollow* = *their interiors.*   The wax prevented leaks.

Parva mora est, epulāsque focī mīsēre calentēs,
nec longae rūrsus referuntur vīna senectae,
dantque locum mēnsīs paulum sēducta secundīs.[1]
Hīc nux, hīc mixta est rūgōsīs cārica[2] palmīs
prūnaque et in patulīs redolentia māla canistrīs   675
et dē purpureīs[3] collēctae vītibus ūvae.
Candidus in mediō favus est; super omnia vultūs
accessēre bonī[4] nec iners pauperque[5] voluntās.

The Miracle of the Wine

Intereā totiēns haustum crātēra[6] replērī
sponte suā per sēque vident succrēscere vīna.   680
Attonitī novitāte pavent manibusque supīnīs[7]
concipiunt Baucisque precēs timidusque Philēmōn
et veniam dapibus nūllīsque parātibus[8] ōrant.

Ūnicus ānser erat, minimae custōdia[9] vīllae;
quem dīs hospitibus dominī mactāre parābant.   685
Ille celer pennā tardōs aetāte fatīgat
ēlūditque diū, tandemque est vīsus ad ipsōs
cōnfūgisse deōs. Superī vetuēre necārī
" dī " que " sumus, meritāsque luet vīcīnia poenās
impia," dīxērunt; " vōbīs immūnibus huius   690
esse malī dabitur.[10] Modo vestra relinquite tēcta

---

[1] *the second course, i.e.* the dessert.   [2] *fig.*

[3] Transferred epithet; in thought with **ūvae.**   [4] *kindly expressions.*

[5] There are nearly thirty direct and indirect references to poverty
between lines 626 and 678. Can you detect them?

[6] Accusative singular (Greek form); subject of **replērī.**

[7] *with upturned palms.*

[8] Dative of the noun : *for their lack of preparation.*

[9] = **custōs.** Ever since the sacred geese saved the Capitol at Rome
from the Gauls in 390 B.C., the goose had been considered an especially
good guardian (**custōs**).

[10] *it will be granted you to be free from.*

ac nostrōs comitāte gradūs et in ardua[1] montis
īte simul." Pārent ambō baculīsque levātī
nītuntur longō vēstīgia pōnere clīvō.

The Wicked Countryfolk Are Drowned by a Flood

695 Tantum aberant summō[2] quantum semel īre sagitta
missa[3] potest; flexēre oculōs et mersa palūde
cētera prōspiciunt, tantum sua tēcta manēre.
Dumque ea mīrantur, dum dēflent fāta suōrum,
illa vetus dominīs etiam casa parva duōbus[4]
700 vertitur in templum; furcās subiēre[5] columnae,
strāmina flāvēscunt, adopertaque marmore tellūs
caelātaeque forēs aurātaque tēcta videntur.

A Strange Metamorphosis

Tālia tum placidō Sāturnius[6] ēdidit ōre:
" Dīcite, iūste senex et fēmina coniuge iūstō
705 digna, quid optētis." Cum Baucide pauca locūtus
iūdicium superīs aperit commūne Philēmōn:
" Esse sacerdōtēs dēlūbraque vestra tuērī
poscimus; et quoniam concordēs ēgimus annōs,
auferat[7] hōra duōs eadem, nec coniugis umquam
710 busta meae videam neu sim tumulandus[8] ab illā."

Vōta fidēs[9] sequitur; templī tūtēla fuēre,
dōnec vīta data est. Annīs aevōque solūtī[10]
ante gradūs sacrōs cum stārent forte locīque
nārrārent cāsūs, frondēre Philēmona Baucis,
715 Baucida cōnspexit senior frondēre Philēmōn.

---

[1] Substantive.   [2] *from the top.*
[3] *an arrow sent once, i.e.* the distance of one arrow flight.
[4] The prose order = **illa casa vetus, parva etiam duōbus dominīs.**
[5] *took the place of.*   [6] *son of Saturn,* i.e. *Jupiter.*   [7] Optative (**376**).
[8] *nor may I have to be buried.*   [9] *fulfillment.*   [10] *broken down.*

Iamque super geminōs crēscente cacūmine vultūs,
mūtua,[1] dum licuit, reddēbant dicta " Valē " que
" Ō coniūnx " [2] dīxēre simul, simul abdita tēxit
ōra frutex.[3] Ostendit adhūc Thȳnēius illīc
incola dē geminō vīcīnōs corpore[4] truncōs.   720

(Met. VIII. 626–720)

Read Bulfinch, pp. 62–65; Gayley, pp. 105–107; Guerber,
pp. 43–44; Sabin, pp. 83–84; Nathaniel Hawthorne, *A Won-
derbook for Boys and Girls.*

Word Study. — What English words are derived from **sēdula**
(640), **cinerem** (641), **suscitat** (642), **cortice** (642), **truncat** (647),
succīncta (660), **lactis** (666), **crātēr** (669), **redolentia** (675).

[1] *to each other.*   [2] *dear mate.*
[3] *growth of foliage.*   [4] *(formed) from the two bodies.*

Fig. 123. Mercury

207.   Atalanta's Race

Venus tells Adonis how Hippomenes, through her aid, won a race from Atalanta and got as the prize a wife. All previous contestants, beaten to the tape by the fleet-footed girl, paid the penalty of failure, death.

The Allurement of the Prize Banishes Fear of Death

560 Forsitan audierīs[1] aliquam[2] certāmine cursūs
　　vēlōcēs superāsse virōs.　Nōn fābula[3] rūmor
　　ille fuit (superābat enim), nec dīcere possēs,[4]
　　laude pedum fōrmaene bonō[5] praestantior esset.
　　Scītantī deus[6] huic dē coniuge, " coniuge," dīxit,
565 " nīl opus est, Atalanta, tibī ;[7]　fuge coniugis ūsum ![8]
　　Nec tamen effugiēs tēque ipsā vīva carēbis."[9]
　　Territa sorte deī per opācās innuba silvās
　　vīvit et īnstantem turbam violenta procōrum
　　condiciōne[10] fugat, " nec sum potiunda,[11] nisi," inquit,
570 " victa prius cursū.　Pedibus contendite mēcum.
　　Praemia vēlōcī coniūnx thalamīque[12] dabuntur,
　　mors pretium tardīs.　Ea lēx certāminis estō."
　　Illa quidem immītis, sed (tanta potentia fōrmae est)
　　vēnit ad hanc lēgem temerāria turba procōrum.

---

[1] Potential subjunctive : *you may have heard.*

[2] Supply **puellam.**

[3] Predicate nominative.

[4] *nor could one say whether.* The double question has no introductory word ; -ne (*or*) connects the two parts.

[5] *excellence.*　　　　　　　　　　　　[6] Apollo.

[7] The final i is sometimes long in poetry.

[8] *the marriage state.*

[9] *you will lose yourself while still alive*, referring to Atalanta's metamorphosis into a lioness.

[10] *by (these) terms.*　　　　　　　　[11] *I am not to be won.*

[12] *wedlock.*

Love at First Sight

Sēderat Hippomenēs cursūs spectātor inīquī 575
et " petitur cuiquam[1] per tanta perīcula coniūnx? "
dīxerat ac nimiōs iuvenum damnārat amōrēs.
Ut faciem et positō corpus vēlāmine vīdit,
quāle meum, vel quāle tuum, sī fēmina fīās,[2]
obstipuit, tollēnsque manūs, " ignōscite,"[3] dīxit, 580
" quōs modo culpāvī. Nōndum mihi praemia nōta
quae peterētis[4] erant." Laudandō concipit ignēs,[5]
et, nē quis iuvenum currat vēlōcius, optat
invidiāque timet. " Sed cūr certāminis huius
intemptāta mihī[6] fortūna relinquitur? " inquit; 585
" audentēs deus ipse iuvat." Dum tālia sēcum
exigit[7] Hippomenēs, passū volat ālite virgō.
Quae quamquam Scythicā nōn sētius[8] īre sagittā
Āoniō vīsa est iuvenī, tamen ille decōrem
mīrātur magis. Et cursus facit ille decōrem. 590
Dum notat haec hospes, dēcursa novissima mēta[9] est, 597
et tegitur fēstā victrīx Atalanta corōnā.
Dant gemitum victī penduntque ex foedere poenās.

Atalanta's Beauty Makes Hippomenes Reckless

Nōn tamen ēventū iuvenis dēterritus hōrum 600
cōnstitit in mediō vultūque in virgine fīxō,
" quid facilem titulum superandō quaeris inertēs?

---

[1] Dative of agent.
[2] Venus is talking to Adonis.
[3] Addressed to the suitors.
[4] Subjunctive because of the implied indirect discourse.
[5] *and as he praised he fell in love.* How literally?
[6] *by me.*   [7] *weighs.*
[8] *not otherwise than.*   [9] *the last lap.*

Mēcum cōnfer ! ” ait. “ Seu[1] mē fortūna potentem
fēcerit, ā tantō nōn indignābere[2] vincī ;
605 namque mihī genitor Megareus Onchēstius, illī
est Neptūnus avus, pronepōs ego rēgis aquārum ;
nec virtūs citrā[3] genus est. Seu vincar, habēbis,
Hippomenē victō, magnum et memorābile nōmen.”
Tālia dīcentem mollī[4] Schoenēia[5] vultū
610 aspicit et dubitat[6] superārī an vincere mālit,
atque ita, “ quis deus hunc[7] fōrmōsīs,”[8] inquit, “ inīquus
perdere vult cāraeque iubet discrīmine vītae
coniugium petere hoc ? Nōn sum, mē iūdice, tantī.[9]
Nec fōrmā tangor (poteram tamen hāc quoque tangī),
615 sed quod adhūc puer est. Nōn mē movet ipse, sed
aetās.[10]
Quid, quod inest virtūs et mēns interrita lētī ?[11]
Quid, quod ab aequoreā numerātur orīgine[12] quārtus ?
Quid, quod amat tantīque putat cōnūbia nostra
ut pereat, sī mē fors illī dūra negārit ?

She Urges Him to Withdraw His Challenge

620 “ Dum licet, hospes, abī thalamōsque relinque cru-
entōs.[13]
Coniugium crūdēle meum est. Tibi nūbere nūlla[14]
nōlet ; et optārī potes ā sapiente puellā.

---

[1] **Seu . . . Seu** (607): *If, on the one hand . . . But if.*
[2] What figure? See **157.** [3] *less than;* lit., *this side of.*
[4] *tender.* [5] *daughter of Schoeneus* (king of Boeotia).
[6] *hesitates whether.* [7] Object of **perdere** and subject of **petere.**
[8] With **inīquus:** *hostile to handsome men.*
[9] *that important;* genitive of indefinite value (**308**).
[10] Which do you think influenced her, **ipse** or **aetās ?**
[11] *fearless of death.* [12] His *watery origin* is from Neptune.
[13] *a marriage fraught with blood.* [14] Supply **puella.**

Cūr tamen est mihi cūra tuī,[1] tot iam ante perēmptīs?
Vīderit![2] Intereat, quoniam tot caede procōrum
admonitus nōn est agiturque in taedia vītae!   625
Occidet hic igitur, voluit quia vīvere mēcum,
indignamque necem pretium patiētur amōris?
Nōn erit invidiae victōria nostra ferendae.[3]
Sed nōn culpa mea est. Utinam dēsistere vellēs![4]
Aut, quoniam es dēmēns, utinam vēlōcior essēs!   630
Ā, quam virgineus[5] puerīlī vultus in ōre est!
Ā, miser Hippomenē,[6] nōllem tibi vīsa fuissem![7]
Vīvere dignus erās. Quod sī fēlīcior essem,
nec[8] mihi coniugium fāta importūna negārent,[9]
ūnus erās cum quō sociāre cubīlia[10] vellem."   635
Dīxerat, utque rudis[11] prīmōque Cupīdine tācta,
quid facit[12] ignōrāns, amat et nōn sentit amōrem.

Iam solitōs poscunt cursūs populusque paterque,[13]
cum mē[14] sollicitā prōlēs Neptūnia vōce
invocat Hippomenēs, "Cytherēa"que "comprecor, ausīs[15]
adsit," [16] ait, "nostrīs et quōs dedit adiuvet ignēs."   641
Dētulit aura precēs ad mē nōn invida[17] blandās,
mōtaque sum, fateor. Nec opis mora longa dabātur.[18]

---

[1] Objective genitive.   [2] Volitive subjunctive (**366**).
[3] *will be one of unbearable odium.*   [4] For mood see **376,** *b.*
[5] *chaste.*   [6] Vocative (Greek form).
[7] *I could wish that I had not been seen by you.*   [8] = **et nōn.**
[9] Refers to the declaration of the oracle in 566.
[10] *join in marriage.*   [11] *inexperienced as she was* (*i.e.* in love).
[12] Indirect questions in the indicative are a survival of the original construction.
[13] *i.e.* Atalanta's.   [14] *i.e.* Venus.   [15] From **audeō:** *undertaking.*
[16] The subject is **Cytherēa** (Venus).   [17] With **nōn:** *willing* (**157**).
[18] In 644–651, not given here, Venus tells how, in answer to Hippomenes' prayer she brings him three golden apples and tells him how they may be of help to him.

Hippomenes Saves His Head and Wins a Wife

652 Signa tubae dederant, cum carcere[1] prōnus uterque
émicat et summam celerī pede lībat harēnam.
Posse putēs[2] illōs siccō freta rādere passū[3]
655 et segetis cānae[4] stantēs percurrere[5] aristās.
Adiciunt animōs iuvenī clāmorque favorque
verbaque dīcentum[6] " nunc, nunc incumbere tempus!
Hippomenē,[7] properā! Nunc vīribus ūtere tōtīs!

Fig. 124. Atalanta and the Golden Apples
From a painting by Poynter.

Pelle moram, vincēs!" Dubium,[8] Megarēius hērōs
660 gaudeat an virgō magis hīs Schoenēia dictīs.
Ō quotiēns, cum iam posset trānsīre, morāta est,
spectātōsque diū vultūs invīta relīquit![9]
Āridus ē lassō veniēbat anhēlitus ōre,[10]
mētaque erat longē. Tum dēnique dē tribus ūnum
665 fētibus arboreīs prōlēs Neptūnia mīsit.

---

[1] *starting-line;* lit., *stall.* The language is that of the circus with its chariot races.

[2] *one might think.*

[3] *soles;* lit., *step.*

[4] *ripe;* lit., *white.*

[5] *skim over the tops of* — so lightly did they float along.

[6] = **dīcentium.**

[7] Vocative.

[8] Supply **est utrum.**

[9] *reluctantly left behind.*

[10] of Hippomenes.

Obstipuit virgō nitidīque cupīdine pōmī
dēclīnat cursūs aurumque volūbile[1] tollit.
Praeterit Hippomenēs : resonant spectācula[2] plausū.
Illa moram celerī cessātaque[3] tempora cursū
corrigit atque iterum iuvenem post terga relinquit,   670
et rūrsus pōmī iactū remorāta secundī
cōnsequitur trānsitque virum.   Pars ultima cursūs
restābat.   " Nunc," inquit, " ades,[4] dea mūneris auc-
    tor ! "
Inque latus campī,[5] quō tardius illa redīret,[6]
iēcit ab oblīquō[7] nitidum iuvenāliter aurum.   675
An peteret, virgō vīsa est dubitāre ; coēgī[8]
tollere et adiēcī sublātō pondera mālō[9]
impediīque[10] oneris pariter gravitāte morāque.
Nēve meus sermō cursū sit tardior ipsō,
praeterita est virgō ; dūxit sua praemia victor.[11]   680
(Met. X. 560–680)

Read Bulfinch, pp. 83–85, 174–177 ; Gayley, pp. 126–128,
139–141 ; Guerber, pp. 100–101, 276–278 ; Sabin, pp. 185–186
179–180.

Word Study. — What English words are derived from **opācās**
(567), **decōrem** (589), **titulum** (602), **taedia** (625), **carcere** (652),
rādere (654), **incumbere** (657), **lassō** (663), **volūbile** (667).

---

[1] Lit., *the rolling gold;* what would we say?
[2] *grandstands.*   [3] *lost.*
[4] Imperative ; Hippomenes is speaking.
[5] *i.e.* off the race-course.
[6] Purpose (**369**).   [7] *at an angle.*
[8] Remember that Venus is talking.
[9] *to the apple when she raised it.*   [10] Supply **eam.**
[11] How much better than the prosaic **puellam in mātrimōnium dūxit** !

LATIN COMPOSITION

EXERCISES FOR PART I[1]

208.   I.

Use of the reflexive pronoun (**288**). Volitive substantive clauses (**370**). Ablative absolute (**335**).

1. (After a meeting of) the senate had been held, the tribunes went[2] to Caesar. 2. (Now that) the die had been cast,[3] they could not be persuaded to remain with Pompey in Rome. 3. Caesar urged his soldiers not to fear but to set out with him. 4. (Upon) hearing his words, all exclaimed that they were ready to defend their commander, and he ordered them to follow him.

209.   II.

Uses of participles (**395–397**). Uses of the gerund (**399**). Uses of the future passive participle (**398**). Subjunctive in **cum** causal clauses (**383**).

1. Domitius said nothing (while) reading the letter. 2. (After) reading it through, he conferred secretly with his friends about the plan to be adopted. 3. Since Pompey was not going to come to their aid, new plans had to be formed for the sake of defending Corfinium. 4. Having placed Domitius in custody, they sent envoys to Caesar to seek peace.

---

[1] Each section is based on the Latin text of the lesson whose Roman numeral it bears.

[2] Use a reflexive expression.

[3] Use ablative absolute.

210. III.

Indirect statements (**402**). Causal clauses (**389**).

1. Caesar said that he did not want to conquer with the sword. 2. For he had formed the hope that he could finish the matter without a battle. 3. His plan is not approved by the soldiers because (they say) they prefer to fight. 4. Since they are losing such an opportunity for victory, they state they will not advance but want to fight immediately.

211. IV.

Dative of possession (**316**). Volitive subjunctive (**366**). Subjunctive in indirect questions (**386**).

1. Vibullius had great influence with Pompey because Pompey knew how much Vibullius had done for (**prō**) his cause. 2. He said to Pompey: " Let us spare ourselves and think what we owe to the republic." 3. Then Pompey interrupted him and asked what need of life he would have if he should accept (*past perf. subj.*) Caesar's kindness. 4. Now that the war is over, let all nations try to bring about (**efficiō**) peace through conferences rather than (**magis quam**) by the sword.

212. V.

Datives of purpose and reference (**310, 311**). Purpose clauses with **ut** and **nē** (**367**). Result clauses with **ut** and **ut nōn** (**378**). Subordinate clauses in indirect discourse (**387**).

1. Sulla came to the aid of Caesar's soldiers in order that they might not retreat. 2. I know that his coming was (for) so great a help to the cohort that the

Pompeians could not bear their attack. 3. The latter thought that if they retreated, our men would pursue. 4. They were so far away from us that they could not be struck by our weapons.

213. VI.

Genitive and ablative of description (**299, 342**). Adversative (concessive) **cum** clauses (**384**).

1. Although these brothers were men of the greatest courage, they were not worthy of honor (*abl.*). 2. They used Caesar's friendship for their own gain, although he had given them money and magistracies. 3. All the cavalrymen went to Caesar and complained because these men were stealing[1] their pay. 4. The brothers therefore went over to Pompey, nor were they ashamed, although no one before this time had deserted to him.

214. VII.

General review of ablative constructions (**326 ff.**).

1. (Now that) Pompey's army has been increased, the hope of his soldiers is strengthened. 2. First they plan how they may be able to use the money. 3. Then they contend in camp in daily disputes about the prizes. 4. But a few days later they are defeated with great slaughter by Caesar.

215. VIII.

Ablative of respect (**345**). Descriptive **cum** clauses (**382**). Dative of agent with future passive participle

---

[1] Subjunctive — why?

and **sum** (**317**). Subjunctive in anticipatory clauses (**385**).

1. When his soldiers were ready in spirit to fight, Caesar thought that he ought[1] to defer his march. 2. But, since Pompey was strong in cavalry, he wished to rout Caesar before a weapon could be thrown. 3. When Pompey had ceased speaking (" made an end of speaking "), Labienus said that they ought[1] to despise Caesar's forces. 4. " We excel in number and ought to swear that we will not return to camp except (as) victors."

216. IX.

General review of dative constructions (**309 ff.**). General review of infinitive tenses and uses (**400–403**).

1. Caesar thought that Crastinus would be (for) an example of courage for the rest. 2. We know that Caesar had placed him in command of the first maniple. 3. Caesar tells us that Crastinus was killed while fighting bravely. 4. He had many men like Crastinus, who trusted and obeyed him.

217. X.

Final review of participles (**395 ff.**) and subjunctive constructions (**366 ff.**). Tense sequence (**359**).

1. Ptolemy, having driven his sister Cleopatra from the kingdom, was now king of Egypt. 2. Pompey, influenced by the fear that he would be killed by his enemies, asked Ptolemy to protect him. 3. But do

---

[1] Use future passive participle.

you know what the king's soldiers did? They killed
the friend of the king's father. 4. Caesar was so
overcome (with grief) when he had heard about Pompey's death that he wept.

EXERCISES FOR PART II

218. I. Selections 1–3[1]

Dative of indirect object (**309**). Volitive subjunctive (**366**).

1. It gives me great pleasure to receive a letter from
you. 2. An old man, a friend of Pliny, will write to
tell us that he is well. 3. Pliny says that an old man
is not a slave to love. 4. Let not avarice concern you,
for you will soon die. 5. I do not know why my
friend wishes to advise others. 6. Do they think
that we are trifling? Old men are not wont to trifle.
7. Let us not envy those who have wealth. 8. Do
you think, Pliny, that all men mourn because they are[2]
not well?

219. II. Selections 4–6

Genitive of description (**299**). Ablative of description (**342**). Volitive substantive clauses (**370**). Sequence of tenses (**359**).

1. Write me how long Pliny and his friend, a man
of the same age, served in the Roman army. 2. We
do not fear that Pliny will not bring back full tablets.

---

[1] Each section is based on the Latin selections whose numbers are
given at the top.

[2] Subjunctive.

3. Pliny wrote that he would not accuse the soldier because of his (the soldier's) words. 4. Let us ask Fannia to go out of her way to (visit) us. 5. Pliny advises us not to despise his method of hunting,[1] because he always brings back[2] full tablets, though[3] his hands are empty. 6. Fannia was not removed from the eyes of the Roman world because she was a woman with a beautiful face, was she? 7. It is remarkable how greatly exercise aids[4] the mind. 8. Laugh, if you want to, but I shall go-hunting with Pliny.

220. III. SELECTIONS 7–9

Ablative absolute (**335**). **Cum** causal clauses (**383**). Descriptive **cum** clauses (**382**).

1. Pliny, who spends the summer in his Tuscan villa, enjoys both hunting and study. 2. But he cannot tell, himself, which is more difficult, catching[5] game[6] or writing. 3. Some people are so accustomed to travel abroad[7] that they overlook sights[8] that lie right-before-them[9] in their own country. 4. Since the master was cruel toward[10] his slaves, the latter seized him by the throat.[11] 5. When the slave had served his master many years, he remained in the villa and persuaded the rest of the slaves not to flee to Rome. 6. Pliny was well off[12] since he had his wife and son with him in his villa. 7. By opening his eyes[13] he indicated[14] that he

---

[1] Gerund.
[2] Subjunctive.
[3] quamvīs with subjunctive.
[4] *is for an aid to*, etc.
[5] Infinitive.   [6] aliquid.
[7] mare trānsmittō.
[8] ea.   [9] sub oculīs.
[10] in.   [11] faucēs invādō.
[12] Literally, *it was well for*, etc.
[13] Ablative absolute.
[14] *confessed.*

was alive. 8. Do not try to persuade Pliny to stay in Rome. When his work is done,[1] he will hasten to his Tuscan villa.

221. IV. SELECTIONS 10–12

Vocative case (**352**). Future passive participle (**398**). Dative of agent (**317**).

1. Zosimus, play[2] the lyre for your master! 2. Pliny ought to treat Zosimus kindly because he[3] is a good slave. 3. Zosimus sometimes read to his master too long and overtaxed[4] his voice. 4. How many times, Pliny, must we listen-to these bad poets (reeite)? 5. He found Zosimus reciting (a poem) as if he were[5] a Roman poet, not a Greek slave. 6. Pliny then praised him for his genius. 7. All slaves are now free, but at that time in Rome many were-the-slaves-of[6] cruel masters. 8. Let us all listen to Zosimus read[7] Pliny's letter.

222. V. SELECTIONS 13–16

Substantive clauses of result (**379**). Substantive **quod** clauses (**365**).

1. It happened that Pliny's eyes were very weak. 2. And so he writes that he studied in a dark bedroom with his ears. 3. Although Pliny did not think that wine injured him, nevertheless he used it very sparingly. 4. The fact that my eyes are weak does not keep me from seeing[8] that my friend has sent me a very fat hen.

---

[1] Ablative absolute. [2] *use.* [3] **hic.** [4] **imperō.**
[5] Subjunctive. [6] **serviō.** [7] Present participle.
[8] For mood see **371.**

5. We must look out that we do not seem to be of doubtful sanity when-we-are-reciting.[1] 6. Let the windows remain closed! The light hurts my eyes! 7. Pliny, I advise you to remain in bed. 8. That Pliny had so many friends made the longest day seem short to him.

223. VI. Selections 17–20

Substantive **quīn** clauses (**371, 372**).

1. There is no doubt that many boys studied at Milan. 2. Do you think that Pliny was able to hire teachers? 3. The fact that there were no teachers made the boys rejoice. 4. It must not be doubted that a few parents sent their children to foreign teachers. 5. Although Pliny had no children, he thought that boys should be educated at Rome rather than sent to Milan. 6. Pliny begged Trajan to grant (the right of) citizenship to a friend of his (Pliny's) doctor. 7. Consequently it happened that this man and [2] several others received (the right of) citizenship. 8. Pliny was not prevented by Trajan from correcting evils in Bithynia.

224. VII. Selections 21–27

Simple conditions (**390, I**). Causal relative clauses (**380, a**).

1. Trajan thought that the people were able to extinguish their own fires. 2. If the citizens of Asia build [3] an aqueduct, they will obtain very good water

---

[1] Participle.　　　[2] **cum.**　　　[3] Not present.

from a spring. 3. Trajan will not grant the right to build an aqueduct to people[1] who have wasted so much money. 4. If Pliny is willing to give a third part of all the money for hiring teachers, we ought to rejoice. 5. If it was cheaper to build a part of brick-work,[2] why did Trajan permit the people to use blocks of stone?[3] 6. There was no doubt that the city should be supplied[4] with water, but the soft ground was not able to support an aqueduct. 7. If the people wish us to provide those things that will aid in extinguishing fires, the houses will not be destroyed. 8. Pliny condemned the people who destroyed the aqueduct when it was unfinished.

225. VIII. Selections 28–29

Future less vivid conditions (**390, III**).

1. Pliny said that he had never been present at the trials of the Christians. 2. Did it avail a Christian to deny that he had worshiped Christ? 3. If these Christians should worship the image of Trajan, pardon would be granted them. 4. If this man was free from crime, he ought not to have been punished. 5. The Christians said that they would not worship Trajan's image. 6. There is no doubt that Pliny did not wish the Christians to be punished. 7. If an accusation should be made, this man would not confess that he is a Christian. 8. It happened that (only) a few denied that they had been Christians.

---

[1] eīs.   [2] testāceum opus.
[3] lapis quadrātus.
[4] *water . . . led-through to the city.*

226. IX. SELECTIONS 30–35

Purpose and result clauses (**367, 378**).

1. What sort of horse was (that) of Seius? 2. He excelled all-other horses in size and was of unbelievable beauty. 3. He was also a horse of such ill (omen) that whoever possessed[1] him perished wretchedly.[2] 4. If the teacher says that the vocative is **ēgregī,** I shall not write **ēgregie.** 5. Regulus had to fight[3] with his whole army in order to overcome a serpent one hundred twenty feet long. 6. If Xerxes should get possession of Athens, he would carry away all the books. 7. The Athenians will carry away their books to a safe place lest the Persians, after burning the city,[4] destroy them. 8. If the horse which he possessed was like mine, he bought it at a very high price.[5]

227. X. SELECTIONS 36–42

Indirect questions (**386**).

1. Can you tell how many men are in the senate? 2. Let us ask the consul whether he is going to call-upon this senator. 3. " Crassus," the censor said, " you have entered the senate in order to discover whom the consul will first call upon." 4. Let him not ask Crassus his opinion, since Crassus is unwilling to tell what he thinks. 5. When these men saw Africanus and Gracchus feasting (as) friends in the temple of Jupiter, they told how often they had disagreed. 6. There is no doubt that this man predicted Caesar's

---

[1] Subjunctive.   [2] *with wretched death.*
[3] See **398,** I.   [4] Ablative absolute   [5] Ablative.

victory in the assembly of the soldiers. 7. Since you know (how) to speak Latin, can you not ask this soldier where the camp of Caesar is? 8. We advised the slave not to buy many books, even if they were cheap.

228.   XI. Selections 42, 45–48

Review.

1. Can we believe that the Scythians had one eye in the middle of the forehead and fed on the bodies of human beings? 2. If you should see certain (people) with no necks and having eyes in their shoulders, how fast would you run? 3. If the prize is lost,[1] we shall all assemble again and try to solve the question. 4. We are accustomed to believe that Niobe had fourteen children, but some writers declare that she had only three. 5. Is it of any concern[2] to us how many children Niobe had, since Apollo and Diana killed them all? 6. Trimalchio feared his wife so much that he believed everything that she said. 7. Let us hasten to see the fire which started[3] in the home of Trimalchio. 8. No doubt Trimalchio's slave started[4] the fire.

229.   XII. Selections 49, 43, 44

Review.

1. If Trimalchio thinks that what he said[5] about the Trojan War is true, he is greatly mistaken. 2. For he said that Diomedes and Ganymede were brothers and that Helen was their sister! 3. The teacher forbade the boys to listen longer to Trimalchio (when

---

[1] Future perfect.
[2] Dative.
[3] **orior**; subjunctive (**388**).
[4] **faciō.**
[5] Subjunctive.

he was) saying such things. 4. If it should seem (best) to Hannibal to exchange prisoners (of war), all Romans would rejoice. 5. Was it not a great disgrace that two prisoners did not return to Carthage? 6. If this noble prisoner said that he would return, he must not deceive Hannibal. 7. The parents of the prisoners will beg them not to return. 8. We do not know why the exchange of the prisoners did not please the senate.

EXERCISES FOR PART III

230. I. Cat. I, Sections 1–2

Direct questions (**287**). Predicate nominative (**296**). Predicate genitive (**298**).

A. 1. Whom did Catiline mark out for murder? 2. The man whom Catiline marked out was consul. 3. Will the senate be held in the temple of Jupiter or in the Forum? 4. The senate will be held in the temple of Jupiter. The Forum is not a very well fortified place 5. Was not Catiline very brave? Yes,[1] but Cicero, who was made consul, was braver. 6. By whose order ought[2] Catiline to have been killed?[3] The consul's. 7. Cicero did not kill Catiline, did he? 8. No, but Catiline was called by Cicero a plague of the fatherland.

B. Catiline will enter the senate and become a participant in public discussion. But Cicero will avoid his mad weapons,[4] and the senate will hurry[5] him away to his death. Will not Catiline's plans be revealed?

---

[1] Repeat the verb: **erat.**   [2] Past tense.   [3] Present tense.
[4] *madness and weapons.*   [5] **dūcō.**

The senate is not ignorant of these plans, is it? Cicero cried-out: O the times, the customs (of us Romans)! We consuls are not doing-our-duty[1] by the republic.[2]"

231. II. Cat. I, Sections 3–5

Indirect questions (**386**). Sequence of tenses (**359**). Genitive of the whole (**300**). Genitive of description (**299**). Ablative of description (**342**).

A. 1. Do you know, Cicero, what harm the republic will receive? 2. We all knew what plan Catiline was adopting. 3. Catiline wondered why the senate had a decree of this kind. 4. We shall ask Catiline why he desired to lay waste the whole world. 5. Can you tell us whether the consul seemed too cruel or Catiline too wicked? 6. The consul was not cruel, but Catiline, who was of most illustrious family, was the most wicked of all (men). 7. Will a man of such worthlessness abandon his (acts of) boldness? 8. No, for he knows what plans the senate has and he does not fear the punishment of that body.

B. The senate knew what Catiline did the night before and what plan he had adopted. But was any one of the senators willing to believe the report?[3] Catiline, in fact, came into the senate and Cicero, the consul, wondered whether he would[4] remain or not.

[1] **satis faciō.**   [2] Dative.
[3] *those (things) said.* What case?
[4] Future active participle + **sum.**

232.   III. Cat. I, Sections 6–7

Infinitive as subject (**400**). Genitive with verbs
(**306**). Dative of possession (**316**).

A. 1. It is difficult for Catiline to hide his wicked
crimes.   2. Did Cicero forget what Catiline tried to
say in the senate?   3. Cicero's enemies will forget, but
Cicero and the rest-of-the senators should remember
Catiline's words.   4. It seemed pleasing to the senate's
leader not to put Catiline to death.   5. It is said that
Cicero had[1] a guard of very brave soldiers.   6. It
seemed (best) to the senate to ask Catiline whether
Manlius was in the senate or outside the city.   7. To
kill the consul in his home was a savage crime.   8. We
now know who is called the enemy of the republic.

B. Catiline does not dare to kill Cicero because the
eyes of the senators are watching him (Catiline).   The
voices of this conspiracy can no longer be restrained
within the walls of the city.   Catiline will soon go, and
it will be pleasing to all of us to see him go.

233.   IV. Cat. I, Sections 8–9

Infinitive as object (**401**). Subordinate clauses in
indirect discourse (**387**). Indirect object (**309**).

A. 1. Catiline wished to seize Praeneste, but he
found that that colony had been fortified by Cicero's
garrisons.   2. Did the consuls see what conspirators
were with Catiline at the home of Laeca?   3. The
consul will tell the senate what the conspirators tried to
do on that night.   4. Catiline distributed parts of Italy

---

[1] Use **sum.**

to the conspirators and placed Manlius in command of the camp. 5. We know that the men whom Catiline left behind at Rome promised to kill the consul. 6. Do you know why the men left behind at Rome by Catiline were unable to kill Cicero? 7. Cicero spared those who tried to kill him, but ordered[1] the senators to watch-out for the safety of the republic. 8. And now,[2] do the immortal gods know where-in-the-world we are?

B. The senators had never seen men of such boldness. These wicked (men) do not deny that they were trying to move against the republic. Moreover Cicero knows that they will not be content with the murder of those who will not flee from the city. But Catiline is no longer quiet and daily plots the destruction of the city.

234. V. CAT. I, SECTIONS 10–15

Simple conditions (**390, I**). Dative with adjectives (**312**). Participles (**395–397**).

A. 1. If Catiline leads[3] out all his comrades, the city will be cleansed. 2. But if Catiline, plotting so often against the consul, remains in Rome, no good (person) will escape destruction. 3. Does it delight Catiline that this disgrace will always cling to his reputation? 4. Catiline, (who is) hostile to the republic, will sometime be driven into exile, unless he ceases[3] to stir up the citizens. 5. Cicero ought not to pass over all these crimes, ought he, (when he is) about to speak of Catiline's private life? 6. A senator asked why Cicero

---

[1] Use **iubeō**. [2] **dēnique.** [3] Future perfect.

had not ordered Catiline (to be) arrested (and) to be killed. 7. Cicero replied: " If I do not kill Catiline now, I shall finally be able to drive both him and his comrades out of the city." 8. Who is opposing Catiline as he delays in the city?

B. If Cicero sees what Catiline is doing, he will not permit him to remain longer in the city. For Catiline is a bold, bad (man), threatening everybody with death and plotting against the consuls and the leaders of the state. A man of such worthlessness ought either to be driven from the city or put to death at once.

235. VI. Cat. I, Sections 16–20

Future less vivid conditions (**390, III**). Proviso clauses (**374**). Accusative of extent (**319**).

A. 1. If Cicero, moved by pity, should permit Catiline to live many years, he (Cicero) would always be in danger. 2. Cicero did not fear Catiline, provided that the latter[1] stayed outside the city. 3. But if Catiline should come into the senate armed, the senators would run, as we think, from the senate-house with great speed. 4. Do you know whether or not Cicero's slaves feared him? 5. A few slaves hated him, but most (of them) respected his authority. 6. If anything[2] should happen to Cicero, the senate would not be able to win the other consul over to the state. 7. Cicero said that the fatherland was the common parent of all Romans. 8. If the fatherland is the parent, Catiline is not a good son.

---

[1] hic. [2] quid.

B. Catiline, having at last departed from the city, has freed us all from fear. Provided that he stays for many years we shall all be happy. But he has not gone, has he? If he awaits longer the spoken[1] opinion of the consul, the senate will lay violent[2] hands on him.

236. VII. Cat. I, Sections 21–27

Conditions contrary to fact (**390, II**). Ablative of separation (**327**). Ablative of place from which (**328**).

A. 1. O Catiline, if fear of prison could recall you from your baseness, it would be worth-the-price[3] to endure unpopularity. 2. Do you think that Catiline shrinks from the slaughter of honorable men? 3. If Catiline cannot[4] longer be deprived of that eagle, he will depart[5] from Rome and hasten to Faesulae. 4. And yet his joy would have been very great, I suppose, if he had seen only wicked men in Rome. 5. Even if Catiline had been killed, we would not be safe now. 6. Marcus Tullius, if you had seen that Catiline was going-to-be a leader in war,[6] would you have allowed this instigator of crime to leave the city? 7. Unless the praetor arrests[5] Catiline's associates and drags them away to prison, we shall never be free from fear. 8. If Cicero has kept Catiline from the consulship, the latter will no longer be able, as he was wont, to harass the republic.

B. Cicero said that he did not know why he was talking about these crimes of Catiline. This wicked

---

[1] Lit., *command of the consul speaking.*   [2] Lit., *violence and hands.*
[3] **tantī.**   [4] Present.   [5] Participle.   [6] *of war.*

citizen ought to be in prison. The ancestors of the
Romans were wont to put to death men of such[1] ambitions. For they were unwilling (for) such men to
plot against the property of good (citizens).

237.   VIII. Cat. I, Sections 28–33

Volitive subjunctive (**366**). Imperative (**393**). Ablative of source (**329**).

A. 1. Let us no longer endure Catiline, (even though
he was) born of illustrious ancestors. 2. Let Catiline
and his comrades go to the Manlian camp. 3. Let
not sleep be dear to you, fellow citizens! Drive Catiline from the city at once! 4. What would the republic have thought, if Catiline had led his comrades
out of all Italy? 5. Let these conspirators confess that
they have tried to blot out the light of the republic.
6 If these robbers had not been (men) of such sluggishness, perhaps they would have been able to conceal
their crimes. 7. Catiline seems to have sprung from
the seed of all evils and to have been born under[2] most
evil omens. 8. Let Catiline remove the torches (which
have been) placed under the senate-house.

B. Show gratitude, Cicero, to the Roman people,
unless you want unpopularity to hang over you in[3] the
future. They are asking what hinders you. Let fear
of any danger be banished from your mind and sluggishness from your body. Let all (of) us senators
promise the people that Catiline shall die in exile.

---

[1] iste.
[2] Without preposition.
[3] of.

238. IX. Cat. II, Sections 1, 17, 18

Deliberative subjunctive (**375**). Ablative of manner (**333**).

A. 1. Where has Catiline gone? He has left the city with the greatest speed. 2. Why should he longer threaten this city with fire and sword? Let him live with his wicked comrades in a distant land! 3. If, fellow citizens, you should see Catiline what would you do? 4. If this can in any way be accomplished, we shall not punish these wicked (men). 5. But how can we cure them? These friends of Catiline do not wish to be won-over to the state. 6. Who is talking with Catiline? I do not know who he is. 7. He did not understand how this could be done, but he said that he would explain what he intended[1] to do. 8. The senators knew that Catiline was wrong when-he-said[2] that he was fighting against wicked men in-behalf-of the state.

B. If Catiline remains longer in Rome, Cicero will discover with whom he converses and in what manner he hopes to destroy[3] the city. But what is he expecting? Why should he hesitate to withdraw something from his money[4] and the returns[5] of his farms and add to his credit? Let him not think that he can increase his wealth by war.

---

[1] Future active participle with **sum.**
[2] Present participle.
[3] Future infinitive.
[4] **argentum.**
[5] **frūctūs.**

239.   X. Cat. II, Sections 19–23

Optative subjunctive (**376**). Ablative of respect (**345**).

A. 1. Oh that this settler had not bought his farm for so high a price![1]   2. Other settlers chose large farms, which they bought at a very small price.   3. Oh that Sulla might be raised from the dead! For if he were here, these men would cease to talk about the expenses of their farms.   4. These robbers excelled the senators in diligence.   5. Others Cicero called herds (of cattle) and hoped that they would perish in their brigandage. 6. This class is last in number and manner of living. For they are even fond of Catiline.   7. Provided that this gladiator combs[2] his hair, we shall let him stay in the city.   8. Oh that that robber, who vowed that he would be king, may not overthrow our government!

B. Do not plan confiscations (of property), Catiline. Your nearest neighbors know that you are a bad debtor[3] and they hope that you, who cannot live uprightly, will perish disgracefully. But why should I warn you? Let your[4] wicked herd of robbers immediately leave the city!

240.   XI. Cat. III, Sections 1–5

Ablative absolute (**335**).

A. 1. If you should explain in the senate what Catiline has done, not all the senators would believe you. 2. Would we be extolling Romulus to-day, if Catiline

---

[1] Ablative.   [2] **pexerit.**
[3] **infitiātor lentus.**   [4] **iste.**

had been able to destroy this city? 3. Do we not know what crimes Catiline committed in the consulship of Cicero? 4. When this city was founded, Romulus because of his kindness was (held) in honor among the Romans. 5. Would the conspirators have dared to do these things in the consulship of Caesar? 6. Oh that Caesar may decide to aid Cicero in behalf of the fatherland! 7. Cicero would be able to expose[1] the conspiracy and save the temples of the gods from wicked men. 8. It remained to explain to the people what seemed best to be done; and when this had been done, the senate ordered the praetors to undertake the business without any delay.

B. After the finding[1] of the letters, Cicero thought that he would be able[2] to arrest Catiline. But Catiline aroused[1] his comrades and fled from Rome. Let him depart, Cicero! It is easy to see that the conspiracy has been exposed.

241. XII. Cat. III, Sections 6–11

Substantive **quīn** clauses (**371, 372**). Ablative of place (**343**). Locative (**351**).

A. 1. There is no doubt that a great disturbance was caused[3] the state. 2. But who will say that this was done rashly? 3. For (even) if nothing should be found in the letters, nevertheless Cicero thought that the senate ought to be called to the temple of Jupiter. 4. We do not doubt that Cicero will give[4] Lentulus an opportunity to speak[5] in the senate. 5. However,

---

[1] Ablative absolute.   [2] Present tense.
[3] **iniciō.**   [4] *make.*   [5] *if he wishes to speak.*

does he[1] know whether he[2] is at home or in the country?　6. When the letters had been read at Rome, there was no doubt that these conspirators would soon confess.　7. Let Lentulus confess how many times he has tried to set fire to the city.　8. You do not doubt, do you, Cethegus, that the praetor brought-away a great number of weapons from your home?

B. May Cicero never[3] fear the unpopularity which Catiline says is threatening him.　For the people all know that Cicero has saved the state.　Moreover, the report will come to the ears of those wicked (men who are) remaining among[4] us in Rome (of) how many times the consul has beaten back the swords (that have been) drawn against our republic.

242.　XIII. CAT. III, SECTIONS 12–16[5]

Gerund (**399**). Future passive participle (**398**). Dative of agent (**317**). Ablative of agent (**330**).

A. 1. Lentulus' training in[6] speaking did not avail him.　2. And for that reason he did not know what he ought to say.　3. If we hope to be able to oppose these conspirators, we shall have to choose men faithful to Cicero.　4. But what should Cicero do first?　He ought to punish these (men) and not let them go. 5. Let us not allow men of this kind to entertain[7] the hope of destroying this beautiful city.　6. Do you think that a man clad-in-the-toga[8] is ready for fighting? 7. They realized that the men chosen by Catiline for-

---

[1] ille.　　　[2] hic.　　　[3] nē . . . umquam.　　　[4] *with.*
[5] Use future passive participle whenever possible in this lesson.
[6] *of.*　　　　　[7] *come into.*　　　　[8] togātus.

the-sake-of accomplishing the conspiracy had failed them. 8. Provided that Catiline is not confined within the walls of the city, he is not to be feared.

B. There is no doubt that the senate was freed from all (religious) scruple in the punishment of Lentulus. For this man, who was almost equal to Catiline, was no longer to be endured. And yet, would that we knew how we might catch[1] Catiline and bring him back to Rome! But let him go! Cicero will soon consult the senate (as to) what shall seem best to be done concerning him.

243. XIV. Cat. III, Sections 17–22

Volitive substantive clauses (**370**). Ablative of time (**344**).

A. 1. The senate ordered[2] Cicero to attend[3] to the setting up of the statue. 2. If Cicero had said that he alone had opposed those who had attempted to destroy the city, he would have attributed too much to himself. 3. We fear that the senate will think that they have joined (themselves) with the conspirators for the sake of destroying the city. 4. If these crimes have been planned by wicked citizens, the city is in great danger. 5. Cicero to-day advised the praetors to lead the conspirators to their punishment. 6. For he was afraid that within a few days the senate would not keep-in-mind the crimes[4] committed by these evil (men). 7. The senate has decreed that the statue of Jupiter shall be set up at this very time. 8. When this had

---

[1] *having been caught.*
[3] cūrō.
[2] Write twice, using **iubeō** and **imperō**.
[4] Accusative.

been done, we could easily see that that which ought to have been done by good citizens had been finally done by the gods.

B. We urge Cicero not to fear Catiline. We know that Catiline is clever in crime, but all men are not like Catiline, and this empire will not be handed over to the Gauls for plundering. However, let us warn the magistrates to be-on-the-watch.

244. XV. CAT. III, SECTIONS 17–22

Substantive clauses of result (**379**). Dative with adjectives and verbs (**312, 313**).

A. 1. It happened that the leaders of the conspiracy were living at Rome. 2. These men at this time were hostile to Cicero and after preparing civil discord hoped to be able to blot out the (leading) lights of the state. 3. Do you not remember with what harmony the knights and the senators were united? 4. Persuade this man not to envy the good citizens. 5. What made the Romans think that they ought to placate the gods? 6. Did Cicero think that all these (things) were accomplished by the nod of the gods (any) more than by his own bravery? 7. But Cicero happened not to believe these things. Why then did he advise the people to obey the gods? 8. If Cicero demands no monument to his praise, will not the people think that he has accomplished nothing worthy of a consul?

B. Cicero tells in the third oration with how great disaster to the state Sulla avenged Marius' cruelty. But if men like Sulla did not wish that there be no republic, why did they hope to be leaders in the city which they were willing to burn? We must look out for (the welfare of) our state! If it is (the part) of human wisdom to save good men, let us drive all men (who are) worthy of death out of the city!

245. XVI. Cat. III, Sections 27–29; IV, 4

Subjunctives of purpose and result (**367–369, 378**).

A. 1. Cicero had to live with those whom he had conquered. 2. If Catiline escapes to the Manlian camp, he will return within three days to slay the senators. 3. Cicero does not think that his deeds will injure him. 4. Oh that all foreign enemies may be joined in harmony with the Roman people! 5. For Cicero has brought it about that all (men) within the city (of) Rome have ceased[1] to carry on war with each[2] other. 6. Will you not aid us, Catiline, in attaining (to) these things? 7. Cicero called the senate together in order to see what the opinions of Silanus and Caesar were. 8. Caesar wants to deprive these assassins[3] of their property in order that they may enjoy life less.

B. These conspirators labored to destroy this beautiful city. But all good men gladly undertook the preservation[4] of the republic and looked out that Catiline should not be able to injure the consul. Let us depart now to our homes that we may defend our wives and children. Caesar will cause[5] the conspirators to be distributed among the municipalities, or Silanus will urge that they be punished with death.

---

[1] Primary sequence.   [2] *among themselves.*   [3] **sīcārius.**
[4] Future passive participle.   [5] *bring about.*

Oh that the gods may free us from the fear of these wicked men!

246.   XVII. Arch., Sections 1-4

Cum clauses (**382-384**).

A. 1. Since Cicero had had much training in speaking, he thought that he could persuade the judges to give Archias citizenship. 2. When the matter had been argued[1] before the praetor, (who was) Cicero's brother, it happened that Archias was added to the number of citizens at Rome. 3. Although the judges and the friends of Cicero wondered that he was using this style of speaking, Cicero spoke as if he knew what ought to be said in behalf of an excellent citizen and learned poet. 4. When Cicero sees his friend Archias on the street, he is so delighted that he talks with nobody else. 5. Did Cicero ask of these very stern judges that they allow him to speak more freely about Archias? 6. Archias must be defended by Cicero that all may know that he is a Roman citizen. 7. Consequently, let us hope that the judges will not consider Cicero's speech annoying. 8. Moreover, if you are able to speak and write well, you will never be separated from the number of your citizens.

B. Rome was once a great city in which Greeks lived and wrote as if they were Roman citizens. And so it happened that since Archias was worthy of citizenship, he obtained it through Cicero's power in[2] speaking. For when the enemies of Lucullus desired to injure him,[3] they said that the friend of Lucullus was not a citizen.

---

[1] agō.   [2] *of.*   [3] ipse.

247.   XVIII. Arch., Sections 5–11

Review.

A. 1. Although Italy was at that time full of Greek arts, the Latin language was cultivated more vigorously here at Rome. 2. While Archias was living at the home of Lucullus, he was pleasing to many famous Romans. 3. Did not these men wait in the atrium until Archias appeared and spoke with them? 4. While Archias was registering[1] before the praetor, an enemy denied that he (Archias) had had a home at Rome. 5. Why does Grattius demand the public records, since he knows that they are often corrupted? 6. When the censor called at Lucullus' home, he sought for Archias in vain. The latter was with the quaestor in Asia. 7. Archias made wills as if he were[2] a Roman citizen. 8. He thought that he was a Roman citizen and had done all that was to be done.

B. Where-in-the-world was Archias? He was waiting for Lucullus outside the city. While he was waiting there Grattius was talking with the praetor. Grattius said to the praetor: " I have no hope of defeating Archias, but I hate Lucullus so much that I am willing to injure Archias."

248.   XIX. Arch., Sections 12–18

Ablative of comparison (**331**). Ablative of measure of difference (**341**).

A. 1. Cicero said that if anyone enjoyed these studies, he would devote himself to them. 2. Cicero

---

[1] **profiteor;** use present tense.   [2] Imperfect subjunctive.

enjoyed these studies more than other Romans. 3. Do you find-fault-with us because we devote more time to (playing) ball than to study? 4. I cannot be persuaded that young men are better trained to-day in culture than the old men. 5. Did you not say, Archias, that your brother was ten years older than you? 6. He was much older and wiser than I. 7. For he was a poet of very great talent and wrote more excellent verses than any man in Antioch. 8. We think that Archias ought to win the love of all those listening (to him) by the unbelievable quickness of his genius.

B. Cicero asked us if we did not think that Archias should be defended by every (possible) means. We think that if Roscius was loved so much, Archias, who is more famous than Roscius and pleasing to the Luculli, ought to be loved by every educated Roman.

249. XX. Arch., Sections 19–25

Place constructions (**320, 328, 343, 351**).

A. 1. At Athens the name of poets was sacred; was this true in Italy? 2. No one knows in what city Homer was born; some think that he was not born at all. 3. Archias came to Rome, Italy, (as) a young man. 4. From Antioch, where he was born, he went to Greece, and from Greece to Italy. 5. If you do not know where Antioch is, I will tell you that it is in Syria. 6. If Archias had remained in Antioch, Syria, would he have been a more famous poet? 7. Archias went to Asia with Lucullus and after he returned to Rome wrote a poem about the Mithridatic war.

8. Did Archias possess greater ability in writing than Cicero?

B. Romans, do not deprive this poet of citizenship! For he is like our Ennius and is most pleasing to the gods. He has lived at Rome for many years. He is famous not only in Italy but also in Athens and Alexandria and the cities of Asia. He came to Rome from the city (of) Heraclea, in which he was a citizen.

250. XXI. ARCH., SECTIONS 26–32.

Descriptive relative clauses (**380**).

A. 1. There is no one who is not influenced by the desire for praise. 2. Archias' case was of the sort which was easy to prove. 3. He advised me not to revere the temple in which the fugitive had been killed. 4. There is no reward which Cicero wants except praise. 5. Archias is one of those who have always been called sacred by the Romans. 6. It is not our custom to crush ourselves with cares that may be avoided. 7. There are some men who are greedy for[1] money, others to whom it is of no concern. 8. The Romans ought to give citizenship to the man who has written poems about Roman victories.

B. Do you know why Archias did not complete this book? Some say[2] that he despised those who sought glory. Others say that he did not consider himself worthy to[3] treat with verses the great deeds which Cicero had accomplished. However, if the subject seemed pleasing to him, he should have completed it.

---

[1] of.　　　[2] There are who say.　　　[3] who should.

251. XXII. Review

1. Defend your homes, citizens; Catiline is about to attack the city. 2. If your consul were not watchful, the city would have been captured by the conspirators. 3. Although I had not seen my friend for many years, I recognized him at once. 4. Cicero said that glory, not money, was to be sought by us. 5. What should we do first to attain it? 6. If your friend should attain glory by writing books, what would you say? 7. It is a republic of great strength which does not remove by death its suppliant enemies. 8. Do not fear your consul; he is trying to deprive these robbers of their booty and keep the citizens safe.

252 XXIII. Review

1. Let not Catiline again threaten the city. 2. Cicero did not ask Catiline what his plans were because he already knew. 3. Can a man who does not know (how) to read be a great poet? 4. When Archias had seen the great cities of Asia and Greece, he decided that he ought to see Italy. 5. Cicero read many books written by Greek poets but he also was fond of Roman writers. 6. There was no temple too sacred for Catiline[1] to plunder. 7. If this poet had been born of noble parents on the Calends of April, would you have expected greater things (of him)? 8. Did the praetor say that a man of so great rashness ought to be hurried away to prison? If he said that, he ought to be praised by all.

---

[1] *which he would not,* etc.

253.   XXIV. Review

1. It is difficult to say whether all men like Catiline deserve death or imprisonment.[1]   2. There is no doubt that under the leadership of Cicero the republic will be saved.   3. It happened that on that night there was a full moon and Catiline had no hope of concealing his wicked crimes.   4. Send a man to bring away from the home of Cethegus whatever weapons may be (there). 5. Cethegus spoke as if he had always been fond[2] of fine weapons.   6. Do you know whether Caesar or Cicero was killed on the Ides of March?   7. When he had journeyed many miles from Rome into the country, he lay down to rest.   8. Since you have refused so many times to purchase this fine house, I shall not ask you again.

FIG. 125. St. Peter's and the Tomb of Hadrian

In the Tiber is a barge carrying a huge monolith to be erected in honor of Mussolini.

---

[1] *prison.*   [2] studiōsus.

254. IMPORTANT DATES IN ROMAN HISTORY

A Chronological Summary of Parts I–IV

B. C.

106–43	Cicero, orator, statesman, man of letters
106–48	Pompey, general, political leader
100–44	Caesar, general, statesman, writer
88–63	Mithridatic Wars
86–35	Sallust, historian
81	Cicero delivers his *Pro Quinctio*, his earliest extant speech
70	Cicero's speeches against Verres
66	Cicero praetor; speech *De Imperio Gnaei Pompei*
63	Cicero consul (with Antonius)
	Conspiracy of Catiline. Cicero's *Four Speeches against Catiline*
62	Cicero's *Defense of Archias*
60	First Triumvirate (Caesar, Crassus, Pompey)
58–50	Caesar in Gaul
58	Cicero banished
57	Cicero recalled
51	Cicero governor of Cilicia
49	Caesar crosses the Rubicon, thus precipitating civil war
48	Battle of Pharsalus — Pompey defeated
	Pompey murdered in Egypt
44	Caesar assassinated, March 15
	Cicero's fourteen *Philippics* against Antony
43	Cicero beheaded by Antony's order
43–A.D. 17	Ovid, poet, author of the *Metamorphoses*
31–A.D. 14	Reign of Augustus
4 ?–A.D. 65	Seneca, Stoic philosopher and writer

A. D.

8	Banishment of Ovid. *Metamorphoses* finished
54–68	Reign of Nero
62–114 ?	Pliny the Younger, author of *Letters*
66	Death of Petronius, the novelist
98–117	Reign of Trajan
130–180 ?	Aulus Gellius, author of *Noctes Atticae*

255. BOOKS FOR COLLATERAL READ-ING OR REFERENCE

PART II

JOHNSTON, H. W., *The Private Life of the Romans*, Scott, Foresman and Company, Chicago (1903).

PART III

ABBOTT, FRANK F., *A History and Description of Roman Political Institutions*, 3d edition, Ginn and Company, Boston (1909).

ABBOTT, FRANK F., *Roman Politics* (Our Debt to Greece and Rome Series), Longmans, Green and Company, New York (1923).

ABBOTT, FRANK F., *Society and Politics in Ancient Rome*, Charles Scribner's Sons, New York (1909).

BOISSIER, GASTON, *Cicero and His Friends*, G. P. Putnam's Sons, New York (1907).

CHURCH, A. J., *Roman Life in the Days of Cicero*, The Macmillan Company, New York (1883).

DAVIS, WILLIAM STEARNS, *A Day in Old Rome*, Allyn and Bacon, Boston (1925).

FOWLER, W. W., *Social Life at Rome in the Age of Cicero*, The Macmillan Company, New York (1909).

LOVELL, ISABEL, *Stories in Stone from the Roman Forum*, The Macmillan Company, New York (1902).

ROLFE, JOHN C., *Cicero and His Influence* (Our Debt to Greece and Rome Series), Longmans, Green and Company, New York (1923).

STOBART, J. C., *The Grandeur That Was Rome*, Sidgwick and Jackson, London (1920).

STRACHAN-DAVIDSON, J. L., *Cicero and the Fall of the Roman Republic*, G. P. Putnam's Sons, New York (1903).

PART IV

BULFINCH, THOMAS, *The Age of Fable*, Thomas Y. Crowell Company, New York (1913).

GAYLEY, CHARLES, *Classic Myths*, Ginn and Company, New York (1911).

GUERBER, H. A., *Myths of Greece and Rome*, American Book Company, New York (1895).

SABIN, FRANCES E., *Classical Myths That Live Today*, Silver, Burdett and Company (1927).

FIG. 126. THE FORUM OF AUGUSTUS, ROME

The temple is that in honor of Mars Ultor. Behind it is the high wall which shut off the view of the slums.

GREEK ALPHABET

Capital	Small	Value	Name
A	α	a	alpha
B	β	b	beta
Γ	γ	g	gamma
Δ	δ	d	delta
E	ε	ĕ	epsilon
Z	ζ	z	zeta
H	η	ē	eta
Θ	ϑ	th	theta
I	ι	i	iota
K	κ	k	kappa
Λ	λ	l	lambda
M	μ	m	mu
N	ν	n	nu
Ξ	ξ	x	xi
O	ο	ŏ	omicron
Π	π	p	pi
P	ρ	r	rho
Σ	σ, ς	s	sigma
T	τ	t	tau
Υ	υ	y	upsilon
Φ	φ	ph	phi
X	χ	ch (as in German)	chi
Ψ	ψ	ps	psi
Ω	ω	ō	omega

Vowel values are those of Latin; upsilon is like French u, German ü; iota subscript (ᾳ, ῃ, ῳ) is not pronounced.

' over initial vowel not pronounced; ' over initial vowel pronounced h.

´ ` ^ are accent marks.

SUMMARY OF INFLECTIONS

NOUNS

257. FIRST DECLENSION

	Singular	Plural
Nom.	via	viae
Gen.	viae	viārum
Dat.	viae	viīs
Acc.	viam	viās
Abl.	viā	viīs
Voc.		

SECOND DECLENSION

	Singular	Plural
Nom.	servus	servī
Gen.	servī	servōrum
Dat.	servō	servīs
Acc.	servum	servōs
Abl.	servō	servīs
Voc.	serve	

Note. — Fīlius and proper nouns in -ius often have -ī in the genitive and vocative singular: fīlī, Cornēlī. The accent does not change.

258. SECOND DECLENSION

	Singular	Plural	Singular	Plural	Singular	Plural
Nom.	ager	agrī	puer	puerī	signum	signa
Gen.	agrī	agrōrum	puerī	puerōrum	signī	signōrum
Dat.	agrō	agrīs	puerō	puerīs	signō	signīs
Acc.	agrum	agrōs	puerum	puerōs	signum	signa
Abl.	agrō	agrīs	puerō	puerīs	signō	signīs

Note. — Nouns in -ium often have -ī in the genitive singular: cōnsilī. The accent does not change.

259. THIRD DECLENSION

	Singular	Plural	Singular	Plural	Singular	Plural
Nom.	mīles	mīlitēs	lēx	lēgēs	corpus	corpora
Gen.	mīlitis	mīlitum	lēgis	lēgum	corporis	corporum
Dat.	mīlitī	mīlitibus	lēgī	lēgibus	corporī	corporibus
Acc.	mīlitem	mīlitēs	lēgem	lēgēs	corpus	corpora
Abl.	mīlite	mīlitibus	lēge	lēgibus	corpore	corporibus

469

I-Stems

	Singular	Plural		Singular	Plural
Nom.	cīvis	cīvēs		mare	maria
Gen.	cīvis	cīvium		maris	marium
Dat.	cīvī	cīvibus		marī	maribus
Acc.	cīvem	cīvēs (-īs)		mare	maria
Abl.	cīve	cīvibus		marī	maribus

260. FOURTH DECLENSION

	Singular	Plural		Singular	Plural
Nom.	cāsus	cāsūs		cornū	cornua
Gen.	cāsūs	cāsuum		cornūs	cornuum
Dat.	cāsuī	cāsibus		cornū	cornibus
Acc.	cāsum	cāsūs		cornū	cornua
Abl.	cāsū	cāsibus		cornū	cornibus

261. FIFTH DECLENSION

	Singular	Plural		Singular	Plural
Nom.	diēs	diēs		rēs	rēs
Gen.	diēī	diērum		reī	rērum
Dat.	diēī	diēbus		reī	rēbus
Acc.	diem	diēs		rem	rēs
Abl.	diē	diēbus		rē	rēbus

262. NOUNS OF IRREGULAR OR DEFECTIVE DECLENSION

	Sing.	Plur.	Sing.	Sing.	Plur.
Nom.	vīs	vīrēs	nēmō	domus	domūs
Gen.	——	vīrium	(nūllīus)	domūs (-ī)	domuum (-ōrum)
Dat.	——	vīribus	nēminī	domuī (-ō)	domibus
Acc.	vim	vīrēs (-īs)	nēminem	domum	domōs (-ūs)
Abl.	vī	vīribus	(nūllō)	domō (-ū)	domibus
Loc.				domī	

ADJECTIVES

263.   FIRST AND SECOND DECLENSIONS

Nom.	magn**us**, *m.*	magn**a**, *f.*	magn**um**, *n.*
Gen.	magn**ī**, *etc.*	magn**ae**, *etc.*	magn**ī**, *etc.*

Nom.	līber, *m.*	līber**a**, *f.*	līber**um**, *n.*
Gen.	līber**ī**, *etc.*	līber**ae**, *etc.*	līber**ī**, *etc.*

(The -e- is retained before -r- throughout)

Nom.	noster, *m.*	nost**ra**, *f.*	nost**rum**, *n.*
Gen.	nost**rī**, *etc.*	nost**rae**, *etc.*	nost**rī**, *etc.*

(The -e- is dropped before -r- throughout)

264.   THIRD DECLENSION

a. THREE ENDINGS

	SINGULAR			PLURAL		
Nom.	ācer, *m.*	ācris, *f.*	ācre, *n.*	ācr**ēs**	ācr**ēs**	ācr**ia**
Gen.	ācr**is**	ācr**is**	ācr**is**	ācr**ium**	ācr**ium**	ācr**ium**
Dat.	ācr**ī**	ācr**ī**	ācr**ī**	ācr**ibus**	ācr**ibus**	ācr**ibus**
Acc.	ācr**em**	ācr**em**	ācr**e**	ācr**ēs** (-**īs**)	ācr**ēs** (-**īs**)	ācr**ia**
Abl.	ācr**ī**	ācr**ï**	ācr**ī**	ācr**ibus**	ācr**ibus**	ācr**ibus**

b. TWO ENDINGS   *c.* ONE ENDING

Nom.	fortis, *m., f.*	fort**e**, *n.*	pār, *m., f.*	pār, *n.*
Gen.	fort**is**, *etc.*	fort**is**, *etc.*	par**is**, *etc.*	par**is**, *etc.*

265.   PRESENT PARTICIPLE

	SINGULAR		PLURAL	
Nom.	parāns, *m., f.*	parāns, *n.*	parant**ēs**	parant**ia**
Gen.	parant**is**	parant**is**	parant**ium**	parant**ium**
Dat.	parant**ī**	parant**ī**	parant**ibus**	parant**ibus**
Acc.	parant**em**	parāns	parant**ēs** (-**īs**)	parant**ia**
Abl.	parant**e** (-**ī**)	parant**e** (-**ī**)	parant**ibus**	parant**ibus**

Note. — The future and perfect participles of all verbs are regularly declined like **magnus, -a, -um.**

266. IRREGULAR ADJECTIVES

Nom.	ūnus, m.	ūna, f.	ūnum, n.	trēs, m., f.	tria, n.
Gen.	ūnīus	ūnīus	ūnīus	trium	trium
Dat.	ūnī	ūnī	ūnī	tribus	tribus
Acc.	ūnum	ūnam	ūnum	trēs	tria
Abl.	ūnō	ūnā	ūnō	tribus	tribus

Nom.	duo, m.	duae, f.	duo, n.	mīlle	mīlia
Gen.	duōrum	duārum	duōrum	mīlle	mīlium
Dat.	duōbus	duābus	duōbus	mīlle	mīlibus
Acc.	duōs	duās	duo	mīlle	mīlia
Abl.	duōbus	duābus	duōbus	mīlle	mīlibus

Note. — Like ūnus are alius, alter, ūllus, nūllus, sōlus, tōtus, uter, neuter, uterque. The plural is regular. The nominative and accusative singular neuter of alius is aliud; for the genitive singular of all genders alterīus, with short i (the genitive of alter), is generally used.

267. COMPARISON OF ADJECTIVES

a. REGULAR

POSITIVE	COMPARATIVE	SUPERLATIVE
altus, –a, –um	altior, altius	altissimus, –a, –um
fortis, forte	fortior, –ius	fortissimus, –a, –um
līber, –era, –erum	līberior, –ius	līberrimus, –a, –um
ācer, ācris, ācre	ācrior, –ius	ācerrimus, –a, –um
facilis, facile	facilior, –ius	facillimus, –a, –um

Note. — Like facilis are difficilis, similis, dissimilis. Adjectives in -er are like līber or ācer.

b. IRREGULAR

POSITIVE	COMPARATIVE	SUPERLATIVE
bonus, –a, –um	melior, –ius	optimus, –a, –um
malus, –a, –um	peior, –ius	pessimus, –a, –um
magnus, –a, –um	maior, –ius	maximus, –a, –um
parvus, –a, –um	minor, –us	minimus, –a, –um
multus, –a, –um	——, plūs	plūrimus, –a, –um
īnferus, –a, –um	īnferior, –ius	īnfimus or īmus, –a, –um
superus, –a, –um	superior, –ius	suprēmus or summus, –a, –um
——	prior, –ius	prīmus, –a, –um
——	propior, –ius	proximus, –a, –um
——	ulterior, –ius	ultimus, –a, –um

268. DECLENSION OF COMPARATIVES

	SINGULAR		PLURAL	
Nom.	altior, m., f.	altius, n.	altiōrēs	altiōra
Gen.	altiōris	altiōris	altiōrum	altiōrum
Dat.	altiōrī	altiōrī	altiōribus	altiōribus
Acc.	altiōrem	altius	altiōrēs	altiōra
Abl.	altiōre	altiōre	altiōribus	altiōribus

	SINGULAR	PLURAL	
Nom.	plūs,[1] n.	plūrēs, m., f.	plūra, n.
Gen.	plūris	plūrium	plūrium
Dat.	——	plūribus	plūribus
Acc.	plūs	plūrēs	plūra
Abl.	plūre	plūribus	plūribus

269. COMPARISON OF ADVERBS

POSITIVE	COMPARATIVE	SUPERLATIVE
altē	altius	altissimē
līberē	līberius	līberrimē
fortiter	fortius	fortissimē
facile	facilius	facillimē
bene	melius	optimē
male	peius	pessimē
multum	plūs	plūrimum
——	minus	minimē
(magnopere)	magis	maximē

PRONOUNS

270. PERSONAL

	SING.	PLUR.	SING.	PLUR.	M.	F.	N.
Nom.	ego	nōs	tū	vōs	is	ea	id
Gen.	meī	nostrum (nostrī)	tuī	vestrum (–trī)	(For declen-		
Dat.	mihi	nōbīs	tibi	vōbīs	sion see de-		
Acc.	mē	nōs	tē	vōs	monstrative		
Abl.	mē	nōbīs	tē	vōbīs	is, 272)		

[1] Masculine and feminine lacking in the singular.

271. REFLEXIVE

meī	tuī	*Gen.*	suī
(declined	(declined	*Dat.*	sibi
like	like	*Acc.*	sē (sēsē)
ego)	tū)	*Abl.*	sē (sēsē)

Note. — Reflexive pronouns can have no nominative case.

272. DEMONSTRATIVE

	SINGULAR				PLURAL	
Nom.	hic, *m.*	haec, *f.*	hoc, *n.*	hī	hae	haec
Gen.	huius	huius	huius	hōrum	hārum	hōrum
Dat.	huic	huic	huic	hīs	hīs	hīs
Acc.	hunc	hanc	hoc	hōs	hās	haec
Abl.	hōc	hāc	hōc	hīs	hīs	hīs
Nom.	is, *m.*	ea, *f.*	id, *n.*	eī (iī)	eae	ea
Gen.	eius	eius	eius	eōrum	eārum	eōrum
Dat.	eī	eī	eī	eīs (iīs)	eīs (iīs)	eīs (iīs)
Acc.	eum	eam	id	eōs	eās	ea
Abl.	eō	eā	eō	eīs (iīs)	eīs (iīs)	eīs (iīs)
Nom.	īdem, *m.*	eadem, *f.*	idem, *n.*	eīdem (īdem)	eaedem	eadem
Gen.	eiusdem	eiusdem	eiusdem	eōrundem	eārundem	eōrundem
Dat.	eīdem	eīdem	eīdem	eīsdem (īsdem)	eīsdem (īsdem)	eīsdem (īsdem)
Acc.	eundem	eandem	idem	eōsdem	eāsdem	eadem
Abl.	eōdem	eādem	eōdem	eīsdem (īsdem)	eīsdem (īsdem)	eīsdem (īsdem)

DEMONSTRATIVE

	SINGULAR		
Nom.	ille, *m.*	illa, *f.*	illud, *n.*
Gen.	illīus	illīus	illīus
Dat.	illī	illī	illī
Acc.	illum	illam	illud
Abl.	illō	illā	illō

(Plur. regular like **magnus**)

INTENSIVE

	SINGULAR		
	ipse, *m.*	ipsa, *f.*	ipsum, *n.*
	ipsīus	ipsīus	ipsīus
	ipsī	ipsī	ipsī
	ipsum	ipsam	ipsum
	ipsō	ipsā	ipsō

(Plur. regular)

273. RELATIVE

	SINGULAR			PLURAL		
Nom.	quī, *m.*	quae, *f.*	quod, *n.*	quī	quae	quae
Gen.	cuius	cuius	cuius	quōrum	quārum	quōrum
Dat.	cui	cui	cui	quibus	quibus	quibus
Acc.	quem	quam	quod	quōs	quās	quae
Abl.	quō	quā	quō	quibus	quibus	quibus

274. INTERROGATIVE

	SINGULAR [1]	
Nom.	quis,[2] *m., f.*	quid, *n.*
Gen.	cuius	cuius
Dat.	cui	cui
Acc.	quem	quid
Abl.	quō	quō

275. INDEFINITE

Nom.	quīdam, *m.*	quaedam, *f.*	quiddam, *n.*
Gen.	cuiusdam, *etc.*	cuiusdam, *etc.*	cuiusdam, *etc.*

Acc. sing. quendam, quandam, quiddam; *gen. plur.* quōrundam, quārundam, quōrundam. The adjective has quoddam for quiddam.

	SINGULAR		SINGULAR	
Nom.	quisquam, *m., f.*	quicquam,[3] *n.*	quisque, *m., f.*	quidque, *n.*
Gen.	cuiusquam	cuiusquam	cuiusque	cuiusque
Dat.	cuiquam	cuiquam	cuique	cuique
Acc.	quemquam	quicquam[3]	quemque	quidque
Abl.	quōquam	quōquam	quōque	quōque
	(Plural lacking)		(Plural rare)	

(The adjective form of quisque is quisque, quaeque, quodque, etc.)

Note. — The indefinite pronoun aliquis, aliquid is declined like the interrogative quis in the sing. and relative quī in the plur. (except aliqua in n. plur., nom. and acc.). The adjective form is aliquī, -qua, -quod, etc. The indefinite pronoun quis (declined like the interrogative) and the indefinite adjective quī (declined like the relative except that the nom. fem. sing. is qua) are used chiefly after sī, nisi, and nē.

---

[1] Plural like that of quī.

[2] Interrogative adjective quī is declined throughout like relative quī.

[3] Or quidquam.

REGULAR VERBS

276. FIRST CONJUGATION

Principal Parts: **parō, parāre, parāvī, parātus**
(Stems: **parā-, parāv-, parāt-**)

ACTIVE VOICE

PASSIVE VOICE

INDICATIVE

PRESENT		PRESENT	
I prepare, etc.		*I am prepared, etc.*	
parō	parāmus	paror	parāmur
parās	parātis	parāris (–re)	parāminī
parat	parant	parātur	parantur

IMPERFECT		IMPERFECT	
I was preparing, etc.		*I was prepared, etc.*	
parābam	parābāmus	parābar	parābāmur
parābās	parābātis	parābāris (–re)	parābāminī
parābat	parābant	parābātur	parābantur

FUTURE		FUTURE	
I shall prepare, etc.		*I shall be prepared, etc.*	
parābō	parābimus	parābor	parābimur
parābis	parābitis	parāberis (–re)	parābiminī
parābit	parābunt	parābitur	parābuntur

PERFECT		PERFECT	
I prepared, I have prepared, etc.		*I was prepared, I have been prepared, etc.*	
parāvī	parāvimus	parātus $\begin{cases} \text{sum} \\ \text{es} \\ \text{est} \end{cases}$ parātī $\begin{cases} \text{sumus} \\ \text{estis} \\ \text{sunt} \end{cases}$	
parāvistī	parāvistis	(–a, –um) (–ae, –a)	
parāvit	parāvērunt (–ēre)		

PAST PERFECT		PAST PERFECT	
I had prepared, etc.		*I had been prepared, etc.*	
parāveram	parāverāmus	parātus $\begin{cases} \text{eram} \\ \text{erās} \\ \text{erat} \end{cases}$ parātī $\begin{cases} \text{erāmus} \\ \text{erātis} \\ \text{erant} \end{cases}$	
parāverās	parāverātis	(–a, –um) (–ae, –a)	
parāverat	parāverant		

FUTURE PERFECT		FUTURE PERFECT	
I shall have prepared, etc.		*I shall have been prepared, etc.*	
parāverō	parāverimus	parātus $\begin{cases} \text{erō} \\ \text{eris} \\ \text{erit} \end{cases}$ parātī $\begin{cases} \text{erimus} \\ \text{eritis} \\ \text{erunt} \end{cases}$	
parāveris	parāveritis	(–a, –um) (–ae, a)	
parāverit	parāverint		

ACTIVE VOICE		PASSIVE VOICE	

SUBJUNCTIVE

PRESENT		PRESENT	
parem	parēmus	parer	parēmur
parēs	parētis	parēris (–re)	parēminī
paret	parent	parētur	parentur

IMPERFECT		IMPERFECT	
parārem	parārēmus	parārer	parārēmur
parārēs	parārētis	parārēris (–re)	parārēminī
parāret	parārent	parārētur	parārentur

PERFECT		PERFECT			
parāverim	parāverimus	parātus $\left\{\begin{array}{l}\text{sim}\\\text{sīs}\\\text{sit}\end{array}\right.$		parātī $\left\{\begin{array}{l}\text{sīmus}\\\text{sītis}\\\text{sint}\end{array}\right.$	
parāverīs	parāveritis	(–a, –um)		(–ae, –a)	
parāverit	parāverint				

PAST PERFECT		PAST PERFECT			
parāvissem	parāvissēmus	parātus $\left\{\begin{array}{l}\text{essem}\\\text{essēs}\\\text{esset}\end{array}\right.$		parātī $\left\{\begin{array}{l}\text{essēmus}\\\text{essētis}\\\text{essent}\end{array}\right.$	
parāvissēs	parāvissētis	(–a, –um)		(–ae, –a)	
parāvisset	parāvissent				

PRESENT IMPERATIVE

2d sing.	parā, *prepare*	parāre, *be prepared*
2d plur.	parāte, *prepare*	parāminī, *be prepared*

FUTURE IMPERATIVE

2d sing.	parātō, *prepare*	parātor, *be prepared*
3d sing.	parātō, *he shall prepare*	parātor, *he shall be prepared*
2d plur.	parātōte, *prepare*	
3d plur.	parantō, *they shall prepare*	parantor, *they shall be prepared*

INFINITIVE

Present	parāre, *to prepare*	parārī, *to be prepared*
Perfect	parāvisse, *to have prepared*	parātus esse, *to have been prepared*
Future	parātūrus esse, *to be going to prepare*	(parātum īrī, *to be going to be prepared*)

PARTICIPLE

Present	parāns, *preparing*	
Perfect		parātus, –a, –um, *prepared*
Future	parātūrus, –a, –um, *going to prepare*	parandus, –a, –um, *(necessary) to be prepared*

GERUND

Gen. parandī, *of preparing, Dat.* parandō, *Acc.* parandum, *Abl.* parandō

SUPINE

Acc. parātum, *in order to prepare   Abl.* parātū, *in preparing*

277. SECOND, THIRD, AND FOURTH CONJUGATIONS

2d Conj.	*3d Conj.*	*4th Conj.*	*3d Conj.* (*-iō*)

PRINCIPAL PARTS

habeō	pōnō	mūniō	capiō
habēre	pōnere	mūnīre	capere
habuī	posuī	mūnīvī	cēpī
habitus	positus	mūnītus	captus

STEMS

habē-	pōne-	mūnī-	cape-
habu-	posu-	mūnīv-	cēp-
habit-	posit-	mūnīt-	capt-

INDICATIVE ACTIVE

PRESENT

habeō	pōnō	mūniō	capiō
habēs	pōnis	mūnīs	capis
habet	pōnit	mūnit	capit
habēmus	pōnimus	mūnīmus	capimus
habētis	pōnitis	mūnītis	capitis
habent	pōnunt	mūniunt	capiunt

IMPERFECT

habēbam, *etc.*	pōnēbam, *etc.*	mūniēbam, *etc.*	capiēbam, *etc.*

FUTURE

habēbō	pōnam	mūniam	capiam
habēbis	pōnēs	mūniēs	capiēs
habēbit	pōnet	mūniet	capiet
habēbimus	pōnēmus	mūniēmus	capiēmus
habēbitis	pōnētis	mūniētis	capiētis
habēbunt	pōnent	mūnient	capient

PERFECT

habuī, *etc.*	posuī, *etc.*	mūnīvī, *etc.*	cēpī, *etc.*

PAST PERFECT

habueram, *etc.*	posueram, *etc.*	mūnīveram, *etc.*	cēperam, *etc.*

FUTURE PERFECT

habuerō, *etc.*	posuerō, *etc.*	mūnīverō, *etc.*	cēperō, *etc.*

SUBJUNCTIVE ACTIVE

PRESENT

habeam	pōnam	mūniam	capiam
habeās	pōnās	mūniās	capiās
habeat	pōnat	mūniat	capiat
habeāmus	pōnāmus	mūniāmus	capiāmus
habeātis	pōnātis	mūniātis	capiātis
habeant	pōnant	mūniant	capiant

IMPERFECT

habērem, *etc.*	pōnerem, *etc.*	mūnīrem, *etc.*	caperem, *etc.*

PERFECT

habuerim, *etc.*	posuerim, *etc.*	mūnīverim, *etc.*	cēperim, *etc.*

PAST PERFECT

habuissem, *etc.*	posuissem, *etc.*	mūnīvissem, *etc.*	cēpissem, *etc.*

IMPERATIVE ACTIVE

PRESENT

2d sing.	habē	pōne	mūnī	cape
2d plur.	habēte	pōnite	mūnīte	capite

FUTURE

2d sing.	habētō	pōnitō	mūnītō	capitō
3d sing.	habētō	pōnitō	mūnītō	capitō
2d plur.	habētōte	pōnitōte	mūnītōte	capitōte
3d plur.	habentō	pōnuntō	mūniuntō	capiuntō

INFINITIVE ACTIVE

Pres.	habēre	pōnere	mūnīre	capere
Perf.	habuisse	posuisse	mūnīvisse	cēpisse
Fut.	habitūrus esse	positūrus esse	mūnītūrus esse	captūrus esse

PARTICIPLE ACTIVE

Pres.	habēns	pōnēns	mūniēns	capiēns
Fut.	habitūrus	positūrus	mūnītūrus	captūrus

GERUND

Gen.	habendī	pōnendī	mūniendī	capiendī

Dat. habendō, *etc.*, *Acc.* habendum, *etc.*, *Abl.* habendō, *etc.*

SUPINE

Acc.	habitum	positum	mūnītum	captum
Abl.	habitū	positū	mūnītū	captū

INDICATIVE PASSIVE

PRESENT

habeor	pōnor	mūnior	capior
habēris (–re)	pōneris (–re)	mūnīris (–re)	caperis (–re)
habētur	pōnitur	mūnītur	capitur
habēmur	pōnimur	mūnīmur	capimur
habēminī	pōniminī	mūnīminī	capiminī
habentur	pōnuntur	mūniuntur	capiuntur

IMPERFECT

habēbar, *etc.*	pōnēbar, *etc.*	mūniēbar, *etc.*	capiēbar, *etc.*

FUTURE

habēbor	pōnar	mūniar	capiar
habēberis (–re)	pōnēris (–re)	mūniēris (–re)	capiēris (–re)
habēbitur	pōnētur	mūniētur	capiētur
habēbimur	pōnēmur	mūniēmur	capiēmur
habēbiminī	pōnēminī	mūniēminī	capiēminī
habēbuntur	pōnentur	mūnientur	capientur

PERFECT

habitus sum, *etc.*	positus sum, *etc.*	mūnītus sum, *etc.*	captus sum, *etc.*

PAST PERFECT

habitus eram, *etc.*	positus eram, *etc.*	mūnītus eram, *etc.*	captus eram, *etc.*

FUTURE PERFECT

habitus erō, *etc.*	positus erō, *etc.*	mūnītus erō, *etc.*	captus erō, *etc.*

SUBJUNCTIVE PASSIVE

PRESENT

habear	pōnar	mūniar	capiar
habeāris (–re)	pōnāris (–re)	mūniāris (–re)	capiāris (–re)
habeātur	pōnātur	mūniātur	capiātur
habeāmur	pōnāmur	mūniāmur	capiāmur
habeāminī	pōnāminī	mūniāminī	capiāminī
habeantur	pōnantur	mūniantur	capiantur

IMPERFECT

habērer, *etc.*	pōnerer, *etc.*	mūnīrer, *etc.*	caperer, *etc.*

PERFECT

habitus sim, *etc.*	positus sim, *etc.*	mūnītus sim, *etc.*	captus sim, *etc.*

PAST PERFECT

habitus essem,	positus essem,	mūnītus essem,	captus essem,
etc.	*etc.*	*etc.*	*etc.*

IMPERATIVE PASSIVE

PRESENT

2d sing. habēre	pōnere	mūnīre	capere
2d plur. habēminī	pōniminī	mūnīminī	capiminī

FUTURE

2d sing. habētor	pōnitor	mūnītor	capitor
3d sing. habētor	pōnitor	mūnītor	capitor
3d plur. habentor	pōnuntor	mūniuntor	capiuntor

INFINITIVE PASSIVE

Pres.	habērī	pōnī	mūnīrī	capī
Perf.	habitus esse	positus esse	mūnītus esse	captus esse
(*Fut.*	habitum īrī	positum īrī	mūnītum īrī	captum īrī)

PARTICIPLE PASSIVE

Perf.	habitus	positus	mūnītus	captus
Fut.	habendus	pōnendus	mūniendus	capiendus

278. DEPONENT VERBS

Deponent verbs are active in meaning but passive in form, conjugated like the passive forms of the conjugations to which they belong: **arbitror,** *I think,* etc. Note, however, active forms and passive meanings in the following:

INFINITIVE		PARTICIPLE	
Pres.	arbitrārī, *to think*	*Pres.*	arbitrāns, *thinking*
Perf.	arbitrātus esse, *to have thought*	*Perf.*	arbitrātus, *having thought*
Fut.	arbitrātūrus esse, *to be going to think*	*Fut. Act.*	arbitrātūrus, *going to think*
		Fut. Pass.	arbitrandus, *(necessary) to be thought*

GERUND

Gen. arbitrandī, etc., *of thinking,* etc.

SUPINE

Acc. arbitrātum, *in order to think*   *Abl.* arbitrātū, *in thinking*

IRREGULAR VERBS

279. Principal Parts: **sum, esse, fuī, futūrus**

INDICATIVE

PRESENT		IMPERFECT		FUTURE	
sum	sumus	eram	erāmus	erō	erimus
es	estis	erās	erātis	eris	eritis
est	sunt	erat	erant	erit	erunt

PERFECT	PAST PERFECT	FUTURE PERFECT
fuī, *etc.*	fueram, *etc.*	fuerō, *etc.*

SUBJUNCTIVE

PRESENT		IMPERFECT	
sim	sīmus	essem [1]	essēmus
sīs	sītis	essēs	essētis
sit	sint	esset	essent

PERFECT	PAST PERFECT
fuerim, *etc.*	fuissem, *etc.*

IMPERATIVE

Pres. es este *Fut. 2d* estō estōte *Fut. 3d* estō suntō

INFINITIVE	PARTICIPLE
Pres. esse	——
Perf. fuisse	——
Fut. futūrus esse (**fore**)	futūrus, –a, –um

280. Principal Parts: **possum, posse, potuī, ——**

INDICATIVE

Pres.	possum	possumus
	potes	potestis
	potest	possunt
Impf.	poteram, *etc.*	
Fut.	poterō, *etc.*[2]	
Perf.	potuī, *etc.*	
Past P.	potueram, *etc.*	
Fut. P.	potuerō, *etc.*[2]	

SUBJUNCTIVE

possim	possīmus
possīs	possītis
possit	possint
possem, *etc.*	
potuerim, *etc.*	
potuissem, *etc.*	

INFINITIVE	PARTICIPLE
Pres. posse *Perf.* potuisse	*Pres.* potēns (adj.), *powerful*

[1] Sometimes **forem, forēs**, etc.

[2] The third plural future is **poterunt**; future perfect, **potuerint**.

281.   Principal Parts: ferō, ferre, tulī, lātus

INDICATIVE

ACTIVE   PASSIVE

Pres.	ferō	ferimus	feror	ferimur
	fers	fertis	ferris (–re)	feriminī
	fert	ferunt	fertur	feruntur
Impf.	ferēbam, etc.		ferēbar, etc.	
Fut.	feram, ferēs, etc.		ferar, ferēris, etc.	

(Perfect system regular)

SUBJUNCTIVE

Pres.	feram, ferās, etc.	ferar, ferāris, etc.
Impf.	ferrem, etc.	ferrer, etc.

(Perfect system regular)

IMPERATIVE

Pres.	fer	ferte	ferre	feriminī
Fut.	fertō	fertōte	fertor	
	fertō	feruntō	fertor	feruntor

INFINITIVE

Pres.	ferre	ferrī
Perf.	tulisse	lātus esse
Fut.	lātūrus esse	(lātum īrī)

PARTICIPLE

Pres.	ferēns, –entis	
Perf.		lātus, –a, –um
Fut.	lātūrus, –a, –um	ferendus, –a, –um

GERUND	SUPINE
Gen. ferendī, etc.	Acc. lātum Abl. lātū

282.   Principal Parts: eō, īre, iī, itus

INDICATIVE

PRESENT		IMPERFECT	FUTURE		PERFECT	
eō	īmus	ībam, etc.	ībō	ībimus	iī	iimus
īs	ītis		ībis	ībitis	īstī	īstis
it	eunt		ībit	ībunt	iit	iērunt (iēre)

PAST PERFECT	FUTURE PERFECT
ieram, etc.	ierō, etc.

SUBJUNCTIVE

PRESENT	IMPERFECT	PERFECT	PAST PERFECT
eam, *etc.*	īrem, *etc.*	ierim, *etc.*	īssem, *etc*

IMPERATIVE

Pres.	ī	īte	*Fut.*	ītō	ītōte
				ītō	euntó

INFINITIVE	PARTICIPLE
Pres. īre	iēns, *Gen.* euntis
Perf. īsse	itus, –a, –um
Fut. itūrus esse	itūrus, –a, –um (*Passive,* eundus)

GERUND	SUPINE
Gen. eundī, *etc.*	*Acc.* itum *Abl.* itū

283. Principal Parts: volō, velle, voluī; nōlō, nōlle, nōluī; mālō, mālle, māluī

INDICATIVE

PRESENT

volō	volumus	nōlō	nōlumus	mālō	mālumus
vīs	vultis	nōn vīs	nōn vultis	māvīs	māvultis
vult	volunt	nōn vult	nōlunt	māvult	mālunt

Impf.	volēbam, *etc.*	nōlēbam, *etc.*		mālēbam, *etc.*
Fut.	volam, *etc.*	nōlam, *etc.*		mālam, *etc.*
Perf.	voluī, *etc.*	nōluī, *etc.*		māluī, *etc.*
Past P.	volueram, *etc.*	nōlueram, *etc.*		mālueram, *etc.*
Fut. P.	voluerō, *etc.*	nōluerō, *etc.*		māluerō, *etc.*

SUBJUNCTIVE

PRESENT

velim	velīmus	nōlim	nōlīmus	mālim	mālīmus
velīs	velītis	nōlīs	nōlītis	mālīs	mālītis
velit	velint	nōlit	nōlint	mālit	mālint

Impf.	vellem, *etc.*	nōllem, *etc.*		māllem, *etc.*
Perf.	voluerim, *etc.*	nōluerim, *etc.*		māluerim, *etc.*
Past P.	voluissem, *etc.*	nōluissem, *etc.*		māluissem, *etc.*

PRESENT IMPERATIVE	FUTURE IMPERATIVE
nōlī nōlīte	nōlītō nōlītōte

INFINITIVE

Pres. velle	nōlle	mālle
Perf. voluisse	nōluisse	māluisse

PARTICIPLE

Pres. volēns   nōlēns

284.   Principal Parts: fīō, fierī, factus sum

INDICATIVE

PRESENT	IMPERFECT	FUTURE	PERFECT
fīō ——	fīēbam, *etc.*	fīam, *etc.*	factus sum, *etc.*
—— ——	PAST PERFECT	FUTURE PERFECT	
fit fīunt	factus eram, *etc.*	factus erō, *etc.*	

SUBJUNCTIVE

PRESENT	IMPERFECT	PERFECT	PAST PERFECT
fīam, *etc.*	fierem, *etc.*	factus sim, *etc.*	factus essem, *etc.*

IMPERATIVE	INFINITIVE	PARTICIPLE
Pres. fī fīte	fierī	
Perf.	factus esse	factus, –a, –um
Fut.	(factum īrī)	faciendus, –a, –um

285.   DEFECTIVE VERBS

Coepī is used only in the perfect system. For the present system **incipiō** is used. With a passive infinitive the passive of **coepī** is used: **Lapidēs iacī coeptī sunt,** *Stones began to be thrown.* **Meminī** and **ōdī** likewise are used only in the perfect system, but with present meaning. The former has an imperative **mementō, mementōte.**

The only forms of **inquam** in common use are found in the present indicative: **inquam, inquis, inquit, inquiunt.**

286.   SPECIAL FORMS

Verbs having perfect stems ending in -āv- or -ēv- are sometimes contracted by dropping -ve- before -r- and -vi- before -s-: **amārunt, cōnsuēsse.** Verbs having perfect stems ending in -vi- drop -īv- before -s- but only -v- before -r-: **audīsset, audierat.**

Four verbs have shortened forms in the singular of the present imperative active: **dīc, dūc, fac, fer.**

SUMMARY OF SYNTAX [1]

287.   QUESTIONS

Some questions are introduced by interrogative pronouns
or adverbs (**quis, ubi,** etc.). Others are introduced as
follows:

1. In questions the answer to which might be either *yes*
or *no* the particle **-ne** is attached to the first word.

    Frāterne venit? *Is your brother coming?*

2. In questions the answer to which is expected to be *yes*
the introductory word is **nōnne** (*i.e.* **nōn** + **ne**; cf. English).

    Nōnne frāter venit? *Is not your brother coming?*

3. In questions the answer to which is expected to be *no*
the introductory word is **num.**

    Num frāter venit? *Your brother is not coming, is he?*

Double questions are introduced by **utrum, -ne,** or nothing
at all and are connected by **an.**

    Frāterne bonus an malus est? *Is your brother good or bad?*

Note. — For *or not* in a double question Latin uses **annōn** or **necne.**

288. REFLEXIVE PRONOUNS AND ADJECTIVES

The personal pronouns of the first and second persons and
the possessive adjectives derived from them may be used
reflexively. It is only in the third person that the Latin
employs a distinct reflexive pronoun, **suī** (adjective **suus**).

---

[1] In this summary only those constructions are included which are relatively more important and which recur repeatedly in the text, or are referred
to in the notes or in the written exercises.

a. Both **suī** and **suus** commonly refer to the subject of the clause in which they stand (" Direct Reflexive ").

Sē suaque omnia dēdidērunt, *They surrendered themselves and all their possessions.*

b. Sometimes **suī** or **suus,** occurring in a subordinate clause, refers not to the subject of its own clause, but to the subject of the main verb (" Indirect Reflexive ").

Petēbant utī Caesar sibi potestātem faceret, *They begged that Caesar give them a chance.*

Note. — In order to avoid ambiguity if it ever becomes necessary to refer to the subjects of both clauses, **ipse** is used as the indirect reflexive, and **suī** (or **suus**) as the direct reflexive.

AGREEMENT

289. Adjectives. — Adjectives and participles agree in number, gender, and case with the nouns which they modify.

290. Adjectives as Substantives. — Sometimes adjectives are used substantively : **nostrī,** *our (men)* ; **malum,** *evil.*

291. Verbs. — Verbs agree in person and number with their subjects.

Note. — (*a*) When two singular subjects are connected by **aut, aut . . . aut, neque . . . neque,** the verb is singular.

(*b*) A plural verb may be used with a singular subject which is plural in thought.

292. Relative Pronouns. — The relative pronoun agrees in gender and number with its antecedent but its case depends upon its use in its own clause.

Note. — (*a*) The antecedent of the relative is often omitted.

(*b*) Sometimes the antecedent is represented by an entire clause, in which case the pronoun is best translated *a thing which.*

293. Connecting Relative. — In Latin a relative pronoun is often used at the beginning of a sentence to refer to the

thought of the preceding sentence. The English idiom calls
for a demonstrative or personal pronoun.

> **quā dē causā,** *for this reason.*

294. Appositives. — Appositives agree in case.

Note. — It is often best to supply *as* in translating the appositive.

> **eōdem homine magistrō ūtī,** *to use the same man as teacher.*

NOUN SYNTAX

NOMINATIVE

295. Subject Nominative. — The subject of a finite verb
is in the nominative case.

296. Predicate Nominative. — (*a*) A noun or adjective
used in the predicate after a linking verb (*is, are, seem,* etc.)
to complete its meaning is in the nominative case.

> 1. **Īnsula est magna,** *The island is large.*
> 2. **Sicilia est īnsula,** *Sicily is an island.*

(*b*) Predicate nouns and adjectives are used not only with
sum but also with **fīō** and the passive voice of verbs meaning
call, choose, appoint, elect, and the like.

> 1. **Caesar dux factus est,** *Caesar was made leader.*
> 2. **Cicerō Pater Patriae appellātus est,** *Cicero was called the Father
> of his Country.*

Note. — In the active these verbs take two accusatives.

GENITIVE

297. Possessive Genitive. — Possession is expressed by
the genitive.

> **īnsulae viae,** *the roads of the island.*

298. Predicate Genitive. — The possessive genitive may
be used in the predicate with **sum** (or **faciō**) (often translated
it is the part of, the duty of, etc.).

> **Sapientiae est vidēre,** *It is the part of wisdom to see.*

299. Descriptive Genitive. — The descriptive genitive, modified by an adjective, is used to describe a person or thing.

viri magnae virtūtis, *men of great courage.*

Note. — The descriptive genitive is largely confined to expressions of measure and number.

spatium decem pedum, *a space of ten feet.*

300. Genitive of the Whole. — The genitive of the whole (partitive genitive) represents the whole to which the part belongs.

1. hōrum omnium fortissimī, *the bravest of all these.*
2. nihil praesidī, *no guard.*

Note. — (*a*) The English idiom is the same except when the genitive is used with such words as nihil, satis, quid, ubi.

(*b*) Instead of the genitive of the whole, the ablative with ex or dē is regularly used with cardinal numerals (except mīlia) and quīdam, often also with other words, such as paucī and complūrēs.

quīnque ex nostrīs, *five of our men.*

301. Subjective Genitive. — The subjective genitive expresses the subject of the verbal idea of the noun on which it depends. If this noun is turned into a verb, the genitive becomes subject :

timor populī, *the fear of the people* (i.e. *the people feared*).

302. Objective Genitive. — The objective genitive expresses the object of the verbal idea of the noun or adjective on which it depends. If this noun or adjective is turned into a verb, the genitive becomes object :

amantissimōs reī pūblicae virōs, *patriotic men* (i.e. *they loved the state*).

303. Genitive of Material. — The noun denoting the material of which something is composed is in the genitive.

talentum aurī, *a talent of gold.*

304. Genitive of Plenty and Want. — Certain adjectives and verbs denoting plenty or want take the genitive; so regularly with **plēnus** and **refertus,** *full of;* **inānis, inops,** and **expers,** *empty, without, devoid of.*

Note. — The ablative is sometimes used with these words (except **expers**).

305. Genitive with *Proprius*. — Certain adjectives of the group which regularly take the dative (**312**) sometimes take the possessive genitive. The most common are **proprius, similis,** and **commūnis.**

    1. **tuī similis,** *like you.*
    2. **proprium populī,** *characteristic of the people.*

306. Genitive with Special Verbs. — **Oblīvīscor** (*forget*), **meminī,** and **reminīscor** (*remember*) take the genitive.

Oblīvīscere caedis atque incendiōrum, *Forget bloodshed and burning.*

Note. — Sometimes the accusative is used with **meminī** and **reminīscor;** regularly so with **recordor** (*remember*).

307. Genitive of the Charge and Penalty. — Verbs of *accusing, condemning,* or *acquitting* take the genitive to denote either the charge or the penalty.

    capitis damnātum, *condemned to death* (lit., *of the head*).
    Accūsō tē inertiae, *I accuse you of inaction.*

308. Genitive of Indefinite Value. — The genitive is used with **sum** and other verbs to express indefinite value.

    1. **Est tantī,** *It is worth that much.*
    2. **parvī esse dūcenda,** *to be considered of little value.*

DATIVE

309. Dative of Indirect Object. — The indirect object of a verb is in the dative. This dative is used with verbs of *giving, reporting, telling,* etc.

    Nautae pecūniam dō, *I give money to the sailor.*

310. Dative of Purpose. — The dative is sometimes used to express purpose.

Locum castrīs dēlēgit, *He chose a place for a camp.*

311. Dative of Reference. — The dative of reference denotes the person concerned or referred to.

sī mihi dignī esse vultis, *if you wish to be worthy in my sight* (lit., *for me*).

a. The dative of reference is often used with the dative of purpose to show the person or thing affected.

Haec castra erunt praesidiō oppidō, *This camp will be (for) a protection to the town.*

312. Dative with Adjectives. — Certain adjectives, as amīcus, idōneus, pār, proximus, similis, ūtilis, and their opposites, govern the dative. In many cases the English idiom is the same.

Hic liber est similis illī, *This book is similar to that.*

313. Dative with Special Verbs. — Certain special verbs, as cōnfīdō, crēdō, dēsum, diffīdō, faveō, imperō, invideō, noceō, parcō, pāreō, persuādeō, placeō, praestō, resistō, serviō, and studeō, govern the dative.

Pārēbisne patrī tuō an eī resistēs? *Will you obey your father or resist him?*

a. These verbs become impersonal in the passive and the dative is retained.

Eī persuāsum est, *He was persuaded.*

b. A neuter pronoun or adjective or an ut clause may be used as a direct object with imperō and persuādeō.

Hoc mihi persuāsit, *He persuaded me of this.*

314. Dative with Compounds. — Certain compound verbs often take a dative, especially when the noun goes closely with

the prefix of the verb.   No general rule can be given.   When
the simple verb is transitive, the compound sometimes takes
both an accusative and a dative.

> **Gallīs bellum intulit,** *He made war against the Gauls.*

315. Dative of Separation. — The dative of separation is
commonly confined to persons and occurs chiefly with
adimō and verbs compounded with **ab, dē,** and **ex.**

> **scūtō mīlitī dētrāctō,** *having seized a shield from a soldier.*

316. Dative of Possession. — The possessor may be expressed by the dative with **sum.**

> **Liber mihi est,** *I have a book.*

317. Dative of Agent. — The dative of agent is used with
the future passive participle to denote the person upon whom
the obligation rests (**398,** I).   It is also often used with the
perfect passive participle and the compound tenses of the
passive.

> **Hoc opus vōbīs faciendum est,** *This work must be done by you.*

ACCUSATIVE

318. Accusative of Direct Object. — The direct object of
a transitive verb is in the accusative.

> **Viam parāmus,** *We are preparing a way.*

319. Accusative of Extent. — Extent of time and space is
expressed by the accusative.

> 1. **Duōs annōs remanēbat,** *He remained two years.*
> 2. **Flūmen decem pedēs altum est,** *The river is ten feet deep.*

320. Accusative of Place to Which. — The accusative with
ad (*to*) or **in** (*into*) expresses place to which.   These prepositions, however, are omitted before **domum, rūs,** and names of
towns and cities.

1. Lēgātōs ad eum mittunt, *They send envoys to him.*
2. Rōmam eunt, *They go to Rome.*

Note. — When the preposition **ad** is used with names of towns it means *to the vicinity of.*

321. Accusative Subject of Infinitive. — The subject of an infinitive is in the accusative.

Puerōs esse bonōs volumus, *We want the boys to be good.*

322. Two Accusatives. — (*a*) With **trādūcō** and **trānsportō** two accusatives are used. In the passive the accusative governed by the prefix is retained.

1. Cōpiās flūmen trādūcit, *He leads his forces across the river.*
2. Cōpiae flūmen trādūcuntur, *The forces are led across the river.*

(*b*) Verbs of *asking, demanding, teaching, warning* may take two accusatives, one of the person and another of the thing.

1. Hōs sententiam rogō, *I ask them their opinion.*
2. Eōs hoc moneō, *I warn them of this.*

Note. — For two accusatives with verbs meaning *call, choose,* etc., see **296** (*b*).

323. Accusative with Prepositions. — Prepositions (except those listed in **350**) take the accusative; **in** and **sub** take the accusative with verbs of motion.

324. Accusative of Exclamation. — The object of the emotion is expressed by the accusative.

Ō fortūnātam rem pūblicam, *O fortunate republic!*
Ō tempora, Ō mōrēs! *O what a time, what a state of affairs!*

325. Accusative of Respect. — In poetry the accusative of respect is used with verbs and adjectives to indicate the part affected :

hirsūta capillōs, *with shaggy hair* (lit., *shaggy as to the hair*).

Note. — Some cases are classed as direct objects of the passive verb used in a middle (reflexive) sense

ABLATIVE

326. Summary. — The uses of the ablative may be grouped under three heads :

I. The **true** or " from " **ablative** (**ab**, *from* and **lātus**, *carried*), used with the prepositions **ab, dē,** and **ex** — if any preposition is used.

II. The **associative** or " with " **ablative**, used with the preposition **cum** — if any preposition is used.

III. The **place** or " in " **ablative**, used with the prepositions **in** and **sub** — if any preposition is used.

327. Ablative of Separation. — The ablative of separation is used without a preposition with certain verbs, as **careō, abstineō, dēsistō, egeō, excēdō, līberō,** and **vacō.**

Note. — (*a*) **Prohibeō,** *keep from,* is commonly used without a preposition, but occasionally with it.

Suīs fīnibus eōs prohibent, *They keep them from their own territory.*

(*b*) Other verbs denoting separation regularly take the prepositions **ab, dē,** and **ex.**

328. Ablative of Place from Which. — Place from which is expressed regularly by the ablative wi'h the prepositions **ab, dē,** and **ex.**

    1. **dē montibus,** *down from the mountains.*
    2. **ex agrīs,** *out of the fields.*

Note. — The preposition is regularly omitted before **domō** as well as before names of towns and cities. When it is used, it means *from the vicinity of.*

329. Ablative of Origin. — Origin is expressed by the ablative with or without a preposition (**ab, dē, ex**).

    amplissimō genere nātus, *born of most illustrious lineage.*

330. Ablative of Agent. — Personal agency with a passive verb is expressed by **ā** or **ab** with the ablative.

    Amāmur ab amīcīs, *We are loved by our friends.*

331. Ablative of Comparison. — After a comparative the ablative is used when **quam** (*than*) is omitted.

Nec locus tibi ūllus dulcior esse dēbet patriā, *No spot ought to be dearer to you than your native land.*

332. Ablative of Accompaniment. — The ablative is used with **cum** to express accompaniment.

Cum servō venit, *He is coming with the slave.*

a. When **cum** is used with a personal, reflexive, or relative pronoun, it is attached to it as an enclitic : **vōbīscum,** *with you;* **sēcum,** *with himself;* **quibuscum,** *with whom.*

b. **Cum** is omitted in certain military phrases denoting accompaniment, if qualified by an adjective other than a numeral.

    1. **omnibus suīs cōpiīs,** *with all his forces.*
    2. **cum tribus legiōnibus,** *with three legions.*

333. Ablative of Manner. — The ablative of manner with **cum** describes how something is done. **Cum** may be omitted, as a rule, only if an adjective is used with the noun.

(**Cum**) **magnō studiō labōrat,** *He labors with great eagerness (very eagerly).*

334. Ablative of Attendant Circumstances. — The ablative, usually with a modifier, is used to indicate the circumstances or conditions under which an act takes place.

hīsce ōminibus, *with these prospects.*

335. Ablative Absolute. — A noun in the ablative case used with a participle, adjective, or other noun and having no grammatical connection with the subject or the predicate is called an ablative absolute.

In translating, an ablative absolute should, as a rule, be changed to a clause expressing *time, cause, condition, means,* or *concession,* according to the context. At other times it may best be rendered by a clause coördinate with the main clause.

Servō accūsātō, dominus discessit, *After accusing the slave* (lit., *the slave having been accused*), *the master departed.*

336. Ablative of Means. — Means (or instrument) is expressed by the ablative without a preposition.

Ratibus trānsībant, *They were trying to cross by means of rafts.*

337. Ablative with Special Verbs. — The ablative is used with **fruor, fungor, potior, ūtor,** and **vēscor,** and their compounds. Their English equivalents govern a direct object.

Castrīs potītī sunt, *They got possession of the camp.*

338. Ablative with *Opus Est*. — This expression, which means *there is need,* may be followed by the ablative.

Pecūniā opus est, *There is need of money.*

339. Ablative with *Contentus* and *Frētus*. — The ablative is used with **contentus,** *satisfied,* and **frētus,** *relying upon.*

frētus vōbīs, *relying upon you.*

340. Ablative of Cause. — The ablative of cause is used especially with verbs and adjectives expressing feeling.

labōrāre iniūriā, *to suffer because of the wrong.*

341. Ablative of Measure of Difference. — The ablative without a preposition expresses the measure of difference. It is used with comparatives or words implying a comparison.

Tribus annīs ante eum vīdī, *I saw him three years ago* (lit., *before by three years*).

342. Ablative of Description. — The ablative of description, like the genitive of description, is used with an adjective to describe a noun. It is regularly used to express physical qualities.

hominēs inimīcā faciē, *men with an unfriendly appearance.*

343. Ablative of Place Where. — Place where is regularly expressed by the ablative with **in** (*in, on*). The preposition is omitted, however, with certain words like **locō, locīs, parte,** and **terrā,** also in certain fixed expressions like **tōtō orbe terrārum,** *in the whole world.* See also **351.**

344. Ablative of Time. — Time when or within which is expressed by the ablative without a preposition.

aestāte, *in summer;* paucīs diēbus, *within a few days.*

345. Ablative of Respect. — The ablative of respect (specification) tells in what respect the statement applies.

Nōs superant numerō, nōn animō, *They surpass us in number, not in courage.*

346. Ablative with *Cōnfīdō.* — Fīdō and cōnfīdō (*trust*) may take the ablative. They regularly take the dative of persons.

cum affīnitāte Pompeī cōnfīderet, *since he trusted in his relationship with Pompey.*

347. Ablative with *Rēfert* and *Interest.* — Rēfert and interest, *it concerns, it is for the interest of,* take the genitive of the person or thing concerned, if a noun ; otherwise they take the feminine ablative singular of the possessive.

1. Rēgis rēfert, *It concerns the king.*
2. Meā videō quid intersit, *I see what is to my interest.*

Note. — The construction originated in such expressions as **Quid meā rē fert?** *What does it bear on my affair?*

348. Ablative of Accordance. — The ablative is used with a few words to express the idea *in accordance with.*

mōre suō, *in accordance with his custom.*

349. Ablative with *Dignus*. — **Dignus** and **indignus** take the ablative.

> **dignus patre,** *worthy of his father.*

350. Ablative with Prepositions. — The ablative is used with the prepositions **ab, dē, ex, prae, prō, sine, cum;** also with **in** and **sub** when used with verbs of rest, not motion.

LOCATIVE

351. Domus and a few other words, as well as the names of towns and cities, require a separate case, called the locative, to express place where. The locative has the same ending as the genitive in the singular of nouns of the first and second declensions; it has the same ending as the ablative in the plural of these declensions and in the third declension.

> **domī,** *at home;* **mīlitiae,** *in the field;* **Rōmae,** *at Rome;* **Athēnīs,** *at Athens.*

VOCATIVE

352. The vocative is used in direct address. Unless emphatic it never stands first.

> **Quid facis, amīce?** *What are you doing, my friend?*

VERB SYNTAX

TENSES

353. The tenses of the indicative in Latin are in general used like those in English, but the following points are to be noted.

354. Present. — The Latin present has the force of the English simple present and of the progressive present.

> **Vocat,** *He calls,* or *He is calling.*

355. Historical Present. — The historical present is often used for vivid effect in place of a past tense in Latin as in English.

> **Rōmam proficīscuntur,** *They depart for Rome.*

356. *Dum* **Clauses.** — In clauses introduced by **dum** meaning *while* not in the sense of *as long as*, the historical present is always used. In translating use the English past.

> **dum haec geruntur,** *while these things were going on.*

Note. — Distinguish carefully from **dum** meaning *as long as* (**364**) or *until* (**385**).

357. Imperfect. — The Latin imperfect expresses continued or repeated action in the past and is usually best translated by the English progressive past, sometimes by the auxiliary *would*, or by a phrase, such as *used to* or *kept on*.

> **Pugnābant,** *They were fighting.*

Sometimes the imperfect has *conative* force and represents the act as *attempted*. Sometimes it has *inceptive* force and represents an act as just *beginning.*

358. Perfect. — The Latin perfect is generally equivalent to the English past, occasionally to the present perfect.

> **Vīcī,** *I conquered,* or *I have conquered.*

359. Sequence of Tenses. — The subjunctive mood is used chiefly in subordinate clauses, in which its tenses are determined by the principle of " sequence of tenses," as shown in the following summary :

(*a*) **Primary tenses**	(referring to the present or future)	
Indicative:	present, future, future perfect.	
Subjunctive:	present, perfect.	
(*b*) **Secondary tenses**	(referring to the past)	
Indicative:	imperfect, perfect, past perfect.	
Subjunctive:	imperfect, past perfect.	

Primary indicative tenses are followed by primary subjunctive tenses, secondary by secondary.

Note. — The " historical " present (**355**), used for vivid effect in describing a past action, is often followed by a secondary tense.

360. Epistolary Tenses. — The writer of a letter some-times puts himself in the reader's place and uses his tenses accordingly from the standpoint of the receiver rather than of the sender. Hence the imperfect or perfect = present, and the past perfect = perfect.

Haec ego scrībēbam hōrā octāvā, *I am writing this at the eighth hour.*

361. Present and Imperfect with *Iam Diū*. — In Latin the present is used with **iam diū, iam dūdum, iam prīdem** where in English we use the progressive perfect. The Latin imperfect with such expressions is equivalent to the English progressive past perfect.

$$\text{iam diū} \begin{Bmatrix} \text{putō} \\ \text{putābam} \end{Bmatrix}, \; I \begin{Bmatrix} \textit{have} \\ \textit{had} \end{Bmatrix} \; \textit{long been thinking.}$$

INDICATIVE MOOD

362. The indicative mood is generally used in Latin as in English. The following points are to be noted.

363. Relative Clauses. — Most relative clauses are in the indicative, as in English. But see **368, 380, 381, 387.**

364. Adverbial Clauses. — Clauses introduced by **post-quam** and **posteā quam** (*after*), **ubi** and **ut** (*when*), **cum prīmum** and **simul ac** (*as soon as*), **dum** (*while, as long as*), **quamquam** and **etsī** (*although*) are in the indicative.

Postquam id cōnspexit, signum dedit, *After he noticed this, he gave the signal.*

365. Substantive Clauses. — A clause introduced by **quod** (*the fact that, that*) is in the indicative and may be used as subject or object of the main verb or in apposition with a demonstrative.

Grātum est quod mē requīris, *It is gratifying that you miss me.*

SUBJUNCTIVE MOOD

366. Volitive Subjunctive. — The volitive (**volō**) subjunctive represents an act as *willed* and is translated by *let*. The negative is **nē**.

> **Patriam dēfendāmus,** *Let us defend our country.*
> **Nē id videat,** *Let him not see it.*

367. Purpose Clauses. — The subjunctive is used in a subordinate clause with **ut** or **utī** (negative **nē**) to indicate the purpose of the act expressed by the principal clause.

> **Venīmus ut videāmus,** *We come that we may see,* or *We come to see.*
> **Fugit nē videātur,** *He flees that he may not be seen.*

368. Relative Purpose Clauses. — If the principal clause contains (or implies) a definite antecedent, the purpose clause may be introduced by the relative pronoun **quī** (= **ut is** or **ut eī**) or by **ubi, unde**, etc., instead of **ut**.

> **Mīlitēs mīsit quī hostem impedīrent,** *He sent soldiers to hinder the enemy.*

369. *Quō* Purpose Clauses. — If the purpose clause contains an adjective or adverb in the comparative degree, **quō** is generally used instead of **ut**.

> **Accēdit quō facilius audiat,** *He approaches in order that he may hear more easily.*
> (For other ways to express purpose see **398** (II), **399, 310.**)

370. Volitive Substantive Clauses. — Clauses in the subjunctive with **ut** (negative **nē**) are used as the objects of such verbs as **moneō, rogō, petō, hortor, persuādeō,** and **imperō.** Occasionally **ut** is omitted.

> 1. **Mīlitēs hortātus est ut fortēs essent,** *He urged the soldiers to be brave.*
> 2. **Helvētiīs persuāsit ut exīrent,** *He persuaded the Helvetians to leave.*

a. **Iubeō** (*order*), unlike **imperō** above, usually takes the infinitive with subject accusative.

1. Iussit eōs venīre, *He ordered them to come.*
2. Imperāvit eīs ut venīrent, *He ordered them to come.*

Note. — Vetō (*forbid*) and cupiō (*desire*) take the same construction as iubeō.

b. The various constructions with the impersonal verb **licet** are as follows :

1. Licet $\begin{Bmatrix} \text{tibi} \\ \text{tē} \end{Bmatrix}$ īre, *You may go.*
2. Licet (ut) eās, *You may go.*

371. Clauses after Verbs of Hindering. — Verbs of hindering and preventing, especially **impediō** and **dēterreō,** take the subjunctive introduced by **nē** or **quō minus** if the main clause is affirmative or by **quīn** or **quō minus** if negative.

Tū dēterrēre potes nē maior multitūdō trādūcātur, *You can prevent a greater host from being brought over.*

Note. — Prohibeō (*prevent*) regularly takes the infinitive.

Caesar prohibuit eōs trānsīre, *Caesar prevented them from crossing.*

372. Clauses with Expressions of Doubt. — **Nōn dubitō, quis dubitat, nōn dubium est,** and similar expressions implying a negative commonly take **quīn** and the subjunctive.

Nōn erat dubium quīn plūrimum Helvētiī possent, *There was no doubt that the Helvetians were the most powerful.*

Note. — When dubitō means *hesitate,* it regularly takes the infinitive.

373. Clauses of Fear. — Verbs of fearing are followed by clauses in the subjunctive introduced by **nē** (*that, lest*) and **ut** (*that not*).

1. Verēbātur nē tū aeger essēs, *He feared that you were sick.*
2. Timuī ut venīrent, *I was afraid that they would not come.*

374. Proviso Clauses. — The subjunctive with **dum, dum modo, modo,** meaning *provided that,* is used to express a proviso (negative **nē**).

> **modo inter mē atque tē mūrus intersit,** *provided that a wall is between you and me.*

375. Deliberative Subjunctive. — In questions of doubt and perplexity where the speaker asks himself or some one else for advice, or in questions or exclamations expressing surprise or indignation, the subjunctive is used, sometimes with **ut.** The negative is **nōn.** The deliberative subjunctive is commonly used in questions which expect no answer, and is therefore purely rhetorical.

1. **Quid fīat?** *What shall be done?*
2. **Cūr ego nōn laeter?** *Why should I not rejoice?*
3. **Tū ut umquam tē corrigās?** *You ever reform?*

376. Optative Subjunctive. — The optative (**optō**) subjunctive represents *a wish.* It frequently is preceded by **utinam** (*would that*). The negative is **nē.**

a. The present (rarely the perfect) is used when the wish can come true :

> **Vīvās fēlīciter!** *May you live happily!*

b. The imperfect expresses a wish contrary to fact in present time :

> **Utinam venīret!** *Oh, that he were coming* (but he is not) !

c. The past perfect expresses a wish contrary to fact in past time :

> **Utinam nē vēnisset!** *Would that he had not come* (but he did) !

377. Potential Subjunctive. — The potential subjunctive expresses the possibility or capability of something being done. The negative is **nōn.** The present and perfect refer to present or future time, the imperfect to past time. It is variously translated by *may, might, can, could.*

1. **Aliquis dīcat mihi,** *Some one may say to me.*
2. **Aurum fluitāre vidērēs,** *You might have seen the gold flowing.*

378. Result Clauses. — The result of the action or state of the principal verb is expressed by a subordinate clause with **ut (utī),** negative **ut nōn (utī nōn),** and the subjunctive.

1. **Tantum est perīculum ut paucī veniant,** *So great is the danger that few are coming.*
2. **Ita bene erant castra mūnīta ut nōn capī possent,** *So well had the camp been fortified that it could not be taken.*

Note. — (*a*) Result clauses are usually anticipated by some word in the main clause meaning *so* or *such* (**ita, tantus, tot, tam,** etc.).

(*b*) A result clause depending upon a secondary tense may have the perfect instead of the imperfect subjunctive.

379. Substantive Clauses of Result. — Verbs meaning *to happen* (**accidō**) or *to cause* or *effect* (**efficiō**) require clauses of result in the subjunctive with **ut (utī)** or **ut (utī) nōn,** used as subject or object of the main verb :

1. **Accidit ut mē nōn vidēret,** *It happened that he did not see me.*
2. **Efficiam ut veniat,** *I shall cause him to come.*

380. Descriptive Relative Clauses. — A relative clause with the subjunctive may be used to describe an otherwise indefinite antecedent. Such clauses are called relative clauses of description (characteristic) and are especially common after such expressions as **ūnus** and **sōlus, sunt quī** (*there are those who*), **nēmō est quī** (*there is no one who*), **quis est quī** (*who is there who*), **quid est quod** (*what is there that*).

a. Sometimes a descriptive clause expresses cause or concession, as follows :

quī (= cum ego) magnō in perīculō essem, *since I was in great danger.*

Cethēgus, quī ante respondisset, repente conticuit, *Cethegus, though he had previously replied, suddenly stopped.*

Note. — A descriptive relative clause with the subjunctive sometimes expresses result.

381. *Quī* **Clauses after** *Dignus.* — A relative clause in the subjunctive follows certain adjectives, as **dignus, indignus, aptus, idōneus.**

> **Dignus est quī mittātur,** *He is worthy to be sent.*

382. Descriptive *Cum* **Clauses.** — In secondary sequence **cum,** *when,* is used with the imperfect or the past perfect subjunctive to describe the situation or the circumstances under which the action of the main verb occurred. Such **cum** clauses are called descriptive **cum** clauses.

> **Cum mīlitēs redīssent, Caesar ōrātiōnem habuit,** *When the soldiers returned, Caesar made a speech.*

Note. — When the **cum** clause simply dates or defines the time of the action of the main verb, instead of describing the circumstances leading up to it, it takes the indicative — often preceded by some definite temporal expression such as **tum** (*then*).

> **tum cum ex urbe eum ēiciēbam,** *at the time when I was trying to drive him from the city.*

383. *Cum* **Causal Clauses.** — A causal clause introduced by **cum,** meaning *since,* is in the subjunctive.

> **Quae cum ita sint, nōn ībō,** *Since this is so, I shall not go.*

384. *Cum* **Adversative Clauses.** — An adversative clause introduced by **cum,** meaning *although,* is in the subjunctive.

> **Cum ea ita sint, tamen nōn ībō,** *Although this is so, nevertheless I shall not go.*

Note. — When **ut** means *although, granted that,* its clause is in the subjunctive.

385. Anticipatory Clauses. — **Dum** (*until*), **antequam,** and **priusquam** (*before*) introduce clauses (*a*) in the indicative

to denote *an actual fact,* (*b*) in the subjunctive to denote an
act *as anticipated.*

1. Silentium fuit dum tū vēnistī, *There was silence until you came.*

2. Caesar exspectāvit dum nāvēs convenīrent, *Caesar waited until the ships should assemble.*

3. Priusquam tēlum adigī posset, omnēs fūgērunt, *Before a weapon could be hurled, all fled.*

386. Indirect Questions. — In a question *indirectly quoted*
or expressed after some introductory verb such as *ask, doubt,
learn, know, tell, hear,* etc., the verb is in the subjunctive.

Rogant quis sit, *They ask who he is.*

a. The first member of a double indirect question is introduced by **utrum, -ne,** or nothing at all, the second by **an.**

Quaerō utrum nūntius vērus an falsus sit, *I ask whether the report is true or false.*

387. Subordinate Clauses in Indirect Discourse. — The
verb of a subordinate clause, ordinarily in the indicative, becomes subjunctive in indirect discourse. If the subordinate
clause is not felt as a corporate part of the quotation but is
merely explanatory or parenthetical, its verb may be in the
indicative.

Dīxit sē pecūniam invēnisse quam āmīsisset, *He said that he found the money which he had lost.*

(For verbs in main clauses in indirect discourse, see **386, 394, 402.**)

388. Subjunctive by Attraction. — A verb in the indicative, occurring in a clause dependent upon a subjunctive or an
infinitive, is frequently " attracted " to the subjunctive, especially if it constitutes a corporate part of the statement.

Dat negōtium hīs utī ea quae apud Belgās gerantur cognōscant, *He directs them to learn what is going on among the Belgians.*

389. *Quod* **Causal Clauses.** — Causal clauses introduced
by **quod** (or **proptereā quod**) and **quoniam,** *since, because,* are

in the indicative when they convey the writer's or speaker's reason, the subjunctive when the reason is presented as that of another person or is rejected.

1. **Amīcō grātiās ēgī quod mihi pecūniam dederat,** *I thanked my friend because he had given me money.*

2. **Rōmānīs bellum intulit quod agrōs suōs vāstāvissent,** *He made war against the Romans because (as he alleged) they had laid waste his lands.*

390.   OUTLINE OF CONDITIONS

a. Subordinate clause (" condition ") introduced by **sī, nisi,** or **sī nōn.**

b. Principal clause (" conclusion ").

I. Simple (nothing implied as to truth)

Any possible combination of tenses of the indicative, as in English.

Sī mē laudat, laetus sum, *If he praises me, I am glad.*

II. Contrary to Fact

1. *Present:* imperfect subjunctive in both clauses.

2. *Past:* past perfect subjunctive in both clauses.

1. **Sī mē laudāret, laetus essem,** *If he were praising me* (but he isn't), *I should be glad* (now).

2. **Sī mē laudāvisset, laetus fuissem,** *If he had praised me* (but he didn't), *I should have been glad* (then).

Note. — Sometimes the indicative is used in the conclusion for greater vividness or to emphasize the certainty of the result if the condition were or had been true.

III. Future Less Vivid (" should," " would ")

Present subjunctive in both clauses.

Sī mē laudet, laetus sim, *If he should praise me, I should be glad.*

Note. — The term " less vivid " is used to contrast with one type of simple condition known as " more vivid " (" shall," " will "), in which the future or future perfect indicative is used in the condition and the future in the conclusion. The present is more common in such conditions in English.

391. REFLEXIVE USE OF THE PASSIVE

Occasionally the passive form of a verb or participle is used in a " middle " or reflexive sense : **armārī,** *to arm themselves.*

392. IMPERSONAL VERBS

(*a*) Some verbs are used only impersonally and therefore have no forms in the first and second persons ; as, **licet** (*it is permitted*), **oportet** (*it is necessary*), **placet** (*it is pleasing*), etc.

> **Licēbit tibi īre,** *You will be allowed to go.*
> **Mē hoc facere oportet,** *It is necessary that I do this.*

(*b*) Other verbs may at times be used impersonally, *i.e.* without a personal subject.

(*c*) Intransitive verbs are used only impersonally in the passive.

> **Ventum erat,** *He* (or *they*) *had come.* See also **313,** *a.*

IMPERATIVE MOOD

393. Affirmative commands are expressed by the imperative ; negative commands by the present imperative of **nōlō** (**nōlī, nōlīte**) and the infinitive.

> **Amā tuōs inimīcōs,** *Love your enemies.*
> **Nōlīte īre,** *Do not go* (lit., *be unwilling to go*).

Note. — The future imperative is rare, being found chiefly in laws, etc.

394. Exhortations (volitive subjunctive, **366**) and commands (**393**), though main clauses, become subjunctive in indirect discourse.

> 1. (Direct) **Īte !** *Go !*
> 2. (Indirect) **Dīxit īrent,** *He said that they should go.*

PARTICIPLE

395. The tenses of the participle (present, perfect, future) denote time *present, past,* or *future* from the standpoint of the main verb.

396. (*a*) Perfect participles are often used as simple adjectives: **nōtus,** *known.*

(*b*) Participles, like adjectives, may be used substantively: **factum,** " having been done," *deed.*

397. The Latin participle is often a *one-word substitute* for a subordinate clause in English introduced by *who* or *which* (relative), *when* or *after* (temporal), *since* or *because* (causal), *although* (adversative), and *if* (conditional).

FUTURE PASSIVE PARTICIPLE

398. The future passive participle (gerundive) is a verbal adjective, having thirty forms. It has two distinct uses:

I. As a predicate adjective with forms of **sum,**[1] when it naturally indicates, as in English, *what must be done.* The person upon whom the obligation rests is in the dative (**317**).

Caesarī omnia erant agenda, *Caesar had to do all things* (lit., *all things were to be done by Caesar*).

II. (*a*) With phrases introduced either by **ad** and the accusative or by **causā** (or **grātiā**) and the genitive to express purpose.

1. **Ad eās rēs cōnficiendās Mārcus dēligitur,** *Marcus is chosen to accomplish these things* (lit., *for these things to be accomplished*).

2. **Caesaris videndī causā** (or **grātiā**) **vēnit,** *He came for the sake o seeing Caesar* (lit., *for the sake of Caesar to be seen*).

Note. — Causā and grātiā are always placed after the participle.

(*b*) In agreement with the object of **cūrō, locō, dō,** etc.

Pontem faciendum cūrat, *He attends to having a bridge built.*

---

[1] The so-called passive periphrastic, a term not used in this book. The term should be avoided because it is not only useless but troublesome.

399.   GERUND

The gerund is a verbal noun of the second declension with only four forms — genitive, dative, accusative, and ablative singular, and has many of the same case constructions as other nouns.

The gerund, like the future passive participle, is used with **ad, causā,** or **grātiā** to express purpose:

1. **Ad discendum vēnimus,** *We have come for learning* (i.e. *to learn*).
2. **Discendī causā** (or **grātiā**) **vēnimus,** *We have come for the sake of learning.*

INFINITIVE

400. The infinitive is a verbal noun, and as such it may be used as the subject of a verb.

1. **Errāre hūmānum est,** *To err is human.*
2. **Vidēre est crēdere,** *To see is to believe.*

401. With many verbs the infinitive may be used as a direct object, like other nouns. (This is sometimes called the complementary infinitive.)

Parat cōpiās movēre, *He prepares to move the troops.*

402. Statements that convey indirectly the thoughts or words of another, when used as the objects of verbs of **saying, thinking, knowing, hearing, perceiving,** and the like, require subjects in the accusative and verbs in the infinitive.

1. (Direct) **Dīcit, " Puerī veniunt,"** *He says, " The boys are coming."*
2. (Indirect) **Dīcit puerōs venīre,** *He says that the boys are coming.*

(*a*) With the passive third singular (impersonal) of these verbs the infinitive is the subject.

Caesarī nūntiātur eōs trānsīre, *It is reported to Caesar that they are crossing.*

403. 1. The present infinitive represents time or action as *going on,* from the standpoint of the introductory verb:

Dīcit **Dīxit** } eōs pugnāre,   *He* { *says* / *said* } *(that) they* { *are* / *were* } *fighting.*

2. The future infinitive represents time or action as *subsequent to* that of the introductory verb :

Dīcit **Dīxit** } eōs pugnātūrōs esse,   *He* { *says* / *said* } *(that) they* { *will* / *would* } *fight.*

3. The perfect infinitive represents time or action as *completed before* that of the introductory verb :

Dīcit **Dīxit** } eōs pugnāvisse,   *He* { *says* / *said* } *(that) they* { *have* / *had* } *fought.*

404. The Historical Infinitive. — The historical infinitive with subject in the nominative has the force of the indicative imperfect or perfect and lends vigor and dash to a narrative passage. Usually two or more such infinitives are used together.

Omnēs obstrepere, hostem atque parricīdam vocāre, *All cried out against him, called him an enemy and traitor.*

405.   SUPINE

The supine, like the gerund, is a verbal noun.   It has only two cases.

(*a*) The accusative in **-um,** used with verbs of motion to express purpose :

Pācem petītum vēnērunt, *They came to seek peace.*

(*b*) The ablative in **-ū,** used to express respect :

difficile factū, *hard to do* (lit., *hard in the doing*).

FIGURES OF SPEECH [1]

406. Hendiadys. — In Latin two nouns are sometimes connected by a coördinate conjunction when one of them is

---

[1] For other figures (treated in **136–157**) see the Index.

in thought subordinate to the other.   This is called hendiadys (a Greek word meaning " one thing through two ").

> **vī et armīs,** *by force of arms.*

407. Metonymy. — The use of a noun in place of another noun related in sense (especially the part for the whole) is called metonymy (" change of name ").

> **Bacchus,** *wine;* **puppis,** *ship.*

408. Oxymoron. — The juxtaposition of contradictory expressions is called oxymoron.

> **Cum tacent, clāmant,** *In being silent, they shout (their opinions).*

409. Zeugma. — The use of a word (usually a verb) to govern two other words when its sense applies strictly only to one of them is called zeugma (" joining ").

> **Locus acervīs corporum et cīvium sanguine redundāvit,** *The place was covered* (lit., *overflowed*) *with heaps of bodies and the blood of citizens.*

FIG. 127.   THE CAPITOLINE HILL AND THE TIBER AT ROME

Many houses were destroyed in 1929–1930 so that the ancient hillside might be clearly visible.   Ruins of ancient houses were discovered.

410. THE ROMAN CALENDAR

The Roman calendar was reformed by Julius Caesar in 46 B.C. This calendar, with relatively slight changes, is the one which is in use to-day. Before that time the Roman year had only 355 days, with a leap year consisting of an additional short month every other year. By this old calendar March, May, July, and October had 31 days, February had 28, and the rest had 29.

The political (consular) year began January 1, and this day had long since become the regular New Year's Day instead of March 1, as in the original calendar. The names of some of the months (**Quīnctīlis,** *July;* **Sextīlis,** *August;* **September,** etc.) go back to the time when March was the first month. The new names July and August were given in honor of Julius Caesar and Augustus. The Romans had no weeks and therefore no names for the days of the week. These came in with the spread of Christianity.

Years were sometimes reckoned from the founding of the city (753 B.C.), but ordinarily the names of the annual consuls were used as the year date.

Our simple system of numbering the days of the month was not in use in classical times. Instead the Romans used as a basis three fixed points in the month. These were :

1. **Kalendae,** *Calends,* first of the month.
2. **Nōnae,** *Nones,* fifth of the month (seventh in March, May, July, and October).
3. **Īdūs,** *Ides,* thirteenth of the month (fifteenth in March, May, July, and October).

Thus in a date the Romans would say:

Kalendīs Septembribus [1] (abbreviated **Kal. Sept.**, etc.), *September* 1.
Nōnīs Mārtiīs (**Nōn. Mārt.**), *March* 7.
Īdibus Novembribus (**Īd. Nov.**), *November* 13.

The days before these fixed points were indicated by **prīdiē**, *day before*, used as a preposition with the accusative :

prīdiē (**pr.**) **Kal. Feb.**, *January* 31 (before the reform of the calendar *January* 29).

In the case of other days the Romans reckoned *back* from the nearest of the three fixed points, counting both ends, so that 1 must be added to 13 (15 in some months) in counting back from the Ides and to 5 (or 7) in counting back from the Nones, and two must be added to the number of days of the month in counting back from the Calends of the next month. [2] Instead of the ablative of time the usual form is the ungrammatical expression **ante diem** (abbreviated **a.d.** [3]), followed by the proper ordinal numeral and the accusative :

a.d. IIII Nōn. Apr. (**ante diem quārtum Nōnās Aprīlēs**), *April* 2, *i.e.* $5 + 1 - 4 = 2$.
a.d. VIIII Kal. Mai., *April* 23, *i.e.* $30 + 2 - 9 = 23$ (*April* 22 before the reform, *i.e.* $29 + 2 - 9 = 22$).
a.d. XVII Kal. Sept., *August* 16, *i.e.* $31 + 2 - 17 = 16$ (*August* 14 before the reform, *i.e.* $29 + 2 - 17 = 14$).

---

[1] The names of the months are adjectives. The ablative is one of time

[2] If you will count the days out on your fingers, you will see the reason for this.

[3] This phrase is sometimes omitted.

SUMMARY OF PREFIXES AND SUFFIXES

411. **PREFIXES**

A great many Latin words are formed by joining prefixes (**prae,** *in front;* **fīxus,** *attached*) to *root* words. These same prefixes, most of which are prepositions, are those chiefly used in English, and by their use many new words are continually being formed.

Some prefixes change their final consonants to make them like the initial consonants of the words to which they are attached. This change is called assimilation (**ad,** *to;* **similis,** *like*).

Many prefixes in Latin and English may have intensive force, especially **con-, ex-, ob-, per-.** They are then best translated either by an English intensive, as *up* or *out,* or by an adverb, as *completely, thoroughly, deeply.* Thus **com-moveō** means *move greatly,* **permagnus,** *very great,* **obtineō,** *hold on to,* **concitō,** *rouse up,* **excipiō,** *catch, receive.*

1. ab (abs, ā), *from:* abs-tineō; *ab-undance, abs-tain, a-vocation.*

2. ad, *to, toward:* ad-iciō ; *ac-curate, an-nounce, ap-paratus, ad-vocate.*

3. ante, *before:* ante-cēdō; *ante-cedent.*

4. bene, *well:* bene-dīcō; *bene-factor.*

5. bi-, bis-, *twice, two:* bi-ennium; *bi-ennial.*

6. circum, *around:* circum-eō; *circum-ference.*

7. con-, *with, together:* con-vocō; *con-voke, col-lect, com-motion, cor-rect.*

8. contrā, *against:* contra-dict.

9. dē, *from, down from, not:* dē-ferō; *de-ter.*

10. dis-, *apart, not:* dis-cēdō; *dis-locate, dif-fuse, di-vert.*

11. ex (ē), *out of, from:* ex-eō; *ex-port, e-dit, ef-fect.*

12. extrā, *outside: extra-legal.*

515

13. **in,** *in, into, against:* **in-dūcō**; *in-habit, im-migrant, il-lusion, en-chant.*

14. **in-,** *not, un-:* **im-mēnsus**; *il-legal, im-moral, ir-regular.*

15. **inter,** *between, among:* **inter-clūdō**; *inter-class.*

16. **intrā,** *within, inside:* *intra-collegiate.*

17. **intrō-,** *within:* *intro-duce.*

18. **male,** *ill:* *male-factor, mal-formation.*

19. **multi-,** *much, many:* *multi-graph.*

20. **nōn,** *not:* *non-sense.*

21. **ob,** *against, toward:* **ob-tineō**; *oc-cur, of-fer, o-mit, op-pose, ob-tain.*

22. **per,** *through, thoroughly:* **per-moveō**; *per-fect.*

23. **post,** *after:* *post-pone.*

24. **prae,** *before, in front of:* **prae-ficiō**; *pre-cede.*

25. **prō,** *for, forward:* **prō-dūcō**; *pro-mote.*

26. **re- (red-),** *back, again:* **re-dūcō, red-igō**; *re-fer.*

27. **sē-,** *apart from:* **sē-cēdō**; *se-parate.*

28. **sēmi-,** *half, partly:* **sēmi-barbarus**; *semi-annual.*

29. **sub,** *under, up from under:* **suc-cēdō**; *suf-fer, sug-gest, sup-port, sub-let.*

30. **super (sur-),** *over, above:* **super-sum**; *super-fluous, sur-mount.*

31. **trāns (trā-),** *through, across:* **trā-dūcō**; *trans-fer.*

32. **ultrā,** *extremely:* *ultra-fashionable.*

33. **ūn- (ūni-),** *one:* *uni-form.*

412. SUFFIXES

Particles which are attached to the ends of words are called suffixes (**sub,** *under, after;* **fīxus,** *attached*). Like the Latin prefixes, the Latin suffixes play a very important part in the formation of English words.

The meaning of suffixes is often far less definite than that of prefixes. In many cases they merely indicate the part of speech.

Suffixes are often added to words which already have suffixes. So *functionalistically* has six suffixes, all of Latin or Greco-Latin origin except the last. A suffix often combines with a preceding letter or letters to form a new suffix. This is especially true of suffixes added to perfect participles whose base ends in -s- or -t-. In the following list no account is taken of such English suffixes as -ant, derived from the ending of the Latin present participle.

1. -ālis (-al), pertaining to: līber-ālis; annu-al.
2. -ānus (-an, -ane, -ain), pertaining to: Rōm-ānus; capt-ain, hum-ane.
3. -āris (-ar), pertaining to: famili-āris; singul-ar.
4. -ārium (-arium, -ary), place where: aqu-arium, gran-ary.
5. -ārius (-ary), pertaining to: frūment-ārius; ordin-ary.
6. -āticum (-age): bagg-age.
7. -ātus (-ate), office: cōnsul-ātus; sen-ate.
8. -āx (-ac-ious), tending to: aud-āx; rap-acious.
9. -culum (-cle), means of: vehi-culum; vehi-cle.
10. -ēnsis, -iēnsis (-ese), place: Athēni-ēnsis; Chin-ese.
11. -ester, pertaining to: equ-ester.
12. -faciō, -ficō (-fy), make: cōn-ficiō; satis-fy.
13. -ia (-y), -cia, -tia (-ce), -antia (-ance, -ancy), -entia (-ence, -ency), condition of: memor-ia, grā-tia, cōnst-antia, sent-entia; memor-y, provin-ce, gra-ce, const-ancy, sent-ence.
14. -icus (-ic), pertaining to: pūbl-icus; civ-ic.
15. -idus (-id), having the quality of: rap-idus; flu-id.
16. -ilis (-ile, -il), -bilis (-ble, -able, -ible), able to be: fac-ilis, laudā-bilis; fert-ile, no-ble, compar-able, terr-ible.
17. -īlis (-ile, -il), pertaining to: cīv-īlis; serv-ile.
18. -īnus (-ine), pertaining to: mar-īnus; div-ine.
19. -iō (-ion), -siō (-sion), -tiō (-tion), act or state of: reg-iō, mān-siō, ōrā-tiō; commun-ion, ten-sion, rela-tion.
20. -ium (-y), -cium, -tium (-ce): remed-ium, sōlā-cium, pre-tium; stud-y, edifi-ce.
21. -īvus (-ive), pertaining to: capt-īvus; nat-ive.
22. -lentus (-lent), full of: opu-lentus; corpu-lent.
23. -men (-men, -min, -me): lū-men; cri-min-al, cri-me.
24. -mentum (-ment), means of: im-pedī-mentum; comple-ment.
25. -ō, from nouns (" denominative "): rēgn-ō.
26. -or (-or), state of: tim-or: terr-or.
27. -or, -sor, -tor (-sor, -tor), one who: scrīp-tor; inven-tor.
28. -ōrium (-orium, -ory, -or), place where: audit-orium, fact-ory, mirr-or.
29. -ōsus (-ous, -ose), full of: ōti-ōsus; copi-ous.
30. -scō (-sce, -sh), begin to (" inceptive "): hebē-scō; fini-sh.
31. -tās (-ty), state of: līber-tās; integri-ty.
32. -timus, pertaining to: fīni-timus.

33. -tō, -sō, -itō, *keep on* ("frequentative"): **dic-tō, prēn-sō.**
dict-itō.

34. -tūdō (-*tude*), *state of:* **magni-tūdō**; *multi-tude.*

35. -tūs (-*tue*), *state of:* **vir-tūs**; *vir-tue.*

36. -ūra, -sūra, -tūra (-*ure, -sure, -ture*): **fig-ūra, mēn-sūra, agricul-**
tūra; *proced-ure, pres-sure, na-ture.*

Fig. 128. Ruins on the Palatine Hill at Rome

WORD LISTS FOR VOCABULARY DRILL

Prescribed for the Third Year by the Revised (1928) New York State Syllabus and by the College Board Latin Word List. The words common to both lists, including those recommended only by the College Entrance Examination Board, are printed in blackface type. College Board words which are not prescribed for the third year by the New York Syllabus are marked with an asterisk (*). New York Syllabus words which are not required by the College Board in the third year are printed in lightface type.

abhorreō	(shudder) shrink from	aliquandō	at some time, at length
accūsō	charge, accuse	aliquot	some
acerbus	bitter	alō	nourish
adeō (*adv.*)	up to this, so	*āmēns	without mind, mad
adhūc	up to here, so far, hitherto	āmentia	insanity, madness
		*amō	love
adimō	take away, deprive	*anima	breath, life, soul
adipīscor	attain, obtain	*antequam	(sooner than), before
admoneō	remind, warn		
adulēscentia	youth	antīquus	ancient, old-time
aedēs	temple; (plu.) house	appetō	strive after
		aptus	fit, suitable
aerārius	belonging to money; neuter, as n., treasury	*āra	altar
		ārdeō	blaze, glow
		argentum	silver, money
aeternus	everlasting	argūmentum	proof
afflīgō	strike down	ars	skill, art, theory
*agitō	drive, pursue	*arx	citadel
agrestis	rustic, boorish	assequor	attain
aiō	say	assiduus	uninterrupted

519

atrōx	cruel, horrible	colō	cherish, worship
attendō	turn attention to, listen to	colōnus	husbandman, settler
auctoɪ	originator, founder	comes	companion
audācia	boldness	comitātus	retinue
*auferō	bear off	comitia	elections
auris	ear	*commendō	intrust
auspicium	auspices, omen	*complector	embrace
avāritia	greed	conciliō	win over
avidus	eager, desirous	concitō	arouse, excite
avus	grandfather	concordia	harmony, agreement
beātus	blessed, happy, wealthy	condō	put together, found, hide
bellō	make war	cōnfiteor	confess
benevolentia	good will, friendship	coniūnx	spouse, husband, wife
bīnī	two each	coniūrātiō	conspiracy
		cōnscientia	consciousness, conscience
caelum	sky, heaven		
carcer	prison	cōnsīderō	consider
careō	be without, do without	cōnstantia	consistency, firmness
cārus	dear, beloved	cōnsulāris	belonging to a consul, ex-consul
caveō	beware		
celeber	crowded, frequent, famous	cōnsulātus	consulship
		cōnsultum	decree
celebrō	crowd, make famous, celebrate	contemnō	despise
		contentus	satisfied
ɪēnseō	assess, propose, estimate, vote	contingō	happen
		cōntiō	assembly
cēnsor	censor	convīvium	banquet
*certāmen	contest, struggle	corrumpō	break, corrupt, bribe
certē	surely, at least		
certō, -āre	struggle	crēdō	give trust, believe, trust
*cervīx	neck, throat		
cīvīlis	belonging to a citizen	creō	make, elect
		crēscō	grow larger
clārus	bright, illustrious	*crīmen	judgment, charge
clēmēns	mild, merciful	cruciātus	torture
cōgitō	think, reflect	crūdēlis	cruel
collēga	colleague	*cruentus	bloody

culpa	blame, guilt
cūnctus	all together, entire
cūra	care, anxiety
cūria	senate house
custōdia	protection, custody, garrison
custōs	guardian, watchman
damnō	condemn
dēbilitō	weaken
dēcēdō	go away, die
decet	it becomes, behooves
dēclārō	make clear
dēdecus	disgrace
dēlectō	give joy, delight
dēleō	destroy
dēlīctum	fault, crime
dēlūbrum	sacred place, shrine
dēmēns	without mind, unreasonable
dēnique	finally, at last
dēnūntiō	announce, give warning
dēprecor	beg off
dēprehendō	seize, surprise
dēsīderō	desire, long for
dēsignātus	marked out, elect
*dēsignō	mark out, appoint
dēsinō	cease, desist
dictitō	keep saying
dignus	worthy, deserving
dīlēctus	conscription, levy
dīligentia	carefulness
dīligō	pick, choose, love
dīripiō	tear apart, plunder
discō	learn
discrīmen	turning point, crisis, peril
dissentiō	disagree
dissimulō	dissemble

diūturnus	lasting, long continued
dīvīnus	of god, divine
dīvitiae	riches, wealth
doctrīna	teaching, learning
dolor	pain, grief
domesticus	belonging to the house, inner
domicilium	residence
*dominus	master
dōnō	make a gift, present
dubius	doubtful
dulcis	sweet, pleasant
ecquis	any one at all
efferō	bear out, lift up
egeō	be in need, want
*equidem	certainly, (w. first person)
ergā	toward
ergō	therefore
errō	wander, make a mistake
ērudiō	educate
etenim	and indeed, for
ēvertō	overturn
exanimō	kill
exaudiō	hear from a distance
excellō	surpass
excelsus	high, distinguished
exemplum	sample, example
exerceō	train
exigō	drive out, exact, collect
eximius	taken out, outstanding
exitium	destruction, ruin
expetō	ask for
exsilium	banishment
exsistō	come out, come into being

exstinguō — put out, quench
exsultō — leap up, exult
externus — outside, foreign
exterus — outside, foreign

facinus — deed, crime
fallō — deceive, fail
falsus — deceptive, false
fānum — shrine
*fās — divine right
fateor — confess, admit
fātum — destiny, oracle
faucēs — jaws, defile
faveō — favor
fax — torch, firebrand
fēlīcitās — luck
*fēlīx — happy
ferrum — iron
*fidēlis — faithful
fingō — mould, invent
flāgitium — outrage
flāgitō — demand
flagrō — burn, flare
flamma — flame, fire
*flectō — bend, turn
flōreō — flourish
foedus (n.) — treaty
formīdō — fear, panic
fors — chance
fortasse — perchance, perhaps
forum — market place
frequēns — crowded
frētus — trusting, relying
frīgus — cold, chill
rūctus — produce, fruit, gain
fruor — enjoy
furō — rave, rage
furor — rage, madness
fūrtum — theft

*gaudeō — rejoice
glōria — renown, glory
gradus — step, rank

*grātulātiō — rejoicing
gravitās — weight, seriousness
grex — herd, crowd

habitō — occupy, dwell in
*haereō — stick
*haud — by no means
hesternus — of yesterday
*hīc (adv.) — here
hinc — hence
hodiē — to-day
hodiernus — of to-day
honestus — honorable, respected
hūmānus — of man, kindly, cultured

iaceō — lie (on the ground)
iactō — throw about, boast
idcircō — therefore
Īdūs — Ides
igitur — therefore, thus
ignōminia — disgrace, degradation
ignōscō — not know, pardon
illūstris — illustrious
illūstrō — light up, honor
imāgō — likeness, picture, portrait
*immānis — immense, savage
immineō — threaten
immō — on the contrary
immortālis — immortal
impendeō — overhang, threaten
imperātor — commander
improbus — not upright, wicked
*inānis — empty
incendium — conflagration
incrēdibilis — unbelievable
index — witness, informer
indicō, -āre — point out, betray, reveal
indīcō, -ere — proclaim, appoint

industria	application	laetor	rejoice
inertia	idleness	*laetus	glad
inferus	below	largior	give abundantly, lavish, bribe
infestus	hostile		
ingenium	inborn gift, talent	*lateō	lie hidden
ingredior	step into, begin	latrō	highwayman, thief
innocēns	guiltless, upright	latrōcinium	robbery
innocentia	uprightness, honesty	*lēgō, -āre	appoint
		*legō, -ere	choose, read
inquam	quoth, say	lēnis	gentle, kind
insidior	lie in ambush, plot	levō	make light, relieve
insigne	badge, device	libenter	gladly
insignis	marked, distinguished	*liber	book
		līberālis	of a freeman, gentlemanly
*intendō	stretch, aim		
interdum	sometimes	libīdō	lust
interitus	destruction, death	locuplēs	wealthy
intersum	be between, be of importance	longinquus	far off, at a distance
		lūdus	play, school; (plu.) games
intueor	gaze upon, admire		
invideō	look upon, envy	*lūgeō	mourn
invidia	envy, hatred, unpopularity	lūmen	light
		lūxuria	extravagance
*īra	anger		
īrāscor	become (be) angry	macula	spot, stain, disgrace
iste	that one (of yours)	maeror	grief, mourning
iterum	again	*magister	master, teacher
iūcundus	pleasant, agreeable	manifestus	plain, visible, manifest
iūdex	judge, juror		
iūdicium	judgment, trial	mánsuētūdō	gentleness
iūdicō	judge, decide	mātūrus	ripe, early
iussū	by order of	mediocris	middle, average
*iuventūs	youth	meminī	remember, recall
iuvō	aid, please	*-met	(intensive suffix)
		mīlitia	military service
Kalendae	first day of the month	*minae	threats
		*minor, -ārī	threaten
		mīror	marvel at
*lābor, lābī	slip, err	mīrus	marvelous, astonishing
lacessō	challenge, harass		
lacrima	tear	misceō	mix, mingle, confuse
laetitia	joyfulness, joy		

misericordia	kindheartedness, clemency, pity	obeō	go against, meet, attend
mītis	kind	oblīvīscor	forget
moenia	fortifications, walls	obscūrus	dark, concealed
molestus	troublesome, annoying	obsecrō	implore
mōlior	put up, plot	*occidō	fall, perish
monumentum	(means of recalling), monument	ōdī	hate
		odium	hate, hatred
morbus	sickness	*ōmen	sign
morior	die	omittō	leave out, pass by
mōtus	commotion, tumult, uprising	opīnor	believe, think
		optō	wish for, pray for
mūnicipium	free town	ōra	shore, district
mūtō	change	orbis	circle
		ōrnāmentum	adornment, equipment
*nauta	sailor	ōrnō	equip, adorn
nāvālis	of a ship, naval	ōs, ōris	mouth, face
*necessārius	necessary	ōtium	leisure, peace
necessitūdō	close relationship		
necō	kill	pactum	agreement
nefārius	unspeakable, criminal	paenitet	(it repents one), repent
neglegō	overlook, neglect	palam	openly
negō	deny, refuse	parēns	parent
nēquitia	worthlessness, shiftlessness	pāreō	obey
		pariēs	wall (of a house)
nervus	sinew, string	pariō	bring forth, bear, gain
nesciō	know not, be unaware	parricīda	murderer (of parent), traitor
nex	slaughter, murder	*parum	too little
nimis	too much	patefaciō	make open, reveal
nimius	exceeding, excessive	patientia	endurance, patience
nōminō	name	*patria	fatherland
Nōnae	Nones	patrius	belonging to a father, inherited
notō	mark		
num	(a question particle)	peccō	injure, do wrong
*nūmen	nod, divine will	penitus	deep within
nūper	newly, recently	percipiō	notice
*nusquam	nowhere	perdō	ruin, destroy
nūtus	nod, command		

perīculōsus	dangerous, risky	**pudet**	(it shames one), be ashamed
perniciēs	destruction, ruin		
pertimēscō	become (be) afraid	**pudor**	shame, modesty
pestis	plague, pestilence, ruin	**pulcher**	beautiful
		pūniō	punish
*pius	dutiful, loyal		
placeō	please	**quaesō**	beg, beseech
plācō	make pleasant, appease	**quaestiō**	inquiry, trial, court
		quaestus	gain, profit
plānus	level, plain	**quālis**	of what kind
plēnus	full	**quamquam**	although, and yet
populāris	of the people, popular, democratic	**quamvīs**	however much, although
*possideō	possess		
*potius,		**quandō**	when
potissimum	rather, preferably	**quasi**	as if
		querēla	complaint
prae	in front of	**quia**	because
praecipuus	special, excellent	quiēs	rest, quiet
praeclārus	very bright, famous	**quiēscō**	come to rest, keep quiet
praedicō, -āre	assert		
praeditus	equipped, endowed	**quisnam**	who indeed
praedō	pirate	**quisquis**	whoever
praeferō	bear before, prefer	**quīvīs**	anyone (you please)
		quō (*conj.*)	that
praetereō	pass by	**quoad**	(up to where), as long as
praetermittō	pass by		
praetor	praetor	**quondam**	at some time, at last
praetūra	praetorship		
pretium	price	**quot**	how many
prīdem	long ago	**quotiēns**	how often
prīvō	deprive		
probō	prove, approve	**recitō**	read aloud
prōdō	put forth, betray	**recordor**	recall
profectō	truly, in truth	**rēctē**	rightly
profiteor	say openly, profess, register	redimō	ransom, redeem
		rēgius	of a king, royal
proinde	therefore	**rēgnō**	be king, rule
proprius	belonging to, characteristic	religiō	scruple, religion
		repetō	seek back, demand, recollect
prōsum	be advantageous, benefit	**reprehendō**	censure, blame
prūdentia	foresight, wisdom	reprimō	repress, check

repudiō	spurn, reject	soleō	be wont,
requīrō	demand		accustomed
restō	remain, be left	*solvo	loose, pay
retardō	keep back, delay	somnus	sleep
reus	defendant	*soror	sister
rōbur	oak, strength	sors	lot, fate
rūmor	talk, gossip	spīritus	breath, pride
*ruō	rush	splendor	brilliance
		spoliō	despoil
*sacer	holy	*spolium	spoil
*sacerdōs	priest	stabilis	steadfast
salvus	safe	stimulus	goad, spur
sānctus	sacred, holy	strepitus	noise, uproar
sānē	truly, indeed	stultus	foolish
sanguis	blood	stuprum	debauch
sānō	make healthy, cure	suādeō	advise
sapiēns	wise	subiciō	throw under,
scelerātus	criminal		conquer
scelus	crime	suffrāgium	ballot, vote
scientia	knowledge	sūmptus	outlay, expense
scīlicet	you may know, of	supplex	bending, suppliant
	course	supplicātiō	thanksgiving
sēcernō	set aside, separate		
secūris	ax	tabella	tablet, letters
sedeō	sit	tabula	board, archive
sēdēs	seat	taceō	keep still
sēmen	seed	tālis	of such kind
senectūs	old age	tametsī	as if, although
senex	old man	tamquam	as if, so to say
sēnsus	feeling	tandem	at length
sepeliō	bury	tantum	so much, only
sermō	talk, conversation	tēctum	roof, building
serviō	serve	temere	rashly
sevēritās	strictness	temeritās	rashness
sevērus	strict	temperantia	self-control
sīca	dagger	templum	ːacred precinct,
silentium	silence		temple
simulō	pretend	tenebrae	darkness
sīn	but if	tenuis	thin, humble
sinō	let, permit	terminus	boundary line,
sīve (seu)	or if, whether		limit
societās	fellowship, alliance	testāmentum	last will

testimōnium	evidence, testimony	vectīgal	tax, tribute
testis	witness	vehemēns	violent
*testor	call to witness	vēndō	sell
togātus	dressed in the toga, civilian	venēnum	poison
		veneror	revere
tolerō	bear, endure	venia	pardon, permission
totiēns	so often	verber	lash, stripes
trāctō	handle	*verbum	word
trānsmittō	send across, cross	versus	line, verse
triumphō	celebrate a triumph	vērum (conj.)	truly, but
triumphus	a triumph	vēstīgium	track, trace
tumultus	uproar, rebellion	*vetō	forbid
*tunc	then	vexō	harass, plunder
turpitūdō	baseness	vidēlicet	you may see, of course
		vigilō	watch
ulcīscor	avenge, punish	*vīlla	farmhouse
umquam	ever	*vinculum	bond, fetter
*urgeō	press on, urge	vindicō	claim, punish
ūsitātus	common, customary	vīnum	wine
		violō	ravish
*usquam	anywhere	virgō	maiden
ūtilitās	usefulness	vīsō	look at, visit
utinam	would that	vitium	fault, vice
utrum	whether	vīvō	be alive
uxor	wife	vīvus	alive
		voluptās	pleasure
varietās	variety	*voveō	vow
varius	different, diverse	vultus	face, countenance

LATIN–ENGLISH VOCABULARY

Verbs of the first conjugation whose parts are regular (*i.e.* like **parō, 276**) are indicated by the figure 1.

The English pronunciation of proper names is indicated by a simple system. The vowels are as follows: ā as in *hate*, ă as in *hat*, ē as in *feed*, ĕ as in *fed*, ī as in *bite*, I as in *bit*, ō as in *hope*, ŏ as in *hop*, ū as in *cute*, ŭ as in *cut*. In the ending *ēs* the *s* is soft as in *rose*. When the accented syllable ends in a consonant, the vowel is short; otherwise it is long.

A

ā! *interj.*, oh!

A., *abbreviation for* **Aulus,** –ī, *m.*, *a Roman name.*

ā, ab, abs, *prep. w. abl.*, from, away from, by.

a. d. = ante diem.

abdicō, 1, disown; *w.* **sē,** resign.

abditus, –a, –um, hidden.

abdō, –ere, –didī, –ditus, put away, bury.

abdūcō, –ere, –dūxī, –ductus, withdraw, lead *or* take away.

abeō, –īre, –iī, –itus, go away *or* off, depart.

abhorreō, –ēre, –uī, —, shrink from, be inconsistent with.

abiciō, –ere, –iēcī, –iectus, throw away *or* down.

abiectus, –a, –um, cast down, dejected.

abluō, –ere, –luī, –lūtus, bathe.

abnegō, 1, refuse, deny.

aborior, –īrī, –ortus sum, arise.

abrumpō, –ere, –rūpī, –ruptus, break off, sever.

absconditus, –a, –um, hidden.

absēns, *gen.* –entis, absent.

absolūtiō, –ōnis, *f.*, acquittal.

absolvō, –ere, –solvī, –solūtus, (loose from), acquit; finish.

abstinentia, –ae, *f.*, self-restraint.

abstineō, –ēre, –uī, –tentus, (hold away), refrain.

abstrahō, –ere, –trāxī, –trāctus, draw away.

absum, –esse, āfuī, āfutūrus, be away, be distant; be absent; *w.* **ab,** fail.

absūmō, –ere, –sūmpsī, –sūmptus, consume, destroy.

abūtor, –ūtī, –ūsus sum, abuse, take advantage of.

ac, *see* **atque.**

accēdō, –ere, –cessī, –cessus, (come to), approach; be added.

accendō, –ere, –cendī, –cēnsus, kindle, inflame.

accidō, –ere, accidī, —, fall (to), happen.

accingō, –ere, –cīnxī, –cīnctus, gird on, equip, arm.

accipiō, –ere, –cēpī, –ceptus, receive, accept; hear.

1

Accius, –cī, *m.,* Accius (Ac'-shius), *a Roman poet.*

acclīvus, –a, –um, rising.

accommodō, 1, adapt, adjust, suit.

accūrātē, *adv.,* carefully.

accursus, –ūs, *m.,* gathering.

accūsātor, –ōris, *m.,* prosecutor.

accūsō, 1, blame, censure.

ācer, ācris, ācre, sharp, keen, fierce, bitter, severe, active.

acerbitās, –tātis, *f.,* severity.

acerbus, –a, –um, bitter, harsh.

acervus, –i, *m.,* heap.

Achaia, –ae, *f.,* Achaia (Akā'ya), Greece.

Achillās, –ae, *m.,* Achillas (Akill'-as), *murderer of Pompey.*

Achillēs, –is, *m.,* Achilles (Akill'ēs), *a Greek hero.*

aciēs, aciēī, *f.,* (keen) edge, battle line.

acquiēscō, –ere, –ēvī, –ētus, find rest.

acquīrō, –ere, –quīsīvī, –quīsītus, add to.

ācriter (*comp.* **ācrius,** *superl.* **ācerrimē**), sharply, eagerly, earnestly, fiercely.

acuō, –ere, acuī, acūtus, sharpen.

acūtus, –a, –um, sharp, keen.

ad, *prep. w. acc.,* to, toward, near; for; until; according to.

adaequō, 1, make equal (to).

Adbucillus, –ī, *m.,* Adbucillus, (Adbusil'us), *an Allobrogian.*

addō, –dere, –didī, –ditus, add.

addūcō, –ere, –dūxī, –ductus, lead to, bring, influence, move.

adeō, –īre, –iī, –itus, go to, approach.

adeō, *adv.,* so, so much; to such a degree, in fact.

adhaereō, –ēre, –haesī, –haesus, stick (to), trail after.

adhibeō, –ēre, –hibuī, –hibitus, (hold toward), summon, admit; use; furnish.

adhūc, *adv.,* up to this time, thus far, still.

adiciō, –ere, –iēcī, –iectus, throw (to), add.

adigō, –ere, –ēgī, –āctus, drive (to), hurl (to).

adimō, –ere, –ēmī, –ēmptus, take away.

adipēs, –ium, *m. and f. pl.,* fat; corpulence.

adipīscor, –ī, –eptus sum, obtain.

aditus, –ūs, *m.,* approach.

adiūmentum, –ī, *n.,* help, aid.

adiungō, –ere, –iūnxī, –iūnctus, join to, add, attach, win over.

adiuvō, –āre, –iūvī, –iūtus, help.

administer, –trī, *m.;* **administra, –ae,** *f.,* assistant, servant, tool.

administrō, 1, conduct, carry on, govern.

admīrātiō, –ōnis, *f.,* wonder; admiration.

admīror, –ārī, –ātus sum, wonder (at), admire.

admittō, –ere, –mīsī, –missus, admit.

admoneō, –ēre, –monuī, –monitus, remind, warn.

admonitus, –ūs, *m.,* suggestion.

admoveō, –ēre, –mōvī, –mōtus, (move to), place near, apply.

admurmurātiō, –ōnis, *f.*, murmuring.

adnotō, 1, (add a note), direct.

adoperiō, –īre, –operuī, –opertus, cover, close.

adōrnō, 1, fit out, furnish.

adstō, –stāre, –stitī, —, stand near.

adsum –esse, –fuī, –futūrus, be near *or* on hand, be present; assist.

adulēscēns, –entis, *m.* and *f.*, youth.

adulēscentia, –ae, *f.*, youth.

adulēscentulus, –ī, *m.*, mere lad.

adulter, –erī, *m.*, adulterer.

adulterium, –rī, *n.*, adultery.

adultus, –a, –um, full-grown.

adūrō, –ere, –ussī, –ustus, set fire to, scorch.

adveniō, –īre, –vēnī, –ventus, arrive.

adventīcius, –a, –um, foreign.

adventus, –ūs, *m.*, approach, arrival.

adversārius, –a, –um, opposed; *as noun, m.*, enemy.

adversus, –a, –um, facing, opposite.

adversus, *adv. and prep. w. acc.*, toward, against.

advertō, –ere, –vertī, –versus, turn to, direct.

advolō, 1, fly *or* hasten to.

aedēs, –is, *f.*, building, temple; *pl.*, house.

aedificium, –cī, *n.*, building.

aedificō, 1, build, erect.

aedīlitās, –tātis, *f.*, aedileship.

Aegaeus, –a, –um, Aegean (Ejē'an).

aeger, –gra, –grum, sick, suffering.

aegrē, *adv.*, with difficulty.

aegritūdō, –dinis, *f.*, sickness.

aegrōtus, –a, –um, sick.

Aegyptiācus, –a, –um, Egyptian.

Aegyptus, –ī, *f.*, Egypt.

Aemilius, –lī, *m.*, Aemilius (Emīl'ius), *a Roman name.*

aequālis, –e, equal.

aequē, *adv.*, equally; *w.* ac, just as.

aequō, 1, make even *or* level.

aequor, –ōris, *n.*, surface of the sea, ocean.

aequus, –a, –um, even, equal, just, right; aequō animō, calmly, with resignation; ex aequō, equally.

āēr, āeris, *m.*, air (*acc.* āera).

aerārium, –rī, *n.*, treasury.

aerumnōsus, –a, –um, wretched.

aes, aeris, *n.*, bronze, money; aes aliēnum, debt.

Aesōpus, –ī, *m.*, Aesopus (Eso'pus), *an actor.*

aestās, –tātis, *f.*, summer.

aestimō, 1, estimate, value.

aestuō, 1, be hot, be excited; burn.

aestus, –ūs, *m.*, heat.

aetās, –tātis, *f.*, age; life.

aeternus, –a, –um, everlasting, endless.

aethēr, –eris, *m.*, upper air, sky.

aetherius, –a, –um, of heaven.

Aethiopēs, –um, *m. pl.*, the Ethio'pians.

Aethōn, –ōnis, *m.*, Aethon

(Ē'thon), *one of the horses of ihe Sun.*

Aetōlī, –ōrum, *m. pl.,* the Aetolians (Ētō'lians).

aevum, –ī, *n.,* time; old age.

affectus, –a, –um, weakened; honored with, affected.

afferō, –ferre, attulī, allātus, bring (to), apply, cause, present, produce.

afficiō, –ere, –fēcī, –fectus, almost finish, afflict with, visit with, wound.

affingō, –ere, –fīnxī, –fictus, add.

affīnis, –is, *m.,* relative (*by marriage*).

affīnitās, –tātis, *f.,* relationship.

affirmō, 1, declare.

afflīctō, 1, afflict.

afflīctus, –a, –um, shattered, ruined.

afflīgō, –ere, –flīxī, –flīctus, strike at, afflict, dishearten.

affluēns, *gen.* –entis, abounding in.

Afrānius, –ī, *m.,* Afrā'nius, *one of Pompey's generals.*

Āfrica, –ae, *f.,* Africa.

Āfricānus, –a, –um, African; **Āfricānus,** –ī, *m.,* Africā'nus, *an honorary name of Scipio.*

Agamemnon, –onis, *m.,* Agamem'non, *king of Mycenae.*

ager, agrī, *m.,* field, land, country.

aggredior, –ī, –gressus sum, attack.

aggregō, 1, gather.

agitātiō, –ōnis, *f.,* exercise.

agitō, 1, stir, excite; plan, act; express.

agmen, agminis, *n.,* line of march, column.

agnōscō, –ere, –nōvī, –nitus, recognize, acknowledge.

agō, –ere, ēgī, āctus, drive, act, do; discuss, speak, plead with *or* for; make; live *or* spend (*of time*); *pass.,* be at stake; **grātiās agere,** thank; *w.* **iter,** pursue a course.

agrestis, –e, rustic, boorish.

agricola, –ae, *m.,* farmer, planter.

Agrippa, –ae, *m.,* Agrip'pa, *a Roman name.*

Ahāla, –ae, *m.,* Ahā'la, *a Roman name.*

aiō, *defective,* say, assert.

āla, –ae, *f.,* wing.

albēns, *gen.* –entis, white.

āleātor, –ōris, *m.,* gambler.

āles, *gen.* –itis, winged; *as noun, m. and f.,* bird.

Alexander, –drī, *m.,* Alexander, *king of Macedonia.*

Alexandrīa, –ae, *f.,* Alexandria, *a city of Egypt.*

Alexandrīnus, –a, –um, Alexandrian.

aliās, *adv.,* at another time; **aliās . . . aliās,** at one time . . . at another time.

alibī, *adv.,* elsewhere; **alibī . . . alibī,** here . . . there.

aliēnō, 1, alienate.

aliēnus, –a, –um, of another, another's, foreign; unfavorable; *as noun, m.,* stranger.

aliōquī, *adv.,* besides, moreover.

ālipēs, *gen.* –pedis, wing-footed.

aliquandō, *adv.*, sometime, at last.

aliquantō, *adv.*, a little.

aliquantum, –ī, *n.*, (some part of), some.

aliquis, aliquid, *indef. pron.*, some one, any one; some, any; something, anything.

aliquot, *indecl. adj.*, some, several, few.

aliter, *adv.*, otherwise.

alius, alia, aliud, other, another; different, else; alius . . . alius, one . . . another; aliī . . . aliī, some . . . others.

allegō, –ere, –lēgī, –lēctus, admit, elect to.

allevō, 1, raise.

alliciō, –ere, –lexī, –lectus, attract.

alligō, 1, tie (to), fasten.

Allobrogēs, –um, *m. pl.*, the Allobroges (Allŏb'rojēs), *a Gallic tribe.*

alloquor, –loquī, –locūtus sum, speak to, address.

alō, –ere, aluī, alitus, feed, support.

Alpēs, –ium, *f.*, the Alps.

Alphēnōr, –oris, *m.*, Alphenor (Alfē'nor), *one of Niobe's sons.*

altāria, –ium, *n. pl.*, altar.

altē, *adv.*, high, deeply.

alter, –era, –erum, the other (*of two*), another, second; alter . . . alter, the one . . . the other.

altitūdō, –dinis, *f.*, height, depth.

altus, –a, –um, high, deep.

alveus, –ī, *m.*, channel, bed (*of a stream*).

amābilis, –e, lovely, attractive.

amāns, *gen.* amantis, fond, loving; *as noun, m.*, lover.

ambō, –ae, –ō, both.

ambrosia, –ae, *f.*, ambrosia, *food of the gods.*

ambulō, 1, walk.

ambūrō, –ere, –ussī, –ustus, scorch.

āmēns, *gen.* –entis, out of one's senses, foolish.

āmentia, –ae, *f.*, madness, folly.

Amerīnus, –a, –um, of Ameria, *a town in Etruria.*

amīcē, *adv.*, amicably.

amīcitia, –ae, *f.*, friendship.

amictus, –a, –um, clothed.

amictus, –ūs, *m.*, mantle.

amīcus, –a, –um, friendly; amīcus, –ī, *m.*, friend.

Amīsus, –ī, *f.*, Ami'sus, *a town in Pontus.*

āmittō, –ere, āmīsī, āmissus, let go, lose.

amnis, –is, *m.*, stream, torrent, river.

amō, 1, love, like.

amoenē, *adv.*, pleasantly.

amoenitās, –tātis, *f.*, delightfulness, charm.

amoenus, –a, –um, pleasant.

amor, –ōris, *m.*, love, affection.

Amphīōn, –onis, *m.*, Amphī'on, *husband of Niobe.*

amplē, *adv.*, fully.

amplector, –ī, –plexus sum, embrace.

amplexus, –ūs, *m.*, embrace.

amplificō, 1, enlarge, increase.

amplitūdō, –dinis, *f.*, greatness.

amplius, *adv.*, more, further.

amplus, –a, –um, great, ample,

generous, illustrious, distinguished.

an, *conj.,* or, *introducing the second part of a double question;* **utrum . . . an,** (whether) *. . .* or; *w. indir. question,* whether; *w.* **vērō,** or indeed.

ancilla, –ae, *f.,* maidservant.

angō, –ere, —, —, trouble.

anhēlitus, –ūs, *m.,* panting.

anīlis, –e, old woman's, feeble.

anima, –ae, *f.,* breath, soul; existence.

animadversiō, –ōnis, *f.,* investigation; punishment.

animadvertō, —ere, —vertī, —versus (give attention to), notice, punish.

animāns, –antis, *n.,* living being.

animōsus, –a, –um, spirited.

animus, –ī, *m.,* mind, heart, spirit, feeling, courage, desire.

anne = an.

Annius, –nī, *m.,* Annius, *a Roman name.*

annuō, —ere, —nuī, —, nod (to), assent to.

annus, –ī, *m.,* year.

ānser, –eris, *m.,* goose.

ante, *adv. and prep. w. acc.,* before (*of time and place*), beforehand, ago.

anteā, *adv.,* before.

antecellō, –ere, —, —, excel.

antepōnō, –ere, —posuī, —positus, place before, prefer.

antequam (ante quam), *conj.,* before.

Antiochīa, –ae, *f.,* An'tioch, *chief city of Syria.*

Antiochus, –ī, *m.,* Antī'ochus, *king of Syria.*

antīquitās, –tātis, *f.,* antiquity.

antīquus, –a, –um, old, ancient.

Antōnius, –nī, *m.,* Antonius, Antony, *a Roman name.*

antrum, –ī, *n.,* cave.

ānulus, –ī, *m.,* ring.

anus, –ūs, *f.,* old woman.

Āonius, –a, –um, Aonian.

aper, aprī, *m.,* wild boar.

aperiō, –īre, aperuī, apertus, open, disclose.

apertē, *adv.,* openly, frankly.

apertus, –a, –um, open, unprotected.

Āpiōn, –ōnis, *m.,* Apion, *a Greek name.*

Apollineus, –a, –um, of Apollo.

apparātus, –a, –um, prepared, sumptuous, magnificent.

apparātus, –ūs, *m.,* preparation, splendor.

appāreō, —ēre, —uī, —itūrus, appear.

appellō, 1, call, speak to, name, address.

Appennīnus, –ī, *m.,* the Apennines.

appetēns, *gen.* –entis, eager for.

appetō, –ere, —petīvī, —petītus, seek for.

Appius, –pī, *m.,* Appius, *a Roman name;* **Appius,** –a, –um, Appian.

approbō, 1, approve (of).

appropinquō, 1, draw near.

Aprīlis, –e, (of) April.

aptē, *adv.,* fitly.

aptō, 1, fit, place carefully.

aptus, –a, –um, suited.

apud, *prep. w. acc.,* at, among,

near, with, before, in the presence of, at the house of.

Āpūlia, -ae, *f.,* Apulia, *a district in Italy.*

aqua, -ae, *f.,* water.

aquaeductus, -ūs, *m.,* aqueduct.

aquila, -ae, *f.,* eagle; legionary standard (*a silver or bronze eagle mounted on a staff*).

āra, -ae, *f.,* altar.

arbiter, -trī, *m.,* witness, judge.

arbitror, -ārī, -ātus sum, think.

arbor, -oris, *f.,* tree.

arboreus, -a, -um, of a tree.

arca, -ae, *f.,* chest, safe.

arcānō, *adv.,* in private, secretly.

arceō, -ēre, -uī, —, keep away, ward off, prevent.

arcessō, -ere, -cessīvī, -cessītus, summon, invite.

Archiās, -ae, *m.,* Archias (Ar′-kias), *a Greek poet.*

architectus, -ī, *m.,* architect.

Arcitenēns, -entis, *m.,* (bow-bearing), Apollo.

arcus, -ūs, *m.,* bow, arch.

ārdēns, *gen.* **-entis,** burning, passionate.

ārdeō, -ēre, ārsī, ārsus, be on fire, burn; be aroused.

ārdor, -ōris, *m.,* burning, glow.

arduus, -a, -um, steep, lofty; *as noun, n. pl.,* heights.

ārea, -ae, *f.,* flat surface; threshing-floor.

ārēns, *gen.* **-entis,** dry.

āreō, -ēre, -uī, —, be parched.

argentum, -ī, *n.,* silver, money.

Argī, -ōrum, *m.,* Argos, *a city in southern Greece.*

argūmentum, -ī, *n.,* proof, argument, subject.

arguō, -ere, -uī, -ūtus, make known, accuse.

āridus, -a, -um, dry, parched.

Arimaspī, -ōrum, *m.,* the Arimaspi, *a Scythian people.*

Arīminum, -ī, *n.,* Rimini, *a town in northern Italy.*

Ariobarzānēs, -is, *m.,* Ariobarzā′nēs, *a king of Cappadocia.*

arista, -ae, *f.,* head of grain.

arma, -ōrum, *n. pl.,* arms, weapons.

armātūra, -ae, *f.,* armor, equipment.

armātus, -a, -um, armed.

Armenius, -a, -um, Armenian; *as noun, m. pl.,* the Armenians.

armentum, -ī, *n.,* cattle, herd.

armō, 1, arm.

arrogantia, -ae, *f.,* arrogance, insolence.

ars, artis, *f.,* skill, art, profession, practice.

artifex, -ficis, *m.,* artist; *w.* **scaenicus,** actor.

artus, -a, -um, close.

artus, -ūs, *m.,* joint; limb.

arvum, -ī, *n.,* field.

arx, arcis, *f.,* citadel.

ascendō, -ere, ascendī, ascēnsus, climb (up), mount, ascend; go aboard.

ascēnsus, -ūs, *m.,* ascent.

ascīscō, -ere, ascīvī, ascītus, admit.

ascrībō, -ere, ascrīpsī, ascrīptus, enroll.

asellus, -ī, *m.,* donkey.

Asia, -ae, *f.,* Asia.

Asiāticus, -a, -um, Asiatic.

aspectus, –ūs, *m.*, appearance, sight.

asper, –era, –erum, rough, harsh, cruel, wild, disagreeable.

aspiciō, –ere, aspexī, aspectus, look at, behold, see.

aspīrō, 1, breathe upon; aspire.

asportō, 1, carry off.

assentior, –īrī, –sēnsus sum, agree with.

assequor, –sequī, –secūtus sum, accomplish, obtain.

asservō, 1, watch over, keep.

assīdō, –ere, –sēdī, –sessus, sit near, sit at the side of, be seated.

assiduē, *adv.*, constantly.

assiduitās, –tātis, *f.*, perseverance.

assiduus, –a, –um, continual, incessant.

assuēfaciō, –ere, –fēcī, –factus, make accustomed.

assuēscō, –ere, –suēvī, –suētus, become accustomed.

assuētus, –a, –um, accustomed.

assūmō, –ere, –sūmpsī, –sūmptus, receive, take.

astō, –āre, astitī, —, stand (near).

astringō, –ere, astrīnxī, astric-tus, bind.

at, *conj.*, but, on the other hand.

Atalanta, –ae, *f.*, Atalanta, *a Boeotian girl.*

Ateius, –eī, *m.*, Atē'ius, *a Roman name.*

āter, ātra, ātrum, black, dark

Athēnae, –ārum, *f. pl.*, Athens.

Athēniēnsēs, –ium, *m. pl.*, the Athenians.

Atīlius, –lī, *m.*, Atĭl'ius, *a Roman name.*

Atlantiadēs, –ae, *m.*, Mercury, *a god.*

Atlās, –antis, *m.*, Atlas, *a giant.*

atque (ac), *conj.*, and, and especially; than.

ātrium, ātrī, *n.*, atrium. hall, house.

atrōx, *gen.* –ōcis, cruel, inhuman.

attendō, –ere, –tendī, –tentus, (stretch toward), direct, give heed (to), listen.

attenuō, 1, make thin, make less formidable.

attingō, –ere, –tigī, –tāctus, touch upon, reach, attain.

attollō, –ere, —, —, lift.

attonitus, –a, –um, astounded.

attribuō, –ere, –uī, –ūtus, assign.

auctiōnārius, –a, –um, of the auctioneer.

auctor, –ōris, *m.*, author, authority, voucher.

auctōritās, –tātis, *f.*, authority, influence, opinion.

audācia, –ae, *f.*, boldness.

audāx, *gen.* –ācis, bold, daring.

audēns, *gen.* –entis, bold, courageous.

audeō, –ēre, ausus sum, *semi-deponent*, dare.

audiō, –īre, –īvī (–iī), –ītus, hear, hear of, listen (to).

audītiō, –ōnis, *f.*, hearing, lecture.

audītor, –ōris, *m.*, hearer, auditor.

auferō, –ferre, abstulī, ablātus, bear *or* take away, remove.

Aufidius, –dī, *m.,* Aufidius, *a Roman name.*

augeō, –ēre, auxī, auctus, increase.

Aulus, –ī, *m.,* Aulus, *a Roman name.*

aura, –ae, *f.,* breeze, air.

aurātus, –a, –um, covered with gold.

aureus, –a, –um, golden, made of gold; *as noun, m.,* gold piece (= $5.00).

aurīga, –ae, *m.,* driver.

auris, –is, *f.,* ear.

aurōra, –ae, *f.,* morning, dawn.

aurum, –ī, *n.,* gold.

auspicium, –cī, *n.,* augury; *pl.,* auspices.

auster, –trī, *m.,* south wind.

aut, or; **aut . . . aut,** either . . . or.

autem, *conj.* (*never first word*), however, but, moreover.

Autrōnius, –nī, *m.,* Autronius, *a Roman name.*

autumnālis, –e, of autumn.

autumnus, –ī, *m.,* autumn.

auxiliārius, –a, –um, auxiliary.

auxilium, –lī, *n.,* help, aid, assistance; *pl.,* reinforcements.

avāritia, –ae, *f.,* greed, avarice.

avēna, –ae, *f.,* reed.

āvertō, –ere, āvertī, āversus, turn away *or* aside; *w.* **domum,** appropriate.

āvia, –ōrum, *n.,* pathless regions.

avidē, *adv.,* eagerly.

avidus, –a, –um, eager.

avis, –is, *f.,* bird.

avītus, –a, –um, of a grandfather.

āvocō, 1, call away *or* aside.

avus, –ī, *m.,* grandfather.

axis, –is, *f.,* axle, chariot; globe.

B

Babylōnius, –a, –um, Babylonian.

bacchor, –ārī, –ātus sum (*from* **Bacchus**), revel.

Bacchus, –ī, *m.,* Bacchus, *god of wine.*

baculum, –ī, *n.,* staff.

Baeticus, –a, –um, of Baetica (Bē'tica), Baetican.

Bagrada, –ae, *m.,* the Bag'rada, *a river in Africa.*

Balbus, –ī, *m.,* Balbus, *a Roman name.*

balineum, –ī, *n.,* bath.

ballista, –ae, *f.,* ballista.

barbaria, –ae, *f.,* savage people.

barbaricus, –a, –um, barbaric.

barbarus, –a, –um, foreign; savage, uncivilized.

barbātus, –a, –um, bearded.

Bassus, –ī, *m.,* Bassus, *a Roman name.*

Baucis, –idis (*acc.* **-ida**), *f.,* Baucis (Bau'sis), *wife of Philemon.*

beātus, –a, –um, happy.

bellicōsus, –a, –um, warlike.

bellō, 1, wage war.

bellum, –ī, *n.,* war.

bellus, –a, –um, charming, civil.

bene, *adv.,* well, successfully; *comp.* **melius,** better; *superl.* **optimē,** best.

beneficium, –cī, *n.,* kindness, favor; honor.

benevolentia, –ae, *f.,* good will, kindness.

benignitās, –tātis, *f.,* kindness.

Berecyntius, –a, –um, Berecyntian.

bēstia, –ae, *f.,* beast.

bibō, –ere, bibī, —, drink.

Bibulus, –ī, *m.,* Bibulus, *a Roman name.*

bicolor, –ōris, two-colored.

bicornis, –e, two-pronged.

bīnī, –ae, –a, two each, two.

bipertītō, *adv.,* in two divisions.

bis, *adv.,* twice.

Bithynia, –ae, *f.,* Bithyn'ia, *a province in Asia Minor.*

blanditiae, –ārum, *f.,* fond words.

blandus, –a, –um, coaxing, caressing.

bonitās, –tātis, *f.,* goodness.

bonus, –a, –um, good; *comp.* **melior, melius,** better; *superl.* **optimus, –a, –um,** best; **bona, –ōrum,** *n.,* goods, property.

Boōtēs, –ae, *m.,* Boō'tēs, *a constellation.*

Boreās, –ae, *m.,* Boreas, *north wind.*

Borysthenēs, –is, *m.,* the Dnieper, *a river.*

bōs, bovis, *m. and f.,* ox, cow; *pl.,* cattle.

Bosporānī, –ōrum, *m.,* people on the Bosporus.

bracchium, –chī, *n.,* arm.

brevī, *adv.,* in a short time, soon.

brevis, –e, short.

brevitās, –tātis, *f.,* brevity.

breviter, *adv.,* briefly.

Britannia, –ae, *f.,* Britain.

brūma, –ae, *f.,* winter.

Brundisium, –sī, *n.,* Brundisium, (Brundizh'ium), *a town in Italy.*

Brūtus, –ī, *m.,* Brutus, *a Roman name.*

bustum, –ī, *n.,* pyre; tomb.

Būthrōtum, –ī, *n.,* Buthro'tum, *a town in Epirus.*

C

C., *abbreviation for* **Gāius.**

cacūmen, –minis, *n.,* peak; tree top.

Cadmus, –ī, *m.,* Cadmus, *founder of Thebes.*

cadō, –ere, cecidī, cāsus, fall

caecus, –a, –um, blind, hidden.

caedēs, –is, *f.,* slaughter, murder, bloodshed; blood.

caedō, –ere, cecīdī, caesus, cut; beat.

caelestis, –e, heavenly; *as noun, m. pl.,* gods.

caelicola, –ae, *m.,* god.

Caelius, –lī, *m.,* Caelius (Sē'lius), *a Roman name.*

caelō, 1, carve, emboss.

caelum, –ī, *n.,* sky; weather.

Caepiō, –ōnis, *m.,* Caepio (Sē'pio), *a Roman name.*

caerulus (–eus), –a, –um, dark blue *or* green.

Caesar, –aris, *m.,* Caesar; emperor.

Caiēta, –ae, *f.,* Caieta (Kayē'ta), *a town in Latium.*

calamitās, –tātis, *f.,* loss, misfortune, defeat, ruin

calamitōsus, –a, –um, unfortunate, disastrous.

calamus, –ī, *m.,* reed, reed-pipe.

calcō, 1, tread.

caleō, –ēre, –uī, –itūrus, be warm *or* hot.

Calestrius, –trī, *m.,* Calestrius, *a Roman name.*

calidus, –a, –um, warm.

calliditās, –tātis, *f.,* shrewdness, cunning.

callidus, –a, –um, crafty.

calor, –ōris, *m.,* heat.

Calymnē, –ēs, *f.,* Calym'ne, *an island in the Aegean.*

Camillus, –ī, *m.,* Camil'lus. *a Roman name.*

campus, –ī, *m.,* plain; the Campus Martius, *a park and place of assembly at Rome.*

candidātōrius, –a, –um, of a candidate.

candidātus, –ī, *m.,* candidate.

candidus, –a, –um, white, clear.

cānēscō, –ere, —, —, grow white.

Canīnius, –nī, *m.,* Canĭn'ius, *a Roman name.*

canīnus, –a, –um, of a dog.

canistrum, –ī, *n.,* reed basket.

canna, –ae, *f.,* reed.

Cannēnsis, –e, of Cannae (Can'ē).

canō, –ere, cecinī, cantus, sing, predict, play.

cantō, 1, sing.

cantus, –ūs, *m.,* song.

cānus, –a, –um, white, hoary.

Capēna (porta), porta Capē'na, *a gate in the wall of Rome.*

capillus, –ī, *m.,* hair; *pl.,* locks, hair.

capiō, –ere, cēpī, captus, take, seize, hold, capture, captivate; suffer.

Capitō, –ōnis, *m.,* Capĭto, *a Roman name.*

Capitōlium, –lī, *n.,* the Capitoline Hill; the Capitol (*temple of Jupiter*).

Cappadocia, –ae, *f.,* Cappadō'-cia, *a country of Asia Minor.*

captīvus, –ī, *m.,* prisoner.

captō, 1, seek to catch.

caput, capitis, *n.,* head.

carbasus, –ī, *f.* (*pl.* –a, –ōrum, *n.*), sail.

Carbō, –ōnis, *m.,* Carbo, *a Roman name.*

carcer, –eris, *m.,* prison.

cardō, –dinis, *m.,* hinge.

careō, –ēre, caruī, caritūrus, be without, lack, be deprived of.

Cāria, –ae, *f.,* Caria, *a province in Asia Minor.*

Cāriō, –ōnis, *m.,* Cario, *a name.*

cāritās, –tātis, *f.,* high price; affection.

carmen, –minis, *n.,* song, poem.

carpō, –ere, carpsī, carptus, pick, seize; *of a road,* pursue, traverse.

Carthaginiēnsēs, –ium, *m. pl.,* the Carthaginians (Cartha-jin'ians).

Carthāgō, –ginis, *f.,* Carthage, *a city in northern Africa.*

cārus, –a, –um, dear.

casa, –ae, *f.,* cottage.

cāseus, –ī, *m.,* cheese.

Cassius, –sī, *m.,* Cassius (Cash'us) *a Roman name.*

castē, *adv.,* purely; conscientiously.

castellum, –ī, *n.,* (little fort), fortress, redoubt, stronghold.

castīgō, 1, punish; censure.
castitās, –tātis, f., purity.
castra, –ōrum, n., camp.
castrēnsis, –e, of the camp, open.
cāsus, –ūs, m., fall, chance, event, misfortune; case.
catapulta, –ae, f., catapult.
catella, –ae, f., little dog, puppy.
Catilīna, –ae, m., Cat'ilīne, the conspirator of 63 b.c.
Catō, –ōnis, m., Cato (Kā'tō), a Roman senator.
Catulus, –ī, m., Cat'ulus, a Roman name.
cauda, –ae, f., tail.
causa, –ae, f., cause, reason; case, pretext; position; causā, for the sake of, for the purpose of.
cautē, adv., cautiously.
cautus, –a, –um, wary, careful.
caveō, –ēre, cāvī, cautus, beware (of), take care.
cavus, –a, –um, hollow.
–ce, enclitic, here, this, that.
cēdō, –ere, cessī, cessus, go away, retreat, retire, yield.
celeber, –bris, –bre, populous, crowded.
celebritās, –tātis, f., throng; renown.
celebrō, 1, throng, celebrate, attend.
celer, –eris, –ere, swift.
celeritās, –tātis, f., speed, swiftness.
celeriter, adv., quickly.
cēlō, 1, hide, keep secret.
celsus, –a, –um, high.
cēna, –ae, f., dinner.
cēnō, 1, dine.

cēnseō, –ēre, cēnsuī, cēnsus, assess, enroll; be of the opinion, think; decree.
cēnsor, –ōris, m., censor.
cēnsūra, –ae, f., censorship.
cēnsus, –ūs, m., census list.
centiēs, adv., a hundred times.
centum, hundred.
centuria, –ae, f., century, company.
centuriō, –ōnis, m., centurion.
cēnula, –ae, f., little dinner.
Cēpārius, –rī, m., Ceparius (Sēpar'ius), a Roman name.
cēra, –ae, f., wax.
cērātus, –a, –um, waxed.
Cereālis, –e, of Ceres.
Cerēs, Cereris, f., Ceres (Sē'res), goddess of agriculture.
cernō, –ere, crēvī, crētus, (separate), see, regard.
certāmen, –minis, n., contest.
certātiō, –ōnis, f., strife, dispute.
certē, adv., certainly, at least; certō, adv., for a certainty.
certō, 1, struggle.
certus, –a, –um, fixed, certain, sure; certiōrem facere, inform (him), certior fierī, be informed.
cerva, –ae, f., hind, deer.
cervīx, –īcis, f., neck; pl., shoulders.
cēterī, –ae, –a, the other(s), the rest; everything else.
Cethēgus, –ī, m., Cethegus (Sethē'gus), a Roman name.
Chiī, –ōrum, m., the Chians (Kī'ans), inhabitants of Chius.
Chīlō, –ōnis, m., Chilo (Kī'lo), a Roman name.

Chrīstiānus, –a, –um, *adj. and n.*, Christian.

Chrīstus, –ī, *m.*, Christ.

cibus, -ī, *m.*, food.

Cicerō, –ōnis, *m.*, Cicero (Marcus Tullius, *the orator;* Quintus, *his brother;* Marcus, *his son*).

Cilicia, –ae,*f.*, Cilicia (Silish'ia), *a province in Asia Minor.*

Cimber, –brī, *m.*, Cimber (Simber), *a Roman name.*

Cimbrī, –ōrum, *m.*, the Cimbri (Sim'brī), *a German tribe.*

cingō, –ere, cīnxī, cīnctus, surround; crown.

cinis, cineris, *m.*, ashes.

Cinna, –ae, *m.*, Cinna (Sin'a), *a Roman name.*

circā, *adv. and prep. w. acc.*, around, about.

circiter, *adv.*, about.

circum, *prep. w. acc.*, about.

circumclūdō, –ere, –clūsī, –clūsus, surround.

circumdō, –dare, –dedī, –datus, put around, surround (with).

circumdūcō, –ere, –dūxī, –ductus, lead around.

circumeō, –īre, –iī, –itus, go around.

circumferō, –ferre, –tulī, –lātus, bear *or* spread around, cast about.

circumscrībō, –ere, –scrīpsī, –scrīptus, bound.

circumsistö, –ere, –stetī, —, take a stand around, surround.

circumstō, –āre, –stetī, —, stand around, surround.

circumveniō, –īre, –vēnī, –ventus, surround.

citerior, –ius, *comp. adj.*, (on this side), nearer, hither.

cithara, –ae, *f.*, cithara, lyre.

cito, *adv.*, quickly.

citus, –a, –um, swift.

cīvīlis, –e, civii.

cīvis, –is, *m.*, citizen.

cīvitās, –tātis, *f.*, citizenship; state; city.

clam, *adv.*, secretly.

clāmō, 1, cry (out), shout.

clāmor, –ōris, *m.*, shout, uproar; applause.

clandestīnus, –a, –um, secret.

clārē, *adv.*, clearly, loudly.

clārus, –a, –um, clear, brilliant, illustrious, loud, famous.

classis, –is, *f.*, fleet.

Claudius, –dī, *m.*, Claudius, *a Roman emperor.*

claudō, –ere, clausī, clausus, shut, close, cut off, bar.

clēmēns, –entis, mild, gentle, merciful.

clēmenter, *adv.*, gently, with forbearance.

clēmentia, –ae, *f.*, forbearance, mercy.

Cleopātra, –ae, *f.*, Cleopā'tra, *queen of Egypt.*

clīvus, –ī, *m.*, slope, hillside.

Clymenē, -ēs, *f.*, Clȳm'enē, *mother of Phaëthon.*

Clymenēius, –a, –um, of Clymene.

Clytaemēstra, –ae, *f.*, Clytaemnestra (Clītemnes'tra), *wife of Agamemnon.*

Cn., *abbreviation for* Gnaeus, –ī, *m.*, Gnaeus (Nē'us), *a Roman name.*

Cnidus, –ī, *f.,* Cnidus (Nīdus), *a city of Asia Minor.*

coarguō, –ere, –uī, —, make known, betray.

coemō, –ere, –ēmī, –ēmptus, buy up.

coeō, –īre, –iī, –itus, come together, assemble, unite.

coepī, coepisse, coeptus (*used only in perf. tenses*), have begun, began.

coeptum, –ī, *n.,* undertaking, task.

coerceō, –ēre, –uī, –itus, check, repress.

coetus, –ūs, *m.,* meeting.

cōgitātē, *adv.,* thoughtfully.

cōgitātiō, –ōnis, *f.,* thought, meditation.

cōgitō, 1, think (of), consider, plan.

cognātiō, –ōnis, *f.,* kinship.

cognātus, –ī, *m.,* kinsman.

cognitiō, –ōnis, *f.,* (learning to know), trial, acquaintance.

cognōscō, –ere, cognōvī, cognitus, become acquainted with, learn; recognize, note; *perf. tenses,* have learned, know.

cōgō, –ere, coēgī, coāctus, (drive together), assemble; force, compel.

cohaereō, –ēre, –haesī, –haesus, cling together, be connected with.

cohibeō, –ēre, –uī, –itus, (hold together), restrain.

cohors, –rtis, *f.,* cohort, *one-tenth of a legion.*

cohortātiō, –ōnis, *f.,* encouragement.

cohortor, –ārī, –ātus sum, encourage, urge.

collābor, –lābī, –lāpsus sum, fall in ruin, sink down.

collātiō, –ōnis, *f.,* collecting.

collaudō, 1, praise, commend.

collēga, –ae, *m.,* colleague.

collēgium, –gī, *n.,* company, brigade.

colligō, –ere, –lēgī, –lectus, collect, infer.

collocō, 1, put, establish, set up.

colloquium, –quī, *n.,* conference, interview.

colloquor, –loquī, –locūtus sum, talk (with), hold a conference.

collum, –ī, *n.,* neck.

colō, –ere, –uī, cultus, cultivate, worship, attend, cherish, honor.

colōnia, –ae, *f.,* colony.

colōnus, –ī, *m.,* farmer; colonist.

Colophōn, –ōnis, *m.,* Cŏl′ophon, *a city of Asia Minor.*

color, –ōris, *m.,* color.

columna, –ae, *f.,* pillar.

coma, –ae, *f.,* hair.

comes, –itis, *m.,* companion.

cōmis, –e, courteous, affable.

comitātus, –ūs, *m.,* escort, company.

cōmiter, *adv.,* affably.

comitium, –tī, *n.,* comitium (comish′ium), *an assembly place in Rome; pl.,* election, assemblies.

comitō, 1, accompany.

commemorātiō, –ōnis, *f.,* remembrance, mention.

commemorō, 1, call to mind, mention.

commendātiō, -ōnis, f., recommendation.

commendō, 1, intrust, commend, approve.

commentārius, -rī, m., notebook, commentary.

commeō, 1, go and come, visit.

commīlitō, -ōnis, m., fellow soldier, comrade.

committō, -ere, -mīsī, -missus, commit, do, intrust; allow.

commodē, adv., well, suitably, comfortably.

commodus, -a, -um, fit, suitable, favorable; as noun, n., advantage.

commoror, -ārī, -ātus sum, linger, remain.

commoveo, -ēre, -mōvī, -mōtus, move, affect, disturb.

commūnicō, 1, share, communicate, consult.

commūniō, -īre, -īvī (iī), -ītus, fortify strongly.

commūnis, -e, common.

commūniter, adv., in general.

commūtō, 1, change, alter.

comoedus, -ī, m., comedian, comic actor.

comparātiō, -ōnis, f., preparing.

comparō, 1, get ready, prepare; collect, provide, constitute; compare.

compellō, -ere, -pulī, -pulsus, drive together, force.

comperiō, -īre, -perī, -pertus, find out, discover.

compescō, -ere, -pescuī, —, check, put out.

competītor, -ōris, m., rival, competitor.

complector, -plectī, -plexus sum, embrace, include.

compleō, -ēre, -ēvī, -ētus, fill (up).

complexus, -ūs, m., embrace.

complūrēs, -a (-ia), several, many.

compōnō, -ere, -posuī, -positus, (put together), compose, settle, arrange; bury.

comprecor, -ārī, -precātus sum, pray to, invoke, implore.

comprehendō, -ere, -hendī, -hēnsus, seize, catch, detect; arrest.

comprimō, -ere, -pressī, -pressus, press together, restrain, repress.

comprobō, 1, approve.

compugnō, 1, fight with, wrangle.

cōnātus, -ūs, m., attempt.

concavō, 1, make hollow, curve.

concēdō, -ere, -cessī, -cessus, give way, retire, yield, concede, grant.

concelebrō, 1, (attend in throngs), celebrate.

concidō, -ere, -cidī, —, fall (together), collapse.

conciliō, 1, win.

concilium, -lī, n., meeting, council.

concipiō, -ere, -cēpī, -ceptus, take up, receive, utter.

concitātē, adv., quickly.

concitō, 1, arouse.

conclāmō, 1, cry out, exclaim, shout.

concordia, -ae, f., harmony, concord.

concors, *gen.* **–cordis,** in harmony.

concubīna, **–ae,** *f.,* concubine.

concupīscō, **–ere, –cupīvī, –ītus,** long (for), desire, covet.

concurrō, **–ere, –currī, –cursus,** run together, rush, flock.

concursus, **–ūs,** *m.,* (running together), gathering, throng.

concutiō, **–ere, –cussī, –cussus,** (strike together), shake up, shake.

condemnō, 1, condemn.

condiciō, –ōnis, *f.,* condition.

condiscō, –ere, –didicī, —, grow accustomed.

condō, **–ere,** **–didī,** **–ditus,** found, establish ; bring to an end ; bury, preserve.

condūcō, –ere, –dūxī, –ductus, bring together, hire.

cōnferō, –ferre, –tulī, –collātus, bring together, join, compare, collect, contest, devote, contribute ; bring upon ; postpone ; **sē cōnferre,** go, proceed.

cōnfessiō, –ōnis, *f.,* confession.

cōnfestim, *adv.,* at once.

cōnficiō, –ere, –fēcī, –fectus, (make up), finish, complete, exhaust ; accomplish ; raise.

cōnfīdō, –ere, –fīsus sum, *semideponent,* trust, be confident, rely on.

cōnfirmō, 1, strengthen, assure, establish, declare.

cōnfiteor, –ērī, –fessus sum, confess, admit.

cōnflagrō, 1, be consumed (by fire).

cōnflīctiō, –ōnis, *f.,* combat.

cōnflīctor, 1, contend with.

cōnflīgō, –ere, –flīxī, –flīctus, (dash together), fight.

cōnflō, 1, (blow up), kindle, excite ; compose.

cōnfluō, –ere, –flūxī, –flūxus, flock (together).

cōnfōrmō, 1, mold, train.

cōnfugiō, –ere, –fūgī, –fugitūrus, flee for refuge.

cōnfūsus, –a, –um, miscellaneous.

congelō, 1, freeze ; stiffen.

congerō, –ere, –gessī, –gestus, bring together, collect.

congregō, 1, collect ; *pass.,* assemble.

coniciō, –ere, –iēcī, –iectus, throw (forcibly), hurl ; aim.

coniectūra, –ae, *f.,* inference.

coniugium, –gī, *n.,* union, marriage.

coniūnctiō, –ōnis, *f.,* uniting, union.

coniūnctus, –a, –um, united.

coniungō, –ere, –iūnxī, –iūnctus, join with, unite.

coniūnx, –iugis, *m. and f.,* husband, wife.

coniūrātī, –ōrum, *m.,* conspirators.

coniūrātiō, –ōnis, *f.,* conspiracy.

cōnor, –ārī, cōnātus sum, attempt, try, endeavor.

conquiēscō, –ere, –quiēvī, –quiētus, find rest ; cease.

conquīrō, –ere, –quīsīvī, –quīsītus, seek out, hunt up, collect.

cōnscelerātus, –a, –um, wicked.

cōnscendō, –ere, –scendī,

–scēnsus, climb, mount, scale, embark.

cōnscientia, –ae, f., consciousness, conscience.

cōnscīscō, –ere, –scīvī, –scītus, resolve upon.

cōnscius, –cī, m., witness.

cōnscrībō, –ere, –scrīpsī, –scrīptus, enroll; patrēs cōnscrīptī, senators.

cōnsecrō, 1, dedicate.

cōnsenēscō, –ere, –senuī, —, grow old together.

cōnsēnsiō, –ōnis, f., agreement, harmony.

cōnsentiō, –īre, –sēnsī, –sēnsus, agree.

cōnsequor, –ī, –secūtus sum, follow (up), pursue; result; obtain, accomplish.

cōnservātor, –ōris, m., preserver.

cōnservō, 1, keep, save, maintain.

cōnservus, –ī, m., fellow slave.

cōnsīderātē, adv., deliberately.

cōnsīderō, 1, consider.

cōnsīdō, –ere, –sēdī, –sessus, sit down, encamp, sink.

cōnsilior, –ārī, –ātus sum, take counsel, consult.

cōnsilium, –lī, n., plan, purpose, prudence, advice, wisdom; council, counsel.

cōnsistō, –ere, –stitī, –stitus, stand still, take one's stand, halt.

cōnsobrīnus, –ī, m., cousin.

cōnsolor, –ārī, –ātus sum, comfort.

cōnspectus, –ūs, m., sight.

cōnspiciō, –ere, –spexī, –spectus, catch sight of, look upon, see.

cōnspicor, –ārī, –ātus sum, catch sight of, see.

cōnspīrō, 1, combine.

cōnstanter, adv., firmly, consistently.

cōnstantia, –ae, f., firmness, consistency.

cōnsternō, 1, terrify.

cōnstituō, –ere, –stituī, –stitūtus, put, establish, settle; appoint, create; determine, decide, agree upon.

cōnstō, –āre, –stitī, –statūrus, stand together, agree; cōnstat, it is evident, it is clear, it is agreed.

cōnstringō, –ere, –strīnxī, –strictus, bind, hold in check.

cōnsuēscō, –ere, –suēvī, –suētus, become accustomed; in perf. system, be accustomed, be wont.

cōnsuētūdō, –dinis, f., custom, habit, practice; intimacy.

cōnsul, –ulis, m., consul.

cōnsulāris, –e, consular, of consular rank; as noun, m., ex-consul, man of consular rank.

cōnsulātus, –ūs, m., consulship.

cōnsulō, –ere, –uī, –sultus, consider, consult, put the question; look out for.

cōnsultātiō, –ōnis, f., mature deliberation.

cōnsultō, 1, take counsel.

cōnsultō, adv., purposely.

cōnsultum, –ī, n., decree.

cōnsūmō, –ere, –sūmpsī, –sūmptus, (take wholly), spend; destroy, consume.

cōnsurgō, –ere, –surrēxī, –sur-rēctus, rise together.

contāctus, –ūs, *m.*, touch.

contāgiō, –ōnis, *f.*, (touch), infection.

contāminō, 1, stain, defile.

contegō, –ere, –tēxī, –tēctus, cover.

contemnō, –ere, –tempsī, –temptus, despise, disregard.

contemptiō, –ōnis, *f.*, contempt.

contendō, –ere, –tendī, –tentus, stretch, hasten; strive, fight, contend; maintain.

contentiō, –ōnis, *f.*, strain, struggle, dispute.

contentus, –a, –um, satisfied, content.

conterō, –ere, –trīvī, –trītus, waste.

conterreō, –ēre, –uī, –itus, terrify.

conticēscō, –ere, –ticuī, —, become silent.

contiguus, –a, –um, adjoining.

continēns, *gen.* –entis, temperate, self-restrained; *as noun,* *f.,* the mainland.

continentia, –ae, *f.*, self-control.

contineō, –ēre, –tinuī, –tentus, hold together, connect, check, keep, contain, confine, control.

contingō, –ere, –tigī, –tāctus, touch, reach; happen, fall to one's lot.

continuus, –a, –um, successive.

cōntiō, –ōnis, *f.*, assembly, meeting.

cōntiōnor, –ārī, –ātus, make an address.

contrā, *adv. and prep. w. acc.*, against, contrary to; to the other side.

contrahō, –ere, –trāxī, –trāctus, draw together; contract.

contrārius, –a, –um, opposite, opposed.

contrōversia, –ae, *f.*, dispute.

contubernālis, –is, *m. and f.,* companion, mate.

contumēlia, –ae, *f.*, insult, abuse.

contundō, –ere, –tudī, –tūsus, beat, bruise, pound.

conturbō, 1, disturb.

cōnūbium, –bī, *n.*, marriage.

convalēscō, –ere, –valuī, —, recover from an illness, regain health.

convellō, –ere, –vellī, –vulsus, tear away; bite.

conveniō, –īre, –vēnī, –ventus, come together, assemble, meet; be suited to; *impers.*, it is fitting *or* agreed.

conventum, –ī, *n.*, agreement.

conventus, –ūs, *m.*, assembly, meeting.

convertō, –ere, –vertī, –versus, turn, change.

convīcium, –cī, *n.*, violent reproach, wrangling.

convīctus, –ūs, *m.*, (living together), intimacy.

convincō, –ere, –vīcī, –victus, prove.

convīvium, –vī, *n.*, feast, banquet.

convocō, 1, call together.

coopertus, –a, –um, steeped in.

cōpia, –ae, *f.*, supply, abundance; fluency; *pl.*, resources, troops, forces.

cōpiōsus, -a, -um, well-supplied, plentiful, rich.

cōpulātus, -a, -um, united.

coquus, -ī, *m.,* cook.

cor, cordis, *n.,* heart.

cōram, *adv. and prep. w. abl.,* face to face; before.

Corduba, -ae, *f.,* Cor'dova, *a city in Spain.*

Corfīnium, -nī, *n.,* Corfĭn'ium, *a town in Italy.*

Corinthus, -ī, *f.,* Corinth, *a city in Greece.*

Cornēlius, -lī, *m.,* Cornē'lius, *a Roman name.*

Cornificius, -cī, *m.,* Cornificius (Cornifish'us), *a Roman name.*

cornū, -ūs, *n.,* horn; wing (*of an army*), flank, tip (*of the moon*).

corōna, -ae, *f.,* wreath, crown.

corpus, corporis, *n.,* body.

corrigō, -ere, -rēxī, -rēctus, improve, reform, correct, change; make up for.

corripiō, -ere, -uī, -reptus, seize.

corrōborō, 1, strengthen.

corrumpō, -ere, -rūpī, -ruptus, corrupt, falsify; waste.

corruō, -ere, -ruī, —, fall together.

corruptēla, -ae, *f.,* corruption.

cotīdiānus, -a, -um, daily.

cotīdiē, *adv.,* daily.

Cotta, -ae, *m.,* Cotta, *a Roman name.*

Crassus, -ī, *m.,* Crassus, *a Roman name.*

Crāstinus, -ī, *m.,* Cras'tinus.

crātēr, -ēris, *m.,* wine bowl.

Cratippus, -ī, *m.,* Cratip'pus, *a Greek name.*

crēber, -bra, -brum, thick, frequent, numerous.

crēdibilis, -e, credible.

crēditor, -ōris, *m.,* creditor.

crēdō, -ere, crēdĭdī, crēditus, believe; suppose; intrust.

cremō, 1, burn.

creō, 1, make, create.

crepitus, -ūs, *m.,* noise.

crēscō, -ere, crēvī, crētus, grow, increase.

Crēta, -ae, *f.,* Crete, *an island south of Greece.*

Crētēnsis, -e, Cretan; *m. pl.,* the Cretans.

crīmen, -minis, *n.,* accusation, charge, crime.

crīminor, -ārī, -ātus sum, charge.

crīnis, -is, *m.,* hair.

Crotōniēnsis, -e, Crotonian, of Croton (*in southern Italy*).

cruciābilis, -e, agonizing.

cruciātus, -ūs, *m.,* torture.

crūdēlis, -e, cruel.

crūdēlitās, -tātis, *f.,* cruelty.

crūdēliter, *adv.,* cruelly.

cruentātus, -a, -um, bloody.

cruentus, -a, -um, bloody.

cruor, -ōris, *m.,* blood.

crūs, crūris, *n.,* leg.

crux, crucis, *f.,* cross.

cubiculum, -ī, *n.,* bedroom, lounging room.

culpa, -ae, *f.,* fault, guilt.

culpō, 1, blame, reproach.

cultūra, -ae, *f.,* tilling.

cultus, -ūs, *m.,* care.

cum, *prep. w. abl.,* with.

cum, *conj.,* when, while, since, although; **cum . . . tum,** not only . . . but also.

Cūmānus, -a, -um, at *or* of Cumae (Cū'mē), *a town in Italy.*

cumulō, 1, (heap up), crown.

cumulus, -ī, *m.,* heap, increase.

cūnctanter, *adv.,* reluctantly.

cūnctātiō, -ōnis, *f.,* hesitancy, uncertainty.

cūnctor, -ārī, -ātus sum, delay.

cūnctus, -a, -um, all together, the whole, all.

cupidē, *adv.,* eagerly.

cupiditās, -tātis, *f.,* desire, greed.

cupīdō, -dinis, *f.,* desire, longing; Love.

cupidus, -a, -um, eager.

cupiō, -ere, -īvī, -ītus, desire, be eager.

cūr, *adv.,* why.

cūra, -ae, *f.,* care, concern, anxiety.

cūrātiō, -ōnis, *f.,* care; cure.

cūria, -ae, *f.,* senate house, curia.

Curicta, -ae, *f.,* Curicta, *an island in the Adriatic.*

Cūriō, -ōnis, *m.,* Curio, *a Roman name.*

cūriōsē, *adv.,* carefully.

Cūrius, -rī, *m.,* Curius, *a Roman name.*

cūrō, 1, care for, look after, attend to; take care, arrange, cause (to be done).

curriculum, -ī, *n.,* course.

currō, -ere, cucurrī, cursus, run; fly.

currus, -ūs, *m.,* chariot.

cursus, -ūs, *m.,* running; race, way, voyage, course, career.

curvāmen, -minis, *n.,* curve.

curvō, 1, curve.

curvus, -a, -um, curved.

cuspis, -idis, *f.,* point; sting.

custōdia, -ae, *f.,* guard, custody, protection, prison.

custōdiō, -īre, -īvī, -ītus, guard, watch.

custōs, -ōdis, *m.,* guard, custodian, parent.

Cynthus, -ī, *m.,* Cynthus, *a mountain on Delos.*

Cytherēa, -ae, *f.,* Venus.

Cyzicēnī, -ōrum, *m.,* the people of Cyzicus (*in Asia Minor*).

D

D., *abbreviation for* **Decimus.**

Daedalus, -ī, *m.,* Daedalus (Dĕd'alus), *a mythical Greek artisan.*

Damasichthōn, -onis, *m.,* Damasich'thon, *one of Niobe's sons.*

Damasippus, -ī, *m.,* Damasip'pus, *a Roman name.*

damnātiō, -ōnis, *f.,* conviction.

damnō, 1, condemn.

damnōsus, -a, -um, harmful.

damnum, -ī, *n.,* loss; fine, penalty; curse.

daps, dapis, *f.,* meal, feast; food.

dē, *prep. w. abl.,* from, down from, concerning, about, for, during.

dea, -ae, *f.,* goddess.

dēbeō, -ēre, dēbuī, dēbitus, ought, owe, should, must, bound to be; *pass.,* be due.

dēbilis, -e, weak, helpless.

dēbilitō, 1, weaken.

dēcēdō, –ere, –cessī, –cessus, depart, die.

decem, ten.

December, –bris, –bre, (of) December.

decenter, adv., becomingly, properly.

dēcernō, –ere, –crēvī, –crētus, decide, decree, vote (for).

dēcerpō, –ere, –cerpsī, –cerptus, pluck.

dēcertō, 1, fight it out.

decet, –ēre, –uit, impers., becomes, befits.

dēcidō, –ere, –cidī, —, fall down, fall.

decimus, –a, –um, tenth; Decimus, –ī, m., Decimus (Des'imus), a Roman name.

dēclārō, 1, show, declare.

dēclīnātiō, –ōnis, f., bending aside, avoidance.

dēclīnō, 1, turn aside.

dēclīvis, –e, sloping downward; as noun, n., slope, descent.

decor, –ōris, m., charm, beauty.

decorō, 1, adorn, honor, embellish.

decōrus, –a, –um, comely, beautiful.

dēcrētum, –ī, n., decree.

dēcurrō, –ere, –cucurrī (–currī), –cursus, run (down), hasten.

decus, –coris, n., honor.

dēcutiō, –ere, –cussī, –cussus, shake or strike down.

dēdecus, –coris, n., disgrace, vice.

dēdicō, 1, dedicate.

dēditiō, –ōnis, f., surrender.

dēdō, –ere, –didī, –ditus, hand over, surrender, devote.

dēdūcō, –ere, –dūxī, –ductus, lead away, conduct, bring.

dēfatīgō, 1, wear out.

dēfectiō, –ōnis, f., failing, exhaustion.

dēfendō, –ere, –fendī, –fēnsus, ward off, defend.

dēferō, –ferre, –tulī, –lātus, bring (down), offer, report; grant, bestow.

dēfessus, –a, –um, wearied.

dēficiō, –ere, –fēcī, –fectus, fail, revolt; animō dēficere, lose courage.

dēfīgō, –ere, –fīxī, –fīxus, fix, plunge.

dēfīniō, –īre, –īvī, –ītus, limit, fix, appoint, define.

dēfīnītiō, –ōnis, f., definition.

dēflectō, –ere, –flexī, –flexus, turn aside.

dēfleō, –ēre, –ēvī, –ētus, weep over.

dēfluō, –ere, –flūxī, –flūxus, flow or sink down.

dēfraudō, 1, cheat out of.

dēiciō, –ere, –iēcī, –iectus, throw down. thrust aside, ward off; rout.

dēierō, 1, swear.

dein, see deinde.

deinceps, adv., one after another, next.

deinde, adv., then, next.

dēlābor, –ī, –lāpsus sum, fall down.

dēlectātiō, –ōnis, f., delight.

dēlectō 1, take delight in, please, charm.

dēlēctus, see dēligō.

dēlēniō, –īre, –īvī, –ītus, allay, charm.

dēleō, -ēre, -ēvī, -ētus, blot out, destroy.

dēlīberātiō, -ōnis, f., deliberation, question.

dēlīberō, 1, think about, consider.

dēlicātus, -a, -um, effeminate.

dēliciae, -ārum, f. pl., delight, pleasure.

dēlīctum, -ī, n., wrong.

dēligō, 1, bind.

dēligō, -ere, -lēgī, -lēctus, pick, choose, esteem.

dēlīrātiō, -ōnis, f., craziness.

Dēlius, -a, -um, Delian, of Delos.

Dēlos, -ī, f., Dē′los, an island in the Aegean.

delphīn, -īnis, m., dolphin.

dēlūbrum, -rī, n., shrine.

dēmēns, gen. -entis, mad.

dēmenter, adv., foolishly.

dēmigrō, 1, go off, depart.

dēminūtiō, -ōnis, f., sacrifice, loss.

dēmissus, -a, -um, downcast; w. crīne, disheveled.

dēmittō, -ere, -mīsī, -missus, let down, lower; plunge.

dēmō, -ere, dēmpsī, dēmptus, take away.

dēmōnstrō, 1, point out, show, mention.

dēmum, adv., at length, at last.

dēnī, -ae, -a, ten each.

dēnique, adv., finally, after all, in short.

dēns, dentis, m., tooth; w. Indus, ivory.

dēnūntiō, 1, threaten.

dēpellō, -ere, -pulī, -pulsus, drive from, avert, remove, overthrow.

dēpereō, -īre, -periī, -peritūrus, go to destruction, be lost.

dēpōnō, -ere, -posuī, -positus, put aside; quench.

dēportō, 1, bring back.

dēposcō, -ere, dēpoposcī, —, demand.

dēpositum, -ī, n., deposit, loan.

dēprāvō, 1, corrupt, tamper with.

dēprecātor, -ōris, m., intercessor.

dēprecor, -ārī, -ātus sum, avert by prayer.

dēprehendō, -ere, -hendī, -hēnsus, catch, detect, discover.

dēprimō, -ere, -pressī, -pressus, (press down), sink.

dēprōmō, -ere, -prōmpsī, -prōmptus, withdraw.

dērelinquō, -ere, -līquī, -līctus, abandon, forsake.

dērigēscō, -ere, -riguī, —, become rigid.

dēscendō, -ere, -scendī, -scēnsus, descend, resort.

dēscrīptus, -a, -um, assigned.

dēserō, -ere, -seruī, -sertus, desert; dēsertus, -a, -um, lonely.

dēsīderium, -rī, n., longing, desire.

dēsīderō, 1, desire, long for; lose, miss, need.

dēsidia, -ae, f., idleness, indolence.

dēsignō, 1, mark out, elect, choose.

dēsinō, -ere, -siī, -situs, cease.

dēsistō, -ere, -stitī, -stitus, (stand away), cease.

dēsōlō, 1, leave alone, desert.

dēspērō, 1, despair (of).

dēspiciō, -ere, -spexī, -spectus, look down on, despise.

dēspondeō, -ēre, -spondī, -spōnsus, promise.

dēstinō, 1, bind; intend, determine.

dēstitūtus, -a, -um, deserted.

dēstringō, -ere, -strīnxī, -strictus, unsheath.

dēstruō, -ere, -strūxī, -strūctus, tear down, destroy.

dēsum, deesse, dēfuī, dēfutūrus, fail, be lacking.

dēsūmō, -ere, -sūmpsī, -sūmptus, undertake.

dēterreō, -ēre, -uī, -itus, deter.

dētrahō, -ere, -trāxī, -trāctus, draw or take from, pull off, remove, withdraw.

dētrectō, 1, reject.

dētrīmentum, -ī, n., loss, defeat.

deus, -ī, m., god; nom. pl. diī or dī.

dēvertō, -ere, -vertī, -versus, turn aside.

dēvinciō, -īre, -vīnxī, -vīnctus, bind, unite.

dēvincō, -ere, -vīcī, -victus, subdue.

dēvocō, 1, call away.

dēvorō, 1, swallow (up), devour.

dēvoveō, -ēre, -vōvī, -vōtus, vow, dedicate; curse.

dexter, -tra (-tera), -trum (-terum), right; comp. dexterior, -ius, right; dextra (-tera). -ae, f., right hand.

Diāna, -ae, f., Dīăn'a, goddess of hunting.

dicāx, -ācis, sarcastic, witty.

diciō, -ōnis, f., authority, sway.

dīcō, -ere, dīxī, dictus, say, speak, tell, call.

dictātor, -ōris, m., dictator.

dictātūra, -ae, f., dictatorship.

dictitō, 1, say often.

dictō, 1, dictate.

dictum, -ī, n., word.

diēs, diēī, m. and f., day.

differō, -ferre, distulī, dīlātus, postpone; differ.

difficilis, -e, hard, difficult; critical.

difficultās, -tātis, f., difficulty, trouble.

difficulter, adv., with difficulty.

diffīdō, -ere, -fīsus sum, semideponent, distrust.

diffugiō, -ere, -fūgī, -fugitūrus, flee in different directions.

diffundō, -ere, -fūdī, -fūsus, spread, scatter.

dīgerō, -ere, -gessī, -gestus, force apart, separate.

digitus, -ī, m., finger.

dignitās, -tātis, f., dignity, worth, position. rank, honor, authority.

dignus, -a, -um, worthy.

diiūdicō, 1, decide, settle.

dīlātiō, -ōnis, f., putting off, postponement.

dīlēctus, -ūs, m., choice, draft, levy.

dīligēns, gen. -entis, careful, scrupulous.

dīligenter, adv., carefully.

dīligentia, -ae, f., care, diligence.

dīligō, -ere, -lēxī, -lēctus, single out, esteem, love.

dīlūcēscō, -ere, dīlūxī, —, grow light.

dīluvium, -vī, n., flood.

dīmētior, -īrī, -mēnsus sum, measure *or* lay out.

dīmicātiō, -ōnis, f., struggle.

dīmicō, 1, fight, contend, struggle.

dīmittō, -ere, -mīsī, -missus, let go, lose, send forth *or* away, dismiss.

dīmoveō, -ēre, -mōvī, -mōtus, move apart, stir.

Diomēdēs, -is, m., Dīomē'dēs, *a Greek hero.*

dīreptiō, -ōnis, f., plundering; loot.

dīreptor, -ōris, m., plunderer.

dīripiō, -ere, -ripuī, -reptus, tear apart, plunder.

dīruō, -ere, -uī, -utus, tear down, destroy.

dīrus, -a, -um, awful.

dīs, *gen.* dītis, rich.

discēdō, -ere, -cessī, -cessus, go away, depart.

discessus, -ūs, m., departure.

disciplīna, -ae, f., training, instruction.

discō, -ere, didicī, —, learn, be taught.

discordāns, *gen.* -antis, opposing, veering.

discordia, -ae, f., strife.

discrībō, -ere, -scrīpsī, -scrīptus, assign.

discrīmen, -minis, n., difference, decision; danger, crisis.

disiūnctiō, -ōnis, f., difference.

dispār, *gen.* -paris, unequal.

dispēnsō, 1, distribute.

dispergō, -ere, -spersī, -spersus, scatter.

dispertiō, -īre, -īvī, -ītus, distribute.

dispiciō, -ere, -spexī, -spectus, consider.

dispōnō, -ere, -posuī, -positus, (place here and there), arrange. dispose.

disputō, 1, discuss, argue.

dissēminō, 1, spread abroad.

dissēnsiō, -ōnis, f., quarrel.

dissentiō, -īre, -sēnsī, -sēnsus, disagree, differ.

dissimulanter, *adv.*, secretly.

dissimulātor, -ōris, m., dissembler.

dissimulō, 1, conceal (the truth), deny.

dissipō, 1, scatter.

dissolūtus, -a, -um, lax, remiss.

distineō, -ēre, -uī, -tentus, keep apart; distract.

distō, -āre, —, —, (stand apart), be distant, be different.

distribuō, -ere, -tribuī, -tribūtus, distribute, assign.

distringō, -ere, -strīnxī, -strictus, distract the attention.

dissuādeō, -ēre, -suāsī, -suāsus, dissuade.

diū, *adv.*, for a long time, long; *comp.* diūtius ; *superl.* diūtissimē.

diūtinus, -a, -um, long, of long duration.

diūturnitās, -tātis, f., length of time, tenure.

diūturnus, -a, -um, long-continued.

dīvellō, –ere, –vellī, –vulsus,
tear away, rend, separate.

dīversitās, –tātis, *f.*, difference.

dīversus, –a, –um, opposite,
different, widely separated.

dīves, *gen.* -vitis, rich.

dīvidō, –ere, –vīsī, –vīsus, divide; extend.

dīvīnitus, *adv.*, providentially.

dīvīnus, –a, –um, divine, god-
like.

dīvitiae, –ārum, *f.*, riches.

dīvulgō, 1, (spread among the
people), divulge, make
known.

dō, dare, dedī, datus, give.

doceō, –ēre, docuī, doctus,
teach, show.

doctor, –ōris, *m.*, teacher, in-
structor.

doctrīna, –ae, *f.*, teaching,
learning.

doctus, –a, –um, learned,
skilled.

Dolābella, –ae, *m.*, Dolabella, *a
Roman name.*

doleō, –ēre, –uī, –itūrus, suffer,
grieve, deplore.

dolor, –ōris, *m.*, pain, suffering;
grief, grievance.

domesticus, –a, –um, private,
domestic.

domicilium, –lī, *n.*, home, residence.

dominātiō, –ōnis, *f.*, mastery,
rule.

dominor, –ārī, –ātus sum, rule.

dominus, –ī, *m.*, master, owner;
voc., Sir.

Domitius, –tī, *m.*, Domitius
(Domish'us), *one of Pom-
pey's officers.*

domō, –āre, domuī, domitus,
tame, subdue, break in.

domus, –ūs, *f.*, house, home,
household; *loc.* domī, at
home.

dōnec, *conj.*, until, as long as.

dōnō, 1, present, give.

dōnum, –ī, *n.*, gift.

Drūsus, –ī, *m.*, Drusus, *a Roman name.*

dubitō, 1, doubt, be in doubt;
hesitate.

dubius, –a, –um, doubtful, uncertain.

ducentī, –ae, –a, two hundred.

dūcō, –ere, dūxī, ductus, lead,
draw, attract, construct;
draw out; consider.

ductus, –ūs, *m.*, leadership.

dūdum, *adv.*, for a long time.

dulcēdō, –dinis, *f.*, sweetness,
charm.

dulcis, –e, sweet.

dum, *conj.*, while, as long as;
provided that (*often w.* modo).

duo, –ae, –o, two.

duodecim, twelve.

dupliciter, *adv.*, doubly.

dūrō, 1, last, remain.

dūrus, –a, –um, hard, cruel,
insensible.

dux, ducis, *m.*, leader, general.

Dyrrachīnus, –a, –um, of *or* at
Dyrrachium (Dyrrā'kium),
*a city in Illyricum, now Du-
razzo.*

E

ē, ex, *prep. w. abl.*, from, out of,
of, after, in accordance with.

ecce ! *interj.*, lo !

ecquis, (**–quae**), -**quid,** (whether) anyone? (whether) anything? any?

ēdīcō, –ere, ēdīxī, ēdictus, declare.

ēdictum, –ī, *n.,* proclamation, order.

ēdō, –ere, ēdidī, ēditus, publish, utter.

ēducō, 1, bring up.

ēdūcō, –ere, –dūxī, –ductus, lead out *or* forth, draw out.

efferō, –ferre, extulī, ēlātus, carry out; bring; exalt, extol.

efficiō, –ere, –fēcī, –fectus, make (out), cause, accomplish, produce.

effigiēs, –ēī, *f.,* copy.

efflō, 1, breathe out.

effluō, –ere, –flūxī, —, flow out; escape.

effodiō, –ere, –fōdī, –fossus, dig up.

effrēnātus, –a, –um, unbridled, unrestrained.

effugiō, –ere, –fūgī, –fugitūrus, escape.

effundō, –ere, –fūdī, –fūsus, pour out *or* forth.

egēns, *gen.* **–entis,** needy.

egeō, –ēre, –uī, —, need, be in need of, lack.

egestās, –tātis, *f.,* poverty.

ego, meī, *pers. pron.,* I; **egomet,** I myself.

ēgredior, ēgredī, ēgressus sum, go *or* march out, go, leave; disembark.

ēgregius, –a, –um, distinguished, excellent.

Egus, –ī, *m.,* Ē'gus, *an Allobrogian.*

ēiaculor, –ārī, –ātus sum, shoot *or* spurt out.

ēiciō, –ere, ēiēcī, ēiectus, throw *or* drive out, reject; *w.* **sē,** rush out.

ēlābor, ēlābī, ēlāpsus sum, slip away, escape.

ēlabōrō, 1, work out, perfect.

ēlegantia, –ae, *f.,* refinement.

ēlegī, –ōrum, *m. pl.,* elegiac verses.

ēlevō, 1, raise.

ēligō, –ere, ēlēgī, ēlēctus, pick out, select.

ēloquentia, –ae, *f.,* eloquence.

ēlūdō, –ere, ēlūsī, ēlūsus, escape; mock, make sport of.

ēmendō, 1, correct, improve.

ēmergō, –ere, ēmersī, ēmersus, rise, emerge.

ēmicō, –āre, –uī, –ātus, dart forth, spurt.

ēmittō, –ere, ēmīsī, ēmissus, let go, send forth, drive out, allow to escape.

emō, –ere, ēmī, ēmptus, buy.

ēmorior, –rī, ēmortuus sum, die.

ēmptor, –ōris, *m.,* buyer.

enim, *conj.* (*never first word*), for; *w.* **at,** but you say.

ēnītor, –ī, ēnīxus (ēnīsus) sum, make one's way.

Ennius, –nī, *m.,* Ennius, *a Roman poet.*

ēnotō, 1, mark out, note down.

ēnsis, –is, *m.,* sword.

eō, īre, iī, itus, go.

eō, *adv.,* there.

eōdem, *adv.,* to *or* at the same place.

Eōus, –ī, *m.,* Eō'us, *one of the horses of the Sun.*

epistula, –ae, f., letter.

epulae, –ārum, f., food.

epulor, –ārī, –ātus sum, hold a banquet.

epulum, –ī, n., feast.

eques, equitis, m., horseman, knight; pl., cavalry.

equester, –tris, –tre, equestrian.

equidem, adv., (w. 1st person), for my part, at any rate.

equitātus, –ūs, m., cavalry.

equus, –ī, m., horse.

ergā, prep. w. acc., toward.

ergō, adv., accordingly, therefore, then.

Ēridanus, –ī. m., the Erid'anus, a river (the Po?).

ērigō, – ere, ērēxī, ērēctus, raise, set up, erect, encourage.

ēripiō, –ere, ēripuī, ēreptus, snatch or take away, rescue from, remove.

errō, 1, wander, be mistaken.

error, –ōris, m., error.

ērudiō, –īre, –īvī, –ītus, teach.

ērudītiō, –ōnis, f., instruction.

ērudītus, –a, –um, educated, learned.

ērumpō, –ere, ērūpī, ēruptus, break out, burst forth.

ēruō, –ere, –uī, –utus, tear out.

ēscendō, –ere, ēscendī, ēscēnsus, climb, ascend.

et, conj., and, even, also, too; et . . . et, both . . . and.

etenim, conj., for truly, and indeed.

etiam, adv., also, even, still; nōn sōlum . . . sed etiam, not only . . . but also; etiam atque etiam, again and again.

Etrūria, –ae, f. Etrū'ria, a district of Italy.

etsī, conj., although.

Eurus, –ī, m., Eurus, southeast wind.

ēvādō, –ere, ēvāsī, ēvāsus, go out, escape.

ēvānēscō, –ere, –uī, —, disappear.

ēvehō, –ere, ēvexī, ēvectus, carry away.

ēveniō, –īre, ēvēnī, ēventus, (come out), turn out, happen.

ēventus, –ūs, m., occurrence; fate.

ēvertō, –ere, ēvertī, ēversus, overthrow, destroy, ruin.

ēvigilō, 1, awake.

ēvītābilis, –e, avoidable.

ēvocātor, –ōris, m., summoner, instigator.

ēvocātus, –ī, m., reënlisted veteran.

ēvocō, 1, call out, summon.

ēvolō, 1, fly or rush forth.

ēvolvō, –ere, ēvolvī, ēvolūtus, unroll (and read).

ex, see ē.

exagitō, 1, disturb, antagonize.

exanimātus, –a, –um, exhausted, lifeless.

exanimis, –e, lifeless, dead.

exārdēscō, –ere, –ārsī, –ārsus, be inflamed.

exaudiō, –īre, –īvī, –ītus, hear (plainly).

excandēscō, –ere, –duī, —, grow hot, burn (with anger).

excēdō, –ere, –cessī, –cessus, go forth, withdraw, depart; leave, preclude.

excellēns, *gen.* **–entis,** superior, remarkable.

excellō, –ere, —, –celsus, be eminent, excel.

excelsus, –a, –um, elevated, high.

excidō, –ere, –cidī, —, fall (out), disappear.

excipiō, –ere, –cēpī, –ceptus, take out *or* up, receive, catch; follow; except; intercept.

excitō, i, arouse; raise.

exclāmō, 1, exclaim.

exclūdō, –ere, –clūsī, –clūsus, shut out.

excolō, –ere, –uī, –cultus, cultivate.

excurrō, –ere, –cucurrī, –cursus, run out *or* up.

excursiō, –ōnis, *f.,* inroad, invasion.

exemplar, –āris, *n.,* copy.

exemplum, –ī, *n.,* example, copy, precedent.

exeō, –īre, –iī, –itus, go *or* come forth, depart.

exerceō, –ēre, –ercuī, –ercitus, train, exercise; conduct; trouble; collect.

exercitātiō, –ōnis, *f.,* training, exercise.

exercitātus, –a, –um, trained.

exercitus, –ūs, *m.,* army.

exhālō, 1, breathe out.

exhauriō, –īre, –hausī, –haustus, draw off, drain.

exhibeō, –ēre, –uī, –itus, (hold forth), show.

exigō, –ere, –ēgī, –āctus, drive out, demand; *of time,* spend, pass.

exiguus, –a, –um, small, slight, narrow.

eximiē, *adv.,* exceedingly.

eximius, –a, –um, extraordinary.

eximō, –ere, –ēmī, –ēmptus, take away, consume.

exinde, *adv.,* thence, then.

exīstimātiō, –ōnis, *f.,* reputation.

exīstimō, 1, think, suppose, consider.

exitiābilis, –e, fatal.

exitiōsus, –a, –um, deadly.

exitium, –tī, *n.,* ruin, destruction, death.

exitus, –ūs, *m.,* outcome, end.

exōrnō, 1, adorn.

exōrō, 1, induce, prevail upon.

expallēscō, –ere, –palluī, —, turn pale.

expediō, –īre, –īvī, –ītus, set free, procure.

expedītus, –a, –um, without baggage, unencumbered, ready.

expellō, –ere, –pulī, –pulsus, drive out, expel; deprive of.

experior, –īrī, –pertus sum, try, test; find.

expers, –pertis, having no share in.

expetō, –ere, –īvī, –ītus, seek (out).

expīlō, 1, plunder.

explicō, 1, unfold, explain; free.

explōrō, 1, investigate, explore.

expōnō, –ere, –posuī, –positus, put out, expose, explain.

exportō, 1, carry out, export.

exprimō, –ere, –pressī, –pres

sus, press out, portray, describe.

expugnātiō, -ōnis, *f.,* storming, capture.

expugnō, 1, take by storm, capture.

expūrgō, 1, clear oneself.

exquīrō, -ere, -quīsīvī, -quīsītus, search out, ascertain.

exsecror, -ārī, -ātus sum, curse.

exserō, -ere, -uī, -tus, thrust forth.

exsilium, -lī, *n.,* exile, banishment.

exsistō, -ere, -stitī, —, stand *or* come forth, appear, arise.

exspectātiō, -ōnis, *f.,* waiting, anticipation.

exspectō, 1, look out for, expect, wait (for).

exstinguō, -ere, -stīnxī, -stīnctus, extinguish, destroy.

exstō, -āre, —, —, stand out, protrude; exist.

exstruō, -ere, -strūxī, -strūctus, heap up, bridge.

exsul, -ulis, *m. and f.,* exile.

exsultō, 1, (leap up), exult.

extendō, -ere, -tendī, -tentus (-tēnsus), stretch out, prolong.

externus, -a, -um, foreign.

exterus. -a, -um, on the outside, foreign.

extollō, -ere, —, —, raise up.

extorqueō, -ēre, -torsī, -tortus, wrest.

extrā, *prep. w. acc.,* outside of, without.

extrēmus, -ā, -um, farthest, last, end of, waning; *as*

noun, n., final outcome; **ad extrēmum,** at last.

exūrō, -ere, -ussī, -ustus, burn (up).

exuviae, -ārum, *f.,* spoils.

F

faba, -ae, *f.,* bean.

faber, -brī, *m.,* mechanic, fireman.

Fabius, -bī, *m.,* Fā'bius; **Fabia, -ae,** *f.,* Fā'bia, *Roman names.*

fabricō, 1, make.

fābula, -ae, *f.,* story.

facētiae, -ārum, *f. pl.,* jest, wit.

faciēs, -ēī, *f.,* appearance, face.

facile, *adv.,* easily, readily.

facilis, -e, easy.

facilitās, -tātis, *f.,* ease, facility; affability.

facinorōsus, -ī, *m.,* criminal.

facinus, -noris, *n.,* deed, crime.

faciō, -ere, fēcī, factus, do, make, form, cause; **proelium facere,** fight a battle.

factiō, -ōnis, *f.,* faction.

factum, -ī, *n.,* deed, act, fact.

facultās, -tātis, *f.,* ability, means, opportunity.

fācundus, -a, -um, eloquent.

Faesulae, -ārum, *f.,* Faesulae, Fiesole, *a town in Etruria.*

fāgus, -ī, *f.,* beechwood.

Falcidius, -dī, *m.,* Falcidius (Falsĭd'ius), *a Roman name.*

Falernum, -ī, *n.,* Falernian wine.

fallō, -ere, fefellī, falsus, deceive, elude, escape the notice of; *w.* **fidem,** break.

falsō, *adv.*, falsely.

falsus, **-a, -um**, false.

fāma, **-ae,** *f.*, report, story; fame, reputation; *w.* **est,** it is said.

famēs **-is,** *f.*, hunger.

familia, **-ae,** *f.*, household, family; slaves.

familiāris, **-e,** (belonging to the family), friendly, private, intimate; *as noun, m.*, intimate friend.

familiāritās, **-tātis,** *f.*, friendship.

familiāriter, *adv.*, intimately.

famulus, **-ī,** *m.*, servant.

Fannia, **-ae,** *f.*, Fannia, *a Roman woman.*

fānum, **-ī,** *n.*, shrine.

fās, *n. indecl.*, divine right; **fās est,** it is right, lawful, *or* fitting.

fascis, **-is,** *m.*, bundle; *pl.*, fasces.

fateor, **-ērī, fassus sum,** confess, admit.

fātifer, **-era, -erum,** death-bringing, fatal.

fatīgō, 1, weary.

fātum, **-ī,** *n.*, fate.

faucēs, **-ium,** *f. pl.*, throat, jaws; pass, defile.

faveō, **-ēre, fāvī, fautus,** be favorable to, favor.

favīlla, **-ae,** *f.*, embers.

favor, **-ōris,** *m.*, favor; cheering.

favus, **-ī,** *m.*, honeycomb.

fax, facis, *f.*, torch.

febris, **-is,** *f.*, fever.

Februārius, **-a, -um,** (of) February.

fēcundus, **-a, -um,** fruitful, rich.

fēlīcitās, **-tātis,** *f.*, good fortune, luck.

fēlīciter, *adv.*, fortunately, successfully.

fēlīx, *gen.* **fēlīcis,** happy, fortunate, productive.

fēmina, **-ae,** *f.*, woman.

fenestra, **-ae,** *f.*, window.

fera, **-ae,** *f.*, wild beast.

ferāx, *gen.* **ferācis,** fruitful, abounding in.

ferē, fermē, *adv.*, almost, about; *w. neg.*, hardly.

fermentum **-ī,** *n.*, leaven.

ferō, ferre, tulī, lātus, bear, carry, bring, direct, produce, obtain; say; *w.* **lēgem,** propose, pass; *w.* **pedem retrō,** start back.

ferōciter, *adv.*, fiercely.

ferōx, *gen.* **-ōcis,** fierce.

ferrum, **-ī,** *n.*, iron; sword, point.

fertilis, **-e,** fertile.

ferus, **-a, -um,** savage, cruel.

fervēns, *gen.* **-entis,** hot, burning.

festīnō, 1, hasten.

fēstus, **-a, -um,** festive.

fētus, **-ūs,** *m.*, offspring; fruit.

fīdē, *adv.*, faithfully, loyally.

fidēlis, **-e,** faithful.

fidēs, **-eī,** *f.*, trust, belief, promise; credit, honor, loyalty; pledge.

fīdūcia, **-ae,** *f.*, confidence, assurance.

fīgō, **-ere, fīxī, fīxus,** fix, set, imprint.

Figulus, **-ī,** *m.*, Figulus, *a Roman name.*

figūra, –ae, *f.*, shape, figure.
fīlia, –ae, *f.*, daughter.
fīliolus, –ī, *m.*, little son.
fīlius, –lī, *m.*, son.
findō, –ere, fidī, fissus, split.
fingō, –ere, fīnxī, fictus, form; imagine, suppose.
fīniō, –īre, –īvī, –ītus, end, finish, bound.
fīnis, –is, *m.*, end, limit; *pl.*, borders.
fīnitimus, –a, –um, neighboring; *as noun*, *m.*, neighbor.
fīō, fierī, factus sum, become, be made, be done, happen.
firmāmentum, –ī, *n.*, support.
firmō, 1, strengthen.
firmus, –a, –um, strong, firm.
fissus, *see* findō.
fistula,–ae, *f.*,(shepherd's) pipe.
fīxus, *see* fīgō.
Flaccus, –ī, *m.*, Flaccus, *a Roman name.*
flāgitium, –tī, *n.*, disgraceful act, crime.
flāgitō, 1, demand, insist upon.
flagrō, 1, burn.
flamma, –ae, *f.*, flame, fire.
flammifer,–fera, –ferum, flame-bearing, fiery.
flāvēns, *gen.* –entis, yellow.
flāvēscō, –ere, —, —, become golden.
flāvus, –a, –um, yellow, golden.
flectō, –ere, flexī, flexus, turn, bend, influence.
fleō, –ēre, flēvī, flētus, weep.
flētus, –ūs, *m.*, weeping.
flexus, *see* flecto.
flōreō, –ēre, –uī, —, bloom, flourish.

flūctus, –ūs, *m.*, wave.
fluitō, 1, float, flow.
flūmen, flūminis, *n.*, river.
fluvius, –vī, *m.*, stream, river.
focilō, 1, revive, keep alive.
focus, –ī, *m.*, hearth.
foederātus, –a, –um, allied.
foedō, 1, stain.
foedus, –a, –um, loathsome, vile, shameful.
foedus, –deris, *n.*, league, alliance; compact.
folium, –lī, *n.*, leaf.
fōns, fontis, *m.*, spring, fountain, source.
fore, forem, *see* sum.
forēnsis, –e, of the Forum, public.
foris, –is, *f.*, door; forīs, *adv.*, out of doors, abroad.
fōrma, –ae, *f.*, shape, beauty; plan.
Formiae, –ārum,*f. pl.*, Formiae, *a town in Italy.*
Formiānus, –a, –um, Formian, at Formiae.
formīdō, –dinis,*f.*, fear, dread.
formīdolōsus, –a, –um, alarming, formidable.
fōrmō, 1, form, compose.
fōrmōsus, –a, –um, handsome, beautiful.
fors, fortis, *f.*, chance.
forsitan, *adv.*, perhaps.
fortasse, *adv.*, perhaps.
forte, *adv.*, by chance.
fortis, –e, strong; brave, valiant, fearless.
fortiter, *adv.*, bravely.
fortitūdō, –dinis, *f.*, fortitude, courage, strength.
fortuitus, –a, –um, accidental.

fortūna, –ae, *f.,* fortune, fate, luck, lot.

Fortūnāta, –ae, *f.,* Fortunā'ia, *Trimalchio's wife.*

fortūnātus, –a, –um, happy, fortunate.

forum, –ī, *n.,* forum, market place; **Forum Aurēlium,** *n., a town in Etruria.*

frangō, –ere, frēgī, frāctus, break, crush; overcome.

frāter, frātris, *m.,* brother.

frāternus, –a, –um, of one's brother.

fraudō, 1, cheat, steal.

fraudulentus, –a, –um, deceitful.

frēnī (–a), –ōrum, *m. or n. pl.,* bridle, rein.

frequēns, *gen.* **–entis,** frequent, full; *pl.,* in throngs.

frequentia, –ae, *f.,* throng, vast number.

frequentō, 1, visit often.

fretum, –ī, *n.,* strait, sea; water.

frētus, –a, –um, relying on.

frīgeō, –ēre, —, —, be cold, freeze.

frīgus, –goris, *n.,* cold, coolness.

frondeō, –ēre, —, —, put forth leaves.

frōns, frondis, *f.,* leaf.

frōns, frontis, *f.,* forehead; front.

frūctus, –ūs, *m.,* enjoyment, fruit; income, benefit, reward, products.

frūgālitās, –tātis, *f.,* thrift.

frūmentārius, –a, –um, of grain; *w.* **auxilium,** granary; *w.* **rēs,** grain supply.

frūmentum, –ī, *n.,* grain.

fruor, fruī, frūctus sum, enjoy.

frūstrā, *adv.,* in vain.

fuga, –ae, *f.,* flight.

fugiō, –ere, fūgī, fugitūrus, flee, avoid, escape.

fugitīvus, –ī, *m.,* runaway slave.

fugō, 1, put to flight, repel.

fulgeō, –ēre, fulsī, —, gleam.

fulmen, –minis, *n.,* lightning; thunderbolt.

Fulvia, –ae, *f.,* Ful'via, *a Roman name.*

Fulvius, –vī, *m.,* Ful'vius, *a Roman name.*

fulvus, –a, –um, yellow.

fūmō, 1, smoke.

fundō, –ere, fūdī, fūsus, pour; rout.

fundus, –ī, *m.,* bottom; estate.

fūnestus, –a, –um, fatal.

fungor, –ī, fūnctus sum, perform.

fūnus, fūneris, *n.,* funeral, death; ruin.

furca, –ae, *f.,* forked pole.

furibundus, –a, –um, raving mad.

furiōsus, –a, –um, insane, furious.

Fūrius, –rī, *m.,* Fū'rius, *a Roman name.*

furō, –ere, –uī, —, rage, be mad.

furor, –ōris, *m.,* madness, fury.

fūrtim, *adv.,* by stealth, furtively.

fūrtum, –ī, *n.,* theft.

fūsilis, –e, molten.

futūrus, –a, –um, *fut. part. of* **sum.**

G

Gabīnius, -nī, *m.,* Gabinius, *a Roman name;* **Gabīnius, -a, -um,** Gabinian.

Gāius, -ī, *m.,* Gā'ius, *a Roman name.*

Galba, -ae, *m.,* Galba, *a Roman name.*

Gallia, -ae, *f.,* Gaul.

Gallicus, -a, -um, Gallic, of Gaul.

gallīna, -ae, *f.,* hen.

Gallus, -ī, *m.,* a Gaul.

Ganymēdēs, -is, *m.,* Găn'ymēde, *cupbearer of the gods.*

gaudeō, -ēre, gāvīsus sum, *semi-deponent,* rejoice.

gaudium, -dī, *n.,* joy, delight.

Gāvius, -vī, *m.,* Gā'vius, *a Roman name.*

gaza, -ae, *f.,* treasure.

gelidus, -a, -um, cold.

geminus, -a, -um, twin; two, both.

gemitus, -ūs, *m.,* groan, lamentation.

gemma, -ae, *f.,* precious stone.

genae, -ārum, *f.,* cheeks.

gener, -erī, *m.,* son-in-law.

genitor, -ōris, *m.,* father.

genitus, *see* **gignō.**

gēns, gentis, *f.,* tribe, family, people, nation.

genū, -ūs, *n.,* knee.

genus, generis, *n.,* birth, race; kind, class, family.

geōmetra, -ae, *m.,* geometrician.

Germānī, -ōrum, *m.,* the Germans.

Germānia, -ae, *f.,* Germany.

gerō, -ere, gessī, gestus, bear, carry on, manage, do, accomplish; hold; *w.* **bellum,** wage war; *w.* **sē,** conduct oneself.

gestō, 1, carry, bear; *pass.,* ride.

gignō, -ere, genuī, genitus, bring forth, produce; *pass.,* be born.

Glabriō, -ōnis, *m.,* Glab'rio, *a Roman name.*

glaciālis, -e, icy.

gladiātor, -ōris, *m.,* gladiator.

gladius, -dī, *m.,* sword.

glaeba, -ae, *f.,* clod.

glāns, glandis, *f.,* acorn.

Glaucia, -ae, *m.,* Glaucia (Glaw'sia), *a Roman name.*

glōria, -ae, *f.,* glory, fame.

glōrior, -ārī, -ātus sum, boast.

Gnaeus, -ī, *m.,* Gnaeus (Nē'us), *a Roman name.*

gnāvus, -a, -um, active.

Gracchus, -ī, *m.,* Gracchus, *a Roman name.*

gradior, -ī, gressus sum, step, walk.

gradus, -ūs, *m.,* step, grade.

Graecē, *adv.,* in Greek.

Graecia, -ae, *f.,* Greece.

Graecus, -a, -um, Greek; *as noun, m. pl.,* the Greeks.

grammaticus, -ī, *m.,* grammarian.

grandis, -e, great.

grātēs, *w.* **agere,** thank.

grātia, -ae, *f.,* gratitude, favor, influence; **grātiās agere,** thank; **grātiam referre,** show one's gratitude; **grātiam habēre,** feel grateful; **grātiā, for** the sake of.

Grattius, -tī, *m.,* Grattius, *a Roman name.*

grātuītō, *adv.,* without pay, freely.

grātulātiō, -ōnis, *f.,* rejoicing, congratulation.

grātulor, -ārī, -ātus sum, congratulate.

grātus, -a, -um, pleasing; **grātum facere,** do a favor.

gravidus, -a, -um, heavy.

gravis, -e, heavy, important, severe, offensive, grave, grievous; august.

gravitās, -tātis, *f.,* weight, dignity, seriousness.

graviter, *adv.,* seriously, strongly.

gravō, 1, make heavy; weigh down; *pass.,* be reluctant.

gressus, -ūs, *m.,* step.

grex, gregis, *m.,* herd.

gubernātiō, -ōnis, *m.,* control.

gubernō, 1, steer, navigate.

gustō, 1, taste, enjoy.

guttur, -uris, *n.,* throat.

H

habēna, -ae, *f.,* rein.

habeō, -ēre, habuī, habitus, have, hold, regard; pay.

Habinna, -ae, *m.,* Habĭn'na, *a name.*

habitātiō, -ōnis, *f.,* dwelling; *pl.,* lodgings.

habitō, 1, live.

habitus, -ūs, *m.,* condition.

haereō, -ēre, haesī, haesus, stick, cling.

haesitō, 1, (stick fast), be undecided, be at a loss.

Hannibal, -alis, *m.,* Hăn'nibal, *a Carthaginian general.*

harēna, -ae, *f.,* sand.

harundō, -dinis, *f.,* reed, rod.

haruspex, -picis, *m.,* soothsayer.

haud, *adv.,* not, by no means.

hauriō, -īre, hausī, haustus, draw; empty.

haustus, -ūs, *m.,* drawing, shedding.

hebēscō, -ere, —, —, grow dull.

Helena, -ae, *f.,* Helen, *wife of Menelaus.*

Helicē, -ēs, *f.,* Helice (Hel'isē), *a constellation.*

Helvētiī, -ōrum, *m.,* the Helvetians (Helvē'shians), *a Gallic tribe.*

Helvidius, -dī, *m.,* Helvĭd'ius, *a Roman name.*

Hēraclēa, -ae, *f.,* Heraclea (Heraklē'a), *a Greek city in southern Italy.*

Hēraclīēnsis, -e, of Heraclea; *as noun, m.,* a Heraclē'an.

herba, -ae, *f.,* plant; *pl.,* grass.

herbidus, -a, -um, grassy, overgrown (with).

Herculēs, -is, *m.,* Her'culēs, *a Greek hero.*

hērēditās, -tātis, *f.,* inheritance.

hērēs, -ēdis, *m. and f.,* heir, heiress.

hērōs, -ōis, *m.,* hero.

Hesperides, -um, *f.,* Hesperidēs, *daughters of Atlas.*

Hesperius, -a, -um, of the west.

hesternus, -a, -um, of yesterday; *w.* **diēs,** yesterday.

heu ! *interj.,* alas !

hīberna, –ōrum, n. pl., winter quarters.

hībernō, 1, pass the winter.

Hibērus, –ī, m., the Ēbro, a river in Spain.

nic, haec, hoc, dem. pron., this, the latter; he, she, it (enclitic –ce added for emphasis).

hīc, adv., here, hereupon, in view of this.

hiems, hiemis, f., winter.

hilaritās, –tātis, f., gayety.

hinc, adv., hence, from this place; hinc . . . illinc, on this side . . . on that.

Hippomenēs, –is, m., Hippŏm'enēs, victor over Atalanta.

hirsūtus, –a, –um, rough, bristling.

Hirtius, –tī, m., Hirtius (Her'-shius), a Roman name.

Hispānia, –ae, f., Spain.

Hispāniēnsis, –e, Spanish.

Hispānus, –a, –um, Spanish; as noun, m., a Spaniard.

historia, –ae, f., history, account.

hodiē, adv., to-day.

hodiernus diēs, this day, to-day.

holus, –leris, n., vegetables.

Homērus, –ī, m., Homer, a Greek poet.

homō, hominis, m., man, person; pl., men, people.

honestās, –tātis, f., honor.

honestē, adv., honorably.

honestō, 1, honor, distinguish.

honestus, –a, –um, honorable.

honor (honōs), –ōris, m., honor, office.

honorātus, –a, –um, honored.

hōra, –ae, f., hour.

hōrologium, –gī, n., sundial.

horreum, –ī, n., granary.

horribilis, –e, dreadful.

hortātus, –ūs, m., urging, encouragement.

Hortēnsius, –sī, m., Horten'-sius, a Roman name.

hortor, –ārī, –ātus sum, urge, encourage.

hortus, –ī, m., garden.

hospes, –pitis, m. and f., stranger, guest; host.

hospita, –ae, f., a stranger.

hospitium, –tī, n., (tie of) hospitality.

hostīlis, –e, an enemy's, hostile.

hostis, –is, m., enemy (usually pl.), (public) foe.

hūc, to this place, to this, here.

hūmānitās, –tātis, f., kindness, sympathy, culture.

hūmāniter, adv., like a man.

hūmānus, –a, –um, human, cultured, refining.

humilis, –e, low, humble.

humus, –ī, f., ground, earth.

Hypaepa, –ōrum, n., Hypaepa (Hypē'pa), a town at the base of Mt. Tmolus.

I

iaceō, –ēre, iacuī, —, lie, be prostrate.

iaciō, –ere, iēcī, iactus, throw.

iactō, 1, throw, hurl, toss; boast of; w. sē, display itself.

iactūra, –ae, f., throwing away, loss.

iactus, –ūs, *m.,* throwing; stroke.

iam, *adv.,* already, now; *w. neg.,* no longer; *of future time,* soon, presently; *w.* **diū, dūdum,** *or* **prīdem,** long ago; *w.* **vērō,** furthermore.

Iānuārius, –a, –um (of) January.

Iavolēnus, –ī, *m.,* Javolē′nus, *a Roman name.*

ibi, *adv.,* there, then.

ibīdem, *adv.,* in the same place.

Īcarus, –ī, *m.,* Ic′arus, *son of Daedalus.*

(īcō, –ere), īcī, ictus, strike.

idcircō, *adv.,* for this (that) reason, therefore.

īdem, eadem, idem, *dem. pron.,* same; also, besides, likewise.

identidem, *adv.,* repeatedly, again and again.

ideō, *adv.,* for this reason, therefore.

idōneus, –a, –um, fit, suitable.

Īdūs, –uum, *f. pl.,* the Ides, (15*th of March, May, July, and October;* 13*th of the other months*).

igitur, *adv.,* therefore, then.

ignārus, –a, –um, not knowing, ignorant.

ignifer, –era, –erum, fiery.

ignis, –is, *m.,* fire.

ignōbilis, –e, unknown, of lowly birth.

ignōminia, –ae, *f.,* disgrace.

ignōrantia, –ae, *f.,* want of knowledge, ignorance.

ignōrō, 1, be ignorant of, not know.

ignōscō, –ere, –nōvī, –nōtus, overlook; forgive.

ignōtus, –a, –um, unknown, strange.

īlex, īlicis, *f.,* oak.

īlia, –ōrum, *n. pl.,* abdomen, groin.

Īlias, Īliadis, *f.,* the Iliad.

Īlioneus, –ī, *m.,* Ili′oneus, *one of Niobe's sons.*

illāc, *adv.,* that way.

ille, illa, illud, *dem. pron.,* that, the former; he, she, it.

illecebra, –ae, *f.,* enticement.

illīc, *adv.,* in that place, there.

illinc, *adv.,* from that side.

illinō, –ere, –lēvī, –litus, smear, cover.

illūstris, –e, brilliant, noble, glorious.

illūstrō, 1, bring to light, reveal, glorify.

Īllyricus, –a, –um, Illўr′ian.

imāgō, –ginis, *f.,* representation, likeness, image, statue; appearance.

imber, –bris, *m.,* rain, storm.

imberbis, –e, beardless.

imitor, –ārī, –ātus sum, imitate.

immānis, –e, vast; savage.

immānitās, –tātis, *f.,* enormity, fierceness, barbarism.

immātūrus, –a, –um, untimely.

immemor, –oris, unmindful, forgetful.

immēnsus, –a, –um, immeasurable, boundless.

immineō, –ēre, —, —, threaten.

imminuō, –ere, –uī, –ūtus, lessen.

immītis, –e, severe; heartless.

immittō, −ere, −mīsī, −missus, send in *or* against, let loose; immissus, −a, −um, flowing.

immō, *adv.*, on the contrary, nay; *w.* vērō, nay more.

immōbilis, −e, immovable.

immoderātus, −a, −um, excessive.

immodicus, −a, −um, beyond measure, excessive.

immorior, −morī, −mortuus sum, die upon.

immortālis, −e, immortal.

immortālitās, −tātis, *f.*, immortality.

immōtus, −a, −um, unmoved; fixed.

immurmurō, 1, murmur into.

impār, *gen.* −paris, unequal; short.

impatiēns, *gen.* −entis, not bearing, impatient.

impediō, −īre, −īvī, −ītus, hinder, prevent.

impellō, −ere, −pulī, −pulsus, urge on, prevail upon, induce to undertake.

impendeō, −ēre, —, —, overhang, threaten.

impendium, −dī, *n.*, outlay, expense.

impendō, −ere, −pendī, −pēnsus, (weigh out), expend.

impēnsē, *adv.*, highly, extravagantly.

imperātor, −ōris, *m.*, commander in chief, general; emperor.

imperātōrius, −a, −um, (worthy) of a commander.

imperfectus, −a, −um, unfinished.

imperītus, −a, −um, inexperienced, ignorant.

imperium, −rī, *n.*, command, control, military power, government, empire.

imperō, 1, command, govern, order.

impertiō, −īre, −īvī, −ītus, share with, bestow.

impetrō, 1, get (one to), gain one's request, obtain.

impetus, −ūs, *m.*, attack, charge, fury, force.

impius, −a, −um, undutiful, wicked.

impleō, −ēre, −plēvī, −plētus, fill, fulfill.

implicō, −āre, −uī, −itus, enfold, involve, unite, attach closely.

implōrātiō, −ōnis, *f.*, entreaty.

implōrō, 1, implore.

impōnō, −ere, −posuī, −positus, place upon, put.

importūnus, −a, −um, unfit; cruel.

improbitās, −tātis, *f.*, baseness, shamelessness.

improbō, 1, disapprove.

improbus, −a, −um, base, wicked.

impudēns, *gen.* −entis, shameless, presumptuous.

impudenter, *adv.*, impudently.

impudentia, −ae, *f.*, shamelessness, effrontery.

impudīcus, −a, −um, shameless.

impūne, *adv.*, without punishment, safely.

impūnītus, −a, −um, unpunished.

impūrus, −a, −um, vile, impure.

īmus, -a, -um, *see* **īnferus.**

in, *prep. w. acc.,* into, to, toward, against, for; *w. abl.,* in, on, upon.

inānis, -e, empty.

inaudītus, -a, -um, unheard of.

incalēscō, -ere, -caluī, —, be kindled.

incēdō, -ere, -cessī, -cessus, advance, proceed.

incendium, -dī, *n.,* fire, burning, conflagration.

incendō, -ere, -cendī, -cēnsus, set on fire, burn.

incēnsiō, -ōnis, *f.,* burning.

inceptum, -ī, *n.,* beginning.

incertus, -a, -um, uncertain.

inchoō, 1, begin.

incidō, -ere, -cidī, —, fall into *or* on.

incīdō, -ere, -cīdī, -cīsus, cut (into).

incipiō, -ere, -cēpī, -ceptus, begin.

incitāmentum, -ī, *n.,* incentive, stimulus.

incitō, 1, urge on, arouse.

inclūdō, -ere, -clūsī, -clūsus, inclose, confine.

inclutus, -a, -um, famous, celebrated.

incognitus, -a, -um, unknown.

incola, -ae, *m. and f.,* inhabitant.

incolumis, -e, unharmed, safe, undefeated.

incommodum, -ī, *n.,* inconvenience, loss, defeat.

incrēdibilis, -e, extraordinary, incredible.

increpō, -āre, -uī, -itus, make a noise.

incrēscō, -ere, -crēvī -crētus, grow, increase.

incultus, -a, -um, untilled, rude.

incumbō, -ere, -cubuī, -cubitus, fall upon, bend to, devote oneself, press on.

incūriōsus, -a, -um, careless, indifferent (to).

incursō, 1, run *or* strike against.

incurvātus, -a, -um, bent.

inde, *adv.,* then, hence.

index, -dicis, *m.,* informer, witness.

India, -ae, *f.,* India.

indicium, -cī, *n.,* testimony, proof, evidence.

indicō, 1, point out, reveal, prove; accuse.

indigentia, -ae, *f.,* need, want.

indignē, *adv.,* unworthily.

indignitās, -tātis, *f.,* unworthiness.

indignor, -ārī, -ātus sum, regard as unworthy, be angry.

indignus, -a, -um, unworthy.

indolēscō, -ere, -doluī, —, be grieved.

indūcō, -ere, -dūxī, -ductus, bring in, draw over; influence.

indulgentia, -ae, *f.,* kindness.

indulgeō, -ēre, -dulsī, -dultus, yield to, indulge, favor.

industria, -ae, *f.,* diligence, care.

industrius, -a, -um, enterprising.

inedia, -ae, *f.,* fasting.

ineō, -īre, -iī, -itus, enter upon, begin; form.

inerrō, 1, wander, roam upon.

iners, *gen.* −ertis, unskilled; sluggish.

inertia, −ae, *f.* (lack of ski'l), inactivity, aversion to labor.

īnfāns, *gen.* −fantis, *m. and f.*, (speechless), infant.

īnfantia, −ae, *f.*, infancy.

īnfēlīx, *gen.* −īcis, unhappy, unfortunate.

īnferior, −ius, *see* īnferus.

īnferius, *adv.*, lower, too low.

īnfernus, −a, −um, of the lower world.

īnferō, −ferre, −tulī, illātus, bring in *or* upon, apply, lay upon; enter (*of an account*); *w.* bellum, wage.

īnferus, −a, −um, below; *as noun, m. pl.*, the dead; *compar.* īnferior, −ius, lower; *superl.* īnfimus, −a, −um *or* īmus, −a, −um, lowest.

īnfestus, −a, −um, hostile, dangerous.

īnfīdus, −a, −um, not to be trusted.

īnfimus, *see* īnferus.

īnfīnītus, −a, −um, endless.

īnfirmitās, −tātis, *f.*, sickness, weakness.

īnfirmō, 1, weaken, refute.

īnfirmus, −a, −um, not strong, weak, sick.

īnfitior, −ārī, −ātus sum, deny.

īnflammō, 1, set on fire, burn; inflame, arouse.

īnflexibilis, −e, unbending, inflexible.

īnflō, 1, blow into; inspire.

īnfluō, −ere, −flūxī, −flūxus, flow in.

īnfōrmō, 1, mold, train.

īnfrā, *adv.*, below.

ingemēscō, −ere, −uī, —, groan, sigh (over).

ingenium, −nī, *n.*, natural capacity, nature, talent, genius, spirit.

ingēns, *gen.* −entis, huge, vast.

ingrātus, −a, −um, ungrateful.

ingredior, −gredī, −gressus sum, (step into), go into, enter (upon).

inhibeō, −ēre, −uī, −itus, restrain; use.

inhonestus, −a, −um, disonorable.

iniciō, −ere, −iēcī, −iectus, throw into, cause, inspire.

inimīcitia, −ae, *f.*, hatred, enmity.

inimīcus, −a, −um, unfriendly, hostile; *as noun, m.*, (personal) enemy.

inīquitās, −tātis, *f.*, unfairness, injustice.

inīquus, −a, −um, unequal, sloping; unfavorable, discontented.

initiō, 1, initiate, consecrate.

initium, −tī, *n.*, beginning.

iniūria, −ae, *f.*, wrong, injustice, injury.

iniūstus, −a, −um, unjust.

innatō, 1, swim *or* float upon, flow over.

innītor, −nītī, −nīxus sum, lean upon.

innocēns, *gen.* −entis, (harmless), upright.

innocentia, −ae, *f.*, blamelessness, honesty.

innoxius, −a, −um, harmless, innocent.

innubus, -a, -um, unwed.

innumerābilis, -e, countless.

inopia, -ae, *f.*, lack (of funds), poverty.

inopīnātus, -a, -um, unexpected.

inquam, *defective*, say; inquis, you say, inquit, said, said he (*inserted parenthetically after one or more words of a direct quotation*).

inquīrō, -ere, -quīsīvī, -quīsītus, inquire (into).

īnscitus, -a, -um, ignorant, stupid.

īnscius, -a, -um, not knowing; ignorant.

īnscrībō, -ere, -scrīpsī, -scrīptus, write upon, inscribe.

īnscrīptiō, -ōnis, *f.*, inscription.

īnsecō, -āre, -secuī, -sectus, cut into.

īnsequor, -sequī, -secūtus sum, follow up *or* closely, pursue.

īnserō, -ere, -seruī, -sertus, thrust into.

īnsideō, -ēre, -sēdī, -sessus, (sit upon), take possession of; dwell, be fixed.

īnsidiae, -ārum, *f. pl.*, snare; plot, danger.

īnsidior, -ārī, -ātus sum, plot against.

īnsigne, -is, *n.*, mark.

īnsimulō, 1, charge.

īnsolenter, *adv.*, arrogantly.

īnsolitus, -a, -um, unaccustomed.

īnsonō, -āre, -uī, —, play on.

īnspectō, 1, look on.

īnspērātus, -a, -um, unlooked for, unexpected.

īnspiciō, -ere, -spexī, -spectus, look at, on, *or* into; inspect, examine.

īnstabilis, -e, unstable.

īnstanter, *adv.*, earnestly.

īnstituō, -ere, -stituī, -stitūtus, establish, decide (upon), begin; train.

īnstitūtiō, -ōnis, *f.*, training, education.

īnstitūtum, -ī, *n.*, custom.

īnstō, -āre, -stitī, —, press on, pursue.

īnstringō, -ere, -strīnxī, -strictus, fasten; set.

īnstrūmentum, -ī, *n.*, implement, tool.

īnstruō, -ere, -strūxī, -strūctus, build, draw up; provide, instruct, equip.

īnsula, -ae, *f.*, island.

īnsum, inesse, īnfuī, —, be in, exist.

integer, -gra, -grum, untouched, unimpaired, fresh, unbroken, irreproachable.

integrē, *adv.*, honestly.

integritās, -tātis, *f.*, integrity.

intellegō, -ere, -lēxī, -lēctus, understand, know, perceive.

intemptātus, -a, -um, untried, unattempted.

intendō, -ere, -tendī, -tentus, stretch; intend.

intentē, *adv.*, earnestly, vehemently.

inter, *prep. w. acc.*, between, among; inter sē, with each other, with one another.

intercēdō, -ere, -cessī, -cessus, go between, intervene.

intercessiō, –ōnis, *f.*, intervention, veto.

interclūdō, –ere, –clūsī,–clūsus, cut off.

interdiū, *adv.*, by day.

interdum, *adv.*, sometimes, at times.

intereā, *adv.*, meanwhile.

intereō, –īre, –iī, –itus, perish, be destroyed.

interest, *impers.*, it is of interest, it concerns.

interficiō, –ere, –fēcī, –fectus, kill, put to death.

interiaceō, –ēre, –uī, —, lie between.

interim, *adv.*, meanwhile.

interimō, –ere, –ēmī, –ēmptus, kill.

interior, –ius, interior; inland.

interitus, –ūs, *m.*, destruction, death.

interius, *adv.*, within.

intermittō, –ere, –mīsī, –missus, interrupt, neglect.

interneciō, –ōnis, *f.*, utter ruin, massacre.

internōdium, –dī, *n.*, space between two joints.

interpellātiō, –ōnis, *f.*, interruption.

interpellō, 1, interrupt.

interpres, –pretis, *m.*, interpreter.

interrogō, 1, ask.

intersum, –esse, –fuī, –futūrus, be between, be present, take part in; be different.

intervāllum, –ī, *n.*, interval, distance.

interveniō, –īre, –vēnī, –ventus, come in (between), interrupt.

interventus, –ūs, *m.*, intervention.

intestīnus, –a, –um, internal, civil.

intimus, –a, –um, inmost.

intonō, –āre, –uī, —, thunder.

intōnsus, –a, –um, unshorn, long-haired.

intrā, *prep. w. acc.*, within.

intremō, –ere, –uī, —, tremble.

intrō, 1, enter.

intrōdūcō, –ere, –dūxī, –ductus, bring in, introduce.

intueor, –ērī, –itus sum, look at *or* upon.

intus, *adv.*, within.

inultus, –a, –um, unpunished.

inūrō, –ere, –ussī, –ustus, burn in, brand.

inūsitātus, –a, –um, unusual.

inūtilis, –e, useless.

invādō, –ere, –vāsī, –vāsus, rush upon, seize.

inveniō, –īre, –vēnī, –ventus, come upon, find, discover, invent.

invēstīgō, 1, track, discover.

inveterāscō, –ere, –erāvī, —, become established.

invictus, –a, –um, unconquered, invincible.

invideō, –ēre, –vīdī, –vīsus, be envious toward, envy.

invidia, –ae, *f.*, envy, jealousy; unpopularity.

invidiōsus, –a, –um, envied.

invidus, –a, –um, envious, hateful.

inviolātē, *adv.*, inviolably.

invīsitātus, –a, –um, (unseen), uncommon.

invīsus, –a, –um, hated, displeasing, detested.

invītō, 1, invite.

invītus, –a, –um, unwilling, against one's will.

invocō, 1, call upon.

involvō, –ere, –volvī, –volūtus, wrap up in, bury.

iocor, –ārī, –ātus sum, jest, joke.

ioculāria, –ium, n. pl., jests, jokes.

iocus, –ī, m. (pl. ioca, n.), joke.

Iovis, Iovī, see Iuppiter.

Īphigenīa, –ae, f., Iphigenia (Ifigenī'a), daughter of Agamemnon.

ipse, ipsa, ipsum, intensive pron., self, himself, etc., very.

īra, –ae, f., anger.

īrāscor, –ī, īrātus sum, be angry at.

īrātus, –a, –um, angry.

irrēpō, –ere, –rēpsī, —, creep in.

irrētiō, –īre, –īvī, –ītus, ensnare.

irrīdeō, –ēre, –rīsī, –rīsus, laugh at, ridicule.

irruptiō, –ōnis, f., invasion, raid.

is, ea, id, dem. pron., this, that; he, she, it.

Ismēnus, –ī, m., Isme'nus, one of Niobe's sons.

iste, ista, istud, dem. pron., that (of yours), such, this; that fellow.

istīc, adv., there.

istinc, adv., from that place.

ita, adv., so, in this (such a) way, thus; as follows; w. ut, just as.

Italia, –ae, f., Italy.

itaque, adv., and so, therefore, accordingly.

item, adv., also, besides, likewise.

iter, itineris, n., journey, march, route.

iterum, adv., again, a second time.

iubeō, –ēre, iussī, iussus, order, command.

iūcundē, adv., pleasantly.

iūcundus, –a, –um, pleasant, agreeable.

iūdex, –dicis, m., judge, juror.

iūdiciālis, –e, judicial.

iūdicium, –cī, n., judgment, decision, opinion, trial; court.

iūdicō, 1, judge, decide.

iugulum, –ī, n., throat.

iugum, –ī, n., yoke; ridge.

Iugurtha, –ae, m., Jugur'tha, king of Numidia.

Iūlius, –a, –um, Julian; as noun, m., Julius, a Roman name.

iūmentum, –ī, n., (yoke animal), pack horse, donkey.

Iūn. = Iūnius, –a, –um, (of) June.

iungō, –ere, iunxī, iūnctus, join, harness.

Iūnia, –ae, f., Junia, a Vestal Virgin.

Iūnō, –ōnis, f., Juno, sister and wife of Jupiter.

Iūnōnius, –a, –um, sacred to Juno.

Iuppiter, Iovis, m., Jupiter, king of the gods.

iūre, adv., justly, rightly.

iūrō, 1, take an oath, swear.

iūs, iūris, n., right, justice, law, authority; iūs iūrandum, iūris iūrandī, n., oath.

iussū, *abl.*, by order.
iussum, –ī, *n.*, order.
iūstitia, –ae, *f.*, justice.
iūstus, –a, –um, just, proper.
iuvenālis, –e, youthful.
iuvenāliter, *adv.*, with youthful strength.
iuvenis, –is, *m.* and *f.*, youth.
iuventūs, –tūtis, *f.*, youth.
iuvō, –āre, iūvī, iūtus, help, aid; please.
iūxtā, *adv. and prep. w. acc.*, near, close to.

K

K., Kal. = Kalendae.
Kalendae, –ārum, *f. pl.*, the calends, *first day of the month.*

L

L., *abbreviation for* Lūcius (Lū′-shius), *a Roman name.*
labefactō, 1, cause to totter, weaken, destroy.
Laberius, –rī, *m.*, Labē′rius, *a Roman name.*
lābēs, –is, *f.*, fall; blot.
Labiēnus, –ī, *m.*, Lăbiē′nus.
labō, 1, be unsteady, roll.
labor, –ōris, *m.*, work, trouble, effort, hardship.
lābor, –ī, lāpsus sum, slip, glide; err.
labōriōsus, –a, –um, industrious.
labōrō, 1, labor, work (for).
lac, lactis, *n.*, milk.
lacer, –era, –erum, shattered.
lacertus, –ī, *m.*, arm.
lacessō, –ere, –īvī, –ītus, provoke, attack.

lacrima, –ae, *f.*, tear.
lacus, –ūs, *m.*, lake.
Laeca, –ae, *m.*, Laeca (Lē′ka), *a Roman name.*
laedō, –ere, laesī, laesus, hurt.
Laelius, –lī, *m.*, Laelius (Lē′-lius), *a Roman name.*
laetitia, –ae, *f.*, joy.
laetor, –ārī, –ātus sum, be glad, rejoice.
laetus, –a, –um, joyous, glad.
laevus, –a, –um, left.
lāmina, –ae, *f.*, (thin) layer.
lancea, –ae, *f.*, lance.
languēscō, –ere, –guī, —, become weak, languish.
languor, –ōris, *m.*, feebleness, lingering illness.
laniō, 1, tear (in pieces).
lapis, lapidis, *m.*, stone.
lāpsus, –ūs, *m.*, gliding, flight.
Lār, Laris, *m.*, Lar, hearth; *w.* familiāris, home.
Larcius, Larcius (Lar′shius), *a Roman name.*
lardum, –ī, *n.*, lard.
largior, –īrī, –ītus sum, be lavish, bestow.
lassus, –a, –um, tired, weary.
lātē, *adv.*, widely, far and wide.
latebrae, –ārum, *f.*, hiding place.
lateō, –ēre, latuī, —, lie hidden, hide, escape notice.
Latīnē, *adv.*, in Latin.
Latīniēnsis, –is, *m.*, Latini-ĕn′sis, *a Roman name.*
Latīnus, –a, –um, Latin.
lātitūdō, –dinis, *f.*, width, breadth.
Latium, –tī, *n.*, Latium (Lā′-shium), *a district of central Italy.*

Lātōna, –ae, *f.,* Latō′na, *mother of Apollo and Diana.*
Lātōus, –a, –um, of Latona.
latrō, –ōnis, *m.,* robber, bandit.
latrōcinium, –nī, *n.,* robbery, brigandage.
latus, lateris, *n.,* side, flank.
lātus, -a, –um, wide, broad.
laudō, 1, praise.
laurus, –ī, *f.,* laurel.
laus, laudis, *f.,* praise.
lavō, –āre, lāvī, lautus, wash, bathe.
laxō, 1, (open), relax.
Lebinthus, –ī, *f.,* Lebin′thus, *an island in the Aegean.*
lēctiō, –ōnis, *f.,* reading.
lēctitō, 1, read eagerly.
lēctus, -a, –um, choice, excellent.
lectus, –ī, *m.,* couch, bed.
lēgātiō, –ōnis, *f.,* embassy.
lēgātus, –ī, *m.,* envoy; legate, lieutenant general.
legiō, –ōnis, *f.,* legion.
lēgō, 1, appoint.
legō, –ere, lēgī, lēctus, gather, choose; read.
Lēnaeus, –a, –um, Lenaean, of Bacchus.
lēniō, –īre, –īvī, –ītus, soften, conciliate.
lēnis, –e, gentle, mild.
lēnitās, –tātis, *f.,* smoothness, leniency.
lentē, *adv.,* slowly.
Lentulus, –ī, *m.,* Len′tulus, *a Roman name.*
leō, –ōnis, *m.,* lion.
lepidus, -a, –um, charming.
Lepidus, –ī, *m.,* Lep′idus, *a Roman name.*

lepōs, –ōris, *m.,* charm, grace.
lētum, –ī, *n.,* death.
levis, –e, light; trivial.
levitās, –tātis, *f.,* lightness, lack of principle.
leviter, *adv.,* lightly, gently.
levō, 1, raise, lift, lighten, relieve.
lēx, lēgis, *f.,* law, condition, bill.
libellus, –ī, *m.,* (little) book, manuscript; indictment.
libenter, *adv.,* gladly, with pleasure.
liber, librī, *m.,* book.
līber, –era, –erum, free, unrestricted, allowed.
līberālis, –e, liberal.
līberāliter, *adv.,* like a free man, liberally, courteously.
līberē, *adv.,* freely; boldly.
līberī, –ōrum, *m. pl.,* children.
līberō, 1, free, set free.
lībertās, –tātis, *f.,* freedom.
lībertīnus, –ī, *m.,* freedman.
lībertus, –ī, *m.,* freedman.
libet, –ēre, libuit *or* **libitum est,** it pleases.
libīdō, –dinis, *f.,* longing, pleasure, lust.
lībō, 1, sip, offer; skim.
lībra, –ae, *f.,* pound.
librārius, –rī, *m.,* secretary.
lībrō, 1, poise.
Libyē, –ēs, *f.,* Libya (*in Africa*).
licentia, –ae, *f.,* liberty, freedom.
licet, –ēre, licuit *or* **licitum est,** it is permitted, one may.
Licinius, –nī, *m.,* Licinius (Lĭsĭn′ius), *a Roman name.*
ligna, –ōrum, *n.,* firewood.
līmes, –mitis, *m.,* path.

līnea, –ae, *f.*, line.

līneāmentum, –ī, *n.*, (line), feature.

lingua, –ae, *f.*, tongue, language.

līnum, –ī, *n.*, string, thread.

liquefaciō, –ere, –fēcī, –factus, melt.

liquidus, –a, –um, flowing, clear.

līquor, –ī, —, —, flow, melt.

littera, –ae, *f.*, letter (*of the alphabet*); *pl.*, letter (*epistle*); literature; learning.

litterātus, –a, –um, lettered, well educated.

litūra, –ae, *f.*, erasure.

lītus, –toris, *n.*, shore.

līvēns, *gen.* –entis, black and blue, bruised.

locō, 1, place.

Locrēnsēs, –ium, *m.*, the Lō'crians.

locuplēs, *gen.* –ētis, rich.

locuplētō, 1, enrich.

locus, –ī, *m.* (*pl.* loca, –ōrum, *n.*), place, room, rank, occasion.

longē, *adv.*, far, far away, by far; long.

longinquitās, –tātis, *f.*, distance, remoteness.

longinquus, –a, –um, remote, distant.

longitūdō, –dinis, *f.*, length.

longius, *see* longē.

longus, –a, –um, long; distant.

loquor, loquī, locūtus sum, speak, talk; say.

lōrum, –ī, *n.*, strap; *pl.*, reins.

lūceō, –ēre, lūxī, —, be light, shine.

luctor, –ārī, –ātus sum, struggle.

lūctus, –ūs, *m.*, sorrow, affliction.

lūculentus, –a, –um, brilliant.

Lūcullus, –ī, *m.*, Lucul'lus, *a Roman name.*

lūcus, –ī, *m.*, grove.

lūdibrium, –brī, *n.*, mockery, jest; abuse.

lūdō, –ere, lūsī, lūsus, play, jest.

lūdus, –ī, *m.*, game, sport; school; *pl.*, public games.

lūgeō, –ēre, lūxī, lūctus, mourn.

lūmen, lūminis, *n.*, light; eye.

lūna, –ae, *f.*, moon.

luō, –ere, luī, —, loose; suffer.

lūstrō, 1, (light up), survey.

lūsus, –ūs, *m.*, playing.

lūx, lūcis, *f.*, light, daylight; life.

lūxuria, –ae, *f.*, extravagance.

Lȳsō, –ōnis, *m.*, Lyso (Lī'sō), *a Greek name.*

M

M., *abbreviation for* Mārcus, –ī, *m.*, Marcus; M.', *abbreviation for* Mānius, –nī, *m.*, Mā'nius, *Roman names.*

Macedo, –ōnis, *m.*, Macedo (Măs'edo), *a Roman name.*

māchinātor, –ōris, *m.*, plotter.

māchinor, –ārī, –ātus sum, devise, plot.

maciēs, –ēī, *f.*, thinness.

mactō, 1, sacrifice, put to death, afflict.

madefaciō, –ere, –fēcī, –factus, soak.

madēscō, –ere, maduī, —, become moist.

madidus, –a, –um, drenched, dripping.

Maecēnātiānus, –ī, *m.,* Maecenatianus (Mēsēnāshiā'-nus), *a name.*

Maelius, –lī, *m.,* Maelius (Mē'-lius), *a Roman name.*

maeror, –ōris, *m.,* grief.

maestus, –a, –um, sad.

magis, *adv.,* more, rather; *superl.* **maximē,** most, especially.

magister, –trī, *m.,* teacher.

magistrātus, –ūs, *m.,* (public) office; magistrate.

magnificus, –a, –um, splendid.

magnitūdō, –dinis, *f.,* greatness, size, importance.

magnus, –a, –um, large, great; *comp.* **maior, maius,** greater; **maiōrēs (nātū),** ancestors, forefathers; *superl.* **maximus, –a, –um,** greatest, very great; **magnō opere,** greatly.

maior, *see* **magnus.**

male, *adv.,* badly, unsuccessfully; *comp.* **peius,** worse; *superl.* **pessimē,** worst.

maledīcō, –ere, –dīxī, –dictus, curse.

maledictum, –ī, *n.,* insult.

maleficium, –cī, *n.,* evil deed, wrong.

malignus, –a, –um, wicked, malicious.

malleolus, –ī, *m.,* firebrand.

Mallius, –lī, *m.,* Mallius, *a Roman name.*

mālō, mālle, māluī, —, prefer.

mālum, –ī, *n.,* apple.

malus, –a, –um, bad, evil; *comp.* **peior, peius,** worse;

superl. **pessimus, –a, –um,** very bad, worst; *as noun, n.,* evil, misfortune.

mancipium, –pī, *n.,* slave.

mandātum, –ī, *n.,* order, instruction, command.

mandō, 1, commit, instruct, intrust.

māne, *adv.,* early in the morning.

maneō, –ēre, mānsī, mānsus, remain, last.

manicātus, –a, –um, long-sleeved.

manifestō, *adv.,* openly, clearly.

manifestus, –a, –um, clear, plain.

Mānīlius, –lī, *m.,* Manīl'ius, *a Roman name.*

manipulāris, –is, *m.,* comrade (*member of the same maniple*).

Mānliānus, –a, –um, of Manlius.

Mānlius, –lī, *m.,* Manlius, *a Roman name.*

mānō, 1, flow, drip.

mānsuētūdō, –dinis, *f.,* gentleness.

manūmittō, –ere, –mīsī, –missus, make free.

manus, –ūs, *f.,* hand, handwriting; force, band.

Mārcellus, –ī, *m.,* Marcel'lus, *a Roman name.*

Mārcius, –cī, *m.,* Marcius (Mar'shius), *a Roman name.*

mare, maris, *n.,* sea.

Marīnus, –ī, *m.,* Marī'nus, *a Roman name.*

maritimus, –a, –um, of *or* on the sea, maritime.

marītus, –ī, *m.,* husband.

Marius, -rī, *m.,* Măr′ius, *a Roman general.*

marmor, –oris, *n.,* marble, stone.

Mārs, Mārtis, *m.,* Mars, *god of war.*

massa, –ae, *f.,* lump (of gold).

māter, mātris, *f.,* ₁nother.

mātrōna, –ae, *f.,* wife, married woman, matron.

mātūrē, *adv.,* early.

mātūrēscō, –ere, mātūruī, —, come to maturity.

mātūritās, –tātis, *f.,* ripeness, maturity.

mātūrus, –a, –um, ripe, mature; early.

maximē, *see* **magis.**

maximus, *see* **magnus.**

Maximus, –ī, *m.,* Maximus, *a Roman name.*

Mēdēa, –ae, *f.,* Medē′a, *daughter of the king of Colchis.*

medeor, –ērī, —, cure, remedy.

medicāmen, –minis, *n.,* medicine.

medicīna, –ae, *f.,* remedy.

medicus, –ī, *m.,* physician.

mediocris, –cre, moderate, ordinary, of ordinary attainments.

mediocriter, *adv.,* slightly, moderately.

meditor, –ārī, –ātus sum, plan, compose.

medius, –a, –um, middle, midst (of), intervening; *as noun, n.,* middle.

Megalēnsia, –ium, *n.,* festival of Cybele (Sĭb′elē).

Megarēius, –a, –um, son of Megareus.

Megareus, –ī, *m.,* Měg′areus, *Hippomenes' father.*

mehercule, meherculēs, *interj.,* by Hercules, truly.

mel, mellis, *n.,* honey.

melius, *see* **bene.**

membrum, –ī, *n.,* limb, member.

meminī, meminisse (*perf. translated as pres.*), remember.

memorābilis, –e, memorable.

memoria, –ae, *f.,* memory.

memorō, 1, call to mind, mention, relate.

mēns, mentis, *f.,* mind, intention, purpose, feeling, heart.

mēnsa, –ae, *f.,* table, banquet.

mēnsis, –is, *m.,* month.

menta, –ae, *f.,* mint.

mentiō, –ōnis, *f.,* (a calling to mind), mention.

mentior, –īrī, –ītus sum, lie, deceive; invent

mercātor, –ōris, *m.,* merchant.

mercēs, –ēdis, *f.,* pay; reward.

mercule, merculēs, *see* **mehercule.**

mereō, –ēre, meruī, meritus, deserve, earn.

mergō, –ere, mersī, mersus, dip; submerge.

merīdiēs, –ēī, *m.,* noon.

meritum, –ī, *n.,* service.

meritō, *adv.,* justly.

merx, mercis, *f.,* goods, merchandise.

Mescinius, –nī, *m.,* Mescinius (Messĭn′ius), *a Roman name.*

Messāna, –ae, *f.,* Messina (Messē′na), *a city in Sicily.*

messis, –is, *f.,* harvest.

–met, *enclitic,* -self.

mēta, –ae, *f.*, goal.
Metellus, –ī, *m.*, Metel′lus, *a Roman name.*
mētior, –īrī, mēnsus sum, measure.
metuō, –ere, –uī, —, fear, dread.
metus, –ūs, *m.*, fear, terror.
meus, –a, –um, my, mine.
micāns, *gen.* –antis, shining.
Midās, –ae, *m.*, Mī′das, *king of Phrygia.*
mīles, mīlitis, *m.*, soldier.
mīlitāris, –e, military.
mīlitia, –ae, *f.*, military service, war.
mīlitō, 1, serve as a soldier.
mīlle, thousand; *pl.*, mīlia.
minae, –ārum, *f.*, threats.
Minerva, –ae, *f.*, Minerva, *goddess of wisdom.*
minimē, *superl. adv.*, least; not at all.
minimus, *see* parvus.
minister, –trī, *m.*, servant, attendant; ministra, –ae, *f.*, deaconess.
ministerium, –rī, *n.*, service, office.
minitor, –ārī, –ātus sum, threaten.
minor, –ārī, –ātus sum, threaten.
minor, *see* parvus.
Mīnōs, –ōis, *m.*, Mīnos, *king of Crete.*
minuō, –ere, –uī, –ūtus, lessen; break up.
minus, *adv.*, less; not.
mīrābilis, –e, marvelous.
mīrābile, –is, *n.*, miracle, wondrous deed.

mīrāculum, –ī, *n.*, wonder, miracle; *pl.*, monsters.
mīrē, *adv.*, wonderfully, strangely.
mīrificus, –a, –um, singular, extraordinary
mīror, –ārī, atus sum, wonder, admire.
mīrus, –a, –um, strange, wonderful, marvelous.
misceō, –ēre, –uī, mixtus, mix, mingle.
Mīsēnum, –ī, *n.*, Mīsē′num, *a town and promontory near Naples.*
miser, –era, –erum, wretched, poor.
miserābilis, –e, pitiable, wretched, deplorable.
misereor, –ērī, –itus sum, have pity.
miseria, –ae, *f.*, wretchedness, trouble.
misericordia, –ae, *f.*, pity, compassion.
miseror, –ārī, –ātus sum, pity.
Mithridātēs, –is, *m.*, Mithridā′tēs, *king of Pontus.*
Mithridāticus, –a, –um, Mithridā′tic.
mītis, –e, mild, kind.
mittō, –ere, mīsī, missus, send.
mixtus, *see* misceō.
mōbilitās, –tātis, *f.*, fickleness.
moderāmen, –minis, *n.*, control.
moderātiō, –ōnis, *f.*, moderation.
moderātus, –a, –um, self-controlled.
moderor, –ārī, –ātus sum, guide.
modestus, –a, –um, moderate, scrupulous.

Modestus, –ī, *m.*, Modes'tus, *a Roman name.*

modicē, *adv.*, discreetly.

modicus, –a, –um, moderate, small.

modius, –dī, *m.*, peck.

modo, *adv.*, only, merely; lately, just now; **nōn modo . . . sed** (*or* **vērum**) **etiam,** not only . . . but also; **modo . . . modo,** now . . . now; *conj.*, provided (that).

modulor, –ārī, –ātus sum, play.

modus, –ī, *m.*, measure; moderation; manner, method, way; **quem ad modum,** how, as; **eius** (*or* **huius**) **modī,** of this kind, such.

moenia, –ium, *n. pl.*, (city) walls.

mōlēs, –is, *f.*, mass, burden.

molestia, –ae, *f.*, worry, vexation.

molestus, –a, –um, troublesome, annoying, disagreeable.

mōlior, –īrī, –ītus sum, strive, plan, undertake; plot.

molliō, –īre, –īvī, –ītus, soften.

mollis, –e, soft; easy, mild.

molliter, *adv.*, softly, gently.

moneō, –ēre, monuī, monitus, remind, advise, warn; suggest.

monitus, –ūs, *m.*, warning.

mōns, montis, *m.*, mountain, hill.

montānus, –a, –um, of the mountains.

monumentum, –ī, *n.*, memorial, monument, remembrance.

mora, –ae, *f.*, delay.

morbus, –ī, *m.*, disease.

moribundus, –a, –um, dying.

morior, morī, mortuus sum, die.

moror, –ārī, –ātus sum, delay, linger.

mors, mortis, *f.*, death.

morsus, –ūs, *m.*, (biting), teeth.

mortālis, –e, mortal, human; *as noun, m.*, a mortal.

mortuus, –a, –um, dead.

mōrum, –ī, *n.*, mulberry.

mōrus, –ī, *f.*, mulberry tree.

mōs, mōris, *m.*, custom, manner; *pl.*, customs, character.

mōtus, –ūs, *m.*, movement, activity.

moveō, –ēre, mōvī, mōtus, move; influence, disturb.

mox, *adv.*, soon, presently.

Mūcius, –cī, *m.*, Mucius (Mū'shius), *a Roman name.*

mūcrō, –ōnis, *m.*, point, edge.

mulier, –eris, *f.*, woman.

multitūdō, –dinis, *f.*, multitude, great number.

multō, 1, punish.

multō, *adv.*, much; by far.

multum, *adv.*, much; **plūs,** more; **plūrimum,** most.

multus, –a, –um, much; *pl.*, many; *comp.* **plūrēs, plūra,** more, several; *superl.* **plūrimus, –a, –um,** most, very many.

mūlus, –ī, *m.*, mule.

Mulvius, –a, –um, Mulvian.

mundus, –ī, *m.*, world, heavens.

mūniceps, –cipis, *m.*, fellow citizen.

mūnicipālis, –e, municipal.

mūnicipium, –pī, *n.*, municipal (free) town.

mūniō, –īre, –īvī, –ītus, fortify, defend.

mūnītiō, –ōnis, ƒ., fortifying, building.

mūnus, mūneris, n., duty, office, service; gift, boon.

Mūrēna, –ae, m., Murē'na, a Roman name.

mūrex, –ricis, m., (shell-fish), purple.

murmur, –uris, n., whisper.

mūrus, –ī, m., wall.

mūs, mūris, m., mouse.

Mūsa, –ae, ƒ., Muse, one of the nine goddesses of the fine arts.

mūtābilis, –e, capable of change.

mūtātiō, –ōnis, ƒ., change.

mūtō, 1, change.

mūtus, –a, –um, mute.

Mytilēnaeus, –a, –um, of Mytilene (Mitilē'nē), a city in Asia Minor.

N

Nāides, -um, ƒ., Nāiads (water nymphs).

nam, conj., for.

namque, conj., for.

nancīscor, nancīscī, nactus (nānctus) sum, get, obtain, find, meet.

nārrō, 1, tell, relate.

nāscor, nāscī, nātus sum, be born; rise.

Nasta, –ae, m., Nasta, a Roman name.

nātālis, –e, of one's birth; nātālis, –is, m., birthday.

nātiō, –ōnis, ƒ., nation, tribe.

natō, 1, swim, float.

nātūra, –ae, ƒ., nature, character.

nātūrālis, –e, natural.

nātus, –a, –um, born; as noun, m. and ƒ., son, daughter; pl., children.

naufragō, 1, be wrecked.

nauta, –ae, m., sailor.

nauticus, –a, –um, of ships, naval.

nāvālis, –e, naval.

nāvicula, –ae, ƒ., small vessel, boat.

nāviculārius, –rī, m., shipowner.

nāvigātiō, –ōnis, ƒ., sailing.

nāvigō, 1, sail; set sail.

nāvis, –is, ƒ., ship, boat.

nē, adv., no, not; nē . . . quidem (emphatic word between), not even, not . . . either; conj., that . . . not, not to, lest, for fear that.

–ne (enclitic), introduces questions; whether.

Neāpolitānī, –ōrum, m., the Neapŏl'itans, people of Naples.

nebula, –ae, ƒ., mist, cloud.

nec, see neque.

necessāriō, adv., from necessity.

necessārius, –a, –um, necessary; as noun, m., relative, friend.

necesse, indecl. adj., necessary.

necessitās, –tātis, ƒ., necessity.

necessitūdō, –dinis, ƒ., necessity; relationship, bond.

necō, 1, kill, put to death, murder.

nefāriē, adv., wickedly.

nefārius, –a, –um, impious, base.

neglegēns, *gen.* –entis, careless.

neglegenter, *adv.*, carelessly.

neglegentia, –ae, *f.*, neglect.

neglegō, –ere, –lēxī, –lēctus, disregard, neglect.

negō, 1, say no, deny, say . . . not.

negōtior, –ārī, –ātus sum, carry on business, be a trader.

negōtium, –tī, *n.*, business, affair, trouble; undertaking; *w.* dare, instruct.

nēmō, *dat.* nēminī, *acc.* nēminem (*no other forms*), no one.

nepōs, –ōtis, *m.*, grandson.

Nepōs, –ōtis, *m.*, Nē′pos, *a Roman historian.*

Neptūnius, –a, –um, of Neptune.

Neptūnus, –ī, *m.*, Neptune, *god of the sea.*

neque (nec), and not, nor; neque . . . neque, neither . . . nor.

nequeō, –īre, –īvī, —, be unable.

nēquīquam, *adv.*, in vain.

nēquitia, –ae, *f.*, worthlessness, neglect.

nervōsus, –a, –um, sinewy.

nervus, –ī, *m.*, sinew, nerve, string.

nesciō, –īre, –īvī, —, not know, be ignorant; *w.* an, I know not whether, very likely.

nēve (neu), *conj.*, and not, nor, and that . . . not.

nex, necis, *f.*, murder, (violent) death.

nexus, –ūs, *m.*, (binding together), embrace.

nī = nisi.

Nīcānor, –oris, *m.*, Nicā′nor, *a name.*

Nīcomēdēnsis, –e, of the Nicomē′dians; *as noun, m. pl.*, Nicomedians.

Nīcomēdīa, –ae, *f.*, Nicomē′dia, *capital of Bithynia.*

nīdus, –ī, *m.*, nest.

niger, –gra, –grum, black.

nihil, nothing; not at all; nihildum, nothing as yet.

nihilō minus, none the less, nevertheless.

nīl = nihil.

Nīlus, –ī, *m.*, the Nile, *a river in Egypt.*

nimis, *adv.*, too much, too.

nimium, *adv.*, too, too much.

nimius, –a, –um, excessive, too (great).

Ninus, –ī, *m.*, Nī′nus, *an Assyrian king.*

Niobē, –ēs, *f.*, Nī′obe, *queen of Thebes.*

nisi, *conj.*, unless, except, if not.

nitidus, –a, –um, shining; sleek.

nītor, nītī, nīxus (nīsus) sum, strive, struggle.

niveus, –a, –um, snow-white.

nix, nivis, *f.*, snow.

nōbilis, –e, well-known, famous, noble.

nōbilitās, –tātis, *f.*, fame; nobility.

nocēns, *gen.* –entis, harmful; guilty.

noceō, –ēre, –uī, nocitus, do harm to, injure.

nocturnus, –a, –um, of *or* by night.

nōlō, nōlle, nōluī, —, be unwilling, not wish.

nōmen, nōminis, *n.*, name.

nōmenclātor,   –ōris,   *m.*, prompter.

nōminātim, *adv.*, by name, expressly.

nōminō, 1, name, call.

nŏn, *adv.*, not.

Nōn. = Nōnae.

Nōnae, –ārum, *f.*, the Nones, *the ninth day before the Ides.*

nōndum, *adv.*, not yet.

Nōniānus, –ī, *m.*, Nōniā'nus, *a name.*

nōscō, –ere, nòvī, nōtus, learn; *in perf. tenses,* have learned, know.

noster, –tra, –trum, our.

nota, –ae, *f.*, mark.

notābilis, –e, noteworthy, remarkable.

notārius, –rī, *m.*, secretary.

nōtitia, –ae, *f.*, knowledge, acquaintance,

notō, 1, mark, note, observe.

nōtus, –a, –um, known, familiar.

novem, nine.

November, –bris, –bre, (of) November.

novēnī, –ae, –a, nine each.

novissimē, *adv.*, quite recently.

novitās, –tātis, *f.*, newness, strangeness.

novus, –a, –um, new, strange; last.

nox, noctis, *f.*, night.

nūbēs, –is, *f.*, cloud.

nūbila, –ōrum, *n.*, clouds.

nūbō, –ere, nūpsī, nūptus, veil oneself, wed.

nūdus, –a, –um, bare, naked, vacant.

nūgae, –ārum, *f.*, trifles.

nūllus, –a, –um, no, none.

num, *interrog. adv. expecting a negative answer; w. indir. questions,* whether.

Numantia, –ae, *f.*, Numantia (Nūman'shia), *a city in Spain.*

nūmen, –minis, *n.*, nod; divine will *or* power; divinity.

numerō, 1, count, number.

numerus, –ī, *m.*, number.

Numidicus, –ī, *m.*, Nūmĭd'icus. *a Roman name.*

nummus, –ī, *m.*, coin, money.

numquam, *adv.*, never.

nunc, *adv.*, now.

nūntiō, 1, announce, report.

nūntius, –tī, *m.*, messenger; message, news, report, order.

nūper, *adv.*, recently.

nūptiae, –ārum, *f.*, wedding.

nūrus,   –ī,   *f.*,   daughter-in-law.

nusquam, *adv.*, nowhere.

nūtriō, –īre, –īvī, –ītus, nourish, keep alive.

nūtus, –ūs, *m.*, nod, will.

nux, nucis, *f.*, nut.

nympha, –ae, *f.*, nymph.

O

ō! *interj.* O! oh!

ob, *prep. w. acc.*, toward; on account of, for; **quam ob rem**, why, wherefore.

obdūcō, –ere, –dūxī, –ductus, draw (over).

obeō, –īre, –īvī, –itus, (go to meet), attend to, engage in; reach.

obiciō, –ere, –iēcī, –iectus, throw before, expose.

oblectō, 1, delight.

obligō, 1, bind (to), put under obligation.

oblinō, –ere, –lēvī, –litus, stain.

oblīviō, –ōnis, f., forgetting, forgetfulness.

oblīvīscor, –ī, –lītus sum, forget.

oboediō, –īre, –īvī, –ītus, give heed to.

obruō, –ere, –ruī, –rutus, overwhelm, bury.

obscūrē, adv., obscurely.

obscūrō, 1, darken, hide.

obscūrus, –a, –um, dark, secret, obscure.

obsecrō, 1, implore.

obsecundō, 1, comply with.

observō, 1, heed, observe.

obses, –sidis, m., hostage.

obsideō, –ēre, –sēdī, –sessus, beset, besiege, hem in.

obsidiō, –ōnis, f., siege.

obsolēscō, –ere, –solēvī, –solētus, grow old, lose force.

obstinātiō, –ōnis, f., stubbornness.

obstinātus, –a, –um, stubborn.

obstipēscō, see obstupēscō.

obstō, –āre, –stitī, —, withstand, stand in the way of.

obstrepō, –ere, –uī, —, drown out (with noise).

obstringō, –ere, –strīnxī, –strictus, bind.

obstruō, –ere, –strūxī, –strūctus, build up; bar.

obstupēscō, –ere, –stupuī, —, be astounded.

obsum, –esse, –fuī, —, be against, injure.

obtemperō, 1, obey, consult.

obtestor, –ārī, –ātus sum, entreat.

obtineō, –ēre, –tinuī, –tentus, hold, obtain.

obtrectātiō, –ōnis, f., disparagement.

obtrectō, 1, object to, oppose.

obviam, adv., in the way; w. veniō, come to meet.

occāsiō, –ōnis, f., opportunity.

occāsus, –ūs, m., going down; downfall; occāsus sōlis, sunset, west.

occidō, –ere, –cidī, –cāsus, fall down; die.

occīdō, –ere, –cīdī, –cīsus, kill, murder.

occulō, –ere, –uī, –cultus, hide.

occultē, adv., secretly.

occultō, 1, hide.

occultus, –a, –um, hidden, secret.

occupātiō, –ōnis, f., business.

occupō, 1, seize, occupy.

occurrō, –ere, –currī, –cursus, run against, meet.

ōceanus, –ī, m., ocean.

Octāvius, –vī, m., Octā'vius, a Roman name.

Oct. = Octōber, –bris, –bre, of October.

octō, eight.

oculus, –ī, m., eye.

ōdī, ōdisse, ōsūrus, defective, hate.

odium, odī, n., hatred.

odōrātus, –a, –um, fragrant.

offendō, –ere, –fendī, –fēnsus, (strike against); come upon, find.

offēnsiō, –ōnis, *f.,* (hitting against), dislike, disfavor; defeat.

offēnsus, –a, –um, offensive.

offerō, –ferre, obtulī, oblātus, (bear to), offer, present, expose.

officiōsus, –a, –um, obliging, dutiful.

officium, –cī, *n.,* duty, service, allegiance.

ōlim, *adv.,* formerly, once; hereafter.

Olympus, –ī, *m.,* Olym'pus, *the home of the gods.*

ōmen, ōminis, *n.,* omen.

omittō, –ere, omīsī, omissus, let go, pass over.

omnīnō, *adv.,* altogether, entirely, at all, to be sure.

omnipotēns, *gen.* **–entis,** all-powerful.

omnis, omne, all, every.

Onchēstius, –a, –um, of Onches'tus, *a city in Boeotia.*

onerāriae (*w.* **nāvēs**), transports, freighters.

onerō, 1, load with.

onus, oneris, *n.,* load, burden, cargo.

onustus, –a, –um, loaded.

opācus, –a, –um, shaded, gloomy.

opera, –ae, *f.,* work, service, assistance, aid; *w.* **dare,** see to it.

operiō, –īre, –uī, opertus, cover.

opifex, –ficis, *m.,* workman.

Opīmius, –mī, *m.,* Opĭm'ius, *a Roman name.*

opīmus, –a, –um, fat, splendid, rich.

opīniō, –ōnis, *f.,* belief, opinion, fancy, expectation.

opīnor, –ārī, –ātus sum, imagine, judge, think.

oportet, –ēre, oportuit, it is fitting *or* necessary, ought.

oppetō, –ere, –īvī, –ītus, meet; *w.* **mortem,** die.

oppidum, –ī, *n.,* town.

Oppius, –ī, *m.,* Op'pius, *a Roman name.*

opportūnē, *adv.,* fitly, opportunely.

opportūnitās, –tātis, *f.,* (fitness), fortunate circumstance.

opportūnus, –a, –um, fit, timely.

opprimō, –ere, –pressī, –pressus, overcome, crush.

oppugnō, 1, attack.

ops, opis, *f.,* aid, might; *pl.,* wealth, resources, influence.

optimātēs, –ium, *m.,* best men, nobility, optimates.

optimē, *see* **bene.**

optimus, *see* **bonus.**

optō, 1, wish, desire.

opus, operis, *n.,* work, labor, task, exercise; **magnō opere,** greatly; **tantō opere,** so greatly.

opus, *n., indeclinable,* need, necessity; **opus est,** it is necessary, there is need.

opusculum, –ī, *n.,* little work.

ōra, –ae, *f.,* shore.

ōrātiō, –ōnis, *f.,* speech, words, eloquence; argument.

orbis, –is, *m.,* circle; *w.* **or** *without* **terrae** *or* **terrārum,** the world (*the circle of lands around the Mediterranean*).

orbus, –a, –um, childless.

ōrdō, ōrdinis, *m.*, row, order, turn, rank, company, body; class.

oriēns, -entis, *m.*, rising sun, east.

Ōriōn, -ōnis, *m.*, Ōrī'on, *a constellation.*

orior, -īrī, ortus sum, arise, descend.

ōrnāmentum, -ī, *n.*, (mark of) distinction, decoration, ornament.

ōrnātē, *adv.*, elegantly.

ōrnātus, -a, -um, adorned, fitted; honorable, distinguished.

ōrnō, 1, adorn, furnish, equip; honor.

ōrō, 1, pray, implore, beg.

ortus, -ūs, *m.*, rising; east.

ōs, ōris, *n.*, mouth, face, expression; lips.

Oscē, *adv.*, in Oscan.

ōsculum, -ī, *n.*, kiss.

ostendō, -ere, ostendī, ostentus, (stretch out), point out, show, declare.

ostentō, 1, hold up, display.

Ōstiēnsis, -e, at Os'tia, *the port of Rome.*

ōstium, -tī, *n.*, mouth.

ōtiōsus, -a, -um, idle, unemployed; peaceful.

ōtium, ōtī, *n.*, leisure, quiet, peace.

ōvum, -ī, *n.*, egg.

P

P., *abbreviation for* Pūblius.

pābulum, -ī, *n.*, pasture.

pācātus, -a, -um, subdued, peaceful.

pacīscor, -ī, pactus sum, agree, appoint.

pācō, 1, make peaceful, subdue.

pactum, -ī, *n.*, agreement; manner.

pactus, *see* pacīscor.

paene, *adv.*, almost.

paenitentia, -ae, *f.*, repentance.

paenitet, -ēre, -uit, *impers.*, it makes regret, it grieves.

palaestra, -ae, *f.*, wrestling place.

palam, *adv.*, openly, publicly.

Palātium, -tī, *n.* the Pal'atīne, *one of the seven hills of Rome.*

palātum, -ī, *n.*, palate.

Palīcānus, -ī, *m.*, Palicā'nus, *a Roman name.*

palla, -ae, *f.*, robe.

pallēscō, -ere, -uī, —, become pale, turn yellow.

palma, -ae, *f.*, palm; date.

palūs, -ūdis, *f.*, swamp.

Pamphȳlia, -ae, *f.*, Pamphyl'ia, *a country in Asia Minor.*

Pān, Pānis, *m.*, Pan, *god of shepherds.*

pānis, -is, *m.*, bread.

panthēra, -ae, *f.*, panther.

Pāpius, -a, -um, Pä'pian.

pār, paris, equal, a match for, like.

parātus, -a, -um, ready, prepared.

parcē, *adv.*, sparingly.

parcō, -ere, pepercī, parsus, spare.

parcus, -a, -um, frugal, saving.

parēns, parentis, *m. and f.*, parent.

Parentīnī, -ōrum, *m.*, the Parentī'nī.

pāreō, -ēre, -uī, -itus, obey.

pariēs, -etis, m., wall (of a house).

parilis, -e, equal.

pariō, -ere, peperī, partus, give birth, produce; gain.

pariter, adv., equally, in like manner, likewise.

Parnāsis, -idis, of Parnas'sus.

parō, 1, get, prepare.

Paros, -ī, f., Pa'ros, an island in the Aegean.

parricīda, -ae, m., parricide, murderer.

parricīdium, -dī, n., parricide, murder.

pars, partis, f., part, rôle; direction; duty.

particeps, participis, m., participant, sharer.

partim, adv., partly; partim . . . partim, partly . . . partly, some . . . others.

partior, -īrī, -ītus sum, divide, share.

parum, adv., little, too little.

parvulus, -a, -um, very small, petty.

parvus, -a, -um, small, little, slight.

pāscō, -ere, pāvī, pāstus, feed, feast.

Passennus, -ī, m., Passen'nus, Roman name.

passim, adv., everywhere.

passus, -ūs, m., step, pace; mīlle passūs, mile.

pāstiō, -ōnis, f., pasturage.

pāstor, -ōris, m., shepherd.

pāstus, -ūs, m., pasture, fodder.

Patāvium, -vī, n., Patā'vium (Padua, a city in Italy).

patefaciō, -ere, -fēcī, -factus, lay open, open (up), expose.

pateō, -ēre, patuī, —, stand or be open, be exposed; patēns, -entis, extending.

pater, patris, m., father; pl., senators, patricians.

paternus, -a, -um, of a father.

patientia, -ae, f., patience; ability to bear.

patior, patī, passus sum, suffer, endure, allow.

Patiscus, -ī, m., Patis'cus, a name.

patria, -ae, f., fatherland, native land, country.

patricius, -a, -um, patrician.

patrius, -a, -um, of a father, ancestral.

patrōcinium, -nī, n., patronage, defense.

patrōnus, -ī, m., patron.

patulus, -a, -um, spreading, wide.

paucitās, -tātis, f., scarcity.

pauculus, -a, -um, very few, very little.

paucus, -a, -um, little; pl., few, only a few.

paulātim, adv., gradually, little by little.

paulisper, adv., for a short time.

paulō, adv., a little.

paulum, -ī, n., a little.

Paulus, -ī, m., Paulus, a Roman name.

pauper, gen. -eris, poor.

paupertās, -tātis, f., poverty.

paveō, -ēre, pāvī, —, be afraid, tremble with fear.

pavidus, -a, -um, quaking.

pavīmentum, -ī, n., floor, pavement.

pāx, pācis, f., peace, truce.

peccātum, -ī, n., mistake.

peccō, 1, sin.

pectus, -toris, n., breast; heart.

pecūlium, -lī, n., savings.

pecūnia, -ae, f., money; pl., riches.

pecus, -coris, n., cattle, flock.

pecus, -udis, f., beast; pl., herds.

pedester, -tris, -tre, on foot, infantry.

peditātus, -ūs, m., foot soldiers, infantry.

pelagus, -ī, n., sea.

pellō, -ere, pepulī, pulsus, beat, drive, put to flight; banish.

Pēlūsium, -sī, n., Pelūs'ium, a city in Egypt.

pendeō, -ēre, pependī, —, hang, hover.

pendō, -ere, pependī, pēnsus, weigh; pay.

penetrō, 1, penetrate, enter.

penitus, -a, -um, remote; penitus, adv., deeply, within.

penna, -ae, f., feather, wing.

pēnsitō, 1, (weigh out), pay.

per, prep. w. acc., through, by, over, among, along, by means of, during; in the name of.

peradulēscēns, gen. -entis, very young.

peragō, -ere, -ēgī, -āctus, complete; obey.

peragrō, 1, traverse.

peramanter, adv., very lovingly.

perambulō, 1, ramble through or over.

perbrevis, -e, very short.

percipiō, -ere, -cēpī, -ceptus, seize; hear, learn, appreciate, obtain.

percontor, -ārī, -ātus sum, inquire.

percutiō, -ere, -cussī, -cussus, strike, pierce, beat.

perditus, -a, -um, lost; desperate, corrupt.

perdō, -dere, -didī, -ditus, lose, waste, destroy.

perdūcō, -ere, -dūxī, -ductus, lead or bring (through).

peregrē, adv., abroad.

peregrīnātiō, -ōnis, f., sojourn abroad, travel.

peregrīnor, -ārī, -ātus sum, go abroad.

perēmptus, see perimō.

perennis, -e, (through the year), unceasing, perpetual.

pereō, -īre, -iī, -itus, perish, disappear.

perexiguus, -a, -um, very small.

perfectus, -a, -um, finished, ideal.

perferō, -ferre, -tulī, -lātus, carry (through), report, bring; endure, suffer.

perficiō, -ere, -fēcī, -fectus, (do thoroughly), finish, carry out, accomplish; cause, bring about.

perfringō, -ere, -frēgī, -frāctus, break through or down, violate.

perfugiō, -ere, -fūgī, —, flee for refuge, go over, desert.

perfugium, -gī, n., refuge.

pergō, -ere, perrēxī, perrēctus, proceed, continue, hasten.

perīclitor, –ārī, –ātus sum, try, risk, endanger.

perīculōsus, –a, –um, dangerous.

perīculum, –ī, *n.*, trial, danger.

perimō, –ere, –ēmī, –ēmptus, destroy.

perinīquus, –a, –um, most unjust.

perītē, *adv.*, skilfully.

perītus, –a, –um, skilled, acquainted with.

perlegō, –ere, –lēgī, –lēctus, read through, examine thoroughly.

permagnus, –a, –um, very large.

permaneō, –ēre, –mānsī, –mānsus, remain.

permātūrēscō, –ere, –mātūruī, —, ripen fully.

permittō, –ere, –mīsī, –missus, (let go through), allow, intrust.

permoveō, –ēre, –mōvī, –mōtus, move deeply, arouse.

permultus, –a, –um, very much; very many.

permūtātiō, –ōnis, *f.*, exchange.

permūtō, 1, exchange.

perniciēs, –ēī, *f.*, destruction, ruin.

perniciōsus, –a, –um, destructive, dangerous.

pernoctō, 1, spend the night.

perofficiōsē, *adv.*, very attentively.

perōsus, –a, –um, loathing.

perpetuō, *adv.*, permanently.

perpetuus, –a, –um, lasting; in perpetuum, forever.

Persae, –ārum, *m. pl.*, the Persians; Persia.

persaepe, *adv.*, very often.

perscrībō, –ere, –scrīpsī, –scrīptus, write out.

persequor, –sequī, –secūtus sum, follow up, pursue, avenge.

Persēs, –ae, *m.*, Per'seus, *king of Macedonia.*

persevērantia, –ae, *f.*, persistence.

persevērō, 1, persist, continue.

perspiciō, –ere, –spexī, –spectus, see (through), perceive, examine.

perstō, –stāre, –stitī, –stātus, continue standing.

persuādeō, –ēre, –suāsī, –suāsus, persuade.

perterreō, –ēre, –uī, –territus, frighten thoroughly, alarm.

pertimēscō, –ere, –timuī, —, become thoroughly alarmed; fear, dread.

pertinācia, –ae, *f.*, obstinacy.

pertineō, –ēre, –tinuī, –tentus, (extend to), pertain to, belong to, concern; tend.

perturbō, 1, disturb, alarm, throw into confusion.

pervādō, –ere, –vāsī, –vāsus, (go through), spread, fill.

pervagor, –ārī, –ātus sum, wander through, spread through, pervade.

perveniō, –īre, –vēnī, –ventus, come (through), arrive reach, attain.

pēs, pedis, *m.*, foot.

pessimus, *see* **malus.**

pestilentia, –ae, *f.*, malaria, fever.

pestis, –is, *f.*, plague, destruction, curse, ruin.

petītiō, –ōnis, *f.*, thrust; canvass.

petō, –ere, petīvī, petītus, seek, ask; attack.

Petraītēs, –ītis, *m.*, Petraī'tēs, *a name.*

Petreius, –ī, *m.*, Petre'ius, *a lieutenant of Pompey.*

pexus, –a, –um, combed.

Phaedimus, –ī, *m.*, Phaedimus, (Fē'dimus), *one of Niobe's sons.*

Phaethōn, –ontis, *m.*, Phaëthon (Fā'ethon), *son of Phoebus.*

pharetra, –ae, *f.*, quiver.

Philargyrus, –ī, *m.*, Philargyrus (Filar'jirus), *a name.*

Philēmōn, –onis, *m.*, Philē'mon, *husband of Baucis.*

Philippus, –ī, *m.*, Philip'pus, *a Roman name;* Philip, *king of Macedonia.*

philosophia, –ae, *f.*, philosophy.

philosophus, –ī, *m.*, philosopher.

Philotīmus, –ī, *m.*, Philotī'mus, *a name.*

Phlegōn, –ontis, *m.*, Phlegon (Fle'gon), *one of the horses of the Sun.*

Phoebē, –ēs, *f.*, Phoebe (Fē'bē), Diana.

Phoebus, –ī, *m.*, Phoebus (Fē'bus), Apollo.

Phrygius, –a, –um, Phrygian (Frij'ian).

pictus, –a, –um, painted.

piget, –ēre, piguit, it grieves.

pignus, –noris, *n.*, pledge.

pigrē, *adv.*, slowly, reluctantly.

pila, –ae, *f.*, ball, ball-playing.

pīlus, –ī, *m.*, first maniple (*of a cohort*).

pinguis, –e, fat, comfortable.

pīnus, –ūs, *f.*, pine tree; ship.

piscis, –is, *m.*, fish.

Pīsistratus, –ī, *m.*, Pīsis'tratus, *tyrant of Athens.*

Pīsō, –ōnis, *m.*, Pī'so, *a Roman name.*

pius, –a, –um, devoted, loyal, loving.

Pius, –ī, *m.*, Pī'us, *a Roman name.*

placeō, –ēre, placuī, placitus, be pleasing to, please; *impers.*, it seems best, (he) decides, it is decided by.

placidus, –a, –um, calm.

placitus, –a, –um, pleasing, acceptable.

plācō, 1, appease.

plāga, –ae, *f.*, blow; disaster.

Plancus, –ī, *m.*, Plancus, *a Roman name.*

plānē, *adv.*, plainly

plangō, –ere, plānxī, plānctus, beat.

plangor, –ōris, *m.*, beating (*of the breast*); shrieks.

plānus, –a, –um, level, plane.

plausus, –ūs, *m.*, clapping of hands, applause.

plēbs, plēbis, *f.*, people, common people.

plēctrum, –ī, *n.*, pick (*for striking the lyre*).

Pleiades, –um, *f.*, Plē'iadēs, *the seven daughters of Atlas.*

plēnus, –a, –um, full, abounding in.

plērīque, –aeque, –aque, most, the majority.

plērumque, usually.

plexus, –a, –um, woven.

Plīnius, –nī, *m.*, Pliny, *a Roman author.*

Plōtius, –tī, *m.*, Plotius (Plō'-shius), *a Roman name.*

plūma, –ae, *f.*, feather.

plūrimum, *adv.*, very much, most, especially.

plūrimus, *see* multus.

plūs, *see* multus.

pōculum, –ī, *n.*, cup.

poena, –ae, *f.*, penalty, punishment.

Poenicus, –a, –um, Carthaginian.

Poenus, –a, –um, Punic; *as noun, m. pl.*, the Carthaginians.

poēta, –ae, *m.*, poet.

poliō, –īre, –īvī, –ītus, polish.

pollex, –icis, *m.*, thumb.

polliceor, –ērī, –itus sum, promise.

Pompeiānus, –a, –um, of Pompey, at Pompeii, Pompeian; Pompeiānī, –ōrum, *m.*, Pompey's followers, the Pompeians.

Pompeiī, –ōrum, *m.*, Pompeii (Pompā'yē), *a town, destroyed in* 79 A.D. *by an eruption of Vesuvius.*

Pompeius, –peī, *m.*, Pompey, *a Roman general and statesman.*

Pomptīnus, –ī, *m.*, Pomptī'nus, *a Roman name.*

pōmum, –ī, *n.*, fruit; apple, berry.

pondus, –deris, *n.*, weight.

pōnō, –ere, posuī, positus, put, place, set, pitch, lay aside.

pōns, pontis, *m.*, bridge.

pontifex, –ficis, *m.*, priest.

pontus, –ī, *m.*, sea.

Pontus, –ī, *m.*, Pontus, *the region south of the Black Sea.*

poples, –litis, *m.*, knee.

populāris, –e, popular, democratic.

populor, –ārī, –ātus sum, consume.

populus, –ī, *m.*, people.

Porcius, –a, –um, Porcian (Por'shian).

porrigō, –ere, –rēxī, –rēctus, stretch out, extend.

porrō, *adv.*, then, moreover.

porta, –ae, *f.*, gate.

portus, –ūs, *m.*, harbor, port.

poscō, –ere, poposcī, —, demand, call for, ask.

possessiō, –ōnis, *f.*, possession.

possideō, –ēre, –sēdī, –sessus, own, possess.

possum, posse, potuī, —, can, be able.

post, *adv. and prep. w. acc.*, behind; after, later, since.

posteā, *adv.*, afterwards.

posteā quam, *conj.*, after.

posteritās, –tātis, *f.*, the future, posterity.

posterus, –a, –um, following, next; in posterum, for the future; *as noun, m. pl.*, descendants.

posthāc, *adv.*, hereafter.

postis, –is, *m.*, doorpost; *pl.*, door.

postpōnō, –ere, –posuī, –positus, put after, esteem less.

postquam, *conj.*, after.

postrēmō, *adv.*, at last, finally; in short.

postrēmus, –a, –um, last.

postrīdiē, *adv.*, the next day.

postulātum, –ī, *n.*, demand.

postulō, 1, demand.

Postumius, –mī, *m.*, Postu'-mius, *a Roman name.*

potēns, *gen.* –entis, strong, powerful.

potentia, –ae, *f.*, power.

potestās, –tātis, *f.*, power, opportunity.

potior, –īrī, –ītus sum, get possession of.

potissimum, *adv.*, especially, above all, in preference to all others.

potius, *adv.*, rather.

pr. = prīdiē.

prae, *prep. w. abl.*, before; in comparison with.

praebeō, –ēre, –uī, –itus, hold out, offer, furnish.

praecēdō, –ere, –cessī, –cessus, go before, precede.

praeceps, –cipitis, headlong, rash; rushing, steep; in **praeceps,** headfirst.

praeceptor, –ōris, *m.*, teacher.

praeceptum, –ī, *n.*, precept, rule; instructions.

praecipiō, –ere, –cēpī, –ceptus, direct, lay down a rule.

praecipitō, 1, rush headlong, sink.

praecipuē, *adv.*, especially.

praecipuus, –a, –um, special.

praeclārus, –a, –um, brilliant, remarkable.

praecō, –ōnis, *m.*, crier, herald.

praecōnium, –nī, *n.*, proclaiming.

praecordia, –ōrum, *n.*, breast, heart.

praecursōrius, –a, –um, preliminary.

praeda, –ae, *f.*, booty.

praedātor, –ōris, *m.*, robber.

praedicātiō, –ōnis, *f.*, proclamation; praise.

praedicō, 1, announce, declare, say, proclaim.

praedīcō, –ere, –dīxī, –dictus, foretell, predict.

praeditus, –a, –um, endowed, possessing.

praedium, –dī, *n.*, farm, estate.

praedō, –ōnis, *m.*, pirate.

praefātiō, –ōnis, *f.*, preface, prologue.

praefectūra, –ae, *f.*, prefecture.

praefectus, –ī, *m.*, overseer, officer, commander.

praeferō, –ferre, –tulī, –lātus, carry before, prefer.

praeficiō, –ere, –fēcī, –fectus, set over, put in command of.

praemittō, –ere, –mīsī, –missus, send ahead.

praemium, –mī, *n.*, reward, prize.

Praeneste, –is, *n.* Praenes'te, *a town near Rome.*

praepōnō, –ere, –posuī, –positus, put before, prefer, place in charge.

praesāgus, –a, –um, ominous.

praescius, –a, –um, foreknowing, foreseeing.

praescrībō, –ere, –scrīpsī, –scrīptus, direct, require of.

praescrīptum, –ī, *n.*, (previous direction), order.

praesēns, *gen.* –entis, present, in person, evident; providential.

praesentia, –ae, f., presence; in praesentiā, for the present.

praesentiō, –īre, –sēnsī, –sēnsus, look forward to.

praesēpe, –is, n., stall.

praesertim, adv., especially.

praesideō, –ēre, –sēdī, —, guard, preside over.

praesidium, –dī, n., guard, garrison, fortification; protection, help.

praestābilis, –e, preëminent, excellent.

praestāns, gen. –antis, outstanding, preëminent.

praestō, –āre, –stitī, –stitus, stand before, excel; guarantee; perform; show; praestat, impers., it is better.

praestō, adv., at hand, ready.

praestōlor, –ārī, –ātus sum, wait for.

praesum, –esse, –fuī, –futūrus, be in charge of.

praeter, prep. w. acc., beyond, contrary to; except.

praetereā, adv., furthermore, besides, moreover.

praetereō, –īre, –īvī, –itus, go or pass by, omit; outstrip.

praetermittō, –ere, –mīsī, –missus, let go, omit, pass over.

praeterquam, conj., except.

praetextātus, –a, –um, wearing the toga praetexta, i.e. young (worn also by magistrates).

praetor, –ōris, m., praetor, a Roman judicial magistrate.

praetōrius, –a, –um, praetorian; as noun, m., ex-praetor.

praetūrā, –ae, f., the praetorship.

prāvus, –a, –um, crooked, vicious, depraved.

precor, –ārī, –ātus sum, entreat, pray.

premō, –ere, pressī, pressus, press, oppress; cover.

prēndō, –ere, prēndī, prēnsus, seize.

pretiōsus, –a, –um, valuable, precious.

pretium, –tī, n., price, reward.

prex, precis, f., prayer, entreaty.

prīdem, adv., long ago; w. iam, now for a long time.

prīdiē, adv., on the day before.

prīmō, adv., at first, first.

prīmum, adv., first, in the first place, at first; w. quam, as soon as possible; w. ut or cum, as soon as.

prīmus, –a, –um, first, foremost. chief; in prīmīs, especially

prīnceps, –cipis, adj. and noun, m., first, chief, leader, emperor.

prīncipātus, –ūs, m., first place, leadership.

prīncipiō, adv., in the first place.

prīncipium, –pī, n., beginning.

prior, prius, former, first; last.

Prīscus, –ī, m., Pris'cus, a Roman name.

prīstinus, –a, –um, former.

prius, compar. adv., before, first.

priusquam or prius quam (often prius . . . quam), conj., before.

prīvātim, adv., privately.

prīvātus, –a, –um, private; as noun, m., private citizen.

prīvignus, -ī, m., step-son.
prīvō, 1, deprive.
prō, *prep. w. abl.*, for, in behalf of, in return for, on account of, instead of, according to.
prō! *interj.*, O!
proavus, -ī, m., great-grandfather.
probō, 1, approve; prove.
probrum, -ī, n., disgraceful conduct.
probus, -a, -um, upright.
Probus, -ī, m., Prō'bus, *a Roman name.*
prōcēdō, -ere, -cessī, -cessus, go forward, advance.
prōcōnsul, -ulis, m., proconsul (*governor of a province*).
procul, *adv.*, far off.
prōcūrātiō, -ōnis, f., management, charge.
prōcurrō, -ere, -cucurrī (-currī), -cursus, run *or* rush forward, charge.
procus, -ī, m., suitor.
prōdō, -ere, -didī, -ditus, give forth, betray, transmit.
prōdūcō, -ere, -dūxī, -ductus, lead forth *or* out, induce, coax (*of a fire*).
proelior, -ārī, -ātus sum, fight.
proelium, -lī, n., battle.
profectiō, -ōnis, f., departure.
profectō, *adv.*, for a fact, certainly, doubtless.
prōferō, -ferre, -tulī, -lātus, bring forth, produce.
prōficiō, -ere, -fēcī, -fectus, accomplish.
proficīscor, -ī, -fectus sum, set out, march, depart, go; begin, proceed.

profiteor, -ērī, -fessus sum, confess; offer, promise; register.
prōflīgātus, -a, -um, corrupt, unprincipled.
profugiō, -ere, -fūgī, -fugitūrus, flee (forth), escape.
profundō, -ere, -fūdī, -fūsus, squander.
prōgeniēs, -ēī, f., offspring, child.
prōgredior, -ī, -gressus sum, (go forward), advance.
prōgressiō, -ōnis, f., advance.
prohibeō, -ēre, -hibuī, -hibitus, prevent, keep from, protect.
prōiciō, -ere, -iēcī, -iectus, throw *or* place under.
proinde, *adv.*, just, therefore.
prōlēs, -is, f., offspring, young; son.
prōmiscuus, -a, -um, without distinction.
prōmissum, -ī, n., promise.
prōmittō, -ere, -mīsī, -missus, (put forth), promise.
prōmulgō, 1, bring forward.
pronepōs, -ōtis, m., great-grandson.
prōnūntiō, 1, announce, declaim, recite, pronounce.
prōnus, -a, -um, headlong, steep.
prōpāgātiō, -ōnis, f., extension.
prōpāgō, 1, extend; grant.
prōpāgō, -ginis, f., offspring.
prope, *adv. and prep. w. acc.*, almost, near.
properō, 1, hasten.
Propertius, -tī, m., Propertius (Proper'shius), *a Roman poet.*

propinquus, –a, –um, near; *as noun, m.,* relative.

propior, –ius, nearer.

prōpōnō, –ere, –posuī, –positus, place *or* set before, publish, propose.

prōpositum, –ī, *n.,* plan.

proprius, –a, –um, one's own, belonging to, proper, characteristic of.

propter, *prep. w. acc.,* on account of, for the sake of; *adv.,* near.

proptereā, *adv.,* on this account; *w.* **quod,** because.

prōpugnō, 1, take the offensive.

prōrsum, prōrsus, *adv.,* forward; certainly.

prōruō, –ere, –ruī, –rutus, overthrow, demolish.

prōscrīptiō, –ōnis, *f.,* proscription.

prōsequor, –sequī, –secūtus sum, follow (after), accompany, pursue.

prōsiliō, –īre, –uī, —, leap forth.

prōspiciō, –ere, –spexī, –spectus, foresee, look forward to, look out for *or* over.

prōsternō, –ere, –strāvī, –strātus, throw down, overthrow.

prōsum, prōdesse, prōfuī, —, benefit, profit, help.

prōtinus, *adv.,* at once.

prōverbium, –bī, *n.,* saying, proverb.

prōvidentia, –ae, *f.,* foresight.

prōvidēns, *gen.* **–entis,** foreseeing, prudent.

prōvideō, –ēre, –vīdī, –vīsus, foresee, provide, take care, look out for.

prōvincia, –ae, *f.,* province.

proximē, *adv.,* most recently.

proximus, –a, –um, nearest, next, last; *as noun, n.,* neighborhood.

prūdentia, –ae, *f.,* foresight, discretion.

pruīna, –ae, *f.,* frost.

pruīnōsus, –a, –um, frosty.

prūnum, –ī, *n.,* plum.

Ptolemaeus, –a, –um, Ptolemaic (Tŏlemā'ic), Egyptian; **Ptolemaeus, –ī,** *m.,* Ptolemy (Tŏl'emy), *general name for the Egyptian kings.*

pūblicānus, –ī, *m.,* publican, tax collector.

pūblicē, *adv.,* publicly, officially.

pūblicō, 1, make public, confiscate.

pūblicus, –a, –um, public, common; *as noun, n.,* public (place), community.

Pūblius, –lī, *m.,* Pub'lius, *a Roman name.*

pudet, –ēre, –uit, *impers.,* it makes ashamed.

pudicē, *adv.,* modestly, virtuously.

pudor, –ōris, *m.,* (sense of) shame, modesty, sense of honor.

puella, –ae, *f.,* girl.

puer, puerī, *m.,* boy, child.

puerīlis, –e, boyish, youthful.

pueritia, –ae, *f.,* boyhood, childhood.

pugillārēs, –ium, *m. pl.,* writing tablets.

pugna, –ae, *f.,* fight, battle.

pugnō, 1, fight.

pulcher, –chra, –chrum, beautiful; honorable, fine.

pulchritūdō, –dinis, f., beauty.

pullus, –a, –um, dark-colored.

pulmō, –ōnis, m., lung.

pulsō, 1, beat.

pulverulentus, –a, –um, dusty.

pulvīnar, –āris, n., shrine.

pulvis, –veris, m., dust.

Pūnicus, –a, –um, Punic.

pūniō, –īre, –īvī, –ītus, punish.

pūrgātiō, –ōnis, f., cleansing.

pūrgō, 1, cleanse.

purpureus, –a, –um, purple.

pūrus, –a, –um, clean, pure.

putō, 1, think.

Pȳramus, –ī, m., Pyr'amus, Thisbe's lover.

Pyroīs, –oentis, m., Pyr'oïs, one of the horses of the Sun.

Q

Q., abbreviation for Quīntus.

quā, adv., where; w. nē, in any way.

quadrāgintā, indecl., forty.

quadrātum, –ī, n., square.

quadrātus, –a, –um, squared.

quadriiugī, –ōrum, m., four-horse team.

quadrupēs, –pedis, m., steed.

quaerō, –ere, quaesīvī, quaesītus, seek, inquire, ask, examine.

quaesō, –ere, ––, ––, beg.

quaestiō, –ōnis, f., question, trial.

quaestor, –ōris, m., quaestor, a Roman official.

quaestus, –ūs, m., gain, profit, business.

quālis, –e, of what sort, what, of such a kind as, such as; w. tālis, as.

quāliscumque, quālecumque, of whatever sort.

quam, adv. and conj., how, as; w. superl., as . . . possible; w. comp., than; quam prīmum, as soon as possible; quam diū, as long as, how long.

quamquam, conj., although; however; and yet.

quamvīs, adv. and conj., however much; although.

quandō, adv. and conj., when; at any time, ever.

quandōque, adv., at some time.

quantulus, –a, –um, how little.

quantum, adv., how much.

quantus, –a, –um, how great, how much, as (great or much as); quantō . . . tantō, the . . . the.

quantuscumque, –tacumque, –tumcumque, however great, however trifling.

quārē, adv., why; wherefore; therefore.

quārtus, –a, –um, fourth.

quasi, adv. and conj., as if, as it were.

quassō, 1, shake violently.

quater, adv., four times.

quatiō, –ere, ––, quassus, shake, flutter.

quattuor, four.

quattuordecim, fourteen.

–que, and.

queō, –īre, quīvī, ––, be able, can.

quercus, –ūs, f., oak; garland.

querēla, –ae, f., complaint.

querimōnia, –ae, f., complaint.

queror, querī, questus sum, complain.

quī, quae, quod, rel. pron., who, which, what, that; interrog. adj., what.

quia, conj., because.

quīcumque, quaecumque, quodcumque, rel. pron., whoever, whatever.

quid, adv., why.

quīdam, quaedam, quiddam (adj. quoddam), indef. pron., a certain one or thing; adj., certain, some.

quidem (follows emphatic word), to be sure; nē . . . quidem, not even.

quiēs, –ētis, f., rest, repose.

quiēscō, –ere, quiēvī, quiētus, be quiet, rest.

quiētus, –a, –um, undisturbed.

quīlibet, quaelibet, quodlibet, indef. pron., (anyone you please), any.

quīn, conj., (but) that; adv., why not; w. etiam, in fact.

Quīnctīlis, –e, (of) July.

quīndecim, fifteen.

quīngentī, –ae, –a, five hundred.

quīnque, five.

quīntus, –a, –um, fifth.

Quīntus, –ī, m., Quintus, a Roman name.

Quirītēs, –ium, m., Quirī'tēs, fellow citizens.

quis, quid, interrog. pron., who, what; quid, again; quid quod, what of the fact that.

quis, quid, indef. pron. and adj., quī, qua, quod, indef. adj., any, anyone, anything (usually after sī, nisi, nē, or num).

quisnam, quaenam, quidnam, interrog. pron., who or what in the world.

quispiam, quaepiam, quidpiam (quodpiam), indef. pron., anyone, any; some one, something.

quisquam, quicquam, indef. pron., anyone, anything, any.

quisque, quidque, indef. pron., each one, each thing, every.

quisquis, quicquid, rel. pron., whoever, whatever.

quīvīs, quaevīs, quidvīs (quodvīs), any you please, any.

quō, adv., where, wherefore; quō usque, how long; conj. (w. compar.), in order that, that.

quoad, conj., as long as.

quōcumque, adv., wherever.

quod, conj., because, that; quod sī, but if.

quondam, once (upon a time).

quoniam, conj., since, because.

quoque, adv., also; even.

quot, indecl. adj., how many; as many as, as.

quotannīs, adv., yearly.

quotiēns, adv., as often as; how often.

quotiēnscumque, adv., as ofter as.

R

radiō, 1, gleam.

radius, –dī, m., rod; ray, beam; spoke.

rādīx, –īcis, f., root, radish.

rādō, –ere, rāsī, rāsus, scrape; skim.

rāmus, -ī, *m.*, branch.
rapidus, -a, -um, fierce, swift.
rapīna, -ae, *f.*, plunder, robbery.
rapiō, -ere, -uī, raptus, seize, carry off, hurry along.
rārō, *adv.*, rarely.
rārus, -a, -um, rare.
ratiō, -ōnis, *f.*, reckoning, account; plan, nature, method, policy; manner, means, reason.
Reātīnus, -a, -um, of Rea'te.
Rebilus, -ī, *m.*, Reb'ilus, *a Roman name.*
recēdō, -ere, -cessī, -cessus, go back, withdraw.
recēns, *gen.* -entis, fresh, recent.
receptus, -ūs, *m.*, retreat, place of refuge.
recīdō, -ere, -cīdī, -cīsus, cut off.
recipiō, -ere, -cēpī, -ceptus, take back, recover, receive, admit; sē recipere, retreat.
recitātiō, -ōnis, *f.*, reading, recitation.
recitātor, -ōris, *m.*, reader, reciter.
recitō, 1, recite, read (aloud).
reclāmō, 1, protest.
recognōscō, -ere, -nōvī, -nitus, recognize; review.
recolō, -ere, -uī, -cultus, renew.
reconciliātiō, -ōnis, *f.*, renewal.
reconciliō, 1, restore, reconcile.
recondō, -ere, -condidī, -conditus, hide; close.
recordor, -ārī, -ātus sum, call to mind.

recreō, 1, recreate, restore; *w.* sē, recover.
rēctā, *adv.*, straightway.
rēctē, *adv.*, rightly, correctly.
rēctor, -ōris, *m.*, ruler, herdsman, pilot.
recuperō, 1, get back, recover.
recurrō, -ere, -currī, -cursus, run back, return.
recūsātiō, -ōnis, *f.*, declining.
recūsō, 1, be reluctant to do.
reddō, -ere, -didī, -ditus, return, render, make, restore, deliver; vomit.
redeō, -īre, rediī, reditus, go back, return.
redigō, -ere, -ēgī, -āctus, bring (back), reduce.
redimō, -ere, -ēmī, -ēmptus, buy back *or* up; ransom.
reditus, -ūs, *m.*, return.
redolēns, *gen.* -entis, fragrant.
redormiō, -īre, -īvī, -ītus, sleep again.
redūcō, -ere, -dūxī, -ductus, bring back, restore.
redundō, 1, overflow, redound.
referō, -ferre, rettulī, relātus, bring *or* carry back, lay *or* bring before, report; reply; grātiam referre, show one's gratitude.
refertus, -a, -um, filled.
reficiō, -ere, -fēcī, -fectus, repair, renew, recruit, reinforce.
refugiō, -ere, -fūgī, -fugitūrus, flee back, flee for safety, escape.
refūtō, 1, repel; refute.
regerō, -ere, -gessī, -gestus, throw back.

rēgiē, *adv.*, despotically.
Rēgīnī, -ōrum, *m.*, the people of Regium.
regiō, -ōnis, *f.*, region.
rēgius, -a, -um, royal.
rēgnō, 1, reign.
rēgnum, -ī, *n.*, royal power, kingdom, throne.
regō, -ere, rēxī, rēctus, guide, rule, control.
regredior, -ī, -gressus sum, go back.
Regulus, -ī, *m.*, Reg'ulus, *a Roman name.*
reiciō, -ere, -iēcī, -iectus, throw, drive back, reject; vomit.
relanguēscō, -ere, -languī, —, sink down.
relaxō, 1, relax.
relēgō, 1, send away, banish.
relevō, 1, lighten, relieve, rest.
religiō, -ōnis, *f.*, scrupulousness, sacredness.
religiōsus, -a, -um, sacred.
relinquō, -ere, -līquī, -līctus, leave (behind), abandon; leave unmentioned.
reliquus, -a, -um, remaining, rest (of); future; **reliquum est,** it remains.
remaneō, -ēre, -mānsī, -mānsūrus, remain (behind).
remedium, -dī, *n.*, remedy.
rēmex, -migis, *m.*, oarsman.
remissiō, -ōnis, *f.*, relaxation, recreation.
remittō, -ere, -mīsī, -missus, send (back), remit; drop.
remoror, -ārī, -ātus sum, hold back, delay.

removeō, -ēre, -mōvī, -mōtus, remove.
renīdeō, -ēre, —, —, shine; smile.
renovō, 1, renew.
renūntiō, 1, report, declare elected.
reor, rērī, ratus sum, reckon; think.
repāgula, -ōrum, *n.*, barriers.
repellō, -ere, reppulī, repulsus, drive *or* push back, repulse, ward off.
repente, *adv.*, suddenly.
repentīnus, -a, -um, sudden.
reperiō, -īre, repperī, repertus, find, discover.
repetō, -ere, -īvī, -ītus, seek again, demand; repeat.
repleō, -ēre, -ēvī, -ētus, fill again.
reportō, 1, bring back.
reposcō, -ere, -poposcī, —, demand in turn.
reprehendō, -ere, -hendī, -hēnsus, (hold back), censure, criticize.
reprimō, -ere, -pressī, -pressus, press back, check, thwart.
repudiō, 1, reject, scorn.
repugnō, 1, fight against, resist.
₁epulsa, -ae, *f.*, refusal.
requiēs, -ētis, *f.*, rest.
requiēscō, -ere, -ēvī, -ētus, rest, repose.
requīrō, -ere, -quīsīvī, -quīsītus, hunt up, search for, inquire; demand; miss.
rēs, reī, *f.*, thing, fact, affair, matter, object; **rēs pūblica,**

the republic, state, public interest; **rēs frūmentāria**, supply of grain, supplies; **rēs gestae**, deeds; **rēs mīlitāris**, art of war, warfare; **rēs novae**, revolution; **rēs familiāris**, means.

rescrībō, –ere, –scrīpsī, –scrīptus, write back, reply (in writing).

resecō, –āre, –secuī, –sectus, cut off.

reservō, 1, keep back, reserve.

resideō, –ēre, –sēdī, —, be left, sit down.

resistō, –ere, –stitī, —, resist.

resonō, 1, resound

respiciō, –ere, –spexī, –spectus, look back (at), look at, consider.

respondeō, –ēre, –spondī, –spōnsus, answer, reply.

respōnsum, –ī, n., answer, reply.

respuō, –ere, –uī, —, (spit back at), reject.

restinguō, –ere, –stīnxī, –stīnctus, extinguish.

restituō, –ere, –stituī, –stitūtus, restore.

restō, –āre, –stitī, —, withstand, be left, remain.

restringō, –ere, –strīnxī, –strictus, (bind back), restrict.

resupīnus, –a, –um, on one's back.

retardō, 1, check, hinder.

rēte, –is, n., net.

reticeō, –ēre, –ticuī, —, be or keep silent.

retineō, –ēre, –tinuī, –tentus, hold back, keep.

retorqueō, –ēre, –torsī, –tortus, turn back.

retrahō, –ere, –trāxī, –trāctus, drag or bring back.

retrō, adv., back, backward.

retundō, –ere, rettudī, retūsus, beat back.

reus, –ī, m., defendant.

revellō, –ere, –vellī, –vulsus, tear away.

revertō, –ere, –vertī, –versus, return (sometimes deponent).

revincō, –ere, –vīcī, –victus, convict.

revivīscō, –ere, –vīxī, —, come to life again.

revocābilis, –e, that can be recalled.

revocō, 1, recall, call back.

rēx, rēgis, m., king.

Rēx, Rēgis, m., Rex, a name.

Rhodiī, –ōrum, m., the Rhodians.

rictus, –ūs, m., jaws.

rīdeō, –ēre, rīsī, rīsus, laugh.

rīdiculus, –a, –um, funny, amusing; absurd.

rigeō, –ēre, —, —, be stiff.

riguus, –a, –um, well-watered.

rīma, –ae, f., crack.

rīpa, –ae, f., bank (of a stream).

rīsus, –ūs, m., laughter.

rōbur, roboris, n., oak; strength.

rōbustus, –a, –um, (of oak), hardy, robust.

rōdō, –ere, rōsī, rōsus, gnaw, eat (away).

rogātus, –ūs, m., request.

rogō, 1, ask, beg; **propose**, pass.

Rōma, –ae, f., Rome.

Rōmānus, –a, –um, Roman;
as noun, m. pl., the Romans.

Rōmulus, –ī, m., Rŏm'ulus,
founder of Rome.

rosa, –ae, f., rose.

Rōscius, –cī, m., Roscius
(Rŏsh'ius), a Roman name.

rota, –ae, f., wheel; pl., chariot.

Roucillus, –ī, m., Roucillus
(Roosil'us), a name.

rubēns, gen. –entis, red.

rubēscō, –ere, rubuī, —, grow
red.

Rubicō, –ōnis, m., the Rubicon,
a river in northern Italy.

rudis, –e, rough.

Rūfus, –ī, Rū'fus, a Roman
name.

rūgōsus, –a, –um, wrinkled.

ruīna, –ae, f., ruin.

rūmor, –ōris, m., hearsay, report; fame.

rumpō, –ere, rūpī, ruptus,
break, pierce.

ruō, –ere, ruī, rutus, fall, go to
ruin, rush.

rūpēs, –is, f., rock, cliff.

rūrsus, adv., again.

rūs, rūris, n., country; farm;
pl., fields.

rūsticānus, –a, –um, rural.

rūsticor, –ārī, –ātus sum, go
into the country.

rūsticus, –a, –um, rustic, of the
country; as noun, m., rustic.

S

sacculus, –ī, m., little sack.

sacer, sacra, sacrum, sacred;
n. pl., sacred rites, ceremonies.

sacerdōs, –ōtis, m. and f.,
priest, priestess.

sacerdōtium, –tī, n., priesthood.

sacrāmentum, –ī, n., solemn
oath, vow.

sacrārium, –rī, n., shrine.

sacrificium, –cī, n., sacrifice.

sacrōsānctus, –a, –um, sacred,
inviolable.

saeculum, –ī, n., generation,
age, reign.

saepe, adv., often.

saevus, –a, –um, fierce, cruel.

sagāx, –ācis, keen.

sagitta, –ae, f., arrow.

sagum, –ī, n., military cloak.

Salamīniī, –ōrum, m., the Sal-
amin'ians, inhabitants of
Salamis, a town in Cyprus.

Sallustius, –tī, m., Sallus'tius, a
Roman name.

saltātiō, –ōnis, f., dance.

saltem, adv., at least.

saltō, 1, dance.

saltus, –ūs, m., leap, bound.

salūbris, –e, healthful, whole-
some.

salūbritās, –tātis, f., health-
fulness.

salūs, –ūtis, f., safety.

salūtātiō, –ōnis, f., greeting.

salūtō, 1, greet, pay one's
respects.

salvus, –a, –um, safe, well,
solvent.

Samarobrīva, –ae, f., Samaro-
brī'va (now Amiens), in
Gaul.

Samos, –ī, f., Sāmos, an island
in the Aegean Sea.

sānciō, –īre, sānxī, sānctus,
(make sacred), ordain.

sānctē, *adv.,* religiously, scrupulously.

sānctitās, **–tātis,** *f.,* virtue, piety.

sānctus, –a, –um, sacred, holy, venerable, upright.

sānē, *adv.,* indeed, truly, of course.

Sanga, –ae, *m.,* Sanga, *a Roman name.*

sanguis, sanguinis, *m.,* blood.

sānitās, –tātis, *f.,* soundness of mind, sanity.

sānō, 1, make sound, cure.

sānus, –a, –um, in one's right mind, sane.

sapiēns, *gen.* **–entis,** wise; *as noun, m.,* philosopher.

sapienter, *adv.,* wisely.

sapientia, –ae, *f.,* wisdom.

Sardēs, –ium, *f. pl.,* Sardis, *capital of Lydia, in Asia Minor.*

Sardinia, –ae, *f.,* Sardinia.

satelles, –litis, *m. and f.,* attendant; accomplice.

satiō, 1, satisfy, sate.

satis, *adv. and indecl. adj.,* enough; quite, sufficiently; *compar.* **satius,** better.

satisfaciō, –ere, –fēcī, –factus, satisfy.

satur, –ura, –urum, full.

satus, *see* serō.

Sāturnālia, –ium, *n. pl.,* the Saturnā'lia, *a festival in honor of Saturn.*

Sāturnīnus, –ī, *m.,* Saturnī'nus, *a Roman name.*

saturō, 1, fill, saturate.

Sauromatae, –ārum, *m.,* the Sarmatians (Sarmā'shians).

saxum, –ī, *n.,* rock, stone.

scaena, –ae, *f.,* theater, stage.

scaenicus, –a, –um, of the stage.

scelerātē, *adv.,* wickedly, impiously.

scelerātus, –a, –um, wicked, accursed, criminal.

scelus, sceleris, *n.,* crime, wickedness.

Schoenēius, –a, –um, of Schoeneus (Skē'neus).

sciēns, *gen.* **–entis,** experienced.

scientia, –ae, *f.,* knowledge.

scīlicet, *adv.,* (one may know), of course, doubtless.

scindō, –ere, scidī, scissus, cut, split.

sciō, scīre, scīvī, scītus, know (how).

Scīpiō, –ōnis, *m.,* Scipio (Sip'io), *a Roman name.*

scītē, *adv.,* cleverly.

scītor, –ārī, –ātus sum, inquire.

Scorpius, –pī, *m.,* the Scorpion, *a sign of the zodiac.*

scrība, –ae, *m.,* clerk.

scrībō, –ere, scrīpsī, scrīptus, write.

scrīptor, –ōris, *m.,* writer.

scrīptūra, –ae, *f.,* writing.

scurrīliter, *adv.,* like a buffoon.

Scythae, –ārum, *m.,* the Scythians (Sith'ians), *wandering tribes beyond the Black Sea.*

Scythicus, –a, –um, Scythian.

sēcēdō, –ere, –cessī, –cessus, go away, retire, withdraw.

sēcernō, –ere, –crēvī, –crētus, separate.

sēcessiō, –ōnis, *f.,* withdrawal, insurrection.

sēcessus, –ūs, *m.*, departure, retirement.

sēcrētō, *adv.*, in private.

secundus, –a, –um, second, favorable, successful.

sector, –ārī, –ātus sum, follow eagerly, pursue.

sectus, –a, –um, cut off.

secundum, *prep. w. acc.*, following, according to, behind, next to.

secundus, –a, –um, second; successful; *w.* rēs, prosperity.

Secundus, –ī, *m.*, Secundus, *a name.*

secūris, –is, *f.*, ax.

sed, *conj.*, but.

sedeō, –ēre, sēdī, sessus, sit, sit down, lie idle.

sēdēs, –is, *f.*, seat; abode, place.

sedīle, –is, *n.*, seat.

sēditiō, –ōnis, *f.*, rebellion, sedition.

sēdō, 1, bring to an end, stop.

sēdūcō, –ere, –dūxī, –ductus, set aside.

sēdulitās, –tātis, *f.*, diligence.

sēdulō, *adv.*, busily, carefully, eagerly.

sēdulus, –a, –um, diligent.

seges, –etis, *f.*, grain field; crop.

sēgregō, 1, exclude.

Sēiānus, –a, –um, of Sēius.

sēiūnctus, –a, –um, separate.

sēiungō, –ere, –iūnxī, –iūnctus, disjoin, separate, sever.

Sēius, –ī, *m.*, Sēius, *a Roman name.*

Seleucus, –ī, *m.*, Seleu'cus, *king of Syria.*

sella, –ae, *f.*, seat, chair.

semel, *adv.*, once.

sēmen, –minis, *n.*, seed.

sēminārium, –rī, *n.*, nursery.

sēmita, –ae, *f.*, footpath.

semper, *adv.*, always.

sempiternus, –a, –um, everlasting, perpetual.

Semprōnius, –a, –um, Sempro'nian.

senātor, –ōris, *m.*, senator.

senātōrius, –a, –um, senatorial.

senātus, –ūs, *m.*, senate.

senecta, –ae, *f.*, old age.

senectūs, –tūtis, *f.*, old age.

senēscō, –ere, senuī, —, grow old.

senex, senis, *m.*, old man.

senīlis, –e, of an old man.

senior, –ius, older; aged.

sēnsus, –ūs, *m.*, feeling; consciousness.

sententia, –ae, *f.*, feeling, opinion; proposal; meaning, sentiment.

sentiō, –īre, sēnsī, sēnsus, feel, realize, perceive, think, know.

sepeliō, –īre, –īvī, –pultus, bury.

septem, seven.

September, –bris, –bre, (of) September.

septēnī, –ae, –a, seven each.

septentriōnēs, –um, *m.*, seven stars (*near the north pole*), north.

Septimius, –mī, *m.* Septim'ius.

septimus, –a, –um, seventh.

septingentī, –ae, –a, seven hundred.

sepulcrum, –ī, *n.*, tomb.

sequor, sequī, secūtus sum, follow.

serēnus, –a, –um, clear.

sēriō, *adv.*, in earnest, seriously.

sērius, –a, –um, grave, serious.

sermō, –ōnis, *m.*, speech, conversation, talk, report.

serō, –ere, sēvī, satus, sow, produce; satus, –a, –um, sprung from.

sērō, *adv.*, late.

serpēns, *gen* –entis, *m. and f.*, serpent.

servīlis, –e, of slaves, servile.

Servīlius, –lī, *m.*, Servil'ius, *a Roman name.*

serviō, –īre, –īvī, –ītus, be a slave (to), serve, have regard for, court.

servitūs, –tūtis, *f.*, slavery.

servō, 1, save, keep, preserve.

servus, –ī, *m.*, slave.

sescentī, –ae, –a, six hundred.

sēstertium, –tī, *n.*, 1000 sesterces ($50.00).

sēstertius, –tī, *gen. pl.* –ium, *m.*, sesterce, *a small silver coin* (= *about* 5¢).

Sēstius, –tī, *m.*, Ses'tius, *a Roman name.*

seu, *see* sīve.

sevēritās, –tātis, *f.*, severity.

sevērus, –a, –um, severe, stern.

sex, six.

sexāgintā, sixty.

Sextīlis, –e, (of) August.

sextus, –a, –um, sixth; sextus decimus, sixteenth.

sexus, –ūs, *m.*, sex.

sī, *conj.*, if.

Sibyllīnus, –a, –um, Sib'yllīne.

sīc, *adv.*, so, in this way, thus.

sīca, –ae, *f.*, dagger.

sīcārius, –rī, *m.*, assassin.

Sicca, –ae, *m.*, Sicca, *a Roman name.*

siccō, 1, dry.

siccus, –a, –um, dry.

Sicilia, –ae, *f.*, Sicily.

sīcut, sīcutī, *adv.*, just as.

sīdus, –deris, *n.*, constellation, star.

Sīgēum, –ī, *n.*, Sigē'um, *a promontory.*

significātiō, –ōnis, *f.*, meaning.

significō, 1, (make signs), show, indicate.

signō, 1, seal, mark.

signum, –ī, *n.*, sign, token, standard; signal; seal, statue.

Sīlānus, –ī, *m.*, Silā'nus, *a Roman name.*

silentium, –tī, *n.*, silence.

sileō, –ēre, –uī, —, be silent, leave unmentioned.

silva, –ae, *f.*, forest, woods.

Silvānus, –ī, *m.*, Silvā'nus, *a Roman name.*

similis, –e, like, similar.

similiter, *adv.*, in like manner.

simplex, –plicis, simple, single.

simpliciter, *adv.*, plainly, openly.

simul, *adv.*, at the same time, at once, together; *w.* atque, *or* ac, as soon as.

simulācrum, –ī, *n.*, likeness, image.

simulātor, –ōris, *m.*, pretender.

simulō, 1, pretend.

simultās, –tātis, *f.*, rivalry, enmity.

sīn, *conj.*, but if.

sincēriter, *adv.*, honestly.

sincērus, –a, –um, pure, chaste.

sine, *prep. w. abl.*, without.

singillātim, *adv.*, singly.

singulāris, –e (–ius, –a, –um), unique, remarkable, separate.

singulī, –ae, –a, *pl. only*, separate, single, each, one after another.

sinister, –tra, –trum, left; *compar.* sinisterior, the left.

sinō, –ere, sīvī, situs, allow.

Sinōpē, –ēs, *f.*, Sinō′pē, *a city of Asia Minor.*

Sinōpēnsis, –e, of Sinope, *a Greek colony;* Sinōpēnsēs, –ium, *m.*, the people of Sinope.

sinus, –ūs, *m.*, fold; bosom; bay.

Sipylus, –ī, *m.*, Sip′ylus, *one of Niobe's sons.*

sistō, –ere, stitī, status, place; stop, check.

sitiēns, –entis, thirsty.

sitis, –is, *f.*, thirst.

situs, –ūs, *m.*, position.

situs, –a, –um, placed; situm est, it lies.

sīve, *or* seu, *conj.*, or if, or; sīve (seu) . . . sīve (seu), whether . . . or, either . . . or.

smaragdus, –ī, *m.*, emerald.

Smyrnaeī, –ōrum, *m.*, the people of Smyrna.

sōbrius, –a, –um, sober.

socer, –erī, *m.*, father-in-law.

societās, –tātis, *f.*, fellowship, alliance.

socius, –cī, *m.*, comrade, companion, associate; *pl.*, allies, provincials.

sodālis, –is, *m.*, companion.

sōl, sōlis, *m.*, sun.

sōlācium, –cī, *n.*, comfort.

soleō, –ēre, solitus sum, *semideponent*, be accustomed *or* wont.

solidus, –a, –um, solid.

sōlitūdō, –dinis, *f.*, solitude.

solitus, –a, –um, customary.

solium, –lī, *n.*, throne.

sollemnis, –e, (annual), customary, appointed, solemn.

sollicitātiō, –ōnis, *f.*, tampering with.

sollicitē, *adv.*, carefully.

sollicitō, 1, disturb, stir, incite to revolt, tamper with.

sollicitūdō, –dinis, *f.*, uneasiness, anxiety.

sollicitus, –a, –um, anxious, worried.

sōlor, –ārī, –ātus sum, comfort.

solum, –ī, *n.*, soil.

sōlum, *adv.*, only, alone; nōn sōlum . . . sed (vērum) etiam, not only . . . but also.

sōlus, –a, –um, alone, only.

solūtus, –a, –um, loose, at large.

solvō, –ere, solvī, solūtus, loose, release, solve.

somnus, –ī, *m.*, sleep.

sonitus, –ūs, *m.*, sound.

sonō, –āre, sonuī, sonitus, resound; sonāns, –antis, clanking.

sordidus, –a, –um, stained.

soror, –ōris, *f.*, sister.

sors, sortis, *f.*, lot; oracle.

sortītō, *adv.*, by lot.

Sp., *abbreviation for* Spurius, –rī, *m., a Roman name.*

spargō, –ere, sparsī, sparsus, scatter, spread.

spatior, –ārī, –ātus sum, take a walk, walk.

spatium, –tī, n., space, time, distance.

speciēs, –ēī, f., sight, appearance.

speciōsus, –a, –um, showy, glittering.

spectābilis, –e, conspicuous, beautiful.

spectātiō, –ōnis, f., sight.

spectātor, –ōris, m., spectator.

spectō, 1, look at or on, see, face.

speculātor, –ōris, m., spy.

speculor, –ārī, –ātus sum, watch.

spērō, 1, hope (for).

spēs, speī, f., hope.

spīritus, –ūs, m., breath, spirit, air; pride.

splendidus, –a, –um, shining, brilliant, distinguished.

splendor, –ōris, m., brightness, splendor.

spolia, –ōrum, n., spoils, booty.

spoliō, 1, deprive.

sponte, of his (their) own accord, voluntarily.

spūmāns, gen. –antis, foaming.

spūmiger, –era, –erum, foaming.

squāleō, –ēre, –uī, ——, be stiff, be filthy.

stabilis, –e, firm.

stāmen, –inis, n., thread, string.

Statilius, –lī, m., Statil'ius, a Roman name.

statim, adv., at once, immediately.

statiō, –ōnis, f., station.

Stator, –ōris, m., Stayer, Protector.

statua, –ae, f., statue.

statuō, –ere, statuī, statūtus, place, decide, determine.

statūra, –ae, f., stature.

status, –a, –um, fixed, appointed.

status, –ūs, m., state, position, condition, status.

stella, –ae, f., star.

sternō, –ere, strāvī, strātus, stretch out, spread.

stilus, –ī, m., stylus (instrument used in writing on wax tablets).

stimulus, –ī, m., goad, spur; incentive.

stīpendium, –dī, n., tribute, pay; campaign.

stirps, stirpis, f., stock, root.

stīva, –ae, f., plow-handle.

stō, stāre, stetī, status, stand.

Stōicī, –ōrum, m., the Stoics.

stolidus, –a, –um, dull, stupid.

stomachus, –ī, m., stomach.

strāmen, –minis, n., straw; pl., thatch.

strātum, –ī, n., cover, horse-blanket.

strēnuus, –a, –um, energetic.

strepitus, –ūs, m., noise.

stringō, –ere, strīnxī, strictus, draw (tight); ruffle.

studeō, –ēre, –uī, ——, be eager for, desire; study.

studiōsē, adv., eagerly.

studiōsus, –a, –um, fond of.

studium, –dī, n., eagerness, desire, interest, zeal; study, pursuit.

stultus, –a, –um, foolish, stupid.

stupeō, –ēre, –uī, —, stand aghast.

stuprum, –ī, *n.*, debauchery.

Stygius, –a, –um, Stygian.

suādeō, –ēre, suāsī, suāsus, urge, advise, persuade.

sub, *prep.*, under, close to, at the foot of, just before (*w. acc. after verbs of motion; w. abl. after verbs of rest or position*).

subdō, –ere, –didī, –ditus, put *or* plunge under.

subiaceō, –ēre, –uī, —, lie below *or* near.

subiciō, –ere, –iēcī, –iectus, throw under, spread beneath.

subigō, –ere, –ēgī, –āctus, subdue.

subinde, *adv.*, from time to time.

subitō, *adv.*, suddenly.

subitus, –a, –um, sudden.

sublātus, –a, –um, *see* **tollō.**

subsellium, –lī, *n.*, bench, seat.

subsequor, –sequī, –secūtus sum, follow up, follow closely.

subsidium, –dī, *n.*, aid, support; sinews.

subsīdō, –ere, –sēdī, –sessus, sit down.

subveniō, –īre, –vēnī, –ventus, come to the rescue, relieve, assist.

succēdō, –ere, –cessī, –cessus, come up, enter, follow, succeed.

succrēscō, –ere, —, —, grow up, be supplied.

succurrō, –ere, –currī, –cursus, run to one's aid, help.

succutiō, –ere, –cussī, –cussus, toss up.

sūcus, –ī, *m.*, juice; moisture.

sūdor, –ōris, *m.*, sweat.

sufficiō, –ere, –fēcī, –fectus, suffice.

suffrāgium, –gī, *n.*, ballot, vote.

suī, *reflexive pron.*, of himself, herself, itself, of themselves.

Sulla, –ae, *m.*, Sulla, *a Roman name.*

Sulpicius, –cī, *m.*, Sulpicius (Sulpish'ius), *a Roman name.*

sum, esse, fuī, futūrus, be, exist.

summa, –ae, *f.*, sum total, chief part, substance; **summa rērum,** general interest; **ad summam,** in short.

summātim, *adv.*, in a general way, briefly.

summittō, –ere, –mīsī, –missus, lower.

summoveō, –ēre, –mōvī, –mōtus, drive away.

summus, –a, –um, highest, greatest, best, eminent; surface of; *as noun, n.*, top, summit.

sūmō, –ere, sūmpsī, sūmptus, take, assume.

sūmptuōsē, *adv.*, extravagantly.

sūmptus, –ūs, *m.*, expense, extravagance.

super, *prep. w. acc.*, above; upon.

superbia, –ae, *f.*, pride, arrogance.

superbus, –a, –um, haughty, proud.

superfundō, –ere, –fūdī, –fūsus, pour over; *pass.*, overflow.

superior, –ius, higher, elder, previous, former, superior.

superō, 1, surpass, overcome, conquer, defeat; pass over.

superstitiō, –ōnis, *f.,* superstition.

supersum, –esse, –fuī, –futūrus, be left over, remain, survive.

superus, –a, –um, above; *as noun, m. pl.,* the gods.

suppeditō, 1, supply.

suppleō, –ēre, –ēvī, –ētus, fill.

supplex, –plicis, *m.,* suppliant.

supplicātiō, –ōnis, *f.,* public prayer, thanksgiving.

supplicium, –cī, *n.,* punishment, torture.

supplicō, 1, kneel down (to), pray, worship.

suprā, *adv. and prep. w. acc.,* above, beyond, before, previously.

suprēmus, –a, –um, last, dying.

surgō, –ere, surrēxī, surrēctus, arise, rise.

surripiō, –ere, –uī, –reptus, steal.

suscēnseō, –ēre, –uī, —, be angry with.

suscipiō, –ere, –cēpī, –ceptus, undertake, incur, suffer.

suscitō, 1, rekindle.

suspectus, –a, –um, suspicious, suspected.

suspiciō, –ōnis, *f.,* suspicion.

suspicor, –ārī, –ātus sum, suspect.

suspīrium, –rī, *n.,* sigh.

sustentō, 1, sustain.

sustineō, –ēre, –tinuī, –tentus, hold up, bear, endure.

suus, –a, –um, *reflexive adj.,* his, her, its, their; his own, her own, *etc.; as noun,* **suī,** his (her, their) men, friends; **sua,** *n.,* his (her, their) possessions.

syllaba, –ae, *f.,* syllable.

Syria, –ae, *f.,* Syria, *a country in western Asia.*

T

T., *abbreviation for* **Titus, –ī,** *m., a Roman name.*

tabella, –ae, *f.,* tablet; *pl.,* letter, ballot, record.

tabellārius, –rī, *m.,* letter carrier.

tabernāculum, –ī, *n.,* tent.

tābēscō, –ere, tābuī, —, melt.

tabula, –ae, *f.,* board, painting; writing tablet; *pl.,* records, accounts.

taceō, –ēre, –uī, –itus, be silent, leave unmentioned.

taciturnitās, –tātis, *f.,* silence.

tacitus, –a, –um, secret, silent.

taedium, –dī, *n.,* weariness, loathing.

taeter, –tra, –trum, foul, revolting.

tālāris, –e, reaching the ankles.

tālis, –e, such.

tam, *adv.,* so, so much.

tamen, *adv.,* yet, still, nevertheless, however.

tametsī, *conj.,* although.

tamquam, *adv.,* as if, as, as it were.

tandem, *adv.,* at last, finally; *in questions,* I ask.

tangō, –ere, tetigī, tāctus, touch, move, reach; partake of.

Tantalus, –ī, *m.,* Tan'talus (1) *Niobe's father;* (2) *son of Niobe.*

tantō, *adv.,* so much.

tantum, *adv.,* so much, so greatly; only, merely; **w. modo,** only, merely.

tantus, -a, -um, so great, so much, such: **tantus . . . quantus,** as much (*or* great) . . . as.

tardē, slowly, late, tardily.

tarditās, -tātis, *f.,* slowness, delay.

tardō, 1, delay, check.

tardus, -a, -um, slow.

Tarentīnī, -ōrum, *m.,* the people of Tarentum.

Tarquinius, -nī, *m.,* Tarquin'ius, *a name.*

Tartara, -ōrum, *n.,* Tar'tarus, *the lower world.*

tēctum, -ī, *n.,* roof; dwelling, home.

tegō, -ere, tēxī, tēctus, cover, conceal; protect.

tellūs, -ūris, *f.,* earth; land.

tēlum, -ī, *n.,* missile, weapon, shaft.

temerārius, -a, -um, rash.

temere, *adv.,* rashly, without reason.

temeritās, -tātis, *f.,* rashness.

tēmō, -ōnis, *m.,* pole (*of a chariot*).

temperantia, -ae, *f.,* self-control.

tempestās, -tātis, *f.,* season; storm, weather.

tempestīvus, -a, -um, timely, suitable; early.

templum, -ī, *n.,* temple.

temptō, 1, try, tempt; attack.

tempus, -poris, *n.,* time, period, temple (*of the head*); **w. ex,** offhand.

tenebrae, -ārum, *f.,* darkness.

teneō, -ēre, -uī, tentus, hold, keep, possess, occupy; restrain.

tener, -era, -erum, tender; young.

tenuis, -e, thin, little; humble.

tenus, *postpositive prep. w. abl.,* up to.

tepeō, -ēre, —, —, be warm.

tepidus, -a, -um, warm.

ter, *adv.,* three times, thrice.

terebrō, 1, pierce.

Terentia, -ae, *f.,* Terentia (Teren'shia), *Cicero's wife.*

tergeō, -ēre, tersī, tersus, wipe, sweep (clean).

tergum, -ī, *n.,* back; side (of pork); **ā tergō,** in the rear.

tergus, -goris, *n.,* back; side (of pork).

terminō, 1, bound, limit; end, close.

terminus, -ī, *m.,* boundary.

terra, -ae, *f.,* land, earth, ground.

terreō, -ēre, -uī, -itus, frighten.

terribilis, -e, terrible.

terror, -ōris, *m.,* alarm, terror.

tertiō, *adv.,* for the third time.

tertius, -a, -um, third.

testa, -ae, *f.,* brick.

testāmentum, -ī, *n.,* will.

testimōnium, -nī, *n.,* testimony, proof.

testis, -is, *m.,* witness.

testor, -ārī, -ātus sum, call to witness.

Tēthys, -yos, *f.,* Tēthys, *wife of Oceanus.*

Teutonī, -ōrum, *m.,* the Teutons, *a people of Germany.*

Themistoclēs, –is, *m.,* Themis'-toclēs, *an Athenian statesman.*

Theophanēs, –is, *m.,* Theophanes (Theof'anēs), *a Greek writer.*

Thessalia, –ae, *f.,* Thes'saly, *part of Greece.*

Thisbē, –ēs, *f.,* Thisbe, *a Babylonian maiden.*

Thrācia, –ae, *f.,* Thrace, *a country north of Greece.*

Thrasea, –ae, *m.,* Thras'ea, *a Roman name.*

Thrāx, –ācis, Thrā'cian.

Thȳnēius, –a, –um, of Thynaeum.

Ti., *abbreviation for* **Tiberius.**

Tiberīnus, –a, –um, of the Tiber.

Tiberis, –is, *m.,* the Tiber, *a river of Italy.*

Tiberius, –rī, *m.,* Tībē'rius, *a Roman name.*

Tīcīnum, –ī, *n.,* Ticinum (Tisī'-num), *a city in Cisalpine Gaul.*

tignum, –ī, *n.,* beam.

Tigrānēs, –is, *m.,* Tigrā'nēs, *king of Armenia.*

timeō, –ēre, –uī, —, fear, be afraid.

timidē, *adv.,* timidly, hesitatingly.

timidus, –a, –um, timid, cowardly.

timor, –ōris, *m.,* fear.

tingō, –ere, tīnxī, tīnctus, wet; color, stain.

Tīrō, –ōnis, *m.,* Tīro, *a name.*

Tītān, –ānis, *m.,* Tītan, *son of Heaven and Earth.*

titulus, –ī, *m.,* inscription; honor.

Tmōlus, –ī, *m.,* Tmōlus, *a mountain in Lydia.*

toga, –ae, *f.,* toga.

togātus, –a, –um, in civilian garb, toga-clad.

tolerō, 1, bear.

tollō, –ere, sustulī, sublātus, raise, take *or* pick up, remove, take away, carry off.

Tolosānus, –a, –um, of Tolō'sa (Toulouse).

tonitrus, –ūs, *m.,* thunder.

tormentum, –ī, *n.,* hurling machine; torture.

Torquātus, –ī, *m.,* Torquā'tus, *a Roman name.*

torqueō, –ēre, torsī, tortus, twist, whirl; torture.

torvus, –a, –um, stern.

tot, *indecl. adj.,* so many.

totidem, *indecl. adj.,* (just) as many.

totiēns, *adv.,* so often.

tōtus, –a, –um, whole, entire.

trabs, trabis, *f.,* beam.

trāctō, 1, handle, treat, conduct; draw into.

trāctus, –ūs, *m.,* (drawing), course.

trādō, –ere, –didī, –ditus, hand over *or* down, deliver, relate.

trahō, –ere, trāxī, trāctus, draw, influence, derive; *w.* **ad sē,** claim.

trāiciō, –ere, –iēcī, –iectus, hurl through, pierce.

trāmittō, –ere, –mīsī, –missus, transmit, hand over.

tranquillitās, –tātis, *f.,* calm, tranquillity.

tranquillus, –a, –um, quiet.

Trānsalpīnus, -a, -um, beyond the Alps, Transalpine.

trānseō, -īre, -iī, -itus, go over, cross; pass.

trānsferō, -ferre, -tulī, -lātus, carry over, transfer.

trānsfuga, -ae, *m.,* deserter.

trānsigō, -ere, -ēgī, -āctus, carry out.

trānsitus, -ūs, *m.,* passage.

trānsmarīnus, -a, -um, beyond the sea.

trānsmittō, -ere, -mīsī, -missus, send across; cross; devote.

Trānspadānus, -a, -um, beyond the Po.

trecentiēs, *adv.,* three hundred times.

tremebundus, -a, -um, quivering.

tremō, -ere, -uī, —, shake, tremble.

tremulus, -a, -um, trembling.

trepidanter, *adv.,* tremblingly.

trepidō, 1, tremble, rush about.

trepidus, -a, -um, trembling.

trēs, tria, three.

tribūnal, -ālis, *n.,* platform, tribunal.

tribūnātus, -ūs, *m.,* tribunate.

tribūnīcius, -a, -um, of a tribune.

tribūnus, -ī, *m.,* tribune.

tribuō, -ere, -uī, -ūtus, bestow, grant, assign.

trīclīnium, -nī, *n.,* dining couch.

triennium, -nī, *n.,* (a space of) three years.

trīgintā, thirty.

Trimalchiō, -ōnis, *m.,* Trimal'chio, *a name.*

triquetrum, -ī, *n.,* triangle.

trīstis, -e, sad.

trīticum, -ī, *n.,* wheat.

trītus, -a, -um, beaten.

triumphō, 1, triumph, celebrate a triumph.

triumphus, -ī, *m.,* triumph, triumphal procession.

Trōiānus, -a, -um, Trojan; *as noun, m.,* the Trojans.

tropaeum, -ī, *n.,* trophy.

trucīdō, 1, butcher, murder.

trūdō, -ere, trūsī, trūsus, thrust, shove forward.

truncō 1, strip.

truncus, -ī, *m.,* trunk (*of a tree*).

tū, tuī, you.

tuba, -ae, *f.,* trumpet.

Tuberō, -ōnis, *m.,* Tu'bero, *a Roman name.*

tueor, -ērī, tūtus sum, watch, defend, maintain.

Tullia, -ae, *f.,* Tul'lia, *Cicero's daughter.*

Tullius, -lī, *m.,* Tul'lius, *a Roman name.*

Tullus, -ī, *m.,* Tullus, *a Roman name.*

tum, *adv.,* then.

tumultus, -ūs, *m.,* disturbance, civil war.

tumulus, -ī, *m.,* hill; tomb.

tunc, *adv.,* then; accordingly.

tunica, -ae, *f.,* tunic.

turba, -ae, *f.,* (turmoil), throng.

turbidus, -a, -um, violent, troubled.

turbulentus, -a, -um, disorderly, violent.

turpis, -e, disgraceful.

turpiter, *adv.,* basely.

turpitūdō, –dinis, *f.,* disgrace, baseness.

tūs, tūris, *n.,* incense.

Tusculānum, –ī, *n.,* Tusculan estate.

tussis, –is, *f.,* cough.

tutēla, –ae, *f.,* charge; guardian.

tūtō, *adv.,* safely.

tūtus, –a, –um, safe.

tuus, –a, –um, your, yours (*referring to one person*).

tyrannus, –ī, *m.,* tyrant.

Tyrius, –a, –um, Tyrian.

U

ūber, –eris, abounding, full.

ūbertās, –tātis, *f.,* richness, fertility.

ubi, *adv.,* where; when; **ubi prīmum,** as soon as.

ubīque, *adv.,* everywhere.

ulcīscor, –ī, ultus sum, avenge, punish.

ūllus, –a, –um, any.

ultimus, –a, –um, farthest, most distant, last.

ultiō, –ōnis, *f.,* revenge.

ultrā, *adv. and prep. w. acc.,* beyond, more.

ultrō, *adv.,* of one's own accord, voluntarily; actually.

ululātus, –ūs, *m.,* wailing, shrieking.

umbra, –ae, *f.,* shade.

Umbrēnus, –ī, *m.,* Umbrē′nus, *a Roman name.*

umerus, –ī, *m.,* shoulder.

ūmidus, –a, –um, moist, dewy.

ūmor, –ōris, *m.,* moisture.

umquam, *adv.,* ever.

ūnā, *adv.,* along with, together, at the same time *or* place (with).

unda, –ae, *f.,* wave; water.

unde, *adv.,* from which (point), whence.

ūndēquīnquāgēsimus, –a, –um, forty-ninth.

undique, *adv.,* from *or* on all sides, everywhere.

ungō, –ere, ūnxī, ūnctus anoint.

unguentum, –ī, *n.,* ointment, perfume.

ūnicē, *adv.,* singularly, devotedly.

ūnicus, –a, –um, only.

ūniversus, –a, –um, all (together), whole, in a body.

ūnus, –a, –um, one, single, alone, sole.

urbānitās, –tātis, *f.,* wit.

urbānus, –a, –um, of *or* in the city; polished; facetious.

urbs, urbis, *f.,* city.

urgeō, –ēre, ursī, —, press hard *or* on.

urna, –ae, *f.,* urn.

ūrō, –ere, ussī, ustus, burn, parch.

ūsitātus, –a, –um, customary.

usquam, *adv.,* anywhere.

usque, *adv.,* even (to), all the time, as far as; **w. adeō,** to such an extent.

ūsūra, –ae, *f.,* use, enjoyment.

ūsūrpō, 1, use, employ.

ūsus, –ūs, *m.,* use, need, advantage; practice.

ut, utī, *conj.,* in order that, that, so that (*w. subjunct.*); as, when (*w. indic.*); *adv.,* how, as.

uterque, utraque, utrumque, each (of two), either, both.

utī = ut.

ūtilis, –e, useful, helpful.

ūtilitās, –tātis, f., usefulness, advantage.

utinam! adv., oh that! would that!

ūtor, ūtī, ūsus sum, use, make use of, employ.

utrimque, adv., on both sides.

utrum, conj., whether; utrum . . . an, whether . . . or; in dir. quest. it cannot be translated.

ūva, –ae, f., grapes.

uxor, –ōris, f., wife.

V

vacillō, 1, stagger.

vacō, 1, be free from, empty, or unoccupied.

vacuēfaciō, –ere, fēcī, –factus, make empty, free, or vacant.

vacuus, –a, –um, empty; without, free.

Vadimōnis (w. lacus), Vadimō'nis, a small lake in Etruria.

vadimōnium, –nī, n., bail-bond, security.

vādō, ere, —, —, go.

vāgīna, –ae, f., sheath.

vagor, –ārī, –ātus sum, wander.

vagus, –a, –um, wandering, uncertain, vague.

valdē, adv., strongly, very (much), exceedingly.

valeō, –ēre, –uī, –itūrus, be well or in good health, be able, strong; have influence, succeed, excel; valē, valēte, farewell.

Valerius, –rī, m., Vale'rius, a Roman name.

valētūdō, –dinis, f., health; sickness.

vallēs, vallis, f., valley.

vāllō, 1, defend (as if by a rampart).

vāllum, –ī, n., rampart, intrenchment.

vānitās, –tātis, f., folly.

variē, adv., in different ways.

varietās, –tātis, f., variety, variation.

varius, –a, –um, diverse, various, changing.

Varrō, –ōnis, m., Varro, a Roman author.

vāstātiō, –ōnis, f., laying waste, destruction.

vāstitās, –tātis, f., devastation.

vāstō, 1, lay waste, destroy.

vāstus, –a, –um, vast, immense.

Vatīnius, –nī, m., Vatin'ius, a Roman name.

–ve, conj., or.

vectīgal, –ālis, n., tax, revenue.

vectīgālis, –e, tributary; as noun, m., tributary.

vehemēns, gen. –entis, violent, rigorous, strong.

vehementer, adv., violently, greatly, earnestly.

vehiculum, –ī, n., carriage.

vel, conj., or; vel . . . vel, either . . . or; adv., even, at least; very; w. superl., the most . . . possible.

vēlāmen, –minis, n., veil, cloak.

vēlō, 1, cover, veil.

vēlōcitās, –tātis, f., swiftness.
vēlōciter, adv., swiftly.
vēlōx, –ōcis, swift.
vēlum, –ī, n., awning; sail.
velut, velutī, adv., just as, like.
vēna, –ae, f., vein.
vēnālis, –e, for sale.
vēnātiō, –ōnis, f., hunting.
vēnātus, –ūs, m., hunting.
vēndō, –ere, –didī, –ditus, sell.
venēnum, –ī, n., poison.
vēneō, –īre, –iī, —, be sold.
venerandus, –a, –um, revered, venerable.
veneror, –ārī, –ātus sum, worship.
venia, –ae, f., favor; pardon.
veniō, –īre, vēnī, ventus, come.
vēnor, –ārī, –ātus sum, hunt.
venter, ventris, m., stomach.
ventus, –ī, m., wind.
Venusīnum, –ī, n., Venu'sian villa.
venustās, –tātis, f., charm.
vēr, vēris, n., spring.
verber, –eris, n., lash; pl., blows.
verberō, 1, beat, strike.
verbum, –ī, n., word.
vērē, adv., truly.
verēcundia, –ae, f., modesty, timidity.
vereor, –ērī, veritus sum, fear; respect.
vēritās, –tātis, f., truth.
vērō, adv., in truth, in fact, indeed; but, however.
Verrius, –rī, m., Ver'rius, a Roman name.
verrō, –ere, verrī, versus, sweep.
versō, 1, turn (often); pass., be engaged in, be employed;

remain, dwell, exist; be skilled; depend on.
versus, –ūs, m., verse.
vertex, –ticis, m., (whirl), head, peak.
vertīgō, –ginis, f., whirl.
vertō, –ere, vertī, versus, turn; sē vertere, wheel about.
vērum, adv., but (in truth).
vērus, –a, –um, true; as noun, n., truth; rē vērā, really.
vēscor, vēscī, —, —, feed, eat.
vespera, –ae, f., evening.
vesperī, at evening.
Vesta, –ae, f., Vesta, goddess of the hearth.
vester, –tra, –trum, your, yours (referring to two or more).
vēstīgium, –gī, n., footstep, track, sole (of the foot); pl., fragments.
vestīmentum, –ī, n., clothing.
vestis, –is, f., clothes, garment, robe.
vetō, –āre, vetuī, vetitus, forbid.
vetus, gen. veteris, old, former, ancient.
vetustās, –tātis, f., old age, age; long standing.
vetustus, –a, –um, old, aged.
vexātiō, –ōnis, f., harassing.
vexō, 1, trouble, harass.
via, –ae, f., way, road, street; journey; viam mūnīre, build a road.
viāticum, –ī, n., traveling money.
vibrō, 1, brandish.
Vibullius, –lī, m., Vibul'lius, a Roman name.
vīcēsimus, –a, –um, twentieth

vīcīnia, –ae, *f.*, neighborhood, nearness.

vīcīnus, –a, –um, neighboring; *as noun, m.*, neighbor.

(vicis), –is, *f.*, change; in vicem *or* vicēs, in turn.

victima, –ae, *f.*, victim.

victor, –ōris, victorious; *as noun, m.*, victor.

victōria, –ae, *f.*, victory.

victrīx, –īcis, victorious; *as noun, f.*, victor.

vīctus, –ūs, *m.*, living.

vīcus, –ī, *m.*, village, street.

vidēlicet, *adv.*, (one may see), evidently; of course, doubtless.

videō, –ēre, vīdī, vīsus, see; *pass.*, seem, seem best.

vigeō, –ēre, –uī, —, be vigorous, thrive.

vigil, –ilis, watchful.

vigilāns, *gen.* –antis, watchful, active.

vigilia, –ae, *f.*, watching, loss of sleep, guarding, watch; sentinel.

vigilō, 1, keep awake, watch.

vīgintī, *indecl.*, twenty.

vīlicus, –ī, *m.*, overseer, steward.

vīlis, –e, cheap.

vīlitās, –tātis, *f.*, cheapness.

vīlla, –ae, *f.*, farmhouse, country home, villa.

villus, –ī, *m.*, shaggy hair.

vinciō, –īre, vīnxī, vīnctus, bind.

vincō, –ere, vīcī, victus, conquer, defeat; exhaust.

vinculum, –ī, *n.*, fastening, chain, bond.

vindicō, 1, avenge, punish; claim, assert one's claim to.

vīnea, –ae, *f.*, vine.

vīnum, –ī, *n.*, wine.

violentia, –ae, *f.*, violence, oppression.

violentus, –a, –um, impetuous.

violō, 1, wrong, dishonor, injure.

vir, virī, *m.*, man; husband.

virēns, *gen.* –entis, green.

virga, –ae, *f.*, twig, rod.

virgō, –ginis, *f.*, virgin, maiden.

viridis, –e, green.

viriditās, –tātis, *f.*, greenness, freshness.

virīlis, –e, manly.

virtūs, –tūtis, *f.*, manliness, courage, virtue, worth, character, ability.

vīs, —, *f.*, force, power, violence, energy; *pl.* vīrēs, vīrium, strength.

vīscera, –um, *n. pl.*, vitals.

vīsō, –ere, vīsī, vīsus, go to see, view.

vīta, –ae, *f.*, life.

vītis, –is, *f.*, vine.

vitium, –tī, *n.*, defect, fault, vice.

vītō, 1, avoid, escape.

vīvō, –ere, vīxī, vīctus, live.

vīvus, –a, –um, alive, living.

vix, *adv.*, hardly, scarcely, with difficulty.

vocābulum, –ī, *n.*, word, substantive.

vocātīvus, –a, –um, vocative.

vōciferor, –ārī, –ātus sum, cry out, exclaim.

vocō, 1, call, summon.

volātus, –ūs, *m.*, flying, flight.

volō, 1, fly.

volō, velle, voluī, —, wish, want, intend.

Volturcius, –cī, *m.,* Volturcius (Voltur'shius), *a conspirator.*

volucer, –cris, –cre, flying, fleet.

volūmen, –minis, *n.,* roll, volume; revolution.

voluntārius, –a, –um, willing, voluntary; *w.* **mīles,** volunteer.

voluntās, –tātis, *f.,* will, good will, wish, loyalty, purpose; consent.

voluptās, –tātis, *f.,* pleasure, satisfaction.

volvō, –ere, volvī, volūtus, turn (over), ponder; *pass.,* roll, be hurled.

vomō, –ere, –uī, –itus, throw out, emit.

vōtum, –ī, *n.,* vow, wish, prayer.

voveō, –ēre, vōvī, vōtus, vow; wish for.

vōx, vōcis, *f.,* voice, cry; word.

Vulcānius, –a, –um, of Vulcan.

vulgō, *adv.,* generally, everywhere.

vulgus, –ī, *n.,* common people, crowd.

vulnerō, 1, wound.

vulnus, vulneris, *n.,* wound.

vultus, –ūs, *m.,* expression, face, looks, features; presence.

X

Xerxēs, –is, *m.,* Xerxēs, *king of Persia.*

Z

Zōsimus, –ī, *m.,* Zo'simus, *Pliny's freedman.*

ENGLISH–LATIN VOCABULARY

For proper nouns and proper adjectives not given in this vocabulary see the Latin-English Vocabulary or the Latin passage on which the English sentence is based.

Verbs of the first and fourth conjugations whose parts are regular are indicated by the figures 1 and 4 respectively.

A

abandon, dēpōnō, –ere, –posuī, –positus.

ability, ingenium, –nī, *n.*

able (be), possum, posse, potuī, —.

about, dē, *w. abl.*

accept, accipiō, –ere, –cēpī, –ceptus.

accomplish, faciō, –ere, fēcī, factus; cōnficiō, –ere, –fēcī, –fectus; gerō, –ere, gessī, gestus.

accusation, crīmen, crīminis, *n.*

accuse, accūsō, 1.

accustomed (be), soleō, –ēre, solitus sum.

add, acquīrō, –ere, acquīsīvī, acquīsītus; ascīscō, –ere, ascīvī, ascītus.

adopt, capiō, –ere, cēpī, captus.

advance, prōcēdō, –ere, –cessī, –cessus; prōgredior, –gredī, –gressus sum.

advise, moneō, –ēre, monuī, monitus; praecipiō, –ere, –cēpī, –ceptus; suādeō, –ēre, suāsī, suāsus.

afraid (be), metuō, –ere, –uī, —.

after (*prep.*), post, *w. acc.*; (*conj.*), postquam.

again, iterum.

against, contrā, in, *w. acc.*; cum, *w. abl.*

age, aetās, –tātis, *f.*

aid (*noun*), auxilium, –lī, *n.*; subsidium, –dī, *n.*; (*verb*), adiuvō, –āre, –iūvī, –iūtus.

alive (be), vīvō, –ere, vīxī, victus.

all, omnis, –e; tōtus, –a, –um; **at all,** omnīnō.

allow, patior, patī, passus sum.

almost, paene.

already, iam.

also, etiam; quoque.

although, cum; quamquam.

always, semper.

ambitions, cupiditās, –tātis, *f.*

among, apud, inter, *w. acc.*

ancestors, maiōrēs, –um, *m. pl.*

and, et; –que.

annoying, molestus, –a, –um.

any, ūllus, –a, –um; **any one,** aliquis, aliquid; quis, quid.

appear, appāreō, –ēre, –pāruī, –pāritūrus.

approve, probō, 1.

aqueduct, aquaeductus, –ūs, *m.*

arm, armō, 1.

army, exercitus, –ūs, *m.*

arouse, concitō, 1.

arrest, comprehendō, –ere, –hendī, –hēnsus.

art, ars, artis, *f.*

as, ut ; **as if,** quasi.

ashamed (be), pudōre addūcor, –dūcī, –ductus sum.

ask, rogō, 1 ; petō, –ere, petīvī, petītus ; quaerō, –ere, quaesīvī, quaesītus ; **ask again,** repetō.

assemble, conveniō, –īre, –vēnī, –ventus.

assembly, cōntiō, –ōnis, *f.*

associate, socius, –cī, *m.*

atrium, ātrium, ātrī, *n.*

attack (*noun*), impetus, –ūs, *m.* ; (*verb*), oppugnō, 1.

attain, assequor, –sequī, –secūtus sum.

attribute, sūmō, –ere, sūmpsī, sūmptus.

authority, auctōritās, –tātis, *f.*

avail, prōsum, prōdesse, prō-fuī, —.

avarice, avāritia, –ae, *f.*

avenge, ulcīscor, ulcīscī, ultus sum.

avoid, vītō, 1.

await, exspectō, 1.

away (be), absum, –esse, āfuī, āfutūrus.

B

bad, malus, –a, –um.

ball, pila, –ae, *f.*

banish, prohibeō, –ēre, –hibuī, –hibitus.

baseness, turpitūdō, –dinis, *f.*

battle, pugna –ae, *f.*

be, sum, esse, fuī, futūrus.

bear, ferō, ferre, tulī, lātus.

beat back, retundō, –ere, ret-tudī, retūsus.

beautiful, pulcher, –chra, –chrum.

beauty, pulchritūdō, –dinis, *f.*

because, quod ; quia ; **because of,** propter, *w. acc.*

become, fīō, fierī, factus sum.

bed, lectus, –ī, *m.*

bedroom, cubiculum, –ī, *n.*

before (*prep.*), prae, *w. abl.* ; ante, apud, *w. acc.* ; (*adv.*), ante, anteā ; (*conj.*), ante-quam, priusquam ; **night before,** proxima nox.

beg, petō, –ere, petīvī, petītus ; rogō, 1.

behalf (in), prō, *w. abl.*

believe, crēdō, –ere, crēdidī, crēditus.

blot out, exstinguō, –ere, –stīnxī, –stīnctus.

body, corpus, corporis, *n.* ; ōrdō, –dinis, *m.*

bold, audāx, *gen.* audācis.

boldness, audācia, –ae, *f.*

book, liber, librī, *m.*

booty, praeda, –ae, *f.*

born (be), nāscor, nāscī, nātus sum.

both . . . and, et . . . et.

boy, puer, puerī, *m.*

brave, fortis, –e.

bravely, fortiter.

bravery, virtūs, –tūtis, *f.*

brigandage, latrōcinium, –nī, *n.*

bring about, efficiō, –ere, –fēcī, –fectus ; perficiō ; **bring away,** efferō, efferre, extulī, ēlātus ; **bring back,** reportō,

1; redūcō, –ere, –dūxī, –ductus.

brother, frāter, –tris, *m.*

build, aedificō, 1.

burn, incendō, –ere, –cendī, –cēnsus.

business, negōtium, –tī, *n.*

but, sed; autem; **but if,** sīn.

buy, emō, –ere, ēmī, ēmptus.

by, ā, ab, *w. abl.*

C

Calends, Kalendae, –ārum, *f.*

call, appellō, 1; vocō, 1; **call at,** vīsō, –ere, vīsī, vīsus; **call together,** convocō, 1; **call upon,** rogō, 1.

camp, castra, –ōrum, *n. pl.*

can, possum, posse, potuī, —.

capture, capiō, –ere, cēpī, captus.

care, cūra, –ae, *f.*

carry away, auferō, –ferre, abstulī, ablātus; **carry on,** gerō, –ere, gessī, gestus.

case, causa, –ae, *f.*

cast, iaciō, –ere, iēcī, iactus.

catch, capiō, –ere, cēpī, captus.

cause, causa, –ae, *f.*

cavalry, equitātus, –ūs, *m.*; equitēs, –um, *m.*

cavalryman, eques, –itis, *m.*

cease, cessō, 1; dēsinō, –ere, –siī, –situs.

censor, cēnsor, –ōris, *m.*

certain, quīdam, quaedam, quiddam.

cheap, vīlis, –e.

children, līberī, –ōrum, *m. pl.*

choose, dēligō, –ere, –lēgī, –lēctus.

citizen, cīvis, –is, *m.*

citizenship, cīvitās, –tātis, *f.*

city, urbs, urbis, *f.*

civil, cīvīlis, –e.

class, genus, generis, *n.*

cleanse, pūrgō, 1.

clever, callidus, –a, –um.

cling, haereō, –ēre, haesī, haesus.

close, claudō, –ere, clausī, clausus.

cohort, cohors, cohortis, *f.*

colony, colōnia, –ae, *f.*

come, veniō, –īre, vēnī, ventus.

coming, adventus, –ūs, *m.*

command, auctōritās, –tātis, *f.*

commander, imperātor, –ōris, *m.*

commit, faciō, –ere, fēcī, factus.

common, commūnis, –e.

complain, queror, querī, questus sum.

complete, perficiō, –ere, –fēcī, –fectus.

comrade, comes, –itis, *m.*; socius. –ci *m.*

conceal, cēlō, 1; dissimulō, 1.

concern (*verb*), sollicitō, 1; (*noun*), cūra, –ae, *f.*

concerning, dē, *w. abl.*

condemn, damnō, 1.

confer, colloquor, –loquī, –locūtus sum.

conference, colloquium, –quī, *n*

confess, fateor, –ērī, fassus sum; cōnfiteor, –ērī, –fessus sum.

confine, contineō, –ēre, –tinuī, –tentus.

confiscation, prōscrīptiō, –ōnis, *f.*

conquer, superō, 1; vincō, –ere, vīcī, victus.

consequently, ergō ; quae cum ita sint.

consider, putō, 1 ; habeō, -ēre, habuī, habitus.

conspiracy, coniūrātiō, -ōnis, *f.*

conspirator, coniūrātus, -ī, *m.*

consul, cōnsul, -ulis, *m.*

consulship, cōnsulātus, -ūs, *m.*

consult, cōnsulō, -ere, -suluī, -sultus.

contend, contendō, -ere, -tendī, -tentus.

content, contentus, -a, -um.

converse, loquor, loquī, locūtus sum.

correct, corrigō, -ere, -rēxī, -rēctus.

corrupt, corrumpō, -ere, -rūpī, -ruptus.

country, patria, -ae, *f.* ; rūs, rūris, *n.*

courage, virtūs, -tūtis, *f.*

credit, fidēs, -eī, *f.*

crime, flāgitium, -tī, *n.* ; scelus, sceleris, *n.*

cruel, crūdēlis, -e.

cruelty, crūdēlitās, -tātis, *f.*

crush, frangō, -ere, frēgī, frāctus.

cry out, clāmō, 1.

cultivate, colō, -ere, coluī, cultus.

culture, doctrīna, -ae, *f.*

cure, sānō, 1.

custody (place in), custōdiō, 4.

custom, mōs, mōris, *m.*

D

daily, cotīdiānus, -a, -um ; (*adv.*), cotīdiē.

danger, perīculum, -ī, *n.*

dare, audeō, -ēre, ausus sum.

dark, obscūrus, -a, -um.

day, diēs, diēī, *m. and f.*

dead, īnferī, -ōrum, *m. pl.*

dear, cārus, -a, -um.

death, mors, mortis, *f.* ; exitium, -tī, *n.*

deceive, fallō, -ere, fefellī, falsus.

decide, statuō, -ere, statuī, statūtus.

declare, dēclārō, 1.

decree (*noun*), cōnsultum, -ī, *n.* ; (*verb*), dēcernō, -ere, -crēvī, -crētus.

deed, factum, -ī, *n.* ; rēs, reī, *f.*

defeat, superō, 1 ; vincō, -ere, vīcī, victus.

defend, dēfendō, -ere, -fendī, -fēnsus.

defer, differō, differre, distulī, dīlātus.

delay (*verb*), moror, 1 ; (*noun*), mora, -ae, *f.*

delight, dēlectō, 1.

demand, postulō, 1 ; flāgitō, 1.

deny, negō, 1.

depart, proficīscor, proficīscī, profectus sum ; excēdō, -ere, -cessī, -cessus ; discēdō.

deprive, prīvō, 1.

deprived (be), careō, -ēre, caruī, caritūrus.

desert, perfugiō, -ere, -fūgī, —.

deserve, mereō, -ēre, meruī, meritus.

desire (*verb*), cupiō, -ere, -īvī, -ītus ; (*noun*), studium, -dī, *n.*

despise, dēspiciō, -ere, -spexī, -spectus ; contemnō, -ere, -tempsī, -temptus.

destroy, absūmō, -ere, -sūmpsī, -sūmptus ; dēstruō, -ere,

–strūxī, –strūctus; dēleō, –ēre, dēlēvī, dēlētus.

destruction, exitium, –tī, *n.*

devote, tribuō, –ere, tribuī, tribūtus.

die (*noun*), ālea, –ae, *f.* ; (*verb*), morior, morī, mortuus sum.

difficult, difficilis, –e.

diligence, dīligentia, –ae, *f.*

disagree, dissentiō, –īre, –sēnsī, –sēnsus.

disaster, calamitās, –tātis, *f.*

discord, dissēnsiō, –ōnis, *f.*

discover, reperiō, –īre, repperī, repertus.

discussion, cōnsilium, –lī, *n.*

disgrace, ignōminia, –ae, *f.* ; dēdecus, –coris, *n.*

disgracefully, turpiter.

dispute, contentiō, –ōnis, *f.*

distant, longinquus, –a, –um.

distribute, distribuō, –ere, –tribuī, –tribūtus.

disturbance, tumultus, –ūs, *m.*

do, agō, –ere, ēgī, āctus; faciō, –ere, fēcī, factus; cōnficiō, –ere, –fēcī, –fectus.

doctor, medicus, –ī, *m.*

doubt (*verb*), dubitō, 1 ; **is no doubt = is not doubtful ; no doubt,** scīlicet.

doubtful, dubius, –a, –um.

drag away, rapiō, –ere, rapuī, raptus.

draw, dēstringō, –ere, –strīnxī, –strictus.

drive, drive from, expellō, –ere, –pulī, –pulsus.

E

eagle, aquila, –ae, *f.*

ear, auris, –is, *f.*

easily, facile.

easy, facilis, –e.

educate, ēducō, 1.

educated, ērudītus, –a, –um.

either . . . or, aut . . . aut.

else, alius, –a, –ud.

empire, imperium, –rī, *n.*

empty, vacuus, –a, –um.

end, fīnis, –is, *m.*

endure, ferō, ferre, tulī, lātus.

enemy, inimīcus, –ī, *m.* ; hostis, –is, *m.*

enjoy, fruor, fruī, frūctus sum ; dēlector, 1.

enter, ingredior, –gredī, –gressus sum ; veniō, –īre, vēnī, ventus.

envoy, lēgātus, –ī, *m.*

envy, invideō, –ēre, –vīdī, –vīsus.

equal, pār, *gen.* paris.

escape, effugiō, –ere, –fūgī, –fugitūrus.

even, etiam.

every, omnis, –e ; **everybody,** omnēs ; **everything,** omnia.

evil, malus, –a, –um ; (*noun*), malum, –ī, *n.*

example, exemplum, –ī, *n.*

excel, praestō, –āre, –stitī, –stitus.

excellent, bonus, –a, –um ; summus, –a, –um.

except, nisi ; praeter, *w. acc.*

exchange (*verb*), permūtō, 1 ; (*noun*), permūtātiō, –ōnis, *f.*

exclaim, (con)clāmō, 1.

exercise, exercitātiō, –ōnis, *f.*

exile, exsilium, –lī, *n.*

expect, exspectō, 1.

expense, sūmptus, –ūs, *m.*

explain, expōnō, –ere, –posuī, –positus.

expose, dēprehendō, –ere, –hendī, –hēnsus.

extinguish, compescō, –ere, –pescuī, —.

extol, tollō, –ere, sustulī, sublātus.

eye, oculus. –ī, *m.*

F

face, faciēs, –ēī, *f.*

fact (in), vērō.

fact that, quod.

fail, dēsum, deesse, dēfuī, dēfutūrus.

faithful, fidēlis, –e.

family, familia, –ae, *f.*

famous, clārus, –a, –um.

far (so), tantum.

farm, praedium, –dī, *n.*

fast (how), quantā celeritāte.

fat, pinguis, –e.

father, pater, patris, *m.*

fatherland, patria, –ae, *f.*

fault (find), *see* **find.**

fear (*verb*), timeō, –ēre, timuī, —; metuō, –ere, –uī, —; vereor, –ērī, veritus sum; (*noun*), timor, –ōris, *m.*; metus, –ūs, *m.*

feast, epulor, 1.

feed, vēscor, vēscī, —.

fellow citizens, Quirītēs, –ium, *m. pl.*

few, paucī, –ae, –a.

fight, dīmicō, 1; pugnō, 1; certō, 1.

finally, aliquandō.

find, reperiō, –īre, repperī, repertus; inveniō, –īre, –vēnī, –ventus; **find fault with,** suscēnseō, –ēre, –cēnsuī, –cēnsus.

fine, bonus, –a, –um; clārus, –a, –um.

finish, cōnficiō, –ere, –fēcī, –fectus; perficiō.

fire, ignis, –is, *m.*; incendium, –dī, *n.*; flamma, –ae, *f.*

first, prīmus, –a, –um; (*adv.*), prīmum.

flee, fugiō, –ere, fūgī, fugitūrus.

follow, sequor, sequī, secūtus sum.

fond (be), amō, 1.

foot, pēs, pedis, *m.*

for (*conj.*), nam, enim; (*prep.*), prō, *w. abl.;* ad, propter, *w. acc.*

forbid, vetō, –āre, vetuī, vetitus.

forces, cōpiae, –ārum, *f. pl.*

forehead, frōns, frontis, *f.*

foreign, aliēnus, –a, –um; externus, –a, –um.

forget, oblīvīscor, oblīvīscī, oblītus sum.

form a plan, cōnsilium capiō, –ere, cēpī, captus; **form the hope,** *see* **hope.**

fortify, mūniō, 4.

found, condō, –ere, –didī, –ditus.

fourteen, quattuordecim.

free (*adj.*), līber, –era, –erum; (*verb*), līberō, 1; **be free,** careō, –ēre, caruī, caritūrus.

freely, līberē.

friend, amīcus, –ī, *m.*; familiāris, –is, *m.*

friendship, amīcitia, –ae, *f.*

from, ā, ab, ex, *w. abl.*; quīn.

fugitive, fugitīvus, –ī, *m.*

full, plēnus, –a, –um.

future, posteritās, –tātis, *f.*

G

gain, quaestus, –ūs, *m.*

garrison, praesidium, –dī, *n.*

genius, ingenium, –nī, *n.*

give, dō, dare, dedī, datus.

gladiator, gladiātor, –ōris, *m.*

gladly, libenter.

glory, glōria, –ae, *f.*

go, eō, īre, iī, itus; abeō; discēdō, –ere, –cessī, –cessus; sē cōnferre; proficīscor, proficīscī, profectus sum; go over, trānseō; go to, adeō.

god, deus, deī, *m.*

good, bonus, –a, –um.

government, rēs pūblica, –ae, *f.*

grant, dō, dare, dedī, datus.

gratitude, grātia, –ae, *f.*

great, magnus, –a, –um; so great, tantus, –a, –um; how great, quantus, –a, –um.

greatly, magnopere.

greedy, avidus, –a, –um.

ground, terra, –ae, *f.*

guard, praesidium, –dī, *n.*

H

hair, capillus, –ī, *m.*

hand, manus, –ūs, *f.*; hand over, offerō, offerre, obtulī, oblātus.

hang over, impendeō, –ēre, —.

happen, accidō, –ere, –cidī, —; contingō, –ere, –tigī, –tāctus.

happy, laetus, –a, –um.

harass, vexō, 1.

harm, dētrīmentum, –ī, *n.*

harmony, concordia, –ae, *f.*

hasten, properō, 1; mātūrō, 1.

hate, ōdī, ōdisse, ōsūrus.

have, habeō, –ēre, habuī, habitus.

he, is; hīc; ille.

hear, audiō, 4.

help, ūsus, –ūs, *m.*

hen, gallīna, –ae, *f.*

herd, grex, gregis, *m.*

here, hīc; be here, adsum, –esse, –fuī, –futūrus.

hesitate, dubitō, 1.

hide, obscūrō, 1.

high, magnus, –a, –um; so high, tantus, –a, –um.

himself (*reflex.*), suī; (*intens.*), ipse.

hinder, impediō, 4.

hire, condūcō, –ere, –dūxī, –ductus.

his (*poss.*), eius; his own (*reflex.*), suus, –a, –um.

hold, habeō, –ēre, habuī, habitus.

home, aedēs, –ium, *f. pl.*; domus, –ūs, *f.*; tēctum, –ī, *n.*; at the home of, apud, *w. acc.*

honor, honor, –ōris, *m.*

honorable, honestus, –a, –um.

hope (*noun*), spēs, speī, *f.*; form the hope, in spem venīre; (*verb*), spērō, 1.

horse, equus, –ī, *m.*

hostile, īnfestus, –a, –um; inimīcus, –a, –um.

house, domus, –ūs, *f.*

how, quem ad modum; quō modō; how great, how much, quantus, –a, –um; how greatly, quantum; how long, quam diū; how many, quot; how many times, how often, quotiēns.

however, autem.

human, hūmānus, –a, –um;
human being, homō, hominis, *m.*
hundred, centum.
hunt, vēnor, 1.
hunting, vēnātiō, –ōnis, *f.*
hurry away, rapiō, –ere, rapuī, raptus.
hurt, noceō, –ēre, nocuī, nocitus.

I

I, ego, meī.
Ides, Īdūs, –uum, *f. pl.*
if, sī.
ignorant (be), ignōrō, 1.
ill, malum, –ī, *n.*
illustrious, clārus, –a, –um.
image, imāgō, imāginis, *f.*
immediately, statim.
immortal, immortālis, –e.
in, in, *w. abl.*
increase, augeō, –ēre, auxī, auctus.
influence (*noun*), auctōritās, –tātis, *f.*; (*verb*), addūcō, –ere, –dūxī, –ductus.
injure, noceō, –ēre, nocuī, nocitus.
instigator, auctor, –ōris, *m.*
interrupt, interpellō, 1.
it, hoc, id.

J

join, (con)iungō, –ere, –iūnxī, –iūnctus.
journey, exeō, –īre, –iī, –itus.
joy, laetitia, –ae, *f.*
judge, iūdex, iūdicis, *m.*

K

keep, dētineō, –ēre, –tinuī, –tentus; servō, 1: **keep**

from, repellō, –ere, reppulī, repulsus; **keep in mind,** meminī, meminisse.
kill, interficiō, –ere, –fēcī, –fectus; caedō, –ere, cecīdī, caesus; occīdō, –ere, –cīdī, –cīsus; necō, 1.
kind, modus, –ī, *m.*
kindly, molliter.
kindness, beneficium, –cī, *n.*; benevolentia, –ae, *f.*
king, rēx, rēgis, *m.*
kingdom, rēgnum, –ī, *n.*
knight, eques, –itis, *m.*
know, intellegō, –ere, –lēxī, –lēctus; sciō, –īre, scīvī, scītus; **not know,** nesciō.

L

labor, labōrō, 1.
land, terra, –ae, *f.*
language, lingua, –ae, *f.*
large, magnus, –a, –um.
last, extrēmus, –a, –um; **at last,** aliquandō.
later, post, posteā.
latter, hic, haec, hoc.
laugh, rīdeō, –ēre, rīsī, rīsus.
lay on, īnferō, īnferre, intulī, illātus; **lay waste,** vāstō, 1.
lead, dūcō, –ere, dūxī, ductus; **lead out,** ēdūcō; **lead through,** perdūcō.
leader, prīnceps, prīncipis, *m.*; dux, ducis, *m.*
learned, ērudītus, –a, –um.
leave, exeō, –īre, –iī, –itus; excēdō, –ere, –cessī, –cessus; **leave behind,** relinquō, –ere, –līquī, –līctus.
less, minus.
lest, nē.

let, patior, patī, passus sum;
  let go, āmittō, -ere, āmīsī,
  āmissus.
letter (epistle), litterae, -ārum,
  f. pl.
lie, pass. of pōnō, -ere, posuī,
  positus; lie down, recubō, 1.
life, vīta, -ae, f.
light, lūx, lūcis, f.; lūmen,
  -minis, n.
like, similis, -e.
listen to, audiō, 4.
live, vīvō, -ere, vīxī, vīctus;
  habitō, 1.
living, vīta, -ae, f.
long, longus, -a, -um; long,
  for a long time, diū; how
  long, quam diū; no longer,
  nōn iam.
look out, prōvideō, -ēre, -vīdī,
  -vīsus.
lose, āmittō, -ere, āmīsī, āmissus.
love (verb), dīligō, -ere, -lēxī,
  -lēctus;(noun), amor,-ōris,m.
lyre, cithara, -ae, f.

M

madness, furor, -ōris, m.
magistracy, magistrate, magistrātus, -ūs, m.
make, faciō, -ere, fēcī, factus;
  efficiō, -ere, -fēcī, -fectus;
  afferō, afferre, attulī, allātus.
man, homō, hominis, m.; vir,
  virī, m.
maniple, pīlus, -ī, m.
many, multī, -ae, -a.
March, Mārtius, -a, -um.
march, iter, itineris, n.
mark out, dēsignō, 1.
master, dominus, -ī, m.

matter, rēs, reī, f.
means, ratiō, -ōnis, f.
method, genus, generis, n.
middle, medius, -a, -um.
mile, mīlle (passūs).
mind, animus, -ī, m.; mēns,
  mentis, f.; keep in mind, see
  keep.
mistaken (be), errō, 1.
money, pecūnia, -ae, f.
monument, monumentum, -ī, n.
moon, lūna, -ae, f.
more, magis; plūs.
moreover, autem.
most, plūrimī, -ae, -a.
mourn, lūgeō, -ēre, lūxī, lūctus.
move, commoveō, -ēre, -mōvī,
  -mōtus; permoveō.
municipality, mūnicipium, -pī,
  n.
murder, caedēs, -is, f.
my, meus, -a, -um.

N

name, nōmen, -minis, n.
nation, populus, -ī, m.
nearest, proximus, -a, -um.
neck, cervīx, -īcis, f.
need (have), opus esse.
neighbor, vīcīnus, -ī, m.
never, numquam.
nevertheless, tamen.
new, novus, -a, -um.
night, nox, noctis, f.
no, nōn; nūllus, -a, -um;
  nobody, no one, nēmō, dat.
  nēminī, acc. nēminem.
noble, nōbilis, -e.
nobody, see no.
nod, nūtus, -ūs, m.
nor, neque, nec.
not, nōn, nē.

nothing, nihil.
now, nunc.
number, numerus, –ī, *m.*

O

O! Ō!
obey, pāreō, –ēre, pāruī, pāri-
tus.
obtain, perdūcō, –ere, –dūxī,
–ductus; obtineō, –ēre,
–tinuī, –tentus.
often, saepe.
Oh! utinam!
old, old man, senex, senis, *m.*
omen, ōmen, ōminis, *n.*
on, in, *w. abl.*
once, ōlim; **at once,** statim.
one, ūnus, –a, –um.
only, sōlus, –a, –um; **not only,**
nōn sōlum.
open, tollō, –ere, sustulī, sublātus.
opinion, sententia, –ae, *f.*
opportunity, occāsiō, –ōnis, *f.*;
potestās, –tātis, *f.*
oppose, resistō, –ere, –stitī, —.
or, aut; an.
oration, ōrātiō, –ōnis, *f.*
order (*verb*), iubeō, –ēre, iussī,
iussus; **by order,** iussū; **in
order to** *or* **that,** ut.
other, alius, –a, –ud; **the
other,** alter, –era, –erum.
ought, dēbeō, –ēre, dēbuī, dēbitus.
our, noster, –tra, –trum.
out of, ex, *w. abl.*
outside, extrā, *w. acc.*
over (**be**), perfectus, –a, –um.
overcome, permoveō, –ēre,
–mōvī, –mōtus; vincō, –ere,
vīcī, victus.

overlook, neglegō, –ere, neglēxī,
neglēctus.
overthrow, ēvertō, –ere, ēvertī,
ēversus.
owe, dēbeō, –ēre, dēbuī,
dēbitus.
own, *see* **my,** *etc.*

P

pardon, venia, –ae, *f.*
parent, parēns, –ntis, *m.*
part, pars, partis, *f.*
participant, particeps, –cipis,
m.
pass over, omittō, –ere, omīsī,
omissus.
pay, stīpendium, –dī, *n.*
peace, pāx, pācis, *f.*
people, populus, –ī, *m.*
perhaps, fortasse.
perish, intereō, –īre, –iī, –itus;
pereō.
permit, patior, patī, passus sum.
persuade, persuādeō, –ēre,
–suāsī, –suāsus.
pity, misericordia, –ae, *f.*
placate, plācō, 1.
place (*noun*), locus, –ī, *m.* (*pl.
n.*); (*verb*), pōnō, –ere, posuī,
positus; **place in command,**
praeficiō, –ere, –fēcī, –fectus;
place in custody, *see* **custody.**
plague, pestis, –is, *f.*
plan (*noun*), cōnsilium, –lī, *n.*;
(*verb*), cōgitō, 1.
please, placeō, –ēre, placuī,
placitus.
pleasing, iūcundus, –a, –um;
be pleasing, placeō, –ēre,
placuī, placitus.
pleasure, voluptās, –tātis, *f.*
plot, mōlior, 4; īnsidior, 1.

plunder, dīripiō, –ere, –ripuī, –reptus; spoliō, 1.
poem, carmen, –minis, *n.*
poet, poēta, –ae, *m.*
possess, habeō, –ēre, habuī, habitus; possideō, –ēre, –sēdī, –sessus.
possession of (get), potior, 4.
power, potestās, –tātis, *f.*
praetor, praetor, –ōris, *m.*
praise (*verb*), laudō, 1; (*noun*), laus, laudis, *f.*
predict, praedīcō, –ere, –dīxī, –dictus.
prefer, mālō, mālle, māluī, —.
prepare, parō, 1.
present (be), intersum, –esse, –fuī, –futūrus.
preserve, cōnservō, 1.
prevent, impediō, 4.
price, pretium, –tī, *n.*
prison, carcer, –eris, *m.*
prisoner, captīvus, –ī, *m.*
private, prīvātus, –a, –um.
prize, praemium, –mī, *n.*
promise, polliceor, poilicērī, pollicitus sum.
property, bona, –ōrum, *n. pl.*
protect, tegō, –ere, tēxī, tēctus.
prove, probō, 1.
provide, prōvideō, –ēre, –vīdī, –vīsus.
provided that, dum (modo).
public, pūblicus, –a, –um.
punish, pūniō, 4.
punishment, supplicium, –cī, *n.*
purchase, emō, –ere, ēmī, ēmptus.
pursue, īnsequor, –sequī, –secūtus sum.
put to death, interficiō, –ere, –fēcī, –fectus.

Q

quaestor, quaestor, –ōris, *m.*
question, quaestiō, –ōnis, *f.*
quickness, celeritās, –tātis, *f.*
quiet (be), taceō, –ēre, tacuī, tacitus.

R

raise, excitō, 1.
rashly, temere.
rashness, temeritās, –tātis, *f.*
rather, potius.
read, legō, –ere, lēgī, lēctus; **read through,** perlegō.
ready, parātus, –a, –um.
realize, intellegō, –ere, –lēxī, –lēctus.
reason (for that), quam ob rem.
recall, revocō, 1.
receive, capiō, –ere, cēpī, captus; accipiō, –ere, –cēpī, –ceptus.
recite, recitō, 1.
recognize, cognōscō, –ere, –nōvī, –nitus.
record, tabula, –ae, *f.*
refuse, recūsō, 1.
rejoice, gaudeō, –ēre, gāvīsus sum.
remain, (re)maneō, –ēre, –mānsī, –mānsūrus; restō, –stāre, –stitī, —.
remarkable, mīrus, –a, –um.
remember, meminī, meminisse.
remove, ēripiō, –ere, ēripuī, ēreptus; auferō, –ferre, abstulī, ablātus.
reply, respondeō, –ēre, –spondī, –spōnsus.
report, nūntius, –ī, *m.*
republic, rēs pūblica, reī pūblicae, *f.*

reputation, fāma, –ae, *f.*

respect, vereor, –ērī, veritus sum.

rest, quiēscō, –ere, quiēvī, quiētus; **rest (of),** cēterī, –ae, –a; reliquus, –a, –um.

restrain, contineō, –ēre, –tinuī, –tentus.

retreat, sē recipere.

return, redeō, –īre, rediī, reditus; revertor, –vertī, –versus sum.

revealed (be), pateō, –ēre, patuī, —.

revere, colō, –ere, coluī, cultus.

reward, mercēs, –ēdis, *f.*

right, iūs, iūris, *n.*

robber, latrō, –ōnis, *m.*

rout, pellō, –ere, pepulī, pulsus.

run, currō, –ere, cucurrī, cursus.

S

sacred, sacer, –cra, –crum.

safe, tūtus, –a, –um; salvus, –a, –um.

safety, salūs, –ūtis, *f.*

sake of (for the), causā.

same, īdem, eadem, idem.

sanity, sānitās, –tātis, *f.*

savage, atrōx.

save, (cōn)servō, 1.

say, dīcō, –ere, dīxī, dictus; aiō.

scruple, religiō, –ōnis, *f.*

secretly, sēcrētō.

see, videō, –ēre, vīdī, vīsus.

seed, sēmen, sēminis, *n.*

seek, seek for, petō, –ere, petīvī, petītus; quaerō, –ere, quaesīvī, quaesītus.

seem, videor, –ērī, vīsus sum; **seem best,** placeō, –ēre, placuī, placitus; videor.

seize, occupō, 1.

senate, senātus, –ūs, *m.* ; **senate house,** cūria, –ae, *f.*

senator, senātor, –ōris, *m.*

send, mittō, –ere, mīsī, missus.

separate, sēgregō, 1.

serpent, serpēns, –ntis, *m.*

serve, mīlitō, 1 ; serviō, 4.

set fire, incendō, –ere, –cendī, –cēnsus; **set out,** proficīscor, –ficīscī, –fectus sum; **set up,** statuō, –ere, statuī, statūtus.

settler, colōnus, –ī, *m.*

several, complūrēs, –a(–ia).

short, brevis, –e.

should, oportet; dēbeō.

shoulder, humerus, –ī, *m.*

show, referō, –ferre, rettulī, relātus.

shrink, abhorreō, –ēre, horruī, —.

since, cum; quoniam.

sister, soror, –ōris, *f.*

size, magnitūdō, –dinis, *f.*

slaughter, caedēs, –is, *f.* ; nex, necis, *f.*

slave, servus, –ī, *m.* ; **be a slave,** serviō, 4.

slay, occīdō, –ere, occīdī, occīsus.

sleep, somnus, –ī, *m.*

sluggishness, inertia, –ae, *f.*

small, parvus, –a, –um.

so, ita, tam; **so great, so high, so much,** tantus, –a, –um; **so many,** tot; **so much,** tantopere, tam; **so many times, so often,** totiēns.

soft, mollis, –e.

soldier, mīles, mīlitis, *m.*

solve, solvō, –ere, solvī, solūtus.

some, some people, quīdam, quaedam, quiddam; aliquis, aliquid; some . . . others, aliī . . . aliī.

something, aliquid.

sometime, aliquandō.

sometimes, interdum.

son, fīlius, -lī, *m.*

soon, brevī; mox.

sort, modus, -ī, *m.*; what sort of, quālis, -e.

spare, parcō, -ere, pepercī, parsus.

sparingly, parcē.

speak, dīcō, -ere, dīxī, dictus; loquor, loquī, locūtus sum.

speech, ōrātiō, -ōnis, *f.*

speed, celeritās, -tātis, *f.*

spend, agō, -ere, ēgī, āctus.

spirit, animus, -ī, *m.*

spring (*noun*), fōns, fontis, *m.*; (*verb*), orior, orīrī, ortus sum.

state (*noun*), cīvitās, -tātis, *f.*; (*verb*), dēclārō, 1; dīcō, -ere, dīxī, dictus.

statue, signum, -ī, *n.*

stay, maneō, -ēre, mānsī, mānsus.

steal, fraudō, 1.

stern, sevērus, -a, -um.

stir up, concitō, 1.

street, via, -ae, *f.*

strength, robur, -oris, *n.*

strengthen, cōnfirmō, 1.

strike, percutiō, -ere, -cussī, -cussus.

strong (be), valeō, -ēre, valuī, valitūrus.

study (*noun*), studium, -dī, *n.*; (*verb*), studeō, -ēre, studuī, —.

style, genus, generis, *n.*

subject, rēs, reī, *f.*

such, tālis, -e; tantus, -a, -um.

summer, aestās, -tātis, *f.*

suppliant, supplex, *gen.* supplicis.

support, sustineō, -ēre, -tinuī, -tentus.

suppose (I), scīlicet.

swear, iūrō, 1.

sword, gladius, -ī, *m.*; ferrum, -ī, *n.*

T

tablet, cēra, -ae, *f.*

talent, ingenium, -nī, *n.*

talk, loquor, loquī, locūtus sum.

teacher, praeceptor, -ōris, *m.*

tell, dīcō, -ere, dīxī, dictus.

temple, templum, -ī, *n.*

ten, decem.

than, quam.

that (*conj.*), quod; ut; quīn; in order that, so that, ut; (*dem. pron.*), ille, -a, -ud; is, ea, id; (*rel. pron.*), quī, quae, quod.

their, (*poss.*), eōrum, eārum, eōrum; (*reflex.*), suus, -a, -um.

then, deinde; tum; igitur.

there, ibi.

therefore, igitur.

thing, rēs, reī, *f.*

think, putō, 1; exīstimō, 1: arbitror 1; opīnor, 1; sentiō, -īre, sēnsī, sēnsus.

third, tertius, -a, -um.

this, hic, haec, hoc; is, ea, id.

threaten, minitor, 1.

three, trēs, tria.

through, per.

throw, iaciō, -ere, iēcī, iactus.

time, tempus, –oris, *n.*; **at that time,** tunc.

times (how many), quotiēns; **so many times,** totiēns.

to, ad, *w. acc.*; (*purpose*), ut.

to-day, hodiē.

too, nimis; **too much,** nimius, –a, –um.

torch, fax, facis, *f.*

train, ērudiō, 4.

training, exercitātiō, –ōnis, *f.*

treat, trāctō, 1; attingō, –ere, attigī, attāctus.

trial, cognitiō, –ōnis, *f.*

tribune, tribūnus, –ī, *m.*

trifle, lūdō, –ere, lūsī, lūsus.

true, vērus, –a, –um.

trust, crēdō, –ere, –didī, –ditus.

try, cōnor, 1; temptō, 1.

twenty, vīgintī.

two, duo, duae, duo.

U

unable (be), nōn possum.

unbelievable, incrēdibilis, –e.

under, sub, *w. abl.*

understand, intellegō, –ere, –lēxī, –lēctus.

undertake, suscipiō, –ere, –cēpī, –ceptus.

unfinished, imperfectus, –a, –um.

unite, coniungō, –ere, –iūnxī, –iūnctus.

unless, nisi.

unpopularity, invidia, –ae, *f.*

until, dum.

unwilling (be), nōlō, nōlle, nōluī, —.

uprightly, honestē.

urge, hortor, 1.

use, ūtor, ūtī, ūsus sum.

V

vain (in), frūstrā.

verse, versus, –ūs, *m.*

very, ipse, –a, –um.

victor, victor, –ōris, *m.*

victory, victōria, –ae, *f.*

vigorously, vehementer.

villa, vīlla, –ae, *f.*

violence, vīs, —, *f.*

vocative, vocātīvus, –ī, *m.*

voice, vōx, vōcis, *f.*

vow, voveō, –ēre, vōvī, vōtus.

W

wait, wait for, moror, 1; exspectō, 1.

walls, moenia, –ium, *n. pl.*

want, volō, velle, voluī, —; dēsīderō, 1; not want, nōlō, nōlle, nōluī, —.

war, bellum, –ī, *n.*

warn, moneō, –ēre, monuī, monitus.

waste, perdō, –ere, –didī, –ditus.

watch, speculor, 1; watch out, be on the watch, vigilō, 1.

watchful, vigilāns, *gen.* –ntis.

water, aqua, –ae, *f.*

way, iter, itineris, *n.*; modus, –ī, *m.*

weak, īnfirmus, –a, –um.

wealth, opēs, –um, *f. pl.*

weapon, tēlum, –ī, *n.*

weep, fleō, –ēre, flēvī, flētus.

well, bene; be well, valeō, –ēre, valuī, valitūrus.

what, quis, quid.

whatever, sī quid.

when, cum.

where, quō; ubi; where in the world, ubinam (gentium).

whether, utrum.

which (of two), uter, utra, utrum.

while, dum.

who (*rel.*), quī, quae, quod; (*interrog.*), quis, quid.

whoever, quisquis, quicquid.

whole, tōtus, –a, –um.

why, cūr.

wicked, improbus, –a, –um; nefārius, –a, –um.

wife, uxor, –ōris, *f.*

will (*noun*), testāmentum, –ī, *n.*; (*verb*), volō, velle, voluī, —.

willing (be), volō, velle, voluī, —.

win, conciliō, 1; **win over,** plācō, 1

window, fenestra, –ae, *f.*

wine, vīnum, –ī, *n.*

wisdom, cōnsilium, –lī, *n.*

wise, sapiēns, *gen.* –ntis.

wish, volō, velle, voluī, —; **not wish,** nōlō, nōlle, nōluī,—.

with, cum, *w. abl.*; apud, *w. acc.*

withdraw, dētrahō, –ere, –trāxī, –trāctus.

within, intrā, *w. acc.*

without, sine, *w. abl.*

woman, fēmina, –ae, *f.*

wonder, mīror, 1.

wont (be), soleō, –ēre, solitus sum.

word, verbum, –ī, *n.*

work, opus, operis, *n.*

world, orbis terrārum; cīvitās, –tātis, *f.*; **where in the world,** ubinam (gentium).

worship, veneror, 1.

worthlessness, nēquitia, –ae, *f.*

worthy, dignus, –a, –um.

wretched, miserābilis, –e.

write, scrībō, –ere, scrīpsī, scrīptus.

writer, scrīptor, –ōris, *m.*

wrong (be), errō, 1.

Y

year, annus, –ī, *m.*

yet (and), quamquam.

you, tū, tuī.

young man, adulēscēns, –ntis, *m.*

your, tuus, –a, –um.

INDEX